Plays Children Love

Plays
Children
Love

A Treasury of Contemporary and
Classic Plays for Children

Edited by

Coleman A. Jennings

and

Aurand Harris

Foreword by Mary Martin

Illustrations by Susan Swan
Original set designs created by Lee Duran

DOUBLEDAY & COMPANY, INC.
Garden City, New York

ISBN: 0-385-17096-3
Library of Congress Catalog Card Number 80–2412
Copyright © 1981 by Coleman A. Jennings and Aurand Harris
All Rights Reserved
Printed in the United States of America
Design by Jeanette Portelli

Grateful acknowledgment is made to:

Anchorage Press, Inc., for permission to reprint *Androcles and the Lion* by Aurand Harris, copyright © 1964 by The Children's Theatre Press (now Anchorage Press); *The Sleeping Beauty* by Charlotte Chorpenning, copyright © 1947 by The Children's Theatre Press (now Anchorage Press); *Tom Sawyer* adapted by Sara Spencer, copyright © 1935 by The Children's Theatre Press (now Anchorage Press); *A Toby Show* by Aurand Harris, copyright © 1978 by Anchorage Press; *Johnny Moonbeam and the Silver Arrow* by Joseph Golden, copyright © 1962 by The Children's Theatre Press (now Anchorage Press); *Step on a Crack* by Suzan Zeder, copyright © 1976 by Anchorage Press; *I Didn't Know That!* by Saldaña, Selber, Moloney and Winfree, copyright © 1980 by Anchorage Press; four plays from *In One Basket* by Shirley Pugh, copyright © 1972 by Anchorage Press; *Yankee Doodle Dandies* from *Yankee Doodle* by Aurand Harris, copyright © 1975 by Anchorage Press.

Dodd, Mead & Company, for permission to reprint *Snow White and the Seven Dwarfs* by Jessie Braham White, copyright © 1913 by Dodd, Mead & Company. Acting edition rights controlled by Samuel French, Inc.

Samuel French, Inc., for permission to reprint *Ming Lee and the Magic Tree* by Aurand Harris, copyright © 1971 by Samuel French, Inc.

The Paper Bag Players, Inc., for permission to reprint *Ma and the Kids* by Judith Martin *et al.*, copyright © 1966 by The Paper Bag Players, Inc.; *Hands Off! Don't Touch!* by Judith Martin, copyright © 1966 by The Paper Bag Players, Inc.

Performance Publishing Co., for permission to reprint *Jack and the Beanstalk* by Robert Rafferty, copyright © 1979 by Performance Publishing Co.

The Dramatic Publishing Company, for permission to reprint *Winnie-the-Pooh* adapted by Kristin Sergel, copyright © 1957 by The Dramatic Publishing Company; *The Buffalo and the Bell* from *Topeng: Tales of Trickery* by Kim Alan Wheetley, copyright © 1980 by The Dramatic Publishing Company.

The Coach House Press, Inc., for permission to reprint *Wiley and the Hairy Man* by Jack Stokes as adapted by Alice Molter, copyright © 1970 by The Coach House Press, Inc.

Plays, Inc., Publishers, for permission to reprint *The Fisherman and His Wife* by Lowell Swortzell, copyright © 1966 by Plays, Inc., Publishers.

Contents

Foreword
Mary Martin

When Sir James M. Barrie wrote the words: "I am Youth, I am Joy, I am Freedom," for Peter Pan to say, for generations to come, he really knew what was in the hearts of *all* children, everywhere, of *all* ages.

The joy of youth, the freedom to express imagination, the art of "playing like" imaginary people belong to all children . . . white, black, yellow, or green. Yes, indeed, it is universal. What grown-up in this world today hasn't said, at *some* time, "Let's play like . . ."? I've been "playing like" for many decades. And what a privilege it has been!

THE most rewarding, thrilling experience of my entire career was that moment, as Peter Pan, when I went down to the footlights and asked for *help* to save Tinkerbell's life by saying, "Do you believe? If you do, clap your hands!" And to hear the waves of sound of a thousand little hands, and BIG hands, clapping, clapping, and voices crying out, "I believe, I believe, Peter, I believe."

And when I was Peter Pan on television, and there was no visible audience for Peter to see, or hear, *that* moment was even greater . . . the chemistry of sixty-five million people came through the ether like an ESP sonic boom!

THAT'S BELIEF. It's almost tangible. Too, it's trust, it's faith, it's love. And it will keep the Land of Make Believe alive and well forever and ever and ever.

I am enjoying a lifetime of gratitude that I have had children who grew up in the theatre world; and they have performed onstage, and are still performing. And that I have grandchildren who are performing, or dreaming of performing. And I am dreaming right along with each one of them. We are privileged people living in the Magic Land.

As my next to youngest grandchild, aged four, reminded me on a recent visit, when I made the foolish statement, "Oh, Mary Devon, you can't do that; it's impossible." And she replied, "Vova [grandmother in Portuguese], it's *not* impossible, not for *me!* You see, I have the powah!"

And she does. I should have known better. And I will always remember what I learned from her.

Thank you, Aurand Harris and Coleman Jennings, and all you young in heart readers, for letting me be a part of your exciting anthology. . . . Let's all read all these plays, alone but out loud, together, and we can all end up feeling together, clapping our hands and saying: "We believe, we believe."

Plays Children Love

Scripts and Royalty Fees
Any group that produces a play for an audience, whether for
paid admission or not, is required by copyright law to purchase enough copies for the entire cast from the publisher
and to pay a prescribed royalty fee for each performance
in advance. An address for buying scripts and paying the
royalty fee precedes each play in this anthology.

Part One:

Plays for
Adult Performers

Introduction

In the United States, plays were not performed for young people until the beginning of this century, and were called children's theatre. Recently, to clarify the label for both the profession and the general public, the national Children's Theatre Association of America (CTAA) officially adopted an expanded definition of terms. The vague description, "children's theatre," was replaced with "Theatre for Young Audiences," which encompasses both "Theatre for Children," plays produced specifically for children from ages five to twelve (elementary school age), and "Theatre for the Young," plays produced for children ages thirteen to fifteen (junior high and high school age). This collection of plays fits into the category of "Theatre for Children."

The plays in Part One have been selected primarily for adults to perform. Part Two is devoted to more informal, improvisational plays that can easily be performed by children for an audience of children. The division of the two groups of plays, however, is not rigid. Certainly many adult groups can perform plays from Part Two, and some young performers may be able to tackle selected scenes from plays in Part One. The eleven plays that have been selected for adults to perform for children represent a spectrum of works now available for producers. Original publication dates range from 1912 to 1980. Within each script are suggested descriptions of scenery, special effects, and staging which may be used or replaced by other ideas, depending on the producers and the production. Following some of the plays are additional notes from the original production.

The plays are combinations of comedy and drama, realism and fantasy. Some are based on other literature; others on fairy tales, myths, and fables. One is a modern revue and another, a story of a modern family. Each has a place in theatre for children and youth.

The main goal of any adult theatre company performing for children is to create a superior production—one that is exciting, meaningful, and excellently staged. In order to achieve this theatrical experience it is essential that the producers and performers have a knowledge of certain special techniques. Here are some important tips about performing for children:

THE CHILD AUDIENCE

The child audience behaves quite differently from an adult audience. As the children wait for the play to begin there is usually much talking and movement. They will probably be excited by such things as the bus ride to the theatre, being out of school, being with many other children, and the anticipation of seeing the play. The sea of motion and noise builds to a climax as the house lights dim and the curtain rises. Something about a dark theatre makes children begin shouting, whistling, and making strange noises—which will subside only after several minutes of action onstage. Therefore, it is important to fade the house lights out and bring the stage lights up almost at the same time so that the audience is not left in a dark auditorium. Once the audience realizes that the play has begun they will become attentive.

As a group, children are uninhibited and will react spontaneously to what is happening onstage. Children will readily join in the action of the play by either impulsively calling out to the characters to give advice and warn them of dangers, or by actually standing up to see better. This participation is a sure sign of a well-staged play because it shows that the children see actors not as performers but as characters in a real situation. It's interesting that these outbursts of emotion are usually ignored by other children in the audience while the adults are often embarrassed or annoyed, and will sometimes try to shush the children.

When they are involved in the story, children are an attentive, appreciative audience for whom performing is exceedingly satisfying. The actors are subliminally aware of their audience's vocal and physical reactions, and will instinctively use the involvement and excitement of this special audience to intensify their own performance.

All child audiences will include adults. When the children outnumber the adults, such as during an in-school performance, the children tend to be more overt in their reactions. The more adults there are the more restraint there will be on children's reactions. But, regardless of the composition of the audience, a good production of a good script will capture the attention and stimulate the imagination of the children *and* adults.

THE PLAYS

Plays presented for children should be of excellent quality. Patronizing, trite, and meaningless scripts have no place in theatre for young people. Instead, children should be challenged to *think*, encouraged to become emotionally *involved*, and they should be provided with a *worthwhile experience*. The play may be a comedy or a drama with a plot based on a fairy tale, modern story, historical event, legend, folk tale, or traditional story, but the plot must tell a compelling story with unexpected consequences always impending. The play may also have an underlying message or theme. The characters, although not particularly complex, must be important to the children; they will automatically become important if they are consistent, interesting, and involved in the action of the plot rather than simply telling about themselves or their situation. Children want to see them in action. The language should stretch imaginations and create a background appropriate for the plot, characters, and theme.

Never underestimate children by simply amusing them. Set out to entertain as well as enlighten them. And never become preoccupied with entertaining the adults; it is a bad production that uses puns, sophisticated jokes, or innuendo to amuse the grown-ups, while going over the heads of the main audience.

One must be aware of what interests children, what amuses them, of their attention spans, their familiarity with a particular plot or background information about a country or culture, their ability to understand certain uses of language, and their probable responses in a theatre in order to create a successful play.

Most of the dramatic literature has been aimed at the target age—students in the late elementary grades, ages ten and eleven—with the assumption that many younger and older students would also be interested in the material. For a variety of reasons, major playwrights have avoided writing for both very young children and children of the junior high school ages. Both groups demand special attention. The younger children need short plays with lots of action and uncomplicated characters and plot; while the junior high age needs plays that are more mature and speak directly or indirectly to them about their own situation. It should be noted, however, that a play which is imaginatively staged will interest a wide age range and will find a strong audience outside the target age.

THE PRODUCTION

Ideally children should have the opportunity to see professional productions—whether performed in their schools by visiting troupes or in a traditional theatre where the support of complete scenery, lighting, and sound effects are possible. Although not essential, unusual stage effects can be quite a treat for children, but only if the effects truly enhance the plot and the characters.

Because the child audience loves action, the play should have constant *motivated movement*. Stationary characters, seated or otherwise, are uninteresting to children. But remember, the physical action must develop from the situation and the characters' behavior; having characters move about for no reason except for the purpose of adding activity is insulting to the audience.

Since playwrights think in terms of characters in action, they usually include some stage directions in their scripts. The abbreviations commonly used in noting stage directions appear in many of the scripts in this collection. The following chart of stage positions is provided to help the reader visualize the action of the play.

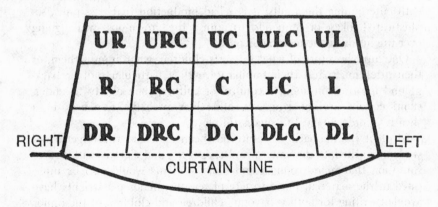

UR	URC	UC	ULC	UL
R	RC	C	LC	L
DR	DRC	DC	DLC	DL

RIGHT — CURTAIN LINE — LEFT

AUDIENCE

An area designated on the stage refers to a general place rather than a specific spot. *Upstage* means away from the audience, *downstage* means toward the audience, and *right* and *left* are used with reference to the actor as he faces the audience. R means *right*, L means *left*, U means *up*, D means *down*, C means *center*, and these abbreviations are used in combination, as: UR for *up right*, RC for *right center*, DLC for *down left center*, etc.

As in the acting, the directing must be believable. The most effective telling of a story is through a variety of stage compositions or picturizations. The actors should visually illustrate the meaning of the scene through their physical arrangement on the stage. For example: (1) two characters who keep their distance from each other during a conflict, literally move toward one another as their problem is resolved; (2) characters are arranged to emphasize the entrance of an important character; (3) the attention of the audience is focused on the spot where the climactic scene between the hero and the villain is taking place by having all other characters facing that action.

In order to have interesting variety in the stage compositions, and to intensify the meaning of the play, the stage floor should include as many different levels on which to perform as possible. This variety can be achieved using steps, platforms, and ramps.

The *playing time* for most full-length plays for children is sixty to eighty minutes. Therefore it is possible, and many think advisable, to present the play without interruptions. Reestablishing the story line and mood after scene shifts and intermissions can be difficult. A well-written and thoughtfully staged script should capture the attention of most of the audience throughout the performance.

A variety of audience-actor relationships, from the traditional proscenium arch auditorium to theatre-in-the-round, can be utilized to draw the audience into the play. When children are in a small theatre and close to the action, their attention and involvement increase considerably. A larger house will demand an expanded, more presentational production to reach the entire audience. With any production in any theatre, however, it is the script and the creative abilities of the director and cast that determine the success of the production.

In any type of production, the actors must portray their characters with vitality and sincerity. Their characterizations must be believable. The actors should not "play at" being the characters but should *become* the characters and devote their full creative energies to realizing the dramatic action of the story.

Literal presentations of costumes and settings are unnecessary. Children are quite willing to accept a costume or a locale suggested by designs which convey the essence of the script requirements. In cos-

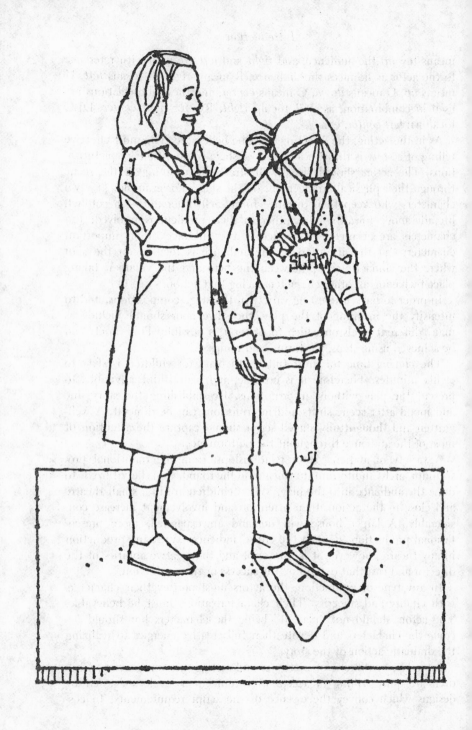

tuming, for example, animal characters can be effectively communicated by using only a few essential elements of the creature. Actors don't need to wear a complete animal suit to appear "correctly" costumed in the eyes of the audience—ears and a tail will convey a mouse, a flat beak and flippers will look like a duck. The children will see the animal that is merely suggested in the costume and the acting.

In scenic design also, suggestion is preferable. Spectacular and complicated settings are seldom necessary in productions for children. To show each locale in detail will definitely hinder the flow of the play. A better solution is to have the actors establish the settings through interaction and their own belief that those settings are real places. If the actors believe in what they're doing, so will the children.

Snow White and the Seven Dwarfs

Jessie Braham White

Adapted from the Brothers Grimm
(*An Abridged Version*)

Snow White and the Seven Dwarfs was first produced on Broadway in 1912 by Winthrop Ames at his Little Theatre. The abridged version in this anthology has been specially prepared to preserve the original plot. Several minor characters, anachronisms, long speeches, and repetitious dialogue have been deleted. Producers who wish to present this edited version may purchase the longer scripts from the publisher and make the adjustments accordingly.

Plot is the most important element in the play and Snow White, a conventional "good" character, is its center. The underlying conflict between the arrogant Queen and the beautiful Snow White is soon apparent. The tension begins to build in the first scene as the Queen heartlessly commands her unwilling Huntsman to kill Snow White. Suspense increases as the safety of the heroine is precariously balanced against the machinations of her adversary. The conflict is finally resolved at the end of the final scene when Snow White is saved, the villainy is foiled, and all receive their just rewards!

Although the story is essentially serious, many of the characters provide a generous leavening of humor. Sir Dandiprat Bombas, the court chamberlain, sets the tone in the initial minutes of the play with a pratfall, while trying to demonstrate a proper court bow to a new Maid of Honor to Snow White. The first scene with the seven dwarfs is also light, brisk comedy which opens with the youngest dwarf being given his daily, obligatory scolding for stealing, along with a lengthy list of goods the other dwarfs expect him to get for them the next day.

Even the villains are amusing. Hex, the Witch, the source of evil magic which the Queen uses against Snow White, is portrayed as an irritable, uncaring, slightly zany, old woman, but not as a frightening villain. Even the Queen's wickedness is softened by making her the object of the Witch's comic ridicule. The denouement reveals the vain Queen made comic in defeat by her metamorphosis into a very ugly woman, and a Witch who has uncharacteristically renounced all spells and charms so she can be a respectable old lady.

In 1912 when the play was written, villains of unmitigated evil were considered too severe for the child audience. By the 1940s that attitude had begun to change as seen in the appearance of a terrifying and malevolent queen in the Walt Disney motion picture of the same story.

The play requires particular attention to the technical production. There are four separate settings and a large cast to be costumed. Since the story is magic fantasy, spectacular effects are important and many special-effects problems must be solved. Notes based on the Winthrop Ames production that suggest possible solutions follow below. Music for the songs in the script is available in the acting editions of the original version.

NOTES TO THE PRODUCER

EFFECTS:

The Appearance of the Witch.

In the professional production the Witch made her first appearance through a circular "trap" cut in the stage floor. If this is not practicable, the Witch should run onto the stage during the moment of darkness, and crouch down under her cloak. When the light returns she rises slowly, thus giving the effect of coming up through the floor. The smoke is imitated by compounds for sale by dealers in theatrical properties.

Entrance of the Dwarfs.

In the professional production the Dwarfs entered through a "trap" cut in the stage floor. But all their entrances and exits may be made, with equal effect, through the door of the hut.

Washing of Quee.

The large barrel in which Quee is supposed to be washed should be set against the side of the set. Holes are cut through both barrel and set, so that Quee may creep out of the barrel, without being seen by the audience, before water is pumped into it. The spout of the pump should run through the wall of the set, so that water can be poured into it from offstage when the pumping begins. The water is caught in an ordinary pail placed in the bottom of the barrel.

The Witch's Pig-tails.

The Witch acquires a head full of pig-tails by merely slipping over her bald wig, as she dips her head into the cauldron, a flesh-colored skull cap, to which is sewed a number of twisted ribbons, stuffed to imitate the small and curly tails of pigs.

The Transformation of the Queen into the Pedlar-Woman.

The Pedlar-Woman is played by a different actress from the Queen. It is desirable that both should be of about the same height. When the Cats begin to chase the Queen, they throw over her a black mantle long enough to completely hide her. At the end of the chase the actress playing the Queen runs just out of sight behind one of the wings which form the walls of the Witch's cave. The actress who plays the Pedlar-Woman stands behind the same wing, completely covered by an exact duplicate of the first mantle. The Cats immediately bring this second covered figure out onto the stage instead of the Queen, who remains in hiding. When the mantle is thrown off and the Pedlar-Woman discovered, the transformation seems magical.

The Transformation from the Pedlar-Woman to Queen Brangomar.

Just before this transformation is to be made, the actress who plays the Queen goes behind the back wall of the scene and stands, hidden from the audience, in the space between the door and the window of the hut. After the Pedlar-Woman has chanted her transforming rhyme, and as she shuts the hut door, the Queen immediately sweeps past the window, in view of the audience, while the Pedlar-Woman remains concealed behind the scene.

Snow White's Coffin.

Snow White's coffin is made like a "show case" (the frame of a box), except that sheets of transparent white gelatine are substituted for glass. The coffin is covered with a pall of flowers so thick that the audience cannot see whether Snow White is in it or not. In fact, she is not in it when it is carried onto the scene by the Dwarfs. As the coffin falls from their shoulders, the Dwarfs, the Maids of Honor, and the Dukes and Duchesses form a group between the coffin and the audience, entirely concealing it. At this moment Snow White creeps in under the curtain at the back of the scene, and lies down beside the coffin as though she had fallen out of it. She is discovered in this position when the concealing group parts. The frame of the coffin should be hinged so as to collapse, as if broken, when it falls.

SNOW WHITE AND THE SEVEN DWARFS

CHARACTERS

Princess Snow White
Queen Brangomar
Rosalys
Amelotte
Ermengarde
Guinivere   } Maids of Honor to Snow White
Christabel
Astolaine
Sir Dandiprat Bombas, the Court Chamberlain
Berthold, the Chief Huntsman
Prince Florimond of Calydon
Blick
Flick
Glick
Snick   } the Seven Dwarfs
Plick
Whick
Quee
Witch Hex
Long Tail
Short Tail   } her Cats
Lack Tail
Page

SETTINGS

SCENE I.   The Throne Room in Queen Brangomar's Palace.
SCENE II.   In the Forest.
SCENE III.   The House of the Seven Dwarfs.
SCENE IV.   Where the Witch Lives.
SCENE V.   The House of the Seven Dwarfs.
SCENE VI.   A Hallway and The Throne Room of the Palace.

SCENE I

The Throne Room in Queen Brangomar's Palace.

(*The Throne Room is a fine apartment, with rich furnishings and a golden throne. A Page enters, stands at attention, and blows the royal trumpet. The five Maids of Honor enter: Rosalys, Amelotte, Ermengarde, Guinivere, and Christabel. They stand in their proper places at the side. Sir Dandiprat Bombas, the Court Chamberlain, enters. Aware of his great importance, he makes an official announcement.*)

SIR DANDIPRAT: I have an important announcement to make. Since Lady Cecily was sent home with the mumps your usual number, six, has been reduced to five. The Queen wishes your number kept complete, so I have brought another young lady to take the vacant place. (*He motions and Lady Astolaine enters.*) The Lady Astolaine. These are the Maids of Honor to the Princess Snow White. (*Lady Astolaine curtsies to the Maids of Honor and they to her.*) You must teach Lady Astolaine all she ought to know. How to dance your minuet. (*And the little man dances a few steps, puffing out the tune meantime.*) And how to make a proper curtsy—so—(*And he tries to make one.*) And how to retire backwards gracefully—so! (*But as he retires backwards he stumbles and falls flat. He is so embarrassed by this mishap that he scrambles out of the room as fast as he can, puffing . . .*) Gracefully, young ladies! Gracefully! (*. . . till he is out of sight. Page exits.*)

ROSALYS: (*Mimicking Sir Dandiprat's voice and strut.*) That's Sir Dandiprat Bombas, Court Chamberlain to the Queen.

ASTOLAINE: Do you have good times here?

ROSALYS: Splendid. Except—(*Confidentially.*)—when the Queen is especially cross.

ASTOLAINE: I don't think I shall like the Queen!

MAIDS OF HONOR: (*Hastily.*) Ssh!

ASTOLAINE: Why, ssh?

ROSALYS: (*Whispering.*) Never say anything uncomplimentary about the Queen!

MAIDS OF HONOR: (*Loudly, intending to be overheard.*) We all *adore* the Queen! (*But they shake their heads, and make little faces to show Astolaine that they don't mean it.*)

ASTOLAINE: But I'm to be Maid of Honor to the Princess Snow White, so I'll take my orders from her.

ROSALYS: (*To the others.*) Oh, do you think we could get Snow White to come and see Astolaine now while we're all alone?

CHRISTABEL: Oh, let's try!

ROSALYS: Where is she?

CHRISTABEL: Kitchen, I think. She said she had to bake some bread, and—

AMELOTTE: I'll go! I'll go! (*And off she darts to the kitchen.*)

ASTOLAINE: (*Wonderingly.*) But what is the Princess doing in the kitchen?

ROSALYS: Of course you don't understand about Snow White yet. (*To the others.*) But I think we ought to tell her before she sees Snow White, or she might think . . . (*They evidently agree, for they begin to speak at once.*)

MAIDS OF HONOR: I'll tell her! . . . No, let me. I know! . . . Snow White was born . . . This Queen isn't her real mother . . . It's like a fairy tale!

ASTOLAINE: (*Stopping her ears.*) I can't *possibly* understand if you all talk at once. I choose—(*She hesitates, and then points to Rosalys.*) —*her* to tell.

ROSALYS: I was so afraid it wouldn't be me! I tell it so much the best. First, Queen Brangomar isn't Snow White's real mother.

ASTOLAINE: Oh, I know *that!*

ROSALYS: (*Continuing.*) One day in winter, before Snow White was born, her real mother was sitting by the window, embroidering at an ebony frame. And she pricked her finger, so she opened the window and shook the drop of blood on the snow outside. And it looked so beautiful that she said, "Oh, how I wish I had a little daughter with hair as black as ebony, skin as white as snow, and lips as red as blood!" and a little while after that a baby daughter was born with . . .

MAIDS OF HONOR: (*Chanting impressively.*) Hair as black as ebony, skin as white as snow, and lips as red as blood.

ASTOLAINE: So *that's* why they named her Snow White.

ROSALYS: But then Snow White's mother died, and I suppose the King thought there ought to be *somebody* to mind the baby, for he married Queen Brangomar, and she's Queen now. But after the King died, then —(*She pauses impressively.*)

ASTOLAINE: Then what?

ROSALYS: Then—she grew awfully jealous of Snow White. First, she pretended that Snow White might grow up vain, so she took away all her princessy clothes and made her wear old, rag-baggedy things.

CHRISTABEL: Then she pretended that she might grow up lazy, so she made her sweep and dust the palace.

ROSALYS: And now Snow White is really like a kitchen-maid, and sleeps in the little closet under the stairs.

ASTOLAINE: Why does Princess Snow White endure it? I wouldn't!

MAIDS OF HONOR: (*Apprehensively.*) Oh, ssh!

ASTOLAINE: Why "ssh"? I never heard anything so "sshy" as this palace.

ROSALYS: But what can Snow White do? The reason it's not safe for anyone to do or say anything against the Queen is—that she might *magic* you.

ASTOLAINE: What do you mean?

ROSALYS: Enchant you, bewitch you—do some terrible magic thing to you!

ASTOLAINE: You don't mean that she's a—Witch! (*The others nod silently.*)

ROSALYS: If she isn't a Witch, she is friends with one. You see, she must really be very old. And she's still the most beautiful woman in the Seven Kingdoms.

CHRISTABEL: And once a maid found a broomstick, the kind that witches ride on, under her bed.

ROSALYS: So you see, if you did anything against her, she might magic you, and turn you into a toad.

ERMENGARDE: Or a caterpillar.

CHRISTABEL: Or something worse.

ASTOLAINE: Oh, I want to go home! I am afraid!

ROSALYS: (*In despair.*) Oh, if Snow White would only come now! Then she wouldn't want to go home. (*Just at this moment Amelotte reappears in the doorway.*)

AMELOTTE: Princess Snow White says she'll come if nobody's here.

ROSALYS: Oh, she's coming! Snow White's coming! Now you'll see!

AMELOTTE: (*Announces.*) The Princess Snow White! (*The Maids of Honor kneel to receive their little Princess. Snow White appears in the doorway. She is dressed in a ragged frock.*)

SNOW WHITE: Is this my new Maid of Honor, Lady Astolaine?

ASTOLAINE: (*Kissing the hand which Snow White holds out to her.*) Yes, yes dear Princess.

ROSALYS: Can you stay just a moment and teach Astolaine our minuet? You do it so much the best. I'll watch and tell you if anybody's coming.

SNOW WHITE: (*To Astolaine.*) Well, Astolaine, you be my partner. It's very simple. Are you ready? Now! (*The Maids of Honor take positions for the Dance; and, as Snow White teaches Astolaine the steps, they sing.*) (*Maids of Honor Dance.*)

SNOW WHITE: Turn to me and curtsy low.

THE MAIDS: One, two, three,
  One, two, three.

SNOW WHITE: Turn away and point your toe.

THE MAIDS: One and two and three.

SNOW WHITE: Turn again, and hand in hand,

THE MAIDS: Hand in hand,
  Hand in hand,

SNOW WHITE: Turn your partner where you stand.

ROSALYS: Look out! Old Dandiprat's coming!

SNOW WHITE: Oh, dear, I must run . . .

ROSALYS: (*Catching her.*) No, don't! He won't stay a minute. Hide behind the throne till he's gone.

MAIDS OF HONOR: Yes, yes! Quick! Get behind the throne! (*Snow White runs behind the throne, and the Maids of Honor spread themselves out before it so that she is quite hidden. But they are not a moment too soon, for Sir Dandiprat enters.*)

SIR DANDIPRAT: I have a most important announcement to make. (*He unrolls an imposing parchment and reads:*) "Whereas, his Highness, Prince Florimond, heir to the Kingdom of Calydon, will call upon the Queen this afternoon to deliver a letter from his royal father, I have arranged the following reception. At four-fifteen this Proclamation will be read. At four-thirty Prince Florimond will arrive, and be shown at once to the throne-room by—ahem—myself. The Maids of Honor will dance to amuse his Highness until the Queen is announced, when they will immediately retire. By order of me, Sir Dandiprat Bombas, Court Chamberlain. "P.S. Her Majesty the Queen regrets that, owing to her duties in the kitchen, Princess Snow White will be unable to attend." You have eight minutes and thirty-one seconds to prepare. (*He exits.*)

ASTOLAINE: Gracious! I can't possibly learn that dance in eight minutes and thirty-one seconds!

CHRISTABEL: And we *must* dance in pairs!

ERMENGARDE: What *shall* we do?

ROSALYS: (*Calling to Snow White, who enters from behind the throne.*) Princess Snow White, what *shall* we do?

ASTOLAINE: (*Struck with an idea.*) Wait! The Queen won't be here when we dance for the Prince? Then why can't the Princess dance in my place?

SNOW WHITE: Oh, I wish it were possible, but my dress!

ROSALYS: Why can't we *all* lend her something?

CHRISTABEL: We have on heaps more than we need.

ROSALYS: She could have my underskirt! (*She pulls it up to show an underskirt almost as elaborate.*)

CHRISTABEL: And my guimpe.

AMELOTTE: And my lace jacket.

ERMENGARDE: And my cap and pearls.

ROSALYS: We could dress her perfectly!

ASTOLAINE: Will you do it, Princess?

SNOW WHITE: I suppose I oughtn't—but I will! (*And she runs behind the throne to dress, with Guinivere to help her. The other little Maids unpin and unhook and twist and turn to reach hard buttons, at a great rate, as you can judge from the things they say.*)

MAIDS OF HONOR: Help me with this skirt. I can't unhook me! . . . These pearls just *won't* untangle! . . . Please come and unpin this . . . No, me first . . . She's ready for the skirt now . . . You unhook while I squeeze. Now: One, two, three! There isn't room for all our fingers on one little hook! . . . Here's the jacket! (*And now they're all behind the throne, helping Snow White on with the new things, except poor Christabel, who is left writhing to reach a pin at the back of her neck.*)

ROSALYS: (*Dancing out, waving Snow White's black frock.*) Here's her little black dress. What shall I do with it?

ASTOLAINE: (*Following.*) Oh, put it anywhere!

ROSALYS: But where *is* anywhere?

ASTOLAINE: Here, stuff it under this cushion on the throne. (*She does so.*)

ASTOLAINE: They'll never find it there. *Won't* it be a joke when the Queen sits on it! (*They run behind the throne again. Snow White is almost dressed now; and the little Maids one after another tiptoe away from the throne, whispering.*)

CHRISTABEL: Oh, she is beautiful.

ROSALYS: Her lips red as blood and her hair black as night!

ASTOLAINE: She's lovely, she's lovely, our Princess Snow White! (*They stand waiting for her. She steps into sight. The Maids sink down in involuntary curtsies at the sight of her.*)

CHRISTABEL: She is lovelier than apple blossoms.

ASTOLAINE: Lovelier than anybody I ever saw.

ROSALYS: (*In a hushed voice.*) More beautiful than the Queen!

CHRISTABEL: (*Whispering.*) The Queen must never see her like this.

GUINIVERE: Never! (*A trumpet sounds.*)

SNOW WHITE: There's the Prince now!

ASTOLAINE: We can't stay here. Let's run into the anteroom.

SNOW WHITE: I ought not to, but I do so want to see him again!

MAIDS OF HONOR: Hurry! (*They hasten off, drawing Snow White with them. They are only just in time before Sir Dandiprat enters.*)

SIR DANDIPRAT: (*Announcing.*) His Highness, Prince Florimond, Heir Apparent to the Kingdom of Calydon. (*The Prince appears.*)

SIR DANDIPRAT: I regret, your Highness, that the Queen hasn't quite finished dressing. But she will be here in a moment. Meantime may the Maids of Honor entertain your Highness with a little dance?

THE PRINCE: It would give me great pleasure. (*Sir Dandiprat motions. Music begins. He exits. The Maids of Honor begin their dance. There is something about Snow White that attracts the Prince from the first; and as the dance progresses he watches her more closely. As the first figure ends, he stands close beside her.*)

THE PRINCE: (*To Snow White.*) Lady, do you think that I
Might dance, too? I'd like to try.

SNOW WHITE: (*Giving him her hand.*) I was hoping you might be
Tempted to join in—with me.

(*Snow White now dancing with the Prince. Once in a while we overhear what they are saying.*)

SNOW WHITE: One would think that you (*we bow*)
Never saw me until now.

THE PRINCE: Is it likely I'd forget
If we two *had* ever met?

Do you know (*I did that bow*)
Steps don't seem important now.

(*The dance ends. Page enters. Trumpet sounds to announce the coming of the Queen. But the Prince still holds Snow White's hand.*)

SNOW WHITE: There's the Queen. She mustn't know!
Please, my hand, sir! I must go!

THE PRINCE: Oh, not yet. I'll take the blame.
I don't even know your name!

SNOW WHITE: Oh, don't keep me. I must fly—!
I'm sorry, but—good-bye!

(*She runs off with the Maids. Sir Dandiprat enters.*)

SIR DANDIPRAT: Her Majesty the Queen! (*To a blare of trumpets Queen Brangomar enters. She is very beautiful. She holds out a jeweled hand for the Prince to kiss, and then sweeps to the throne.*)

THE QUEEN: So you are Prince Florimond? I'm sorry you chose today to come. I'm not looking my best.

THE PRINCE: I have always heard of Queen Brangomar as the most beautiful . . .

THE QUEEN: (*Interrupting rudely.*) Of course, of course! I am told you bring me a message from your father. What is it?

THE PRINCE: This letter. He said it was confidential.

THE QUEEN: (*Reading the letter.*) M-m-m-m-m . . . wretched handwriting . . . "My son Florimond, now of an age to marry . . ."

THE PRINCE: (*Startled.*) Marry?

THE QUEEN: So your foolish old father is intending to marry you off. What's this? "To marry the Princess Snow White"! Snow White! (*She rises in anger.*) Snow White! (*Then, trying not to betray her jealousy, she reseats herself with a bitter laugh.*) Really, my dear Florimond, Snow White isn't a *possible* choice. She is most ill-tempered; and so vulgar that she prefers to associate with kitchen maids.

Indeed, I believe she's in the kitchen at this moment. She wouldn't do for you at all.

THE PRINCE: Your Majesty has made me very happy!

THE QUEEN: Happy?

THE PRINCE: Five minutes ago what you say would have made me miserable, for even as a little boy I always dreamed of marrying Snow White when I grew up. But *now—!* You see, I've fallen in love with someone else meantime.

THE QUEEN: Meantime? When?

THE PRINCE: Here, just now, in this very room.

THE QUEEN: (*With a pleased laugh.*) Oh, my poor boy! Really, I'm so much older than you . . .

THE PRINCE: She's one of Snow White's Maids of Honor.

THE QUEEN: A Maid of Honor! Summon *all* the Maids of Honor. (*She motions to Sir Dandiprat, who hurries off.*) I am curious to know your taste. Stand here by me and point her out when she comes. (*Sir Dandiprat reappears, and introduces the Maids of Honor; and as each is named she curtsies to the Prince.*)

SIR DANDIPRAT: The Lady Rosalys. The Lady Amelotte. The Lady Ermengarde. The Lady Guinivere. The Lady Christabel. The Lady Astolaine.

THE PRINCE: But she's not there! There was another—!

THE QUEEN: Another? Six—that's all.

THE PRINCE: But there *was* another!

THE QUEEN: (*Suspiciously.*) Another? What was she like?

THE PRINCE: Her hair was black as ebony; her skin was whiter than snow; her lips were redder than a drop of blood.

THE QUEEN: (*In a terrible voice.*) Snow White! Summon Snow White! (*Snow White appears timidly in the entrance as if she had been listening behind the curtains.*)

SNOW WHITE: Your Majesty?

THE PRINCE: That is she! And oh, is she Snow White? You are Snow White!

THE QUEEN: (*Anger quite overcoming her as she sees Snow White's changed appearance.*) Snow White! You! You dared . . . (*She rushes toward the Princess; but suddenly, halfway, she falters, gives a cry, and falls fainting.*)

SIR DANDIPRAT: (*Hopping about in great excitement.*) The Queen has fainted! The Queen has fainted! Oh, this is most important! Oh, Princess, see what you've done! Take her away, take her away! (*The Maids of Honor hurry Snow White away; and Sir Dandiprat turns to the astonished Prince.*) It's most distracting. Air, air! Out of the room! Give her air! (*The Prince hurries out. Page exits. But no sooner is the Queen alone with Sir Dandiprat than she recovers from her pretended swoon.*)

SIR DANDIPRAT: Shall I fan your Majesty?

THE QUEEN: Where is the Prince?

SIR DANDIPRAT: On the terrace, your Majesty.

THE QUEEN: Keep him there till I ring. Guard the doors. Go. Get out, you idiot! (*Sir Dandiprat exits.*)

THE QUEEN: (*Alone.*) The Witch! Witch Hex! I must summon her. She must help me now. (*In a hushed, mysterious voice she chants:*)

THE SPELL

From my eyebrow pluck a hair,
  E—burrimee *boo*-row.
Blow it high up in the air,
  E—burrimee hock.
Where it lands a circle trace,
  E—burrimee *boo*-row.
Three times pace about the space,
        and
      Knock, knock, knock!

(*As she knocks smoke rises from the circle she has traced with a pointed finger, and there is a sound of distant thunder.*)

Thunder says the spell grows warm,
  E—burrimee *boo*-row

Now I speak the mystic Charm,
  E—burrimee boo!

THE CHARM

Ee Eye-*sof*-o-gos. Ee Eye-sof-a-giddle!
Ee Eye-*sof*-o-gos. Ee Eye-sof-a-giddle.
  Ee Eye-*sof*-o-gos!
Eee Eye-sof-o-*lof*-o-gos!
  Ee Eye-*sof*-o-gos!
  Ee Eye-sof-a-giddle!

(*The Charm sounds like nonsense, but it must be true magic, for the smoke increases as she chants it, and the thunder comes nearer.*)

The spell's wound up, the charm is clear!
I summon thee, Witch Hex, appear!

(*Lo! through the floor Witch Hex does appear. She looks exactly like the witches in all fairy-tale pictures, with her pointed hat, red cloak, and crutched stick. It is evident that she is in a bad temper.*)

THE WITCH: Help me out, help me out! (*The Queen helps her out of the smoking circle.*) What's the meaning of this? I'm getting tired of being called up by you night and day. I was an idiot ever to teach you that spell. Well, what is the matter now?

THE QUEEN: Don't be angry, dear godmother. You know how much I love you!

THE WITCH: Stuff! You don't love me. You don't love anybody but yourself. That's the matter with you. If you only knew the trouble I have to keep you beautiful! Your disposition keeps wearing through. If I should once say, "Bang! No more charms for that wretched Brangomar," how would you look then? (*She chuckles at the thought.*)

THE WITCH: I believe you'd be uglier than I am.

THE QUEEN: I know, I know, dear Hex, but you wouldn't.

THE WITCH: Don't be too sure. Just summon me once too often, and you may find yourself the *ugliest* woman in the Seven Kingdoms, for a change.

THE QUEEN: Oh, tell me I am still the most beautiful!

THE WITCH: You look all right yet. But I warn you! I'm using my strongest magic now. You'd be much safer if you'd try to be good once in a while. Well, who are you jealous of *this* time?

THE QUEEN: Snow White.

THE WITCH: Snow White? She's only a child!

THE QUEEN: So I thought till today, when I saw her for the first time prettily dressed.

THE WITCH: Well, why did you dress her up?

THE QUEEN: I didn't. She tricked me.

THE WITCH: Who thought she was fairer than you?

THE QUEEN: Prince Florimond. He wants to marry her.

THE WITCH: Florimond? Pooh! Mere boy! Probably said it to plague you, knowing your wretched vanity. But I've brought something with me that may help to keep you quiet. Just had time to snatch it when I felt you spelling away. It's a Magic Mirror. (*She takes from her pocket a hand Mirror, carved from a single crystal, that glows and gleams like an opal.*)

THE QUEEN: (*Seizing the Mirror and gazing into it.*) Magic! . . . (*But suddenly she cries out in horror.*) Oh!

THE WITCH: Ah, you see! Reflects you as you really are. If I stopped my spells that's what you'd look like. Now it makes me quite decent looking. That's because my character's better.

THE QUEEN: Oh, the hateful thing! I never saw anything so terrible. Take it away! Take it away!

THE WITCH: Wait! That's not all its magic. Hold it in your hand and say:

> Mirror, Mirror, in my hand,
> Who's the fairest in the land?

and it will answer truthfully.

THE QUEEN: (*Snatching it.*) Oh, let me try! (*Shutting her eyes that she may not see her reflection, she asks:*)

> Mirror, Mirror, in my hand,
> Who's the fairest in the land?

THE WITCH: Listen! (*There is a faint strain of Music, and then a far-away voice that sounds like crystal bells sings:*)

THE MIRROR

You who hold me in your hand,
You were the fairest in the land;
But, today, I tell you true,
Snow White is more fair than you!

(*With a scream of rage the Queen starts to dash the Mirror to the floor. The Witch rescues it just in time.*)

THE WITCH: Stop! Stop! Gracious! Listen to me now! If you ever break that Mirror you will become as ugly as you really are—and for life too!

THE QUEEN: (*Pacing up and down, weeping with rage.*) But Snow White is more beautiful than I!

THE WITCH: (*Mocking her.*) "Snow White is more beau-hoo-hoo-tiful than I!" Stop that wawling.

THE QUEEN: I can't bear it! Make a spell and turn her ugly—as ugly as a toad.

THE WITCH: Won't! Refuse to make any more bad spells. If you can't bear the sight of her, why not send her away somewhere—to be tutored.

THE QUEEN: But she'd come back.

THE WITCH: Why should she? Suppose she got croup or mumps.

THE QUEEN: Oh, I see! You'll make a spell and give her the disease.

THE WITCH: No, no, no! Won't do any more bad magic, I tell you. You must contrive to have her lost on the way and then just tell some tar-radiddle to explain why she doesn't come back—and there you are! Everything permanently settled, and a little peace for me, I hope.

THE QUEEN: I might. I could send Berthold, my Huntsman, . . . and there . . . oh! . . . in the deep forest . . . (*She whispers.*) . . . he shall put her to death.

THE WITCH: (*Starting.*) Goodness—gracious—mercy—me! I never suggested anything like *that!* Why, I hear she's quite a nice child.

THE QUEEN: I shall never know a happy hour while she's alive.

THE WITCH: Well, there's no arguing with *you*. But can you trust your Huntsman?

THE QUEEN: I know a way to make him obey.

THE WITCH: Glad you know something! And look here! If you're *resolved* to have Snow White killed, there's a little favor you might do me. I'm making a new spell that's really *hard* magic! A hair restorer that will really restore hair. Want it for my own personal use. (*She pops off her cap and shows a partially bald head.*) I'd about given it up for want of the last ingredient—the heart of a nice young girl. Now I wouldn't harm a nice young girl myself for anything; but if you're determined to dispose of Snow White, I'd be obliged for her heart.

THE QUEEN: I promise. Berthold shall bring it to me as a proof. And now good-bye, dear Hexy. I must summon him at once.

THE WITCH: Hm! It's always, "Good-bye, dear Hexy," as soon as I've done what you want. But I'm as glad to go as you are to have me. Say the "Quick Spell" and get me off. Ready? (*The Queen and the Witch join hands, shut their eyes and chant in chorus:*)

THE QUICK SPELL

Bangaboo-bar;
Bangaboo whack;
    Crow eat sun,
    Make all black!
    Mar-*oom*-bah!

(*Everything suddenly becomes dark, and in the darkness the two voices are heard still chanting:*)

Bangaboo-bar;
Bangaboo whack,
    Mole dig hole,
    Witch go back,
    Mar-*oom*-bah!

(*There is a queer sound, something like a very small earthquake. Then only the Queen's voice is heard:*)

THE QUEEN: Bangaboo-bah!
    Bangaboo whack!
        Witch is gone,

Sun come back,
Mar-*oom*-bah!

(*The light returns as suddenly as it went. The Witch has vanished. Quite calmly the Queen goes to the bell cord.*)

THE QUEEN: Let me see. I ring three times for the Huntsman. (*She rings; but it is Sir Dandiprat who enters.*)

SIR DANDIPRAT: Your Majesty rang for me?

THE QUEEN: Not for you, idiot, for Berthold. Give me a minute alone with him, and then summon the Prince and Snow White. Off with you! (*Sir Dandiprat hurries away just as Chief Huntsman Berthold enters. Berthold is tall and big. He has a kind, ruddy face.*) Berthold, I have a task for you—a task you must carry out with absolute obedience. Come nearer. The Princess Snow White is to set away this afternoon. You will conduct her. At the Western Gates, you will take the old road that turns to the left . . .

BERTHOLD: But, your Majesty, that road leads into the deep wood.

THE QUEEN: You will take *that* road. When you have come to the very heart of the forest, then—(*And she hisses the words.*)—you will kill the Princess.

BERTHOLD: (*Springing back.*) Never, your Majesty, never! I would slay myself first. Pray dismiss me. (*He turns to go.*)

THE QUEEN: (*In a terrible voice.*) Wait! I know how to make you obey. You have six small children, I believe?

BERTHOLD: (*Wonderingly.*) Yes, your Majesty.

THE QUEEN: Suppose I lock them up in the Great Gray Tower.

BERTHOLD: Oh, no, your Majesty!

THE QUEEN: Think! Can you not hear their voices calling to you from the dark? "We are hungry, Papa!" they will cry, and they will beat on the door with their little hands.

BERTHOLD: No!

THE QUEEN: At last they will be too weak to cry. Then when all has grown still within the Tower, I will say: "Berthold, here is the key. Go and see how Queen Brangomar punishes disobedience."

BERTHOLD: Oh, I will obey, your Majesty! I cannot let my children starve.

THE QUEEN: That's *much* better, Berthold. You must bring me Snow White's heart before midnight, as a proof. Here comes the Prince. Do try to look more pleasant. (*Prince Florimond returns, ushered in by Sir Dandiprat, and followed by the Maids of Honor.*)

THE PRINCE: I hope your Majesty has recovered.

THE QUEEN: Quite, thank you. I beg everybody's pardon. (*To Sir Dandiprat.*) Where is the Princess Snow White?

SNOW WHITE: (*Appearing.*) I am here, your Majesty.

THE QUEEN: My dear Snow White, Prince Florimond has come to ask your hand in marriage. What do you say?

SNOW WHITE: (*Drooping her head.*) What may I say?

THE QUEEN: I was obliged to tell him how unfitted you are at present to become a Queen. Indeed, I've long been thinking of sending you away to be tutored. This seems the opportunity. You will remain away for a year and a day . . .

THE PRINCE: Oh, no, your Majesty!

THE QUEEN: (*Firmly.*) And the Prince must promise not to see or write to you until the end of that time. Otherwise, I shall refuse my consent. Do you agree?

THE PRINCE: Since I must.

THE QUEEN: Then *that's* settled! Return here one year and one day hence, and we can then—(*And here she means more than she says.*) —discuss the engagement. Now, Snow White, bid farewell to Prince Florimond. (*The Prince starts forward to kiss Snow White's hand, but the Queen intervenes.*) No, no! A respectful bow and a curtsy will be quite sufficient. Good-bye, Prince Florimond. Give my regards to your father. (*So the poor Prince bows himself out, but he looks back at Snow White as long as he can see her.*)

THE QUEEN: Now, Snow White, I've arranged everything. You must leave immediately. Berthold will conduct you. So say your good-byes quickly.

SNOW WHITE: (*Turning to the Maids of Honor.*) Good-bye, Amelotte and Ermengarde and Christabel and Rosalys. Don't cry, Rosalys; it will only be a year. I kiss you all! (*She blows them a kiss. Then, slipping her little hand into Berthold's big one, says:*) Now, Berthold! (*And Berthold and the Princess Snow White go off toward the deep forest, as—*)

THE CURTAIN FALLS

SCENE II

In the Forest.

(*In front of a curtain. Snow White runs in, following an imaginary bird.*)

SNOW WHITE: It is a little brown bird. (*She whistles an imitation of the bird's call.*) Where are you trying to lead us? (*She calls back to Berthold.*) Berthold, the brown bird seems to be trying to get me to follow him. He's perched on that tree now.

(*The bird calls again, and Snow White tries to imitate the call in words.*) "Come, Snow White! Come Snow White!" I'm coming! (*And she runs on, following the bird.*) (*Berthold comes into sight. As he sees how lonely the spot is he halts.*)

BERTHOLD: It may as well be here as anywhere. Mile after mile I have put it off till the next turn or some more shadowed spot. But that is no kindness to the Princess. It must be here! (*He calls after Snow White.*) Princess! Come back!

SNOW WHITE: What is it, Berthold? (*She runs back to him.*)

BERTHOLD: Oh, dear Princess . . . (*But he cannot go on.*)

SNOW WHITE: Why are you so pale? Have you hurt yourself?

BERTHOLD: Oh, forgive me, Princess! (*He kneels before her.*)

SNOW WHITE: (*Wonderingly.*) Forgive you? For what? What is it, Berthold?

BERTHOLD: Don't look at me, Princess! Don't look at me!

SNOW WHITE: Oh, whatever it is, tell me!

BERTHOLD: The Queen . . .

SNOW WHITE: The Queen?

BERTHOLD: The Queen . . . has commanded me to . . . kill you . . . here . . . in this forest . . . now!

SNOW WHITE: (*Looking down at him in wonder.*) Kill me? I don't understand. Look at me! No, look at me! (*Slowly she raises his head. She reads the truth in his face, and with a cry springs from him.*) Oh, it's true! That was why the Queen . . . ! But you won't, will you? You won't hurt me, will you?

BERTHOLD: If it were my life alone that were at stake, I would suffer any torture rather than harm you. But the Queen . . .

SNOW WHITE: Oh, you mean—that the Queen will kill you, unless . . .

BERTHOLD: Not me, Princess, but my children. She has shut them up in the Gray Tower, and she will starve them to death unless . . .

SNOW WHITE: Oh, Berthold! Yes, she would do it too. (*With sudden resolution.*) I'll turn away and shut my eyes. But please be quick!

BERTHOLD: (*Staggering to his feet, he makes a fumbling movement for his knife.*) I cannot, Princess, I cannot! I will find some way—some way.

SNOW WHITE: Berthold, considering the way the Queen has behaved, do you think it would be very wrong to tell her a story?

BERTHOLD: Wrong?

SNOW WHITE: Because, if it weren't wrong, mightn't you *tell* her that you'd killed me without doing it?

BERTHOLD: But the proof! She has commanded me to bring her your—heart—before midnight.

SNOW WHITE: My heart?

BERTHOLD: Why not the heart of some beast? I might catch a wild pig here in the forest, and . . . . But I couldn't leave you here alone.

SNOW WHITE: But if you don't take the heart to the Queen before midnight, you know what she will do. And you must catch the wild pig before it is too dark to see.

BERTHOLD: No! I dare not leave your Highness!

SNOW WHITE: (*Pretending to be struck with a new idea.*) Berthold, could you find this place again?

BERTHOLD: Find it? Every inch of the way is branded on my brain!

SNOW WHITE: Then, tomorrow, hide some food in your tunic and come back again and we can plan.

BERTHOLD: (*Slowly.*) I might . . . but . . .

SNOW WHITE: Hurry. It's getting darker every moment. Until tomorrow.

BERTHOLD: My Princess! Heaven keep you! Until tomorrow! (*He hastens away.*)

SNOW WHITE: (*Calling after him.*) Good-bye, dearest Berthold! (*Then to herself.*) Poor Berthold, does he think the Queen will ever let him out of her sight again? She will shut him up in prison for fear he might tell. He will never come back! Good-bye forever, Berthold! (*A sudden terror seizes her.*) Oh, it's good-bye forever, *everybody!* (*She starts after him, crying.*) Berthold, come back! (*But remembering, she clasps her hands over her mouth to stifle the cry.*) What shall I do? I'm afraid— afraid! (*The call of the brown bird is heard, almost overhead. At first Snow White does not hear, and the bird repeats the cry that sounds almost like "Come, Snow White!" Snow White looks up in wonder.*) Oh, little bird, are you still here? (*The bird flies off a little way, and then perches and repeats his call.*) Are you telling me to follow you? But where? I have nowhere to go. (*Again the bird calls, and Snow White follows where he flies.*) Yes, I will follow. (*She runs out of sight among the trees, calling as she goes.*) I am coming! I am following you.

THE CURTAIN FALLS

SCENE III

The House of the Seven Dwarfs.

(*The Dwarfs' House is very tiny. It has a single wide window and one low door. Along one side of the room are ranged seven small beds of different sizes. On the other is a stone fireplace for cooking, and a pump with a barrel under the spout. In the middle of the floor stands a table with seven places laid for supper. The brown bird flies past and perches on a branch just outside, still calling for Snow White to follow. She runs up to peep in through the window.*)

SNOW WHITE: Oh, was it toward this little house you were leading me, brown bird? Please let me thank you. He's gone. (*She looks cautiously through the window into the house.*) What a queer little room! Seven beds and all so small. There must be lots of children in the family. (*She calls.*) May I come in? (*As there is no answer she knocks at the door, then opens it a crack.*) Please, may I come in to rest just for a moment? I'm lost in the forest. (*Still no answer. She steals into the room and looks about.*) Nobody at home. But they couldn't mind if I sat down just a minute. Oh, there's the children's supper all laid out. I'm so hungry! If I took just a tiny bit from each place, I'm sure they wouldn't mind. (*She goes to the table, and as she nibbles a morsel at each place she sings to herself.*)

EATING SONG

A drink of water from this cup,
Of porridge just a single sup;
Of honey just a drop to spread
Over this bit of crusty bread.
One corner of this barley-cake,
One nut—and for dessert I'll take
A single cherry of these four,
And not a single mouthful more,—
No, not a single mouthful more!

Now I ought to do something to pay for my supper. There's plenty to be done. It isn't at all a tidy house. (*She yawns; and then, shaking herself.*) Wake up, Snow White! You mustn't get sleepy yet; not till the people come home. (*But she cannot stifle another yawn.*) There's a broom. I can sweep a little. (*She begins.*) Dear me, this floor needs a good scrubbing. I might make up the beds. (*She goes to the biggest bed, but she is so tired that she sits down on it a moment before beginning.*) This one looks as if it hadn't been made for years and years and years. I wonder if it's as humpy to lie on as it is to sit on. (*She lies down to try it.*) Oh, it's more . . . It's humpy and bumpy . . . and bumpy and humpy . . . and . . . (*Her voice trails away into silence. She has fallen asleep.*) (*From afar is heard the marching of six Dwarfs as they return home. They pass the window, then file into the room. They are very small—the tallest hardly above your waist—but they are very old and their beards are long and gray. Each carries a heavy sack over his shoulder. As soon as the last is in the room, they form in line, with Blick, the eldest, at the head.*)

BLICK: Now, brothers, evening roll-call. (*He calls his own name.*) Blick! (*And answers.*) Here! (*Then he calls each of the others by name—Flick! Glick! Snick! Plick! and Whick! and each answers, "Here!" Last of all Blick calls.*) Quee! (*There is no answer. Blick shakes his head sadly.*) Late, as usual! He's been stealing again. Whatever shall we do with that boy? (*All the Dwarfs sigh, and hang their heads with shame at Quee's conduct. But Blick goes on.*) Well, brothers, what result of today's work? Half a ton of gold nuggets for mine. (*He takes a handful of enormous nuggets from his sack. The others also exhibit their treasures as they name them.*)

FLICK: A hundred weight of silver dust.

GLICK: Fifty pounds of diamonds.

SNICK: A bushel of rubies.

PLICK: A gallon of emeralds.

WHICK: A peck of opals.

BLICK: Fair, fair! But we ought to work longer hours.

FLICK: Yes, what's the good of coming home—except to sleep.

GLICK: And have supper.

FLICK: (*With scorn.*) Oh, that supper!

BLICK: I know. It's wretched. If we cook it at night, it's too hot to eat; if we cook it in the morning, it's cold and dusty by night. But what else can we do?

GLICK: And I'd rather sleep underground than in those beds.

ALL: So would we!

BLICK: I know! They haven't been made for years. But it doesn't pay to take time from digging diamonds to make beds, so what can we do?

ALL: (*Sighing.*) Nothing.

SNICK: But if we didn't come home to supper we wouldn't have to wash.

BLICK: (*Shocked.*) Oh, brothers! Washing is a duty. Hush! I think I hear Quee. (*They all cock their heads sidewise, like robins, and listen.*)

Yes, that's Quee. He *has* been stealing again! We must scold him soundly.

FLICK: It never does any good.

BLICK: But we must bring him up in the way he should go. He is the youngest of us; he's only ninety-nine next April. Clear away and ready for him. (*They pile their sacks in a corner and stand ready. Quee enters at door and stands timidly in the center. He is much the smallest, but gray bearded like the others.*)

BLICK: Quee, you are late again. (*Quee nods.*) Been stealing as usual, I suppose? (*Quee nods.*)

ALL: (*Shaking their fingers at him reprovingly.*) Oh!

BLICK: You know it's wrong!

ALL: Very, very wrong! (*Quee nods.*)

BLICK: Did anybody catch you at it? (*Quee shakes his head.*) That's good—as far as it goes.

FLICK: Did you get me a mouse trap? (*Quee nods.*)

GLICK: And my candles? (*Quee nods.*)

FLICK: And a pin? (*Quee nods.*) I'm glad of that. I've always wanted a pin.

BLICK: Of course you understand, Quee, that stealing is a sin, and that your conduct makes us very sad?

ALL: Very, very sad!

BLICK: Will you promise to reform and . . .

FLICK: (*Interrupting hastily.*) Wait, wait! Give him the list of things to get tomorrow first!

BLICK: Dear me, I almost forgot! Quee, tie a string round your finger to remember by. Now, what do you all want?

THE DWARFS: (*Speaking in rapid succession; each names one article.*)
A chain. A plane. A weather-vane.
A hat. A mat. A pussy-cat.
A pound of brass.
A pane of glass.
A crock. A lock. An eight-day clock.

A can. A pan. A palm-leaf fan.
A tack. A sack. An almanac.
  A can of soup.
  A chicken-coop.
A map. A cap. A snappy trap.

A pole. A bowl. A baker's roll.
A rake. A cake. A pound of steak.
  A peck of meal.
  A pickled eel.
A slate. A plate. A ten-pound weight.

BLICK: That's all for tomorrow. But remember, young man, if "It's a sin to steal a pin," how much worse it must be to steal a ten-pound weight. You realize that? (*Quee nods sadly.*) Brothers, we shall have to correct him again tomorrow night. He is incorrigible.

ALL: (*Mournfully.*) In-cor-rig-ible!

BLICK: Now for the evening washing. Get the basin, Quee. (*Glad that his daily scolding is over, Quee runs cheerfully and fetches a basin of water, a big sponge and a towel. "No flinching now, brothers," cries Blick. "Line up! Right faces!" All except Quee stand close together, and thrust their faces over one another's shoulders, with eyes closed. Running down the line, Quee washes all their right cheeks with one long sweep of his sponge. "Reverse!" cries Blick. They all turn and face in the opposite direction; and Quee, running back up the line, washes all their other cheeks. "Right faces!" cries Blick. With a single sweep of his towel, Quee dries all their right cheeks; and when Blick commands "Reverse," he dries the opposite sides in the same neat and speedy way. And so the Evening Washing is finished.*)

BLICK: There! That's over for another twenty-four hours.

ALL: Thank goodness!

BLICK: Oh, come! It's quick and comparatively painless. Only—Quee gets dirtier and dirtier every year.

FLICK: *Somebody* must wash the others.

GLICK: He's the youngest.

WHICK: It's his duty.

BLICK: Nevertheless, he's a disgrace to the family. (*Quee bows his head in shame.*)

GLICKS: And now—(*With a heavy sigh.*)—supper!

ALL: (*Sadly.*) Supper!

FLICK: No hurry! It's been getting cold ever since breakfast. (*With lagging feet they march to the table, and are about to eat, when Blick starts back in surprise.*)

BLICK: I say!
Someone's been drinking from my cup!

FLICK: Someone has eat my porridge up!

GLICK: And took my honey!

SNICK: See, they spread
It all across my crust of bread!

PLICK: Someone's been at my barley-cake!

WHICK: Eaten my nut—and dared to take
The biggest cherry of Quee's four!

ALL: And, goodness-gracious! how much
more?

(*They gaze at each other in amazement.*)

BLICK: (*Whispering.*) Brothers, there must be robbers in the house!

FLICK: Or pirates!

GLICK: Or burglars!

BLICK: Probably burglars. If so, they're under the beds; burglars always are. Hush! Let every man look under his own bed. (*Each Dwarf creeps to his bed and peers cautiously under it. Then, one after the other, they rise, shaking their heads and saying: "Nobody under my bed!" Blick is the last. But as he rises he sees Snow White, and exclaims in a tense whisper, "But—there's something in it! Look, brothers!" The Dwarfs creep about Blick's bed, and holding their lanterns high, gaze down upon the sleeping Snow White.*)

GLICK: (*Whispering.*) What is it?

FLICK: I know! It's a child.

BLICK: No, it's a girl. I saw one once.

FLICK: Well, girl or child, it's the most beautiful thing I ever saw.

GLICK: Is it tame, or will it fly away like a bird when it wakes up?

FLICK: Oh, children are tame—and they can talk.

ALL: (*In rapture.*) Oh!

BLICK: But this isn't a child, it's a girl. I don't think *girls* can talk. (*They all heave a sigh of disappointment.*)

FLICK: I wish she'd stay with us just so that we could look at her.

BLICK: She won't.

GLICK: Why not?

BLICK: Of *course* she won't. Are we handsome, or young, or tall? In fact, aren't we dwarfs? (*They all hang their heads.*)

FLICK: But if we didn't tell her that?

BLICK: Flick, I wonder at you! Besides, she might find it out.

GLICK: She's beautifully white and clean. Look, she's been trying to sweep.

FLICK: I can't bear to think of her leaving us.

BLICK: I'm going to stay up all night just to watch her.

GLICK: Do you think there's any way we could persuade her to stay?

BLICK: I'm afraid not.

FLICK: Even if we laid presents on her bed?

BLICK: What kind of presents? Gold and diamonds?

FLICK: Oh, not common things like that! Really valuable things like— my jack-knife!

BLICK: Oh, things like *that!* It might. But I'm afraid not.

FLICK: We might try, anyhow. Let each man give the most valuable thing he has in the world.

BLICK: (*Collecting the gifts. Each names his present lovingly as he takes it from his pocket.*) My thimble!

SNICK: My almanac.

PLICK: My empty bottle.

GLICK: And—my pet frog.

BLICK: (*Laying the gifts gently on the foot of Snow White's bed.*) There, that may help. But no! It's no use, brothers. There is Quee!

ALL: (*Hopelessly.*) Yes! There is Quee!

FLICK: We might hide him?

BLICK: She'd be sure to find him sooner or later.

GLICK: He might reform.

BLICK: But we never could pretend he wasn't dirty. He hasn't been washed for fifty years.

FLICK: (*With a sudden inspiration.*) Brothers, why not wash him now?

GLICK: We might!

ALL: We *will!*

BLICK: It must be done at once or he won't be dry by morning. Get the utensils.

BLICK: (*Marching to the pump.*) Here's the pump to douse him with!

SNICK: (*Fetching the basin.*) Here are suds to souse him with!

FLICK: (*Bringing the sponge.*) Here's the sponge to sop him with!

PLICK: (*Hurrying with the broom.*) Here's the broom to mop him with!

GLICK: (*Running with the soap.*) Here's the soap to scrub him with!

WHICK: (*Waving the towel.*) Here's the cloth to rub him with! (*They surround Quee.*)

BLICK: Quee, you are going to be . . .

ALL: (*In a tremendous whisper.*) Washed! (*They carry him to the barrel, plump him in with a great splash and pump on him. Then, as they scrub and rub and soap and stir him about in the water, they chant in chorus:*)

THE DWARFS: Here's the pump to *douse* him with!
　　Here are suds to *souse* him with!
　　Here's the sponge to *sop* him with!

Here's the broom to *mop* him with!
Here's the soap to *scrub* him with!
Here's the cloth to *rub* him with!
Rub! Scrub! Mop! Sop! Souse! Douse!
  Rub!
    Scrub!
      Mop!
        Sop!
          Souse!
            Douse!

(*In their excitement they forget to be quiet. Snow White stirs in her sleep; then wakes and sits up.*)

SNOW WHITE: Where is this? Oh, there are the children that live here. Why, they're *not* children. They're little old men. They'll never let me stay with them. (*She rises, and standing by the bed says shyly:*) I beg your pardon. (*The Dwarfs turn suddenly. Snow White makes a little curtsy.*) I'm sorry if I've disturbed you; but I was lost in the forest, and when I saw your house I was so tired and hungry I came in and took a little food—without asking. Then I'm afraid I fell asleep. (*She waits for an answer, but the Dwarfs gaze at her in silence, so she falters on.*) I'd pay for it, but I haven't any money. (*She stops. Again a silence.*) So all I can do is to say, "Thank you—and—good night!" (*She moves reluctantly to the door. The Dwarfs sigh deeply. She turns for a farewell curtsy.*) Thank you *very* much. Good night! (*There is no answer except another heavy sigh from the Dwarfs. With sudden pity she bursts out:*) Oh, you're not dumb, are you?

BLICK: (*Clearing his throat.*) No, we're not dumb; but you're a girl, aren't you?

SNOW WHITE: (*Wonderingly.*) Yes—I'm a girl.

BLICK: Or a child?

SNOW WHITE: Well, I'm not very old.

BLICK: We don't know how to talk to young people.

SNOW WHITE: Well, most grown people begin, "Why, how you've grown." And usually the next thing is, "How do you like your school?"

BLICK: "How you've grown."

FLICK: "How do you like your school?"

SNOW WHITE: (*Smiling, but a little embarrassed.*) Well—perhaps it *is* a little late for conversation. It's long past bedtime, isn't it?

BLICK: Long past.

SNOW WHITE: There are six of you and—seven beds, aren't there?

BLICK: (*Hastily putting the cover on the barrel.*) Yes, there are seven beds.

SNOW WHITE: Oh, before I go, perhaps I ought to tidy the one I slept in. (*She goes to the bed.*) What are these things on it? Oh! One's a frog. It's alive!

BLICK: (*Edging toward her eagerly.*) They were meant to be presents.

SNOW WHITE: Oh—somebody's birthday?

FLICK: No, it's nobody's birthday.

SNOW WHITE: Then I don't see—?

BLICK: They were meant to be presents for you.

SNOW WHITE: For me?

FLICK: We were afraid you wouldn't like them.

SNOW WHITE: But I *do* like them. Do you mean that you're not angry with me?

FLICK: Angry with you!

BLICK: We think you're the most wonderful thing we've ever seen!

SNOW WHITE: Oh, you darlings! Oh, I beg your pardon. Perhaps that wasn't respectful.

BLICK: Nobody ever called us "darlings" before, so we don't know.

FLICK: But it *sounds* nice.

SNOW WHITE: And you wouldn't mind if I should stay tonight—only just tonight?

BLICK: We wouldn't mind if you should stay forever—only just forever!

SNOW WHITE: Forever?

FLICK: Oh, will you?

SNOW WHITE: Oh, will you let me? Please let me live with you. I could be so useful.

BLICK: But our housekeeping . . .

SNOW WHITE: That's just how I could be useful. I can cook and sweep and make beds, and—oh, lots of things.

BLICK: (*Solemnly.*) Will you excuse us a moment, please? (*He beckons the Dwarfs together and whispers:*) Did I hear right? Did she say she would stay?

ALL: (*Eagerly.*) She did!

BLICK: Whatever shall we say?

ALL: (*Perplexed.*) We don't know.

BLICK: (*Turning to Snow White.*) Er—could you tell us what it's usual to say when you're so glad that it almost *bursts* you?

SNOW WHITE: Would "Hip, hip, hurrah!" do?

BLICK: It *sounds* right. (*Slowly.*) Hip, hip, hurrah.

ALL: (*Solemnly trying the new word.*) Hip, hip, hurrah. (*Then deciding that it does fit their feelings, they shout it in a joyous outburst.*) Hip, hip, hurrah!

SNOW WHITE: (*Clapping her hands.*) Oh, please, may I say "Hip, hip, hurrah!" too? I am so glad and grateful.

ALL: Hip, hip, hurrah!

SNOW WHITE: (*Remembering.*) But—you may not want me when I tell you who I am. It may be dangerous . . .

BLICK: (*Hopefully.*) Do *you* steal?

SNOW WHITE: No, not so bad as that. My name is Snow White. This morning I was a princess. (*She sits on Blick's bed to tell her story. She is getting sleepy again.*)

FLICK: What's a princess?

SNOW WHITE: Why, the daughter of a king and queen. My stepmother is Queen Brangomar. She hates me so much that I'm afraid there must be something horrid about me . . . (*She is very drowsy now.*) But I'm sure Prince Florimond liked me . . . away . . . (*She sinks back onto the bed and her eyes close. The Dwarfs put their fingers to their lips. Then she revives a little and murmurs:*)—for a year and a day . . . Oh, I'm so sleepy. Please mayn't I tell you tomorrow morning? All I can think of now is "good night."

BLICK: (*Softly.*) Good night, Snow White!

SNOW WHITE: (*Almost asleep.*) Good night!

FLICK: Good night, Snow White.

SNOW WHITE: Good—night.

GLICK: Good night, Snow White.

SNOW WHITE: Good . . . (*There is a silence.*)

BLICK: (*Whispering.*) Brothers, she's asleep. But she'll stay!

ALL: (*Whispering.*) Hip, hip, hurrah!

FLICK: I'm so happy I'm sad!

GLICK: (*Wiping away a tear with his beard.*) I'm so happy it's making me cry!

SNICK: We're all so happy! (*They all wipe their eyes with their beards.*)

BLICK: We mustn't wake her. Not a sound now. We'll be quietest in bed. (*Each Dwarf creeps toward his bed.*)

BLICK: But she's in my bed! Well, I'll take Flick's. (*He moves to the next bed, jumps in and pulls the clothes over his head—Dwarfs always sleep with the bedclothes over their heads. So each of the others has to move up one bed. As they pop in, one after another, and cover their heads, they cry:*)

FLICK: I'll take Glick's.

GLICK: I'll take Snick's.

SNICK: I'll take Plick's.

PLICK: I'll take Whick's.

WHICK: I'll take Quee's.

BLICK: (*Sitting up suddenly.*) Brothers, we've forgotten Quee! (*They all sit bolt upright. Then in a whisper they call:*)

ALL: Q—u—e—e! (*The cover over the water barrel is pushed up and Quee's head appears. He is very wet, but washed as clean as a new doll.*)

BLICK: Quee, she'll stay, but you'll have to sleep in the barrel.

QUEE: Hip, hip, hurrah! (*He disappears again into the barrel, and—*)

THE CURTAIN FALLS

SCENE IV

Where the Witch Lives.

(*In front of a curtain. A fire blazes in the middle of the floor, and over it stands a boiling cauldron. The Witch's three Cats, Long Tail, Short Tail, and Lack Tail are watching the cauldron, and occasionally stir the brew. They are extraordinarily large for cats—almost as large as little boys.*

After a moment, Witch Hex flies home, riding her broomstick, a basket on her arm.)

THE WITCH: (*Entering and setting her broomstick away.*) There! Glad to be home at last. Where is Queen Brangomar? I thought she'd be here before me with Snow White's heart. I had to go halfway to the Moon for the other ingredients for that magic hair-restorer; but I've got them all—safe in my basket. Now help me mix it. We must put all the other ingredients in before Brangomar comes. (*The Witch and her Cats dance round and round the cauldron in a mystic circle; and as Hex throws the various things she has collected into the brew she chants:*)

THE MAGIC MIXTURE

THE WITCH: A hair from the tail of the ride-a-cock Horse;
    A lace from the Old Woman's shoe,
      A bit of the tuffet
      Of Little Miss Muffet;
    The blast that the Little Boy Blue.
  A tear of the Kittens who lost all their mittens
      When they began to cry.
      A sniff from Miss Mary

When she was contrary;
The plum from Jack Horner's pie.
A slice of green cheese from the Man in the Moon;
The tails of the Three Blind Mice;
A bone from the cupboard
Of Old Mother Hubbard;
And little girls' sugar and spice.

(*When she has finished the mixture, the Witch sniffs the steam from the cauldron, and then sips a little of the brew from the ladle.*)

THE WITCH: Tastes good, and hot enough. Yes, the ladle is red hot. Now that's all except the heart. Set the kettle away to cool. (*The Cats take the cauldron from the fire and set it in a corner.*)

THE WITCH: I'm chilly! It's cold up by the Moon. (*She tucks up her skirts and sits down comfortably on the blazing fire.*) Ah, that feels good! Nothing to do now but wait for Snow White's heart. But *then* you shall see what you shall see—a beautiful head of long, wavy hair for me. Ah, here's Brangomar at last! (*Queen Brangomar enters. The Cats bow low to her.*)

THE QUEEN: Sorry to be late, dear Hexy, but Berthold didn't return till morning, and then I personally had to see that he was locked up in the Gray Tower.

THE WITCH: Did he bring the heart?

THE QUEEN: Yes, here it is. Oh, how I hated that child!

THE WITCH: Hair restorer's just ready for it. Help me up. Now the heart. (*She takes it and hobbles to the cauldron.*) Receipt says that when I add this the brew will turn a beautiful pink. Then I dip my head, and presto! long and lovely hair. Now watch! (*She drops the heart into the cauldron, which steams vigorously.*)

THE WITCH: (*Dancing with delight.*) See it steam!

THE QUEEN: But it's turning green, not pink.

THE WITCH: So it is! Still, there can't be any mistake; I was most careful. Well, here goes for a handsome head of hair. You'll hardly know me when you see me again. (*She dips her head into the steaming cauldron, and then raises it proudly.*) How's that? Pretty fine, eh? (*Something has surely sprouted on the Witch's bald pate. The Queen looks carefully, and then bursts into a peal of laughter; and the Cats roll on the ground with mirth.*)

THE WITCH: What are you laughing at? Feels very thick and curly. Stop that cackling!

THE QUEEN: (*Hardly able to speak.*) Oh, my dear Hex! Ha, ha, ha! You have—ha, ha, ha!—a headful of pig-tails!

THE WITCH: Pig-tails? (*She feels them.*) Nonsense! It's short and curly.

THE QUEEN: Not pig-tails, Hexy! Your head is covered with little white, curly tails of pigs!

THE WITCH: Tails of pigs? Tails of pigs? (*She feels the growth carefully.*) By hopscotch, they *are* pigs' tails! Stop laughing! If the joke's on anybody, it's on *you*. Instead of a *human* heart, your precious huntsman has brought back the heart of a pig; and Miss Snow White is alive at this moment. Ha, ha, for *you*!

THE QUEEN: (*Her laughter broken off short.*) What? Snow White alive?

THE WITCH: If these are pigs' tails, that was a pig's heart. Ask your Magic Mirror if Snow White's not alive.

THE QUEEN: (*Seizing the Mirror which hangs from her girdle.*) Mirror, mirror, in my hand,
    Who's the fairest in the land?

THE MIRROR: (*Answering.*) You, who hold me in your hand,
    You *were* the fairest in the land;
    But today, I answer true,
    Snow White is more fair than you.

THE QUEEN: Snow White alive! (*She starts to dash the Mirror to the ground.*)

THE WITCH: (*Seizing it.*) Be careful of that Mirror, I tell you!
    Mirror, Mirror, truly tell,
    Where does Princess Snow White dwell?

THE MIRROR: 'Mid the ancient forest dells
    With the Seven Dwarfs she dwells.

THE WITCH: You see? It's perfectly clear. That huntsman of yours let Snow White escape, and brought back a pig's heart to fool us with.

Snow White has found the house of the Seven Dwarfs—and there you are, my merry lady!

THE QUEEN: The Seven Dwarfs? Who are they?

THE WITCH: Rather nice little men; sort of gnomes. Live all alone.

THE QUEEN: (*Wrapping her cloak about her.*) Where?

THE WITCH: Oh, ho! Intend to deal with Snow White yourself this time, do you?

THE QUEEN: Where do they live?

THE WITCH: The usual way is about twenty miles over the mountains, but there's a short cut I know.

THE QUEEN: Give me a knife or a dagger, quickly!

THE WITCH: What? Walk into the Dwarfs' house, knife in hand, and crown on your head like that? *I'd* sooner dance on a hornet's nest.

THE QUEEN: But what shall I do? She's alive! She's more beautiful than I! Tell me some way!

THE WITCH: There's only one safe way . . .

THE QUEEN: Yes?

THE WITCH: First, I must transform you into a different-looking person altogether.

THE QUEEN: And then?

THE WITCH: And then give you some means of disposing of Snow White. Long Tail, fetch me the magic Killing Things.

THE QUEEN: Yes—yes! (*The Cats fetch a box full of strange articles from offstage.*)

THE WITCH: (*Examining them.*) The dancing slippers. When you put those on you dance yourself to death. But they're too big for her. The doll you stick pins in. That would take too long. Oh, here are two good ones. The poisoned apple. (*She holds it up.*) Beautiful, isn't it? The red side is poisoned, but the other is perfectly good. If they swallow the least bit of the red side, down they drop. Then, if they lie still while you count one hundred, they're as dead as a tombstone. Or, here's the poisoned comb.

THE QUEEN: Let me see it! (*She seizes the jeweled comb.*)

THE WITCH: Put that in Snow White's hair and all's over with her. It works instantly. Which do you want?

THE QUEEN: Let me have both. If I fail with one, I'll try the other. Oh, how my fingers itch to set this in her black hair! Now what disguise?

THE WITCH: Disguise? Oh, yes! Long Tail, bring me the Trans-formation Mixtures. (*Long Tail brings an odd-shaped bottle filled with purple liquid.*)

THE WITCH: I'll read the label. (*She reads.*) "One teaspoon before eating." Well, I declare, I've written out the dose most carefully, but totally forgotten what it changes people into. But that's easily remedied. A drop in the cauldron, and you'll see for yourself. Now watch! (*She pours a few drops into the cauldron. Instantly a cloud of steam rises.*)

THE WITCH: Ah, see! The Old Pedlar-Woman disguise. Just the thing! You could pretend to be selling Snow White the comb.

THE QUEEN: I'd hate to look so ugly.

THE WITCH: Vanity is always getting in your way. Well, it's all I've got. (*She produces a spoon and uncorks the bottle.*)

THE QUEEN: (*Hesitating.*) Is the taste very bad?

THE WITCH: Vile! Really, one of the nastiest tastes I ever made. Open your mouth.

THE QUEEN: (*Shrinking.*) Er—is being transformed painful?

THE WITCH: No—o-o-o, but unpleasant. Feels as though you were being turned inside out like a glove. Open your mouth.

THE QUEEN: I think I'll wait till tomorrow.

THE WITCH: Oh, ho! Here, Cats, here's sport for you. Get the black mantle. (*The Cats get a large black cloth and advance toward the Queen.*)

THE QUEEN: What are they going to do?

THE WITCH: Wrap you up so that you can't scratch while I pour this down your throat.

THE QUEEN: But I'm not ready! I must go home first! (*She makes a dash for the door, but the Cats are before her. Then begins a lively chase, the Queen running and dodging, the Cats following and trying to throw the mantle over her head. The Witch enjoys it all hugely, crying: "Run, Brangomar!" "Catch her, Lack Tail!" and slapping her knees with delight till she is quite out of breath. At last the Cats succeed in cornering the Queen, and throw the mantle over her head. She runs again—darting offstage, back on stage.*)

THE WITCH: Well done, Cats, well done! Trip her up and hold her down. (*This the Cats do. Then the Witch sits on the squirming Queen; and humming happily to herself, pours out a spoonful of the mixture.*)

THE WITCH: Now, where *is* her mouth?

THE QUEEN: (*In a smothered voice.*) I won't take it! I won't!

THE WITCH: Oh, *there* it is! Thank you, Brangomar. (*She pours the dose through the cloth into the Queen's mouth; and as the Queen writhes she goes on.*) I know it tastes bad, but nothing to make such a fuss about. (*Suddenly she holds up a warning finger.*) I feel her changing! Do you? (*The Cats nod.*) Done! Up with her, off with the mantle, and let's see the result. (*The Cats draw off the mantle. Lo! the Queen has been transformed into the likeness of the old Pedlar-Woman.*)

THE WITCH: Splendid! Wouldn't recognize you myself, Brangomar. Wasn't half as bad as you thought it would be, was it?

THE PEDLAR-WOMAN: (*Crossly.*) It was awful! Why—is this *my* voice?

THE WITCH: Of course. Different voice with every disguise.

THE PEDLAR-WOMAN: I'm all cramps too. How do I change back?

THE WITCH: Dear me; lucky you thought to ask. I might have forgotten. Just sing:
"Peas porridge hot,
    Peas porridge cold—"
but sing it backwards, like this:
    "Old days nine,
    Pot the in porridge peas,
    Cold porridge peas,
    Hot porridge peas."
That turns you right side out again.

THE PEDLAR-WOMAN: I must remember. Let me see:—"Old days nine . . ." (*But the Witch claps her hand over Brangomar's mouth.*)

THE WITCH: Gracious woman, don't say it yet! We'd have all this to do over again. Really, you are the most senseless—! Here, take the apple and the comb and be off with you. I've had quite enough of you for one day.

THE PEDLAR-WOMAN: Now for Snow White! Oh, Hex, once I see her lying dead—dead before my own eyes . . .

THE WITCH: (*Interrupting.*) If you use the apple, don't forget to count to one hundred!

THE PEDLAR-WOMAN: It will be the happiest moment of my life!

THE WITCH: Nasty disposition!

THE PEDLAR-WOMAN: (*Going to the door.*) You shan't escape me this time, my little beauty! You have no foolish Berthold to deal with now, but Brangomar, Brangomar her very self! (*And off she strides toward the house of the Seven Dwarfs. Left alone with her Cats, the Witch goes to the blazing fire and again sits down upon it.*)

THE WITCH: Poor little Snow White! I'm really sorry for her. I don't bear her any ill will in spite of my pigs' tails. Long Tail, my looking-glass. (*Long Tail brings the looking-glass, and Witch Hex studies her new appearance carefully.*)

THE WITCH: Oh, not so bad, after all! They're quite becoming.

THE CURTAIN FALLS

SCENE V

The House of the Seven Dwarfs.

(*The room is the same as before, but tidy. The Dwarfs stand in line ready to march to work. Snow White kisses Quee, who is at the end of the line.*)

SNOW WHITE: There! Now you are all ready. Off you go!

BLICK: Couldn't you please give us all another kiss?

SNOW WHITE: (*Merrily.*) No, indeed!

GLICK: A *little* one?

BLICK: You see none of us, ever, er—should I say "ate" or "tasted"?—a kiss till you came; so perhaps we *are* a little eager about them.

SNOW WHITE: I should say you were! Why, you're perfect children about kisses and games. And that reminds me, you're not to come home in the middle of the morning to play. Now not a moment before five today, because—(*She beckons them together and whispers.*)—this is a secret—I'm going to make a cake with pink sugar frosting for supper. Now, off with you!

BLICK: Well, brothers, ready! Today we go into the forest for firewood. March! (*In their usual military file the Dwarfs march off into the forest. Snow White stands in the doorway, waving her hand after them till they are out of sight. Then with a sigh of content she returns to the room.*)

SNOW WHITE: Oh, I'm so happy here. Of course, I miss my dear Maids of Honor and the others; but the Dwarfs are so funny and loving and kind. (*She looks out of the door again.*) It's a beautiful day. (*With a little pensive sigh.*) I wonder if I shall ever see Prince Florimond again. (*But she checks herself sharply.*) You wonder about him much too often! Remember, you're not a Princess anymore, only just housekeeper to the Seven Dwarfs. Now for that cake! (*As she turns away Queen Brangomar, disguised as the old Pedlar-Woman, peers cautiously through the window. Seeing that Snow White is alone, she leans over the sill.*)

THE PEDLAR-WOMAN: Good morning, dearie.

SNOW WHITE: (*Her hand springing to her heart.*) Oh—!

THE PEDLAR-WOMAN: Did I frighten you, dearie? No harm in an old Pedlar-Woman. I've come a weary way. I'm that worn and footsore . . .

SNOW WHITE: Oh, *do* come in!

THE PEDLAR-WOMAN: (*Entering.*) Thank you, dearie. I'll just bar the door behind me for fear of the rheumatic drafts. *You'll* buy some little thing, my pet; some pretty thing?

SNOW WHITE: I'm sorry, but . . .

THE PEDLAR-WOMAN: Don't any of my wares tempt you?
Here's ribbons and laces,
And gentlemen's braces,
A feather as white as foam;
An outfit for cross-stitch,
The egg of an ostrich,
And oh, what a beautiful comb,
That comb!
Just see, what a beautiful comb!

SNOW WHITE: I've no money.

THE PEDLAR-WOMAN: You gave me kind words and bid me in friendly.
I'll tell you what, if you've no money I'll make you a free gift, sweetheart.

SNOW WHITE: I couldn't really!

THE PEDLAR-WOMAN: I'm set on it, my lamb, set on it! Name your choice and yours it shall be. Now what do you say to this comb?

SNOW WHITE: That? Why, that's the *finest* thing you have.

THE PEDLAR-WOMAN: Just why I give it to you, my dear. And lovely it will look, a-shining in your black hair.

SNOW WHITE: (*Shrinking away.*) No, no! I couldn't take anything so valuable!

THE PEDLAR-WOMAN: Come, dearie, just let me put it in for you, and *then* if you don't like the look of it—well, I'll say no more and be on my way.

SNOW WHITE: I *should* like to see how it looks—

THE PEDLAR-WOMAN: That's my sweetheart. Now sit you down— (*Snow White sits on a stool.*)—and shut your eyes so you shan't peep till it's in. Are they shut?

SNOW WHITE: (*Laughing.*) Yes, tight shut!

THE PEDLAR-WOMAN: Then here goes! (*But just as she is about to insert the comb, Snow White springs up again.*)

SNOW WHITE: No! I'd better not even see how it looks. I'd be tempted to keep it, and I mustn't. No-thank-you-very-much!

THE PEDLAR-WOMAN: Wait, wait! I've something better than that. Look—a lovely apple, with a cheek as red as your own! Here, you eat the pretty red half. Taste it, dearie.

SNOW WHITE: Well, thank you. (*She bites the apple. Suddenly she grasps her throat, whirls about once, falls, and then lies quite still.*)

THE PEDLAR-WOMAN: (*Watches her for a moment, then cries exultingly.*) Ah, ha! So, my dear step-daughter, Queen Brangomar laughs last, after all! Now to count one hundred while the poison works. (*And she begins to count.*) One, two, three, four, five—(*Suddenly she stops to listen.*) What's that? (*Steps are heard outside the little house. They come nearer. There is a knock at the door.*)

BLICK: (*Outside.*) Snow White, it's us, the Dwarfs. Open the door. (*He knocks again.*)

THE PEDLAR-WOMAN: (*In terror.*) The Dwarfs! I must hide her! Where, where? (*She looks about for a place to hide Snow White, then drags the big table over her and pulls the tablecloth down. Meantime the Dwarfs are knocking more and more impatiently.*)

BLICK: Please open, Snow White. We haven't come back for games, honestly. We want to go down into the mines. (*The Pedlar-Woman crouches along the wall, looking for some way to escape.*)

FLICK: (*Outside, calling.*) Snow White!

ALL THE DWARFS: (*Calling together.*) Snow White!

BLICK: Brothers, there's something wrong! The window! (*The Dwarfs run to the window and look in. They see the crouching Pedlar-Woman.*)

THE PEDLAR-WOMAN: (*Realizing that she is caught, ducking and curtsying.*) Oh, it's you, my little gentlemen!

BLICK: Open the door!

THE PEDLAR-WOMAN: Yes, indeed, your honors! At once, your honors! (*But as she goes to unbar the door she continues to count under her breath.*) Twenty-one, twenty-two, twenty-three, twenty-four . . .

BLICK: (*Beating on the door.*) Quickly, I tell you!

THE PEDLAR-WOMAN: Yes, your honors! (*She throws the door open. The Dwarfs rush in fiercely, their knives drawn, and surround her.*)

BLICK: What are you doing here?

FLICK: Where is Snow White?

THE PEDLAR-WOMAN: But I've scarce breath to tell you. Just give me thirty seconds—or thirty-one or thirty-two or thirty-three . . .

BLICK: What are you mumbling?

THE PEDLAR-WOMAN: I was passing by with my basket o' wares— (*Blick makes a threatening gesture and she hurries on with a little cry—*)—just passing—when your sweet little lady calls me to step in.

BLICK: Where is she now?

THE PEDLAR-WOMAN: She went into the forest on an errand, and bid me mind the house till she got back.

FLICK: How long has she been gone?

THE PEDLAR-WOMAN: A matter of seconds, your honor. Fifty seconds, maybe, or fifty-one or fifty-two or fifty-three or fifty-four . . .

BLICK: Well, you need stay no longer. Go!

THE PEDLAR-WOMAN: Yes, your honors. Certainly, your honors. (*She goes curtsying to the door, but turns to say:*) Could you tell a poor peddling body how far it might be to the next town? Is it fifty-five miles now, or fifty-six, or fifty-seven, or . . .

BLICK: (*Starting toward her fiercely.*) Be off, or we'll lay hands on you! (*With a little scream the Pedlar-Woman darts out and shuts the door; but she sticks her head in again to say:*)

THE PEDLAR-WOMAN: Before I go, my kind little gentlemen, let me give you an old gypsy-woman's blessing. It's a little rhyme, like. (*And she chants:*)
"Old days nine,
  Pot the in porridge peas,
  Cold porridge peas,
  Hot porridge peas."

(*As she says the last words she claps the door shut. But the transforming charm works instantly; and it is Queen Brangomar in her royal robes who, with a mocking laugh, sweeps past the window and rushes off into the forest, still counting as she goes: "Fifty-eight, fifty-nine, sixty . . ." till her voice dies away in the distance. For a moment the Dwarfs stand amazed. Then Blick cries out:*)

BLICK: Brothers! That wasn't a pedlar-woman!

FLICK: It looked like a queen!

BLICK: Was it magic? Brothers, something is wrong! (*Suddenly he spies something on the floor near the table. It is one of Snow White's slippers that came off when she fell.*)

BLICK: What's that? Her slipper! She is here! Here is her slipper! Search the house! (*The Dwarfs rush back into the room and begin to seek under the beds and behind the pump; but Flick pulls up the table-cloth and cries out:*)

FLICK: Look! Here she is! (*They move the table away and kneel about Snow White. Blick raises her head to his knee.*)

GLICK: Is she hurt?

PLICK: She has fainted.

BLICK: Is she breathing? There is no hope, my brothers. There is nothing we can do. Our Snow White is dead.

FLICK: Yet, see, her lips have not paled, and her skin is still as fair as snow. I cannot bear to think of hiding her away in the black ground.

WHICK: Nor I.

BLICK: Brothers, let us make her a coffin all of crystal, so that we may see her always.

FLICK: Yes. And set it in the dell where she used to go for flowers.

BLICK: And watch over her there, day and night, all our lives long.

FLICK: This we will do.

BLICK: We will never leave you, Snow White! (*One by one they kneel about her silently.*)

AGAIN THE CURTAIN FALLS

SCENE VI

A Hallway and The Throne Room of the Palace.

(*In front of a curtain. Sir Dandiprat is standing in the middle, surrounded by all the Maids of Honor. He looks puzzled and distressed.*)

ROSALYS: (*To Sir Dandiprat.*) Of *course* it's today that Snow White is coming home. That's why we're wearing our best clothes.

AMELOTTE: It's a year and a day today.

CHRISTABEL: She went away on the twentieth of June.

ROSALYS: Last year.

ASTOLAINE: And today is the twenty-first.

ROSALYS: This year.

CHRISTABEL: So it *must* be a year and a day today.

ROSALYS: Prince Florimond comes today too.

SIR DANDIPRAT: What? Prince Florimond *too*?

ASTOLAINE: Of course—to be engaged to Snow White.

SIR DANDIPRAT: The Prince coming, and nothing arranged—nothing! Nobody ever tells me anything at this Court. He may be here any moment, and all the army out hunting for Berthold. I shall go distracted! I shall go distracted! (*He hurries out.*)

ASTOLAINE: I didn't really believe a year and a day would *ever* be over. Did you?

CHRISTABEL: I hope she gets here before the Prince does. What do you think he'll say to Snow White when he does come?

ROSALYS: Why, of course he'll say, "Princess, I love you to distractedness. I should like to marry you at once, please."

GUINIVERE: Oh! And what will *she* say?

ROSALYS: Probably she'll say: "I should be very much obliged."

ASTOLAINE: And that's that! (*Trumpets are heard off. Sir Dandiprat rushes in.*)

SIR DANDIPRAT: The Prince is here! The Prince is here! We're keeping his Highness waiting! Quickly, quickly, to the Throne Room. (*Curtains open. The Throne Room. The Maids and Sir Dandiprat take their proper places. Prince Florimond enters. All bow low.*)

SIR DANDIPRAT: I'm sorry to have kept your Highness waiting. I'll inform the Queen at once. She's been expecting you all the morning. Just a moment, your Highness. (*He exits.*)

THE PRINCE: Has the Princess returned?

ROSALYS: (*Curtsying.*) Not yet, your Highness, but we expect her every moment.

THE PRINCE: Is she well?

ROSALYS: I don't know, your Highness. She hasn't written to us since she went away.

THE PRINCE: Not a single letter? (*Sir Dandiprat reappears and announces:*)

SIR DANDIPRAT: Her Majesty, the Queen. (*Page enters and sounds trumpet. Queen Brangomar enters; and with a haughty nod to the Prince, sweeps to the throne.*)

THE QUEEN: I totally forgot you were coming today, Florimond. Poor boy, I've sad news for you. I deeply regret to say that Snow White is dead.

THE PRINCE: Snow White—dead . . . ! Snow White . . . dead . . . ?

THE QUEEN: I sent at least eighteen doctors, but it was useless. Everything possible has been done. I built a splendid monument over her grave. (*Suddenly she sees the stern figure of Berthold. He has been standing silent and unnoticed in the doorway. She cries out.*) Berthold!

BERTHOLD: (*Advancing.*) Yes, Berthold! Berthold, come to punish you!

THE QUEEN: Seize him! Arrest him! Dandiprat, the soldiers!

SIR DANDIPRAT: The soldiers are all out hunting for him!

BERTHOLD: I fear neither your soldiers nor your witchcraft. No army, no court, no kingdom will be yours when I have told my tale.

THE QUEEN: (*Shrieking.*) Don't listen to him! He is mad! I imprisoned him because he went mad.

BERTHOLD: No, for fear that I should tell of your wickedness. But I escaped, and fled back to the forest to search for Snow White. Last night, in a secret dell, I found—(*His voice falters.*)

THE PRINCE: You found her?

BERTHOLD: Yes. But she lay in a coffin all made of shining crystal, as fair as if she were but asleep. And guarding her, day and night, were Seven Dwarfs.

THE QUEEN: But she is dead?

BERTHOLD: Yes, and you did the deed! Look! (*The Seven Dwarfs bearing Snow White's crystal coffin covered with a pall of flowers appear.*)

THE QUEEN: The Dwarfs! Merciful stars, what are they bringing? No! No! Take it away! You shall not bring her here! You shall not! (*Rushing from the throne, the Queen hurls herself on the Dwarfs to prevent their setting down the coffin. So sudden is her onslaught that they cannot resist; and with a crash of crystal the coffin is overturned. With a cry of horror the Dwarfs surround it. For a moment the Queen stands apart. She seizes the Magic Mirror that hangs at her girdle, and with trembling lips whispers:*)

Mirror, Mirror, in my hand,
Who's the fairest in the land?

(*What the Mirror answers will never be known, for hardly has it begun to speak when, with a cry of rage, the Queen dashes it into a thousand pieces on the floor. Suddenly she clasps her hands over her face, sinks to her knees with a moan, and draws her veil close. And now there is a gasp of wonder from the Maids.*)

ROSALYS: Oh, look! Snow White! She's breathing! (*The group parts, and Snow White, half supported by the Dwarfs, is seen to stir.*)

THE PRINCE: (*Rushing to her.*) Snow White! (*He kneels beside her and raises her head.*)

SNOW WHITE: (*With a deep sigh.*) Oh, it was such a long dream. I dreamed that I was dead. It was all dark and still. Then, just now, came a great crash, and this loosened in my throat—why, see! It's a little piece of apple!—and I woke up. Or am I dreaming now? Where am I? (*With a cry of fear she struggles to her feet.*) This is the palace! The Queen will find me! Hide me, brothers, I'm afraid!

BERTHOLD: (*Pouncing upon the cowering Queen.*) She shall never harm you again, my Princess! What shall her punishment be? Let us starve her in the Gray Tower as she would have starved my children.

BLICK: I'll make her a pair of red-hot iron shoes to dance at your wedding. (*But the Queen, writhing from Berthold's grasp, creeps to Snow White and makes an imploring gesture.*)

SNOW WHITE: Hush, please. I think she wants to speak to me.

THE QUEEN: Yes, to you alone!

SNOW WHITE: She wants to speak to me alone.

BERTHOLD: Be careful, Princess!

SNOW WHITE: I'm not afraid anymore. (*The others withdraw a little, leaving Snow White and the Queen together.*

THE QUEEN: (*In a muffled voice.*) Oh, Snow White, my punishment has come! I broke the Mirror, and my beauty is gone forever! Let me go away where no one can ever see my face. You shall be Queen now. Here is the crown. (*She thrusts it into Snow White's hand.*) You don't believe me? Then look—but oh, let no one else see! (*She lifts her veil a little, so that Snow White alone can see her face.*)

SNOW WHITE: Oh, how dreadful! (*She turns to the others.*) Please let the Queen go away.

BERTHOLD: (*Barring the way.*) Unpunished? Never, your Highness!

ALL: Never, never! (*Witch Hex enters. She looks very different now. Instead of her red cloak and pointed hat she wears a neat black-silk dress and bonnet. On her arm she carries a basket in which are three ordinary-sized black cats.*)

THE WITCH: (*Stopping the Queen.*) Highty-tighty, what's all this?

THE QUEEN: (*Clinging to her.*) Oh, Witch Hex!

ALL: (*In consternation.*) Witch Hex! The Witch!

THE WITCH: Don't be frightened; not Witch Hex anymore! Just Miss Hex now. Gave up magic for good and all day before yesterday, burned all my charms, shrunk my cats to their normal size, and retired. Perfectly respectable old lady now.

THE QUEEN: Oh, Hex, I broke the Magic Mirror.

THE WITCH: And turned ugly, eh? Well, serves you right. Let's see. (*She tries to lift the Queen's veil.*)

THE QUEEN: (*Preventing her.*) Oh, no, no, no!

THE WITCH: Oh, yes, yes, yes! You were fond enough of showing your face before. Turn about's fair play. (*She snatches off the veil.*) (*The Queen has surely turned ugly, but it is a funny kind of ugliness. None of her features have changed except her nose, but that has grown enormous—almost a foot long, and very red.*)

THE WITCH: (*Cackling with laughter.*) My stars and garters! What a nose! *What* a nose!

THE QUEEN: Oh, Hex, can't you help me?

THE WITCH: Afraid not. The only way to be beautiful is to be good.

THE QUEEN: Oooooooh!

THE WITCH: You must be Snow White. And you are Prince Florimond, of course. I can guess why *you're* here. Well, is the betrothal all arranged? Where's the ring, young man? Oh, come! I'll wager you've been carrying it about for a year. (*Prince Florimond produces the ring.*) Give him your hand, Snow White! Put the ring on, Florimond. (*The Prince does so.*) Now, lead her to the throne and crown her properly. (*With stately grace the Prince leads Snow White to the throne, and reverently sets the crown on her head. Then he kneels before her, and all follow his example, and all the trumpets in the palace blare. Rising and unsheathing his sword, the Prince cries:*)

THE PRINCE: Love and homage to our new Queen! (*The Dwarfs have withdrawn shyly, but now Blick, clearing his throat and summoning all his courage, cries:*)

BLICK: Brothers! March! (*In military order the Dwarfs march to the throne.*)

BLICK: (*Stammering.*) Your—er—er—your—(*He gives it up, and bursts out:*) Please tell us what to call you? You see, we've never met a Queen before.

SNOW WHITE: Oh, brothers, call me only Snow White—always and always!

BLICK: Snow White, may we go now? To fetch our wedding present—all our gold and jewels.

SNICK: And then back to our lonely house.

FLICK: And those suppers!

GLICK: And those beds!

SNOW WHITE: No, no! You must stay with me always. There are no braver men in my kingdom! You shall be my bodyguard, and Berthold shall be your Captain.

BLICK: What do you say, brothers?

QUEE: *I* say, "Hip, hip, hurrah!"

ALL THE DWARFS: Hip, hip, hurrah!

THE WITCH: Dear me! I quite enjoy being respectable! And *I* can't see why you shouldn't live happily ever after. (*Music.*)

THE PRINCE: Do you remember the first words I ever said to you?
"Lady, do you think that I
Might dance too? I'd like to try."

SNOW WHITE: And I answered:
"I was hoping you might be
Tempted to join in—with me."

(*She gives him her hand, and they all whirl off into a gay and happy Dance; even the Dwarfs—who never could learn—hopping for joy, as—*)

CURTAIN

Androcles and the Lion
Aurand Harris

A play for the young, based on the Italian tale of
"Androcles and the Lion," and written in the style of
Italian *commedia dell'arte*

Original music by Glenn Mack

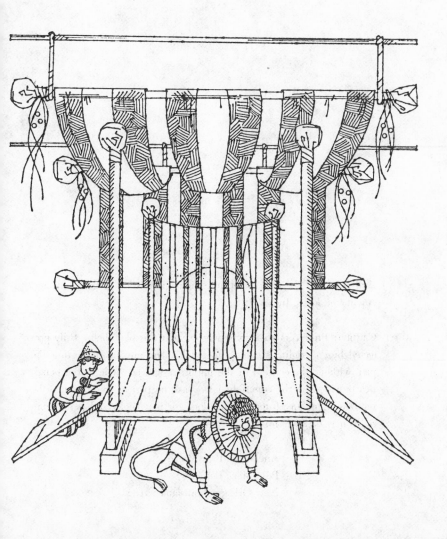

Based on an old Aesop's fable, Aurand Harris' *Androcles and the Lion* is written in the *commedia dell'arte* tradition. A group of strolling players set up the stage and then become stock characters from the *commedia* who enact the tale.

Since the comic story is presented by characters who are immediately established as actors, the script is a play-within-a-play, a form which is maintained from beginning to end by devices directly from the *commedia* tradition. The strolling players become the stock characters of Pantalone, the lovers (Isabella and Lelio), the Captain, and Arlequin (Androcles). The Lion is the only character not from the *commedia* tradition, but he is integrated into the group of stock characters by first playing the Prologue, who is the spokesman of the players.

Other elements derivative of the *commedia* tradition are several references by the actors to a scenario on the scroll posted onstage, instances of direct address to the audience, and the setting of some locales by actors' pronouncements immediately preceding the scenes. The old tradition also included broad, physical comic action, chase scenes, and use of the slapstick, all of which are in plentiful supply in *Androcles and the Lion*.

The play is a comedy of wit and good humor which proclaims the message, "Every man must be free to be himself," within a story of several conflicts. Androcles, a good-natured Roman slave, wins his freedom from his miserly master, but not before helping Isabella escape from the imprisonment of her guardian, befriending a hurt lion, and facing a beast in the arena.

The plot is carefully constructed and the action proceeds to its inevitable conclusion through scenes that quickly shift from fast-moving comedy to slower, serious moods of reflection. The madcap opening scene, for example, is immediately followed by Androcles' lament of his lot as a slave, which furnishes a few minutes of quiet relief after the excitement.

Comic suspense and dramatic irony are used in several scenes to create an anticipation of the outcome in the audience. The final instance of the device in the play occurs when Androcles, with head in sack, faces Lion in the arena, and neither realizes his adversary is an old friend. Not until the latter pulls off the sack to begin his meal "at the top . . ." is the ironic coincidence, which the audience has known and been enjoying from the beginning of the confrontation, revealed to the characters.

Even though Androcles, the hero, is the character with whom the young audience identifies, Lion is equally important as a character. Although he understands all that is said by the human characters of the play, Lion never uses words to communicate with those who speak to him, but answers with roars, noises, pantomime, and facial expressions.

The sparse dialogue sometimes includes rhyme for its amusing effect. The end of one character's short line rhymes with that of the next to speak. The humor is produced not only by the sudden occurrence of obvious rhyme in the dialogue but by the unexpected combination of rhymed words which come within a rapid exchange between characters and sometimes even within a single line.

The music is an essential element. The lyrics of the songs are woven into the structure of the play. Each character's song is an expression of personality and feelings and occurs as part of the plot. Other musical effects may be used to intensify the play, especially to enhance mood and create atmosphere, such as trumpet calls to add majesty to the imagined presence of the Emperor.

The technical production may be as simply executed as that which the original *commedia* troupes did. The play opens on a bare stage which the actors prepare by selecting items from a trunk of properties and pulling a painted backdrop across the stage. The four shifts in setting are managed swiftly by the performers within the dialogue and action.

ANDROCLES AND THE LION

CHARACTERS

Androcles
Pantalone
Isabella
Lelio
Captain
Lion and Prologue

SETTING

The improvised stage of a *commedia dell'arte* troupe of strolling players in Italy.

TIME

The sixteenth century.

ACT ONE

The curtains open on a bare stage with the cyclorama lighted in many colors. There is lively music and the Performers enter, playing cymbals, flute, bells, and drums. They are a commedia dell'arte group.

Arlequin, dressed in his traditional bright patches, leads the parade. Next are Lelio and Isabella, the romantic, forever-young lovers. Next is Pantalone, the comic old miser. Next is the Captain, the strutting, bragging soldier. And last is the Prologue, who wears a robe and who later plays the Lion.

After a short introductory dance, they line up at the footlights, a colorful troupe of comic players.

PROLOGUE: Welcome!
  Short, glad, tall,
  Big, sad, small,
  Welcome all!

(*Actors wave and pantomime "Hello."*)

We are a troupe of strolling players,
With masks, bells, and sword,

(*Actors hold up masks, ring bells, and wave sword.*)

A group of comic portrayers
Who will act out upon the boards
A play for you to see—
A favorite tale of Italy,
Which tells how a friend was won

By a kindness that was done.
Our play is—"Androcles and the Lion."

(*Actors beat cymbals, ring bells.*)

The players are: Arlequin—

(*Arlequin steps forward.*)

Who will be Androcles, a slave.

(*Arlequin bows, steps back, and Pantalone steps forward.*)

Pantalone, stingy and old,
Who thinks only of his gold.

(*Pantalone holds up a bag of gold, bows, steps back; and Isabella and Lelio step forward and pose romantically.*)

Isabella and Lelio, two lovers
Whose hearts are pierced by Cupid's dart.

(*They bow, step back, and Captain marches forward.*)

It is the bragging Captain's lot
To complicate the plot.

(*Captain waves his wooden sword, bows, and steps back.*)

There is one more in our cast—
The Lion! He, you will see last.
Set the stage—

(*Actors quickly set up small painted curtain backdrop.*)

Drape the curtains—raise the platform stand!
Here we will make a magic circle—
Take you to a magic land—
Where love is sung, noble words are spoken,
Good deeds triumph, and evil plots are broken.

(*Holds up long scroll.*)

Our story is written on this scroll which I hold.
What happens in every scene here is told.

(*Hangs scroll on proscenium arch at L.*)

Before we start, I will hang it on a hook
So if someone forgets his part

And has the need, he may have a look
And then proceed.
All the words in action or in song
We will make up as we go along.
All is ready! Players, stand within.

(*Actors take places behind curtain.*)

For now I bow and say—the play—begins!

(*He bows.*)

In ancient Rome our scene is laid,
Where the Emperor ruled and all obeyed.

(*Points to curtain, which is painted with a street in the middle and with a house on either side.*)

A street you see, two chariots wide,
With a stately house on either side.
In one lives Pantalone—rich, stingy, sour,

(*Pantalone leans out the window flap on the house at R and scowls.*)

Who counts and recounts his gold every hour.

(*Pantalone disappears.*)

With him lives his niece Isabella, who each day

(*Isabella leans out the window.*)

Looks lovingly—longingly—across the way

(*Lelio leans out the window of the house at L.*)

At the other house, where Lelio lives, a noble sir, who looks across lovingly—longingly—at her.

(*Lelio sighs loudly. Isabella sighs musically, and they both disappear. Androcles enters from R, around the backdrop, with broom.*)

And all the while Androcles toils each day.
A slave has no choice but to obey.

(*Prologue exits at R.*)

ANDROCLES: (*Music. He sweeps comically, in front of the door, over the door, then down the "street" to footlights. Sings.*)

Up with the sun,
My day begins.
Wake my nose,
Shake my toes,
Hop and never stop.
No, never stop until I—
Off to the butcher's,
Then to the baker's,
To and from the sandalmaker's.
Hop and never stop.
No, never stop until I—
Spaghetti prepare
With sauce to please her.
Dust with care
The bust of Caesar.
Hop and never stop.
No, never stop until I—drop.

Some masters, they say, are kind and good. But mine . . . ! He cheats and he beats—he's a miser. Never a kind word does he say, but shouts, "Be about it!" And hits you a whack on the back to make sure. I'm always hungry. He believes in *under* eating. I'm fed every day with a beating. I sleep on the floor by the door to keep the robbers away. My clothes are patched and drafty because my master is stingy, and cruel, and crafty! When—oh when will there ever be a Roman Holiday for me!

(*Sings.*)

Will my fortune always be,
Always be such drudgery?
Will hope ever be in my horoscope?
Oh, when will I be free?

PANTALONE: (*Enters around R of backdrop, counting money.*) . . . twenty-two, twenty-three, twenty-four, twenty-five . . . (*Androcles creeps up behind him, and, playing a trick, taps Pantalone on the back with broom. Pantalone jumps.*) Who is there?

ANDROCLES: Androcles.

PANTALONE: Be about it! Be off! Go! Collect my rents for the day. Everyone shall pay. (*Androcles starts R.*) Lock the windows tight. Bolt the doors. (*Androcles starts L.*) My stool! Bring me my stool. (*Andro-*

cles exits R.) Lazy stupid fool! There will be no supper for you tonight. Oh, I will be buried a poor man yet—without a coin to put in my mouth to pay for ferrying me across the River Styx. (*Androcles runs in R with stool.*) My stool!

ANDROCLES: (*Places stool behind Pantalone and pushes him down on it roughly. Pantalone gasps in surprise.*) Yes, my master.

PANTALONE: Go! Collect my rents. Make them pay. Bring me—my gold. Away!

ANDROCLES: Yes, O master. I run! (*He starts "running" to L at top speed, then stops, looks back impishly, and then slowly walks.*)

PANTALONE: (*Brings out bag and starts counting.*) Twenty-six, twenty-seven, twenty-eight, twenty-nine, thirty . . .

ISABELLA: (*At the same time, she leans out the window, calls, stopping Androcles.*) Androcles . . . Androcles! (*He runs to her UR. She gives him a letter.*) For Lelio. Run! (*Androcles nods and smiles, pantomimes "running" to painted house on curtain at L, pantomimes knocking. There is music during the letter scene.*)

LELIO: (*Appears at his window, takes letter.*) Isabella! (*Androcles smiles and nods. Lelio gives him a letter. Androcles "runs" to Isabella, who takes letter.*)

ISABELLA: Admired! (*Gives Androcles another letter. He "runs" with leaps and sighs to Lelio, who takes it.*)

LELIO: Adored! (*He gives Androcles another letter. He "runs," enjoying the romance, to Isabella, who takes it.*)

ISABELLA: Bewitched! (*She gives him another letter—they are the same three sheets of parchment passed back and forth—which he delivers. This action is continued with a letter to each lover, and with Androcles "running" faster and faster between them.*)

LELIO: Bewildered!

ANDROCLES: And she has a dowry. The gold her father left her. (*"Runs" to Isabella with letter.*)

ISABELLA: Enraptured!

LELIO: Inflamed!

ISABELLA: Endeared! (*Holds letter.*)

LELIO: My dear! (*Holds letter.*)

ANDROCLES: My feet! (*Androcles sinks exhausted to ground. Isabella and Lelio disappear behind the window flaps. Music stops.*)

PANTALONE: (*Picks up the dialogue with his action, which has been continuous.*) . . . one hundred three, one hundred four, one hundred five, one hundred six . . . (*Bites a coin to make sure.*) one hundred seven . . . one hundred . . .

LELIO: (*Enters from L, around backdrop.*) Signor Pantalone.

PANTALONE: (*Jumps from stool in fear.*) Someone is here!

LELIO: A word with you, I pray.

PANTALONE: (*Nervously hides money.*) What—what do you wish to say?

LELIO: I come to speak of love. I come to sing of love! (*Reads romantically from a scroll he takes from his belt.*) "To Isabella."

PANTALONE: My niece?

LELIO: "Oh, lovely, lovely, lovely, lovely flower,
Growing lovelier, lovelier, lovelier every hour . . .
Shower me your petals of love, O Isabella,
I stand outside—with no umbrella."
Signor, I ask you for Isabella. I ask you for her hand in marriage.

PANTALONE: Marry—Isabella?

LELIO: (*Reads again.*)
"My life, my heart revolve around her;
Alas, I cannot live without her."

PANTALONE: (*Happy at the prospect.*) You will support her?

LELIO: I ask you—give me Isabella. (*Pantalone nods gladly.*) Give us your blessing. (*Pantalone nods eagerly and raises his hand.*) Give her—her dowry.

PANTALONE: (*Freezes.*) Money!

LELIO: The gold her father left her.

PANTALONE: Gold! It is mine—to keep for her.

LELIO: But hers when she marries.

PANTALONE: How did he find out? No. She shall not marry you. Never! Part with my gold! Help! Androcles! (*Androcles runs to him.*)

LELIO: Part with Isabella? Help! Androcles! (*Androcles, between them, runs from one to the other as their suffering increases.*)

PANTALONE: My heart is pounding.

LELIO: My heart is broken.

PANTALONE: Quick! Attend!

LELIO: Lend!

PANTALONE: Send!

LELIO: Befriend!

ANDROCLES: (*To Lelio.*) There is hope.

PANTALONE: I am ill.

LELIO: Amend!

ANDROCLES: (*To Lelio.*) Elope!

PANTALONE: I have a chill!

LELIO: (*Elated with the solution.*) Transcend! (*Exits around L of backdrop.*)

PANTALONE: I will take a pill! (*Exits around R of backdrop.*)

ANDROCLES: (*To audience.*) The end! (*Comes to footlights and sings.*)
They are my masters and I obey.
But who am I? I often say.
"Androcles!" They ring.
"Androcles!" I bring.
But who am I?
A name—I am a name they call,
Only a name—that's all.

(*Speaks simply and touchingly.*)

My father's name was Androcles. We lived on a farm by the sea. Free to be in the sun—to work the land—to be a man. One day when my father was away, a ship came in the bay. "Pirates," my mother cried. I helped her and my sisters hide, but I was caught and brought to Rome —and sold—for twenty pieces of gold. I thought I would run away!

But when they catch a slave they decree a holiday. The Emperor and everyone come to watch the fun of seeing a runaway slave being beaten and eaten by a wild beast. Personally I don't feel like being the meal for a beast. So I stay . . . just a name . . . (*Sings.*)

"Androcles!" They ring.
"Androcles!" I bring.
But who am I?
If I were free
Who would I be?
Maybe . . . maybe . . .
A doctor with a degree,
A poet, a priest, a sculptor, a scholar,
A senator—emperor with a golden collar!
I want to be free
So I can find—me.

PANTALONE: (*Calls off, then enters UR.*) Androcles! Androcles!

ANDROCLES: You see what I mean.

PANTALONE: Androcles!

ANDROCLES: Yes, my master.

PANTALONE: Quick! Answer the bell. Someone is at the gate. (*Androcles picks up stool and crosses to R.*) Then come to me in the garden by the wall. (*Holds up a second bag of gold, different colors from the first.*) I am going to bury—to plant—this bag of—stones.

ANDROCLES: Plant a bag of stones?

PANTALONE: Be off! To the gate! (*Androcles exits DR. Pantalone holds up bag, schemingly.*) Ah, inside this bag are *golden* stones! It is Isabella's dowry. (*There is a loud crashing of wood off R, announcing the entrance of the Captain.*) Who is at the gate? I have forgot. (*Hurries to scroll hanging by the proscenium arch, reads—announcing in a loud voice.*) "The Captain enters!"

CAPTAIN: (*He struts in DR, wooden sword in hand. His voice is as loud as his look is fierce.*) Who sends for the bravest soldier in Rome? Who calls for the boldest Captain in Italy!

PANTALONE: I—Pantalone. (*Goes to him, speaks confidentially.*) I will pay you well—(*Looks away. It breaks his heart.*)—in gold—(*Then anxiously. Androcles peeks in at R.*) to guard my niece. I have learned today she wishes to marry. You are to keep her lover away. Stand under her window. Station yourself at the door. Isabella is to be kept a prisoner forever more. (*No reaction from Captain.*)

ANDROCLES: A prisoner? She will be a slave—like me.

PANTALONE: What do you say?

CAPTAIN: (*Pompously.*) I say—she who is inside is not outside.

ANDROCLES: (*To audience.*) I say—no one should be held a slave. This is treachery! (*Exits UR around backdrop.*)

CAPTAIN: (*Struts.*) I have guarded the royal Emperor. I have guarded the sacred temple. I can guard one niece—with one eye shut. (*Shuts one eye and marches L.*)

PANTALONE: No, no. The house is over there. (*Points R.*) And that is her window. (*Isabella leans out of window.*)

CAPTAIN: Someone is there! Death to him when he tastes my sword! (*Advances with sword waving.*)

PANTALONE: No! No! It is she! (*Whispers.*) It is—Isabella.

ISABELLA: (*Sings happily.*)
Oh, yellow moon,
Mellow moon,
In the tree,
Look and see
If my lover
Waits for me.

PANTALONE: (*Softly.*) Keep watch. Keep guard. She must not meet her lover. (*Captain salutes, clicks his heels, turns, and with thundering steps starts to march. Androcles slips in from around backdrop UL and listens.*) Sh! (*Captain marches with high, silent steps to window and stands at attention. Pantalone speaks to audience.*) I must go to the garden! In this bag is the gold her father left her. I gave my oath to *keep* it—for her. To keep it safely—and for me. I will bury it deep, deep in the ground. Never to be found. (*He hurries off DL.*)

ANDROCLES: (*To audience.*) More trickery that's wrong. The gold belongs to Isabella.

ISABELLA: (*Aware someone is outside.*) Lelio?

CAPTAIN: (*Laughs.*) Ha ha ha—no.

ISABELLA: Oh!

CAPTAIN: I am the Captain!

ISABELLA: Oh?

CAPTAIN: I guard your door. You cannot come or go.

ISABELLA: Oh.

CAPTAIN: Do not despair. I will keep you company. Observe how handsome I am—fifty women swooned today.

ISABELLA: (*Calls softly.*) Lelio . . . ?

CAPTAIN: Know how brave I am—on my way to the barber two dragons I slew!

ISABELLA: Lelio . . . ?

CAPTAIN: Hear what a scholar I am—I say, "He who is sleeping is not awake."

ISABELLA: Lelio-o-o-o. (*Cries daintily. Captain makes a sweeping bow to her.*) No! (*She disappears, letting the flap fall.*)

CAPTAIN: She sighs. (*Louder crying of musical "o's" is heard.*) She cries. Ah, another heart is mine! Fifty-*one* women have swooned today! (*Poses heroically.*)

ANDROCLES: I must do something! She cannot be put in bondage. No one should be. Everyone should be free. But how—(*Beams with an idea, looks at scroll by proscenium arch and points.*) Ah, look and see! (*He quickly reads scroll at side.*)

ISABELLA: (*Appears at window, sings sadly.*)
Oh, lonely moon,
Only moon,
Do you sigh,
Do you cry
For your lover
As—as I?

ANDROCLES: Yes, here is the plan I need! (*Clasps hands and looks up in prayer.*) Oh, gods of the temple, please give me the courage to succeed. (*Makes a grand bow to Captain.*) Signor Captain! (*Captain jumps.*) It is said that you are so fierce the sun stops when you frown.

CAPTAIN: That is true. (*Makes a frightening frown, turns, and frightens Androcles.*)

ANDROCLES: And that the tide goes out whenever you sneeze.

CAPTAIN: That is true. (*Screws up his face comically, puffs up and up his chest, then sneezes.*) A-a-a-achew!

ANDROCLES: (*Circling in front of Captain, going to R, toward window.*) Oh, brave and mighty Captain, I shake before you. (*Bows, back to audience shaking.*)

CAPTAIN: Yesterday I swam five hundred leagues.

ANDROCLES: I heard you swam one thousand.

CAPTAIN: One thousand leagues I swam into the sea.

ANDROCLES: I heard it was into the ocean.

CAPTAIN: The ocean! To meet a ship—

ANDROCLES: A fleet of ships.

CAPTAIN: To meet a fleet of ships! (*Captain suddenly huffs and puffs as he starts pantomiming how he swam in the ocean, his arms pulling with great effort.*)

ANDROCLES: (*At the same time, whispers to Isabella.*) I have a plan to set you free; listen—carefully. (*Whispers, pointing to Captain. Pantomimes dropping handkerchief and fanning himself.*)

CAPTAIN: (*Suddenly starts coughing and waving his arms.*) Help! Help! I am drowning! Drowning!

ANDROCLES: (*Rushes to him, hits him on back.*) Save him. Throw out a rope. Man overboard!

CAPTAIN: (*Sighs in relief, then dramatically continues with his adventure.*) I was saved by a school of mermaids—beautiful creatures—and all of them swooned over me.

ANDROCLES: Then you swam on and on—

CAPTAIN: (*Swimming on L, comically.*) And on—

ANDROCLES: (*Pushing him to exit.*) And on—

CAPTAIN: And on—

ANDROCLES: And on—

CAPTAIN: And on—(*Exits L, "swimming."*)

ANDROCLES: (*Quickly speaks to Isabella.*) Do as I say and you can escape. We will trick the Captain. Wave your handkerchief. Get his attention. Then say the night is so warm—fan yourself. As he becomes warmer, he will shed his cape and hat and sword—and you will put them on. You will be the Captain.

ISABELLA: I?

ANDROCLES: (*On his knees.*) Try.

ISABELLA: The Captain's cape and hat will cover me, and I will be free to go—to Lelio.

CAPTAIN: (*Re-enters at L.*) After I had sunk the fleet of ships—

ANDROCLES: And brought the treasure back.

CAPTAIN: Treasure?

ANDROCLES: You awoke.

CAPTAIN: Awoke?

ANDROCLES: And found—it was but a dream. (*Isabella waves her handkerchief, then drops it coyly. Captain sees it and smiles seductively.*)

CAPTAIN: Ah! She signals for me to approach. Signora—your servant. (*Androcles, behind him, motions for Isabella to begin the trick.*)

ISABELLA: (*Accepts handkerchief with a nod.*) The night is so warm. The air is so still, so stifling. There is no breeze.

CAPTAIN: I will command the wind to blow a gale.

ISABELLA: The heat is so oppressive.

CAPTAIN: I will command the wind to blow a hurricane!

ANDROCLES: My nose is toasting.

CAPTAIN: I will call the wind to blow a blizzard!

ANDROCLES: My ears are roasting.

ISABELLA: The heat is baking. (*Captain, between them, looks at each one as each speaks. Captain becomes warmer and warmer. The dia-*

logue builds slowly so the power of suggestion can take the desired effect on the Captain.)

ANDROCLES: Sweltering.

ISABELLA: Smoldering.

ANDROCLES: Simmering.

ISABELLA: Seething. (*Captain begins to fan himself.*)

ANDROCLES: Stewing!

ISABELLA: Parching!

ANDROCLES: Scalding!

ISABELLA: Singeing! (*Captain takes off his hat, which Androcles takes, as Captain mops his brow.*)

ANDROCLES: Scorching!

ISABELLA: Smoking!

ANDROCLES: Sizzling!

ISABELLA: Blistering! (*Captain, growing warmer and warmer, removes his cape and sword, which Androcles takes.*)

ANDROCLES: Broiling!

ISABELLA: Burning!

ANDROCLES: Blazing!

ISABELLA: Flaming!

CAPTAIN: Help! I am on fire! Blazing! Flaming! I am on fire! (*Captain goes in a circle, flapping his arms, puffing for air, fanning, hopping, and crying, "Fire! Fire!" At the same time, Androcles quickly gives hat, cape, sword to Isabella.*)

ANDROCLES: (*Comes to Captain, who is slowing down.*) Throw on water! Throw on water!

CAPTAIN: (*Stops, dazed.*) Where am I? (*Isabella, dressed in Captain's hat, cape, and sword, marches from R and imitates Captain with comic exaggeration.*)

ANDROCLES: (*Salutes her.*) Signor Captain! What is your philosophy for the day?

ISABELLA: (*Poses and speaks in low loud voice.*) I say—he who is outside—is not inside.

ANDROCLES: Yes, my Captain.

CAPTAIN: Captain?

ISABELLA: I am off to fight a duel. Fifty-four I slew today. Fifty more I will fight—tonight!

ANDROCLES: Yes, my Captain.

CAPTAIN: Captain? Captain! *I* am the Captain. (*They pay no attention to him.*)

ANDROCLES: Your horse is waiting. (*Pantomimes holding a horse.*) Your horse is here. Mount, O Captain, and ride away. (*Isabella pantomimes sitting on a horse, holding reins.*)

CAPTAIN: I am the Captain!

ISABELLA: Did you hear the wind blow?

CAPTAIN: I am the Captain!

ANDROCLES: (*Listening and ignoring Captain.*) No.

ISABELLA: I will ride a thousand leagues—

ANDROCLES: Two thousand—

ISABELLA: Three—

CAPTAIN: I am the Captain!

ISABELLA: Is that a shadow—there? (*Points sword at Captain.*)

ANDROCLES: A shadow . . . ? (*Takes sword and slashes the air, making Captain retreat fearfully.*) No one is here . . . or there . . . or anywhere.

CAPTAIN: (*Almost crying.*) But I am the Captain.

ANDROCLES: To horse! Away—to the woods.

ISABELLA: To the woods!

ANDROCLES: But first, a bag of stones—by the garden wall, yours to take before you go.

ISABELLA: And then—to Lelio!

ANDROCLES: Yes, my Captain.

CAPTAIN: (*Crying comically.*) But I am the Captain. Look at me. Listen to me.

ISABELLA: To the woods! (*Starts pantomiming riding off L.*) Ride, gallop, trot, zoom!

ANDROCLES: Hop, skip—jump over the moon! (*They "ride" off UL.*)

CAPTAIN: (*Crying.*) But I . . . I am the Captain. (*Then, horrified.*) If that is the Captain—then—who—who am I?

PANTALONE: (*Enters DL.*) Captain . . . Captain.

CAPTAIN: Someone calls. Oh, Pantalone . . . Pantalone! Can you see me? (*Waves his hands in front of Pantalone, then shouts in his ear.*) Can you hear me?

PANTALONE: Yes.

CAPTAIN: Am I . . . I here?

PANTALONE: (*Peers at him.*) Yes.

CAPTAIN: Ah, I live. I breathe again. (*Breathes vigorously.*) I am the Captain. (*Struts.*) Look on my hat and shudder. Look at my cape and shiver. Feel my sword—(*Realizes he has no hat, cape, or sword.*) It is gone! Ah, your slave took it. Androcles! It was a trick of his. After him!

PANTALONE: My slave? Ha ha, a trick on you.

CAPTAIN: And another one dressed in my clothes!

PANTALONE: (*Laughing, stops immediately.*) Another one?

CAPTAIN: One who came from your house.

PANTALONE: From my house? (*Runs to house, UR, then turns.*) Isabella!

CAPTAIN: Ha ha, a trick on you.

PANTALONE: (*In a rage.*) Fool, stupid, simpleton! You have set Isabella free!

CAPTAIN: I set Isabella free?

PANTALONE: Fathead, saphead, noodlehead! It was she who left the house in disguise—and is off to meet her lover. Stop them! Which way? Which way?

CAPTAIN: He said—(*Thinks, which is difficult.*) to the woods!

PANTALONE: Bonehead, woodenhead, blockhead! Quick! Save her! Before she is wed! To the woods! (*Starts R.*)

CAPTAIN: He said—(*Thinks.*) first, take a bag of stones by the wall.

PANTALONE: A bag of stones—the gold! Muttonhead, pumpkin head, cabbage head! To the garden! Before he finds it. (*Starts to L, as Captain starts R.*) Forget Isabella. Save the gold! (*Pantalone exits DL. Captain salutes and marches after him. Lights may dim slightly. There is music as the Wall enters DR and crosses to C. Wall is an actor (Lion) with a painted "wall" hanging on his back and short enough to show his feet. The back of his head is masked by a large flower peeping over the wall. He stands at C, feet apart, back to audience. He puts down a bag of gold and then puts a rock over it. Androcles, followed by Isabella, tiptoes in UL. They circle around to DR. Androcles starts feeling for the wall.*)

ANDROCLES: The gold is buried—by the wall—(*Flower on the Wall nods vigorously.*) buried under a stone—(*Flower nods again.*) Look— feel—find a stone—a stone—a stone—(*Wall stomps his foot, then puts foot on top of stone, but Androcles passes by it.*)

ISABELLA: (*Wall again taps foot and points it toward stone. Isabella sees stone and points to it.*) A stone!

ANDROCLES: Ah, I see it! Pray that this will be it! (*Slowly lifts stone.*) Behold! (*Holds up bag.*) A bag of gold! (*Jumps up, sings, and dances.*) We've found it! We've found it! We've found the gold! Yours to keep! To have! To hold!

ISABELLA: Sh!

ANDROCLES: You are free—go! Off to Lelio, who implores you—adores you. Quick, do not hesitate. Run—before it is too late.

ISABELLA: Thank you. Some day may you be set free, too. (*Kisses her finger and touches his nose with it.*) Good-bye. (*Exits DL.*)

ANDROCLES: (*Thrilled that she has touched him.*) Fly—arrivederci. (*Sees he has the gold.*) Wait! The gold! Isabella forgot the gold! Isabella! Isabella! (*He exits after her DL. At the same time, Pantalone, followed by Captain, tiptoes in UL, circling DR, where they stop.*)

PANTALONE: (*Peering and groping.*) It is so dark I cannot see.

CAPTAIN: (*Also peering and groping.*) Wait . . . wait for me.

PANTALONE: The gold—by the wall—under a stone—find—find—

CAPTAIN: You look in front. I'll look behind.

PANTALONE: (*He turns R, Captain turns L. Each peers and steps in the opposite direction on each word.*) Search—scratch—dig around it.

CAPTAIN: (*Still peering, they now step backward toward each other on each word.*) Feel—touch—crouch—(*They bump into each other from the back.*)

PANTALONE: Ouch!

CAPTAIN: (*Grabs and holds Pantalone's foot.*) I've found it! I've found it!

PANTALONE: Knucklehead of soot! You've found my foot! (*Kicks free and creeps toward C.*) Here . . . there . . . oh, where . . . where is my gold? The stone . . . the stone . . . where has it flown? Quick . . . on your knees . . . search . . . find . . . use your nose . . . and not to sneeze. (*He and Captain, on their knees, comically search frantically.*) Pat . . . pound . . . comb . . . the ground . . . chase . . . race . . . find the place. (*He finds stone.*) I have found it! Ah, to gods in prayer I kneel. The stone is here. My gold is back. (*Reaches between feet of Wall, then freezes in panic.*) What do I feel? There is no sack! (*Rises in a frenzy.*) I have been robbed! Thieves! The gold is gone!

CAPTAIN: (*Rises.*) It was the slave who took it! Androcles!

PANTALONE: He is a robber. He is a thief! He will pay for this—with his life!

CAPTAIN: I will find him . . . bind him . . . bend . . . make an end of him!

PANTALONE: He has run away! To the woods! Catch him! Hold! (*Captain stomps to R.*) To the woods! Before his tracks are cold. (*Captain stomps to L.*) Follow! Follow! My bag of gold! (*Pantalone exits DL. Captain salutes and follows him. Wall picks up stone, then he pulls the street scene curtain to one side, revealing another curtain behind it and painted like a forest. Over his shoulder, back still to audience, Wall announces, "The forest," and exits quickly at R. Chase music begins. Isabella and Lelio run in from L, look about.*)

ISABELLA: The forest paths will guide us.

LELIO: The forest trees will hide us.

(*They exit UR around the backdrop.*)

ANDROCLES: (*Runs in from L.*) Isabella! Lelio! I cannot find you. You have left the gold behind you. (*Exits off UR around backdrop.*)

CAPTAIN: (*Enters DL.*) After them! I say—follow me! This way! (*Exits UR behind backdrop.*)

PANTALONE: (*Enters, wheezing, trying to keep up, from L.*) We are near him. I can hear him—and my gold. (*Pantalone exits UR around the backdrop. Isabella and Lelio run in UL from behind the backdrop, start to R, but suddenly stop, frightened at what they see offstage R.*)

ISABELLA: Oh, what do I see?

LELIO: It is a—quick! We must flee! (*Isabella and Lelio exit UR behind the backdrop. Captain enters UL around the backdrop, starts to R.*)

CAPTAIN: This way! This way! Follow me! Onward to—(*Stops, horrified at what he sees offstage R.*) What is that behind a tree? It is a—Oh, no! We must never meet. The order is—retreat! (*Captain runs off UR behind backdrop. Pantalone enters UL around the backdrop.*)

PANTALONE: Find him. Fetch him. Catch him. My gold has run away. (*Stops and looks offstage R.*) What is that? Can that be he? (*Starts to call.*) Andro—No! It is a—Help! It is a *lion*—coming after me! (*There is a loud roar off R. Pantalone sinks to his knees and, quickly walking on his knees, exits L. Music of Lion's song. Lion enters at R, a most appealing creature. He dances to C and sings.*)

LION: Have you roared today,
   Told the world today how you feel?
   If you're down at the heel
   Or need to put over a deal,
   Happy or sad
   Tearful or glad
   Sunny or mad,
   It's a great way
   To show the world how you feel!
   Without saying a single word
   Your meaning is heard.
   "Good morning" is dull,

But a roar is musical!
Happy or sad
Tearful or glad
It's a great way
To show the world how you feel!

(*He gives a satisfied low roar, then looks about and speaks.*)

The sun is up. It is another day—(*Yawns.*) to sleep. Hear all! The King speaks. No birds are allowed over my cave—chirping and burping. No animals are allowed near my cave—growling and howling. Silence in the woods. The King is going to sleep. (*Actors offstage imitate animal sounds, loud buzzing, barking, etc. Or actors may in simple disguise with masks enter as animals, dance, and make sounds.*) Silence! (*All noise and motion stops.*) The King says, "Silence." (*Noise and motion increases, Lion becomes angry, puffs up and roars like thunder, stalking about in all directions.*) R-r-r-r-r-roar! (*There is absolute silence. If actors are onstage, they run off.*) You see—(*Sings.*)

A roar's a great way
To show the world how you feel!

(*He roars and exits majestically into cave—a split in the painted backdrop.*)

ANDROCLES: (*Enters from around backdrop UR. He runs to C. He looks around anxiously to R and to L, and calls softly.*) Isabella . . . ? Lelio . . . ? They are lost in the woods. I am lost in the woods. I have run this way—I have run that way—I have run—(*A terrible thought strikes him.*) I have run—away! I am a runaway slave! No! (*Calls desperately.*) Isabella! Lelio! Where will I go? My master will hunt me. He will track me down. He will take me back. I will be thrown to the wild beasts! (*Sees bag he holds.*) The gold—my master will say I stole it. A runaway slave—and a thief! No, I was only trying to help. (*Calls.*) Isabella! Help *me*, Lelio.

PANTALONE: (*Off L, loudly.*) Oh, beat the bushes. Beat the ground. Find my slave. Find my gold!

ANDROCLES: My master! What shall I do? Where shall I go? Hide—(*Runs behind imaginary tree R.*) Behind a tree—(*Runs to imaginary bush UL.*) Under a bush—he can see. (*Points at cave.*) What is that? Ah, a cave! I will hide—inside the cave and pray he never finds me. (*Quickly he goes into cave, gives a loud "Oh!" and quickly backs out again.*) It is someone's house.

CAPTAIN: (*Off.*) Follow me. I say—this way!

ANDROCLES: (*Knocks at cave in desperation.*) Please! Please, may I come in? I am—

PANTALONE: (*Off.*) I think—I hear him!

ANDROCLES: I am—in danger. (*Androcles quickly goes into cave. Pantalone enters UL, followed by Captain. They are in hot pursuit.*)

PANTALONE: (*Crosses to R.*) My gold! Find the slave. Bind him! Bring him to me.

CAPTAIN: (*Circles DC.*) I will look in every brook and nook and hollow tree!

PANTALONE: Fetch—catch my gold! (*Exits DR.*)

CAPTAIN: Follow me! (*He exits DL. From inside the cave, a long loud roar is heard, and Androcles calls, "Help!" Another and louder roar is heard. Androcles runs out of cave to DL and cries "Help . . . help!" Lion runs out of cave to DR and roars.*)

ANDROCLES: It is a lion!

LION: It is a man! He will try to beat me.

ANDROCLES: He will try to eat me. (*They eye each other. Lion springs at Androcles with a roar. Androcles backs away.*) I am sorry I disturbed you. (*Lion roars. Androcles holds up bag.*) I—I will have to hit you if you come closer.

LION: Hit—hit until he kills—that is man.

ANDROCLES: Leap—eat—that is a lion. (*Lion roars and then leaps on him. Androcles struggles and fights, but soon he is held in a lion-hug.*) Help! Help! (*Lion roars. Androcles gets his arm free and bangs Lion on the back with bag of gold. Lion roars with surprise and releases Androcles. Androcles, thinking he is free, starts off, but Lion holds on to his pants. Androcles, at arm's length, runs in one spot. Androcles gets loose, turns, lowers his head, and charges, butting into Lion's stomach. Lion roars. Androcles runs to L and hides behind imaginary tree. Lion, angry, roars and slowly starts to creep up on him. Androcles looks around "tree," one side, then the other, shaking with fearful expectation. Lion springs at him in front of "tree." Androcles leaps and runs back of "tree." Lion turns and runs after him. Androcles tries to escape, running in figure-eights around the two "trees." They stop, each facing opposite directions, and start backing toward each other. Andro-cles turns, sees Lion, jumps, then cautiously tiptoes toward him and kicks the bent-over approaching Lion. Lion roars and circles. Androcles laughs at his trick. Lion comes up behind him and grabs him, holding Androcles around the waist and lifting him off the ground. Androcles kicks helplessly. Lion throws Androcles on ground. Lion, above him, roars, raises his paw, and gives a crushing blow. But Androcles rolls over and the paw hits the ground. Lion immediately roars and waves his paw in pain. Androcles cautiously slides away and is ready to run. He looks back at Lion, who, with tearful sob-roars, is licking and wav-ing his paw.)*

ANDROCLES: He is hurt. I can run away. (*He starts, but stops when Lion sobs.*) He is in pain. Someone should help. No one is here. No one but one—I—am here. (*Lion roars in frustration. Androcles turns away in fear. Lion sobs sadly. Androcles looks back at him.*) If I go—I maybe can be free! If I stay—(*Lion growls at him.*) he may take a bite out of me! (*Androcles starts to leave. Lion sobs. Throughout the scene the Lion "talks" in grunts and groans almost like a person in answering and reacting to Androcles. Androcles stops.*) When someone needs your help, you can't run away. (*Trying to be brave, he turns to Lion, opens his mouth, but can say nothing.*) I wonder what you say—to a lion? (*Lion sobs appealingly.*) Signor—(*Lion looks at him. Androcles is afraid.*) My name is Androcles. (*Lion roars, looks at his paw, and roars louder.*) Have you—have you hurt your paw? (*Lion grunts and nods.*) If you—will sit still—I will try to help you. (*Lion roars defiantly. Androcles backs away.*) Wait! If we succeed, we will need to —cooperate! (*Lion looks at him suspiciously and grunts.*) You don't trust me—(*Lion roars.*) and I don't trust you. But someone must take the first step—greet the other, or we will never meet each other. (*Cau-tiously Androcles takes a step sideways, facing audience. Lion cau-tiously takes a step sideways, facing audience.*) That is a beginning— (*Lion roars. Androcles holds his neck.*) But what will be the ending? (*Each raises a leg and takes another sideways step toward the other.*) I don't want to hurt you. I want to help you. (*He slowly holds out his hand. Lion "talks" and slowly shows him his paw.*) It's a thorn. You have a thorn stuck in your paw. (*Lion breaks the tension, crying with the thought of it, and waving his injured paw.*) I know it hurts. (*Talks slowly as if explaining to a small child.*) Once I stepped on a thorn. My father pulled it out. (*Lion grunts and reacts with interest.*) My father—on the farm—by the sea. I will pull it out for you—as my father did—for me. (*Lion grunts, undecided, then slowly offers his paw. Androcles nervously reaches for it.*) It—it may hurt a little. (*Lion draws back and roars in protest.*) I thought a lion was brave—not afraid of anything. (*Lion stops, then grunts in agreement and with great bravery thrusts out his paw.*) Now—hold still—brace yourself. (*Lion begins to tremble violently.*) Get ready—(*Lion shakes more.*) One—(*Lion shakes both of them.*) Two—(*Lion cries and tries to pull away. Androcles is stern, with pointed finger.*) Don't move about! (*Lion tries to obey, meekly.*) Three! (*Lion steps backward.*) It's out!

LION: (*Looks at his paw, looks at Androcles, then roars joyfully and hops about. Sings.*)

Let me roar today
Let me say today
We feel great!
Celebrate!
Exhilarate!
Congratulate!
It's a great way
To show the world how you feel.

ANDROCLES: (*Lion rubs against Androcles and purrs softly. Androcles, being tickled by Lion's rubbing, giggles and pets him.*) You—you are welcome.

LION: (*To audience.*) He looks tired. I will get a rock. (*Quickly picks up a rock off R and holds it high.*)

ANDROCLES: He is going to crush me! (*He starts to defend himself, but Lion shakes his head and grunts, and shows Androcles that he should sit.*) For me? (*Lion nods, trying to talk, and dusts the rock with his tail.*) He wants me to sit. (*Lion, delighted, grabs Androcles to help him and seats him roughly.*) Thank you.

LION: (*To audience.*) He looks hungry. (*Roars, shows teeth, and chews.*)

ANDROCLES: He is going to eat me! (*Lion shakes his head and "talks," points to Androcles and indicates from his mouth down into his stomach.*) He wants me to eat. (*Lion agrees joyfully.*) I am hungry. I am always hungry.

LION: (*Thinking.*) What was for breakfast today? A man's skull in the cave—his liver down by the river—(*Embarrassed at what he has thought.*) Oh, I beg your pardon. (*Roars with a new idea, motions Androcles to watch. Lion hums and purrs lightly as he comically pantomimes picking fruit from a tree and eating and spitting out the seeds.*)

ANDROCLES: Fruit! (*Lion, encouraged, purrs happily and hops about pantomiming filling a basket with berries from bushes.*) Berries! (*Lion, elated with his success, buzzes loudly and dances in ballet fashion like a bee.*) What? (*Lion buzzes and his dancing is bigger.*) Honey from the bee! (*Lion agrees loudly.*) Oh, that will be a banquet for me.

LION: (*Speaks to audience.*) A new twist in history! Man and beast will feast together. Celebrate! Sit—wait! I'll be back with cherries and berries for you—and a bone or two, before you can roar—*e pluribus unum*! (*Roars happily and exits R.*)

ANDROCLES: (*Sits alone on rock, looks around, smiles, and speaks quietly.*) I am sitting down. I am being served. I am being treated like a person. I—have a friend. This is what it is like to be free. To be—maybe—(*Sings.*)
   Maybe
   A doctor with a degree,
   A poet, a priest, a sculptor, a scholar,
   A senator—emperor with a golden collar!
   I want to be free
   So I can find—me.

PANTALONE: (*Off.*) Hunt—hunt—search and find my slave. Find my gold!

ANDROCLES: My master has come. My freedom has gone.

PANTALONE: (*Off R.*) Ah, his footprints are on the ground! I have found him!

ANDROCLES: (*Calls quickly.*) Oh, Lion, I must be off before we have fed. I must run—or it is off with my head! (*He starts DL but sees Captain.*) Oh! The Captain! Where will I hide? In the cave! (*Quickly hides in cave.*)

CAPTAIN: (*Enters L with fishing net and a slapstick.*) Beware slave, wherever you are. I shall leap and keep and capture you. In this net—I will get you. (*Holds net out ready.*)

PANTALONE: (*Enters R, peering at the ground, crosses to L.*) His footprints are on the ground. Toe-heel, heel-toe. This is the way his footsteps go.

CAPTAIN: (*To audience.*) The trap is set.

PANTALONE: Lead on—lead me to him.

CAPTAIN: Ha, caught in the net! (*Throws net over Pantalone, who has walked into it.*)

PANTALONE: Help! Help!

CAPTAIN: You stole my hat! (*Hits Pantalone over the head with slapstick.*)

PANTALONE: Oh!

CAPTAIN: My sword. (*Hits him again.*)

PANTALONE: No!

CAPTAIN: My cape! (*Hits him again.*)

PANTALONE: Let me loose!

CAPTAIN: What?

PANTALONE: You squawking goose!

CAPTAIN: Who speaks?

PANTALONE: (*Pulling off the net.*) I—Pantalone.

CAPTAIN: Pantalone? Oh, it was my mistake.

PANTALONE: It was my head!

CAPTAIN: Where is the slave? The runaway? Where is Androcles?

PANTALONE: He is—with my gold.

CAPTAIN: (*Struts.*) I will drag him back to Rome. The Emperor will honor me—decree a holiday—so all can see the slave fight a wild and hungry beast. And after the fun is done and the slave is eaten, all will cheer the Captain of the Year.

PANTALONE: Before you count your cheers, you have to catch one slave —Androcles!

CAPTAIN: (*They start searching, a step on each word. Captain circles to L and upstage. Pantalone circles to R and upstage.*) Search.

PANTALONE: Seek.

CAPTAIN: Track.

PANTALONE: Trail.

CAPTAIN: Use your eyes.

PANTALONE: Scrutinize!

CAPTAIN: (*Stops.*) Think—if you were a slave . . . ?

PANTALONE: I?

CAPTAIN: Where would you hide?

PANTALONE: Inside.

CAPTAIN: (*Sees and points.*) A cave! (*They tiptoe to entrance, hold net ready, whisper excitedly.*) Clap him.

PANTALONE: Trap him.

CAPTAIN: (*Nothing happens.*) The problem is—how to get him to come out.

PANTALONE: Poke him?

CAPTAIN: Smoke him?

PANTALONE: I have a great idea! You will call to him in a voice like Isabella.

CAPTAIN: I—I speak like Isabella?

PANTALONE: You will cry for help in a soft sweet voice. He will think you are her. He will come to Isabella.

CAPTAIN: (*In a high voice, comically.*) Help! Oh, help me. I am Isabella. (*They look at cave entrance.*) I heard—

PANTALONE: Something stirred.

CAPTAIN: (*Falsetto again.*) Andro-o-cles. Come out, ple-e-ese. (*They look at cave and excitedly hold net ready.*) Ready.

PANTALONE: Steady. (*Androcles, behind backdrop, roars—long and loud!*) It is a lion in the cave! (*Runs DR and hides behind a "tree."*)

CAPTAIN: (*Androcles roars again, up and down the scale, louder and louder. Even the backdrop shakes. Captain jumps and runs to Pantalone and hides behind him.*) It is two lions in the cave! (*They stand shaking with fright.*)

ANDROCLES: (*Peeks out of cave, then comes out.*) They have gone. Ran away from a noise. I have learned that a roar is a mighty thing. No wonder a lion is a king. (*He enjoys another roar.*)

PANTALONE: (*Still hiding.*) We are undone!

CAPTAIN: Run! Crawl!

PANTALONE: I cannot move at all. (*Androcles roars again with joy.*) I have an idea. You—you will call in a voice like a lion. He will think you are another lion—a brother.

CAPTAIN: I—roar like a lion?

PANTALONE: Our only chance is to answer back. (*Captain gulps, and then roars.*)

ANDROCLES: (*He is startled. He hides behind "tree" at L.*) It is another lion. (*Pantalone, helping, gives a roar.*) It is two lions! (*With an idea, he roars back.*) Ro-o-o-hello.

CAPTAIN: (*He and Pantalone look at each other in surprise. Captain answers.*) Ro-o-o-hello.

ANDROCLES: (*Now Androcles looks surprised.*) Ro-o-o-lovely-da-a-ay.

CAPTAIN: (*He and Pantalone look at each other and nod, pleased with their success.*) Ro-o-o-have-you-seen—ro-o-o-ar-a-runaway slave? (*Androcles is startled, then he peeks around "tree."*)

PANTALONE: Named-Andro—(*Captain nudges him to roar.*)—roar—cles?

ANDROCLES: It is my master and the Captain. They have come for me. (*He roars loudly.*) Ro-o-oar-he-went—roar-r-r-r-that-away.

CAPTAIN: (*They nod.*) Ro-o-o-thank-you. (*He and Pantalone start to tiptoe off R.*)

ANDROCLES: (*Too confident.*) Ro—o-ar. You are welcome.

PANTALONE: It is his voice. It is my slave, Androcles.

CAPTAIN: It is another trick of his.

PANTALONE: Nab him.

CAPTAIN: Grab him. (*They start back to get him.*)

ANDROCLES: (*Unaware he has been discovered, continues to roar gaily.*) Ro-o-oar. Good-bye. Ro-o-o-ar. Happy eating.

PANTALONE: (*Confronts Androcles on R.*) Eat, cheat, thief! I will beat you! (*Androcles turns to L and walks into net held by Captain.*)

CAPTAIN: Slide, glide, inside. I have you tied! (*Androcles is caught in the net over his head.*)

PANTALONE: (*Grabs his bag of gold.*) My gold!

CAPTAIN: My captive!

ANDROCLES: Help! Help!

CAPTAIN: You stole my hat! (*Hits Androcles over the head with slapstick.*) You stole my sword! (*Hits him.*) You stole my cape! (*Hits him.*) This time you will not escape.

PANTALONE: (*Takes stick from Captain and swings it.*) Robber. Traitor. Thief! Let me hit him. (*Pantalone, in the mix-up, hits Captain several times on his head.*)

CAPTAIN: Help! (*He drops the rope of the net.*)

ANDROCLES: (*Runs to R.*) Help!

PANTALONE: Help! He is running away!

CAPTAIN: (*Quickly catches Androcles and holds the rope.*) Back to Rome. To the Emperor you will be delivered!

PANTALONE: Into the pit you will be thrown.

CAPTAIN: Where the wild beasts will claw, gnaw, and chew you! (*They start to lead him off, marching—Captain, Androcles, and last Pantalone.*) Munch!

PANTALONE: Crunch!

ANDROCLES: I will be eaten for lunch! Help! Lion! Signor Lion, set me free. Come and rescue me! Oh, woods, echo my cry for help. Echo so the Lion will know I am in trouble. Roar—roar with me. Echo from tree to tree! (*He roars, and the Ushers—and the children—help him roar, as he is led off L.*) Roar! Roar!

LION: (*He leaps in at R and roars.*) Someone roars for help? Androcles! (*Off, Androcles cries "Help!"*) He calls for help. (*Sings.*)
Oh, roar and say
Shout out without delay,
Which way, which way, which way?

Oh, roar me a clue,
Roar me two.
I have to know
Which way to go before I start.
Oh, roar, please,
An-dro-cles.
Give a sigh,
Give a cry,
Signify!
I'll sniff—I'll whiff—
Smell (*Sniffs.*)—Tell (*Sniffs.*)
Fe, fi, fo, fum.
Here—

(*Shouts.*)

I come!

(*He exits L.*)

ISABELLA: (*She and Lelio run in from R.*) Oh, Androcles, what has happened to you?

LELIO: (*To audience.*) That you will see in Act Two. Now—we must bow and say, "Our play is half done." This is the end of Act One. (*They bow.*

The curtains close.)

A Short Intermission

(*Or, if played without an intermission, omit the last speech of Lelio's and continue with his first speech in Act Two.*)

ACT TWO

(*Music: Reprise of "Oh, Roar and Say." The curtains open. The scene is the same. Isabella and Lelio stand in C. Music dims out.*)

ISABELLA: Androcles. What has happened to you?

LELIO: I heard his voice, calling in the woods.

ISABELLA: He has followed us to bring the gold—my dowry, which I left behind. (*Calls.*) Androcles?

LELIO: Androcles! (*Lion roars as he enters UR. He sees the lovers and watches.*)

ISABELLA: It is a lion!

LELIO: Do not fear.

ISABELLA: Androcles is alone—unarmed. What if he should meet a lion? Androcles! Androcles!

LELIO: Androcles!

LION: Someone else roars "Androcles." I will stay and hear who is here. (*Lion hides his head behind the small rock.*)

ISABELLA: Androcles! Androcles!

LELIO: We are alone. (*Lion's head pops up behind rock.*) Together. It is time to speak—to sing of love! (*He turns aside, takes scroll from belt.*)

ISABELLA: (*Not looking at him.*) Please, speak no prepared speech, but sing true words that spring freely from your heart.

LELIO: (*Looks surprised, glances again at scroll, then sings.*)
Oh, lovely, lovely flower,
Growing lovelier every hour,
Shower on me petals of love, Isabella—

(*Lion, enjoying the music, nods his head in rhythm.*)

ISABELLA: So unrehearsed—so sincere.

LELIO: (*Sings.*)
My life, my heart revolve about you.
Say yes, I cannot live without you.

(*Lion, unable to refrain, lifts his head and roars musically on Lelio's last note—unnoticed by the lovers—then hides his head behind the rock.*)

ISABELLA: Oh, Lelio—(*Turns to him and speaks or sings.*)
My answer is—can't you guess?
Yes, yes, yes, yes, yes!

LELIO: (*In ecstasy.*) Oh, woods abound with joyous sound! Melodies sing in the trees—

(*Music sound. Lion rises up and listens to R.*)

Bells ring in the breeze—

(*Music sound. Lion stands up and listens to L.*)

Let the lute of the lily lying in the pond—

(*Music sound. Lion stands and begins to move his arms like an orchestra conductor.*)

Let the flute of the firefly's fluttering wand—

(*Music sound. Lion motions to R.*)

And let the flight of the nightingale—

(*Music sound. Lion motions L.*)

Harmonize!

(*Music sounds blend together. Lion holds up paw, ready to begin directing an orchestra.*)

The moment we will immortalize!

(*Music of all sounds plays a folk dance. Lion leads, dramatically, the unseen musicians. Isabella and Lelio do a short dance. At the conclusion, they hold their pose, and Lion bows to audience.*)

ISABELLA: (*Points to ground.*) Look! Footprints—boots and sandals.

LELIO: (*Examines them.*) The Captain's boots—Pantalone's sandals. The Captain and Pantalone were here—following us—following Androcles.

ISABELLA: His cry was for help. He ran away. He is—a runaway slave! And they have found him—

LELIO: Bound him—

ISABELLA: Taken him back to Rome.

LELIO: To the pit!

ISABELLA: We must stop them.

LELIO: If we can.

ISABELLA: We must help him.

LELIO: All we can.

LION: (*Jumps on rock heroically.*) And—we can! (*Roars.*)

ISABELLA: Help!

LELIO: Run! (*Lovers run off DR.*)

LION: Lead the way. I will follow you. To Androcles! To—the rescue! (*Lion roars, picks up rock, and runs off DR. Chase music begins— repeated. But the running is reversed, going around in the opposite direction. Lovers enter from UR and run across. At C, they look back, "Oh!" and exit UL behind backdrop. Lion runs in UR. At C, roars, and exits UL behind backdrop. Lovers enter UR from behind backdrop, running faster. At C, they look back in great fright, "OH!" and exit UL behind backdrop. Lion follows. At C, roars majestically, and shouts: "Andr-roar-cles! Here we come!" Lion exits after lovers. Lovers enter UR from around backdrop. Lelio pulls the curtain of the woods scene back to L, showing the street scene again. Chase music dims out.*)

LELIO: (*Breathless.*) Safe at home—I hope. What does the scroll say?

ISABELLA: (*Reads scroll on proscenium arch.*) The next scene is—a street in Rome.

LELIO: Ah, we can stay.

ISABELLA: (*Reads, announcing.*) "The Captain enters." (*Clashing of slapstick is heard off L; Isabella runs to C.*) He will find us here.

LELIO: Do not fear. We will hide—behind a mask. Quick! We will hide behind another face, and reappear in the Market Place. (*They exit R.*)

CAPTAIN: (*Enters at L.*) Make way, make way for the hero of the day! Bow, salute, kneel, and gaze upon the hero. Raise your voice with praise for the hero. The hero passes by. The hero is—I! (*Lelio and Isabella enter R. Each holds a long, sad beggarman's mask on a stick in front of his or her face. They walk and act and speak like beggars.*)

LELIO: Help the poor. Help the blind.

ISABELLA: Alms for the cripple. Alms for the old.

CAPTAIN: Away, beggars! The Emperor comes this way. It is a holiday!

LELIO: What senator has died? What battle have we won?

CAPTAIN: None! We celebrate today the capture of a runaway.

ISABELLA: A slave? (*They look at each other and speak without their masks; and at the same time, the Captain speaks. They all say together, "Androcles!"*)

CAPTAIN: Today all Rome will celebrate! A wild beast was caught outside the wall, clawing the gate as if he could not wait to come into the city. Now in the pit the beast is locked and barred, waiting to be released—waiting to eat a juicy feast.

LELIO AND ISABELLA: (*They nod to each other and say:*) Androcles!

CAPTAIN: Ah, what a sporting sight to see—a fight—man eaten by a beast. Then I, who caught the slave, will appear. Women will swoon, men will cheer, and I will be crowned the hero of the year! (*Shouts rapidly and marches quickly.*) Hep, hep, ho! Step, step, high. Hail the hero. I, I, I! (*Exits R.*)

ISABELLA: (*They take their masks away.*) Poor, poor Androcles.

LELIO: We must try and save him. Quick, before it is too late. We will go to the Arena—

ISABELLA: Yes!

LELIO: We will go to the Royal Box! Implore the Emperor with our plea!

ISABELLA: Yes!

LELIO: For only he by royal decree can save—our Androcles. (*Lelio and Isabella run off L. There is music. Captain, leading Androcles by the rope, and Pantalone, following, march in from R. As they march, they sing.*)

PANTALONE AND CAPTAIN: Off to the pit we three. Who will be left?

ANDROCLES: Just me.

PANTALONE AND CAPTAIN: Who will be left alone, shaking in every bone?

PANTALONE: Just—

CAPTAIN: Just—

ANDROCLES: Me!

CAPTAIN AND PANTALONE: Off to the pit we three. Who will be left?

ANDROCLES: Just me.

CAPTAIN AND PANTALONE: Who will the animal meet? Who will the animal eat?

PANTALONE: Just—

CAPTAIN: Just—

ANDROCLES: (*Shouts.*) Just a minute. I want to be an absentee! (*Music ends as he speaks.*) I want to be free—to be—just me!

CAPTAIN: To the Arena! Forward march! (*Music: Reprise of Introductory Music of Act One. Captain, Androcles, and Pantalone march across the front of the stage or across down in the orchestra pit. At the same time, Lelio and Isabella, disguised with masks, dance in UL carrying colorful banners, one in each hand, and on stands. They set the banners down in a semicircle in front of the backdrop to indicate the Arena. They dance off as music stops, and the three marchers arrive in the middle of the scene.*)

CAPTAIN: Halt! We are at the Arena! The slave will step forward.

PANTALONE: Step forward.

ANDROCLES: Step forward. (*Frightened, he steps forward.*)

CAPTAIN: The slave's head will be covered. (*He holds out left hand to Androcles, who holds out left hand to Pantalone.*)

PANTALONE: Covered. (*He gives a cloth sack to Androcles, who gives it to Captain, who puts it over Androcles' head.*)

CAPTAIN: (*Trumpets sound.*) The Emperor's chariot draws near. (*Trumpets.*) The Emperor will soon appear. (*Trumpets.*) The Emperor is here! (*A royal banner is extended from the side DL, indicating the Royal Box.*) Bow!

PANTALONE: Now! (*Captain and Pantalone bow low toward Royal Box, facing DL. Androcles, groping with his head covered, turns and bows facing R.*) Turn around! (*Androcles turns around.*) To the ground! (*Androcles bows to ground.*)

CAPTAIN: Most noble Emperor—(*Pushes Androcles' head down, making him bow.*) Most honored Emperor—(*Pushes Androcles, who keeps bobbing up, down again.*) Most imperial Emperor—(*Pushes Androcles down again. He stays down.*) The guilty slave stands before you. Stand!

(*Androcles quickly straightens up.*) As punishment for a slave who runs away, he will today fight a wild beast in the Arena for all Rome to see. (*Androcles shakes his head under the sack.*) He will battle for his life—to survive. There will be but one winner—the one who is left alive. (*Androcles, courageously, draws his fists and is ready to strike. Captain, growing more eloquent, begins to strut.*) I have fought and slain a hundred wild beasts. (*Androcles, visualizing the animals, starts hitting the air.*) With fiery eyes, with gnashing teeth, they charged at me. Fight! The crowd cried, fight! (*Androcles, ready, starts to fight, hitting wildly for his life, hitting the Captain, who is near and whom he cannot see.*) Help! Stop! I am not the wild beast. (*At a safe distance, he regains his bravery.*) I—I am the Captain, the boldest, bravest fighter in Rome—in all Italy! Go—stand at the side. Appear when you hear the trumpets blow. (*Captain points to L. Androcles starts to R.*) No. The other way!

ANDROCLES: (*He turns and starts to L. Loud trumpets blow. He stops, faces R, ready to fight.*) The trumpets! Now?

PANTALONE: No! (*Androcles, groping, exits UL. Pantalone bows to Royal Box.*) Most Imperial Emperor, I am Pantalone, master of the slave. From me he ran away. From me he stole. I am told you plan to reward me for this holiday with a bag of gold.

CAPTAIN: I tracked and captured him. I am sure you will confer a title of bravery on me. (*Trumpets blow.*)

ANDROCLES: (*Enters UL, ready to fight.*) The trumpets! Now?

CAPTAIN: No! (*Androcles turns and exits.*) Ah, the Emperor waves. It is the signal. Open the gates. Let the wild beast in!

PANTALONE: Let the entertainment begin! (*Captain and Pantalone quickly go DR, where they stand. Drum rolls are heard. Then loud roars are heard off UR. Lion, roaring, angrily stalks in from UR.*)

LION: Barred—locked—caged! I am—outraged! (*Roars and paces menacingly.*)

PANTALONE: What a big lion! I am glad he is below.

CAPTAIN: I could conquer him with one blow.

LION: Captured! Held in captivity! Robbed of my liberty! Only man would think of it. Only man would sink to it. Man—man—little—two-legged—tailless thing. Beware man, I am a King! (*Roars.*) The first man I meet I—will eat! (*Trumpets blow.*)

ANDROCLES: (*Enters, head still covered.*) The trumpets! Now?

LION: (*Sees him.*) Ah, a man! A chew or two and a bone to pick. (*Roars.*)

ANDROCLES: (*Frightened and groping.*) Oh! I am not alone. I must get out quick. (*Drum starts beating in rhythm to the fight. Androcles starts walking, then running, the Lion after him. The chase is a dance-mime, fast, comic, with surprises and suspense. It ends with Lion holding Androcles in his clutches.*)

LION: Caught! Held! (*Shakes Androcles like a rag doll.*) Flip—flop. I will start eating at the top! (*Takes off Androcles' headcovering.*)

ANDROCLES: No hope ever to be free. This is the end of me! (*Lion looks at Androcles, is surprised, and roars questioningly. Androcles, frightened, freezes, then slowly feels his neck, his face and nose. He looks at Lion and he is surprised. Lion tries to "talk."*) You? (*Lion nods and roars, pantomimes pulling out a thorn from his paw, and points to Androcles, who nods.*) Me. (*Lion "talks" and points to himself.*) You! (*Lion nods and roars happily.*) Signor Lion! (*Lion "talks" and roars, and they embrace each other joyfully.*)

PANTALONE: Let the fight begin! Beat him! (*Lion stops and looks at Pantalone.*)

CAPTAIN: The Emperor waits to see who wins. Eat him!

ANDROCLES: He is my master—who bought me. He is the Captain— who caught me.

LION: Slave-makers! Taker of men! I will beat you! I will eat you! (*Roars and starts to C.*)

PANTALONE: Help! The lion is looking at me. Draw your sword! (*Hides behind the Captain.*)

CAPTAIN: (*Shaking.*) I am afraid his blood will rust the blade.

PANTALONE: Show you can do what you say—slay him with one blow!

CAPTAIN: I suddenly remember—I have to go! (*Starts off R. At the same time, Lion leaps with a roar and attacks the two.*)

PANTALONE: Help! Guards! Save, attend me!

CAPTAIN: Help! Someone defend me! (*There is an exciting and comic scramble, with Lion finally grabbing each by the collar and hitting their heads together. Then he holds each out at arm's length.*)

LION: Listen and learn a lesson: only a coward steals and holds a man. (*Roars. Shakes Pantalone.*) Only a thief buys and sells a man. And no one—can—own another man! (*Roars.*) The world was made for all—equally. Nod your heads if you agree. (*Lion shakes them and makes their heads nod violently. Then he releases them, and the two drop to the ground.*) The vote is "Yes"—unanimously! (*Trumpets sound. Offstage voices shout, from R and L and from the back of the auditorium: "Kill the lion. The lion is loose. Club him. Stone him. Kill the lion. Kill! Kill!" etc. Captain and Pantalone crawl to R. Hands appear off R and L shaking clubs and spears. This is a tense moment. The Arena has turned against the Lion. Lion is frightened. He crouches by Androcles, who stands heroically by him.*)

ANDROCLES: Stop! Stop! Hold your spears and stones and clubs. Do not kill the lion. You see—he is not an enemy. He remembers me and a kindness which I did for him. Today that kindness he has returned. He did not eat my head, which would have been the end. Instead—he is—my friend. (*He offers his hand to Lion. Lion takes it. Music begins, and the two start to waltz together. Pantalone and Captain crouch and watch in amazement. Hands and weapons disappear from the sides at R and L. Androcles and Lion's waltz becomes bigger, funnier, and happier. Trumpets sound. Music and dancing stop. Lelio enters DL by royal banner.*)

LELIO: The Emperor has spoken. His words will be heard. (*All bow low toward the Box as Lelio holds up a royal scroll.*) The Emperor is amazed, astounded, and astonished—with delight—at this sudden sight. A fight unlike any in history. Indeed it is a mystery. Two enemies —man and lion—dancing hand in hand! To honor this unique occasion, the Emperor has issued this command: today shall be, not one of fighting, but of dance and revelry! (*Trumpets play and people cheer.*) The Emperor gives to the master of the slave—

PANTALONE: That is I, Pantalone. How much gold does he give?

LELIO: The Emperor gives this order; *you* will give twenty pieces of gold to Androcles.

ANDROCLES: To me!

LELIO: A sum he has well earned.

PANTALONE: Give twenty pieces of gold! Oh, I shall die a poor man. No. No! (*Lion starts toward him and growls loudly.*) Yes—yes, I will pay. (*Quickly takes bag from pocket and begins counting.*) One—two —three—

LELIO: Furthermore: the Emperor decrees to the Captain who caught the slave—

CAPTAIN: Ah, what honor does the Emperor give to me?

LELIO: You will command a Roman Legion in a distant land. You will sail to the Isle of Britain, where even the boldest man must fight to keep alive, where it is so dangerous only the bravest survive.

CAPTAIN: (*Shaking violently.*) Danger? Fight? Me?

LELIO: Because of your boasted bravery.

CAPTAIN: I would prefer to stay, please. A cold climate makes me sneeze. (*Lion starts and roars loudly.*) I will go. (*Lion follows him roaring.*) I am going! I am gone!

LELIO: And to me—the Emperor has given me the lovely, lovely Isabella—(*Isabella enters DL.*) and has blessed our marriage which soon will be.

ISABELLA: For me, the Emperor decreed, Pantalone shall pay without delay my dowry which he holds for me.

PANTALONE: Pay more gold! Oh, no—no! (*Lion roars at him loudly.*) Yes—yes. I will pay. It is here, my dear.

LELIO: And finally: (*Trumpets blow.*) The Emperor has ruled that both lion and slave today have won a victory unequaled in history. So —both lion and slave are hereby—set free!

ANDROCLES: Free? I am free.

LION: The way the world should be!

ANDROCLES: Free—to find my family—to work the best I can—to raise my head—to be a man. To find out—who I am! (*Music. They all sing.*)

Let us roar today,
Let us say today
We feel great.
Celebrate!
Exhilarate!
Congratulate!

PANTALONE AND CAPTAIN: (*Dejected.*) We don't feel great.

ALL: It's a great way
To show the world how you feel.
When in need—find a friend.
Laws will read—have a friend.
We feel great.
Don't eat, but meet.
Why wait, make a friend.
Extend!
Do your part, make a start.
Roar today. Show the world today.
It's a great way
To show the world how you feel.

(*All the actors bow; then Androcles comes forward.*)

ANDROCLES: Our story is told. The lovers are joined in happiness. The bragger and the miser are undone. And a friend was won by kindness. Our masks and bells and curtains we put away for another day. And we go our way—a group of strolling players. We say—

LION: (*Points at audience.*) Be sure you roar today!

ALL: Arrivederci! (*They all bow low and the music swells.*)

CURTAIN

The Sleeping Beauty
Charlotte B. Chorpenning

Adapted from the Brothers Grimm

The Sleeping Beauty, created from the old fairy tale, was dramatized by Charlotte B. Chorpenning for production at the Goodman Memorial Theatre in Chicago and was originally published in 1947. The script works better onstage today if the director deletes redundant lines and shortens longer speeches. The plot can be preserved if the editing is done judiciously.

The play is dominated by the story line in which evil is pitted against good and the struggle is resolved only in the final moments. The conflict to come between Frytania, the evil fairy, and the four good fairies is implied from the opening scenes when the king and queen discover that the evil one has not received an invitation to the special party for their infant daughter. They fear her revenge "will know no bounds."

As in the original story, the evil fairy suddenly appears at the party, and her "gift" to the princess is a spell of death—on her sixteenth birthday, the child will prick her finger with a spindle and die from the wound. The last good fairy, however, who has yet to bestow her gift on the infant princess, announces that she will try to change the death sentence to one hundred years of sleep. Such an imposing villain as Frytania with her spells is not readily vanquished. The suspense begins. The other characters' subsequent attempts to defeat Frytania sustain the tension.

The playwright has intensified the conflict by casting the character of Elano into the central position in the story. A young page of princely rank, Elano sets the conflict in motion with his desperate fear of Frytania. It is only he who can weaken her hold over the princess. To win the struggle, he must overcome the fear of Frytania. The entire plot hinges on his responses to the demands made of him, first when the princess is sixteen years old, and finally at the end of the century of sleep.

Even though Elano is central to the action of the plot, the story is actually about the princess, Sleeping Beauty, and how the action affects her fate. Each of the three acts of the play takes place at a specific time relevant to the princess: one month after she was born, sixteen years later, and one hundred years after her sixteenth birthday.

The play makes several valid observations about life. Although they are openly stated by characters, the ideas are even more convincingly expressed as events in the plot. Underlying the whole play is the theme that states, "To achieve maturity one must directly confront one's fears." Other universal messages include the essential importance of loving others and the desirability of having the courage to follow one's curiosity. With this we learn that young people need the freedom to learn for themselves; they cannot be protected from all harm and danger.

Creating three satisfactory settings for the plot will require a high level of technical expertise. The play needs full technical support to create settings which embrace the fantasy and magic of the story, and costumes which separate royalty from servants and human from supernatural beings.

THE SLEEPING BEAUTY

CHARACTERS

Elano, the Queen's page
King
Queen
Gort, the King's attendant
Ella, maid in waiting to the Queen
Five Fairies
    Una
    Freona
    Cordia
    Belita
    Frytania
Beauty
Norbert, a kitchen boy

SETTINGS

Act One: A room in the palace. The day of the Fairies' gifts.

Act Two: SCENE 1. The same room, sixteen years later.

SCENE 2. Ella's spinning room in the tower, five minutes later, and the edge of the enchanted forest.

Act Three: At the edge of the enchanted forest and Ella's room in the tower.

ACT ONE

A room in the palace. Upstage center, approached by two or three steps, there is a wide, draped opening, leading to the rest of the palace. Up right, facing the audience diagonally, are two throne chairs, for the King and Queen. Below these, along the right wall, is a pleasant window. The wall at stage left runs down toward the audience, then makes a right-angle jog, directly facing the audience, into which is set the small, narrow door leading to the tower, later overgrown with cobwebs. Since the action that takes place about this door is essential to the story, it is important that the audience should have a clear, uninterrupted view of it. When this door is opened, a steep, narrow flight of stairs is visible, leading up to the tower. A refectory table stands left center, with two or three stools grouped about it. Down right is the baby's cradle.

When the curtain rises, Elano, the Queen's herald, is gently rocking the cradle. The King and Queen enter up center. The King is carrying a stool.

ELANO: Sh-h—she is asleep.

KING: (*Softly.*) Where shall I put this stool? It is for the First Fairy.

QUEEN: Call Ella. She will know. (*King starts to the bell cord. The Queen checks him.*) Not there. She is high in the tower. She has spun the thread for a new cloth and woven it ready for the fairies' feast, up there. Call her to fetch it. (*King opens the stair door and calls.*)

KING: Ella—fetch the new cloth. We are making the table ready for the fairies.

ELLA: (*Off.*) I'm bringing it now. (*She enters proudly from the tower, carrying a folded cloth. She spreads it on the table.*) I'm sure the fairies will like this. I have woven a pattern of stars in it. And see! At each fairy's place is her name in silver threads. (*Elano looks up. He has something on his mind.*)

QUEEN: That will surely please the fairies!

ELLA: Their gifts to the baby will be more wonderful if they are pleased.

QUEEN: (*To Ella.*) Ring for Gort to bring the food. (*To King.*) And fetch the plates and goblets which were wrought from gold for the fairies to use today. They are in the lowest room in the tower. (*Ella pulls the cord and the King exits up the tower stairs. Gort enters, with dishes of food on a tray.*)

ELLA: Are you sure you have what the fairies will like?

GORT: Of course I am. In this pot is honey made by wild bees. And here is dew which was shaken from flowers in a fairy ring, under the moon. And here is bread, made from wheat which grew without plowing or planting by men. That is what fairies always eat at christenings. All the village knows that.

KING: (*Entering.*) Here are the plates and goblets. (*They set them around.*) Now for the stools. (*He lifts the one he brought.*)

QUEEN: (*Pointing to the cloth.*) Here is the name of the First Fairy— Una. (*King sets the stool there. Gort and Ella bring the others, and the King a fourth.*)

ELLA: Here is the place for the Third—Cordia.

QUEEN: Freona is over here. She is the Second.

KING: And Belita—the Fourth. (*He backs away in consternation.*)

QUEEN: Now we are ready.

ELLA: What's the matter with the King?

QUEEN: What are you staring at?

KING: There are only four places.

QUEEN: Four?

KING: There are five fairies. (*Elano looks up again, frightened.*)

QUEEN: Set the fifth place quickly. Fetch the other plate and goblet.

KING: There isn't any other plate and goblet. I brought all there were.

QUEEN: (*To Gort.*) Didn't you order the goldsmith to make five plates and goblets?

GORT: No, four. You ordered me to have a plate and goblet made for each fairy that sent a flower as a sign she would come. There were only four flowers.

KING: You surely knew there would be five fairies!

ELLA: Indeed, no, your majesty. There were only four flowers. That is why I wove four names into the cloth. I did what I was told to do.

QUEEN: There are only four names in the cloth!

KING: Which one is missing?

QUEEN: (*Counting places.*) The First Fairy—

KING: Where is the second?

ELLA: Here.

KING: Why didn't you put them in order?

ELLA: I didn't want to make any one seem more important than the others. A fairy may be angry if she is ranked below another. I have heard that an angry fairy may make a wicked gift to a baby at a christening.

GORT: It is only Frytania who makes wicked gifts. All the wise ones know she wants to have more power over men than the others. If parents at a christening pay more honor to another than to her, she gets angry.

ELANO: (*To himself.*) Then she makes a wicked gift to the baby.

GORT: Yes.

KING: We must find out quickly which one is left out.

ELLA: (*Pointing hastily.*) I remember—the Second, the First, the Fourth, the Third—

KING: The Fifth! Where is Frytania's name?

ELLA: It isn't here . . .

KING: It is Frytania who is left out!

QUEEN: You have made the worst mistake that could be made!

GORT: It was not my mistake. It was Ella's. She did not weave the name into the cloth.

ELLA: It was Elano's. He didn't give me the flower for the Fifth Fairy.

KING: Elano!

ELANO: (*He stands up, trembling.*) Yes, sire—

KING: Come here. How many flowers did you give Ella?

ELANO: I gave her—(*He is tempted to lie, but doesn't.*)—four—your majesty.

KING: You were ordered to bid five Fairies to the christening.

ELANO: Yes, your majesty.

KING: Did Frytania refuse to come? Stand up straight and look at me. Did she refuse?

ELANO: She didn't refuse.

KING: Did you lose her flower?

ELANO: No, your majesty.

KING: Where is it?

ELLA: Why didn't you give it to me? Now I haven't enough names in the cloth.

GORT: And I haven't enough plates and goblets.

QUEEN: And it is time for the fairies to come!

KING: Answer me, Elano! Where is Frytania's flower?

ELANO: I—there isn't any.

KING: What do you mean by that?

ELLA: You said she accepted the King's invitation to the christening.

ELANO: I didn't say that.

KING: I asked you if she refused. You said no.

GORT: Now you say she didn't accept.

KING: Which answer is true?

ELANO: Both.

GORT: You told a lie one time or the other.

ELANO: I did not! I am the Queen's page, and of royal blood. I do not tell lies.

QUEEN: (*Gently.*) Come here, Elano. I think I know what happened—you didn't invite Frytania at all—is that true?

ELANO: Yes, your majesty.

KING: You disobeyed my orders!

GORT: You left out the only wicked one of them all!

ELLA: You have put our baby in terrible danger!

QUEEN: (*Gently.*) Did you forget the Fifth Fairy, Elano?

ELANO: I didn't forget her.

QUEEN: Then why didn't you give her the King's invitation?

ELANO: (*Crushed.*) I was afraid.

KING: Afraid! You! With royal blood in your veins! The bravest of all the pages of my court! You can disarm a knight twice your age. You can ride the wildest horse in the stables. Only yesterday you saved my life from a wounded bear, in the hunt, at the risk of your own. What sort of an excuse is this? You couldn't be afraid!

ELANO: All those things I know about. It is easy to face such things.

QUEEN: What were you afraid of, Elano?

ELANO: The place where she lives. The other Fairies live in lovely places.

QUEEN: What frightened you in hers?

ELANO: The sky was so strange. It felt as if it were night, at noon. It seemed to me the clouds had faces in them. They threatened me. They laughed at me. The trees were all twisted, and the wind in them sounded like people crying and screaming, the way it sounded to me when I was very little, and alone in the dark. Hark! You can hear it now. (*Frytania is seen outside the window, moving her wand. Very faint crying and moaning like a wind is heard as Elano stands shuddering at the memory. The others lift their heads to listen and hear nothing, as is shown by their superior smiles.*)

QUEEN: There is no crying in the wind, Elano. You just imagine it.

KING: You should be ashamed to act like a frightened child.

GORT: A great boy like you.

ELLA: The queen's own page. (*The sound fades away.*)

ELANO: I was ashamed to be afraid, and I made my feet go on. The path went into a cavern. It was black in there. There began to be a voice, like a big bell, only it made words.

ELLA: (*Frightened.*) What did it say? (*Elano intones the words like the bell.*)

ELANO: Things like: "It's no use.—Trust no one—No one at all." Then the bells changed and began to say: "Come—Come in—Come—" But when I started to go on, the air laughed at me—I ran, till I came to the sunlight.

QUEEN: And you never went back?

ELANO: I couldn't.

KING: And you never told us.

ELANO: I didn't think you'd want such a dreadful fairy at the christening!

KING: Why didn't you ask me whether I did or not? (*Elano stands speechless.*)

QUEEN: Why don't you answer the King?

ELANO: I am ashamed.

KING: Speak up!

ELANO: I was afraid you'd send me back again.

KING: Of course I will!

QUEEN: It may not be too late!

KING: Go at once! (*Elano stands panic-stricken. Gort pushes him toward the door.*)

GORT: Quick! Every moment you stand here afraid you add to Frytania's power.

ELANO: (*Twisting away.*) No!—No!—How?

GORT: All the wise ones in the village know that. She strives with the Others for power over men. Every time she can put fear in a heart her power grows. If she can make the power of fear in the world great enough, all the gifts of all the other fairies will come to nothing! Go! Go!

QUEEN: Before it is too late!

ELLA: It will be your fault if she makes a wicked gift to the baby!

ELANO: (*Struggling with Gort.*) No! No!

QUEEN: (*At the window.*) The fairies are here! They are coming through the gates. (*Silence falls.*)

KING: How many?

QUEEN: (*Pause.*) Four. Frytania did not know about the christening! (*Elano rushes to kneel by the cradle.*)

ELANO: You are safe—

KING: We must never let her know she was left out!

QUEEN: Go out and meet the Fairies, Elano. Bring them through the front hall and announce them as they come. (*Elano runs out, radiant. The King and Queen sit.*)

GORT: We must finish the table!

ELLA: I'll put honey on each plate.

GORT: And bread.

KING: Pour the dew into the goblets. (*They arrange the table in great excitement.*)

ELLA: (*Beaming.*) Everything is perfect. (*Elano enters, leaving the door ajar. The First Fairy enters, the others following in turn. Elano announces each, with a deep court bow.*)

ELANO: The Fairy Una.

UNA: We were told a child is newly come to this place.

KING: (*Indicating the cradle.*) She is here.

QUEEN: She is asleep.

UNA: In her sleep wait as many fates as there are seeds in the earth in winter.

ELANO: The Fairy Freona.

FREONA: How many days have you had this child?

QUEEN: She is a whole month old, today. That is why you are bid to her christening.

FREONA: A month is a very little part of a life.

UNA: Her fate has not yet been written in her.

FREONA: We are in time.

ELANO: The Fairy Cordia.

CORDIA: Who will teach this child?

QUEEN: She will have many teachers.

KING: The most learned in the kingdom.

CORDIA: There are many things the learned do not know.

KING: She will be guarded from every danger.

CORDIA: No one can ward off another's danger.

UNA: Each must meet his dangers for himself.

QUEEN: (*Low.*) What do they mean?

ELANO: The Fairy Belita.

BELITA: Who is there to love this child?

ELANO: I love her!

KING: I am her father.

QUEEN: I am her mother.

BELITA: Who will be her friends and playfellows?

GORT: I will! I will carry her in the sunshine. She shall run and play in my garden. All the wise ones in the village shall be her friends.

QUEEN: Prince Elano will be her page. He will play with her.

ELANO: I will never be afraid! (*Una speaks to the other fairies.*)

UNA: Come and taste this food that is set out for us, that the power of the gift may come on you. (*They cross to the table.*)

FREONA: Here is my name in the cloth!

BELITA: All our names are in the cloth!

UNA: This is beautifully done.

ELLA: I did it, for love of the child. I thought it might please you and stir you to make some wonderful gift to the baby.

UNA: It pleases us very much. (*They sit at the table and each takes a bit of the food, in succession. It is a ceremony and must be concerted action, but not slow.*) Here is honey gathered by wild bees. A drop of it will give you the power of all things that shed sweetness under sun and rain. . . . Here is bread made from wheat that grew without plowing or planting by men. A crumb of it will give you the power that makes a growing seedling split a rock. . . . Here is dew, shaken from flowers in a fairy ring under the moon. A sip of it will give you the power that draws the sea in tides and holds the stars in place.

BELITA: I am ready to make my gift!

CORDIA: The power of the gift is in me!

FREONA: And me!

UNA: Take away the table and set the cradle in its place.

KING: Elano. (*Elano and Gort move the table and chairs. Elano sets the cradle in place. The Fairies stand ready for the gifts. Their movements are swift and silent. The court people return to their places filled with awe.*)

UNA: Who wishes to be first?

FREONA: Let me speak first. If my gift is not great enough, one of you can add to it. Our gifts must have power to overcome all the fears in the world.

BELITA: Let the First Fairy speak last of all. Her power is more than ours. She can change our gifts as she understands more than we do.

UNA: Begin. (*She stands at one side. The Fairies approach the cradle in turn, each indicating the quality of her gift by her attitude and action. A silver bell sounds after each gift.*)

FREONA: I give you love. Your heart shall go out to everyone and (*Bell.*) everyone's heart shall go out to you. (*She bends low to kiss the baby.*)

CORDIA: I give you beauty. It shall be wrought from within. It shall be the light of your spirit, shining through your looks and ways. (*Bell.*)

BELITA: I give you courage. Howsoever much you are watched and tended, you shall never learn to be afraid. You shall have the will to find out for yourself. All the teachings in the kingdom shall not dull the edge of it. (*Bell.*)

FRYTANIA: (*Appearing in the doorway, wand uplifted, the picture of vengeance.*) I give you, on your sixteenth birthday, DEATH! (*A deep echoing bell sounds. Una has slipped out of sight, behind the throne, or the other fairies.*)

GORT: It is Frytania!

ELANO: Not that! No! No!

KING: Take away your gift!

QUEEN: Have pity on us!

ELLA: Take away your terrible gift.

GORT: Take it away!

FRYTANIA: You should not have left me out of the christening.

ELANO: It was not their fault!

FRYTANIA: Who wove four names in the cloth?

ELLA: I wove them. No one gave me your name.

KING: We didn't know your name had been left out till we spread the cloth just now.

FRYTANIA: You all forgot about me! I will make you remember! I heard your gifts. I listened till you were done so I should be the last to speak.

FREONA: You cannot take away our gifts.

CORDIA: No Fairy has the power to take away another's gift.

FREONA: Even the First Fairy can't do that!

FRYTANIA: I can't take away your gifts, but I can use them! Your gifts shall bring mine to pass. You have given her a heart which goes out to everyone. It shall go out to me! You have given her the will to find out for herself! Through these very gifts, on her sixteenth birthday she shall prick her finger on that accursed spindle you used to spin these silver threads. Of that prick she shall die.—And that you may remember this table, with only four names in the cloth, you shall hear four strokes on my bell before the doom falls. On the fifth stroke your child's life shall end. (*Ella slips out through tower door.*)

ELANO: I will save her! What must I do? Tell me!

FRYTANIA: Nothing.

ELANO: It was all my fault! I was afraid.

FRYTANIA: (*Exultant.*) You ran from your fear. At every step my power grew greater. At last, I have more power than you, sisters!

ELANO: I will go back! I'll face it!

FRYTANIA: It is too late. The last gift is spoken. The bell has struck.

UNA: (*Appearing.*) I have not made my gift.

FRYTANIA: You can't change my spell, this time! The power of this boy's fear is in it. You can't overcome it.

UNA: The boy can overcome it.

ELANO: How?

UNA: Your fear gave her this power. Your courage can take it away.

FRYTANIA: Not for sixteen years!

QUEEN: In sixteen years Elano will not be a page! He will be a prince, and a strong man.

FRYTANIA: The man can't take away the power the boy gave me!

UNA: That is true. Come here, Elano. (*Holding her wand over him.*) That you may have the chance to face the fear you ran from, the years shall pass you by. (*Bell.*)

ELANO: Do you mean—I shall not get older?

UNA: Not for sixteen years. If then you face the fear you ran from, it may be I can change her gift of death to sleep.

ELANO: I will face it! Do not say maybe. Say you will. (*Frytania raises her wand. Her voice is like the deep bell.*)

FRYTANIA: Elano! Come here.—Come—Come—(*Elano goes toward her, cowering, looking back at the First Fairy appealingly.*) The frightened child is in him still. It shall always be so. (*Elano looks around; his eyes rest on the cradle and he straightens.*)

ELANO: No—

FRYTANIA: The boy's fear, and the fear the child will feel when she faces my gift, together will take away all your power to change my spell.

UNA: We shall see. At this hour on her sixteenth birthday, we shall try again whose power is greater, yours or ours.

FRYTANIA: On her sixteenth birthday. (*She exits.*)

UNA: We must take our leave of this life which is just beginning. (*They pass around the cradle and off, each pausing to make her own movement over the baby. Ella comes running from the tower. She is holding a spindle.*)

KING: What is that you have?

ELLA: It is the spindle the Fifth Fairy cursed. I will break it to pieces! She cannot prick her finger on it on her birthday if we destroy it now. Take it, Elano. . . . It is too strong for me. (*Elano seizing it, tries in vain to break it, growing more and more afraid as he fails.*)

ELANO: I'll break it. . . . Do you think the fairies know what we do here?

ELLA: (*Also afraid.*) Fairies always know.

GORT: Bah! You are afraid again, Elano. Let me have it. Anyone can break up such a trifle!

KING: Yes, Gort. Break it to bits. (*Gort tries in vain, at first astonished, then going to great acrobatic lengths in his determination. He finally gives up, and holds it gingerly away from his body.*)

QUEEN: There is something strange about this.

KING: We must hide it, where the Princess can never find it when she grows up.

QUEEN: It shouldn't be in the palace. Gort must throw it away.

GORT: How do we know who might pick it up?

ELANO: I will ride to the edge of the kingdom with it!

KING: No! Some one might find it and bring it back.

ELLA: Yes. It has the royal mark on it.

KING: The safest thing is to lock it high in the tower.

ELLA: There is a box with a key in my spinning room at the top of the tower.

QUEEN: Lock it in that, and lock all the doors below.

KING: Yes! Bring the spindle, Ella. (*They exit through tower door left.*)

QUEEN: How can we make sure no one breaks in and brings it where she can see it?

GORT: There must be no more spinning in the kingdom.

QUEEN: Let every spindle in the land be destroyed! Anyone caught with a spindle shall lose his life.

GORT: Let no one even speak about it. The very word must be forbidden.

QUEEN: Yes! The princess must never even know there is such a thing.

ELANO: Won't the people talk about it all the more, in secret?

GORT: They are like that.—We must be sure that no one can ever get up to the tower.

QUEEN: There is a lock on the door, here, but I never saw a key for it.

ELANO: There is a key above it there—that may fit the lock. It's too high for me to reach. Lift me on your shoulder, Gort.—There!—I have it. (*Ella and King enter.*)

ELLA: The spindle is locked in the box and the box is locked in the room.

KING: The room below that is locked and every room below that. This door I will lock before you all. (*Elano hands him the key and he locks the door and tries it.*)

GORT: Let me try it, too, for safety.

KING: This key must be destroyed. The lock must never be turned again till she is safe past her sixteenth birthday.

QUEEN: Let the dust gather on it and the cobwebs remain untouched. They will be proof that no one has entered here.

KING: Gort, take this key to the goldsmith and tell him to grind it to powder.

QUEEN: And then send messengers to every part of the kingdom to proclaim that there shall be no more spinning in the land.

KING: Anyone found with a spindle shall be put to death!

QUEEN: Elano, do not leave the baby till we return. (*Exit King, Queen, Gort, Ella—Elano, left alone with the cradle, stares at the door, then kneels by the cradle.*)

ELANO: The King thinks he can get ahead of the Fifth Fairy. I do not think so.—You are laughing. You do not know about your sixteenth birthday. I wish it were here. I will not be afraid! She waved her wand over me—I will save you for all that. (*He is motionless, beside the cradle, the lullaby sounding softly.*)

CURTAIN

ACT TWO

SCENE 1. *The scene is the same as Act One. It is sixteen years later and all the characters in this scene are aged by sixteen years, except Elano and the fairies. A cobweb covers the door to the tower. The table and cradle are gone. At curtain the room is empty. A panel in the wall opens and the Fifth Fairy enters, looks around, goes to the tower door and waves her wand. The cobweb draws up and the door opens. She goes up the stairs. The door closes and the cobweb returns to place. Elano enters, looks around with satisfaction, and goes to look at the cobweb.*

ELANO: Nothing has touched it. (*He turns to the door center, and finds the fairies, who have entered as the door swung open of itself.*) Oh!—You have come!

UNA: Isn't this the Princess' sixteenth birthday?

ELANO: Yes. All day I have done nothing but guard this door to the tower and wait to tell the King and Queen you are here! I listened every instant for the trumpet. It was to sound when you were at the gates. No one but you was to be allowed to enter. I didn't hear the trumpet. It isn't the hour yet.

UNA: There was no trumpet.

BELITA: Gates do not matter to us.

UNA: We came early because we wish to see the King and Queen before the Princess comes to us.

CLANO: I will call them.

UNA: Gort is bringing them. He met us in the garden. I think I hear them now. (*Ella and Gort enter and bow to the fairies and turn to bow in the King and Queen.*)

GORT: The King—(*Norbert slips in, beaming. Gort is shocked.*) What are you doing here? You belong in the kitchen. (*Norbert evades him and slips behind Ella because the entrance of the King and Queen sends Gort into a bow.*)

KING: It is wonderful that you are here before Frytania.

QUEEN: You will help us guard the Princess from her.

UNA: We wish to put the Princess to a test before Frytania comes.

KING: (*Very proud.*) Put her to any test you like.

QUEEN: She will not fail.

KING: She will dance, or play the harp, or answer learned questions, or anything you wish.

ELLA: Ask her to embroider you a scarf in bright silks. You will see more skill with the needle than you ever dreamed a young girl could have.

GORT: Ask her to show you her garden.

KING: Flowers bud and bloom for her as if she used some magic.

CLANO: I think it is because she loves them so.

GORT: Walk with her among the people. You will see how everybody loves her.

ELLA: Even the cook's boy here, thinks her the apple of his eye.

NORBERT: She lets me talk to her. She knows what I think about. (*Gort checks the impulse to box his ears.*)

GORT: Keep to your place boy.

NORBERT: (*Chuckling.*) She doesn't say that.

UNA: None of those are the test we want.

KING: What is it, then?

UNA: Isn't this her birthday?

QUEEN: Isn't that why you've come? She is sixteen years old today.

FREONA: We wish to tell her she may have anything she chooses as a birthday gift. (*All exchange frightened glances in the shock of this. There is a pause.*)

KING: Anything?

UNA: We wish to know what she will choose. It will tell us how our gifts have worked in her.

KING: Will you give her what she asks for?

ALL FAIRIES: Of course.

CORDIA: Why do you look so frightened?

FREONA: Can't you trust her to make a good choice?

QUEEN: Oh, yes—only—

KING: Will you give it to her today?

UNA: At once.

KING: What if—

QUEEN: Yes—

UNA: You do not trust her after all.

ELANO: It is the spindle they are thinking of.

QUEEN: She is always asking about a spindle.

UNA: How did that happen?

KING: We don't know. There isn't a single spindle in the kingdom.

ELLA: Except the one locked in the Tower. Only we five know about that.

QUEEN: Everyone has always been forbidden to speak of a spindle before her. Yet somehow, she heard the name.

ELLA: And she wants to see one. She wants to have one.

ELANO: I think it is because everyone made such a secret of it.

KING: It would be terrible if she asked for a spindle today.

QUEEN: This is the last day. At midnight the time of the course will be past.

ELLA: We have been rejoicing about it all day.

KING: I beg you to wait until tomorrow to ask her what she wants for her gift.

UNA: Tomorrow it will be too late for me to change Frytania's gift from death to sleep.

FREONA: It is today the curse will fall.

BELITA: It is today we must know what she will choose.

GORT: After all, what does that matter? She can't prick her finger unless she has a spindle. She can't have a spindle unless you give her one. There's not one in the palace.

KING: There's not one in the whole kingdom—except the one we locked high in the tower. And no one has been up there since that day. There's a cobweb across the door.

QUEEN: But what if she chooses a spindle for your gift?

UNA: If you have taught her to want a spindle you can't protect her from one.

QUEEN: We didn't teach her to want one.

CORDIA: Are you sure?

ELLA: We've even kept it a secret that there was such a thing.

GORT: Even the stories the people tell about spinning have been kept from her.

QUEEN: It happened in spite of all we did.

KING: Perhaps it happened because of the fairy's gift of the courage to find out for herself.

QUEEN: I think the gift of love is even stronger in her. Surely she will not choose a thing she knows we do not like to have her even speak about.

UNA: Bring her and we shall know.

KING: Bring her, Elano. (*Elano exits.*)

ELLA: When she comes we must tell her it is a very important choice.

GORT: We must warn her to think carefully before she chooses.

UNA: There must be no warning.

CORDIA: This is her choice, not yours.

QUEEN: Only to guide her a little.

FREONA: Not a word. Not a look, even.

NORBERT: (*Peeking out of door.*) She is coming. (*They wait in tense silence, the Fairies with interest, but impersonal. Beauty is ushered in by Elano. She stands on the step an instant in awe of what is coming. Then she sees the fairies and her awe gives way to delight. The fairies are pleased with her.*)

BEAUTY: Oh-h-h-h—how wonderful they are! I was a little afraid when Elano told me I was to see the fairies. Now I am not afraid. It makes me happy just to look at you. Elano, I want to give them something to show them what love they call up in me. Father, what is good enough to give the fairies?

FREONA: You have given us love already. There is no better gift than that in the world.

UNA: And now we have a birthday gift for you.

CORDIA: You are to choose it for yourself.

BEAUTY: Choose my own gift?

BELITA: You may have anything you want.

CORDIA: Anything you ask for.

FREONA: Anything at all.

BEAUTY: Mother! What shall I choose?

UNA: You mustn't ask her what you want.

CORDIA: You mustn't ask anyone but yourself.

FREONA: It must be the thing you want most of all.

BEAUTY: Elano, help me think.

BELITA: It isn't Elano's choice.

CORDIA: You must think alone.

BEAUTY: It's exciting!—Now I will choose.—There are three things I want to know, and two things I want to do, and one thing I want to have. Three things—two things—one thing. I've wanted that one thing as long as I can remember, and now I can have it!—You won't be sad about it, Mother?

QUEEN: (*Under the eyes of the fairies.*) No—no, Beauty—it's your gift.

BEAUTY: You won't be angry, Father?

KING: Make your own choice.

BEAUTY: It will surprise you, Elano. You won't mind?

ELANO: You must do as the fairies say.

BEAUTY: (*Laughing.*) I choose—to be all alone for a little while! I have never been alone in all my life. May I have that?

UNA: Of course. It is your choice.

BEAUTY: (*In ecstasy.*) All alone? Without Elano, even?

UNA: Without anyone at all.

BEAUTY: It will be a little strange. I have never had the chance to find out something all by myself, in my whole life.

UNA: How long will you have?

ELLA: What will you do all by yourself?

QUEEN: You may get a little tired of it.

UNA: That is her affair.

BEAUTY: (*Running to the window.*) You must wait by the sundial in the garden, there. When the sun falls straight across it, you may come back. Good-bye, Mother, good-bye, Father. (*King and Queen exit, unwilling, embracing her first.*) Good-bye, Ella. (*Ella exits. Norbert starts to say good-bye to Beauty and Gort stops him.*)

GORT: Back to the kitchen!

BEAUTY: No! Good-bye, Norbert. You must come back with the others.

NORBERT: (*To the fairies.*) See? (*Norbert exits.*)

BEAUTY: Good-bye, Fairies. Thank you for your wonderful gift.

UNA: When your time is up, we will come back and see what use you have made of it. (*Fairies exit.*)

BEAUTY: Hurry up, Gort. You are using up my time.

GORT: (*Going.*) I'll watch outside the door. You will be all alone and no one shall bother you. Come Elano. (*Gort exits.*)

BEAUTY: (*To Elano, in sudden panic.*) Wait, Elano . . . It won't seem so sudden if you wait a little.

ELANO: I shall be thinking of you.

BEAUTY: I will tell you all about it—everything I do, everything I think, even. I have never been alone with my thoughts before.

ELANO: Sometimes I have seen you listening to your own thoughts when we were all around you.

BEAUTY: (*Chuckling.*) Yes. I had to keep them to myself.

ELANO: And last night—there by the window . . . what were you thinking then?

BEAUTY: Will you promise not to tell?

ELANO: What was it you were keeping to yourself?

BEAUTY: I was thinking that there were lights so far away that they looked like lights you just remembered and every one of them was giving light to people—and—(*She stops, almost afraid to tell him.*)

ELANO: That wasn't all, was it?

BEAUTY: No!

ELANO: What was the rest of it?

BEAUTY: I thought I'd like to go alone and see those people.

ELANO: Alone—

BEAUTY: Yes. I'd like to go alone and have them for my friends. . . . You may go now Elano. I'm ready to begin—(*At the doorway Elano pauses and turns back, but Beauty has turned away, thinking he has gone.*) No one to say "You mustn't!" No one to say "Be careful." Oh, I like it! (*Whirling in her joy she suddenly sees Elano. He darts back to kneel looking up at her, and then exits. Beauty laughs and half dances as she explores the room, then suddenly she stops.*) I'm alone! I wonder what is up in the tower—I wonder why I mustn't touch the cobweb—I wonder what a spindle is. I wish I could find out. (*Her eyes turn toward the cobweb, her head follows, then she goes to stare at the cobweb. She puts her hand out, then turns away without touching it.*) Father would be angry. Mother wouldn't like it. It would make Elano sad . . . (*She drops her hand, the joy gone from her.*) I'm not alone, after all. (*She drops into a chair, dispirited. Low music fills the air. She looks up, listening.*) It comes from up in the tower! I want to go up and dance to it! (*She begins to move to the music.*) It makes me feel as if I could go right through the cobweb, and through the door and up a hundred stairs and find out something! (*She works into a dance of growing joy, daring and wonder; a voice is added to the music, and she stops, listening. She drops into the Queen's chair.*) I'll play queen. That's a different tune and someone is singing—(*As the deep humming grows in volume the other music fades out. Words come clear after a bit.*)

FRYTANIA: (*Off singing.*)
    See how my spindle flies through the air.
    See how I turn and whirl it about.
    Threads of fate I'm spinning.
    Of ending and beginning.
    Open the door.
    Look all about.
    Come and find out.

BEAUTY: Spindle—(*She draws near the door.*)

FRYTANIA: See how I weave the threads on the loom.
    Threads from my spindle, high up the stairs.
    Threads of fate I'm weaving

Of doubting and believing.
Open the door.
Climb to the tower.
This is your hour.

BEAUTY: This is my hour—(*She runs to look out the window, back to the door and hesitates.*)

FRYTANIA: See how I weep, spinning alone. (*Beauty repeats word "weep."*)
See how my tears fall on my thread. (*Beauty repeats word "tears."*)
None for me is caring.
None for me is daring.
To open the door
And come where I moan,
Weeping alone.

BEAUTY: (*As the voice dies away in sobs.*) I care! I dare! I'm coming!
(*Before she can sweep the cobweb out of her way, it makes room for her as it did for Frytania. The door opens, and both close behind Beauty as she runs up the stairs.*)

CURTAIN

ACT TWO

SCENE 2. *Ella's spinning room, high in the tower. There is a window, overlooking the garden, and a door to the stairway. Bright-colored skeins of flax hang on the walls. A couch, a table on which stands the box holding the spindle and a chair are necessary furniture; if practical, a spinning wheel adds color to the set, though hand spinning can be made to afford all necessary action. Frytania is standing by the door, at curtain, singing. She stops to listen intently, nods as she hears Beauty's footsteps, hastens to the box, over which she waves her wand. It opens without her touching it. She lifts up the spindle, exulting, replaces it, waves her wand to close the box, and hastens to the couch, where she sits, waiting. Beauty appears in the doorway.*

FRYTANIA: (*Glowing.*) How do you do, my dear.

BEAUTY: You are happier now. Why! you are a Fairy. But you are not like the others.

FRYTANIA: No. I'm not quite like the others. . . . You have come at last.

BEAUTY: Why do you say at last?

FRYTANIA: I have waited a long time.

BEAUTY: I came as soon as I heard you sing.

FRYTANIA: I have often sung before.

BEAUTY: I never heard you.

FRYTANIA: It wasn't time for you to hear me. People do not hear things till they are ready to hear them. I sang to you when you were very little.

BEAUTY: Did you know about me then?

FRYTANIA: All the kingdom knows when a princess is born.

BEAUTY: Why did you sing to me before I could hear you?

FRYTANIA: It made you wonder what was behind the cobweb—what was up in the tower.

BEAUTY: Oh, yes. I wondered and wondered. But they didn't like to have me talk about the tower. So I stopped asking about it.

FRYTANIA: But you didn't stop thinking about it.

BEAUTY: Oh, no. I thought all the more. But they were my private thoughts. They were my real thoughts.

FRYTANIA: I knew if you wondered enough when you were little you would find out when you were big.

BEAUTY: (*Laughing with excitement.*) I'm glad I'm big enough to find out things for myself. This is my first time. Did you know this is my sixteenth birthday?

FRYTANIA: Yes, I knew. Why don't you come in?

BEAUTY: I think perhaps I ought to go back. If they knew I had come up here they would be frightened. They have always been afraid of the cobweb and the tower. I don't want to frighten them. I'll go down and tell them I am safe. Then I'll come back again. (*She turns and takes a step down.*)

FRYTANIA: (*Calling after her.*) I shan't be here again.

BEAUTY: (*Off.*) Never?

FRYTANIA: Never. You will never find out how to use my spindle. (*A silence, then Beauty appears in the door.*)

BEAUTY: Did you say—spindle?

FRYTANIA: Yes.

BEAUTY: I have never seen a spindle.

FRYTANIA: There is one in that box.

BEAUTY: I'd like to see it.

FRYTANIA: Open the box.

BEAUTY: (*Trying.*) It's locked. There isn't any key.

FRYTANIA: (*Waving her wand.*) Try again. (*The box comes open. Beauty peers in and steps back.*)

BEAUTY: Why should anyone be afraid of that?

FRYTANIA: I'm not afraid of it. I have spun all these threads on it.

BEAUTY: How do you spin threads?

FRYTANIA: Bring it to me. I'll show you. (*Beauty's hand goes out for it and comes back, two or three times.*)

BEAUTY: I keep thinking of Father and Mother—and Ella and Gort and Elano. They wouldn't want me to touch it.

FRYTANIA: Why not?

BEAUTY: They are afraid of a spindle. I don't know why.

FRYTANIA: Find out for yourself. Show them how foolish they are to be afraid—lift it up. (*Beauty lifts the spindle from the box with great care. In spite of her eager interest she is full of unreasoning terror. Her face grows radiant as nothing bad happens. She carries it around the room, across her two hands, triumphing over her deep fear. She finally lays it in the Fairy's lap.*)

BEAUTY: I carried it all around!

FRYTANIA: That is not the right way to hold it.

BEAUTY: Show me the right way.

FRYTANIA: Straight up, like this . . . and this is the way it works. (*Frytania throws it out and back, as a hand spinner does.*) Try it.

BEAUTY: I carried it all around but I don't think I'd like to throw it like that. (*She moves away, uneasy, and finds herself near the window.*)

FRYTANIA: Why not?

BEAUTY: (*Looking down.*) Why! They are all under this window! How little they look. Father and Mother are talking to Gort and Ella. Elano is watching the sundial. Oh! My time is almost up. I can see the sun straight across it. Elano sees it, too. He is looking up! He sees me! (*She waves.*) He's afraid! He's running toward the palace door. And all the time I'm safe and happier than I have ever been in my life!

FRYTANIA: Take the spindle. Give them a surprise. Let them see you learning how to spin.

BEAUTY: I will sing your song. I remember it! May I change the words a little?

FRYTANIA: Sing anything you like. But use the spindle—so. (*Beauty throws the spindle a little clumsily, singing. If there is a spinning wheel, Frytania shows her how to use it, otherwise throwing it out and back will answer.*)

BEAUTY: Now I'll sing—
　　See how my spindle flies through the air.
　　See how I turn and twist it about.
　　Threads of fate I'm spinning.
　　Of ending and beginning—

(*Sound of the crashing door, off.*)

Elano has broken in the door! Now he's coming! I'm going to change the words! (*She springs across the room, facing the door, holding the spindle out in triumph, still singing.*)
　　I opened the door,
　　I climbed up the stairs,
　　I came and found out!

(*Elano bounds in, and stands frozen an instant, as she ends her song, laughing.*)

ELANO: Beauty! Let me have it! (*He tries to seize it; she eludes his chase, laughing. Finally he gets it from her.*)

BEAUTY: Elano, I've had such a wonderful time! I've found out what a spindle is. And I have a new friend. That is a spindle. And this is my new friend. She is teaching me how to spin. Give it back to me. (*Shouts and footsteps on the stairs, off. Frytania snatches the spindle from Elano as he holds it behind him to keep it from Beauty. She tries to pass it to Beauty, over and under Elano's frantic guard. The King, Queen, Gort, and Ella enter from the stairs, the Fairies appearing back at the same time through an invisible panel. The court people start to help Elano, with cries of warning. The Fairies lift their wands, forbidding.*)

UNA: This is Elano's hour! (*They stand frozen, watching as Frytania motions to Beauty, secretly, to move back, and when she does, throws the spindle to her over Elano's head. He leaps high in the air to catch it.*)

BEAUTY: Elano, you are splendid!

FRYTANIA: (*Suddenly threatening, her hand outstretched.*) Put it in my hand. (*As he shrinks back she moves toward him.*)

ELANO: (*His voice choked with fear.*) You can't have it! I know who you are now. I won't let you hurt her.

FRYTANIA: You can't stop me. You are afraid of me.

ELANO: (*Trembling.*) No. It was the child in me.

FRYTANIA: The child is in you still. You feel his heart beat fast. He wants to run. You want to run.

ELANO: (*Straightening.*) I will not run!

FRYTANIA: The child is afraid. You are afraid. You can't breathe. You can't move. You can't put out your hand to stop me—Come, Princess. Feel of it. The point is very smooth and sharp. Feel. Find out for yourself. (*Beauty takes a step toward it. Elano springs between them, his arms out.*) It's no use. You have no power against me.

ELANO: I have! You only hate her! I love her! (*Frytania suddenly hurls the spindle toward Beauty, who is moving to reach for it. Elano tries to stop Beauty, but she snatches it from Frytania with her other hand. Gort, King, and Elano all try to get it away from Beauty. Norbert enters, watching, bewildered.*)

BEAUTY: (*Dropping the spindle.*) Oh—you made me prick my finger. (*Frytania's bell sounds. There is silence. Beauty runs to show her finger to the Queen.*)

FRYTANIA: How do you do, sisters! Your gifts worked well. Her heart went out to me because I wept. She climbed the stairs to comfort me. She stayed to find out what a spindle was. Your gifts brought mine to pass.

KING: (*To Una.*) Elano faced her, this time. You can change her gift!

ELANO: (*To Fairies.*) Yes—yes!

QUEEN: That was only the first bell. Change it quickly!

ELLA: Speak! Speak!

ELANO: (*To Frytania.*) You could not make me afraid. The power of my fear has left you.

FRYTANIA: She cannot change my gift, for all that. Some gifts have more power than others. Nothing has more power over men than my gift of death.

UNA: Are you sure?

FRYTANIA: You will see, now that the end of her choice has fallen on her. (*To Belita.*) Your gift of beauty will turn to ugliness. (*To Cordia.*) The will to find out to the terror of knowing. (*To Freona.*) All her love will turn to hate.

UNA: We are waiting to know.

BEAUTY: What are they talking about? What was that bell? Why are they all afraid? Elano?

FRYTANIA: I will tell you! At your christening party, sixteen years ago, I was left out. I put you under a curse.

BEAUTY: A curse?

FRYTANIA: She is afraid!

BEAUTY: Is there a curse on me? Mother! Father! Is there a curse on me? Ella! Gort! Fairies! Tell me it isn't so! (*Her face is distorted with horror.*)

FRYTANIA: (*To Freona.*) Look! Which is stronger in her, your gift or mine? (*To Beauty.*) Shall I tell you what it is?

BEAUTY: No! No!

ELANO: Beauty!

KING: Have courage! (*They start toward her. Una checks them, with uplifted wand.*)

UNA: She must face it alone.

FRYTANIA: I will tell you what your curse was. (*Picks up spindle.*) It was to prick your finger on this spindle on your sixteenth birthday, and of that wound to die.

BEAUTY: Die!

FRYTANIA: The bell meant that the curse has come upon you. Four times more you will hear it. On the fifth stroke, your life will end.

BEAUTY: Only because I pricked my finger?

FRYTANIA: Because it was my christening gift. (*Bell sounds.*)

BEAUTY: Yours?!

FRYTANIA: That is two.

BEAUTY: You were my friend.

FRYTANIA: I never said so.

BEAUTY: Did you mean harm all the time? Were you only trying to make me prick my finger?

FRYTANIA: I was working my will in you. It was easy, because I used my sisters' christening gifts.

BEAUTY: It was easy because I didn't know! (*In sudden fury to the Queen.*) Why didn't you tell me? I begged and begged to know. You left me in the dark. I needn't have done it—you made me prick my finger! I hate you! I hate you all!

ELANO: (*As Frytania laughs in triumph.*) Don't say that!

BEAUTY: I hate you most of all, Elano! You knew all the time and you went away and left me alone. You could have told me, and you just looked up at me.

QUEEN: We wanted to protect you.

BEAUTY: You took away the rest of my life because you were afraid to tell me!

FRYTANIA: *You* were afraid! You are afraid now!

BEAUTY: All the things I'll never see! Beautiful things! Exciting things! All the people I'll never know. I want them! I want to go on living! I want to find out everything! I want to be grown-up! (*She flings herself onto the couch in a passion of grief. Elano turns to Frytania, desperately.*)

ELANO: It was my fault. Let me die in her place!

QUEEN: No! It was mine. I kept her from knowing! I made her bring the curse on herself!

KING: And I!

GORT: (*Beside himself.*) The Fairy warned us at the christening. "No one can ward off another's danger," she said. "Each must face his danger for himself." Yet we would not let her know. I was a fool! I was so sure we could keep her safe! I would listen to no one but myself!

ELLA: I believe she asked me a hundred times! What is a spindle, Ella? Why won't you tell me? Why can't I touch the cobweb?

QUEEN: Now all our love has turned to hate in her! (*The bell sounds. Beauty does not seem to hear it. The others are rigid with dread. Frytania's triumph mounts. The other fairies watch, their wands held in two hands, passive.*)

GORT: That is three! She has a right to hate us! (*He breaks into sobs. Beauty looks up, first at Gort, then around at the stricken faces, as the echoes of the bell die away. Her face is flooded with love and courage.*)

BEAUTY: What was that you said, Gort?

GORT: I said—you have a right to hate us.

BEAUTY: (*Going to him.*) I don't hate you. That was silly talk. It was just because I was so surprised. At first, I felt angry and afraid because I was so surprised. Lift up your head, Gort. Dear old Gort. Look! Now I'm not angry. And I'm not afraid. Ella! Don't moan and cry. It's all right! That's what you used to say to me. Now I'm saying it to you. It's all right!

ELLA: It's not all right. It's all my fault.

KING: No. Ours. We forbade you to tell her.

BEAUTY: No, Father! Mother! You didn't know my private thoughts. How could you know you ought to tell me? Listen, all of you. I'm not sorry now! I've found out something wonderful! I've found out how much I love you all! I never knew, before. I never felt like this! I think I've got grown-up! See, Mother? Elano, look! I don't mind any more!

CORDIA: My gift works well. (*She lifts her wand. Belita does the same.*)

BELITA: Which is stronger in her, sister—your gift or mine?

FREONA: (*Motions to Beauty, who stands radiant.*) Look! (*She lifts her wand.*)

QUEEN: How can we give her up?

BEAUTY: Mother! I've found out something else. You won't really give me up at all. When you left me there alone, I wasn't really alone at all! You were all there, too, inside my mind. I shall always be with you like that. Yes, Gort! I shall be running around in your mind the way I used to do in your garden. And I shall be laughing, mind! Do you hear that, Mother? Do you, Elano? Father? Ella? Gort? And you must all laugh with me, in your thoughts. Laughing together, when you love each other, is one of the very best things in the world! (*The bell sounds.*)

ELANO: Four—

BEAUTY: (*Full of the spirit of adventure.*) Now it's coming! Stand where I can see you all. It's something new! Elano, stay close to me until the last bell sounds. We always did the exciting things together.

UNA: (*Lifting her wand, facing Frytania.*) All our gifts have had more power than yours. I change your gift of death to one hundred years of sleep. (*All the four fairies raise their wands against Frytania. She gradually lowers hers and moves back, and off, defeated. Beauty's wonder grows.*)

BEAUTY: One hundred years—

UNA: And because Freona's gift of love has had more power in you than all the others, it shall be a kiss from one you love that calls you awake.

ELANO: Let it be mine!

BEAUTY: Let it be Elano's.

UNA: You began it, you shall end it. (*Beauty holds out a hand to Elano, who, at a sign from Una leads her to the couch. She sits. He lowers her to the pillow. She closes her eyes. Her hand falls; he lifts it and lays it on the couch. Una touches her with her wand and the silver bell sounds. A soft sigh and Beauty lies in smiling stillness. Throughout this no one else moves, all eyes on Beauty. The lighting changes slowly and beautifully.*) That her waking may not be more strange than she can bear, these she loves shall sleep with her and wake when she wakes. And that she may be safe till her waking comes, this palace shall become invisible. A fairy forest shall stand around it. No one but Elano shall have power to make way through it. (*She moves swiftly from one to another who are fixed in their attitudes by a touch of her wand. Just as she approaches Gort, Norbert comes to them, eager.*)

NORBERT: Me too! (*Gort lifts a hand to box his ear; Norbert dodges and they are caught so by Una's spell. There is an instant of tableau, with changing light.*)

UNA: Prince Elano—Stand away from her. (*He moves front, to kneel, with bowed head, eyes covered in grief. She moves her wand in a slow half circle, and from each side the fairy forest comes, upstage of the two of them. The lights fade behind it, and come up front. Una and Elano are alone, with the forest behind them. Elano has not looked up during the change.*

ELANO: (*He looks up and around in amazement.*) Beauty—The palace—

UNA: It is invisible. Around it this enchanted forest keeps guard. It will allow no one but you to reach her.

ELANO: When the hundred years is past! It will be too late for me to waken her!

UNA: Here you shall wait, in sleep as deep as hers for the one last instant that my spell has power. Only in that little point in endless time can your kiss end her sleep.

ELANO: What if I should wake too late!

UNA: When the time is at hand, my bell shall end your sleep. Four times more you will hear it, as you heard the four strokes on Frytania's bell that put the spell of death on Beauty. On the fifth stroke, your kiss can waken her.

ELANO: Only while your bell is sounding?

UNA: Only then. If you do not waken her before its echoes die away, she will sleep forever.

ELANO: How can I find her?

UNA: The forest will part and let you through. The palace and all in it will appear again. You will see her sleeping and kiss her for love of her beauty. Of that kiss, she will wake. Till then, rest here. (*She leads him to clump of flowers or bushes, behind which he lies down. She moves her wand over him. Her bell sounds. She leaves. The lights dim.*)

CURTAIN

ACT THREE

Before the enchanted forest, as at the end of Act Two. Elano is still asleep, probably unseen. Frytania is bending over him, moving her wand at the end of a spell. She turns to the forest as her bell's echoes die away, and waves her wand as she speaks.

FRYTANIA: Enchanted forest, round about
  If mortal touch you anywhere,
  On earth or air,
  Root or tree top,
  Leaf or bark,
  Swift as lightning cleaves the night
  Strike him with pain, shake him with fright.

(*She holds her wand still, listening, and makes a swift exit as the other fairies enter from the other side.*)

UNA: Instant by instant the centuries pass—

OTHERS: Instant by instant—

UNA: And this is the year—

BELITA: And the day—

FREONA: And the hour—

CORDIA: And the instant of danger is drawing near—

ALL: When Beauty must be called awake
   Or the power of our gifts be lost forever.

FRYTANIA: (*Entering, carrying a cape.*) Your gifts will be lost! Elano will be too late!

UNA: My bell will sound and waken him, in time. That is my spell.

CORDIA: You cannot change it.

FRYTANIA: I cannot change it. But I have made it useless by another. He will waken. But he will remember nothing—not who he is, or why he's here or what it is he must do.

UNA: Though you blotted out his memory, you could not blot out what he is.

FREONA: Deeper than memory in him lives his love.

CORDIA: And stronger lives the courage to do and know, which overcame the clutch of fear on his heart.

FRYTANIA: He will not remember how he overcame it. His heart will be like the heart of a little child. The finger of fear can write on it what it will.

UNA: No. Everything he has felt and done is part of him, whether he holds it in memory or not.

FRYTANIA: Yet I will make him afraid again. I have put a spell of pain and terror on your forest here.

BELITA: Though he feel the pain, he will remember Beauty.

FRYTANIA: He cannot remember.

CORDIA: Though he feels the terror he will defy it.

UNA: Then the power of your spell will fade. Ghosts of memory will pass before his mind.

CORDIA: He will dwell on them till he finds out what they mean.

FRYTANIA: I will appear to him in this cape, as a woman of the village. I will warn him of the dangers of this spot. He will flee with me to the village. I will hold him there, with fear till the instant when he can waken Beauty is past. You have no spell to save him.

UNA: It lies in him. He must save himself.

CORDIA: Every time he defies fear, your spell will grow weaker. He will remember more.

FRYTANIA: Every time he feels afraid, my spell will grow stronger. He will remember less.

UNA: We will wait, invisible, in the forest here, and listen. Lies are the language of fear as hate and killing are the fruits of it. If your lies can overcome the truth of what he is, your power is more than ours and Beauty will sleep forever. If the truth of what he is can overcome your lies, our power is more than yours and he will waken her. Farewell. We shall see. (*The fairies exit, Una stopping by Elano to lift her wand. Her bell rings. Elano stirs, and sits up slowly, half awake. Frytania wraps herself in her cape, and seizes the hand he moves.*)

FRYTANIA: Sir! Young sir! Waken!—Quickly!—Why do you stare so?

ELANO: Your pardon. I have been very sound asleep.—I heard a bell. It seemed to call to me.

FRYTANIA: You must get away from here.—At once!

ELANO: (*Still dazed.*) Away?

FRYTANIA: There is danger here!—Frightful danger!

ELANO: (*Suddenly alert.*) What danger?

FRYTANIA: I will tell you as we flee. Come away! (*Almost off, following her, Elano turns back, looking uncertainly around.*) Why do you delay?

ELANO: Something tells me I should stay.

FRYTANIA: Come! This instant!

ELANO: I feel as if there's something I should do. Where am I? Who am I?

FRYTANIA: You are a prince of another land. In your travels you fell asleep on the edge of this enchanted forest.

ELANO: (*Touched with fear.*) Enchanted? When did I come here? I can't remember coming to this place. I can't remember any other land.

FRYTANIA: This forest takes away your memory. It will come back as soon as you are safely far from here. Make haste. If you linger here the spell that holds you now will end in death.

ELANO: Death—Some memory moves like a shadow in me at that word—There is something I must do.

FRYTANIA: You will be horribly slain by the forest, if you linger. (*Una's bell sounds.*)

ELANO: What is that bell? It seems to have some message for me. I can't remember what it is.

FRYTANIA: It marks how your time passes.

ELANO: My time for what? For the thing that I must do? For the thing I can't remember?

FRYTANIA: Time to save yourself. It marks how a hundred years draws toward its end. If that end comes before you break the spell you're under, it will last forever. (*She tries to pull him along, but he breaks from her, almost at exit.*)

ELANO: What is it holds me here? Why do I feel I must be doing something? It's like a trumpet call that echoes in me from the past. Why can't I remember? I will not go until I do!

FRYTANIA: Mad youth! Put your finger on a leaf or twig of the forest, and feel what fate is waiting for you! (*He touches a bit of a branch and leaps away, distorted with the shock of pain and fear.*)

ELANO: I never knew such pain and terror haunted this earth!

FRYTANIA: Obey the terror! Flee!

ELANO: First I must know why some inner voice keeps saying, "Stay."

FRYTANIA: The forest is waiting! Come!

ELANO: I will not run from fear!—Wait! Dim shapes and sounds stir in me, like leaves in the wind on a moonlight night!—Sh-h-h—I'm kneeling by a cradle—There's music—and a throne in the room. Everyone is happy—No! Something terrible has happened! And it's my own fault! My fault!

FRYTANIA: You were afraid!

ELANO: It was long ago. Long, long ago.

FRYTANIA: You are still afraid! Come!

ELANO: Now I'm remembering again. I am running in the sunshine. Someone is running with me. There's something she mustn't even see or hear about. I can't remember what—

FRYTANIA: You never will remember. Why do you waste this precious time?

ELANO: (*Cutting her off.*) Things are getting clearer. We are looking out a window—high above the trees. The world is spread out before us. She is saying "There are lights so far away they seem like lights you just remember. And every one of them is giving light to people. I'd like to go alone," she says "and talk to all those people and have them for my friends." I'm afraid because she says "alone." I must never let her be alone. I can't remember why. I hear her voice, but I can't remember how she looks! Why can't I see her clearly?

FRYTANIA: Because you never saw her. Your memories are false.

ELANO: (*Waving an impatient hand for silence.*) Don't talk. It makes everything go whirling round. Now I'm in a garden looking at a window, high above. I'm afraid! There's something about a cobweb, and winding stairs that go up and up. And people shouting, and calling to me. And something flying through the air. And dreadful echoes, like a great bell tolling. And an old man sobbing, like a little child.—Everything is quiet.—Someone is asleep. Someone I love.—She lies so still in her beauty.—Beauty! That's it! That's what I must do. Something for her! Who is she? And where? And what is it I must do?

FRYTANIA: You poor enchanted youth. Those are not real memories. They are false visions. They fill the minds of all the youths who stay by this forest edge too long.

ELANO: Have there been others here?

FRYTANIA: Many.

ELANO: Do they all have shadowy memories of other days?

FRYTANIA: False memories, meant to give the forest's spell more power.

ELANO: Do they see a princess sleeping?

FRYTANIA: They see what you see.

ELANO: And feel there is something they must do for her?

FRYTANIA: They feel what you feel. (*Una's bell sounds.*) Hark! How fast your time flies!

ELANO: That bell. It echoes in me. It seems to say, "Be quick!"

FRYTANIA: Will you come—quick—or stay and perish like the others? (*Elano starts to run off, but whirls at exit, to face her.*)

ELANO: Who are you? How do I know you speak the truth?

FRYTANIA: You hear the bell. You have felt the trees. Come to the village. Ask the old folk there. They will tell you fearful tales of this place, handed down for a hundred years. (*Una enters during the above, listening. She also wears a cape, hiding her wand, and speaks with a disguised voice.*)

UNA: Good-day, neighbor.—Why are your eyes so full of question, stranger? It's true we have tales without number hereabouts. Magic tales—of an invisible palace beyond the forest's edge.

ELANO: Invisible—I have heard it spoken somewhere—when my heart was full of something I must do—(*While he speaks, his eyes closed in the attempt to recall his haunting memory, the two fairies lift their wands, their eyes locked. They return their wands to hiding under their cloaks as he speaks.*) Invisible palace—

UNA: It is told that there's a sleeping princess in it—

ELANO: A ghost of memory showed her to me!

UNA: And that she will sleep forever unless some youth from far—from very far—goes through this enchanted forest to waken her.

FRYTANIA: Those tales were spread to lure mad youths like you to perish in the forest.

ELANO: What if they are true?!

FRYTANIA: They are all false, like the memories that deceive you.

UNA: Some call them false. Others call them true.

ELANO: You. Which do you call them?

UNA: I call them neither. I wait for proof.

FRYTANIA: There is no proof!

UNA: Except to enter the enchanted forest—(*To Elano.*)

FRYTANIA: And perish there in the pain and terror that you felt!

UNA: *Or* bring back word of the sleeping princess.

ELANO: Did no one ever dare to do it?

FRYTANIA: Never! And never will!

ELANO: Then I must dare! Suppose my memory is real—suppose what the stories say is true and there is an invisible palace yonder and somewhere in it the sleeping princess my shadows showed me, waiting to be called awake! (*Una's bell sounds. Elano stands listening, deeply stirred.*) It calls to me. What does it say?

FRYTANIA: It says "Beware! Your time goes by faster and faster."

UNA: The gossips in the village say your sleeping beauty is under a fairy spell, and that there's only one brief instant in which it can be broken. And they say a fairy bell will sound four times as that little point in endless time draws near. On the fifth bell they say, the princess must be called awake, or sleep forever.

ELANO: There have been four already! What if they are right?

UNA: She must be wakened in that flash of time, they say, or never.

ELANO: What if that is it!—the thing I can't remember, yet know I must do! You said, some youth from far away?

UNA: One whose memories are of another place, and long ago.

ELANO: Mine are like that. If only I were sure they do not deceive me!

FRYTANIA: They do!

UNA: There is only one way to find out.

ELANO: (*Shudders as he looks at the forest edge, then masters his fear.*) I will take it.

UNA: (*Her voice changes to her fairy tones.*) Neighbor. His heart defies the clutch of fear.

ELANO: (*Startled.*) Your voice! I heard it once before—somewhere—sometime.—"This palace shall become invisible—" And before that, the same voice saying "Let it be Elano's." Elano! That's who I am! I remember!—Beauty!—Now I know! I must waken you! (*Una goes off,*

*fting her wand in triumph against Frytania, who darts between Elano
nd the forest. She also speaks in her own voice.*)

RYTANIA: Too late! Four bells have sounded. The fifth will be too
ate!

LANO: Your voice! Now I know you!

RYTANIA: My wand will hold you here, with pain and terror, till the
fth bell sounds. (*Waving her wand over him.*) Kneel to me, and I
vill make it less.

LANO: I will not kneel!—I will end your power.

RYTANIA: You cannot. I am timeless. I will always use my wand to
ule the hearts of men. There can be no end to me.

LANO: There can be an end to your rule over men. I will take away
our wand! (*He seizes her wrist with both hands and they whirl and
truggle, she with cries of anger, he with shouts of triumph, until he
inally wrests the wand from her and either breaks it, or if there is to be
oo long a run to have a new wand for every performance, hurls it off
tage. At the same time the lights flicker and the enchanted forest
noves off; lights come up on the tower room, revealing the same scene
n which the forest closed. Elano has disappeared with the forest, but
s the lights come to fullness he darts in, looking around in bewilder-
nent an instant, then sees Beauty and reaches her side just in time to
ft her hand and bend down to give her the awakening kiss as the fifth
ell sounds. Beauty sits up, radiant with the feeling with which she fell
sleep. The fairies enter with Elano, and watch with wands uplifted.*)

EAUTY: (*Joyful.*) Elano!

LANO: You are awake!

EAUTY: Of course! (*She looks around. Each of the others is stirring,
lowly waking out of the grief and wonder in which they fell under
Jna's spell. Beauty runs to kiss the King on either cheek.*)

EAUTY: Wake up, Father! Wide awake!

ING: Elano did it!

EAUTY: Of course!

ING: (*To Queen, whose eyes are just opened.*) Look!

UEEN: We didn't lose you!

BEAUTY: Of course not!

ELLA: (*Moaning.*) It was my fault—

BEAUTY: (*Running to shake her awake.*) It's all right, Ella! It's all right!

ELLA: You are laughing!

BEAUTY: Of course! (*Gort wakens enough to finish his box on Norbert's ear. Norbert jerks awake, rubs his eyes, sees Beauty, runs to jump over the couch to reach her.*)

NORBERT: I'm here! I waited for you!

BEAUTY: Of course! (*Gort comes to her in wide-eyed ecstasy and Beauty swings him around and around. They laugh, joyfully.*)

GORT: (*Suddenly terrified.*) The fairies will never let Beauty stay with —fools—like us! We don't know how to take care of her.

BEAUTY: Of course you do! This isn't a hundred years ago! This isn't even yesterday! This is today! (*All the fairies' bells sound gaily, as the fairies dance around the people, their wands high, everyone laughing.*)

CURTAIN

The Birthday of the Infanta
Stuart Walker

Adapted from Oscar Wilde

The Birthday of the Infanta, as adapted by
Stuart Walker, was first published in 1916.
An extensive search to locate the current
copyright holders has proved unsuccessful.

Based on the short story of the same title by Oscar Wilde, *The Birthday of the Infanta* was dramatized by Stuart Walker in 1921 for the repertoire of his touring Portmanteau Theatre of New York City.

The plot, inspired by the subject of Velázquez's painting *Maids of Honor*, is a fictional episode at the Spanish court of the mid-seventeenth century. It is the birthday of the princess. Most of all, she wants the attention of a loving father, but overwhelming grief for his dead wife has for years kept the king from showing the affection his daughter so desperately needs. Except on formal occasions, she seldom sees him. Instead of being loved, the little girl is entertained, given lavish gifts, and waited upon by a somber court.

As a special entertainment for her twelfth birthday, the Chamberlain has brought to the palace a "fantastic," an ugly, dwarfed boy, whom he found innocently dancing and singing in nearby woods quite unaware of his grotesque appearance. The impoverished father of the disfigured youth was easily persuaded to sell him to the courtiers.

The plot is the meeting of these two children: one, spoiled, arrogant, unhappy, and surrounded by wealth; the other, naïve, poor, even happy, but absurdly deformed. Of the two, the beautiful princess of the sophisticated, civilized court is the more severely crippled because she lacks human compassion. Her inhumanity destroys him. When he dies broken-hearted before her eyes, she is irritated that she can see him dance no more and haughtily insists that all who come to play with her in the future shall have no hearts. Has she understood nothing of his suffering, or is it too nearly like her own to admit?

The technical support will require attention. The two essential items of the setting, which should suggest a hall in the palace, are a large, curtained mirror and an elegant chair for the princess. Costuming, however, is the more important aspect of the technical production. The actor playing the fantastic must be made to appear bent and deformed. A harness that holds the body in a curved position and restricts the actor's normal movement may be worn beneath the costume to aid an actor who has difficulty retaining the bent posture. The clothing should indicate the differences in social status among the princess, the courtiers, the servants, and the fantastic. Although he would not be in dirty rags because he was bathed and given clean garments before being presented at court, the status of the fantastic's clothing would likely be no higher than that of an unimportant servant. Designs for the courtiers and princess may be derived from mid-seventeenth-century dress at the Spanish court.

THE BIRTHDAY OF THE INFANTA

CHARACTERS

The Infanta of Spain
The Duchess of Albuquerque
The Count of Tierra Nueva
The Chamberlain
The Fantastic
A Moorish Page
Another Page

SETTING

A royal balcony overlooking a garden in Spain.

TIME

The sixteenth century.

The opening of the curtains discloses a balcony overlooking a garden. The grim stone arch frames a brilliant sky. Gay flowers and a few white roses cover the railing. A bit of gaudy awning which can be lowered over the arch flutters in the breeze. At the right is a large mirror so draped that the dull, black hangings can be lowered to cover the mirror entirely. The hangings are of velvet, powdered with suns and stars. At the left similar hangings adorn a doorway. There are rich floor cover-ings and several formal chairs.

A Moorish attendant in black and yellow livery enters and arranges the chairs, and stands at attention.

The Infanta enters, followed by the Duchess of Albuquerque. The Infanta is dressed in gray brocade, very, very stiff and stately. She is small, with reddish hair and a settled air of self-possession and formal-ity. Occasionally her eyes twinkle and her feet suggest her childishness, but she soon recovers herself under the watchful eye of the Duchess, and she never really forgets that she is the Infanta of Spain.

The Infanta bows, if the slight inclination of her head can be called bowing, to the Moorish attendant. The Duchess also inclines her head and stands in the doorway.

INFANTA: I would be alone.

DUCHESS: Your Highness—

INFANTA: I would be alone. (*The Duchess turns in the doorway and speaks to those behind her.*)

DUCHESS: Her Highness would be alone. (*Then to the Infanta.*) This is unheard of.

INFANTA: My birthday is rare enough to be almost unheard of, your Grace of Albuquerque. I would be alone on my birthday—and I'm going to be alone! (*Then to the attendant.*) You may go! . . . But wait. . . . (*She stands admiringly before the mirror.*) Hold back the curtain. (*The attendant lifts the curtain. She preens herself.*) Why do I not look so well in my own suite? See how wonderful this is here. Look at the gold in my hair.

DUCHESS: That is vanity, your Highness.

INFANTA: Can I not admire myself on my birthday? Have I so many birthdays that I must live them as I live every other day?

DUCHESS: What is wickedness on other days is also wickedness on your birthday.

INFANTA: (*Taking a white rose from the balustrade and trying it in her hair and at her waist.*) See—see—I like it here. (*The Duchess, out-raged, speaks to the attendant.*)

DUCHESS: You may go.

INFANTA: No, no—stay—draw the curtains across the mirror!

DUCHESS: What will your father say? (*The Infanta is quite beside her little self.*)

INFANTA: Draw the curtains across the mirror and hide me from myself as those curtains hide my dead mother's room!

DUCHESS: Please—

INFANTA: I have spoken, your Grace. The curtains are to be drawn. We shall have no mirror today. (*The attendant closes the curtain.*) You may go! (*The attendant exits. The Infanta goes to the balustrade and looks into the gardens below. The Duchess, quite at a loss about what to do, finally crosses to the Infanta.*)

DUCHESS: Your Highness, I am compelled to remonstrate with you. What will his Majesty, your father, say?

INFANTA: My father will say nothing. He does not seem to care.

DUCHESS: Oh—Oh—Oh—

INFANTA: And my uncle wishes that I were dead. . . . No one cares. I have to be a queen all the time, and I can never be a little girl like the little girl I saw in Valladolid. She just played . . . and no one corrected her every moment.

DUCHESS: You play with the finest dolls in the world.

INFANTA: But I do not have mud like hers!

DUCHESS: Mud!

INFANTA: I'd like to smear my face!

DUCHESS: Oh!

INFANTA: And I'd like to climb a tree!

DUCHESS: Oh, your Highness, you fill me with horror! You forget that you are the daughter of a king!

INFANTA: Well, it's my birthday—and I'm tired of being a wooden body. (*She seats herself most unmajestically on the footstool.*)

DUCHESS: Such wickedness! I shall have to call the Grand Inquisitor. There is a devil in you!

INFANTA: Call him! I'll rumple my hair at him.

DUCHESS: He'll forbid you to enjoy your birthday.

INFANTA: What is it for my birthday—the same old story.

DUCHESS: (*Mysteriously.*) Who knows?

INFANTA: (*Not so surely.*) When I was ten, they had dancing in the garden, but I could not go amongst the little girls. They played and I looked on.

DUCHESS: An Infanta of the house of Aragon must not play with children.

INFANTA: And when I was eleven they had dancing in the garden and a shaggy bear and some Barbary apes; but I could only sit here. I couldn't touch the bear, even when he smiled at me. And when one of the apes climbed to this balustrade, you drew me away.

DUCHESS: Such animals are very dangerous, your Highness.

INFANTA: And here I am—twelve years old today—and still I must stay up here like a prisoner.

DUCHESS: Your Highness is very ill-tempered today.

INFANTA: I do not care. I do not want to be an Infanta.

DUCHESS: You are the daughter of Ferdinand, by grace of God, King of Spain!

INFANTA: Will my father come to me today? And will he smile?

DUCHESS: This is all for you alone.

INFANTA: Will not my sad father then come to me today? And will he not smile?

DUCHESS: He will see you after the surprise.

INFANTA: A surprise?

DUCHESS: Yes, your Highness.

INFANTA: What is it?

DUCHESS: I cannot tell.

INFANTA: If I guess?

DUCHESS: Perhaps.

INFANTA: It's hobbyhorses!

DUCHESS: No. (*They almost forget their royalty.*)

INFANTA: It's an African juggler with two green and gold snakes in a red basket.

DUCHESS: No.

INFANTA: In a blue basket?

DUCHESS: No.

INFANTA: (*Ecstatically.*) Three snakes?

DUCHESS: Not at all.

INFANTA: (*Dully.*) Is it a sermon by the Grand Inquisitor?

DUCHESS: No.

INFANTA: (*With new hope.*) Is it a troupe of Egyptians with tambourines and zithers?

DUCHESS: No.

INFANTA: Is it something I've never seen before?

DUCHESS: Never in the palace.

INFANTA: (*Screaming.*) It's a fantastic!

DUCHESS: Who knows?

INFANTA: Oh, it's a fantastic. It's a fantastic! (*She dances about.*)

DUCHESS: Your Highness forgets herself.

INFANTA: It's a fantastic! It's a fantastic! (*She suddenly regains her poise.*) Where is my cousin, the Count of Tierra Nueva? I shall tell him that I am to be entertained on my birthday by a fantastic. And I shall let him come here to see it. (*The Moorish attendant steps inside the door and holds the curtain aside.*)

Your Grace, inform the Chamberlain that I shall have the fantastic dance for me in my balcony. The sun in the garden hurts my eyes. Besides, I want to touch his back. (*She goes out, every inch a queen.*)

DUCHESS: She has guessed. Tell the Chamberlain to send the fantastic here.

ATTENDANT: The fantastic is waiting in the antechamber, your Grace. (*The Duchess exits after the Infanta. The Attendant crosses to antechamber.*)

Her Grace, the Duchess of Albuquerque, bids you enter. Inform the Chamberlain that her Highness, the Infanta, is ready for the dance. (*The Fantastic and an Attendant enter. The Fantastic is a hunchback, with a huge mane of black hair and a bright face that shows no trace of beauty, but great light and wonder.*

The Fantastic looks about the balcony. It is all so strange to him. As he goes about touching the things in the place the Attendant follows him closely, watching him with eagle eyes. As the boy nears the mirror and lays his hand upon the black velvet hangings, the Attendant steps in front of him and prevents his opening the curtains. The little boy then sits—a very small, misshapen little creature—on the steps of the balcony. The Chamberlain enters. He is a middle-aged man, with some tenderness left in his somewhat immobile face, and when he addresses the little boy there is a note of pathos that is almost indefinable.)

CHAMBERLAIN: Little grotesque, you are to see the King's daughter!

FANTASTIC: (*Almost overcome.*) Where is she?

CHAMBERLAIN: Come now, you must not be afraid.

FANTASTIC: I have never seen a king's daughter.

CHAMBERLAIN: You must smile.

FANTASTIC: Is she very big—and all bright and shiny?

CHAMBERLAIN: Smile! You did not have such a long face yesterday. That is why we bought you.

FANTASTIC: Will she smile upon me?

CHAMBERLAIN: You must make her smile.

FANTASTIC: Will she beat me if I do not make her smile?

CHAMBERLAIN: You shall be beaten if you displease her. This is her Highness's birthday. And you are to dance for her to make her happy.

FANTASTIC: I have never danced for a king's daughter before.

CHAMBERLAIN: You must dance bravely before her as you danced when we found you in the woods yesterday.

FANTASTIC: I am afraid of the King's daughter.

CHAMBERLAIN: We cannot have fear on the Infanta's birthday. We must have happiness.

FANTASTIC: I wish my father had not sold me.

CHAMBERLAIN: Your father was very poor, and he wanted you to make the Infanta happy.

FANTASTIC: My father did not care for me.

CHAMBERLAIN: You shall make the Infanta happy.

FANTASTIC: If you had a son would you sell him?

CHAMBERLAIN: You were sold to the Infanta.

FANTASTIC: Have you a son?

CHAMBERLAIN: No.

FANTASTIC: My father had seven sons.

CHAMBERLAIN: I had a little boy once.

FANTASTIC: And did you sell him?

CHAMBERLAIN: No. He went away. . . . He died.

FANTASTIC: Could he make the Infanta smile?

CHAMBERLAIN: I think he could.

FANTASTIC: Did he dance for her?

CHAMBERLAIN: No, he rode a hobbyhorse in the mock bull fight.

FANTASTIC: What is a hobbyhorse?

CHAMBERLAIN: A hobbyhorse is a make-believe horse—like the stick that you ride through the woods.

FANTASTIC: Oh, can't I ride a hobbyhorse in a bull fight?

CHAMBERLAIN: Sometime. . . . If you make the Infanta happy on her birthday I'll give you a hobbyhorse.

FANTASTIC: Can I ride it today—for her?

CHAMBERLAIN: No. You'll have to dance for her.

FANTASTIC: Is she terrible?

CHAMBERLAIN: Not if you are good.

FANTASTIC: I think—I'm afraid.

CHAMBERLAIN: Afraid? You were not afraid of the woods.

FANTASTIC: They would not hurt me. I did not have to make them smile.

CHAMBERLAIN: What will you do when you see the Infanta?

FANTASTIC: I don't know. That man who dressed me up said I must smile and bow. My smile was very funny, he said, and my bow was funnier. I didn't try to be funny.

CHAMBERLAIN: Some boys are funny even when they don't try to be.

FANTASTIC: I don't feel funny. I just feel happy, and when I am happy people laugh. . . . Did she smile upon your son when he rode the hobbyhorse?

CHAMBERLAIN: She threw a rose to him.

FANTASTIC: Do you think she'll throw a rose to me? I like roses. . . . Am I like your son?

CHAMBERLAIN: My son was tall.

FANTASTIC: I would be tall and strong, too; but I broke my back, and my brothers say I am very crooked. . . . I do not know. . . . I am not as strong as they are, but I can dance and sometimes I sing, too. . . . I make up my songs as I go along. And they are good songs, too, I know, because I've heard them.

CHAMBERLAIN: How did you hear them, Señor Merry-Face?

FANTASTIC: Someone sang them back to me.

CHAMBERLAIN: A little girl, perhaps?

FANTASTIC: Someone. . . . When I sang in the valley she would mock me.

CHAMBERLAIN: Who was it? . . . Tell me.

FANTASTIC: It was Echo.

CHAMBERLAIN: Echo? And does she live near your house?

FANTASTIC: She lives in the hills—and sometimes she used to come into the woods when it was very still.

CHAMBERLAIN: Did you ever see Echo?

FANTASTIC: No. You can't see her. . . . You can only hear her.

CHAMBERLAIN: Would you like to see her?

FANTASTIC: I always wonder if Echo might not mock my face as she mocks my voice?

CHAMBERLAIN: Who knows?

FANTASTIC: I go into the hills and I sing a song and then Echo sings back to me—just as I sing. . . . But when I go into the woods Echo doesn't stand in front of me—just as I look.

CHAMBERLAIN: Haven't you ever seen yourself?

FANTASTIC: No, but I would like to. I always make people happy when they look at me. They always laugh. Would I laugh if Echo mocked my face?

CHAMBERLAIN: I do not know.

FANTASTIC: Am I really happy looking?

CHAMBERLAIN: You are a fantastic.

FANTASTIC: That sounds happy.

CHAMBERLAIN: I hope it always will be.

FANTASTIC: Have you ever seen yourself?

CHAMBERLAIN: Yes.

FANTASTIC: Did your son see himself?

CHAMBERLAIN: Yes.

FANTASTIC: Where?

CHAMBERLAIN: In a mirror.

FANTASTIC: Is that Echo's other name?

CHAMBERLAIN: Yes.

FANTASTIC: Can I see myself sometime?

CHAMBERLAIN: Yes.

FANTASTIC: I'll sing, too. (*The Attendant enters.*)

ATTENDANT: Her Royal Highness, the Infanta of Spain! (*The Fantastic is very much frightened.*)

CHAMBERLAIN: Go behind the door there. . . . Wait. . . . Be brave. . . . Smile. . . . And do not speak until you are asked to. (*The Infanta enters sedately, followed by the Duchess and the Count of Tierra Nueva, an unpleasant-looking boy of sixteen. The Chamberlain bows very low and kisses the Infanta's stiffly proffered hand.*)

INFANTA: (*Regally.*) My lord Chamberlain, this is our royal birthday, and in accord with the wish of our father, the King of Spain, we are to be entertained with some mirthful sport (*suddenly a little girl*)—and I know what it is. It's a fantastic.

CHAMBERLAIN: Your Highness, it is the pleasure of the Chamberlain to His Majesty, your father, the King of Spain, to offer my felicitations this day on which God has deigned to send happiness and good fortune to Spain in your royal person. His Majesty the King through me desired to surprise you with mirth this day.

INFANTA: Is our royal father well? And does he smile today?

CHAMBERLAIN: His Majesty does not smile, your Highness. He cannot smile in his great grief.

INFANTA: Let the surprise be brought to us. But I guessed what it was! . . . It must be very ugly and very crooked and very, very funny to look at—or we shall be highly displeased. (*She settles into her royal place and takes on a manner. The Fantastic, having been summoned by the page, barely enters the door. The Infanta, looking royally straight before her, does not turn her head.*

After a moment.)
Well?

CHAMBERLAIN: Here is the surprise, your Highness. (*The Fantastic is the picture of grotesque misery. He looks first at the Chamberlain and then at the Infanta. Finally she turns to him, and he tries a timid smile and an awkward bow. The Infanta claps her little hands and laughs in sheer delight. The Fantastic looks desperately at the Chamberlain.*)

INFANTA: Go on. . . . Isn't he funny!

CHAMBERLAIN: (*To Fantastic.*) Bow again and then begin to dance.

FANTASTIC: (*Joyfully.*) She is only a little girl, and I've made her happy!

CHAMBERLAIN: What will you dance, Señor Merry-Face?

FANTASTIC: I'll dance the one I made up and no one ever saw or heard it except Echo. It's the dance of the autumn leaf. I'll show you what the autumn leaves do and I'll tell you what they say.

INFANTA: How do you know, you comic little beast?

FANTASTIC: I know because I live in the woods, up in the hills, and I dance with the leaves—and I have two pet wood-pigeons.

INFANTA: Where is the music?

FANTASTIC: I sing—it's happier that way.

INFANTA: Dance! Dance! (*The Fantastic bows in an absurdly grotesque way—his idea of stateliness and grace.*) I've never seen such a monstrous fantastic.

COUNT: We must touch his back before he goes—for good luck. (*The Fantastic begins to sing and dance "The Song of the Autumn Leaf."*)

FANTASTIC: (*Singing.*)
All summer long
I cling to the tree,
Merrily, merrily!
The winds play and play,
But I cling to the tree,
Merrily, merrily!
The summer sun
Is hot and gold,
Cheerily, cheerily.
But I hang on
In the August heat,
Wearily, wearily!
I am not free,
For I have to hang
Wearily, wearily!
Until autumn frosts
Release my grasp,
Cheerily, cheerily!
Then I'm free,

All crumpled and brown
Merrily, merrily!
I roll and I blow
Up and around,
Merrily, merrily!
All crumpled and brown
In my autumn coat,
I dance in the wind,
I hide in the rain,
Dancing and blowing
And waiting for winter,
Cheerily, cheerily,
Merrily, merrily,
Wearily, wearily.

(*He falls like a dead leaf on to the floor. The Infanta is delighted.*)

INFANTA: I'm going to throw him a rose!

DUCHESS: Your Highness!

INFANTA: See—like the Court ladies to Caffarelli, the treble. (*The Fantastic has risen and bowed in his grotesque way. The Infanta tosses the rose to him. He takes it up and, bowing absurdly, presses it to his lips.*)

DUCHESS: (*Who has never smiled.*) Your Highness, you must prepare for your birthday feast.

INFANTA: Oh, let him dance again! The same dance!

DUCHESS: Think of the birthday feast, your Highness. Your father, the King of Spain; your uncle, the Grand Inquisitor; the noble children.

INFANTA: Once more!

DUCHESS: Your Highness, you must see the huge birthday cake with your initials on it in painted sugar—and a silver flag. . . .

INFANTA: Very well. He can dance again after my siesta. . . . My cousin, I trust that you will see the next dance.

COUNT: I'll ride a hobbyhorse and he'll be the bull. It will be very funny with such a funny bull. (*He kisses her hand and exits the opposite way. The Infanta, followed by the Duchess, exits, and as she goes she looks once more at the Fantastic and breaks into a laugh. The Fantastic is delighted and stands looking after her.)*

CHAMBERLAIN: Come!

FANTASTIC: (*Putting out his hand.*) I think she liked me.

CHAMBERLAIN: The Infanta of Spain is the daughter of the King of Spain. You have made her smile. Come! (*They go out. The Attendant crosses and closes the awning. He draws the curtains from the mirror and preens himself a bit, looking now and then until he disappears. A sunbeam coming through the fluttering awning, strikes the mirror, and reflects on to the tessellated floor. There is a short intermezzo. Far-away harps and violins echo the Fantastic's little song. The Fantastic enters furtively, looking about. He takes the rose from his bosom.*)

FANTASTIC: I think I'll ask her to come away with me when I've finished my dance. (*He crosses to her door and listens. Then smiles and skips a step or two. He sees the sunbeam through the awning and goes to it. He again takes the rose from his coat and holds it in the sunlight. Again he dances to the door and listens, then he turns facing the mirror for the first time. He breaks into a smile, but first hides the rose hastily. He waves his hand.*) Good morrow! . . . You are very funny! . . . You are very crooked! . . . Don't look that way! . . . Why do you frown at me? . . . Can't you talk? . . . You only move your lips. . . . Oh, you funny little boy! (*He puts his hands on his sides and breaks into a great laugh.*)

If you could see yourself, you'd laugh still more. (*He makes a mocking bow and breaks into shouts. He plays before the mirror. The mockery is too clever.*)

You mock me, you little beast! . . . Stop it! Speak to me. . . . You make me afraid. . . . Like night in the forest. (*He has never known anything like this. He is in turn enraged, terrified. He runs forward and puts out his hand. He rubs his hand over the face of the mirror and the cold, hard surface mystifies him. He brushes the hair from his eyes. He makes faces. He retreats. He looks about the room. He sees everything repeated in the mirror—the awning, the chairs, the sunbeam on the floor.*)

(*Calling.*) Echo!

(*He strains for an answer. He hides behind a chair. He makes a plan.*)

I know, miserable little monster. You sha'n't mock me.

(*He takes the rose from his coat.*)

She gave me this rose. It is the only one in the world. . . . She gave it to me—to me.

(*He emerges from behind the chair and holds out the rose. With a dry sob he shrinks away and, fascinated, stares at the mirror. He compares the rose, petal by petal, terror and rage rising in him. He kisses it and presses it to his heart. Suddenly he rushes to the mirror with a cry. He touches the glass again, then with a cry of despair he hurls himself sobbing on the floor. Once more he looks upon the picture and then, covering his face with his hands, he crawls away like a wounded animal, lies moaning in the shadow and beating the ground with his impotent hands.*

The Infanta enters, followed by the Count. At the sight of the Fantastic the Infanta stops and breaks into a laugh.)

INFANTA: His dancing was funny, but his acting is funnier still. Indeed he is almost as good as the puppets. (*His sobs grow fainter and fainter. He drags himself toward the door, trying to hide his face. Then with a sudden gasp he clutches his side and falls back across the step and lies quite still. The Infanta waits a moment.*)

That is capital; it would make even my father, the King of Spain, smile. . . . But now you must dance for me:

Cheerily, cheerily!
Merrily, merrily!
Wearily, wearily!

COUNT: Yes, you must get up and dance and then we'll have a bull fight and I'll kill you. (*The Fantastic does not answer.*)

INFANTA: (*Stamping her foot.*) My funny little fantastic is sulking. You must wake him up and tell him to dance for me.

COUNT: You must dance, little monster, you must dance. The Infanta of Spain and the Indies wishes to be amused. (*Then to a page.*) A whipping master should be sent for. (*The page goes out.*)

COUNT: Let's touch his back (*As the children touch his hump.*) and make a wish.

INFANTA: I *wish* he would dance. (*Enter the Chamberlain and the Duchess.*)

DUCHESS: Your Highness!

INFANTA: Make him dance or I shall have him flogged. (*The Chamberlain rushes to the body. He kneels. Feels the heart—sees the sunbeam and the exposed mirror—shrugs his shoulders—rises.*)

CHAMBERLAIN: Mi bella Princess, your funny little fantastic will never dance again.

INFANTA: (*Laughing.*) But why will he not dance again?

CHAMBERLAIN: Because his heart is broken.

INFANTA: (*Thinks a moment, then frowns.*) For the future let those who come to play with me have no hearts. (*She passes out, not deigning to look back, every inch the queen—the disappointed, lonely, shut-in little queen.*

The others follow her properly according to rank; but the Chamberlain, remembering a little boy who would ride hobbyhorses no more in mock bull fights, returns and throws the Infanta's mantilla over the little warped body. It is a moment of glory. The Chamberlain again starts to follow his Mistress; but memory is stronger than etiquette. He goes to the Fantastic and takes up the little hand which clutches something precious. He opens the fingers and finds the rose. He holds it out and lets the petals flutter to the floor. That is all.)

CURTAIN

Tom Sawyer
Sara Spencer

Adapted from Mark Twain

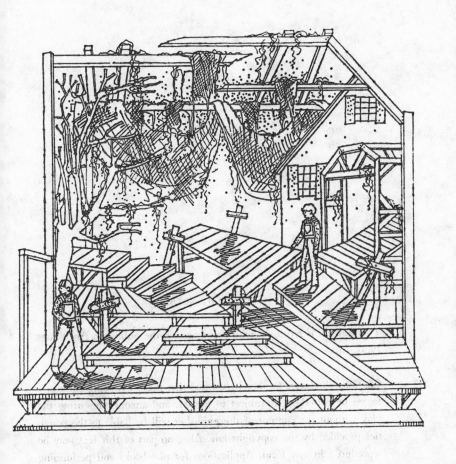

... provided by the copyright law. Above, no part of this text can be
reprinted in any ... Final Application for all stock and performing
rights time permitting ...

Anchorage Press, Inc.
Post Office Box 8067
New Orleans, Louisiana

Based on events and characters from the novel by Mark Twain, *Tom Sawyer* was dramatized in four acts by Sara Spencer in 1935. Although the plot has been made stageworthy, its source will still be apparent to those of the audience familiar with the famous novel.

The plot of the play is episodic in form, but the use of conflict and overlapping action gives the sense of a continuous story. In a series of unrelated conflicts among the children, Aunt Polly, and the schoolmaster, the first act creates Tom's everyday world. In the first scene of the second act, when Tom and Huckleberry Finn see both a murder in a graveyard and the situation set for an innocent man to be falsely charged, the longest thread of the dramatic action in the play begins. That episode is resolved in the second scene of the last act with Injun Joe's death, but not before a new episode has begun in which Becky Thatcher and Tom lose their way in a cave. The reappearance in town of Tom and Becky resolves the last crisis in the final scene of the play.

The action moves ahead with devices to insure the audience's attention. Suspense mounts when the villainous Injun Joe is looking for someone or as Becky and Tom realize that they are truly lost in the enormous cave. Comic scenes, such as the fence white-washing and the pipe-smoking lesson, change the pace and relieve the tension created by Tom's risky encounters with danger.

The several scenes of Tom's interaction with his friends are filled with portraits of three-dimensional child and adult characters in amusing incidents very similar to their prototypes in the novel. When possible, the playwright has incorporated bits of the novelist's dialogue which help delineate the characters even more clearly.

Settings should be simple so that the action will flow quickly and easily. Outside the jail and the courthouse, a street, a bedroom, a cave, etc., should only be suggested using flats to represent walls of a room, or props that indicate a specific place, such as a bed, a fence, or large papier-mâché rocks. Costumes are the working clothes of small-town mid-America a century ago.

TOM SAWYER

CHARACTERS

Tom Sawyer
Sid Sawyer
Alfred Temple
Ben Rogers
Jim Hollis
Huckleberry Finn
Joe Harper
Amy Lawrence
Janie Hardin
Gracie Miller
Susan Harper
Becky Thatcher
Aunt Polly
Mrs. Thatcher
Schoolmaster
Muff Potter
Injun Joe
Dr. Robinson
Preacher
Sheriff

SETTINGS

Act One
    SCENE 1. Tom Sawyer's bedroom.
    SCENE 2. A village street.
    SCENE 3. The Schoolroom.
Act Two
    SCENE 1. The graveyard.
    SCENE 2. A village street.
Act Three
    SCENE 1. Jackson's Island.

TIME

The nineteenth century.

ACT ONE

SCENE 1. *Tom's bedroom. A double bed, a wash stand, a motto on the wall.*

(*Tom and Sid are asleep, Tom snoring vociferously, Sid snoring like a steam whistle.*)

AUNT POLLY: (*Offstage.*) Tom! Oh, Tom! Monday!

TOM: (*Opens his eyes dazedly, yawns, then comes alert.*) Monday! (*He sighs drearily, then begins to plan. Feels around over his body for ailments, coughing experimentally, rejecting a loose tooth, etc. Finally he unties the rag around his sore toe, and falls to groaning.*) Oh-h-h! (*But Sid snores on.*) Ohh-h-h-h! Oooh-h-h-h! (*No response from Sid. Tom reaches over and shakes him.*) Sid! Sid! Ohhhhh-h-h-h! Ooooh-h-h-h!

SID: (*Waking up.*) Tom! Say, Tom!

TOM: Ohhhhhh-h-h-h-h! Ooooooh-h-h-h!

SID: (*Shaking him.*) Here, Tom. Tom! What's the matter, Tom?

TOM: Oh, don't, Sid. Don't joggle me.

SID: Why, what's the matter, Tom? I must call Auntie.

TOM: No, never mind. It'll be over by and by, maybe. Don't call anybody. Ohhhhhhhhh-h-h-h-h-h!

SID: But I must. Don't groan so, Tom. It's awful! How long you been this way?

TOM: Hours. Ouch! Don't stir so, Sid. You'll kill me. Ohhhhhh-h-h-h!

SID: Tom, why didn't you wake me sooner? Oh, Tom, don't! It makes my flesh crawl to hear you.

TOM: I forgive you everything, Sid. Ohhh-h-h-h-h! Everything you ever done to me.

SID: Oh, Tom, you ain't dying, are you? Don't, Tom. Oh, don't! Maybe—

TOM: I forgive everybody, Sid. Tell 'em so, Sid. And Sid, you give my brass knob and my cat with one eye to Joe Harper. And tell him—Ohhh-h-h-h!

SID: (*Making for the door.*) Oh, Aunt Polly! Come quick! Tom's dying!

AUNT POLLY: (*Offstage.*) Dying?

SID: Yes'm. Don't wait. Come quick!

AUNT POLLY: (*Still offstage.*) Rubbage! I don't believe it. (*But she rushes in, just the same, and finds Tom on the bed, writhing.*) You, Tom! Tom, what's the matter with you?

TOM: Oh, Auntie, I'm—Oh-h-h-h!

AUNT POLLY: What's the matter? What is the matter with you, child?

TOM: Oh, Auntie—my sore toe's mortified!

AUNT POLLY: (*Sinking on the bed with relief, and chuckling.*) Tom, what a turn you did give me! Now you shut up that nonsense and climb out of this.

TOM: (*Quite subdued.*) Aunt Polly, it seemed mortified. And—and it hurt so, I never minded my tooth at all.

AUNT POLLY: Your tooth, indeed. What's the matter with your tooth?

TOM: One of 'em's loose, and it aches perfectly awful. Oh-h-h-h-h!

AUNT POLLY: There, now, don't begin that groaning again. Open your mouth. Well, your tooth is loose, but you're not going to die about that. Sid, get me a hot iron off the kitchen stove. (*Sid gleefully rushes off, as Aunt Polly pulls a spool of thread from her apron pocket, and attaches one end of it to the bedpost. The other end she attaches to Tom's tooth.*)

TOM: (*Shrinking away.*) Oh, please, Auntie, don't pull it out. It don't hurt anymore. I wish I may never stir if it does. Please don't, Auntie. I don't want to stay home from school.

AUNT POLLY: Oh, you don't, don't you? So all this was because you thought you'd get to stay home from school and go a-fishing. Oh, Tom, you'll be the death of me yet. Here, Sid. (*Sid has reentered with the iron, and gives it to her, gloating at Tom's misery. Aunt Polly thrusts the iron close to Tom's face. Tom jerks back, and the tooth is dangling by the bedpost.*)

SID: Goody, that's what you get.

AUNT POLLY: Now you boys get your clothes on, and come on here to breakfast. I have an errand for you, Tom, before you go to school. (*Aunt Polly goes out.*)

SID: (*Pulling on his pants underneath his nightshirt.*) Didn't you think you was smart now?

TOM: (*Peeling off his nightshirt and disclosing himself fully dressed underneath.*) You go to grass.

SID: A lot of good it did you.

TOM: (*Experimenting.*) I can spit!

SID: You better not spit in here. I'll tell Auntie on you.

TOM: (*Detaching the tooth from the bedpost.*) All right, tattletale. You're just riled because I can spit and you can't.

SID: What you goin' to do with that tooth?

TOM: Keep it awhile. Then I'll trade it.

SID: What'll you take for it?

TOM: Nothing you got, sissy. Maybe I'll trade it to Ben Rogers for that window sash of his.

SID: Go ahead and do it. See if I care.

AUNT POLLY: (*Offstage.*) Tom! Come on here. You'll be late.

TOM: Yes'm, Aunt Polly. I'm comin'. (*He turns for a last word to Sid.*) Smarty. (*And goes out, dodging the pillow that Sid throws.*)

SCENE 2. *A village street. A white board fence. A barrel.*
(*School bell is heard, off. Ben Rogers enters, walking carefully as he*

balances books, slate, and dinner pail on his head. Sid Sawyer comes in behind him, deliberately jostles him, knocking the things to the ground. Amy Lawrence enters, jumping rope. Susan Harper and Becky Thatcher enter, admire Amy's jumping rope. May take a few trial jumps. Gracie Miller and Janie Hardin enter. Janie proudly exhibits a bandaged finger, and enjoys a momentary fame, as all the girls cluster around. Jim Hollis enters, balancing a straw on his nose. Tom Sawyer dashes in, pointing off to a vision behind him. The vision enters, Alfred Temple, walking primly, and wearing a hat, shoes, and spectacles. The girls are impressed, the boys either envious or resentful. Tom yanks his jacket as he passes. Alfred turns in umbrage. From the opposite direction, Muff Potter enters, the town tramp, fishing pole over his shoulder. The scene should be covered by indistinguishable school-child chatter. The second school bell is heard off, insistently. Muff Potter shambles off toward the river. The children bustle off toward school. As Alfred Temple starts out, Tom purposely slings his books so as to strike Alfred in the small of the back. Alfred turns to glare at him.)

ALFRED: That's the second time.

TOM: I can lick you.

ALFRED: I'd like to see you try it.

TOM: Well, I can do it.

ALFRED: No you can't, either.

TOM: Yes I can.

ALFRED: No you can't.

TOM: I can.

ALFRED: You can't.

TOM: Can!

ALFRED: Can't!

TOM: What's your name?

ALFRED: 'Tisn't any of your business maybe.

TOM: Well, I 'low I'll make it my business.

ALFRED: Well, why don't you?

TOM: If you say much, I will.

ALFRED: Much, much, much! There, now.

TOM: Oh, you think you're pretty smart, don't you? I could lick you with one hand tied behind me, if I wanted to.

ALFRED: Well, why don't you? You say you can do it.

TOM: Well, I will—if you fool with me.

ALFRED: Oh, yes. I've seen whole families in the same fix.

TOM: Smarty! You think you're some now, don't you? Oh, what a hat!

ALFRED: You can lump that hat if you don't like it. I dare you to knock it off. And anybody that will take a dare will suck eggs.

TOM: Say, if you give me much more of your sass, I'll light into you.

ALFRED: Oh, of course you will.

TOM: Well, I will.

ALFRED: Well, why don't you do it, then? What do you keep on saying you will for? Why don't you do it? It's because you're afraid.

TOM: I ain't afraid.

ALFRED: You are.

TOM: I ain't!

ALFRED: You are!

TOM: Get away from here.

ALFRED: Go away yourself.

TOM: I won't!

ALFRED: I won't either! (*Joe Harper enters on the run, late for school, but stops to watch this drama.*)

TOM: (*Drawing a line on the path with his toe.*) I dare you to step over that, and I'll lick you till you can't stand up. And anybody that would take a dare will steal sheep.

ALFRED: (*Stepping over it promptly.*) Now you said you'd do it. Let's see you do it.

TOM: Don't you crowd me. You better look out.

ALFRED: Well, you said you'd do it. Why don't you do it?

TOM: By jingo, for two cents, I would do it.

ALFRED: (*Holding out two pennies.*) There, mister. There's your two cents. (*Tom strikes the two pennies to the ground, and the two boys come to grips. The fight does not last long. In a few moments Tom is astride of the new boy, pounding him with both fists.*)

TOM: Holler 'nuff.

ALFRED: (*Struggling and crying.*) I won't.

TOM: (*Pounding on.*) Holler 'nuff!

ALFRED: 'Nuff! 'Nuff!

TOM: (*Letting him go.*) There, that'll learn you. Better look out who you're fooling with next time.

ALFRED: (*Crying, as he brushes himself off.*) Never you mind, mister. You just see what I do to you the next time I catch you out. (*He starts off to school, snuffling, but when Tom's back is turned, he picks up a stone and flings it at Tom, then takes to his heels as Tom makes a show of starting off in pursuit.*)

JOE: Hey, watch out! Gee whillikers, Tom, what was that all about?

TOM: I didn't like his airs.

JOE: Well—you better come on. It's late.

TOM: (*Flushed with victory.*) It's too hot to hurry. (*The final bell is heard, off.*)

JOE: (*Bolting off.*) There's the bell! (*He exits.*)

TOM: Wait for me, Joe! (*Automatically, Tom starts to bolt off after Joe, and turns to pick up his books. But just at this point, Huckleberry Finn meanders in, swinging a dead cat by the tail. Tom is lost in admiration.*) Huckleberry!

HUCK: H'lo.

TOM: What's that you got?

HUCK: Dead cat.

TOM: Lemme see him, Huck. My, he's pretty stiff. Where'd you get him?

HUCK: Bought him off'n a boy.

TOM: What'd you give?

HUCK: I give a piece of lickerish, and a bladder that I got at the slaughterhouse.

TOM: Say—what is dead cats good for, Huck?

HUCK: Good for? Cure warts with.

TOM: Cure warts with? I know other ways—but how do you cure them with dead cats?

HUCK: Why, you take your cat, and go and get in the graveyard about midnight, where somebody that was wicked has been buried. And when it's midnight, a devil will come—or maybe two or three. But you can't see 'em. You can only hear 'em. And when they're takin' that feller away, you heave the cat after 'em and say, "Devil foller corpse, cat follow devil, wart foller cat, I'm done with ye!" That'll fetch any wart.

TOM: Sounds right. When you going to try it, Huck?

HUCK: Tonight. I reckon they'll come after old Hoss Williams tonight.

TOM: But they buried him on Saturday. Didn't the devils get him Saturday night?

HUCK: Why, how you talk! How could their charms work till midnight, and then it's Sunday. Devils don't slosh around much of a Sunday, I don't reckon.

TOM: That's so, I bet. Hey, lemme go with you.

HUCK: All right—if you ain't afeared.

TOM: Feared? 'Tain't likely. Will you meow under my window?

HUCK: Yes. And you meow back if you get the chance.

TOM: I will—if Aunt Polly ain't awake. Well, so long, Hucky.

HUCK: You ain't goin' to school now, are you? You'll get a lickin' for bein' late.

TOM: I have to.

HUCK: Why?

TOM: Sid'll tell on me if I don't.

HUCK: (*Drawing something from his pocket with a great show of unconcern.*) Suit yourself.

TOM: What's that?

HUCK: Nothing but a tick.

TOM: Where'd you get him?

HUCK: Out in the woods.

TOM: What'll you take for him, Huck?

HUCK: I don't know. I don't want to sell him.

TOM: Oh, all right. It's a mighty small tick anyway.

HUCK: Oh, anybody can run down a tick that don't belong to you. I'm satisfied with it. It's a good enough tick fer me.

TOM: Sho, there's ticks a-plenty. I could have a thousand of 'em if I wanted to.

HUCK: Well, why don't you? Because you know mighty well you can't, that's why. This is a pretty early tick, I reckon. It's the first one I've seen this year.

TOM: Say, Huck, I'll give you my tooth for him.

HUCK: Less see it.

TOM: (*Showing it proudly.*) There!

HUCK: Is it genuwyne?

TOM: Genuwyne? Watch! (*And showing the cavity, he spits through it.*)

HUCK: All right. It's a trade.

TOM: (*Sadly.*) I haven't even had the chance to show that tooth to anybody yet.

HUCK: You can show 'em the hole.

TOM: That's so. Well, so long, Huck. I might as well go on and get my lickin'.

HUCK: Don't forget tonight.

TOM: (*Going off.*) I won't. (*He leaves.*)

HUCK: So long. (*He watches Tom off, then looks the tooth over appreciatively, and pockets it. He looks down at the dead cat on the ground.*) Here, kitty, kitty. (*He gathers the cat up by the tail, and swings off with it.*)

SCENE 3. *The schoolroom. Two long benches on each side. The master's desk. A hat rack, hung with bonnets, hats, and dinner pails.* (*The girls are seated on one side of the room, the boys on the other.*)

MASTER: Fourth Reader! (*Amy Lawrence, Gracie Miller, and Ben Rogers approach the Master's desk.*) Amy Lawrence, you may recite.

AMY: (*Sing-songing it off.*) Shameful Death.
There were four of us about that bed.
The mass-priest knelt at the side—

MASTER: You may not go on, Amy, until you can deliver that piece with the proper expression.

AMY: (*Using broad gestures.*) There were four of us about that bed.
The mass-priest knelt at the side.
I and his mother stood at the head.
Over his feet lay the bride.
We were quite sure that he was dead,
Though his eyes were open wide.
He did not die in the night,
He did not die in the day,
But in the morning twilight—

(*But Tom Sawyer appears at the door, and all action is suspended.*)

MASTER: Thomas Sawyer!

TOM: Sir?

MASTER: Come up here. Now, sir, why are you late again, as usual?

TOM: I—uh—I—

MASTER: Speak up.

TOM: Well—uh—I—I—(*Defiantly.*)—I stopped to talk with Huckleberry Finn!

MASTER: (*Horrified.*) You—you did what?

TOM: Stopped to talk with Huck Finn.

MASTER: Thomas Sawyer, this is the most astounding confession I have ever listened to. No mere ruler will answer for this. Take off your jacket. (*Tom does. The Master takes up a switch from the desk, and goes to the door.*) Now, come here, sir. (*They go out, and we hear the switching offstage, while the children flock to the doorway to see it. But when the Master comes back, they are all sitting primly in their seats again. The Master returns, propelling Tom ahead of him.*) Now, sir, go and sit with the girls! And let this be a warning to you. (*The room titters, and Alfred Temple looks justified, as Tom takes a seat beside Becky Thatcher.*) The Fourth Reader will continue with its lesson. Amy Lawrence, you will finish learning the poem for tomorrow. Benjamin Rogers!

BEN: It was the schooner Hesperus—

MASTER: You will announce the title of your piece, Benjamin.

BEN: The Wreck of the Hesperus.
It was the schooner Hesperus
That—that—

MASTER: (*Prompting.*) That sailed.

BEN: That sailed—that sailed—that sailed the windy sea.

MASTER: The wintry sea. (*While the recitation continues in pantomime, Tom puts a peach in front of Becky Thatcher. She thrusts it away. He puts it back.*)

TOM: Please take it. I got more. (*Becky pretends to be absorbed in her book.*) I'll draw you a picture.

BEN: Blue were her eyes—blue were her eyes—

MASTER: (*Prompting.*) As the.

BEN: Blue were her eyes as the—

MASTER: Zero, Benjamin. You may spend the rest of the hour studying the poem. Grace Miller!

GRACIE: A Lament.
O world! O time! O life!

MASTER: (*Correcting.*) O world, O life, O time.

GRACIE: O world! O life! O time!
On whose last steps I climb—

(*This continues silently, while we hear Tom's conversation with Becky.*)

BECKY: (*Trying to see Tom's slate.*) Let me see it.

TOM: (*Showing it.*) It's not much.

BECKY: It's nice. Make a man.

TOM: (*Dashing off a man in a few strokes.*) All right.

BECKY: It's a beautiful man. Now make me coming along.

TOM: Here you are. Only that's not pretty enough.

BECKY: Silly, it's ever so nice. I wish I could draw.

TOM: It's easy. I'll learn you.

BECKY: Oh, will you? When?

TOM: At recess. Do you go home for dinner?

BECKY: I'll stay if you will.

TOM: Good. That's a whack.

BECKY: What are you drawing now?

TOM: I'm not drawing. I'm writing.

BECKY: What are you writing?

TOM: Oh, it ain't anything.

BECKY: Yes it is.

TOM: No it ain't. You don't want to see.

BECKY: Yes I do. Please let me.

TOM: You'll tell.

BECKY: No I won't. Deed and double deed I won't.

TOM: You won't tell anybody at all? Ever, as long as you live?

BECKY: No, I won't ever tell anybody. Now, let me.

TOM: Oh, you don't want to see.

BECKY: Now that you treat me so, I will see! (*She pulls the slate away from him, but is overcome with shyness when she reads it.*) Oh, you bad thing! (*The Master at this point bears down on Tom, and leads him by the ear to his own seat, beside Joe Harper.*)

MASTER: Now, Thomas Sawyer, we'll see if you can behave yourself a little better in your own seat. Fifth Reader! (*Susan Harper, Jim Hollis, and Alfred Temple approach the Master's desk.*) James Hollis, what is the capital of the state of Missouri?

JIM: The capital of the state of Missouri is—the capital of the state of Missouri—

MASTER: Zero. Susan Harper, what is the capital of the state of Missouri?

SUSAN: Saint Louis.

MASTER: Zero. Alfred Temple.

ALFRED: The capital of the state of Missouri is Jefferson City.

MASTER: Correct. There, boys and girls, is an example of how a question should be answered. James Hollis, name another important city in the state of Missouri. (*While this goes on in pantomime, Tom at his seat pulls out his tick. Joe Harper is promptly interested.*)

JOE: What's that you got, Tom?

TOM: It's a tick. What'd you think it was?

JOE: What you going to do with him?

TOM: Just play with him.

JOE: Suppose he crawls away from you.

TOM: (*Placing the tick on his slate.*) I'll turn him back with my pencil.

JOE: He's coming over my way.

TOM: Don't let him go off, Joe. Turn him back.

JOE: Mighty lively little tick, ain't he?

TOM: Sure is. He's the first one this year, too. Quit proddin' him. Let him come over to my side.

JOE: Let me play with him a little.

TOM: Tell you what. I'll draw a line. Now as long as he's on your side of the slate, you can stir him up, and I'll leave him alone. But if you let him get away and get on my side, you're to leave him alone as long as I can keep him from crossing over.

JOE: All right. Go ahead. Start him up. (*The tick scene proceeds in pantomime.*)

MASTER: James Hollis, what are the chief products grown in the state of Missouri?

JIM: The chief products grown in the state of Missouri are—are—fishing—

MASTER: Susan Harper, what are the chief products grown in the state of Missouri?

SUSAN: Corn.

MASTER: Corn and what else?

SUSAN: Just corn.

MASTER: (*With a bland assurance that here at last will come the exemplary answer.*) Alfred Temple, what is produced in the state of Missouri besides corn?

ALFRED: Whiskey.

MASTER: Ahem! Will you all open your books to page 165, and read just what it says. (*The Fifth Reader turns pages industriously, while our attention is drawn to Tom and Joe again.*)

JOE: Tom, you let him alone.

TOM: I only want to stir him up a little, Joe.

JOE: No sir, it ain't fair. You just let him alone.

TOM: Blame it, I ain't going to stir him much.

JOE: Let him alone, I tell you.

TOM: I won't. (*The whole room is watching the tick scene now, for the Master is descending on the two boys.*)

JOE: You shall. He's on my side of the line.

TOM: Look here, Joe Harper, whose is that tick?

JOE: I don't care whose tick he is. He's on my side of the line, and you shan't touch him.

TOM: Well, I just bet I will, though. He's my tick, and I'll do what I blame please with him, or die. (*But here the Master interferes, and both boys receive a sounding whack across the shoulders.*)

MASTER: What is that thing?

TOM: Only just a tick. (*The Master, after one helpless, horrified glance, gingerly picks up the tick, and throws it out the door.*)

MASTER: Let that be the end of that nonsense, Thomas Sawyer. Now. Everybody will get out your copybooks. Open them to the page you have prepared for today. (*Everybody does, and the Master passes from one to the other, looking them over as he goes.*) Alfred Temple—ah! I should like to show the whole room just what a perfect page can look like. Compare that, for example, with this one. Thomas Sawyer, there are five big blots on this page, three words misspelled, and the writing is very irregular. You will remain during the recess period, and rewrite the whole lesson. The rest of you may put away your books. We now adjourn for recess. (*There is a general rush for the dinner pails, and then the door. Tom joins the movement, and whispers to Becky.*)

TOM: Put on your bonnet and let on you're going home. Then when you get to the corner, give the rest of 'em the slip, and come back through the lane.

BECKY: All right.

MASTER: Thomas Sawyer! Come back here. You are to spend your recess period working on your writing lesson, while the rest of the school is out playing. Now get out your book, sir, and go to work. (*Tom goes through the motions. The Master goes to the door.*) If you finish before the time is up, you may step outside for a few minutes of fresh air. (*The Master leaves, and the room is empty, except for Tom. He works feverishly on his writing lesson, closes the book, and gets up, going to the door to look for Becky. Then, going behind the Master's desk, he is elated to find the key in the drawer, and looking carefully around, he opens the drawer, slips a book out, and starts looking through it. Hearing a step outside, he hastily slips it back. Becky comes in.*)

TOM: Becky! What a turn you did give me! I thought you were old Dobbin. Look! (*He shows her the key to the drawer.*)

BECKY: What is it?

TOM: Old Dobbin's left the key in his drawer.

BECKY: What's in it?

TOM: His book. The Book of Mystery. He never has let anyone look at it. Shall we peep?

BECKY: I'm 'most scared to, Tom.

TOM: Oh, all right. I'd rather talk to you, anyway. Do you love rats?

BECKY: No! I hate them!

TOM: Well, I do, too—live ones. But I mean dead ones, to swing around your head on a string.

BECKY: No, I don't care much for rats anyway. What I like is chewing gum.

TOM: I should say so. Wish I had some now.

BECKY: Do you? I've got some. I'll let you chew it awhile, but you must give it back to me.

TOM: Thanks. We'll take turns. Was you ever at a circus, Becky?

BECKY: Yes, and my pa's going to take me again sometime, if I'm good.

TOM: I'm going to be a clown in a circus when I grow up.

BECKY: Oh, are you? That'll be nice. They're so lovely—all spotted up.

TOM: Yes, and they get slathers of money—'most a dollar a day, Ben Rogers says. Say, Becky, was you ever engaged?

BECKY: What's that?

TOM: Why, engaged to be married.

BECKY: No.

TOM: Would you like to be?

BECKY: I reckon so. I don't know. What is it like?

TOM: Like? Why, it ain't like anything. You only just tell a boy you won't ever have anybody but him—ever, ever, ever,—and then you kiss, and—and that's all. Anybody can do it.

BECKY: Kiss? What do you kiss for?

TOM: Why, that, you know, is to—well, they always do that.

BECKY: Everybody?

TOM: Why, yes, everybody that's in love with each other. Do you remember what I wrote on the slate, Becky?

BECKY: Ye—yes.

TOM: What was it?

BECKY: I—I shan't tell you.

TOM: Shall I tell you?

BECKY: Ye—yes—but some other time.

TOM: No. Now.

BECKY: No, not now. Tomorrow.

TOM: Oh no, now. Please, Becky. I'll whisper it. I'll whisper it ever so easy. (*Becky hangs her head, and Tom softly whispers in her ear.*) Now you whisper it to me—just the same.

BECKY: No, Tom.

TOM: Yes, Becky.

BECKY: Well, you turn your face away, so you can't see, and then I will. But you mustn't ever tell anybody, will you, Tom? Now you won't, will you?

TOM: No, indeed. Indeed I won't, Becky. Now! (*Becky leans toward him timidly, and whispers.*) Now, Becky, it's all done—all but the kiss. (*Becky covers her face with her hands.*) Aw, don't you be afraid of that. It ain't anything at all. And you ain't ever to love anybody but me, Becky. And you ain't ever to marry anybody but me, never, never, and forever. Will you?

BECKY: No, I'll never love anybody but you, Tom, and I'll never marry anybody but you—and you ain't ever to marry anybody but me, either.

TOM: Certainly. Of course. That's part of it. And always coming to school, or when we're going home, you're to walk with me—when there ain't anybody looking. And you choose me, and I choose you at parties. Because that's the way you do when you're engaged.

BECKY: It's so nice. I never heard of it before.

TOM: Oh, it's ever so gay! Why, me and Amy Lawrence—

BECKY: (*Shocked.*) Tom!

TOM: I mean—

BECKY: (*Crying.*) Oh, Tom! Then I ain't the first you've ever been engaged to!

TOM: Oh, don't cry, Becky. I don't care for her anymore.

BECKY: (*Sobbing.*) Yes you do, Tom. You know you do. (*Tom tries to comfort her, but she shakes him off.*)

TOM: Becky, I—I don't care for anybody but you. Honest. (*Becky sobs. Tom pulls a brass and iron knob out of his pocket, and looks at it sadly.*) Becky, this is the very best thing I've got. Please, Becky, won't you take it? (*Becky strikes it to the floor. Tom gathers up his pride, and marches out through the door. Becky cries on for a minute, then lifts her head, and looks all about. No Tom. She runs to the door.*)

BECKY: Tom! Tom! Come back, Tom! (*No response. Her heart is broken, and she falls to sobbing again, laying her head on the Master's desk. In the midst of her tears, her attention is drawn to the key in the drawer. Drying her eyes, but still sobbing spasmodically, she opens the drawer and gets out the Book of Mystery. She has just opened it when Tom rushes in the door. In her haste to hide the book, she tears a page.*)

TOM: Did you call me, Becky?

BECKY: (*Wailing.*) You made me tear it! I hate you, Tom Sawyer!

TOM: Becky!

BECKY: You're just as mean as you can be, to sneak up on a person like that.

TOM: How could I know you was looking at old Dobbin's book? I was clear down the road, and thought I heard you call me.

BECKY: You ought to be ashamed of yourself, Tom Sawyer. You know you're going to tell on me, and oh, what shall I do? I'll be whipped, and I never was whipped in school!

TOM: Never been licked in school? Shucks, what's a licking?

BECKY: Be so mean if you want to. I hate you. I hate you!

TOM: Who cares, Miss Smarty? (*And he flings out, with his head held high, retrieving his precious knob as he goes. Becky's misery is now complete. She sinks to the floor beside the Master's desk, rocking with a despair too great for utterance. Alfred Temple peers cautiously into the room, and finding it apparently empty, makes a beeline for Tom's seat, where he spatters ink in his copybook. Becky looks up in time to see him.*)

BECKY: Alfred Temple, what are you doing?

ALFRED: Oh-h! Uh—nothing.

BECKY: You are so, too. You're splattering ink on somebody's copybook.

ALFRED: Well—what of it?

BECKY: It's the meanest thing a boy can do—that's what of it. And I've a good notion to tell on you.

ALFRED: Oh, don't tell on me, Becky. He had it coming to him. He gave me a licking this morning.

BECKY: Who?

ALFRED: Tom Sawyer.

BECKY: Is that Tom Sawyer's copybook?

ALFRED: Yes. He has it coming to him.

BECKY: He certainly has something coming to him.

ALFRED: Then you won't tell, will you, Becky?

BECKY: I'm not promising.

ALFRED: You must like Tom Sawyer.

BECKY: I don't! I hate him!

ALFRED: Here comes old Cross-Patch. Recess is over, I guess. Remember, don't tell. (*Alfred leaps for his books, and when the Master enters, he is deep in study. Becky is in her own seat.*)

MASTER: Well, Master Temple. This is very fine—very fine indeed, to see you spend even your recess time in studying.

ALFRED: Yes, sir. Books are my only companions.

MASTER: That is a very elevated thought. Becky, school is about to take in. Have you had any fresh air?

BECKY: Yes sir.

MASTER: Well, perhaps you can do me a favor by rounding the rest of the school in. (*The Master rings the bell, and Becky goes to summon the children.*) Alfred, since you are such an interested student, perhaps you would like to write a composition, and deliver it before the parents at the Examination Exercises.

ALFRED: I am always glad to do anything to improve my mind, sir.

MASTER: If you will speak to me about it at recess tomorrow, we may decide upon a subject for the composition. (*By this time, the pupils have all returned, hung up their dinner pails, and seated themselves.*) You may have the next fifteen minutes for a study period. Thomas Sawyer, have you completed that work in your copybook?

TOM: Yes sir.

MASTER: Bring it up here. (*Tom presents the book with some show of assurance, but when the Master opens the book, his expression changes.*) Is this the work you call completed?

TOM: (*Gaping at it.*) I didn't leave it that way, sir.

MASTER: That's very likely, isn't it? Hold out your hand, sir. (*Tom takes his punishment with the ruler.*) Now, sir, you will stay this evening, after school, and rewrite that whole lesson twenty times. Sit down, sir, and I hope I shall not have to speak to you again today. (*Tom returns to his seat.*)

JOE: Less see it, Tom. Craminee! Tom, you are the messiest boy I ever did see. How anybody could make that much mess with just a little old pen—

TOM: (*Scratching his head, puzzled.*) I don't remember doin' it, Joe. Honest Injun, I don't.

MASTER: (*With a roar—he has just opened his Book of Mystery.*) Ahem!!! WHO TORE THIS BOOK? (*Dead silence.*) Benjamin Rogers, did you tear this book?

BEN: No sir.

MASTER: Joseph Harper, did you?

JOE: No sir.

MASTER: Amy Lawrence, did you tear this book?

AMY: No sir.

MASTER: Gracie Miller?

GRACIE: No sir.

MASTER: Susan Harper, did you do this?

SUSAN: No sir.

MASTER: Rebecca Thatcher, did you—no, look me in the face—did you tear this book? (*Becky cannot speak.*)

TOM: I done it! (*An electric silence lasts for a moment.*)

MASTER: (*With gathering wrath.*) You again, Master Sawyer! Come up here, sir. School is dismissed for the day! (*The Master is rolling up his sleeves as the scene ends.*)

END OF ACT ONE

ACT TWO

SCENE 1. *The graveyard. Three or four tombstones. An eerie light.*
(*Tom and Huck creep stealthily in, carrying their dead cat. An owl hoots mournfully. A dog howls offstage.*)

TOM: Here's the grave, Hucky.

HUCK: We have to hide, though. The devils won't come if they see any humans around. Here. (*They settle themselves behind one of the tombstones.*)

TOM: Hucky, do you believe the dead people like it for us to be here?

HUCK: I wish I knowed. It's awful solemn-like, ain't it?

TOM: I bet it is. Say, Hucky, do you reckon Hoss Williams hears us talkin'?

HUCK: O' course he does. Least, his sperrit does.

TOM: I wisht I'd said *Mister* Williams. But I never meant any harm. Everybody called him Hoss.

HUCK: A body can't be too partickler how they talk about these dead people, Tom.

TOM: Sh-h-h!

HUCK: What is it?

TOM: Listen!

HUCK: Oh, my! What a turn you did give me. That ain't nothin' but the wind.

TOM: Oh, I'm mighty glad to hear it. I thought it was the sperrits.

HUCK: Don't go grabbin' me so sudden like that, Tom.

TOM: Sh-h-h! There it is again. Didn't you hear it?

HUCK: I—

TOM: There! Now you hear it!

HUCK: Lord, Tom, they're comin'! They're comin' sure! What'll we do?

TOM: I dunno. Think they can see us?

HUCK: Oh, Tom, they can see in the dark, same as cats. I wisht I hadn't come.

TOM: If we keep perfectly still, maybe they won't notice us.

HUCK: I'll try to, Tom. But Lord, I'm all of a shiver!

TOM: Look! See there? They've got a light. What is it, Hucky?

HUCK: It's devil-fire. Oh, Tom, this is awful.

TOM: Here they come!

HUCK: It's the devils, sure enough! Three of 'em! Lordy, Tom, we're goners! Can you pray?

TOM: I'll try, but don't you be afeared. Now I lay me down to sleep—

HUCK: Sh-h-h-h!

TOM: What is it?

HUCK: They're humans! One of 'em is, anyway. One of 'em's old Muff Potter's voice.

TOM: No, 'tain't so, is it?

HUCK: I bet I know it. Don't you stir nor budge. He ain't sharp enough to notice us.

TOM: Is he drunk again?

HUCK: Ain't he always? The old rip.

TOM: All right. I'll keep still. Now they're stuck. Can't find it. Here they come again. Now they're hot. Red hot! They're pointing right this time. Say, Huck, I know another of them voices. It's Injun Joe!

HUCK: That's so—that murderin' half-breed. Lordy, Tom, I'd druther they was devils a dern sight. What kin they be up to?

TOM: And the third one is young Dr. Robinson. He took dinner with us last Sunday. What's he doing with them two? (*The three men come in. Dr. Robinson is carrying a lantern. Injun Joe is carrying two spades. Muff Potter is pushing a wheelbarrow containing a rolled-up blanket.*)

DR. ROBINSON: Here it is. Now. Muff, spread the blanket out on the ground.

MUFF: It's tied.

DR. ROBINSON: Cut the rope. (*Muff fumbles through his pockets for his knife, but lurches as he tries to cut the rope.*) Damn you, Muff Potter! Did you have to spend the whole evening in the tavern?

INJUN JOE: Here, Potter. Give me the knife. (*He takes Potter's knife, quickly cuts the rope, and spreads the blanket on the ground.*)

DR. ROBINSON: Now hurry and get to work, men. The moon might come up at any moment.

uff: I'm not a-diggin' up no ghosts, Sawbones, without more pay. ou'll just out with another five, or there she stays.

¡JUN JOE: That's the talk!

R. ROBINSON: Look here, what does this mean? You required your pay 1 advance, and I've paid you.

NJUN JOE: Yes, and you done more than that. Five years ago, you rove me away from your father's kitchen one night, when I come to sk for something to eat. You said I warn't there for no good, and hen I swore I'd get even with you if it took a hundred years, your fa-her had me jailed for a vagrant. Did you think I'd forgot? The Injun lood ain't in me for nothin'. And now I've got you, and you've got to ettle, you know. (*He shakes his fist in the Doctor's face. The Doctor nocks him to the ground.*)

IUFF: Here, now, don't you hit my pard. (*Muff lurches toward the*)*octor, and grapples with him, but after a few rounds the Doctor nocks him out. Injun Joe has Muff's knife in his hand, and has been reeping, catlike and stooping, around the combatants, seeking an op- ortunity to use it. Now, as the Doctor flings himself free of Muff, njun Joe springs on him, and drives the knife into the Doctor's breast. he Doctor gasps, reels, then falls, partly upon Potter, and lies still.*)

NJUN JOE: That score is settled, damn you. (*He stoops, to rifle the*)*octor's pockets, transferring the money to his own. Then, seeing Muff till unconscious, he puts the fatal knife in Muff's right hand, sinks*)*ack on his heels to wait a few moments, then begins to rouse Muff.*) 'otter! Here, Potter! (*Muff begins to stir and groan. He sits up* uickly, pushing the body from him, and taking in the dreadful scene.*)

MUFF: Lord, how is this, Joe?

NJUN JOE: It's a dirty business. What did you do it for?

MUFF: I? I never done it.

INJUN JOE: Look here. That kind of talk won't wash.

MUFF: You mean I stabbed the Doctor?

INJUN JOE: It's your knife, ain't it? And it's in your hand.

MUFF: (*Casting the knife away from him.*) I thought I'd got sober, Joe. I'd no business to drink tonight. But it's in my head yet—worse than when we started. Can't recollect anything of it hardly. Tell me, Joe—honest, now, old feller—did I do it? I never meant to. 'Pon my soul and honor, I never meant to. Tell me how it was, Joe. Oh, it's awful! And him so young and promising.

INJUN JOE: Why, you two was scuffling, and he fetched you an awful blow under the chin, and you fell flat. Then up you come, all reeling and staggering like, and snatched the knife and jammed it into him, just as he fetched you another clip. And here you've laid, dead as a wedge till now.

MUFF: Oh, I didn't know what I was a-doing. I wish I may die this minute if I did. It was all on account of the whiskey, I reckon. I never used a weepon in my life before, Joe. I've fought, but never with weepons. They'll all say that. Joe, don't tell. Say you won't tell, Joe— that's a good feller. I've always liked you, Joe, and stood up for you. Don't you remember? You won't tell, will you, Joe?

INJUN JOE: No, you've always been fair and square with me, Muff Potter, and I won't go back on you now. There now, that's as fair as a man can say.

MUFF: Oh, Joe, you're an angel! I'll bless you for this the longest day I live.

INJUN JOE: Here, now, that's enough of that. This ain't any time for blubbering. You be off yonder way, and I'll go this. Move now, and don't leave any tracks behind you.

MUFF: I will, Joe. I will. I never meant to do it. 'Pon my soul, I didn't. (*He starts trotting off, then exits running.*)

INJUN JOE: (*Watching him off.*) If he's as fuddled as he looks, he won't think of the knife until too late. Chicken-heart! (*He goes out in the opposite direction. The two boys, who have watched this scene with frozen horror, peer cautiously out from their hiding place, and are pulled irresistibly to the dead body.*)

TOM: Is he dead, Hucky?

HUCK: Dead as a door nail.

TOM: Are you sure?

HUCK: Ain't a spark of life in him, Tom.

TOM: Huckleberry, what do you reckon'll come of this?

HUCK: I reckon hangin'll come of it.

TOM: Do you, though?

HUCK: Why, I know it, Tom.

TOM: Who'll tell? Us?

HUCK: What are you talking about? Suppose something happened, and Injun Joe didn't get hung. Why, he'd kill us sometime or other, just as sure as you live.

TOM: That's just what I was thinking to myself. Hucky, are you sure you can keep mum?

HUCK: Tom, we got to keep mum. You know that. That Injun devil wouldn't think any more of drownding us than a couple of cats, if we was to squeak about this, and they didn't hang him. Now look-a-here, Tom, less take and swear to one another—that's what we got to do. Swear to keep mum.

TOM: I'm agreed. Would you just hold hands and swear that we—

HUCK: Oh, no, that wouldn't do for this. That's good enough for little rubbishy things, but there orter be writing about a big thing like this— and blood!

TOM: That's just what I think. Hand me that shingle there. (*And taking a piece of charcoal from his pocket, Tom laboriously writes the oath on a piece of pine shingle.*)

HUCK: Gee, Tom, I didn't know you could write that good. What's it say?

TOM: (*Reading as he writes.*) Huck Finn and Tom Sawyer swears they will keep mum about this, and wish they may drop down dead in their tracks if they ever tell and rot.

HUCK: Now we got to sign it in blood. (*He pulls a pin from his lapel, and starts to prick his finger.*)

TOM: Hold on. Don't do that. A pin's brass. It might have verdigrease on it.

HUCK: What's verdigrease?

TOM: It's p'ison, that's what it is. You just swallow some of it once. You'll see. Here, use a needle. (*Both boys prick their finger with Tom's needle, and make their mark on the shingle.*)

HUCK: Tom, does this keep us from ever telling—always?

TOM: Of course it does. It don't make any difference what happens, we got to keep mum. We'd drop down dead—don't you know that?

HUCK: Yes, I reckon that's so. (*A dog howls offstage.*) Tom! Listen to that dog! Which of us does he mean?

TOM: I dunno. Peep out and see. Quick!

HUCK: No, you, Tom.

TOM: I can't—I can't do it, Huck.

HUCK: Please, Tom. There it is again.

TOM: (*As the dog howls again.*) Oh, Lordy, I'm thankful! It's Mr. Harbison's bulldog. I know his voice.

HUCK: (*Much relieved.*) Oh, that's good. I tell you, Tom, I was scared to death. I'd a bet anything it was a stray dog. (*The dog howls again.*) Oh, my, that ain't no Harbison's bulldog! Do look, Tom. I just know it's a stray dog!

TOM: (*Screwing up his courage, and peering off in the direction Muff Potter took.*) Oh, Huck, it is!

HUCK: Quick, Tom! Which of us does he mean?

TOM: Huck, he must mean us both. We're right together.

HUCK: Oh, Tom, I reckon we're goners.

TOM: It's a sure sign, Huck.

HUCK: I reckon there ain't no mistake about where I'll go. I been so wicked.

TOM: (*Beginning to sniffle.*) Dad fetch it! This comes of playing hookey, and doing everything a fellow's told not to do. I might 'a been good, like Sid, if I'd 'a tried. But no, I wouldn't, of course. But I lay, if I ever get off this time, I'll just waller in Sunday schools!

HUCK: (*Sniffling too.*) You bad? Confound it, Tom Sawyer, you're just old pie, alongside of what I am. Oh, Lordy, Lordy, I wisht I only had half your chance.

TOM: Look, Hucky, he's got his back to us!

HUCK: Well, he has, by Jingoes! Did he before?

TOM: Yes, he did. But I, like a fool, never noticed. Oh, this is bully, you know. Now who can he mean?

HUCK: Tom, Muff Potter went off that way.

TOM: Geeminy! It's him!

HUCK: And a stray dog don't mean just bad luck, Tom. It means sure death.

TOM: Huck, let's get home.

HUCK: Keep mum.

TOM: You just bet I'll keep mum.

HUCK: Sh-h-h-h!

TOM: Sh-h-h-h! (*Giving the dead body a wide berth, they go off together.*)

SCENE 2. *A village street. A high board fence. A barrel on one side.*
(*Tom appears with a bucket of whitewash and a long-handled brush. Surveying the endless reaches of fence, he sighs despairingly, then dips his brush and passes it along the topmost plank once or twice. Comparing the insignificant whitewashed streak with the far-reaching continent of unwhitewashed fence, he sits down on the barrel, discouraged. Aunt Polly marches in briskly, takes in the scene.*)

AUNT POLLY: (*Whacking Tom on the seat with her slipper.*) Is this the way you paint the fence? (*Tom leaps to his feet, and starts whitewashing with vigor.*)

TOM: I was just gettin' ready to start.

AUNT POLLY: Remember, this is only the first coat.

TOM: (*Stopping his exertions.*) First coat?

AUNT POLLY: I want three coats on this fence, Tom.

TOM: Aunt Polly, this is a holiday. Can't a boy play on a holiday?

AUNT POLLY: When you finish your work.

TOM: All the other boys are playin' this morning. We was goin' to have a big battle over on Cardiff Hill. Joe Harper's army and mine.

AUNT POLLY: You heard what I said, Tom.

TOM: Well, can't I paint the inside today, 'stead of the outside?

AUNT POLLY: What difference does that make?

TOM: Everybody in tarnation'll see me here on the sidewalk.

AUNT POLLY: Well, what of it?

TOM: I just told you, none of the other boys have to work on a holiday.

AUNT POLLY: (*Going.*) You wouldn't either, if you'd do your work on other days. Three coats, now. (*She leaves.*)

TOM: Jeehosophat! And look comin'! (*Out of his despair is born an inspiration. He falls to whitewashing with elaborate care, handling the brush with an artist's touch, then standing back to get the full effect of it. Alfred Temple comes in.*)

ALFRED: (*Chewing on an apple.*) Hee-eee! Lookit Tom Sawyer! Tom has to paint his Aunt Polly's fence on a holiday! Hee-eee! Tom's up a stump, ain't you, Tom? You got to work, haven't you, Tom?

TOM: (*Turning around to look at him with an air of surprise.*) Why, it's you, Alfred. I warn't noticin'.

ALFRED: I'm going swimming, I am. Don't you wish you could? But of course you'd rather work, wouldn't you? 'Course you would.

TOM: What do you call work?

ALFRED: Why, ain't that work?

TOM: Maybe it is, and maybe it ain't. All I know is, it suits Tom Sawyer.

ALFRED: Oh, come now, you don't mean to let on you like it?

TOM: Like it? Well, I don't see why I oughtn't to like it. Does a boy get a chance to whitewash a fence every day?

ALFRED: Well, no, I guess he doesn't.

TOM: Well, then.

ALFRED: Say, Tom, let me whitewash a little.

TOM: No—no. I reckon it wouldn't hardly do, Alfred. You see, Aunt Polly's awful partickler about this fence—right here on the street, you know.

ALFRED: Oh, come, now. Lemme try. Only just a little.

TOM: Alfred, I'd like to, honest Injun. But Aunt Polly's so partickler. If you was to tackle this fence, and anything was to happen to it—

ALFRED: Oh, shucks, I'll be just as careful. Now lemme try. Say, I'll give you the core of my apple when I finish eating it.

TOM: Well—no. No, Alfred. Now don't. I'm afeared—

ALFRED: I'll give you all of it, Tom.

TOM: (*Taking the apple.*) Well, all right. I'll let you brush for just a minute. Now be mighty careful.

ALFRED: I will.

TOM: Go slow around the edges now. I can't have any splatters on my fence.

ALFRED: Is that all right?

TOM: (*His mouth full of apple.*) Better. Be sure to fill in all those cracks. Well, here comes Joe Harper. Hi, Joe! Lookin' for me?

JOE: (*Entering.*) You're a fine commander. Don't even come to your own battle.

TOM: That's so. We were goin' to fight today weren't we?

JOE: You don't mean to say you forgot?

TOM: Well, I sort of thought of it early this morning, but when Aunt Polly said she wanted me to paint this fence, why, everything else just sort of slipped my mind.

JOE: You mean you wanted to paint this fence?

TOM: 'Course. It's very partickler work. I'm just lettin' Alfred work on it for a few minutes.

JOE: What you givin' him for doin' your work?

TOM: You mean what'd he give me for lettin' him? He gave me this apple.

JOE: (*Impressed, watches Alfred a moment.*) Tell you what. I got a kite I'll give you if you'll let me paint awhile.

TOM: Aren't you goin' to have the battle?

JOE: We've already had it. Beat your army to pieces.

TOM: Well I tell you, Joe. I wasn't aimin' to let anybody else work on that fence, but now that I let Alfred—your home-made newspaper kite, without any string?

JOE: I'll help you make the string.

TOM: Well, I guess maybe you can take a few strokes, soon as Alfred gets through. You have to be awful careful, you know, Joe, on account of this is the front fence, right on the sidewalk, and Aunt Polly said— (*Ben Rogers and Jim Hollis burst in.*)

BEN: Hey, Tom, why didn't you come to the battle?

JIM: How do you expect us to fight without any general?

BEN: The boys want to get another general.

JIM: Well, by hokey, lookit Alfred Temple. What's he doin', Tom?

TOM: He's just paintin' until Joe Harper gets his turn.

BEN: No! Is it fun?

TOM: Fun? It's fun enough for Tom Sawyer to miss a battle on account of.

JIM: No—really? Is that why you didn't come to the battle, Tom?

TOM: I reckon it is.

BEN: Let me have a turn, Tom, after Joe.

JIM: Ah, no. Let me. I'm your adjutant general.

BEN: Tom, you owe me a good turn. I let you copy my 'rithmetic last week.

TOM: Wait a minute. Don't you think I want to paint a little myself?

JIM: Well, you might just let us try it, mightn't you?

TOM: No—no. I don't think I better. Why, you all might ruin that fence.

JIM: Please, Tom.

BEN: You let Alfred and Joe paint on it, didn't you?

TOM: Well—Alfred give me an apple for his turn. And Joe give me his kite.

BEN: Oh.

JIM: (*Ransacking his pockets for treasure.*) I'll give you a handle off a leather grip.

BEN: I'll give you a key, Tom. It won't fit nothin', but it's brass. And I'll throw in a piece of blue bottle glass to look through.

TOM: Oh, all right. But see what you boys have let me in for. If anybody else comes along, I won't get a chance to paint myself. (*Sid rushes in, breathless.*)

SID: Hey, fellows, listen! You know young Doc Robinson? He's been found killed over in the graveyard! (*The boys drop everything, and mill around him. Tom hangs nervously on the edge, where Huck Finn has slipped in unobtrusively, and joined him.*)

JOE: Sid, you don't mean it!

JEFF: How'd it happen?

ALFRED: Who killed him?

BEN: Did you see it?

SID: I saw the Sheriff go by, with a bunch of men, on their way to the graveyard. So I went along. And when we got there—

MRS. HARPER: (*Offstage.*) Joe! Joe!

JOE: Ma'am?

MRS. HARPER: (*Off.*) You come right here this minute!

JOE: Oh, Mom, I can't. I'm busy.

MRS. HARPER: (*Off.*) You march yourself right home, young man. Or I'll come and get you!

JOE: (*Going reluctantly.*) Now what have I done?

BEN: Go on, Sid. What happened?

SID: There was a big crowd standin' around. Everybody was there. But I pushed around till I saw it—and oh, it was awful! The grass was all over blood. He'd been stabbed with a knife!

JIM: Don't they know who done it?

SID: It was Muff Potter's knife!

BOYS: Old Muff Potter?

SID: And then the Preacher he spied Muff Potter kind of skulkin' behind a tree, and the Sheriff went and got him, and he was a-shakin' all over, and when they made him look at the dead Doctor, he just covered up his face and cried.

BEN: Didn't he say nothin'?

SID: No, he just cried. And then the Sheriff told Injun Joe to put the body in the wagon, and—and—

ALFRED: What?

BEN: Go on.

SID: And—and just as he picked it up, the wound bled a little! (*There is a horrified hush from the little group.*)

TOM: Don't that kind of look like Injun Joe did it?

HUCK: (*Intensely, to Tom.*) Sh-h-h!

SID: Listen. The body was in three feet of Muff Potter when it done it!

BOYS: How awful!

ALFRED: Well—what can you expect of a low character like that?

JIM: He's onery, all right—but I wouldn't have figgered him for a killer.

BEN: And why would he want to kill the Doctor?

SID: Look! Here they come!

TOM: Hucky, the Sheriff's got him!

HUCK: And that half-breed, Injun Joe, right behind 'em. (*The Sheriff enters, ostentatiously leading a cringing Muff Potter by the arm, and followed by the townspeople in an angry mood, Injun Joe among them.*)

MUFF: (*Sobbing.*) I didn't do it, friends. 'Pon my word and honor, I didn't. I never done it.

SHERIFF: This is a serious business, Potter.

MUFF: Oh, Sheriff, it's awful! But I didn't do it.

SHERIFF: Who's accused you?

MUFF: Oh, Joe, you promised me you'd never—

SHERIFF: Is that your knife?

MUFF: Oh, Lordy! I shouldn't have left it there. Tell 'em, Joe. Tell 'em. It ain't any use anymore.

INJUN JOE: Do you want me to, Muff?

MUFF: Yes. Tell 'em. No use tryin' to keep it down now.

INJUN JOE: Well, Sheriff, you see, the young Doctor, he asked me to help him do a little job. I didn't know what kind of a job it was, but I'll do anything to turn an honest penny. Well, he told me to bring some help, and I rounded up Muff Potter. Last night, when we met him, he give us spades and a wheelbarrow, and we all started out for the graveyard. When I finally found that he wanted us to rob Hoss Williams' grave, I stood right up and said I wouldn't do it. And then the young Doctor he doubled up his fists and knocked me down. But I heard Potter here say, "Don't you hit my pard!" And when I got up, the young Doctor was lying on the ground, and Potter had his knife out, dripping blood.

SHERIFF: Will you say all this on oath, Joe?

INJUN JOE: Yes sir.

SHERIFF: Come along to the courthouse. (*The little procession moves off, followed by all but Tom and Huck.*)

TOM: (*Gasping for breath.*) Did you hear Injun Joe tell that whopper, Huck? And it didn't even thunder and lightning!

HUCK: You know why?

TOM: No. Why?

HUCK: (*Mysteriously.*) He's sold himself to the devil!

TOM: No! Is that so?

HUCK: Old Mother Hopkins says so. And she's a witch.

TOM: Huck, have you told anybody about that?

HUCK: 'Course I haven't.

TOM: Never a word?

HUCK: Never a solitary word, so help me.

TOM: They couldn't anybody get you to tell, could they, Huck?

HUCK: Get me to tell? Why, if I wanted that half-breed Injun to kill me, they could get me to tell maybe. They ain't no different way.

TOM: Are you sure, Huck?

HUCK: 'Course I'm sure. Long as I'm in my right mind. What's the matter with you, Tom?

TOM: Huck, Sid says I talk in my sleep!

HUCK: Tom!

TOM: Aunt Polly won't let me sleep by myself.

HUCK: Tom, you better leave home.

TOM: Where would I go? (*Joe Harper marches in, with vengeance in his eye. The boys spring apart, guiltily.*)

JOE: Tom, I just wanted to tell you boys good-bye.

TOM: Good-bye? Where you goin'?

JOE: I'm going to run away. It's very plain that my mother is tired of me, and wants me out of the way. Tell her I hope she'll be happy, Tom, and never be sorry that she drove me out into the great world.

TOM: Joe, where you goin'?

JOE: I don't know. But don't forget me, Tom. Nor you either, Huck.

TOM: Forget you? I'm comin' along. And so is Huck. Ain't you, Huck?

HUCK: Sure, I'll come. Where to?

JOE: You mean you fellows want to run away, too?

TOM: Sure, it's just the ticket. Only yesterday Aunt Polly whacked me for feedin' the cat some medicine I was supposed to take. Maybe when she doesn't have me here to fuss at, maybe then she'll be sorry.

HUCK: This'll be fun. Where'll we go?

JOE: Let's go out in a desert somewhere, and be hermits, and live in a cave. And after while, we'll die of cold and hunger, and then they'll be sorry. And maybe next time, Mother won't whip her boy for drinkin' cream that he never even saw.

TOM: I got a better idea than that. Let's be pirates, and lead a life of crime!

HUCK: What's pirates?

TOM: They're a kind of robber gang that holds up ships and things. Listen, let's sneak out a raft and go over to Jackson's Island. That's about three miles down the river. We better take a few supplies with us. Can you get anything, Joe?

JOE: I'll try. Anyway, we can always catch fish over on Jackson's Island.

HUCK: I can bring some tobacco.

TOM: We'll meet at the old wharf at midnight. And we better have a password, so's to 'dentify each other.

HUCK: A password? What you want a password for?

TOM: Why, pirates always have to have a password. Now everybody think. (*They all think hard for a minute.*) I know! Blood!

JOE: That's good!

HUCK: Say, what's the use to put on all that stuff? Everbody'll be down in the village tonight for the fireworks. There won't be anybody at the wharf.

TOM: How you talk! If we're goin' to be pirates, we got to act like pirates, don't we?

HUCK: How do pirates act?

TOM: (*Dramatizing it.*) They go—"Hist! If the foe stirs, let him have it to the hilt, for dead men tell no tales!" Now, let's swear allegiance. (*They cross hands in a mysterious way, known only to them.*) I, Tom Sawyer, the Black Avenger of the Spanish Main—

JOE: I, Joe Harper, the Terror of the Seas—

HUCK: I, Huck Finn, the—the—

TOM: (*Prompting him.*) Huck Finn the Red-Handed—

HUCK: Huck Finn the Red-Handed—

ALL THREE: Swear to be a faithful pirate to the death! . . . Blood! (*And they go off in different directions, with many piratical gestures to keep mum.*)

END OF ACT TWO

ACT THREE

SCENE 1. *Jackson's Island. A practical hollow tree stump, two or three rocks, some practical bushes and loose branches, a campfire. Afternoon light.*
(*The three boys are sitting contentedly around the fire, Huck smoking a corn-cob pipe.*)

JOE: Ain't it gay?

TOM: It's nuts! What would the boys say if they could see us?

JOE: I reckon they'd just die to be here, eh, Hucky?

HUCK: I reckon so. Anyways, I'm suited.

TOM: It's just the life for me. Ain't you glad you decided to be a pirate, Joe, 'stead of a hermit?

JOE: Oh, a heap sight. I'd a good deal rather be a pirate, now that I've tried it.

HUCK: What do pirates have to do?

TOM: Oh, they have just a bully time—take ships and burn 'em, and get the money and bury it. And kill everybody on the ships—make 'em walk the plank.

JOE: And they carry off the women. They don't kill the women.

TOM: No, they don't kill the women. They're too noble. And the women's always beautiful, too.

JOE: And don't they wear the bulliest clothes! All gold and silver and diamonds!

HUCK: Who?

JOE: Why, the pirates.

HUCK: (*Looking at his own bedraggled appearance.*) I reckon I ain't dressed fitten fer a pirate, but I ain't got none but these.

TOM: Oh, the fine clothes will come fast enough, after we begin our adventures.

JOE: These clothes'll do to start with, though rich pirates generally start with the regular costume.

TOM: Listen! (*A deep, sullen boom is heard in the distance.*)

JOE: What is it?

TOM: I wonder.

HUCK: 'Tain't thunder, because thunder—

TOM: Hark! Listen, don't talk!

JOE: Let's look. It's on the river. (*They all strain off, in the direction of the river. Tom gets up on the tree stump, to see better.*)

TOM: It's the ferryboat. Look at all the people on it.

HUCK: Is there a picnic or something? (*The boom is heard again.*)

TOM: I know! Somebody's drownded!

HUCK: That's it! They done that last summer when Bill Turner got drownded. They shoot a cannon over the water, and that makes him come to the top.

TOM: Yes, and they take loaves of bread and put quicksilver in 'em, and set 'em afloat. And wherever there's anybody that's drowned, they'll float right there and stop.

JOE: Yes, I've heard about that. I wonder what makes the bread do that.

TOM: Oh, it ain't the bread so much. I reckon it's mostly what they say over the bread before they start it out.

HUCK: But they don't say anything over it. I've seen 'em, and they don't.

TOM: Well, that's funny. But maybe they say it to themselves.

JOE: That must be so, because how could an ignorant lump of brea[d] find a drowned person, unless it had a spell set on it to send it to th[e] very place?

HUCK: Who do you reckon is drownded?

TOM: (*Looking off toward the boat again.*) By jings, I wish I was ove[r] there now.

HUCK: I do, too. I'd give heaps to know who it is.

JOE: Nobody was drownded before we left last night, was they?

HUCK: It must have happened this morning.

TOM: Boys! I know who's drownded! It's us!

HUCK: Us? We ain't drownded.

JOE: But they think we are. Glory be!

HUCK: Shucks, sure enough?

TOM: Of course it is. Who else could it be? They've just had time t[o] miss us.

JOE: Just think, to get the big ferryboat out, just for us!

TOM: Let's celebrate! What shall we do?

JOE: I know. Let's smoke!

TOM: Bully. Will you give us a pipe, Huck?

HUCK: Sure. Plenty of corn-cobs, and I've got a whole sheaf of leaf t[o]bacco.

TOM: I smoked a cigar made out of grapevines onct.

HUCK: Shucks, that ain't nothin' to a corn-cob pipe. Here, light u[p] (*The two boys, with awed spirits, light their pipes at the fire.*)

JOE: (*Coughing a little.*) The smoke tastes kind of hot, but I like it.

TOM: Why, it's just as easy. If I'd a knowed this was all, I'd 'a learn[ed] long ago.

JOE: So would I. It's just nothing.

TOM: Why, many a time I've looked at people smoking, and though[t] "Well, I wish I could do that." But I never thought I could.

JOE: That's just the way with me, ain't it, Huck? You've heard me talk just that way, haven't you, Huck? I'll leave it to Huck if I haven't.

HUCK: Yes, heaps of times. (*He looks off toward the ferryboat.*) They're followin' the shore pretty close. Reckon they thought we got drownded in swimmin'.

TOM: They haven't missed the raft yet, I guess.

JOE: I believe I could smoke this pipe all day. I don't feel sick.

TOM: Neither do I. I bet I could smoke all day. But I bet you Ben Rogers couldn't.

JOE: Ben Rogers? Why, he'd keel over with just two draws.

TOM: 'Deed he would. Say, Joe, I wish the boys could see us now.

JOE: So do I.

TOM: Say, boys, don't say anything about it. And sometime when they're around, I'll come up to you and say, kind of loud—"Joe, got a pipe?" And you'll say, kind of careless-like, as if it warn't anything, you'll say—"Yes, I got my old pipe, and another one, but the tobacco ain't very good." And I'll say—"Oh, that's all right, if it's strong enough." And then you'll out with the pipes, and we'll light up, just as calm. And then, just see 'em look.

JOE: By jings, that'll be gay. I wish it was now.

TOM: So do I. And when we tell 'em we learned when we was off pirating, won't they wish they'd been along!

JOE: I just bet they will. (*But neither Tom nor Joe is feeling quite so easy now, and after a few agonized glances offstage—*) I've lost my knife. I reckon I better go and find it.

TOM: I'll help you. You go over that-a-way, and I'll hunt around by the spring.

HUCK: I'll come along if you want.

JOE: No, never mind.

TOM: We can find it. (*And Joe and Tom vanish rather suddenly, leaving Huck alone by the campfire, puffing away on his corn-cob pipe. The lights dim out on this scene.*)

SCENE 2. *On the Island, the fourth day out. Early morning.*
(*A frying pan is on the campfire. Huck is up on the tree stump, shading his eyes, and looking off toward the river. Joe's voice can be heard offstage, calling for Tom.*)

JOE: (*Off.*) Tom! Tom! (*Huck, unsuccessful in his search, goes to tend the fish. Joe comes in.*) Where would he go? In four days on this island, we've explored all the places. Huck, do you reckon he's deserted?

HUCK: No. Tom's true-blue, Joe. He wouldn't desert. That'd be a disgrace for a pirate.

JOE: (*Thoughtfully.*) I don't know.

HUCK: It is awful lonesome.

JOE: It sure is. Fish ready?

HUCK: Almost.

JOE: Tom left his rubber ball, and three fish hooks, and a white alley. I reckon they are ours, aren't they?

HUCK: The writin' says they are if he ain't back in time for breakfast. (*Tom strides grandly in.*)

TOM: Which he is!

HUCK: Tom!

JOE: What have you been up to, Tom Sawyer?

TOM: I'll tell you when I've had some breakfast.

HUCK: Fish is 'most ready.

JOE: I hate fish.

TOM: Smells good. Oh, ain't this gay?

JOE: Tom, your hair's wet. Have you been over to mainland?

TOM: Been swimmin'. Here Huck, I'll help you.

JOE: Breakfast is about over, I reckon, over there.

TOM: Not such a breakfast as this. Just look.

JOE: I want to go home.

TOM: Ah, Joe, you don't mean it. Why, home ain't shucks to pirating.

HUCK: Fish is ready, Joe. Here, you can have the biggest one.

JOE: Oh, boys, let's give it up. I want to go home.

TOM: Ah, Joe, eat some breakfast. You'll feel better by and by.

JOE: (*Blinking back the tears.*) It's so lonesome.

TOM: Just think of the fishing that's here.

JOE: I don't care for fishing. I want to go home.

TOM: But Joe, there ain't another such swimming place anywhere.

JOE: Swimming's no good. I don't care for it, somehow, when there ain't anybody to say I shan't go in. I mean to go home.

TOM: Oh, shucks. Baby! You want to see your mother, I reckon.

JOE: (*Snuffling.*) Yes, I do want to see my mother. And you would too, if you had one. I'm no more baby than you are.

TOM: Well, we'll let the little cry-baby go home to his mother, won't we, Huck? Poor thing—does it want to see its mother? And so it shall. You like it here, don't you, Huck? We'll stay, won't we?

HUCK: (*Without conviction.*) Well—I reckon so.

JOE: (*Openly crying now.*) I'll never speak to you again as long as I live. There, now, Tom Sawyer.

TOM: Who cares? Nobody wants you to. Go 'long home and get laughed at. Oh, you're a fine pirate. Huck and me ain't cry-babies. We'll stay, won't we, Huck? Let him go if he wants to. I reckon we can get along without him, perhaps.

JOE: Never you mind, Tom Sawyer. Just wait till I get my things. (*He stamps off.*)

TOM: (*To his departing back.*) Go ahead, Smarty. (*But Huck, too, has picked up Joe's mood, and is quietly whistling, while he eyes Joe's preparations offstage.*) Don't worry, Huck. We don't need him. (*Huck, still whistling, rises to keep Joe under observation offstage.*) Here, let's divide this fish. (*Huck declines with a gesture, without interrupting his whistling. Tom eats the fish without appetite.*) Anyway, Joe'll change his mind, I expect, by the time he gets dressed.

HUCK: (*Breaking his ominous silence.*) What if he don't?

TOM: Well—but he will.

HUCK: (*After a painful pause.*) I want to go, too, Tom.

TOM: What?

HUCK: Oh, Tom, it's gettin' so lonesome, and now it'll be worse, with Joe gone. Let's us go, too, Tom.

TOM: I won't. You can all go, if you want to. I mean to stay.

HUCK: Tom, I better go.

TOM: Well, go along. Who's hendering you?

HUCK: I wisht you'd come, too, Tom.

TOM: Well, you wish wrong, that's all. (*Huck turns sorrowfully away, and starts off toward Joe, but stops at Tom's exclamation.*) Listen!

HUCK: What is it?

TOM: Sh-h-h-h! There, hear it? That ain't Joe, is it?

HUCK: No. Joe went off that-a-way. Oh, my! (*Tom gets up on the tree stump, and looks toward the river.*) Who is it, Tom?

TOM: It's a man. He's getting out of a boat. Cover up the fire, Hucky. He's comin' this way. (*They hide the pan of fish under a pile of leaves, and cover the fire with green branches.*)

HUCK: Come on, Tom. Let's run.

TOM: Keep still. We'll be safer under this bush.

HUCK: But Tom, suppose Joe was to march right onto him?

TOM: Craminee! That's so. Let's run!

HUCK: (*Pulling him down under the bush.*) Too late. Here he comes.

TOM: Huck, look. It's Injun Joe! We should 'a run, like you said.

HUCK: Lordy! I wisht we was out of this.

TOM: Sh-h-h! Don't breathe. (*Injun Joe enters, looks back toward the river, then spits scornfully.*)

INJUN JOE: Pesky town! (*He looks searchingly all around him.*) Now, which tree stump was it? 'Twas more inland than this. Ah! (*He strides purposefully off.*)

TOM: He's lookin' for a tree stump.

HUCK: I'm glad it warn't that one.

TOM: But suppose he finds Joe. He'd kill him.

HUCK: I'll try to crawl out, and warn him.

TOM: We dassen't. Here he comes back. (*Injun Joe reenters, still searching.*)

INJUN JOE: That's funny. Maybe 'twas this one, after all. (*He goes directly to the tree stump the boys have been using all along, reaches into a hollow place in it. A look of satisfaction spreads over his face.*) Ah-h-h! (*He draws out a bag that clinks cheerfully, as he holds it up in exaltation.*) Six hundred dollars! (*He hugs it to him, gloating, then sobers as he thinks back to the hollow in the stump.*) Wait a minute. (*He peers back into the stump.*) Hello. What's this? (*He reaches inside with one hand, and feels. Then he goes to work seriously with both hands, tugging and struggling, finally lifts out a heavy old wooden box.*) Man! (*Drawing out his knife, he goes to work prying the box open, then gasps.*) It's money! (*He dumps out a mound of gold coins.*) Gold money! There must be thousands of dollars here! Part of the swag from Murrell's gang, I reckon. Tree, you sure know how to keep a secret. (*He starts scooping the gold back into the box, then eyes the tree stump again.*) Reckon you're the safest hiding place, after all. (*He starts to put the heavy box back into the hollow, then stops as he sniffs.*) I smell fire. (*Covering the box and the money bag with his jacket, he begins looking for the campfire. The boys, who have watched this scene with bulging eyes, are now frozen with terror. Injun Joe locates the campfire, and kicks the branches off.*) There's somebody on this island. Somebody's camping here. (*Drawing his knife, he searches all around, circling the bush where the boys are hidden. He peers into the far distance in all directions, then shrugs, and puts his knife away.*) Well, let them. They'll never know I've been here. But old tree, I'm not leaving the money here, for them to find. Not exactly. (*Straining, as he picks up the heavy treasure box, and the money bag.*) Old tree, you've been a good friend. But now, this'll be safer in the cave. (*He carries his burden off toward the river. The boys crouch close, listening for his departure. Finally, Tom ventures out, and climbs cautiously on the tree stump to look off.*)

HUCK: Is he gone?

TOM: He's puttin' the treasure box in the boat. Don't move yet. He's coverin' it up with his jacket. Now he's got in. He's pushin' off. He's gone.

HUCK: (*Creeping out into the open.*) Whew, that was close! By jings, Tom, why didn't we think to look in that holler?

TOM: Ain't that the rottenest luck! Here we been playin' around over that stump every day. He's out in the current now. (*Climbs down from his perch. Huck is examining the hollow in the stump.*)

HUCK: Don't reckon there could be anything more in here.

TOM: Nah, 'tain't likely. Huck, did you hear him say he was goin' to put that money in the cave?

HUCK: Yes—and there ain't but one cave around here, and that's Mac-Dougall's.

TOM: Yes, but that cave is five miles long. And there's parts of it nobody's ever been into.

HUCK: I'd hate to go in there lookin' for it, and run into him.

TOM: Oh, Lordy, Huck, don't say it.

HUCK: I'd ruther be poor, a dern sight. (*Joe enters, his trousers pulled over his trunks, ready to swim for the mainland. He carries a partially consumed ham.*)

JOE: Well, good-bye, Huck.

TOM: You can't go yet, Joe. 'Tain't safe.

JOE: (*Pointedly ignoring Tom.*) I'm leavin' this for you, Huck.

HUCK: Wait till that boat gets across. Look.

JOE: (*Mounting the tree stump, looks toward the river.*) What of it? I don't care if he sees me. The whole town'll see me soon enough.

TOM: Joe, that's Injun Joe in that boat. (*Joe is impressed, but ignoring Tom, he looks to Huck.*)

HUCK: Really.

JOE: No!

HUCK: If you'll wait till he gets away, Joe, I'll come with you.

TOM: Hucky!

HUCK: Oh, come on, Tom. Let's all go back.

TOM: No!

HUCK: You think it over, Tom. We'll wait for you when we get to shore.

TOM: Well, you'll wait a blame long time, that's all.

JOE: Come on, Huck. Let him be stubborn if he wants to. (*Huck slowly rolls up his over-long pants.*) We can lay low in the sand till Injun Joe is out of sight. (*He stamps off. The tension between Tom and Huck is terrible. Tom is torn, but his pride will not let him back down.*)

HUCK: (*Sadly.*) So long, Tom. (*He departs after Joe.*
  Until now, Tom has made a great show of unconcern. But left by himself, his inner turmoil becomes painfully evident. All is very lonely and still. Tom dashes his sleeve across his eyes, then hardens himself.)

TOM: I won't! They won't have the nerve to go through with it, anyway. (*He climbs up on the stump, to follow their progress.*) They're wadin' out! (*Pride loses.*) Hey, fellows, wait, wait! (*He dashes off, in their direction. Off:*) I want to tell you something!

HUCK: (*Off.*) Joe! Hold on! Tom's a-comin'!

TOM: (*Off.*) Come back! I got somethin' to tell you!

JOE: (*Off.*) What?

TOM: (*Off.*) Something big. Hurry! (*Tom pulls a reluctant Joe in, followed by Huck.*)

JOE: Looky here, Tom Sawyer. You ain't a-holdin' me here. I mean to go home.

HUCK: Me, too.

TOM: And so do I. But we can't go now!

HUCK: What's to keep us?

JOE: Why not?

TOM: 'Cause they think we're drownded, and they're goin' to have a funeral for us, that's why!

JOE: What?

HUCK: A funeral? For us?

JOE: How can they?

HUCK: It makes you feel right creepy. You ain't makin' this up, are you, Tom?

JOE: Listen, Tom Sawyer, how do you know this?

TOM: (*A little ashamed.*) Last night, after you fellows went to sleep, I slipped off and hooked a ride over to the mainland.

HUCK: Tom, you didn't!

JOE: I knew you was up to something.

HUCK: Didn't they see you?

TOM: 'Course not. What do you take me for? I hid.

JOE: Then how'd you find out about the—the funeral?

TOM: I crawled under Aunt Polly's bed, and I heard 'em talk about it. Now, listen, fellows. I'll tell you my plan. And if you don't think it's the best you ever heard, I'll go back with you right now. (*The scene begins to fade out.*) They plan to have the funeral Sunday morning. Now this being Friday—(*The scene closes on three plotting pirates.*)

SCENE 3. *The village church. A pulpit, pews, a stained-glass window.*
(*The schoolchildren are clustered together, talking of the tragedy. While they talk, the pews fill up with other townspeople.*)

AMY: And I was a-standin' just so—just as I am now. And as if you was him, I was as close as that. And he smiled just this way, and he said, "Never you mind. You just wait. I know something that's going to happen." And I never thought what he meant.

BEN: I got a busted balloon that I traded Joe onct for a fish hook.

GRACIE: I got some writing of Tom's in one of my books.

BECKY: Could I see it, Gracie, if I come over to your house today?

ANIE: My brother's got an old stick of Joe Harper's, that they used to ay war with.

M: Onct I played hookey with Huck Finn. And Tom and me, we ole a watermelon last summer.

LFRED: Well, Tom Sawyer, he licked me once! (*They all scoff.*)

EN: Most of us can say that.

MY: Sh! Here comes the families. (*The children yield place to the ief mourners. Aunt Polly and Sid come in together, followed by Mrs. arper and Susan. The two women are sobbing.*)

D: Don't take on so, Aunt Polly. I hope Tom's better off where he is, ut if he'd been better in some ways—

UNT POLLY: Sid! Not a word against my Tom, now that he's gone. He as the best-hearted boy that ever was, though he tormented the life ut of me, almost.

RS. HARPER: It was just so with my Joe. Always full of mischief, but ust as unselfish and kind as he could be.

UNT POLLY: Oh, Sereny, I don't know how to give Tom up. He was ach a comfort to me.

RS. HARPER: It's hard—oh, it's so hard. Only last Saturday, my Joe usted a firecracker right under my nose, and I knocked him sprawling. ittle did I know then how soon—Oh, if it was to do over again, I'd ug and bless him for it.

UNT POLLY: I know just how you feel, Sereny. Just the day before he ft, my Tom took and filled the cat full of Pain-Killer medicine, that I ave him to take himself, and I thought the cat would tear the house own. And—God forgive me!—I cracked Tom's head with my thimble. oor boy—poor, dead boy. But he's out of all his troubles now. And e last words I ever heard him say was—

D: Sh, Aunt Polly. Here comes the Preacher. (*The Preacher enters, nd stalks ponderously to his pulpit. A hush falls over the congre- ation, and the weeping is subdued. But as the Preacher's address pro- eds, fresh sobs break out, and all are so preoccupied with their grief at nobody notices three bedraggled pirates creep in to listen.*)

REACHER: My friends, we are met here to mourn together over the assing of three young souls that have departed from our midst in the past week. Never before has this village suffered such a blow as now, in the loss of these three high-minded, brave, fearless young boys. Oh, my friends, a great orator once said, "The good that men do in this world is oft interred with their bones, but the evil lives after them." Let that not be true of these three young boys. Let us recall only the sweet, generous natures that led them to do noble and beautiful deeds, and let us ask forgiveness for the hard thoughts we have nourished against them, in their moments of innocent pleasure and fun. My friends, Joe Harper was once known to give away some tokens to a poor German lad that enabled him to earn a Bible. And before their tragic disappearance, Tom Sawyer and Huckleberry Finn visited the county jail, to bring comfort and cheer to the unhappy prisoner, Muff Potter, who is held there for murder. Pardon me, my friends, I cannot hold back a tear— (*But by this time, the whole church is reduced to muffled sobs. The moment has come for the three boys to reveal themselves. As they creep forward, the minister raises his streaming eyes, and stands transfixed, then other eyes follow his.*)

AUNT POLLY: Oh, me! I can even see his sperrit in the broad daylight.

MRS. HARPER: I can see my Joe, too—just as plain as if he was alive.

BEN: Is it real?

ALFRED: It's ghosts, that's what it is!

BECKY: Tom!!!

TOM: Hello, Becky.

PREACHER: They're alive! (*The boys are suddenly surrounded, everybody shouting at once.*)

AUNT POLLY: Tom! What a turn you do give a body! I thought I'd never see you alive.

MRS. HARPER: Joe! Is it really you? I'd given you up.

AUNT POLLY: Tom, I don't care what new mischief you've been into—oh, Tom!

TOM: Aunt Polly, it ain't fair. Somebody's got to be glad to see Huck.

AUNT POLLY: And so they shall. I'm glad to see him, poor thing. (*And poor Huck, who was just about to escape to freedom, is hauled back and kissed, just like any civilized child.*) Huck Finn, you shall come straight home with us to dinner. And Sid, you run ahead and tell Mary to put some ice cream in the freezer.

PREACHER: (*Shouting above the hubbub.*) Praise God! Sing! And put your hearts in it! (*He leads off with "Old Hundred," in which the congregation joins heartily.*)

END OF ACT THREE

ACT FOUR

SCENE 1. *Outside the Courthouse, adjoining the jail. A flight of steps leading to the Courthouse entrance. A brick wall, with barred window, set at an angle to it. A barrel.*

(*Tom, in thoughtful mood, is sitting on the Courthouse steps. Sheriff enters from the direction of the jail.*)

SHERIFF: Why, Tom, you here again?

TOM: Yes sir.

SHERIFF: Well, you can't sit here on the Courthouse steps. People will be coming for the trial.

TOM: Yes sir. I know. Sheriff, are they going to hang Muff Potter?

SHERIFF: It looks mighty bad for him, Tom. And he don't deny the killing. Just says he can't remember doin' it.

TOM: Sheriff, Muff Potter ain't never hurt anybody.

SHERIFF: That's not for us to decide, my boy. Run along now. I have to open up the Courthouse. (*Sheriff unlocks the door, and goes inside the Courthouse. Tom waits till he is safely out of earshot, then crosses to the barrel.*)

TOM: You can come out now, Huck.

HUCK: (*Climbing out of the barrel, somewhat more disreputable than usual.*) By jings, Tom, I don't mind when they throw their potato peels over me—but some joker tumped in a bucket of clinkers.

TOM: Did you bring the tobacco?

HUCK: I got it.

TOM: Come on. The Sheriff'll be out in a minute. (*They cross to the barred window of the jail.*) Pss-s-st! Muff! Muff Potter! (*No answer. The boys exchange apprehensive glances.*)

HUCK: You don't reckon they've already taken him away, do you?

TOM: Muff! Muff! Are you there? (*Muff's head appears at the window.*)

MUFF: Is that you, boys? Oh, bless you. You ain't forgot poor old Muff.

TOM: Hucky here, he's brought you something.

HUCK: It's only a little tobacco.

TOM: And here's some lucifer matches.

MUFF: Boys, you've been so good to me.

HUCK: Oh, shucks, it ain't nothin'.

MUFF: Yes it is. It means a big lot to a man in trouble, when everybody else has turned against him.

TOM: Oh, Muff, don't say so!

HUCK: You never killed anybody, Muff.

MUFF: Oh, boys, you're the only friends I got. Get up on one another's backs, and let me shake your hands. That's it. Yourn'll come through the bars, but mine's too big. Little hands and weak, but they've helped me a power—and I know they'd help me more if they could. Yes, if they could. (*Sheriff comes out of the Courthouse.*)

SHERIFF: Here, you boys, what are you doing there talking to the prisoner? Get down from there!

TOM: Yes sir. We was only—

SHERIFF: Get along home now. It's nearly time for Court. Muff, are you ready?

MUFF: I'm ready, Sheriff. Good-bye, boys. You've been mighty good to me, and I won't forget it. I know you'd help me if you could.

SHERIFF: Go along now—and don't let me catch you lurking around this jail again. (*The boys make a show of leaving, and Sheriff goes off in direction of the jail.*)

TOM: (*Close to tears.*) Did you hear what he said, Huck?

HUCK: I heerd.

TOM: He said he knew we'd help him if we could—and Huck, we can!

HUCK: Jee-hosophat! What are you a-thinkin' of, Tom? We wouldn't be alive two days if we told.

TOM: Well, he won't be alive two days if we don't.

HUCK: But Tom, we swore. Don't you know that if you tell, you'll drop down dead and rot?

TOM: Oh, Hucky, what are we goin' to do? (*Janie Hardin skips in, gay and excited, followed shortly by Ben Rogers and Jim Hollis.*)

JANIE: We're going on a pick-a-nick! We're going on a pick-a-nick! Tom! Tom! We're all invited on a picnic!

BEN: Shucks, what's a picnic? (*Becky Thatcher, Susan Harper, and Gracie Miller enter, chattering animatedly.*)

JIM: We been on picnics before, I reckon. (*Joe Harper enters.*)

GRACIE: But this is a big, all-day picnic, down the river, on the ferryboat!

JOE: On the ferryboat?

SUSAN: You tell them, Becky.

BECKY: My ma's going to let me give a picnic party next Saturday. And you are all invited.

BEN: Are we really going on the ferryboat, Becky?

BECKY: Yes. Down the river, all the way to MacDougall's Cave.

TOM: MacDougall's Cave?

BECKY: Yes. That's where we'll have our lunch.

JOE: By jings! And after lunch, we can go exploring in the cave. (*Tom and Huck exchange significant glances. Amy Lawrence and Alfred Temple enter.*)

AMY: You ought to be ashamed of yourself, Alfred Temple. And if you're going to say such things, I won't listen to you.

ALFRED: All I said was he's the bloodiest-looking villain in the country.

JIM: Who? (*Aunt Polly enters, with Sid.*)

ALFRED: Why, Muff Potter. It's a wonder he wasn't hung long before now. The whole town says so.

AUNT POLLY: Well, I don't say so, young man. I've known Muff Potter all my life, and I never knew him to harm a fly. (*Mrs. Harper enters with Preacher and Schoolmaster.*)

SID: But Aunt Polly, Injun Joe saw him kill the Doctor.

AUNT POLLY: Mph! I don't believe that sneaky Injun. How do, Brother Walters, Mr. Dobbin. Oh, Sereny, ain't it awful?

BEN: My pa said if he was to get loose, they'd lynch him.

JOE: And I bet they would, too.

MRS. HARPER: Joe Harper, you just hush right up with that kind of talk.

JOE: Gee Whillikers, Mom, I—I—

MRS. HARPER: Many's the time you boys have been glad enough to go off fishing with Muff Potter, whenever you got the chance.

JOE: Well, Jiminee, how was I to know he was a killer?

JANIE: (*Beginning to cry.*) He ain't a killer. He mended my dolly.

ALFRED: He is too a killer—ain't he, Mr. Dobbins?

SCHOOLMASTER: There is good reason to believe that he did kill the young Doctor, ladies.

AUNT POLLY: On the say-so of that heathen Injun?

SCHOOLMASTER: Well, not entirely. Ahem. I have evidence of my own to support Injun Joe's testimony. And so has Brother Walters here.

AUNT POLLY: Preacher!

MRS. HARPER: You don't mean it, Brother Walters!

PREACHER: Sister Harper, it is like you soft-hearted ladies to pity anybody in trouble. It is the nature of women, God bless them. And Muff Potter needs pity, poor wretch—yes, and prayer, too. For there is no question in any reasonable mind, that under the influence of that demon drink, he did kill young Dr. Robinson.

AUNT POLLY: Oh, Preacher, how can you be so sure?

PREACHER: Aunt Polly, I saw him that night with my own eyes.

MRS. HARPER: You saw the killing?

PREACHER: Not the killing. But I saw him wash off the bloodstains in the branch.

AUNT POLLY: No!

PREACHER: It was about midnight, and bright moon, and I was on my way home from visiting the sickbed of Brother Hopkins, up the branch. Muff Potter came slipping out from behind the trees, kind of moaning to himself. I thought he was just drunk as usual. And he knelt down beside the water, and washed his hands.

SCHOOLMASTER: Now why would he do that, unless they had blood on them?

BEN: 'Tain't like Muff Potter to wash hisself, I reckon.

ALFRED: Unless he's got a reason.

PREACHER: And in the bright moonlight, I could see dark splotches on his shirt.

ALFRED: You see? He done it all right.

JOE: If he didn't do it, Mom, why don't he say so?

AUNT POLLY: Oh, Preacher, you wouldn't think harsh of a man for washin' himself, would you?

MRS. HARPER: And he's always got splotches on his shirt.

PREACHER: But ladies, that's not all. Mr. Dobbin here can identify the knife.

JOE: The knife?

SCHOOLMASTER: Yes, ladies. I've been called to testify to this point in court. Ahem. The day before the murder, I was addressing an envelope in the post office when my pencil point broke. Muff Potter was loafing around there, and I borrowed his knife to sharpen it.

PREACHER: It was the same knife that killed the Doctor, ladies.

SCHOOLMASTER: It was a distinctive knife. I'd know it anywhere. It was the same one.

MRS. HARPER: If that's so, he's as good as gone.

PREACHER: Yes, I'm afraid he's a goner. (*Injun Joe enters, and crosses silently toward the Courthouse. The children shrink from him in fear, whispering to each other about him. The adults hold themselves aloof. In this hostile climate, the Preacher confronts him at the Courthouse steps.*) My man, what you are about to swear to, in that Courthouse, may send an unfortunate man to his death. Are you prepared to have this on your conscience?

INJUN JOE: Milksop! (*Sheriff enters, leading Muff Potter, from the jail.*)

SHERIFF: Stand back, folks, and let the prisoner come through. Come along, Muff. (*Muff is chained, and downcast. He shrinks from the accusing and pitying faces, as he makes his way to the Courthouse steps. There, he turns to face them.*)

MUFF: Oh, folks, I done an awful thing, but I beg you not to think so hard of me. I didn't do it a-purpose. I liked the young Doctor. I liked all my neighbors, and I loved their chillun, and tried to befriend 'em what I could. It was the drink that did it, friends, and I reckon I'm a-going to pay for it. It's only right I should. But when I'm dead, folks, don't forget me. You bring your chillun to my grave, and you warn 'em about the evils of drink. And tell 'em what happened to poor Muff Potter. And Preacher, you pray for my soul. (*All are visibly moved. Muffled sobs are heard.*)

SHERIFF: That'll do, Muff. Come along now.

TOM: I can stop this hangin'—and by jings, I'm a-goin' to! (*Pulling away from the terrified Huck, he makes his way to the Courthouse steps. Huck moves as far away as possible from Injun Joe, but eyes him watchfully throughout the scene.*) Sheriff! Muff Potter never done it. I saw it happen!

SHERIFF: What? (*Sensation in the crowd. Injun Joe stands staunch, staring Tom down.*)

TOM: (*Losing his nerve.*) Y-y-yes sir. I saw the killin'. I was there.

SHERIFF: Where?

TOM: (*Timidly.*) In—in—in the graveyard.

SHERIFF. The night of the murder, around midnight?

TOM: Y-y-y-yes sir.

INJUN JOE: He's lying.

SHERIFF: Were you anywhere near Hoss Williams' grave?

TOM: Yes sir.

SHERIFF: How near?

TOM: Near as I am to you. But I was hid.

SHERIFF: Where?

TOM: Behind the next tombstone. (*Injun Joe eyes the crowd, for an avenue of escape.*)

SHERIFF: Why?

TOM: Well—we—I—I—

SHERIFF: Speak up, my boy, if you are telling the truth.

TOM: We—ah—I—I was aimin' to bury a dead cat.

SHERIFF: (*Thundering.*) A dead cat?

TOM: (*Whispering.*) Y-y-yes sir. (*A ripple of mirth in the crowd.*)

SHERIFF: And what happened?

TOM: Well, sir, we dropped the cat. I reckon its carcass is still there. But we saw it all, Sheriff. And Muff Potter never done it. Muff was knocked out cold. But he took Muff's knife and—(*He points a finger toward Injun Joe.*)—and he done it!

SHERIFF: Catch him! (*But Injun Joe has sprung through the crowd. Huck, ever so innocently, trips him. And Preacher and Schoolmaster make a show of grabbing at him. But shaking them off easily, he is up and gone, pursued by the Sheriff, Preacher, and Schoolmaster. Tom is making to join in the pursuit, but is hauled back abruptly by Huck. The rest of the crowd swarms affectionately around Muff Potter.*)

HUCK: They'll never catch him, Tom. Them Injuns can go like the wind, and leave no tracks. He'll come back and kill us, sure.

TOM: How can he, Huck? If they catch him, he'll be locked up. And if he gets away, he won't dare show his face around here again.

HUCK: He's got treasure hid somewheres around here. He ain't goin' to leave here without that.

TOM: That's so. Lordy, Huck, what'll we do?

HUCK: Stay out of sight, I bet you. (*He starts sneaking away.*)

TOM: Wait for me! (*Becky breaks away from the group surrounding Muff Potter.*)

BECKY: Oh, Tom, how could you be so brave!

AUNT POLLY: Tom, you done the right thing, for once. I'm proud of you. (*An admiring public gathers around the frightened boy.*)

SCENE 2. *MacDougall's Cave. Rocky silhouettes. Stalactites and stalagmites. A high boulder, which must be practical. Dim light. The sound of water dripping slowly.*

(*Injun Joe enters, panting. Flattens himself against the boulder, and listens.*)

INJUN JOE: Drat those kids! All through the cave, curse 'em. But they won't have the nerve to venture this far, I reckon. (*He listens a moment, then climbs the boulder. At the top, he stands precariously balanced on a narrow ledge, but lights a candle, improving the light.*) Good thing I had one of those lucifer matches. (*Carrying the candle, he locates a position, and tugs at a loose rock, which he finally removes.*) Ah-h-h-h! (*He draws out of hiding the wooden money box, and lets a few coins filter through his fingers. His eyes glisten with greed.*) Money! If Injun Joe has to go, he takes you with him. (*At the sound of a shout offstage, he claps the box shut, and turns quickly.*)

TOM: (*Offstage.*) Yoo—oo—oo! (*Echo.*)

BECKY: (*Offstage.*) Yoo—oo—oo! (*Echo.*) (*In his haste, Injun Joe loses his balance on the narrow ledge. He tries to catch himself, but too late. We see him fall to the ground. He writhes a few moments, then lies still. Tom and Becky grope their way in, carrying candles.*)

TOM: This must be an entirely new part of the cave, Becky. None of the others have been here at all.

ECKY: Tom, it seems ever so long since I heard any of the others.

OM: Come to think, Becky, we're way down below them, and I don't now how far north or south or east, whichever way it is. We couldn't ear them here.

ECKY: I wonder how long we've been here, Tom. We better start ack.

OM: (*Looking for possible exits.*) Yes, I reckon we better. Perhaps we etter.

ECKY: Can you find the way, Tom? It's all a mixed-up crookedness to 1e.

OM: I reckon I could find it—but then the bats. If they put out our andles, it will be an awful fix. Let's try some other way, so as not to go hrough there.

ECKY: Well, but I hope we won't get lost. It would be too awful.

OM: (*Groping in different directions.*) Oh, it's all right. This ain't he way, but we'll come back to it right away.

ECKY: Oh, Tom, never mind the bats. Let's go back that way. We eem to get worse and worse off.

OM: Listen. Yoo—oo—oo! (*Echo.*)

ECKY: Oh, don't do that again, Tom. It's too horrid.

OM: It is horrid, but I better, Becky. They might hear us, you know.

ECKY: Tom, you didn't make any marks, to trace our way back by!

OM: Becky, I was such a fool. Such a fool! I never thought we might ʋant to come back. No, I can't find the way. It's all mixed up.

ECKY: We're lost. We're lost! We can never get out of this awful lace! Oh, why did we ever leave the others?

OM: Don't cry, Becky. It's all my fault.

ECKY: Don't say that, Tom. Let's try again.

OM: We mustn't go far. Here, Becky. Let me blow out your candle. Ve may need it, later.

ECKY: Tom!

TOM: Maybe not, though. We'll look some more.

BECKY: Oh, Tom, it's not a bit of use.

TOM: 'Course it is, Becky. Don't give up. We'll find a way.

BECKY: No we won't, Tom. We never will. Oh Tom, last night I dreamed of the most beautiful country you ever saw. I reckon we are going there, Tom.

TOM: Maybe not. Cheer up, Becky. Here, sit down and rest a minute.

BECKY: Oh no, Tom. Let's move on and look some more.

TOM: Becky, can you bear it if I tell you something?

BECKY: I'll try to, Tom. What is it?

TOM: Well, then, Becky, we must stay here, where there's water to drink. This is our last bit of candle.

BECKY: Tom!

TOM: I'm sorry, Becky.

BECKY: Well, all right. We might as well stay here as anywhere. We're going to die anyway, and it doesn't make much difference where.

TOM: Becky, don't talk like that. We're not going to die.

BECKY: Yes we are, too. I know we're going to die, and I'm all ready for it.

TOM: Becky, here. I've got a kite line in my pocket. Now you hold one end of it, and I'll take the other and explore some of the side passages. If you get scared waiting here, just give a little pull on this string, and I'll come a-running.

BECKY: All right, Tom. But it's not a bit of use. I'll just wait here and die. It won't take long. But Tom, come back every once in a while and speak to me. And when the awful time comes, stay by me and hold my hand till it's over, will you, Tom?

TOM: 'Course I will. But don't you worry, Becky. We ain't goin' to die in here. Now here. I'll be back in a little while. Wait for me. (*Leaving Becky, he fumbles his way around by candlelight, toward the boulder. He almost stumbles over Injun Joe's body.*) Lordy! It's Injun Joe! (*He turns to flee, then stops, and returns fearfully, holding his shaking candle so as to see better.*) That's funny. That ain't no natural way to sleep. (*Cautiously, he kneels to look closer, then after a false start, brings himself to touch the body. When there is no response, he musters his courage to feel the heart.*) Craminee! He's dead! (*Awed, he stands up, and extends his candle to explore the location, spies the ledge at the top of the boulder. He gropes his way to climb the boulder, by the route Injun Joe used earlier, but does not venture to stand on the narrow ledge.*) By jings, the treasure! So this is where he's been hidin' out. (*With sudden resolution, he climbs back down, takes off his jacket and covers the dead face, then hastily gropes his way back to Becky.*) Becky, I—I—

BECKY: Tom, what's the matter? You're shaking! Where's your jacket? What is it, Tom?

TOM: Becky, I—I think we better explore somewhere else. We don't want to stay here.

BECKY: But what about the water, Tom?

TOM: We'll have to find some in another place. We can't stay here. Come on.

BECKY: Tom, they'll miss us, won't they?

TOM: Yes, they will. Certainly they will.

BECKY: Maybe they're hunting for us now, Tom.

TOM: Why, I reckon maybe they are. I hope they are.

BECKY: When would they miss us, Tom?

TOM: Why, when they got back to the boat, I reckon.

BECKY: Tom, it might be dark then. Would they notice we hadn't come?

TOM: I don't know. But anyway, your mother would miss you, soon as they got home.

BECKY: Oh, Tom! She thinks I'm staying all night with Susie Harper!

TOM: Good Lord, Becky!

BECKY: (*Crying.*) Oh, Tom! Tom, we'll never be found! We're in here forever and ever!

TOM: Aw, don't cry, Becky. Let's get away from this fearsome place. (*As the scene ends, two frightened children are groping their way off.*)

SCENE 3. *The village church.*

(*The Preacher is just dismissing the congregation. The Preacher lifts his hand in benediction.*)

PREACHER: Amen. (*The people rise and break up into little groups. Preacher comes down from the pulpit to greet his flock.*)

MRS. HARPER: Good morning, Mr. Dobbin.

AUNT POLLY: Good morning, Sheriff.

SHERIFF: Morning, Aunt Polly.

AUNT POLLY: Good morning, children. I'm glad to see the picnic didn't keep *you* from comin' to church this morning. (*The children mumble greetings.*)

BEN: No'm. Ma made me.

AUNT POLLY: That's more than I can say for my Tom.

PREACHER: I didn't see your Tom in Sunday School this morning, Aunt Polly.

AUNT POLLY: Oh, he turned up missing from the picnic, Preacher. I reckon he stayed with the Harpers last night, and now he's afraid to come to church. I've got to settle with him.

MRS. HARPER: Good morning, Aunt Polly.

AUNT POLLY: Good morning, Sereny. Is my Tom going to sleep all day at your house?

MRS. HARPER: Your Tom?

AUNT POLLY: Yes. Didn't he stay with you last night?

MRS. HARPER: Why, no. Was he supposed to?

AUNT POLLY: (*Anxious.*) Well, where else could he be?

MRS. HARPER: I was expecting Becky Thatcher for the night, but Susan came home without her. Reckon she changed her mind, and went home.

GRACIE: Becky ain't home, Mrs. Harper. I stopped by for her this morning, and her mother said she was spending the night at your house.

MRS. HARPER: (*Alarmed.*) But she didn't. Oh, my! (*Their concern spreads through the congregation in whispers. All attention is focused on the two women.*)

AUNT POLLY: Joe Harper, have you seen my Tom this morning?

JOE: No'm.

AUNT POLLY: When did you see him last?

MRS. HARPER: When did you see Becky last, Susan?

JOE AND SUSAN: (*Scared.*) I don't remember.

SHERIFF: (*Taking charge.*) Look here, didn't they come back on the ferryboat with the rest of you?

JOE: I don't remember seein' 'em.

SUSAN: It was dark when we got on, and we were so tired goin' through the cave—

SHERIFF: (*To the children, who are thinking startled thoughts.*) Do any of you children remember seeing them on the ferryboat? (*The children answer him with dumb silence.*) Did they go into the cave?

JOE: Yes sir. We all went into it together. And then we got to chasin' through some of the side passages, and—and—

SHERIFF: Yes, go on.

JOE: Well, sir, Tom and Becky had a candle apiece, and they took a different turning from us, 'cause they said they was goin' to find something new.

PREACHER: Oh, Sheriff, could it be—is it possible they—they are still in the cave? (*Aunt Polly falls to crying, and wringing her hands. Mrs. Harper tries to comfort her. The children are frozen with horror.*)

SHERIFF: Joe, you run as fast as you can to the town hall and ring the bell. Tell all the men to meet me at the ferryboat landing in ten minutes. Ben, you find old Mr. Harrison, and tell him to open up the store, and let you have all the candles he has in stock. We'll need twine, too, to track our own way through the cave. You men come with me to the wharf, and we'll arrange for boats to carry us over. Don't fear, Aunt Polly. If they are in the cave, we'll find them. (*All are rushing about on one errand or another, as the scene closes.*)

SCENE 4. *A village street. Board fence. Covered barrel.*

(*Aunt Polly enters, downcast, carrying a pan of trash. Stops to stroke the board fence, wipes away a tear, then carries the trash to the barrel. As she lifts the lid, she gasps.*)

AUNT POLLY: Huckleberry Finn! (*Huck's head appears.*)

HUCK: Yes'm.

AUNT POLLY: You climb right out of there. (*Meekly Huck climbs out. Aunt Polly empties the trash, and sets her pan on the lid of the barrel.*) Just look at you! After all the Widow Douglas has done to make a nice, clean, respectable boy of you!

HUCK: Yes'm.

AUNT POLLY: Why are you skulking around like this anyway? . . . Don't stop to think up one of your fibs now. What have you done wrong?

HUCK: Aunt Polly, ain't they found Tom yet?

AUNT POLLY: Oh, Huck, no! Nor Becky neither. They've about give up. They say nobody could be alive in that cave after three days.

HUCK: Tom could. Tom's smart.

AUNT POLLY: Two hundred men have searched that cave, day and night, and all they found was Becky's hair ribbon. Now most of them have come home. (*Joyful shouting is heard off, followed by a wild peal of bells.*) Mercy on us! Who's ringing the town bell?

VOICES: (*Off.*) Turn out! Turn out, everybody! They're found! They're found!

HUCK: (*Bounding off.*) It's Tom! It's Tom and Becky! Tom! (*Aunt Polly stands trembling, adjusting her spectacles. Schoolmaster runs in.*)

SCHOOLMASTER: Aunt Polly! They're found! They're found!

AUNT POLLY: I can't believe it. Tom! Tom! Becky!

SCHOOLMASTER: (*Shouting in all directions.*) Turn out! Turn out, everybody! They're found! (*Muff enters, bearing Tom on his shoulder. Preacher follows with Becky on his, both children looking a little the worse for their experience. Accompanied by Janie, Jim, Gracie, and Ben, all shouting, waving, blowing toy horns, etc. Huck tags along shyly, on the fringe.*)

AUNT POLLY: (*Seizing Tom as Muff sets him down.*) Tom, boy! Tom! (*Joe and Susan Harper rush in, followed by Sid.*)

SUSAN: Oh, Becky! Oh, Tom! (*Sid picks up Aunt Polly's pan and bangs on it.*)

JOE: (*Shouting everywhere.*) Turn out, everybody! Here they are! They're found! They're found! (*Mrs. Harper enters, followed by Alfred.*)

MRS. HARPER: Well, bless my soul! Becky, child!

AUNT POLLY: Becky, your mother is nearly dead from grief. We made sure you two had fallen into one of them crevices in the cave.

PREACHER: The Sheriff has gone to tell your mother, Becky.

SCHOOLMASTER: Your father is still in the cave, with the searching party. (*Sheriff enters.*)

BECKY: Searching party?

SHERIFF: We've sent a skiff over to the cave, to take the news to the searching party.

TOM: We never saw any searching party.

AUNT POLLY: Tom, you don't mean—how did you ever get out, then?

TOM: Well, Aunt Polly, we'd been in there a week or so, I guess. Maybe more. And Becky, she was all wore out. So I left her resting a minute, while I went on explorin' a little bit. I had my kite line along, and I made her hold one end of that, while I followed a little path as far as the line would reach. I tried that out on three different alleys, and I was just about to give up and turn back, when I thought I saw a tiny speck, way off, that looked like daylight. I dropped the kite line, and pushed my way toward it, and first thing you know, I was lookin' right out on the river.

BEN: Craminee!

JOE: Tom! Just suppose it'd been night.

TOM: Don't think it, Joe. And then I went back for Becky, and told her.

BECKY: He was wonderful, Aunt Polly. I didn't do anything but cry. But Tom just kept looking for new places, and if it hadn't been for him, we never would have got out, I reckon.

AUNT POLLY: (*All choked up.*) Becky, child!

TOM: Aw, shucks, that warn't nothin'. But when I showed Becky the little speck of daylight, she nearly died of joy. And then we climbed out of the hole, and were just sittin' there cryin' for gladness when some men came by in a skiff. We told them who we were, but they wouldn't believe us at first, because they said we were five miles down the river below the cave. But anyway they took us aboard, and rowed us to their farm, and gave us some breakfast. And then the old man brought us here in his spring wagon.

CHILDREN: Hoo—ray! 'Ray for Tom, and 'ray for Becky!

SCHOOLMASTER: Let's have a parade! (*All but Huck marching off, shouting, banging, horn-blowing, etc. But as Huck hangs back the hero of the parade stops to coax his friend.*)

TOM: Come on, Huck. Join the fun.

HUCK: I can't, Tom. I'm layin' low.

TOM: What for?

HUCK: The Widow Douglas wants to adopt me. For keeps. And make me wash, and educate me, and everything. And I can't stand it, Tom.

TOM: Hucky, you don't need it. You're rich. I found the treasure!

HUCK: Tom! Where?

TOM: It's in the cave, and when we get the chance, you and me'll snake over there and get it.

HUCK: And run onto Injun Joe? Not me.

TOM: Hucky, you don't ever need to worry about Injun Joe anymore. He's dead.

HUCK: Dead? Lordy! Are you sure?

TOM: Sure. He fell off'n a high ledge where the treasure is. I run onto him in the cave, all spraddled out, dead.

HUCK: Geeminy!

TOM: Now come on. We've got something to parade about! (*They start off together.*)

HUCK: Tom, what'll we do with all that money?

TOM: We'll play robbers, of course. Tom Sawyer's Gang—don't that sound splendid? And we'll buy swords and pistols and things that a robber has to have—and waylay people . . . (*And the play ends while we are still caught up in the dreams of childhood—oh, how beautiful they are, and how perishable.*)

CURTAIN

Winnie-the-Pooh
Kristin Sergel

Adapted from A. A. Milne

Based on A. A. Milne's children's book, *Winnie-the-Pooh* by Kristin Sergel brings Christopher Robin and his toy animals to life in a series of their most famous episodes.

The action of the play begins with Pooh's looking for honey and Piglet's announcing that a strange animal is coming to the forest. Suspense builds about the identity of the newcomer as each character who enters reveals an additional bit of information which everyone considers increasingly ominous. When Kanga and Roo finally make their innocent appearance, the animals are terrified.

Their arrival and Pooh's constant search for honey are the main concerns of the plot. From them spring several familiar scenes from Milne's classic: Pooh's retrieving honey from a tree while he is hoisted aloft by a balloon, his getting stuck in Rabbit's hole after overindulging himself in his host's honey, Piglet's being bathed under protest, and Pooh's attempt to rescue the kidnapped Piglet, and Pooh's own bath and discovery of Kanga's wonderful medicine.

The charm of the play lies in the strengths and foibles of the animal characters who seem very human indeed as they react to disappointments, are frightened, and try to help each other with varying degrees of success. Their subtle interactions with each other reveal believable people even to a child audience.

Their brief lines, many from the original source, create much of the amusement as the characters naïvely reveal themselves. One wants to be a good friend, another talks in words too obscure for the others to understand, still another is gloomy and irritable. One can only jump and hop when he is excited, another wants to mother them all, and still another feels he is treated too much like a child. When he is hungry, Pooh finds it difficult to think of anything but eating honey.

Since, except for Christopher Robin, the characters are stuffed toys which have come to life in their own special world, costumes are the important aspect of technical production. Full animal suits of plush or figured fabrics with the necessary padding are a possible solution. A simpler approach is to use appropriate details such as ears, tails, or feet that have been added to T-shirts and drawstring trousers. Each character has his own distinct human personality and his costume should enhance that.

The setting, an open space in the forest, must provide plenty of room for the animals to move. A background of neutral drapes with added details such as a tree stump, along with a border of painted leaves above the stage, would work very well.

WINNIE-THE-POOH

CHARACTERS

Christopher Robin	*a small boy*
Winnie-the-Pooh	*a teddy bear*
Piglet	*a small pig*
Owl	*an owl*
Eeyore	*a donkey*
Kanga	*a mother kangaroo*
Roo	*her child*
Rabbit	*a rabbit*
Animal 1	*a small rabbit*
Animal 2	*a little skunk*
Animal 3 } Animal 4 }	*two more small rabbits*
Voice	*the narrator*

Extras (*other residents of the forest*) may be added

SETTING

A forest.

ACT ONE

BEFORE RISE OF CURTAIN: *Christopher Robin enters in front of the curtain DR. He is pulling a teddy bear along by one paw. Christopher Robin is heading for a hassock placed at DR.*

CHRISTOPHER ROBIN: (*Talking to the bear in a matter-of-fact way.*) What would you like to do this evening? Play a game of some sort? (*After looking closely for a response, Christopher Robin sits down. He speaks toward the audience.*) Winnie-the-Pooh doesn't feel like playing a game. He wants to sit quietly and—(*Looks at the bear again, then up.*) What about a story?

VOICE: (*Narrator, offstage.*) What about a story?

CHRISTOPHER ROBIN: Couldn't you very kindly tell him one? Please?

VOICE: (*After a slight pause.*) What sort of story does he like?

CHRISTOPHER ROBIN: (*Eagerly.*) About himself. He's that sort of bear.

VOICE: I suppose he goes in for a good bit of adventure?

CHRISTOPHER ROBIN: (*Nodding.*) The only thing he likes better than adventure is eating honey. (*Amends this, in response to the bear.*) And marmalade.

VOICE: Very well, then—I'll tell you a story about adventure *and* eating honey. (*His voice grows ominous.*) A story about how a frightening animal came to the forest—and about the terrible things that happened afterwards.

CHRISTOPHER ROBIN: Is it a scary story? Will I be able to sleep tonight?

VOICE: That depends. Let's get to the story. (*Pause.*) Once upon a time, a very long time ago—

CHRISTOPHER ROBIN: How long?

VOICE: About last Friday—

CHRISTOPHER ROBIN: Oh.

VOICE: Winnie-the-Pooh lived in the forest under the name of Sanders.

CHRISTOPHER ROBIN: What does "under the name" mean?

VOICE: (*After pause.*) It means he had the name over the door in gold letters, and he lived under it.

CHRISTOPHER ROBIN: (*Nodding to indicate Pooh.*) He wasn't quite sure.

VOICE: One day he was out walking in the forest, when he came to an open place. And right on the edge of it, he saw a large oak tree. He stopped to listen . . .

CHRISTOPHER ROBIN: What was he listening to?

VOICE: A strange buzzing noise was coming from the top of the tree.

CHRISTOPHER ROBIN: A buzzing noise?

VOICE: Yes. If you'd stop interrupting, you'd be able to hear it. (*The sound of buzzing starts offstage, softly at first.*)

CHRISTOPHER ROBIN: I can! I wonder what it is?

VOICE: So did Winnie-the-Pooh . . . (*The curtain rises. The scene for the play is a bare stage with a curtain or neutrally painted background of flats against the back wall of the stage. At DL, protruding from the wings, is part of the trunk of a tree. This may be painted on the edge of a flat. A painted branch with perhaps some leaves on it should show just before the tree disappears behind the proscenium. Attached well up on the tree is a sign with gold letters on it saying "Sanders." Underneath it is a nursery-size rocking chair if such an item is available. If not, any small straight chair will do. It should definitely be a child's chair, however. DR is another similar tree, but without the sign. URC, against the back of the stage, is another tree. The stage should be well lighted. Christopher Robin goes out R as the curtain rises. Onstage, Winnie-the-Pooh, at DR, is staring intently upward at something.*)

VOICE: He sat down, put his head between his paws, and began to think. (*Pooh goes to hassock DR and sits down.*) He said to himself, "That buzzing noise means something. If there's a buzzing noise, somebody's making it—and the only reason for buzzing that I know of is because you're a bee—" (*Winnie-the-Pooh has adopted the "thinking position" above described.*) Then he thought another long time and said, "The only reason for being a bee that I know of is to make honey—"

WINNIE-THE-POOH: (*Rising and speaking for himself this time.*) And the only reason for making honey is so *I* can eat it. (*At the thought of doing so, Pooh rubs his paws together, licks his lips, and looks quite rapturous with anticipation. He makes a gurgling sound.*) Honey . . . (*Accompanies this with a couple of skipping steps in the direction of the tree DR.*) M-m-m . . . (*Stands still, struck by the thought.*) Funny, my liking it so much . . . (*Then he turns this into a song with a vague tune.*) Isn't it funny . . . (*Dances a step now and then, keeping time.*) How a bear likes honey . . . Buzz, buzz, buzz . . . I wonder why he does . . . (*Then he stops and frowns, beset by a problem. He goes over close to the tree and looks up.*) The question is: How do I get to the honey? (*Puts his chin on his hand and supports the elbow with the other hand.*) First, I'll have to climb the tree—(*Another upward look.*)—which will be a problem. And once I get to the *top* of the tree—(*He spots the hassock left by Christopher Robin, gets it, places it under the tree, and tries to reach the honey. When this doesn't work, he tumbles it over toward URC.*) (*As if in answer to this, the buzzing gets quite loud for a moment—an angry tone about it. Pooh is rather startled by this and backs away from the tree toward DC. As he is thinking it over, Piglet enters from DL, looking rather excited.*)

PIGLET: (*Calling to him.*) There you are, Pooh!

POOH: (*Preoccupied.*) Hello, Piglet.

PIGLET: (*Importantly, pausing at DLC.*) I've got some news—(*Expecting a big reaction.*) A strange animal is coming to the forest.

POOH: (*Abstractedly, still looking at honey tree.*) Piglet, old friend . . .

PIGLET: (*Upset, moving to DC.*) I said, a *strange animal* is coming to the forest!

POOH: Hm-m-m-m—

PIGLET: (*After a pause, going up close behind Pooh and insisting.*) Aren't you going to ask *questions*?

POOH: (*Finally facing around to Piglet.*) About what?

PIGLET: (*Rather wounded.*) You weren't listening.

POOH: Yes, I was. (*Points up at the tree.*) That's how I can tell it's up there.

PIGLET: (*Looking.*) What is?

POOH: Honey. (*Faces tree again.*)

PIGLET: *I* don't see honey. Just a lot of bees flying around—

POOH: Exactly.

PIGLET: (*Catching on.*) Oh.

POOH: There must be quite a lot of it—and freshly made—(*As he says this, he works himself up to a frenzy of hungry anticipation, walking around in a circle.*)

PIGLET: (*A gently admonishing tone.*) Pooh. You're forgetting.

POOH: (*Carried away.*) One delicious mouthful after another—

PIGLET: (*Tugging at his arm.*) Your diet!

POOH: (*Pausing beside Piglet.*) What's that?

PIGLET: I thought you were going on a diet.

POOH: I am going on a diet. But not now. (*Resumes his hungry pacing, glancing up the tree occasionally.*)

PIGLET: Why not?

POOH: (*Lamely.*) Because—right *now* I'm hungry. (*More firmly.*) That's not a good time to go on a diet.

PIGLET: (*Dubious.*) Oh. (*Then, since he is a true friend who says what Pooh would like to hear.*) I suppose tomorrow—after a good night's rest?

POOH: (*Agreeing, with relief.*) And a good breakfast. (*Pauses under the tree.*)

PIGLET: Yes. (*Crosses to DR and looks up at the tree.*) How are you going to get up there?

POOH: Just what I've been wondering. If I could just reach one of those branches—

PIGLET: If you were three feet taller—

POOH: (*Sadly.*) Which I'm not—

PIGLET: (*Bravely.*) Shall I give you a boost? (*Pooh looks hopeful.*) If you stood on my shoulders—(*He stops.*)

POOH: If I stood on your shoulders, I still couldn't reach it. (*Eyes the height for a moment.*)

PIGLET: We'll think of something.

POOH: Thank you for offering, Piglet. You're a true friend. (*Piglet beams with pleasure. Pooh pats his arm fondly. He tries to find a solution.*) Now, there must be—(*He is interrupted by the entrance of Rabbit, who bustles in from DL, looking agitated.*)

RABBIT: (*Muttering.*) I don't like it. I don't like the sound of it—(*Rabbit is followed by several friends and relations, who are dogging his steps.*)

RABBIT: (*Hailing briskly from C.*) Pooh—Piglet!

POOH: Hello, Rabbit—(*When Rabbit stops walking, the youngsters behind him bump into each other. He turns to them.*)

RABBIT: Now, run along and play. (*They all clamor.*)

ANIMAL 1: But, Uncle Rabbit—

ANIMAL 2: What about the game?

ANIMAL 1: You *promised*—

RABBIT: Later, later. There's an important matter I'll have to attend—

ANIMAL 1: But you *said*—

RABBIT: (*Shaking finger and raising his tone.*) I said—I'm busy. Run along and play! (*They know when he means business; they turn and leave at DL, reluctantly.*) Now, then. (*Crosses to RC.*) I suppose you've heard?

POOH: (*From DR.*) I'm not sure.

RABBIT: That a strange animal is coming to the forest—

PIGLET: (*At DC.*) I've heard.

RABBIT: (*Disappointed.*) Oh, you have.

PIGLET: (*Pouring it out.*) That's what I was trying to tell you, Pooh. Her name is Kanga—(*Building this.*) She's one of the Fiercer Animals—

RABBIT: She's very tall—

PIGLET: *Enormous!*

POOH: (*Thinking this over very calmly, asking in a quiet tone.*) Any family?

RABBIT: I believe she has one offspring.

PIGLET: Is that all?

RABBIT: Its name is Roo. (*After pause.*) Imagine having a family of one! (*He is scornful of the idea.*)

POOH: How many in yours, Rabbit?

RABBIT: Hm-m-m . . . Sixteen.

PIGLET: Isn't it seventeen?

RABBIT: Perhaps. It's hard to keep *exact* count. (*Drops the subject.*) The important thing is, Kanga is coming—and she's . . .

POOH: (*Interrupting.*) I make it fifteen.

RABBIT: What?

POOH: Your family.

RABBIT: (*Impatiently.*) Never mind them!

POOH: I thought—

RABBIT: (*Cutting him off.*) *The important thing* is—Kanga is coming to live in the forest.

PIGLET: Yes!

POOH: And bringing an offspring named Roo—(*Looks up at the honey.*)

RABBIT: Yes—

POOH: And what's all the excitement about?

RABBIT: Because—Baby Roo isn't all she's bringing.

PIGLET: What else?

POOH: (*Hopefully.*) Groceries?

RABBIT: (*Hushed, fearful tone—after looking back over his shoulder.*) A bathtub.

PIGLET: (*Stuttering with fright.*) A b-bath—*bathtub?* What for?

RABBIT: (*Explaining, in a patronizing tone.*) Surely you know what a bathtub is for? You fill it with water—you get in—

PIGLET: I do *not!*

RABBIT: (*Rather enjoying Piglet's nervous state.*) We hope not, Piglet. We *hope* not. (*Folds his arms and stares into space.*)

PIGLET: (*Crossing to Pooh.*) You wouldn't let that happen to me, would you?

POOH: (*Firmly.*) You can count on me.

RABBIT: Now you see what the excitement is about. You see the necessity for taking action—

POOH: When is she supposed to arrive?

RABBIT: (*Hasn't any idea; pausing to think.*) Presently.

POOH: Does that mean she isn't here yet?

RABBIT: Of course.

POOH: What a relief. There was another little matter . . . (*A loud moan is heard offstage DL.*)

PIGLET: Help! (*Clings wildly to Pooh. Pooh and Rabbit stare in the direction of the sound.*)

VOICE: (*Offstage DL.*) Miserable. Miserable!

RABBIT: Someone's saying "miserable."

POOH: It must be Eeyore. He generally is. (*Eeyore enters DL. He is talking glumly to himself, but it sounds as if it were a continuation of Pooh's speech.*)

EEYORE: *Utterly* miserable. (*Stands off at DL, waiting to be recognized.*)

POOH: (*Brightly.*) Good morning, Eeyore. (*Crosses to LC.*)

EEYORE: (*Raising his head, reluctantly.*) Good morning, Pooh Bear— (*Hangs his head down again.*) If it is a good morning—(*Gives his head a slight shake.*)—which I doubt.

RABBIT: (*Crossing to C.*) Surely it isn't that bad.

EEYORE: Perhaps not now. (*Flings his head up, says with more emphasis.*) But it *will* be—when *she* gets here!

PIGLET: (*Hurrying to a place between Pooh and Rabbit.*) He must mean Kanga.

EEYORE: Ah—you've heard.

RABBIT: About Kanga—yes.

POOH: And Baby Roo—

PIGLET: (*The topper.*) *And* the bathtub!

EEYORE: (*Continuing.*) And the soap? (*Eeyore turns his back while the others digest this new bombshell. He talks in the other direction.*) I found out by chance.

POOH: Soap?

EEYORE: No one would bother to tell *me*.

PIGLET: (*In a faint, squealing voice.*) Soap?

EEYORE: (*Turning.*) You didn't know about it?

RABBIT: What soap?

EEYORE: You didn't know she carries a cake of the stuff in her pocket? (*To himself again.*) Well, none of us knows *everything*. (*Begins to munch on a thistle he has been carrying.*)

RABBIT: (*To the others.*) This is terrible!

PIGLET: Awful!

RABBIT: It couldn't be worse!

EEYORE: It could be *much* worse. And probably will be. (*He chews dolefully.*)

RABBIT: (*Annoyed.*) Eeyore, *must* you eat thistles?

EEYORE: All donkeys eat them. And I happen to be *especially* fond of them.

RABBIT: No wonder you're so gloomy. (*Eeyore stares steadily at him.*) How anyone can help seeing the dark side of things, if they eat thistles all the time . . .

EEYORE: (*Very wounded, lying down on his stomach, burying his head in his arms and speaking sobbingly.*) That's right. Deprive me of the only pleasure I have left. Why not give up *everything*? (*He is so broken that Rabbit gives a sigh of "what can you do?"*)

POOH: (*Crossing to DL, where Eeyore is lying.*) He didn't mean it.

RABBIT: (*Crossing to just upstage of Eeyore.*) I didn't mean it! I apologize! (*Tries harder, as Eeyore just sniffs disconsolately.*) Eat thistles—please! (*Eeyore sits up and takes out another thistle, and after wiping his eyes on his arm, begins to munch.*)

EEYORE: (*After a pause.*) Very well. It's terribly kind of you. (*Takes another bite. Rabbit wipes his forehead with relief.*)

RABBIT: (*Moving back to C.*) Now. Where were we?

PIGLET: (*Who has been too nervous to bother about Eeyore's persecution-mania and who has moved to C.*) Soap . . . (*He says it shakily.*)

RABBIT: Yes. I'm afraid the time has come—(*He lets this statement hang ominously and looks over to Pooh, who is still standing by Eeyore, watching his chewing with fascination. Pooh turns and asks suddenly:*)

POOH: What time is it, by the way?

RABBIT: Eleven o'clock.

POOH: Just as I thought. I generally have a little something around eleven . . . (*Crosses to DRC and looks up at the honey.*)

RABBIT: When I say "The time has come," I don't mean eleven o'clock. I mean that danger is threatening!

POOH: Danger?

PIGLET: The bathtub . . . the soap . . .

RABBIT: Yes!

POOH: (*Thoughtfully.*) That sort of thing is unpleasant. But dangerous? (*A voice is heard from UR. It is Owl. He speaks from just onstage UR, from where he has entered slowly during the last few speeches. He has a sonorous, booming voice.*)

OWL: What about the bottle of poison?

RABBIT: (*Not noticing who has said this, arguing with Pooh.*) Yes! What about the—(*He stops.*)

PIGLET: (*Looking around.*) Who said that?

OWL: (*Coming further onstage to RC.*) Who, indeed?

RABBIT *and* POOH: Owl!

EEYORE: I wish he *wouldn't* . . . this barging in suddenly—

OWL: (*Coming downstage.*) I didn't barge in. I've been here for some time.

EEYORE: Then why not speak up sooner?

OWL: (*Frowning at Eeyore.*) There was nothing whatever to say.

PIGLET: But you said "bottle of poison"!

OWL: (*Nodding slowly.*) I did. Because she has one. A small bottle—filled with brown stuff.

POOH: How do you know it's—

OWL: (*Talking over this.*) *Clearly* written on the label is the word "Poison."

RABBIT: I can't believe it! (*Rabbit, Pooh, Piglet, and Eeyore form a compact group at DLC.*)

PIGLET: It must be true—he knows how to read—

POOH: And write—

RABBIT: And spell—

EEYORE: (*Scoffing.*) Spell his name, perhaps. . . . W-O-L . . . that's not so hard. He goes to pieces over words like "measles" or "buttered toast" . . . (*As they all regard Owl doubtfully, he draws himself up and continues.*)

OWL: In addition to the word "Poison" on the label, there was a picture.

POOH: What sort of picture?

OWL: The bones of some dead creature.

RABBIT: Bones!

POOH: Who would want that sort of picture?

RABBIT: Who would want a bathtub!

EEYORE: Or soap . . .

OWL: Or a bottle of poison.

PIGLET: Kanga! She must be a terrible Monster—

OWL: The evidence clearly indicates that she is Up To No Good.

(NOTE: *When "talking in capitals," one talks slowly, importantly, and with great emphasis, enunciating each word with clarity and dignity and allowing a slight pause between each word.*)

PIGLET: What shall we do?

RABBIT: (*Hopping up and down.*) Do? We must organize. Deal with the matter—

EEYORE: The worst is yet to come.

RABBIT: (*Ignoring him.*) Take action—we must—

OWL: (*Advancing a step or two toward them.*) Stop! Listen to me. We shall follow the Customary Procedure. (*The others look mystified, but are quiet.*) In other words—(*They look at him now, hopeful they can understand the "other words."*)—we'll Have a Meeting.

RABBIT: A Meeting?

OWL: One can't take Action without first having a Meeting.

RABBIT: (*Interrupting with a protest and taking a step toward Owl.*) I still think—

OWL: (*Cutting him off severely.*) As you all know. (*Rabbit is properly squelched and scuttles back to the safety of the crowd. Owl continues.*) We'll begin now. (*He raises a wing majestically.*) The Meeting will come to order! (*Rabbit sits down beside Eeyore, who has been sitting throughout.*)

POOH: (*An anxious whisper to Piglet.*) How?

PIGLET: (*Responding in a whisper.*) I think we sit down. (*Points to Eeyore and Rabbit.*)

POOH: Oh. (*He and Piglet sit down. Pooh sits in a spot toward DC.*)

OWL: (*Who is in his element.*) Now, then . . . (*He looks down at the ground.*) Let me see . . . Ahem . . . (*The looks of disgust on everybody's faces increase, and Rabbit stirs restlessly. Eeyore makes a loud smacking sound over a thistle, and Pooh looks longingly at him. As he does this, the lights dim. Owl drones on and on, and the buzzing of the bees increases until it nearly drowns him out. Pooh turns his gaze from Owl toward the top of the tree as if pulled by a magnet.*) Whereas . . . Hum—I daresay we should start with the first order of business, which is . . . (*His voice fades to an indistinct mumble. Pooh rises and walks off toward the tree DR as if he were in a trance. After his exit DR, the buzzing gradually dies down. Owl is still talking, and the other three animals have gone from sitting positions to being sprawled on the ground. Eeyore stifles a yawn. The lights brighten.*)

OWL: (*Speaking audibly again.*) And, as I was saying—

RABBIT: What *were* you saying? (*Animal 3 and Animal 4 stick their heads onstage at DL and listen.*)

EEYORE: That's what I'd like to know.

RABBIT: (*Getting up resolutely.*) If you *ask* me—

OWL: (*Crushing him again.*) If we ask you—what will happen? (*Rabbit continues to hop up and down.*) Excitement. A good deal of hopping up and down. (*Rabbit stops.*) Commotion. (*Owl shakes his head, satisfied.*) The important thing is to remain calm—(*A faint cracking sound is heard offstage DR. The two young animals who have been peeking out from DL look up sharply. The noise comes from high up.*) —to keep our heads. (*Another cracking sound. One young animal points up at it.*)

PIGLET: (*Nervously, getting up.*) What was that? (*Eeyore rises also.*)

RABBIT: I heard something!

OWL: Above all, to follow Customary Procedure—

POOH: (*A faint cry from high up, offstage DR.*) Oh, help!

RABBIT: Help?

PIGLET: Help! She's coming—Kanga's coming! (*Begins to shake all over.*)

OWL: She can't come now. We haven't finished the Meeting.

RABBIT: (*Quickly.*) I suggest we finish it somewhere else!

OWL: (*Very quickly.*) A very good suggestion. (*Rabbit, Owl and Eeyore start off, trying to move with calmness and dignity, but looking nervously behind them. Animal 3 and Animal 4 have disappeared off L.*)

EEYORE: Aren't you coming, Piglet?

PIGLET: (*At DLC.*) I can't—c-can't move—(*The cracking sound gets very loud, and turns into a loud crash. The animals abandon their pretense of calm, and all run out DL with a leap except for Piglet, who throws himself flat on his face and covers his head with his arms. After a pause, Pooh enters. He is limping slightly, brushing himself off, and looking annoyed.*)

POOH: (*As he wanders to R.*) Bother!

PIGLET: (*Uncovering one eye, and peeking out.*) Is that you?

POOH: Yes. At least, most of me seems to be here.

PIGLET: (*Uncovering the other eye.*) Wh-what happened?

POOH: A slight accident. (*As Piglet struggles up.*) You noticed the small tree, growing very close to the large one—the one with the honey at the top—

PIGLET: What small tree?

POOH: It fell over.

PIGLET: That dreadful noise—was a small tree falling over?

POOH: I was *in* the small tree.

PIGLET: (*An exclamation of relief.*) Oh!

POOH: I thought if I could get to the top, I might just reach over and —(*In illustrating this, Pooh stands on one foot, with one paw outstretched. He looks at this paw; an idea occurs.*) I wonder . . . (*He raises his paw higher, as if holding something.*) It might . . . (*Raises the paw even higher, as if something were pulling him up in the air.*) Could it?

PIGLET: Could it what?

POOH: (*Coming DC.*) There's only one way to find out. Piglet, do you have such a thing as a balloon about you?

PIGLET: A *balloon*? (*Shakes head, mystified.*) No.

POOH: Christopher Robin! If I know anything at all, Christopher Robin will have a balloon! (*Starts for DL.*)

PIGLET: Wait. Where are you going?

POOH: To borrow it.

PIGLET: Don't leave me here alone. I mean, I'm coming with you!

POOH: That's very kind of you, Piglet. (*As Piglet joins him, he turns suddenly.*) By the way, what happened to the others?

PIGLET: Others?

POOH: Owl and Rabbit and Eeyore. Is the Meeting all over?

PIGLET: They decided to continue the Meeting somewhere else.

POOH: Oh. Perhaps you'd rather join them—

PIGLET: No! I'd rather stay with you. (*Amending.*) To keep you company.

POOH: Splendid!

PIGLET: And would it be too much—if I held onto your hand—

POOH: Not at all. (*He goes out DL with Piglet clinging to his hand and looking back nervously. Pooh is in good spirits, and starts to sing again as he trots off.*) "Isn't it funny—how a bear likes honey—" (*His voice fades off.*) (*Two of Rabbit's young relations enter DL. One is very small. The other is—if possible—a skunk.*)

ANIMAL 1: (*The smaller, strolling onstage with Animal 2, looking back DL over his shoulder and pouting indignantly.*) It's not fair. Uncle Rabbit said he was too busy to play a game with us—

ANIMAL 2: (*The skunk.*) But he can't be very busy! (*Pauses at UC. Animal 3 comes onstage after the other two, with Animal 4 beside him.*)

ANIMAL 3: A lot you know about it.

ANIMAL 1: We just saw him running a race with Eeyore and Owl.

ANIMAL 4: (*In a superior tone.*) That wasn't a race. (*He is at LC.*)

ANIMAL 2: You should have seen them! I never saw Uncle Rabbit run so fast! (*Demonstrates by running to UR and back to RC.*)

ANIMAL 1: And Eeyore . . . I never saw him run at *all*.

ANIMAL 3: (*At UC.*) Ha! They thought Kanga was chasing them.

ANIMAL 1: Kanga?

ANIMAL 2: What's that?

ANIMAL 4: Never mind. I'll bet there's no such thing.

ANIMAL 3: Me, too!

ANIMAL 4: All that about soap—and bathtubs—and poison—

ANIMAL 3: Who ever heard of stuff like that! (*Animals 1 and 2 look rather anxious.*)

ANIMAL 1: Did you?

ANIMAL 2: No—(*As they are finishing saying the above, Rabbit enters hurriedly from DL and crosses toward DR, saying:*)

RABBIT: We went the wrong way. (*He keeps glancing fearfully behind him as he makes this cross and goes out DR.*)

ANIMAL 4: (*Gesturing after him.*) What's the matter with him?

ANIMAL 3: He's just a fraidy cat. (*Owl enters DL and hastens along from DL to DR.*)

OWL: Hurry! It's coming—it's coming! (*He hastens out DR.*)

(PRODUCTION NOTE: *If extra characters are available and it is desired to use them, this scene may be staged by having one or more animals take the place of Rabbit. A mother animal with several young animals may take the place of Owl, and one or more different animals may take the place of Eeyore in their flight across the stage, in which case the Rabbit's line about going the wrong way should be replaced by one of the animals saying, "Better hurry, it's coming!" Also, the earlier exit of Rabbit, Owl, and Eeyore should be made DR if the extra characters are used.*)

(*The four onstage look at each other. Then the skunk holds up his paw as he sniffs the air.*)

ANIMAL 2: Something *is* coming—

ANIMAL 1: What?

ANIMAL 2: Something *strange*—

ANIMAL 3: (*Skeptically.*) How do *you* know?

ANIMAL 2: I'm very sensitive to unpleasant smells. And I've never come across anything like *this* before—

ANIMAL 1: Is it a Kanga?

ANIMAL 3: Oh, sure! When there isn't any such thing? (*Eeyore enters from DL and crosses to exit DR saying:*)

EEYORE: Oh, I'll never make it. I'll be caught and then—Oh, dear! (OPTIONAL: *Another flock of animals runs across the stage, including a snake—a plastic one can be pulled across by a wire.*)

ANIMAL 4: (*To Animal 3.*) Maybe Uncle Rabbit wasn't fooling.

ANIMAL 3: Sure he was—he made the whole thing up.

ANIMAL 1: He wouldn't do that.

ANIMAL 4: (*To Animal 3.*) He doesn't know everything . . .

ANIMAL 3: (*Bristling.*) He knows more than you do!

ANIMAL 4: And more than you do—and that's not much—

ANIMAL 3: You take that back!

ANIMAL 4: Make me! (*At this point, they begin to fight—wrestling about, making grunting noises, etc., as they roll on the ground at LC.*)

ANIMAL 1: (*Crossing to URC.*) Shouldn't we stop them?

ANIMAL 2: Remember what Christopher Robin says—(*Moves to URC, too.*) "Never interfere in other animals' business." (*Another animal may go by, at this point, from DL to DR, waving its arms and shouting, "It's coming! It's coming!"*)

ANIMAL 1: (*To Animal 2.*) I just happened to remember an old badger hole about four miles from here—Look, a flock of birds! (*Points overhead DL and moves his pointing finger across to DR, as if the flock of birds at which he is pointing were rapidly flying from DL to DR.*)

ANIMAL 2: (*As they follow the flight with their eyes.*) Is it a large hole?

ANIMAL 1: Large enough for both of us, anyway. (*They join hands and run off DR. It seems now that the exodus is over, as there is general quiet. Animal 3 and Animal 4 are still scuffling quietly. At last Animal 3 is on top of Animal 4.*)

ANIMAL 3: Give up?

ANIMAL 4: (*Panting.*) All right—(*They are intent on each other, and don't notice when Kanga enters DL. She is carrying a round tin wash-tub in her right hand and pulling Baby Roo along with her left hand. She stops at DL and looks at the two wrestlers and frowns.*)

ANIMAL 4: What were we fighting about?

ANIMAL 3: I forget.

ANIMAL 4: Something about a—a—(*Sees Kanga.*)

ANIMAL 3: Only there wasn't any such thing—(*Also sees Kanga.*)—any such—(*Animal 4 leaps up and scampers away off DR, and Animal 3 does the same.*)

KANGA: (*A tone of matronly disgust.*) Well! (*She walks to C.*) Disgraceful. Perfectly disgraceful.

ROO: (*Eagerly.*) Mama, can I go play with them? (*Starts after them, pulling across Kanga till her hold on his hand stops him.*)

KANGA: (*Pulling him back to her left side.*) Certainly not, Roo.

ROO: But you said when we came to the forest, I'd have someone to play with. (*Points after animals.*) And I haven't *seen* anybody but them. Maybe nobody else lives here!

KANGA: Nonsense. There are plenty of animals in the forest.

ROO: Then where are they? (*Holds out his hands, looking around.*)

KANGA: (*Frowning, saying in puzzled tone.*) I simply can't understand it. (*To Roo.*) But never mind—you wouldn't want to play with those two filthy creatures—

ROO: Well—

KANGA: (*Shaking her head with disgust.*) Looking as if they never had a bath in their lives—

ROO: (*Muttering to himself.*) Darn it!

KANGA: (*Startled, putting down the washtub near the hassock with a clang, bending down and looking at him ominously.*) What did you say?

ROO: (*Hanging his head.*) Nothing.

KANGA: I heard it, Roo. (*She drags him to where the hassock is, sits on it and reaches into the washtub. Roo still hangs his head.*) And you know what that means. (*She pulls out a soapy washrag—clean washrag with whipped cream from a pressure can.*) When our mouth says ugly things, we must wash it. Mustn't we, Roo? (*All of this is said in a calm, pleasant but very maternal tone.*) There we are—(*She is washing out his mouth. Roo squirms, but she has a nice grip on him. Roo makes a horrible face. Then Kanga notices something on his knee and points to it.*) My goodness, what did you do to your knee? (*Roo burbles something through his mouthful of soap.*) A nasty scratch, dear. (*She reaches into her pocket and pulls out a bottle of iodine. At the sight of it, Roo begins to burble frantically.*) We'll have to put something on it.

ROO: (*As Kanga opens the bottle.*) Wow-w-w—

KANGA: We don't want it to get infected, do we?

ROO: Not *iodine!* Not—

KANGA: (*Dabbing the knee with iodine.*) Just a touch—

ROO: Ouch!

KANGA: There's a brave little Roo. (*Puts the bottle away as Roo struggles about, hopping up and down.*) Think how lucky you are. You wouldn't want to be like *those* poor creatures—with no one to look after you properly. Aren't you thankful? (*Roo mumbles something.*)

KANGA: (*Sharply again.*) What was that?

ROO: Thankful.

KANGA: If only something could be done for them. If I could just get hold of them for one day—

ROO: Would they have a bath?

KANGA: Plenty of soap and good hot water—

ROO: (*Wiping his face carefully.*) *Then* could I play with them?

KANGA: (*Hesitating.*) After a touch of disinfectant powder.

ROO: Would they have oatmeal for breakfast?

KANGA: And a big spoonful of Strengthening Medicine—(*Carried away.*) Oh, the things I could do with them!

ROO: Would they be thankful, too?

KANGA: (*After a momentary hesitation.*) Perhaps not at first. Not right away. But no use thinking about it. I couldn't take care of all the animals in the forest, wherever they are . . .

ROO: How about just one?

KANGA: (*Looking around the stage.*) Dear little Roo—we'll see.

ROO: (*Wistfully.*) One that's my own size. It would be so nice—

KANGA: Maybe we can arrange for you to have a playmate—(*She stops and looks at tree at C.*) I think this will do nicely.

ROO: What will?

KANGA: For our new home.

ROO: Are we going to live here?

KANGA: Let's see. . . . It has shade—privacy—plenty of water in that stream. . . . (*As she goes up to the tree, Roo wanders off toward UL and picks up something.*)

ROO: (*Delighted, squealing.*) Here's a caterpillar!

KANGA: (*Turning suddenly.*) Goodness, don't touch! (*Roo puts it down quickly, with a look of dismay.*) If you touch it, you'll need a bath. (*Roo hides his hands behind his back.*) And there's so much to do, what with sweeping this place out—(*As Kanga goes back to the tree, Roo watches the caterpillar crawl away. It takes the direction of all the other refugees. Roo walks slowly behind it, watching it with mournful eyes.*)—getting settled—

ROO: (*Hearing something.*) Mama—(*There is a faint sound in the distance DL: Pooh's voice, singing, "Isn't it funny—How a bear likes honey—"*)

KANGA: Don't bother me now, dear.

ROO: Somebody's coming!

KANGA: Really?

ROO: I hear them—and that means somebody lives in the forest! (*Kanga listens, hears something, too.*)

KANGA: Then stay near me, Roo.

ROO: Why?

KANGA: (*Rolling her eyes to heaven, and lifting her hands with a typical parental gesture.*) One must be patient, and explain everything . . . (*Looks at Roo and says in a "patient" tone.*) Because if they see you, they'll know we live here. And if they know we live here, I shall have to invite them to tea. And I don't want to have company yet, because everything is a mess. And—(*Goes off DL, or off UC if practical.*)

ROO: (*He can't bear it.*) All right, I'm coming. I just asked. (*Follows her off DL, or off UC, whichever way Kanga went.*) (*Pooh enters DL, singing jovially, with Piglet and Christopher Robin. Christopher Robin carries a large blue balloon and a popgun.* NOTE: *If filled with air, the balloon should be held as if it were helium-filled and quite buoyant.*)

POOH: (*Singing.*) "Buzz, buzz, buzz—I wonder why he does—"

PIGLET: Ssh!

POOH: (*Starting the song over, with great vigor.*) "Isn't it funny—how a bear likes honey—" (*They pause at RC and face about toward the honey tree at DR.*)

PIGLET: (*Tugging at him.*) Please! I wish you wouldn't sing so loudly.

POOH: (*Near tree DR.*) "Buzz, buzz, buzz—" (*Shrugs, then accedes to Piglet's request.*) Rum-tum-tiddle-um-tum. (*This is a sort of finisher to the song, uttered quietly.*)

CHRISTOPHER ROBIN: (*Fondly, by Pooh.*) Silly old bear!

POOH: Are you still feeling jumpy, Piglet?

PIGLET: (*From C.*) I hate to be cowardly, but I couldn't help noticing —as we were coming this way, everybody else was going *that* way . . . (*Points in the direction of the general exodus.*)

POOH: I noticed, myself.

CHRISTOPHER ROBIN: They were, were they?

POOH: It's all this talk about Kanga.

CHRISTOPHER ROBIN: Where did you hear about Kanga? (*Kanga peeks out at the mention of her name.*)

POOH: You know how it is—stories get about in the forest—you can't believe everything you hear—(*Takes a few waltzing steps toward his tree DR.*)

PIGLET: (*Confidential tone.*) Christopher Robin—

CHRISTOPHER ROBIN: Yes?

PIGLET: Is there a Kanga coming to the forest?

CHRISTOPHER ROBIN: You'll have to find out for yourself, Piglet.

PIGLET: You mean—

POOH: If Christopher Robin knows a secret, you don't expect him to tell, do you?

PIGLET: (*After thinking a moment, rushing wildly to Pooh.*) Let's get out of here. Let's go that way! (*Waves frantically DR.*)

POOH: As soon as I reach that honey. After all, if we're going on a journey I've got to have a little something to sustain me.

PIGLET: (*With pathetic despair.*) If I weren't such a coward, I'd go alone!

POOH: Stop worrying, Piglet. You're safe as long as you're with me. (*A cajoling tone.*) Don't I always keep you out of trouble?

PIGLET: What about that time we—

POOH: (*Interrupting him.*) Don't I *usually* keep you out of trouble?

PIGLET: Well—

POOH: You can depend on me.

PIGLET: You're sure?

POOH: Quite sure. (*Crosses to RC near Christopher Robin and looks at the balloon speculatively.*) Now let me see—

CHRISTOPHER ROBIN: Do you really think it will work?

POOH: I think—when you go after honey, it's very important not to let the bees know you're coming. If you have a blue balloon, they might think you're only part of the sky and not notice!

CHRISTOPHER ROBIN: Wouldn't they notice *you* underneath the balloon?

POOH: You never can tell, with bees . . . (*Thinks a moment, then lies down on the ground, rolling about.*)

CHRISTOPHER ROBIN: What are you doing?

POOH: (*Rubbing dirt all over his arms and face.*) I'll try to look like a small black cloud. (*At the sight of all this, Kanga, who has come a step onstage to see this, makes a terrible face of disapproval and steps back again.*)

POOH: That will deceive them.

CHRISTOPHER ROBIN: (*As Pooh reaches for the balloon.*) Well, good luck . . . (*Pooh takes balloon and is immediately pulled. He takes a few running steps and a leap as he is pulled up and offstage. Piglet ducks around to C to keep out from under.*)

POOH: (*As he leaps.*) Here—I—go! (*He is apparently leaving the ground as he disappears off DR. A ladder from which he can give his next few lines will help the illusion of height. Christopher Robin and Piglet watch him float upward, their heads tilting back as they follow the ascent.*)

CHRISTOPHER ROBIN: (*Grinning at the sight.*) Hooray!

POOH: (*Offstage voice DR, calling.*) Isn't this fine? What do I look like?

CHRISTOPHER ROBIN: You look like a bear holding on to a balloon.

POOH: (*Offstage DR, after a pause, in worried tone.*) Not—like a small black cloud in a blue sky?

CHRISTOPHER ROBIN: Not very much.

PIGLET: I wish he'd hurry up.

POOH: Perhaps from up here it looks different . . .

CHRISTOPHER ROBIN: Can't you get any closer to the tree? You're at least ten feet away from it—and a bit too high.

POOH: I'm trying . . .

CHRISTOPHER ROBIN: Maybe a breeze will come along, and blow you a bit closer . . .

POOH: When?

CHRISTOPHER ROBIN: You'll just have to wait.

PIGLET: (*With anxiety.*) We can't wait long—(*As Piglet and Christopher Robin watch Pooh, Roo comes in and approaches Piglet, looking fascinated.*)

ROO: (*Tugging at Piglet's arm.*) What's your name?

PIGLET: (*Not registering, but answering automatically.*) Piglet.

ROO: (*Calling to Kanga excitedly.*) Mama—I've found a playmate!

CHRISTOPHER ROBIN: (*Turning and patting him fondly.*) Hallo there, Roo—(*Crosses back to DR to watch Pooh.*)

PIGLET: Roo . . . (*He turns.*) Roo? (*Kanga comes in quickly.*)

KANGA: (*With an approving smile.*) Isn't that nice? He's just the right size.

PIGLET: (*With growing horror.*) Roo!

ROO: That's my name.

PIGLET: But if you're Roo—she must be—(*Looks at Kanga, who is moving toward him purposefully, and takes one step backwards before he stops and begins to tremble.*)

KANGA: (*To Christopher Robin, in a tone of reprimand.*) You haven't introduced us properly.

CHRISTOPHER ROBIN: Kanga—

PIGLET: *Kanga!*

CHRISTOPHER ROBIN: (*Continuing.*)—and Roo, this is Piglet. (*Points at Pooh.*) And Pooh.

POOH: Did you call me?

PIGLET: (*Calling him.*) Pooh, I think you'd better come down!

KANGA: I hadn't intended to have company just yet, but Roo seems so anxious—

ROO: Give him a bath right now, Mama, so I can play with him!

KANGA: Very well. (*She gets a good grip on Piglet. To Roo.*) Run and get some water. (*Roo hurries off DL.*)

PIGLET: A bath? Me—a bath—

KANGA: The tub is all ready. What are you squirming for?

CHRISTOPHER ROBIN: He—ah—never had a bath before.

KANGA: Well! Then it's about time!

CHRISTOPHER ROBIN: It may be a shock. That is, he won't like it . . .

KANGA: How do you know—when he's never had one?

CHRISTOPHER ROBIN: I suppose you're right . . .

PIGLET: (*As Kanga starts calmly to drag him to washtub at URC.*) Pooh! You've got to come down—right now!

POOH: I know, Piglet—but how can I get down?

PIGLET: Help! Let go of the balloon!

POOH: If I let go, I won't be of much help to anyone . . .

PIGLET: (*Holding Kanga to a standstill by exerting all his force.*) Christopher Robin—please! *Shoot* the balloon—

POOH: Yes—if you can shoot the balloon, I might float down gradually—

KANGA: (*Referring to her struggle with Piglet.*) Honestly, such a time . . .

CHRISTOPHER ROBIN: I'm not supposed to interfere—(*Takes a sympathetic look at the struggling Piglet.*) But I'll try—(*Takes aim and fires the popgun.*)

POOH: *Ow!*

CHRISTOPHER ROBIN: Did I miss?

POOH: You didn't exactly miss, but you missed the *balloon*—

PIGLET: Try it again.

CHRISTOPHER ROBIN: I'm out of ammunition.

PIGLET: Oh-h-h!

KANGA: I've never seen *any*thing like it—

GLET: (As he is dragged farther and farther URC.) Pooh, you've got
come down! You said you'd protect me—you said you'd keep me out
trouble—

OH: But I can't! I can't get down! (As Piglet is forced into the bath-
b.) Oh, dear! (Roo comes rushing on with a pitcher of water and
nds it to Kanga.)

GLET: You promised—you—(As the water is poured over him, he wails
ournfully.)

HRISTOPHER ROBIN: I'll go and get more ammunition.

OH: Hurry!

HRISTOPHER ROBIN: I'll try—(He hurries out DR, with one last worried
ok in the direction of Piglet.)

ANGA: Now stop wiggling. Or you'll get soap in your eyes. This is just
e beginning—first the bath—then the diet—the Strengthening Medi-
ine—This is the beginning, that's all—(The curtain starts down.)

GLET: Wowww—blub-blub—Pooh, this is your fault—all your—Pooh!
elp! Help! (His protests turn into a gurgling sound, as:)

CURTAIN

ACT TWO

The footlights go up. Christopher Robin is once again sitting on the
assock DR at the same spot he was at the start of Act One, holding
is teddy bear—and looking sad and worried.)

OICE: (Narrator, offstage.)—And while you went home to look for
nore ammunition, Pooh stayed up in the air holding on to his bal-
oon . . .

HRISTOPHER ROBIN: And what about Poor Piglet—

OICE: (A sober, sympathetic tone.) Yes, poor Piglet . . . (A sigh.)
Ie'd never been clean before.

HRISTOPHER ROBIN: Did it take me very long to get more ammunition?

OICE: Quite a while. By the time you got back—and shot the balloon—

HRISTOPHER ROBIN: I didn't miss the next time?

VOICE: No.

CHRISTOPHER ROBIN: I'm glad of that.

VOICE: Pooh floated down to the ground—but he'd been holding on to that balloon for such a long time that his arms stayed up in the air.

CHRISTOPHER ROBIN: Like this? (*Holds the teddy bear's paws up over its head.*)

VOICE: Like that.

CHRISTOPHER ROBIN: Wasn't he uncomfortable?

VOICE: Very uncomfortable. But after all, it was his own fault. There was his best friend, in grave difficulty—and where was Pooh? Up in the air. All because he wanted to eat honey. You'll have to admit it served him right.

CHRISTOPHER ROBIN: (*Wagging a reproachful finger at the teddy bear.*) I'm afraid it *did* serve you right!

(*The curtain goes up as Christopher Robin goes out R. The scene for Act Two is the same as for Act One—the forest. However, it is a different part of the forest, so the sign "Sanders" has been taken down from the tree, and the tree that was URC has been moved to LC and a gnarled aerial root which forms a medium-size hole has been attached to the C side of this tree. Over it is a sign saying "Rabbit Hole." A small rocking chair should be placed UC, and against the back wall at URC is a small cupboard. As in Act One, there are trees DR and DL framing the stage. Owl is standing unobtrusively at the UR corner of the stage. Pooh enters from DL, his arms held up in the air as though still clinging to the balloon.*)

POOH: It serves me right! (*Continues to reproach himself.*) Pooh Bear —how could you do a thing like that? (*Owl echoes Pooh from his place at the rear of the stage.*)

OWL: How *could* you?

POOH: (*Answering, thinking it's himself.*) I don't know.

OWL: (*Coming a few steps toward DRC.*) Of course, you were hungry . . .

POOH: (*From DLC.*) Yes, I was hungry . . .

OWL: But being hungry is no excuse for Deserting Your Best Friend.

POOH: (*In an agony of self-reproach.*) Not even if you're *terribly* hungry?

OWL: No excuse.

POOH: Practically *starving!*

OWL: At any rate, it's a very bad excuse. (*Eeyore peeks out from DR.*)

EEYORE: A hard fall, was it?

POOH: What's that, Eeyore?

EEYORE: (*Coming on stage to DR.*) One often talks to oneself after a bad fall. Landed on your head, perhaps?

POOH: I landed in a sitting position.

EEYORE: (*Walking around him slowly.*) Any severe pain?

POOH: No.

EEYORE: (*Shaking his head pessimistically.*) I was afraid of that. The worst sort of injuries—no severe pain—no pain at *all* . . .

POOH: The only trouble with me is, I can't get my paws back to where they belong. And I *must* get them down. Something has to be done about Piglet—right away!

OWL: Piglet.

EEYORE: Poor little Piglet.

POOH: You see, Kanga captured him—*quite by accident*—He's in a terrible predicament. (*He crosses to RC.*)

EEYORE: In hot water?

POOH: How did you know?

EEYORE: A-ha.

POOH: He must be rescued, right away.

OWL: (*Nodding.*) Immediately.

EEYORE: (*Also nodding.*) Without wasting a minute.

POOH: The only question is, how shall we rescue him? (*Eeyore backs up till he is at DR.*)

EEYORE: We?

OWL: (*Still at RC.*) How shall *you* rescue him?

EEYORE: Yes, *that's* the question.

OWL: (*Advancing a step toward Pooh.*) Since Piglet is your best friend, we know *you* want to be the one.

POOH: Oh. (*He thinks this over with a good bit of surprise. His arms drop, at last.*)

EEYORE: (*Also advancing a step toward Pooh.*) Especially since the whole thing was your fault. (*A distant squeal is heard, from Piglet.*)

PIGLET: (*Voice from off L.*) No! No-no-no—o-o-o! (*It is cut off suddenly. All three look in the direction of the noise.*)

OWL: You'd better hurry.

EEYORE: If it isn't too late . . . which it probably is.

POOH: But how? What shall I do?

EEYORE: *Much* too late.

OWL: Why not go to Kanga—explain the situation—

POOH: How?

OWL: Just say, "Kanga, you have something that doesn't belong to you. That isn't *your* Piglet—that's *our* Piglet—" And then—

POOH: (*Warily.*) Then what?

OWL: She'll have to let Piglet go. At least, she *ought* to.

POOH: There's a difference between "*ought* to" and "*have* to."

EEYORE: And Kangas are generally regarded as one of the Fiercer Animals.

OWL: Quite true.

POOH: I wouldn't want to do anything foolish.

OWL: You've already done something foolish. And I just happened to remember—

POOH: What?

OWL: Bears are *also* regarded as one of the Fiercer Animals.

POOH: Bears?

OWL: Very fierce.

POOH: Me?

OWL: They snarl—growl—do all sorts of nasty things. Can't *you* growl, Pooh?

POOH: I don't know.

OWL: Try.

POOH: (*Venturing a cosy sort of growl, or even a purr.*) Gr-r-r. (*Eeyore and Owl frown.*) How was that?

EEYORE: It wasn't much.

POOH: (*Improving it slightly.*) Gr-r-r.

OWL: Let's have just a little snarl.

POOH: (*Baring his teeth this time.*) Gr-r-r-r-r!

OWL: (*To Eeyore.*) Better, don't you think?

EEYORE: A growl ought to be bloodcurdling.

POOH: (*Really putting some stuff in it.*) Gr-r-r—

OWL: (*Signaling that this is it.*) Ah!

POOH: (*Carried away.*) Gr-r-R-R-R!!! (*As Eeyore and Owl recoil, Pooh shakes himself and looks around, quite startled.*)

OWL: What's the matter?

POOH: (*Slightly injured tone.*) I frightened myself.

OWL: That's a good sign.

POOH: The question is, will I frighten Kanga?

OWL: Certainly. There's no doubt in my mind.

EEYORE: And a good thing, too. Here she comes! (*Gestures off DL, in which direction he has been looking.*)

POOH: Who?

OWL: Where?

EEYORE: Kanga. She's coming this way.

OWL: Come, Eeyore—

POOH: (*As Eeyore starts off toward DR with Owl.*) You aren't going?

EEYORE: We'll be around if you need us.

POOH: Around where?

OWL: (*As he and Eeyore hasten off DR.*) Somewhere . . . (*Pooh starts to go after them, but at the edge of the stage he hesitates, turns around and then braces himself. He practices a snarl, which reassures him. He stands firmly ready to confront Kanga.*
Kanga enters at DLC with Roo and Piglet, one holding each hand.)

KANGA: Now then, chins up—chests out—make the most of every step. (*She has each one by the hand. Piglet is practically unrecognizable. If possible, he has on snowy white coveralls, and there is a huge bow tied around his neck.*)

ROO: (*Puffing.*) I can't go any faster—

KANGA: Nonsense.

PIGLET: (*Calling out at the sight of Pooh.*) Pooh—it's Pooh! (*Lunges forward in Pooh's direction, but Kanga retrieves him with a firm grasp.*)

KANGA: Why, so it is.

PIGLET: At last—(*Pooh crosses to C and, crossing his arms over his chest, assumes a wide stance, facing Kanga.*)

KANGA: Would you mind? You're blocking the path.

POOH: Er—um—

KANGA: After all, it doesn't belong to you—does it?

POOH: (*Unfolding his arms so he can gesture freely.*) That's what I wanted to explain. You have something that doesn't belong to you—I mean—

KANGA: Whatever *is* he talking about!

POOH: Piglet.

PIGLET: Poo-oo-oh!

POOH: You are Piglet?

PIGLET: Of course I am!

POOH: I just wanted to be sure. You don't *look* like Piglet. (*Piglet tries to pull loose from Kanga.*)

KANGA: Now, now—mustn't let go of my hand.

POOH: But you ought to let him go. He isn't your Piglet. He's our Piglet—

KANGA: *Well!* No wonder he was in such a state. *Your* Piglet!

POOH: So if you'd kindly give him back—

KANGA: I'll do no such thing! What an idea. The poor little thing is having proper care for the first time in its life. Now move aside!

POOH: Gr-r-r.

KANGA: Out of the way—(*Advances to just in front of Pooh.*)

POOH: G-r-r-r!

KANGA: What was that?

POOH: (*Giving it all he has.*) GR-R-R-R!!!

KANGA: (*Agitated, backing away from him toward DLC.*) Oh, dear—oh, *dear!*

POOH: (*Advancing proudly, in a sort of gorilla fashion.*) Gr-rr-rr-r—(*But he has become rather hoarse, and ends up with a coughing sound.*) Ug —ugh!

KANGA: (*Very much agitated, backing away toward L.*) Now keep away from us! Don't you come near us! (*Continues to hold on to Piglet and Roo.*)

ROO: (*Awed by Pooh.*) Oo-o-oh!

POOH: Frightening, isn't it?

KANGA: Dreadful. *Simply* dreadful!

POOH: (*Remembering to snarl.*) Gr-r-row-w-w—(*Again he coughs slightly.*)

KANGA: I've never heard anything like it.

POOH: (*Advancing again.*) And I'll keep it up until you let Piglet go.

KANGA: (*Shaking a finger at him, letting go of Roo.*) You'll keep it up until you do something about it. That's the worst cold I've ever seen—

POOH: (*Stopping.*) Cold?

KANGA: Down in your chest, too. (*This time she advances, still shaking her finger at him.*) Take my advice—go *straight* to bed!

POOH: I do *not* have a cold. (*But his voice breaks.*)

KANGA: (*Continuing to advance, still clutching Piglet, toward DRC.*) And I suppose you make dreadful noises like that just for fun? Or to frighten us? Ha, ha! (*Pooh makes a strangled sound in his throat.*)

KANGA: (*Fumbling for something in her pocket.*) If you've any sense at all, which you probably haven't—you'll take some of this cough medicine. (*She thrusts a bottle at him, and he jumps at the sight of it.*) One spoonful every half hour.

POOH: No, thank you!

ROO: (*Gleefully.*) Drink it all! It tastes like poison! (*Pooh retreats to R, shuddering slightly.*)

KANGA: (*Sighing.*) Foolish bear . . . (*Puts the bottle back.*) But we can't help those who won't help themselves. (*Takes Roo's hand.*) Come, Roo and Piglet. We'll finish our walk. Then a bath—and a little nap—(*Roo crosses to her and takes hold of her hand, but with great reluctance.*)

POOH: Wait—wait a minute—

KANGA: (*Hustling them out DR.*) Chin up, Piglet. (*Gives him a little jerk.*) One, two—(*Voice fades after they go out.*) One, two—(*Pooh takes a feeble step or two DR in their direction, then stands dejectedly still. He is shaken by an involuntary cough, and stares ahead of himself, much frightened, clutching his chest.*)

POOH: Owl! Eeyore! (*After a moment's pause, Owl and Eeyore come creeping on stage from DR, peering back over their shoulders as they come.*)

OWL: What happened?

EEYORE: Was she frightened?

POOH: (*Crossing to C.*) I don't feel very well. It's gone to my chest . . . (*Eeyore and Owl from DR exchange puzzled looks.*)

OWL: (*Severely, to Pooh.*) Apparently Kanga walked off with Piglet while you just stood there. (*Pooh hangs his head in shame.*)

EEYORE: (*Moving to DRC.*) Perhaps it all happens for the best, and it's useless to struggle . . .

POOH: (*Turning to face them.*) Why can't we all go after them? If we *all* surrounded her—

OWL: I don't think much of that idea.

POOH: But you should have *seen* Piglet. He's turned a different color— and there's a bow tied around his neck! It can't go on. Piglet is *miserable!*

EEYORE: *I'm* miserable. And it goes on—and on—

POOH: If we were to take action—all of us, *together*—

OWL: I'd love to, old fellow. But I have a previous engagement.

EEYORE: (*Crossing to beside Owl at DR.*) So have I.

OWL: (*Helpfully.*) Why don't you ask Rabbit?

POOH: Rabbit?

OWL: He said a good deal about taking action.

POOH: Where will I find him?

OWL: He's probably at home. Try knocking. (*Owl and Eeyore go out DL.*)

POOH: It's a good idea. Rabbit does things. (*Hesitates.*) Anyway, he says he does things. (*Pooh crosses to LC and knocks on tree. After a moment's wait for an answer, he knocks again and calls.*) Rabbit? (*Rabbit comes onstage, from either UR or UL, in his house which is the entire upper third of the stage—cautiously and with an alarmed expression on his face. He stands at URC.*)

POOH: Is anybody home? (*Rabbit shakes his head "no" but makes no sound. Pooh puts a paw to his ear.*) What I said was, "Is anybody home?"

RABBIT: (*Looking desperately around, saying in a shrill, disguised tone.*) No!

POOH: Bother! (*Turns toward DC and thinks a minute, then speaks over his shoulder.*) Isn't there anybody at all?

RABBIT: (*Same tone.*) Nobody!

POOH: (*Thoughtfully, to himself.*) There must be somebody there—because somebody said "nobody"—(*Calls again.*) Hello. Could you kindly tell me where Rabbit is?

RABBIT: He's gone to see his friend, Pooh Bear.

POOH: Oh. (*Turns back.*) But this is me! Pooh.

RABBIT: Oh, well, then—come in. (*Nervously retreats to UR. Pooh struggles through the small opening, into Rabbit's house.*)

RABBIT: (*As Pooh crawls in.*) It *is* you. I'm glad.

POOH: (*Standing at UC.*) Who did you think it was?

RABBIT: Well, you know how it is lately—you can't be too careful—can't have just anybody coming in . . .

POOH: Piglet's got to be rescued from Kanga. And I can't seem to do it alone. So if you'll come with me—

RABBIT: Right now?

POOH: You *do* like to take action, don't you?

RABBIT: Certainly!

POOH: Owl and Eeyore won't do anything. They're afraid of her—

RABBIT: (*Contemptuously.*) A-ha!

POOH: Not like *you*—

RABBIT: Not at all!

POOH: So let's go right now. (*Starts for Rabbit Hole entrance.*)

RABBIT: (*Hesitating where he is and trying wildly to think of something.*) Ah—Pooh?

POOH: (*Turning back to reprove him for not coming at once.*) We don't want to waste time—

RABBIT: Wait a moment. I nearly forgot—

POOH: What?

RABBIT: (*Taking a step toward cupboard URC.*) Lunch. (*Pooh pauses —this word registers.*)

POOH: (*Shaking himself firmly.*) No time for that—

RABBIT: (*Restraining him.*) Imagine my forgetting to eat lunch. Won't you join me?

POOH: No, no!

RABBIT: (*Turning around, reaching for a pot.*) Fancy—I didn't know I had all this honey. (*Looks inside.*)

POOH: But Piglet—

RABBIT: Nearly a full pot, wouldn't you say? (*Holds it out under Pooh's nose.*)

POOH: Piglet—(*Catches the scent, almost sways toward the pot and away from the door.*) Honey—

RABBIT: (*Going a step closer to Pooh.*) Quite full, I'd say . . .

POOH: Honey . . .

RABBIT: (*Handing the pot to Pooh.*) Help yourself. Or would you prefer marmalade? (*Produces a pot of this from top of cupboard.*)

POOH: (*Eyeing the honey, then the marmalade; bursting out after an internal struggle.*) Both! (*Sits in chair, takes a spoon from his pocket and begins to eat furiously.*)

RABBIT: (*Putting the marmalade beside him.*) Here we are.

POOH: (*Between mouthfuls.*) I really shouldn't—(*Gulp.*)—take the time—(*Gulp.*)—must rescue Piglet—

RABBIT: One does better at rescuing after a bite to eat.

POOH: (*Eating voraciously, putting down empty honey pot and starting on the marmalade.*) Much better . . .

RABBIT: One needs strength.

POOH: (*Setting down the empty marmalade pot beside the empty honey pot.*) I do feel stronger! And now—

RABBIT: Have some more?

POOH: (*Looking into the pots.*) There isn't any more.

RABBIT: I have another, someplace—(*Roo runs onstage from DR at this point, looking over his shoulder.*)

POOH: No, thank you—

RABBIT: (*Producing another pot from cupboard.*) Here it is.

POOH: I really couldn't . . . (Roo *has been looking around the stage for a place to hide.*)

RABBIT: (*Waving the opened pot under Pooh's nose.*) Just a *nibble?*

KANGA: (*Voice, calling anxiously from off DR.*) Roo! Roo—where *are* you? (Roo *darts around frantically.*)

POOH: (*Weakening.*) Perhaps just—a—very—tiny—(*Grabs the pot and digs in.*)

KANGA: (*Off DR.*) Roo—come back here this minute! Do you hear me? (*A wrathful tone.*) Wait till I catch you, you naughty thing— (Roo *spots Rabbit's house, finds the doorway, and dives in.*)

RABBIT: (*Startled at the sudden arrival, retreating to UR.*) Help!

POOH: Why, it's Roo!

ROO: Hello.

RABBIT: It can't be—not Kanga's Roo! (*Kanga enters from DR, searching wildly, and dragging Piglet.*)

KANGA: Roo—Roo-oo-oo! (*Her tone changes from anger to concern.*) Oh, dear, is the little thing lost? Oh, dear me— (*Pauses at DLC.*)

ROO: (*As Pooh and Rabbit listen to this.*) Sh-h-h!

RABBIT: (*From UR.*) Playing hide-and-seek, perhaps? (Roo *nods with great vigor.*)

ROO: (*At URC.*) Sh-h-h!

KANGA: (*Quite desperate.*) Oh, the poor baby—what will become of him! (*To Piglet.*) We *must* find him!

PIGLET: Yes, we must.

KANGA: The things that might happen—

PIGLET: I have an idea.

KANGA: What is it?

PIGLET: Why don't you look for Roo over there—(*Points in one direction.*)—and I'll look for him over *there.* (*Points in the opposite direction.*)

KANGA: And have you getting lost, too? (*Clutches Piglet closer to her side, as he makes a face.*) My goodness, no. I wouldn't dare let you out of my sight—not for a minute! (*Drags him off again, calling:*) Roo—Roo, my precious! (*They go out DL.*)

ROO: I'm not really lost. I ran away.

POOH: You did?

ROO: I've always wanted to run away.

RABBIT: Youth will be youth.

ROO: (*Delightedly.*) Look! I'm all dirty! And I have germs *all over* me! (*Rabbit and Pooh look puzzled.*)

RABBIT: (*Feeling he must do something.*) How about a piece of candy?

ROO: (*Eagerly.*) Candy!

RABBIT: (*Offering him a box from the cupboard.*) Have one.

ROO: I'm supposed to never eat candy before supper! (*Takes one.*) Can I have more?

RABBIT: Of course.

ROO: (*Going at the candy with energy.*) This is fun. I like it here! (*As Roo munches the candy delightedly, Pooh notices Rabbit looking very sober about the whole thing. Pooh struggles from his chair with difficulty because of his weight—he may have stuffed a small pillow into his shirt if this can be managed unobtrusively.*)

POOH: (*To Rabbit.*) Why are you frowning like that?

RABBIT: Sooner or later, she's going to find out.

POOH: Kanga?

RABBIT: And there's bound to be a—(*Tremulous tone.*)—disturbance.

ROO: It's all gone!

RABBIT: (*Absently handing him another box.*) Have some more. (*Roo grabs, and Rabbit turns back to Pooh.*) "Where have you been?" she'll ask—"At Rabbit's house," he'll answer—(*Rabbit shudders.*)

POOH: On the other hand, she'll be glad to see him.

RABBIT: Oh, yes.

POOH: (*Crossing to UR.*) She thinks he's lost. And losing one's offspring causes a good bit of worry—

RABBIT: (*Flinging up his paws.*) I've been through it myself. Perfect agony!

POOH: When he *does* turn up safe and sound—won't she be happy?

RABBIT: Terribly happy!

POOH: (*Thoughtfully.*) Do you suppose she might offer a reward—to somebody who brought Roo home safe and sound—

RABBIT: She might very well—

POOH: And if that somebody were *me*—and I could have a reward— that reward might be—

RABBIT: Piglet!

POOH: (*Quietly triumphant.*) Piglet.

ROO: (*Looking up at them suspiciously.*) Who said anything about bringing me home?

POOH: After all, sooner or later—

ROO: I don't *want* to go home!

RABBIT: I'm glad to have you come and visit, of course. But your mother—think how she misses you—

ROO: She has Piglet—she won't miss me so much. She has to give him so many *baths!* (*Pooh's and Rabbit's faces darken.*) And that medicine—

POOH: What medicine?

ROO: You should have seen it. She had to try five spoonfuls before she got him to swallow it. (*Pooh and Rabbit shudder.*) And then he *said* something—

RABBIT: What? (*Roo crosses and whispers something to Rabbit, who looks startled.*)

ROO: So then she had to wash out his mouth with *soap*—(*Roo crosses to chair and sits.*) So I don't have to go home.

POOH: (*Crossing to his side.*) Come, Roo.

ROO: But—

POOH: I hate to do it, but you're going home.

ROO: I am not! (*Sits firmly and rocks chair.*)

RABBIT: (*Crossing to Roo and trying a more diplomatic approach.*) Go ahead, Pooh—we'll follow. Hurry! (*Pooh prepares to go out the doorway LC.*)

POOH: There's not a moment to lose—(*Stops, head and shoulders out of the doorway.*)—to—oof!

RABBIT: What's the matter?

POOH: (*Trying to get through.*) Nothing . . .

RABBIT: (*Crossing to L where he can push.*) Hurry up. You're blocking the door. (*Pooh grunts with the struggle.*) You're not stuck? (*Pooh makes a frantic effort, with no result.*)

ROO: He *is* stuck! (*Rabbit puts his paw to his forehead.*)

RABBIT: But we can't get out—

ROO: (*Overjoyed.*) We *can't*? (*He leaps up and cavorts and dances URC and UR while Rabbit tries frantically to push Pooh through the doorway.*) Whee! I don't have to go home! (*He bounces up and down.*) Hurrah! (*Rabbit gives up.*)

POOH: Bother!

ROO: (*Loud and shrill.*) Wheeeeee!

POOH: (*Calling out in an irritated tone.*) It all comes of not having front doors big enough.

RABBIT: It all comes—(*Crosses and looks sadly into the empty pots of honey.*)—of eating too much! (*Kanga enters from DL, still dragging Piglet, who looks a little frazzled by all this. She looks anxiously around.*)

ROO: (*Continuing his squeals of ecstasy.*) Whee—ee—

POOH: (*As he sees Kanga.*) Sh-h-h!

KANGA: (*From DL.*) I heard him. I'm sure I heard him. Roo? Roo, dear? (*Roo, having grabbed another piece of candy, is silent as he eats it.*)

PIGLET: I did, too. A squealing sound.

KANGA: Roo? Where are you?

PIGLET: (*Leading the way to Rabbit's house LC.*) It seemed to be coming from Rabbit's—(*Takes a look at Pooh, uncomprehendingly.*) —Rabbit's house . . .

KANGA: Roo, are you in there?

POOH: (*Quickly.*) No.

KANGA: What are you doing in the doorway?

POOH: (*Desperately, assuming an appropriate pose.*) Oh, resting—and thinking—

ROO: (*At URC, finished with the candy, demanding more from Rabbit.*) Isn't there any more?

RABBIT: (*Who has been listening nervously to what goes on outside.*) Sh—hhh—

ROO: I want more! More! M—(*Rabbit cuts it off by putting his paw over Roo's mouth.*)

KANGA: (*Frantically.*) It's Roo! He is in there. Roo, Roo? (*To Pooh.*) Get out of the way, you absurd creature—

POOH: Well, you see—

KANGA: (*Interrupting.*) Hurry up!

POOH: That is to say—

PIGLET: He's stuck.

KANGA: What? You can't be stuck in a doorway, and my Roo inside! (*Grabs one of Pooh's ears and tugs on it.*) My precious—my baby— (*She is quite hysterical now.*)

POOH: Oh, help!

RABBIT: (*Grabbing Pooh's hind feet.*) I'll try to pull you back! (*Kanga lets go of Piglet, who remains spellbound. She grabs Pooh's forepaw and also starts to pull.*)

KANGA: (*Wildly.*) We'll see about this—(*She pulls one way, Rabbit pulls the other.*)

POOH: (*Roaring.*) Let me go-o-o-o!

RABBIT: (*Calling.*) I'm trying to get you in—somehow—

KANGA: You wretched bear, I'll get you out—

POOH: But not—not *both!* (*Rabbit gives up, exhausted. Kanga pulls the first thing she can find—a washrag—out of her pocket and starts whacking Pooh over the head with it. She is completely unstrung.*)

KANGA: You're just doing this to be stubborn!

POOH: (*Covering his head, trying to protest.*) No—no—(*Curtain starts down.*)

KANGA: (*Continuing to whack at him wildly.*) My Roo in that dreadful place—and you won't let him out—nasty, stubborn thing! Take that—and that—and that! (*She is whacking him with the washrag, as:*)

CURTAIN

ACT THREE

(*The footlights come up, and once more Christopher Robin is sitting in front of the curtain. This time he is holding the teddy bear tightly, with an anxious expression on his face.*)

VOICE: (*Narrator, offstage.*) And there they were—Rabbit and Roo trapped inside Rabbit's house, Pooh stuck in the doorway, Kanga too upset to realize it was no use whacking him over the head with a washrag—(*The tone changes.*) My word.

CHRISTOPHER ROBIN: Go on—

VOICE: I didn't realize—it's past your bedtime.

CHRISTOPHER ROBIN: Oh, *please*—

VOICE: Shall we finish another time?

CHRISTOPHER ROBIN: But we can't *possibly* sleep—not unless you finish the story—

VOICE: (*Ominously.*) Suppose it has a bad ending?

CHRISTOPHER ROBIN: (*He hadn't thought of this possibility.*) It couldn't—everything always comes out all right—

VOICE: I wonder what Eeyore would say to that.

CHRISTOPHER ROBIN: (*Alarmed.*) Doesn't it? I mean, somehow Pooh got out of Rabbit's doorway—he'd get thinner and thinner, and then—

VOICE: (*A touch of asperity.*) Who is telling this story?

CHRISTOPHER ROBIN: Oh! I'm truly sorry.

VOICE: As a matter of fact, he did get thinner. But it took time.

CHRISTOPHER ROBIN: And Kanga? Excuse me—

VOICE: She calmed down a good bit when Rabbit promised to take very good care of Roo. He had a box of oatmeal—and that made Kanga feel *much* better. Of course, Rabbit forgot to mention that the box was empty. . . . After about a week, Pooh was thin enough to be pulled out. It was a great day—

CHRISTOPHER ROBIN: I should think so!

VOICE: It was his birthday, too. . . . MOST OF RABBIT'S FRIENDS HAD COME 'ROUND, HOPING THERE'D BE A PARTY. They all helped pull. . . . (*The capitalized speech may be used if extras are available and have been used in the earlier scenes. Otherwise, the Voice should say, "It was his birthday, too. Everyone was there—Eeyore, Owl, and all the others."*)

(*Curtain goes up, and Christopher Robin goes out R. The scene in Act Three is simply another part of the forest, a little to the "west" of Rabbit's house. The same trees DR and DL frame the stage, and there is a third tree against the back wall ULC. There is a long line, consisting of Owl, Eeyore, Animal 1, Animal 2, Animal 3, and Animal 4, extending from offstage DR in a diagonal line back toward UL. Each is pulling at the waist of the one in front of him. The front person in the line, who is offstage, has hold of Pooh and is pulling him out of the rabbit hole. NOTE: Any and all extra characters used in the flight across the stage at the end of Act One may be used instead of Owl, Eeyore, and Animals 1, 2, 3, and 4.*)

VOICE: A long line of them—they waited for the signal.

ANIMAL: (*Shouting signal, offstage.*) One—two—three—

VOICE: Then pulled—(*The animals all strain backward, pulling like anything.*) And, finally—(*A loud pop is heard. One by one, the animals fall over backward, with the release of Pooh. Cries of "Hurrah"— "We did it"—"He's out"—are ad libbed by the young animals.*)

OWL: (*Looking severe, from a position C.*) Hush. Hush! (*They calm down.*) Not so much noise. (*The animals group themselves in a semicircle from UC to DLC, facing Owl.*)

ANIMAL 1: Why?

ANIMAL 2: We're celebrating!

ANIMAL 3: After all, we pulled Pooh out—

ANIMAL 4: And it's his birthday, too!

ANIMAL 3: Yes!

ANIMAL 2: Isn't there going to be a party?

OWL: Sh-h-h! This is no time for parties and celebrations. Now run along! (*Points offstage DR, and they reluctantly go out DR, leaving only Owl on stage.*) (*Pooh enters past them, looking weak and thin.*)

POOH: (*All business, from RC.*) She doesn't know?

OWL: Not yet.

POOH: Good. Rabbit is taking Roo to a safe place.

OWL: A good distance away? (*Pooh nods.*) I expect you know the procedure. . . . (*Pooh looks puzzled. Owl explains.*) What to do . . .

POOH: (*As if repeating a lesson.*) I go to Kanga. (*Shudders.*)

OWL: (*With asperity.*) You *confront* Kanga—

POOH: She'll naturally ask where Baby Roo is—

OWL: Yes, yes—

POOH: And I say, "A-ha."

OWL: (*Nodding with satisfaction.*) *That* will give her the idea.

POOH: How? After all, "A-ha" could mean almost anything.

OWL: Pooh, you haven't any brain. "A-ha" means that Baby Roo is hidden in a secret place, and we'll tell her where it is if she'll let Piglet go.

POOH: "A-ha." (*Dubiously.*) It *does?*

OWL: (*Looking off DR in the direction of Rabbit's house.*) I hope Rabbit gets his part right. Can he manage Roo?

POOH: (*Nodding.*) They got on beautifully. Roo enjoyed his visit *very* much.

OWL: (*A touch of annoyance.*) Rabbit ought to know how to amuse youngsters.

POOH: (*With sincere enthusiasm for Rabbit's talent.*) Oh, yes! He gave him peppermints—and gumdrops—and sometimes licorice—

OWL: Plenty of experience, Rabbit's had.

POOH: Roo liked jelly beans the best. (*Sighs.*) It's a shame he has to go home at all.

OWL: No doubt he'll make quite a fuss. (*Roo enters from DR, followed by Rabbit.*)

POOH: If it weren't for Piglet—(*Roo is in bad shape. His expression is of one green with an upset stomach—and he clutches that part of himself in agony.*)

ROO: Oo-o-o-o-ooh! (*He wanders around, making a circuit of the stage and stopping the second time he reaches DLC.*)

POOH: Why, Roo!

OWL: What are you doing here?

RABBIT: I can't do a thing with him.

ROO: Ooh-oh-oh-oh-oooo—

RABBIT: He wants to go home.

POOH: But he can't—not *yet*—

OWL: (*To Rabbit.*) Think of *something!*

RABBIT: (*Crossing to Roo, holding out a little bag.*) Here, little fellow—the last bag of jelly beans—

ROO: (*Taking one look and sitting down weakly on the floor.*) Na-a-ooo-o-owl

RABBIT: (*Turning to the others.*) I simply don't understand! (*To Roo.*) Now tell Uncle Rabbit—what *would* you like?

ROO: (*A weak, pathetic tone.*) Some—some castor oil—

OWL: (*Motioning to Rabbit.*) That's enough. You'd better hustle him off right away—

ROO: I want to go home! (*Rabbit reaches for him, but Roo gets up and plunges off DL, wailing in agony.*) I want to be put to bed! (*Goes out DL.*) I want my mama-a-a-a. . . . (*They all watch his exit. Pooh and Owl turn and look at Rabbit somewhat reproachfully. Rabbit finally turns to face them, shrugs and makes a helpless gesture with his paws.*)

RABBIT: Well—that's that.

OWL: I don't like to mention it—but in view of your family experience, one would hope you'd do a *little* better—

RABBIT: I can't help it. He got sick!

POOH: I wonder why. Did he eat anything strange?

RABBIT: (*Pacing up and down from ULC to DLC.*) Anything besides peppermint—jelly beans—gumdrops—licorice? (*Thinks it over.*) Nothing else.

POOH: I don't understand it.

OWL: But there it is—

POOH: (*Hollow tone.*) There it is. (*Crosses to DR.*)

RABBIT: I suppose Piglet will have to stay with Kanga forever.

OWL: Which is a long time.

POOH: It will *seem* long—to Piglet—(*They all stare dolefully into different directions of space.*) (*Eeyore comes in from DR as they are doing this.*)

EEYORE: (*Who has an unaccountably cheerful manner.*) Good morning, Owl—and Rabbit—*and* Pooh—

RABBIT: *Good* morning?

POOH: (*Gazing DR.*) I don't think it's a good morning—

OWL: Quite the opposite. (*Looks off DL, while Rabbit looks at his feet.*)

EEYORE: (*At RC.*) Pooh Bear—I've come to wish you a happy birthday.

POOH: (*Absently, not looking at him.*) It is?

EEYORE: (*Very proud of himself.*) I'd been so afraid I'd forget all about it. But I didn't.

POOH: (*Turning to Eeyore.*) What?

EEYORE: Forget your birthday.

POOH: Oh.

EEYORE: (*Looking at all of them with some annoyance.*) What's everyone so *gloomy* about? If there's one thing I can't bear, it's a gloomy attitude. . . .

POOH: I'm sorry, Eeyore. (*Owl begins to pace back and forth between C and L.*)

EEYORE: Now my entire day is ruined. (*With the usual sigh.*) But so it goes—

POOH: (*To himself, very sadly.*) My birthday. (*Faces toward DC.*)

RABBIT: What a shame you can't have a party.

POOH: Not without Piglet.

RABBIT: He was so fond of parties—

POOH: With refreshments—and songs—and games—

EEYORE: "Here-we-go-round-the-mulberry-bush—"

POOH: (*Practically in tears.*) "London Bridge" was his favorite.

RABBIT: All because Kanga must have someone to put in her bathtub!

OWL: (*Echoing.*) Yes, she must have someone . . .

POOH: Hm-m-m . . . (*Getting an idea.*) I suppose—anyone would do. . . .

EEYORE: I can't help wondering why it wasn't me. I always get the dirty end of things.

POOH: (*Wrapped in his own train of thought, exclaiming suddenly.*) Yes! It's the—the pro—(*Fumbles with the word.*)—cedure.

OWL: Whatever are you talking about?

POOH: The Thing To Do.

RABBIT: What is?

POOH: (*Advancing to DC.*) If *anyone* can—(*Gulps.*)—take baths, and all that—well, anyone could offer—to take Piglet's place.

OWL: But who—

POOH: (*Bravely.*) I will. (*There is a stunned silence.*)

EEYORE: (*Finally, shaking his head.*) I believe I'm hearing things. I thought Pooh said—

RABBIT: He did. (*Pooh stands looking upward in an exalted manner. He is oblivious for the moment. The others go into a brief huddle at URC, whispering to each other. Finally Owl steps over to Pooh.*)

OWL: Ahem . . . Pooh, have you considered this carefully? We feel terrible about Piglet, and friendship is all very well—

RABBIT: But think of it! Baths—and soap—and oatmeal—

EEYORE: Life isn't *much* around here, but won't you miss it?

POOH: (*Moving to LC, turning to them, nodding soberly.*) I shall. I'll miss a great many things—(*Reminiscent sigh.*)—a peaceful walk in the forest—humming, or just thinking—visiting a friend—now and then having a little something—It's hard to give it all up. A pleasant sort of life—(*Sadly shakes his head.*)—but not a very useful life—(*They are all very much moved.*)

EEYORE: Just—(*A sob.*)—happy—

POOH: (*Ready to go.*) Farewell!

RABBIT: Not now—not on your *birthday!*

OWL: It's highly improper to give up everything on your birthday!

POOH: But—

OWL: (*Interrupting.*) It wouldn't *look* right. (*Kanga enters from DL, storming along and pulling Piglet by the hand, of course.*)

KANGA: So—*there* you are! (*Pooh backs up a few steps toward the others at URC.*)

POOH, OWL, EEYORE, *and* RABBIT: Kanga! (*She pauses.*)

KANGA: (*From LC.*) Rabbit—(*Marches in his direction.*) Rabbit, in-deed! I'm going to give you a piece of my mind! (*But Rabbit doesn't want it. He walks, with the others, at a faster and faster pace, till they are running the last few steps offstage DR. Pooh starts to run, also, but turns back as he reaches DR. Kanga advances to C and calls after them.*) Little Roo has *never* been in such a condition. (*She sees it is no use pursuing them.*)

PIGLET: (*To Pooh, in a strange, faraway voice.*) Hello, Pooh . . .

POOH: Hello, Piglet. I suppose you feel terribly angry at me—

PIGLET: No—I don't—

POOH: Really?

PIGLET: (*A numb tone.*) I don't seem to feel *anything* . . . not anymore—

POOH: (*As Kanga turns to lead Piglet away DL.*) Oh, *Piglet!* (*He is beside himself.*) Birthday or no birthday—I can't stand it any longer—(*He runs around between Kanga and DL.*)

KANGA: What do *you* want?

POOH: I'm going with you!

KANGA: (*With immense disgust.*) You? You most certainly are not!

POOH: Oh, dear me—

KANGA: Nasty, dirty creature! Come, Piglet.

POOH: (*Stopping her.*) Wait! You're right. I *am* dirty—

KANGA: At least you admit it.

POOH: Maybe you don't know how *very* dirty—(*He holds out his paws.*)

KANGA: (*Looking at them.*) Tsk, tsk—(*Takes another look, and becomes interested.*) Heavens!

POOH: Aren't they terrible? And just see—(*Cups an ear, leaning over so she can inspect it.*)

ANGA: (*Becoming more interested.*) My word—

OOH: And the teeth—(*Opens his mouth.*) Ah-h-h—

ANGA: (*Jumping back, so dreadful is this sight.*) Ee-e-e-e!

OOH: They've never been brushed.

ANGA: (*Fascinated.*) Never?

OOH: And my fur—full of burrs, and snarls—

ANGA: (*Really with him now.*) A good combing! Wouldn't I love to o over you with a steel comb—

OOH: You would?

ANGA: And then a bath—

OOH: (*Hollow voice.*) Yes. A bath. When shall we begin?

ANGA: What?

OOH: Well, you just said—

ANGA: I'd love to. But what with Roo feeling sick—and I can't neglect 'iglet—

OOH: Oh, Piglet could go home. You'd have *me*.

ANGA: (*Frowning.*) Piglet—go home? (*Pooh nods, leaning forward 'ith suspense.*)

ANGA: But I'm fond of Piglet. I doubt if I could get very fond of you. *Pooh cups his ear again, temptingly. Kanga's eyes light up again.*) I an't resist. Such a challenge—I've never seen *anything* so dirty!

OOH: (*Modestly.*) Thank you.

ANGA: Piglet, you'll have to be brave—(*Piglet, at C, looks up from his aze, startled a bit.*) From now on, you'll have to take care of yourself. *Lets go of his hand. Piglet doesn't seem to understand what's happen-ig.*) But remember, dear—whenever you need a bath, come over and e'll manage, somehow—(*Takes Pooh's hand.*)

OOH: (*Waving.*) Good-bye, Piglet. (*Kanga tugs at him toward DL. Je takes a last look in the other direction, then pulls himself together nd bravely marches off DL with Kanga.*
Piglet, left alone, begins to come to his senses. He shakes himself—

then pinches himself—looks around, and smiles—then grabs off the bow about his neck. He begins to skip around as the others enter from DR—first Owl, then Rabbit, Eeyore, and Animals 1, 2, 3, and 4. They all pause in wonder between RC and DR, watching Piglet cavort.)

RABBIT: *(Pointing at Piglet.)* Look—he's done it! *(Piglet lies on the ground LC and rolls over a few times.)*

OWL: Whoever would have thought—

EEYORE: *(To Piglet, approvingly.)* That's right, Piglet—getting back your old color again . . .

ANIMAL 1: *(Crossing cautiously to DL and peering in the direction Pooh and Kanga went.)* I can see them!

ANIMAL 2: *(Joining Animal 1 at DR.)* Have they gotten to Kanga's house?

ANIMAL 1: Yes!

ANIMAL 3: *(Also joining them.)* Look—she's putting water in the tub!

RABBIT: Already?

ANIMAL 4: *(Also joining the other three at DR.)* Ooooh—there's smoke coming out of the water!

ANIMAL 3: Steam, silly!

ANIMAL 1: He's saying something to Kanga!

PIGLET: *(Knowingly, as he sits on the floor at LC.)* He's telling her the water is too hot.

ANIMAL 1: Now she's saying something to Pooh—

PIGLET: *(Looking DC.)* Telling him it's all his imagination.

ANIMAL 1: Oh, oh—he's getting in—*(The observers stare in excited horror. At the moment when Pooh presumably gets in, it's too much—they all turn their heads or avert their eyes in horror. There is a silence.)*

OWL: *(Advancing to RC, finally, in an uncomfortable tone.)* Of course, Pooh has no one but himself to blame.

EEYORE: That's some consolation.

RABBIT: When one has bad habits—like overeating—

OWL: And *very* little brain—

EEYORE: Hardly any at all.

ANIMAL 1: (*Who has taken another peek.*) She's scrubbing him—with a great big brush! (*The other three at DR go back to watching the procedure.*)

RABBIT: Of course, he *did* have ideas.

OWL: Interesting ideas.

EEYORE: Rather good company, too. . . .

PIGLET: (*Suddenly overwhelmed at what has happened.*) He was my best friend—(*He sprawls on the floor to sob with his head in his arms.*)

RABBIT: There, there, Piglet.

OWL: Baths don't last forever.

PIGLET: (*Sitting up and drying his eyes.*) But afterward comes—comes the Strengthening Medicine—(*They shake their heads sadly.*)

RABBIT: Does it taste bad?

PIGLET: A big spoonful—*horrible*—ugh!

ANIMAL 1: Oh—look out! (*Turns and starts to run to DR.*)

EEYORE: What's the matter?

ANIMAL 2: (*Also running to DR.*) She's coming—

ANIMAL 3: Run! (*Everybody on stage clusters at DR as Pooh dashes in DL. He is clutching a large bath towel around his middle. If possible, handfuls of soap suds are sticking to him. Kanga runs in DL, chasing him with a bottle and teaspoon.*)

POOH: Oh, no—not that—

KANGA: (*From L.*) Come here—(*Very sharply.*) Pooh! (*This brings him to a halt in the middle of the stage.*) You haven't tasted it yet. How do you know you won't like it?

POOH: Just—one spoonful?

KANGA: One. (*She pours it and advances to C to administer it.*)

POOH: All right. (*Opens his mouth, and she pops it in—as there is a horrified gasp from the crowd of animals. Pooh swallows. Then he be-*

gins to react. There is much whispering among the watchers. Pooh's expression of distaste turns blank. Then he opens his eyes very wide. Then he begins to smile in a surprised fashion.) A strange thing—(He looks at the bottle.)—it tastes like—honey!

KANGA: Naturally! Honey is one of the ingredients.

POOH: It is?

KANGA: You see, honey is very strengthening.

POOH: I've always thought so! (Reaches for bottle with both paws.) Could I please have another—

KANGA: (Handing it to him, rather pleased.) It's good for you!

POOH: (After one more spoonful.) An unusual sort of honey—but just the same—(He then drinks it out of the bottle, gulping it down.)

KANGA: What are you doing? (Worried.) You needn't drink it all. (As he keeps on.) Think of Baby Roo—he needs to be strengthened, too. Give me that bottle!

POOH: (Handing it back, empty.) Ah-h-h.

KANGA: (Furious.) Empty!

POOH: I don't suppose you have any—more?

KANGA: No! (Steps away from him, toward DL.) At any rate, you're not going to have any more. (Pooh follows, and she waves him back.) Stay where you are!

POOH: (From DLC.) Aren't I supposed to go with you?

KANGA: I'm sorry. I'd like to take care of you—(Waves her arm around, to indicate the others.)—and all the rest of them—(Then she looks at the bottle.)—but I have Roo to think of, I can't do everything. (Turns and goes off with righteous indignation, muttering.) A whole bottle— my word, indeed—(Goes out DL.)

POOH: (Staring after her.) Bother.

RABBIT: (As they all begin to come forward several steps.) Bother?

POOH: (Turning to face them.) Until I tasted that medicine, I didn't realize how hungry I am . . .

OWL: Pooh, it didn't seem possible that your appetite could be useful.

POOH: It is? (*Puzzled.*) How?

OWL: (*Shaking his head.*) Very little brain. But you got rid of Kanga. You saved your friend, Piglet. And everything can be the way it was again—all because of Pooh! (*On this, they all cheer, shouting "Hooray for Pooh!" etc. Christopher Robin comes in from DL, pulling a wagon on which is a cake with candles on it, a present, and some assorted candy.*)

CHRISTOPHER ROBIN: Here we are. Surprise! (*Pulls wagon to C.*)

PIGLET: Christopher Robin!

CHRISTOPHER ROBIN: Happy Birthday, Pooh! (*Indicates wagon.*)

RABBIT: (*As he and others cluster around the wagon.*) Look—a birthday cake!

EEYORE:—with candles—

PIGLET: And all sorts of refreshments!

CHRISTOPHER ROBIN: (*To Pooh.*) And here's a present—because you sacrificed yourself for your friend—because you're such a good bear after all. (*Hands Pooh a package, and they all cheer again.*) Many happy returns . . .

POOH: Thank you!

CHRISTOPHER ROBIN: I didn't know what you wanted, so I just got you something useful—(*As he says this, Pooh unwraps the present. It is a large pot with "Honey" written on it in large letters.*)

POOH: (*Overwhelmed.*) I don't know what to say.

OWL: In that case, I suggest you pass the refreshments.

CHRISTOPHER ROBIN: A good idea! (*Pooh takes a basket of candy—the sort that is individually wrapped—and starts passing out the candy. The young animals clamor "Me!" "Don't forget me!" etc.*)

POOH: (*Anxiously, to Christopher Robin.*) Is there enough?

CHRISTOPHER ROBIN: Plenty—for everybody!

POOH: (*Grinning.*) Well, in that case—I want everyone to have some— (*He comes up to the footlights and begins tossing the candy to the audience.*) A little something for everybody—(*As he comes to the end of the candy, he adds regretfully.*) There doesn't seem to be any more— (*The curtain starts falling.*) So this is the end.

CURTAIN

A Toby Show
Aurand Harris

A TOBY SHOW
is a National Endowment for the
Arts children's play.

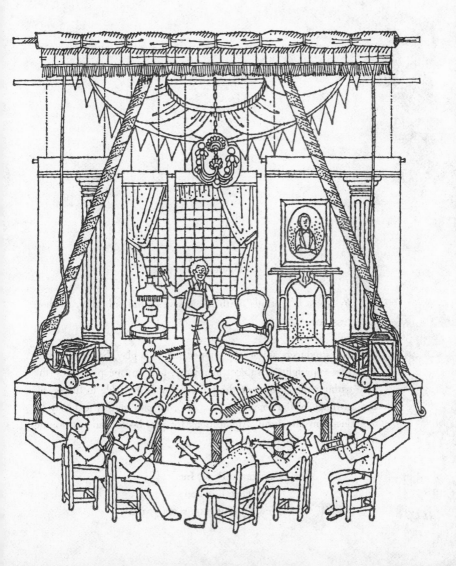

A *Toby Show* by Aurand Harris is a re-creation of a type of American entertainment that began in the early years of the twentieth century and precipitously declined after the Great Depression. Before the development of radio, talking pictures, and television, traveling actors brought live entertainment into rural areas of the country, especially the Midwest and South. Playing in local opera houses and in tents, these repertoire companies performed three-act plays that were supplemented by vaudeville between acts as well as an orchestra or band. (A list of authentic acts is included to indicate the wide variety of numbers used in old-fashioned tent shows.) From the entertainment of these companies emerged a truly American folk character named Toby. Toby was a red-headed, freckle-faced country comedian, who outsmarted the city slicker. He gradually developed into the chief attraction of the rural Toby troupes. Toby manipulated the plot, cracked standard jokes, ad-libbed, talked directly to the patrons, and generally ingratiated himself with audiences.

A *Toby Show* is set in 1915, a time when tent repertoire, melodrama, farce, and Toby's forthright honesty, naïveté, and homespun humor were eagerly accepted by audiences. The plot is the Cinderella story with Toby participating in the action as the "fairy godmother." In Act One the familiar device of mistaken identity is employed to generate comic conflict. In Act Two, Toby discovers an injustice and, as the champion of righteousness, sets about righting the wrongs. In Act Three, as he always does, Toby foils the villain and brings about a happy ending.

Traditional situations, jokes, and stage business are used to contribute to the theatrical style. The same holds for the stock characters: Mrs. Van Undersquire, the "heavy"; Cindy and Burtock, the ingenue and the juvenile; Colonel Dinwiddie, an old man, with a white beard and a squeaky voice; and, of course, Toby.

Traditionally, Toby welcomes the audience at the beginning of the play, introduces the first specialty number between each act, and then before the curtain rises again reminds the audience what problems the characters are facing. When Toby tells his jokes or speaks aside, he plays directly to the audience. His lines are filled with play-on-words and humorous comparisons.

The play is composed of the traditional three acts, each ending with the customary, funny incident and fast curtain. An orchestra provides the overture, plays curtain music at the opening and closing of each act, and accompanies the specialty performers.

Important to the total entertainment of the show are the short vaudeville numbers between the acts. Any act which is short, colorfully costumed, performed in the style of the period, and which is entertaining to children is suitable. The songs and music should be satisfyingly simple and may include such favorites as "Oh, Susannah!," "Turkey in the Straw," and "In the Good Old Summertime." None of the actors in the cast should perform in the specialty numbers or play in the orchestra, because such doubling can be confusing and disillusioning for a child audience.

In addition to appropriate period costumes, the technical support should include a setting that suggests a bright, early twentieth-century drawing room and reveals part of a terrace upstage. The entertainment between the acts is performed on the forestage in front of the closed curtain.

A TOBY SHOW

CHARACTERS

Toby
Cindy
Mrs. Van Undersquire
Sophia
Mauderina
Burtock
Colonel

TIME

A summer day, 1915.

SETTING

The parlor of the Van Undersquire mansion.

There are Specialty Numbers between the Acts.

ACT I

*After a short overture by a small orchestra at the right side of the stage
—traditionally a march and a popular song of the day, i.e. "O Susannah!"—the house lights dim as the footlights come up, and Toby steps
out in front of the curtains lighted with a follow spot. His entrance
music is "Turkey in the Straw." Toby is a likable, fun-loving, country
rube comic with red freckles, red wig, and country clothes. He talks,
jokes, and laughs freely with the audience.*

TOBY: Howdy, folks. Glad to see you. (*To front row.*) Glad you got
here early and got a front row seat. (*To back row.*) And howdy do to
you, way back there. Lady, will you please remove—(*Grins.*) Will all
the ladies, and gentlemen, too, please remove their hats. No hats, no
smoking, and if the baby cries, please take it out. (*Lively.*) Today
Toby comes to town! If you don't know Toby, I'll tell you who he is.
He's a country fellow. Some folks call him a hayseed, but you can bet
your bottom dollar he can outsmart any city slicker. He's got red hair
on his head and red freckles on his nose. And he's about as high as a
chicken sitting on a roosting-pole. (*Measures his own height with his
hand.*) And he likes to crack a joke, like—like telling about his Uncle
Bub at church, and the deacon said to him, "No smoking." "I ain't
smoking," said Uncle Bub. "You've got a pipe in your mouth, ain't
you?" Uncle Bub said, "So—I've got shoes on my feet, but I ain't walking." (*Laughs.*) Yup, Toby is a cracker-upper! Now I want to introduce you to him. (*At side.*) Proudly I present America's own favorite,
funny fellow—Toby! (*Spotlight moves to side of proscenium arch. No
one enters. Spotlight moves back to Toby, who grins and waves.*) He's
standing right in front of you. Yup, I'm Toby, You're dang tootin' I'm
Toby. And we're going to give you a humdinger of a rip-snorting Toby
show! (*Closer.*) In this play, you're going to see, there is a girl who
has a stepmother—Oh, hoity-toity! (*Poses comically and wiggles hips.*)
And she makes the girl do all the work while her own two daughters
primp and get ready for a party. And at the ball that night there's a

Prince who—I ain't going to tell no more. You just hold on to your seats and see what happens. I have to lickity-split now, because I'm on my way to this swell-elegant house. I've come to the big city—all dressed up in my best bib and tucker—to get me a job. And here it is. (*Takes newspaper clipping from pocket.*) "Rich lady wants handyman for light work." I'm handy and a man and the lighter the work the better! (*Laughs.*) So I'm aheading that away. I ain't going to gallop, but I'll do some fancy trotting. (*Enjoys whooping, and trot-running across stage to other side.*) Whoa! Hold the horses. Here we are. (*Reads imaginary address on curtain.*) Number One—o—o Grand Avenue. This is the place where it's all going to happen. Pull the curtains and let the show begin!

(*Music for the opening of the curtain. Scene: elegant drawing room, 1915. Ornate double doorway, DR. Smaller doorway DL. Three open French doors, or open archways, at back, elevated on a one-step platform. Terrace exterior backing. Ornate fireplace with large portrait above it on left wall. Ornate mirror with console table beneath on the right wall. Sofa with table behind it at R. Chair by fireplace at L. Toby is awed by the grandness.*)

TOBY: Take a look at that. Swell-elegant! I'll bet she's so rich she has four cars, one to drive in each direction. (*Laughs.*) (*Telephone rings.*) Something is ringing. Cowbell! Church bell? Fire bell! Oh, it's one of them new tel-E-phones. (*Rings.*) No one is around. (*Rings. Toby starts to phone, stops, excited.*) If I was in there . . . Hello! But I ain't. Whoa, hold the horses! Someone answer the tel-E-phone!

CINDY: (*Off.*) I'm coming. I'm coming. Just a minute. I'm coming.

TOBY: (*By proscenium arch.*) Somebody's coming. (*Rings.*) (*Cindy enters L, running and carrying a dress. She is young, pretty, and is dressed plainly. Although she is treated like a servant, she is always vital, cheerful, and sometimes spunky. She speaks into telephone.*)

CINDY: Hello. The Van Undersquire residence. Who is calling, please? The Society editor of the News! She'll be here. She's coming. She's here. Mrs. Van Undersquire. (*Mrs. Van Undersquire enters L. She is elegantly dressed, haughty, commanding, and comically affected in her speech and manner.*)

TOBY: Hoity-TOITY! I'll bet she's so rich she has a different dentist for every tooth! (*Laughs.*)

MRS. V: (*Stands, holding the telephone.*) Mrs. Van Undersquire? Yes, Mrs. Van Undersquire is speaking?

TOBY: It's Mrs. Van UnderSKIRT.

MRS. V: Oh, the society editor! Yes, I am giving a dance tonight—a masquerade ball—in honor of his Royal Highness Prince Burtock. (*Laughs affectedly.*) He's a real live prince. (*To Cindy.*) Hurry and finish my dress. (*Into telephone.*) His mother was a friend of my late second husband. She married a Balkan prince, and now her son—no throne of course—is honoring us with a visit. (*To Cindy.*) Hang the lanterns in the garden, get the chairs for the orchestra, and—(*Cindy starts to R, then L, drops dress.*) My dress! Oh, you nitwit! (*Into telephone.*) No, no, not you—not you! (*Glares at Cindy.*) My stepdaughter.

CINDY: I can't do everything at once.

MRS. V: Well, someone do something!

TOBY: Hold the horses! I'm a-coming! (*Exits at side.*)

MRS. V: Yes, the Prince is young, handsome, and very rich. I haven't seen him, but he is arriving today. We are expecting him at any minute, expecting the bell to ring at any moment. (*Doorbell rings.*) Oh, the bell! He's here. The Prince is here! (*To Cindy.*) Put on the apron and cap. (*Points to them on table.*)

CINDY: Apron and cap?

MRS. V: The maid's apron and cap.

CINDY: But I'm not the maid.

MRS. V: You will be the maid while the Prince is here. The cap—the apron—ON! (*Doorbell rings. Cindy gets apron and cap.*) He's waiting. You half-wit! (*Into telephone.*) No, no, no, not you!

TOBY: (*Enters R, and shouts happily.*) Howdy, folks. The door was open and here I am!

MRS. V: (*Freezes, her back to Toby.*) He's here. (*Puts telephone down. Cindy freezes, cap over eyes. Mrs. V regains her composure, turns slowly and speaks with great affectation, and curtsies.*)

MRS. V: How do you do. I am Lizzenna—(*Swallows.*)—Lizzenna Smythers Van Undersquire.

TOBY: (*Shakes her hand vigorously.*) Howdy do. Glad to meet you, Lizzie. (*Mrs. V is shocked.*) I'm harnessed, hitched, and ready to give you a hand. (*Turns and sees Cindy.*) And look who else is here. Howdy do to you. (*Shakes hands vigorously.*)

MRS. V: (*Gasps in astonishment.*) We have been waiting—to see your countenance.

TOBY: See my what? (*Alarmed.*) Is it showing?

MRS. V: We are honored that you will inhabit our unostentatious domicile.

TOBY: You want to trade that big word for two little ones?

MRS. V: (*Surprised, then laughs with forced affection.*) What? Oh-oh-oh, how clever. What an original—royal—sense of humor. You do understand English?

TOBY: Sure. If you can speak it.

MRS. V: I shall call my daughters. They are so anxious to meet you.

TOBY: They are?

MRS. V: (*To Cindy.*) Tell Sophia and Mauderina to come at once. Hurry. (*Cindy exits R.*)

MRS. V: If I may take the liberty, I have something to whisper in your ear.

TOBY: (*Quickly cleans out ear with finger and tilts head.*) Let her whisp.

MRS. V: My daughters in YOUR presence may be a bit shy—overcome with modesty.

TOBY: Aw, shucks, fetch 'em in. My sister, she's modest, too. Yessirree. My sister is so modest that she blindfolds herself when she takes a bath. (*Laughs. Mrs. V is startled, then affectedly joins the laughing.*)

TOBY: Poor Sis. Poor Sis, she is sick now.

MRS. V: She is ill?

TOBY: Yup. She thinks she is a chicken.

MRS. V: A chicken? You've put her in a hospital?

TOBY: Nope, can't afford to. We need the eggs. (*He laughs. Again Mrs. V joins him, laughing affectedly. They build the laughing, each topping the other. Cindy enters R.*)

CINDY: The girls are ready. (*Cindy exits R.*)

TOBY: Girls? Girls! (*Fixes himself up for the fair sex.*)

TOBY: My ears are up and I'm biting at the bit. Herd 'em in.

MRS. V: Entrez-vous. (*Sophia enters R and stands. She is comically overdressed, imitates her mother's affectation.*)

MRS. V: May I present my older daughter, Sophia.

TOBY: Howdy do. Glad to meet you, Soffee. (*Shakes hands vigorously.*)

SOPHIA: (*She ALWAYS speaks musically, up and down the scales, holding certain notes with melodic tremors.*) How do you do. How do you do.

TOBY: Listen at her talk. She sounds prettier than the church organ.

MRS. V: Sophia is precociously musical.

SOPHIA: (*Speaking very very musically.*) Be at home here—now, please do-oo-oo-oo. How do you do. How do you do.

TOBY: (*Imitates her comically, with the same musical rhythm and notes.*) I'm at home when I hear a cow—moo-oo-oo-oo. (*Laughs.*)

MRS. V: And now may I present my second daughter. (*Waves.*) Entrez-vous-hoo. (*Mauderina enters R, and stands. She is also comically overdressed, but the two daughters look nothing alike. She is also comically affected.*)

MRS. V: My younger daughter, Mauderina.

TOBY: Howdy do. Glad to meet you, Maud. (*Shakes hands vigorously.*)

MAUDERINA: (*She ALWAYS speaks in verse, stressing clearly and loudly each rhyming word.*) A welcome BOUQUET of words we SAY, and wish you MAY enjoy your STAY.

TOBY: Listen at her talk! Fancy words that rhyme like a book.

MRS. V: Mauderina is lyrical, versical, and poetical. Recite a poem, my dear.

MAUDERINA: (*Takes poetic stance and recites.*) "A mouse! A mouse!" cried Miss DOWD. She shook with fright and screamed ALOUD. Then she thought of a WAY To scare it AWAY; She opened her mouth and—MEOWED.

TOBY: (*Laughs.*) That's pretty good. Now I'll prime my pump and see what words come out—the spout. (*Takes comic stance and recites.*) There was a girl named Nellie, who fell in the bath and wet her— knees.

MRS. V: That doesn't rhyme.

TOBY: The water wasn't deep enough. (*Laughs.*)

MRS. V: Come, girls. Show him to the garden and do take a peep at my gazebo.

TOBY: Peep? (*Aside.*) I'll take a goldarn good look.

SOPHIA: A summer house is a place for a rendezvous. (*Sophia exits L.*)

TOBY: For who?

MAUDERINA: Turtle doves FLY—BY—and bill and COO. (*Mauderina exits L.*)

TOBY: They do? (*Looks after girls and shouts.*) Hot diggitty-dog! Hold the horses! I am a-coming! (*Makes a fast funny exit, stops, waves.*) Tootle-doo. (*Exits. Cindy enters R. There is a loud sound offstage of a flying machine.*)

CINDY: What is that? It sounds like a machine in the air. (*Runs to French doors at back. Points in air, excitedly.*) It is. It's a flying machine.

MRS. V: What is all the noise?

CINDY: An aeroplane. He's circling around.

MRS. V: Tell him to fly away.

CINDY: (*Motions.*) Go away. He's waving back. (*Waves.*) Hello.

MRS. V: Tell him to GO AWAY.

CINDY: Go away. Away.

MRS. V: Flying in the air! What will they think of next?

CINDY: He's coming back.

MRS. V: I will tell him to leave. (*Mrs. V goes to French doors.*) Go away! Away! and stay away! (*Sounds dim out quickly.*) There. (*Romantically.*) Tonight—in the moonlight, the Prince will dance with Sophia and Mauderina.

CINDY: I hope he will ask me to dance.

MRS. V: You to dance? You!

CINDY: I like to dance.

MRS. V: You are plain with no beauty or proper clothes.

CINDY: But I—

MRS. V: You will stay in the kitchen. (*Points. Cindy starts.*) You and the Prince. (*Laughs.*) For you it is pots and pans. (*Mrs. V exits R.*)

CINDY: Pots and pans . . . apron and cap . . . press her dress . . . (*Angrily throws dress on chair, then with spunk puts her chin up.*) If my real mother were here . . . (*Looks at portrait over mantel.*) If my father . . . if you were still alive . . . I'd go to the ball. I would wear . . . (*Grabs the dress.*) . . . a beautiful dress, (*Holds dress up in front of her.*) and the Prince would look right at ME. I'd be—a razzle-dazzle. (*Sings and dances a fast fox-trot. Stops and then pantomimes talking to Prince.*) Oh, I would be charmed to dance, your highness—if you can tango. (*She sings and does a funny tango. Burtock enters at back at French doors. He is young, handsome, and a Prince. He wears coveralls, helmet with goggles which are pushed up. His face is smeared with dirt and there is a small cut on his forehead. Cindy ends her dance, curtsies, and smiles at imaginary partner.*) Thank you, your highness. You dance very well.

BURTOCK: So do you.

CINDY: (*Does a double take.*) What? Who? (*Sees Burtock.*) Where did you come from?

BURTOCK: I—I fell out of the sky. (*Takes off helmet and comes into room.*)

CINDY: It's you! In the aeroplane!

BURTOCK: (*Nods and smiles.*) Yes.

CINDY: Oh, how I would like to fly.

BURTOCK: I'll take you up. It's a two-seater.

CINDY: You will! (*Startled, points.*) You're bleeding!

BURTOCK: I bounced a little as I landed on the drive.

CINDY: I'm very good at first aid. Hold still. (*Wipes his face with apron.*)

BURTOCK: It's nothing.

CINDY: You can't bleed to death. Not until you take me up in your flying machine. Besides your face is dirty. (*Wipes it vigorously.*)

BURTOCK: (*Face to face. He smiles.*) Your face is—very pretty.

CINDY: (*Resigned, states facts cheerfully.*) No. I am plain and have no beauty. The Prince will never dance with me.

BURTOCK: The Prince?

CINDY: Tonight.

BURTOCK: I think he would. I know he would.

CINDY: I'll be in the kitchen. Miss Pots and Pans, that's me.

BURTOCK: You are expecting a Prince?

CINDY: He just arrived.

BURTOCK: How did you know that I was—

CINDY: The Prince is in the garden.

BURTOCK: (*To audience.*) He is?

CINDY: But he—he isn't like my prince.

BURTOCK: Your prince?

CINDY: My prince is dressed in shining armor and he will come riding on his white horse to rescue me.

BURTOCK: That's quite a prince.

CINDY: When you're an orphan you make things up—use your imagination.

BURTOCK: Are you an orphan? I am, too.

CINDY: No mother? No father?

BURTOCK: Just a grandfather.

CINDY: Just a stepmother.

BURTOCK: Then that makes us—well, we're a-a-a-a-a—

CINDY: Yes, we are! We're both a-a-a-a—Shake!

BURTOCK: Shake! (*They shake hands.*) Did you ever imagine a prince in goggles who came in a flying machine?

CINDY: (*Laughs.*) No. I never read a story like that. (*Mrs. V is heard singing loudly off R.*) Here she comes. You have to go! She TOLD you to go away.

BURTOCK: But I was invited.

CINDY: Invited? Oh, no! When I waved I didn't mean for you to come down. Please go. (*Mrs. V enters singing loudly and comically.*)

MRS. V: "Here comes the bride. Here comes Sophia—or Mauderina—" (*Sees Cindy.*) You still here! Off to the kitchen! and who—who is this?

BURTOCK: I am—(*Mrs. V looks him over with her lorgnette.*)

MRS. V: I can see. You are the new handyman.

BURTOCK: I—

MRS. V: Never mind your name. You look strong—if untidy. Take him to the kitchen and show him—

BURTOCK: But—

MRS. V: Both of you—out, out, out!

CINDY: Come on. I'll wash your face. (*She starts to pull him toward the kitchen.*)

BURTOCK: (*Amused, smiles to audience.*) All right. (*Doorbell rings.*)

MRS. V: The doorbell! Answer the door. (*Cindy holding Burtock's arm starts R.*) No, no, take him out. (*Cindy starts L.*) Hang the lanterns. Dump the garbage! (*Doorbell rings.*) I'm coming. (*Hurries*

Cindy off.) Out! Out! Out! (*Cindy and Burtock exit L. Colonel enters R. He is a comic old man—"G-string Man"—with a white beard and he is hard of hearing. He uses a cane. Mrs. V turns and sees him.*)

MRS. V: Who are you?

COLONEL: (*Speaks in a funny squeaky voice—it sounds like a G-string of the violin.*) I know who I am. Who are you?

MRS. V: I am Lizzenna Smythers Van Undersquire.

COLONEL: Eh?

MRS. V: (*Louder.*) I am Lizzenna Smythers Van Undersquire.

COLONEL: I am pleased to meet you, Mrs. Van UnderWATER.

MRS. V: Undersquire. Squire!

COLONEL: Fire? Fire!

MRS. V: No, no!

COLONEL: Please don't shout. You will frighten Ulysses. (*To imaginary dog to whom he speaks throughout the play.*) Quiet, Ulysses. That's a good boy . . . good boy. We have found the right house—Mrs. Van UnderSHIRT. (*Pets imaginary dog.*)

MRS. V: Ulysses?

COLONEL: (*Plays with dog.*) Sit, Ulysses, sit. See how well he sits. (*Shakes dog's paw.*)

MRS. V: You mean, there is a dog in my house?

COLONEL: Eh?

MRS. V: A dog! Dog! DOG!

COLONEL: Three dogs? Just one. Ulysses. Happy, happy boy. That's right, wag you tail, waggy waggy.

MRS. V: Dogs, I do not perMIT.

COLONEL: Eh?

MRS. V: Do not perMIT.

COLONEL: Sit? Thank you. (*Colonel sits.*)

MRS. V: You do not underSTAND.

COLONEL: Stand? (*Colonel stands. Mrs. V draws herself up to full height.*)

MRS. V: I am Mrs. Van Undersquire and I do not—

COLONEL: I AM pleased to meet you, Mrs. Van UnderGROUND.

MRS. V: Take your dog out, out, out! (*There are three loud long dog barks. She gasps.*)

COLONEL: Good boy. (*Pets dog.*) Now that Ulysses has said hello, I will tell you why I am here. I am here because of my grandson, Prince Burtock.

MRS. V: Prince Burtock! Your grandson!

COLONEL: It was a long march, but I made it . . . made it . . . made it. (*He goes to sleep standing up.*)

MRS. V: You are here because—(*Colonel snores and whistles.*) He's gone to sleep standing up! Colonel, wake up! (*Stomps her feet. There are long and loud dog barks. She jumps.*) Oh! Oh! Oh!

COLONEL: (*Opens his eyes and points.*) You stepped on Ulysses' paw.

MRS. V: (*Looks about confused.*) Oh, excuse me. Excuse me, Ulysses.

COLONEL: My grandson, Prince Burtock—

MRS. V: (*Eagerly.*) Prince Burtock?

COLONEL: Is here for a special reason.

MRS. V: A special reason?

COLONEL: He is to choose a wife.

MRS. V: Choose a wife?

COLONEL: Is your hearing bad? His mother, my daughter, married a foreign title—

MRS. V: Yes, I know.

COLONEL: And when she died she left a will.

MRS. V: A will?

COLONEL: The Prince to inherit his fortune must marry . . . must marry . . . (*Goes to sleep. Snores loudly.*)

MRS. V: Yes, marry . . . marry? (*Colonel snores and whistles.*) Oh, he's snoring again. Colonel, wake up. Oh, Ulysses, Ulysses, where are you? (*Whistles and gives a heavy stomp. There is a loud and long barking of a dog.*)

COLONEL: (*Points.*) You stepped on Ulysses' tail. The Prince, to inherit his fortune, must marry a daughter of his mother's friend, Mr. Charles Van Under . . .

MRS. V: Yes, I am MRS. Van Undersquire.

COLONEL: I am glad to meet you, Mrs. Van UnderTAKER.

MRS. V: I have two daughters.

COLONEL: Eh?

MRS. V: Daughters. I have TWO.

COLONEL: A FEW? No, he can only marry one. I am here to see that he marries and inherits his fortune.

MRS. V: And I will see that you are victorious!

COLONEL: (*Salutes.*) Good soldier. Were you in the Civil War, too?

MRS. V: The Prince is already here.

COLONEL: Here?

MRS. V: In the gazebo.

COLONEL: Come on a zebra?

MRS. V: No, no. He—look. Oh, he is hidden by the SHRUB.

COLONEL: In the bathTUB.

MRS. V: He is with my two daughters.

COLONEL: Three of them—in the bathTUB.

MRS. V: In the garden!

COLONEL: He got here first. Oh, shooty-tooty. In the war I was first . . . first . . . (*Colonel sleeps, snores, and whistles.*)

MRS. V: (*Elated.*) The Prince must marry a Van Undersquire daughter. (*Mrs. V talks to portrait on wall.*) Oh, Mr. Van Undersquire, how fortunate that I made you adopt my two daughters. Now one of them will be a Princess. I must alert them. (*Goes to L, waves, calls sweetly.*) Sophia . . . Mauderina. Of course there is his daughter, Cindy. But the Prince would never look at her. And—(*Scheming.*)—she is dressed like a servant, and I will keep her in the kitchen. (*Sophia enters L.*)

SOPHIA: Yes, Ma-maw. (*Mauderina enters L.*)

MAUDERINA: My NAME. I CAME.

MRS. V: I have just learned from his grandfather—(*Points. Girls look. Colonel snores and whistles.*) Why the Prince is here. He is to pick a bride. (*Girls giggle.*) And the bride must be you—(*Mauderina giggles.*) Or you. (*Sophia giggles.*)

MAUDERINA: It will BE—ME.

SOPHIA: No. Me.

MAUDERINA: You can't write a simple rhyme.

SOPHIA: You cannot sing in three-four time. (*Girls make faces at each other.*)

MRS. V: Girls! You must charm the Prince with your wit and beauty. (*Girls react.*) Sparkle in conversation. Walk with grace. (*Mrs. V demonstrates.*) And—remember—in time of trouble—a lady can always faint. (*She faints on sofa. Loud and long dog barks are heard.*)

COLONEL: (*Opens eyes and points.*) You are sitting on top of Ulysses. (*Angry dog barks are heard. Mrs. V screams, jumps up, runs, as if dog is snapping at her heels. Girls scream and run.*)

MRS. V: OH! Oh! Help! Help! (*Toby rushes in L.*)

TOBY: Whoa! Hold the horses! (*To audience, enjoying the confusion, laughs.*) Listen at the chickens cackling in the hen house.

MRS. V: (*Controlling herself.*) Oh, thank heavens you are here. You have arrived just in time.

TOBY: In time for what?

MRS. V: There is someone here to see you.

TOBY: To see me?

MRS. V: Colonel, he is here.

COLONEL: Eh?

MRS. V: Happy surprise! (*Toby and Colonel look at each blankly.*)

TOBY: Who's he?

COLONEL: Who is he?

MRS. V: Your grandson.

COLONEL: My grandson? No.

MRS. V: No.

COLONEL: He's not even my grandDAUGHTER.

MRS. V: Not the Prince? Then who are you?

TOBY: Toby.

MRS. V: Toby?

TOBY: Your new hired man.

MRS. V: A servant? A servant! Oh, oh, oh! I am going to faint. (*She sways and gasps like a chicken cackling.*)

MRS. V: Cluck . . . cluck . . . cluck . . . cluck . . . (*Sophia and Mauderina also cackle in hysteria.*)

COLONEL: Don't sit on Ulysses! (*Dog barks.*)

TOBY: (*Enjoying it.*) Cackle! Cackle! The chicks are clucking again! (*Cindy and Burtock enter.*)

CINDY: What's going on?

BURTOCK: What has happened? (*All noise stops. Mrs. V looks at Burtock.*)

MRS. V: You—you? (*She points to Toby.*) If he is Toby, then who— (*She points to Burtock.*) are you?

BURTOCK: I am—

COLONEL: Burtock!

BURTOCK: Grandfather!

CINDY: The Prince! In the kitchen, washing dishes! No! (*Cindy exits.*)

BURTOCK: Cindy! (*Burtock exits after her.*)

MRS. V: The Prince! In the kitchen! DUMPING GARBAGE!! Oh, h, oh! (*She sways and starts to faint, clucking. Girls squeal.*)

OBY: The old hen is cackling again! (*Mrs. V faints in his arms. He is urprised.*) Whoa! (*Toby laughs.*) Pull the curtains before she lays an gg! (*He laughs. Dog barks. Girls squeal. Quick curtain. Orchestra plays ast curtain music, "Turkey in the Straw."*)

END OF ACT ONE

BETWEEN ACT ONE AND ACT TWO

Toby appears in front of the main curtain, lighted by a follow spot.)

OBY: Well, that was sure a whooping, mixed up, dingeroo! (*Laughs.*) And there's l—o—t—s MORE to come. But before the next act, we're oing to let you wiggle and give yourself a scratch—even if you don't tch. (*Laughs.*) Because we're going to entertain you with some singing nd dancing. Proudly I present our first song bird who will chirp to you er favorite song, entitled: Don't kiss a girl under the mistletoe. It's nore fun under the nose. And here she is! (*He exits as entertainer nters at opposite side.*)

NOTE: *Any short entertaining specialty act can be used, with an appro-riate introduction by Toby. A special curtain, or painted drop, should e used for background. The first performers introduce the next per-ormers.*

After the second number, the main curtain closes, and with run-on nusic Toby steps out in front. He can applaud or comically imitate the ast performance, or have dialogue relating to it. Then he starts his cur-ain speech for Act Two.*

OBY: Now you're going to see the second act of our Toby Show. The ctors are all ready and waiting. Mrs. Hoity-toity—you ought to see er! She's all dolled up in a highfaluting hat. She says the latest fash-on is to wear clothes that match your hair. If Uncle Bub wore clothes hat matched his hair, he'd be in a heck of a pickle, 'cause Uncle Bub s BALD headed. He'd be walking around in his bare skin! (*Laughs.*) ll right! We're going to begin. So get your feet in the stirrup and ang on to the saddle. Ready, set, let'er go!

ACT TWO

Curtain music as curtain opens. Scene: the same. A round table with a fancy cover of ruffles, lace, etc., and a tea service is at center, and a chair is by it. Cindy enters L with a plate of doughnuts.

TOBY: There's the table all set for the tea party. And here comes Cindy bringing in the eats. She baked up a whole batch of little cakes. I asked her, do you know what is the best thing to put in a cake? Then I told her—your teeth. (*Laughs.*) While you're chewing on that I'll—(*Burtock appears, dressed in conventional clothes.*) Oh, oh. Somebody's coming. Two's company, and three is—when you put your ear to the keyhole and listen. (*Toby listens downstage by proscenium arch.*)

BURTOCK: Cindy.

CINDY: (*Startled.*) I almost dropped a cup.

BURTOCK: Why did you run away? What is wrong?

CINDY: You.

BURTOCK: Me?

CINDY: Excuse me. I am very busy. (*Cindy starts to exit.*)

BURTOCK: Wait a minute. Why won't you talk to me?

CINDY: I don't like to be laughed at, to be made a joke of.

BURTOCK: Made a joke of?

CINDY: Why else would you talk to me?

BURTOCK: Because I like you.

CINDY: (*Surprised and pleased.*) You do? (*Worried again.*) But how could you? You're a Prince and I—I am—nobody.

BURTOCK: Prince? Prince! That's all I am to people, a title. But for once, you—you didn't know who I was. It was ME you liked.

CINDY: But I had you washing dishes! And I washed your face!

BURTOCK: And behind the ears.

CINDY: Because they were dirty.

BURTOCK: (*Laughs.*) You see—

CINDY: I'm all mixed up.

BURTOCK: I hope I'll see you again—tonight?

CINDY: You will be at the ball. I'll be in the kitchen.

BURTOCK: I'll help you.

CINDY: All right! But if I let you work, you promise you'll take me up in your aeroplane?

BURTOCK: Shake!

CINDY: Shake! (*They shake hands. Mrs. V is heard, off.*) She's coming. I have to run. (*Runs to L, stops.*) I have to serve tea—to your highness. (*Curtsies and exits L. Burtock stands looking after her.*)

TOBY: Hot diggety-dog! You know what he's thinking? He's thinking he never met a girl like Cindy. He's wondering if—if he would paint his aeroplane white, if she would think it was a white horse. Oh, oh, here comes Mrs. Van UnderPAY. (*Mrs. V enters R, humming. She wears an elaborate hat with flowers on top. Burtock, seeing her, quickly goes to French doors and tip-toes out of sight.*)

MRS. V: Toby!

TOBY: Yes m'am.

MRS. V: Come inside. Come inside. Are your feet dirty?

TOBY: Yes m'am. But I've got my shoes on. (*Laughs and steps into "scene." Mrs. V looking down at him through lorgnette.*)

MRS. V: Now that I know you are the handyman—and I have to have one for tonight—I must ask you a few questions.

TOBY: Fire away.

MRS. V: You were born in this country? (*Toby nods.*)

MRS. V: What part?

TOBY: (*Grins.*) All of me.

MRS. V: I suppose you go to bed with the chickens and wake up with the chickens?

TOBY: No m'am. I sleep in my own bed. (*Laughs.*)

MRS. V: Have you any physical disabilities?

TOBY: Well, I couldn't see much until I was fourteen, then I got haircut. (*Toby laughs, enjoying the interview more and more, whi Mrs. V becomes more and more exasperated.*)

MRS. V: Oh, oh! You are trying my patience! Tell me, are you neat ai tidy? Do you sweep behind the door?

TOBY: OH, yes m'am. I sweep EVERYTHING behind the doc (*Laughs. Cindy enters L with waiter's jacket.*)

CINDY: Here is the jacket you wanted.

MRS. V: It is for him. (*Cindy gives it to Toby.*)

CINDY: Put it on. (*He does.*)

MRS. V: (*To Cindy.*) Quick, run and help the girls. Sophia's hair won stay up, and Mauderina's hat slides down. Hurry! (*Cindy exits R. Does it fit? (*Toby looks at himself in mirror, impressed.*)

TOBY: I look like one of them doctor-fellows that op-er-ated on Uncl Bub. They rushed him to the hospit-title and said he had appendiciti But when they opened him up, he didn't have appendicitis.

MRS. V: What did they do?

TOBY: They sewed him up again and marked him "Opened by mi take." (*Laughs.*)

MRS. V: Oh, I do believe you are next door to a simpleton.

TOBY: Oh. Then I'll move away from you.

MRS. V: YOU are not smart enough to talk to a half-wit.

TOBY: All right. I'll send you a letter! (*Laughs. Sophia off, calls.*)

SOPHIA: Ma-maw. Ma-maw.

MRS. V: (*Looks off R, cries with joy.*) It's Sophia! All dressed for tea (*Sophia enters R, wearing elaborate comic hat.*)

SOPHIA: I am ready, Ma-maw . . . Ma-maw.

MRS. V: Oh my dear, you look beautiful. (*To Toby.*) Tell me, she i beautiful, is she not?

TOBY: Yes, she is not.

MRS. V: (*Looks off R, cries with joy.*) And Mauderina. Come in, my dear. (*Mauderina enters R, also wearing a comic hat.*)

MAUDERINA: Mirror, mirror on the WALL, Tell me THAT My HAT is fairest of them ALL.

MRS. V: It is enchanting, exquisite. Each of you will be the apple of his eye.

TOBY: Yup, the Apple Sisters, Cora 'n' Seedy. (*Mrs. V motions girls to L.*)

MRS. V: Now take your places. You will sit on my left and he will sit on the sofa. (*Girls hurry L, holding hats.*)

TOBY: The sheep on the right and the goats on the left.

MRS. V: (*Sternly to Toby.*) And you—out! And stay out. Off to the kitchen!

TOBY: Food! (*Starts eagerly.*) Yes m'am. (*Stops.*) And if you don't mind, I'll have a ham sandwich.

MRS. V: (*Waves him out.*) With pleasure!

TOBY: Oh, no. With mustard! (*Toby laughs and exits L.*)

MRS. V: Footsteps. The Prince! Ready, girls. Radiate. (*They smile.*) Scintillate. (*They pose hands.*) And gravitate. (*All curtsy low.*) (*Loud dog barks are heard. Colonel enters R, running and holding imaginary leash which pulls him forcefully.*)

COLONEL: Stop, Ulysses. Stop, Ulysses. Ulysses, stop. He is chasing a rat! (*There is loud confusion. All speak at once. Mrs. V holds skirt and hops in a circle.*)

MRS. V: A rat! E-e-ek!

SOPHIA: A rat! Hel-l-lp! (*Her voice goes up the scales as she goes up on footstool.*)

MAUDERINA: A rat! Where's the cat! (*Colonel stops by Mrs. V. All is suddenly quiet.*)

COLONEL: No, Ulysses. She is not a rat. (*Dog barks questioningly.*) She is Mrs. Van UnderWEAR. (*Dog barks and there is bedlam again. Girls squeal. Colonel is pulled about.*) Stop, Ulysses. (*Burtock and Toby enter at back. Colonel, at back, stops. All noise stops.*) Burtock!

MRS. V: The Prince!

SOPHIA: The Prince!

MAUDERINA: The Prince! (*Mrs. V and girls quickly take positions, smile, and curtsy.*)

MRS. V: Radiate . . . Scintillate . . . Gravitate. (*Burtock and Toby come into room.*)

BURTOCK: We fixed the propeller on the aeroplane. Thank you, Toby. (*Shakes hands.*)

TOBY: You're welcome—Prince. You know, Prince, you've a mighty fine handshake. Pa said you can tell a good man by a good grip.

MRS. V: (*Waving her lorgnette.*) You are excused, Toby. Hang the lanterns. Water the flowers. All the things you have to do. Au revoir.

TOBY: She wants me to leave. (*Toby starts to side, picks up doughnut and fork from table.*) Yes m'am. I'm a going. I'm going to do—(*Imitates Mrs. V's affected voice and holds doughnut up on fork like a lorgnette and looks at her.*)—to do all the things I have to do. Olive oil. (*Starts to exit at back. All start to sit, but Toby stops and comes back to C.*) I forgot to tell you how Pa shakes your hand. Pa has milked so many cows that now when he shakes hands, he shakes your fingers one at a time. (*Demonstrates, laughs, and starts to back. All start to sit, but Toby quickly comes back to center again.*) AND—I forgot to tell you that Pa's favorite cow has got the hiccups. Yup, she's got the (*Does it.*) hic—cups, and now—now that dang cow—churns her own butter. (*Laughs. Holds up doughnut on fork, imitates Mrs. V.*) Olive oil. (*Toby exits at back. Cindy enters L.*)

CINDY: Tea is ready. (*Cindy goes to table, pours two cups of tea, one for Mrs. V and one for Burtock. Mrs. V motions to Burtock. All start to sit.*)

MRS. V: Please, everyone be seated.

BURTOCK: After you. (*All start to sit.*)

MRS. V: No, after you. (*All start to sit.*)

BURTOCK: After you. (*All start to sit. Toby enters and watches.*)

MRS. V: No, no, after you. (*All start to sit.*)

BURTOCK: After you!

TOBY: Hold the horses! FIT your seat to the seat and SIT! (*All sit. He puts hands together in prayer.*) Amen—and pitch in. (*Cindy serves tea to Mrs. V.*)

MRS. V: I was reading in the paper that in New York there is a man run over every five minutes.

TOBY: Somebody ought to tell him. He'll get killed. (*Laughs. Exits at back.*) (*Cindy takes tea to Prince.*)

MRS. V: Sophia and Mauderina will entertain us with a bit of artistic diversion. I am sure, Prince Burtock, you are a connoisseur of the arts.

BURTOCK: (*Looking into Cindy's face.*) Yes; yes. I recognize beauty when I see it.

MRS. V: Mauderina—stand up, dear. Mauderina will recite and declaim a favorite poem. (*Cindy exits L. Mauderina steps forward and in comic elocution fashion recites. Sophia goes to drum, which is at the back, and beats it for dramatic and comic effects.*)

MAUDERINA: "The Song of Hiawatha" by Henry Wadsworth Longfellow. (*Sophia hits several loud bangs on drum. Colonel jumps up and shouts.*)

COLONEL: Attack! Charge! Rally around the flag. (*Burtock rises.*)

BURTOCK: The war is over.

COLONEL: Eh?

BURTOCK: The war is won.

COLONEL: Victory! At ease. (*Salutes. They sit. Sophia beats drum at times for dramatic effects.*)

MAUDERINA: By the shores of Gitchie Gumme

  (*Gestures. Drum beat.*)

  By the shining Big-Sea-Water.

  (*Gestures. Drum beat.*)

  Stood the wigwam of Nokomis. Wrinkled old Nokomis, who
    nursed, And taught the growing Hiawatha.

  (*Mauderina measures his height, each inch up with a drum beat.*)

  He heard the whispering of the trees, Minne-wawa . . .
    Minne-wawa . . .

(*Sophia echoes the whispering.*)

And heard the owls hoot at midnight. Who-oo-oo-oo.

(*Sophia echoes the Who-oo-oo-oo. Pause. Then there is an answering dog's loud and prolonged bray in the same key. All look at Colonel. He pets dog.*)

COLONEL: Down, Ulysses, down. (*Another long, loud howl of a dog.*)

MAUDERINA: Then time had come for him—(*She looks at Burtock.*)—to find a wife.

(*Toby enters on terrace, backward. He holds the end of a LONG string of Japanese lanterns. He stops, listens, and enjoys the poem.*)

He sought the ancient Arrow-maker, Who dwelt with his
   dark-eyed daughter.

(*She speaks each syllable loud and flat.*)

Min-ne-ha-ha-ha-ha.

(*Toby starts across the back, pulling the front end of the LONG string of lanterns which continues, taut, after him.*)

'O Arrow-maker,' said Hiawatha, 'Give me as my wife your
   daughter Min-ne-ha-ha-ha-ha.'

(*Toby exits at L. The lanterns, however, continue after him, crossing seemingly by themselves.*)

From the wigwam they departed

(*She steps with drum beats.*)

Sang the bluebird, 'Happy are you, Hiawatha.'

(*Sophia vocalizes cheerful notes up and down the scale.*)

Sang the robin: 'Happy are you Laughing Water.'

(*Sophia vocalizes again.*)

And happily they lived together.

(*Toby enters AT OTHER SIDE, R, now holding the END of the long string of lanterns.*)

Min-ne-ha-ha-ha-ha and brave Hiawatha.

(*Toby at exit, puts hand to mouth, and gives a happy Indian war cry and exits.*)

COLONEL: (*Rises.*) Indians! It must have been the French and IN-DIAN war. (*Mrs. V goes to Mauderina.*)

MRS. V: Beautifully recited, my dear. (*Stands with her at L. Sophia puts drum away. Burtock at R, confidentially to Colonel. Alarmed.*)

BURTOCK: She is one—one of the daughters that I have to marry?

COLONEL: Eh?

BURTOCK: To marry—according to the will.

COLONEL: The Battle of Bunker Hill! (*They continue talking.*)

MRS. V: (*Confidentially to Mauderina.*) He is whispering—about you. Look! Cupid's arrow has pierced his heart. (*Burtock looks at Mauderina and then at audience horrified.*) And now the second surprise— (*Burtock and Colonel sit as one, with frozen amazed expressions.*) Sophia will entertain with a vocal rendition of her favorite song. (*Sophia steps forward, prepares her voice by vocalizing notes of the scale, while Mauderina gets recorder. She accompanies Sophia's comic singing and gesturing.*)

SOPHIA: "Listen to the Mocking Bird" by Alice Hawthorne. (*Sings with abandonment.*)

Listen to the mocking bird.

(*Toby enters at back with sprinkling can. He waters potted plants.*)

Listen to the mocking bird, The mocking bird is singing o'er her grave;

(*Toby sees flowers on Mrs. V's hat, looks and points at hat, looks and points at sprinkling can, steps behind her.*)

Listen to the mocking bird, Listen to the mocking bird, Still singing where the weeping willows wave.

(*Toby sprinkles hat quickly, looks at flower, sprinkles again, looks at flower which grows up in the air.*)

Listen to the mocking bird, The mocking bird is singin o'er her grave. Listen to the mocking bird, Listen to the mocking bird, Still singing where the weeping willows wave.

(*All applaud politely. Toby indicating his blooming flower, bows, then exits quickly at back. Mrs. V rises and goes to Sophia.*)

MRS. V: Melodious, my dear, attuned with harmony.

BURTOCK: She is the other one? The other daughter?

COLONEL: Eh?

BURTOCK: I have to choose between those two?

COLONEL: You do.

BURTOCK: No. (*They argue.*)

MRS. V: The Prince is growing more and more—enamored. (*Burtock looks at girls, then at audience.*)

BURTOCK: *I am APPALLED.*

MRS. V: (*Elated with her eavesdropping.*) ENTHRALLED! Oh, he has been smitten, bitten by the love bug.

COLONEL: You must announce your bride at the ball tonight.

BURTOCK: Neither one! (*Looks.*) Never! (*Looks.*) Ever!

COLONEL: Then it is good-bye to all your money.

BURTOCK: No.

COLONEL: Good-bye to your aeroplane.

BURTOCK: (*Weaker.*) No.

COLONEL: Yes. (*Burtock opens his mouth to speak but nothing comes out. He walks to girls, mouth opens wider in a gasp. He can only gulp and stammer, and exits quickly at back.*)

COLONEL: Tonight the Prince will choose his bride.

MRS. V: It will be an announcement ball!

COLONEL: A victory ball! May I have this dance?

MRS. V: Dance?

COLONEL: The victory waltz! (*Colonel sings loudly, takes her firmly in his arms and dances; suddenly stops, asleep, and snores.*)

MRS. V: He's asleep. (*She tries to wriggle free.*)

MRS. V: Call Cindy. Call Toby. (*Colonel suddenly awakes, starts dancing again, singing the tune. They dance off R.*)

MRS. V: Clear the tea table. Oh, oh, oh—help! (*Cindy enters L, goes to tea table.*)

SOPHIA: The Prince looked at me.

MAUDERINA: I felt ROMANCE in his GLANCE.

CINDY: (*Carrying tea tray, speaks cheerfully.*) The Prince asked me to ride in his flying machine.

SOPHIA: You?

MAUDERINA: YOU! It isn't TRUE.

CINDY: Me. (*Tosses her head.*) I'll wave to both of you. (*Cindy exits with tray at L. Mrs. V enters R.*)

MRS. V: The orchestra has just arrived.

SOPHIA: Ma-maw! Cindy is going to fly with the Prince.

MAUDERINA: It is not PROPER. You must STOP HER.

MRS. V: Cindy with the Prince? She will stay in the kitchen. He will not see her again. Now hurry! Dress in your finest and look your prettiest at the ball. (*Sophia goes R.*)

SOPHIA: I will be the one he chooses. (*Sophia exits R. Mauderina goes R.*)

MAUDERINA: You will SEE. He will choose ME. (*Mauderina exits R.*)

MRS. V: Oh, tonight will be a royal occasion! I must sparkle and shine. Yes, I will wear all my jewels. I'll get them from the safe. (*Looks at portrait.*) Ah, Mr. Van Undersquire, tonight there will be a royal proposal. The only question is, which daughter will be the bride. (*Looks around cautiously.*) Good. There is no one about to spy. (*The picture above the fireplace is hinged on one side. She swings the picture away from the wall, revealing a small wall safe; works dial lock and opens door of safe.*) Turn to six, back to four, and . . . I will wear the diamonds tonight. The diamonds which were Cindy's mother's, but which now are mine. (*Takes out and opens deposit box.*) Now let me see . . . Oh, all these papers . . . marriage certificate . . . birth certificates. . . . (*Looks around, holds up blue legal paper, speaks confidentially.*)

The will! Mr. Van Undersquire's last will—which I must keep a secret. No one—no one must ever read it. (*Off R, an ornate screen moves slowly through the doorway into room. She sees it, gasps, and drops all the papers.*) What . . . who is it? (*Toby is behind the screen and moving it. He peeks around the side.*)

TOBY: Toby.

MRS. V: Oh. Put the screen on the terrace for the musicians. (*She picks up papers, but overlooks the blue one which is left on floor.*)

TOBY: Yes m'am. (*His head disappears. He sings loudly "She'll Be Comin' Round the Mountain," and moves screen.*)

MRS. V: What are you doing? (*Toby steps out in front of screen.*)

TOBY: I'm practicing my singing so I can help you entertain the folks at the big whingding tonight! (*He sings again.*)

MRS. V: You will be in the kitchen. (*Smiles with an idea.*) Yes! You have a special duty tonight. Now listen carefully. You must keep your eye on Cindy! (*He nods.*) Do not let her speak to anyone. (*He nods.*) Especially NOT to the Prince. (*Toby starts to nod, then shakes head.*) She is to say not—a—word! (*Toby gives his head a shake on each word. She holds up jewelry.*) I haven't worn this necklace since my last birthday. I always wear it on my birthday.

TOBY: Your birthday? (*Mrs. V puts box back in safe and swings picture back in place.*)

MRS. V: I am looking toward my next. My thirty-fifth birthday.

TOBY: Her thirty-fifth! She's facing the wrong direction. When you get to be her age, the candles cost more than the cake. (*Laughs.*)

MRS. V: Quick, be about your work. Put the screen outside. Take away the tea table. Pick up, tidy up the room. And—remember your special duty. Nothing can stop my plans. Nothing WILL stop my plans. I will triumph tonight! (*Mrs. V exits R.*)

TOBY: Whoa now. Hold the horses. Keep my eye on Cindy. Don't let Cindy speak to nobody. Nothing will stop what plans? Something is going on here that ain't right. I may be from the country but I know right from wrong. And I'm beginning to smell a rotten apple in the barrel. Yessirree, there's a mouse in the milk bucket. A fish in the fruit dish! A skunk in the woodpile! (*Toby points after Mrs. V. Cindy enters L.*)

CINDY: What are you shouting about?

TOBY: Monkey-business! And it's about you.

CINDY: Me?

TOBY: I'm going to do a little detectin'. How long have you been working here? (*Cindy picks up pink napkin from floor.*)

CINDY: I don't work here. I live here. (*Cindy hands him napkin. Toby puts napkin into pants pocket.*)

TOBY: How long have you been living here? (*Cindy picks up blue paper.*)

CINDY: I was born here. (*Cindy hands him blue paper.*)

TOBY: Born here! (*Toby puts paper into pants pocket.*)

CINDY: It's my father's house. (*Cindy points to portrait.*) That's his picture.

TOBY: Is he—was he your Pa? Then who is she—(*Toby wiggles and imitates Mrs. V.*) Mrs. Hoity-toity!

CINDY: (*Laughs.*) She is my stepmother.

TOBY: And she's got two daughters. She makes YOU stay in the kitchen—Ding-dang it! I keep thinking I've heard this before.

CINDY: Heard what before?

TOBY: Like—like in a story.

CINDY: A story?

TOBY: (*Beams with his discovery.*) Yup, that's it! It's just like a story I read. And at the ball the Prince will—YOU have to go to the ball tonight.

CINDY: Oh, no.

TOBY: OH, YES! You're dang tootin' she HAS to go. And you HAVE to dance with the Prince. And you have to lose your—

CINDY: Dance with the Prince! (*Defeated.*) No. She'd see me.

TOBY: It's a dress-up masquerade, ain't it?

CINDY: I could wear a mask. YES! (*Depressed.*) No. My voice.

TOBY: Don't talk. Yup, that's it. That's my orders! Don't talk to no-body. You are to say—(*Repeats business of shaking head.*) not—a—word.

CINDY: Maybe . . . maybe I can go! I wouldn't stay long.

TOBY: That's right! Just like the story. (*Impresses the fact.*) Yessirree, you HAVE to leave before the clock strikes twelve.

CINDY: Yes! NO!

TOBY: Now what?

CINDY: I don't have a dress—a beautiful dress.

TOBY: Now that's a twisteroo! How in the heck—in the story—did she get a dress!

CINDY: I have the shoes! My mother's wedding slippers.

TOBY: Go get 'em.

CINDY: Yes! They shine like gold and they just fit me. (*Cindy runs off L.*) (*Toby speaks to audience. Scene can also be played with him in the aisles with a follow spot.*)

TOBY: Now how and where am I going to get a dress? (*Grins with an idea.*) Anybody out there got an extra one? Anybody wearing TWO dresses? (*Points or goes up the aisle in auditorium.*) There's a pretty one. Would you like to loan that—oh, you want to keep it on. All right. (*Points.*) What about your dress? Would you stand up and take it off and—oh, you'd rather keep it on. All right. But we got to rig her up. A coat! A raincoat. (*Points.*) I bet YOU don't even have a PETTI-COAT! (*Back on stage.*) We got to get a party dress. A long dress! An evening gown! A NIGHTGOWN! (*Cindy runs in with shoes.*)

CINDY: Here are the slippers.

TOBY: Put 'em on. (*She does. He takes off jacket.*)

TOBY: I got to get her to the ball. I got to get her a dress. Where there's a will there's a way—even if you don't know the way. You have to take the bull by the horns . . . put your shoulder to the wheel . . . you have to milk the cow to fill the bucket. (*Toby sees tea table, points, yells with an idea.*) Whoa! Hold the horses! What's your favorite color?

CINDY: Pink.

TOBY: I've got the saddle on the right horse! Get behind that screen and start undressing.

CINDY: Undressing!

TOBY: SO you can start putting on your pink party dress. (*Cindy goes to screen.*)

CINDY: What party dress?

TOBY: The one I'm going to make, like in the story.

CINDY: What are you doing?

TOBY: I'm waving my magic wand. Scoot! (*She goes behind screen. Toby, beside tea table, waves hand over it and sings a square-dance call.*)

Dos-a-dos. Your partner to the right; Here's your dress, For tonight!

(*With a flourish, he pulls off the lace, ruffled, circular pink tea table-cloth. Holds it around his waist—a perfect skirt. He twists and sings: Tune, "She'll Be Comin' Round the Mountain."*)

"Oh, she'll be wearin' lace and ruffles at the ball, She'll be wearin' lace and ruffles at the ball . . ." Put it on!

(*Tosses skirt over the screen. Thinks and points at his own body.*)

She's got shoes, and a skirt—waist! She needs a waist. Waist. Waist.

(*Looks about room, grins when he sees long beautiful silk table runner on table behind sofa.*)

AH, a waist!

(*Waves hand over runner.*)

Dos-a-dos, Sashay to the fiddle; And hope to heck it fits around the middle.

(*Pulls off runner, wraps it around his chest like a bodice. Sings.*)

"Oh, she'll be wearin' a sash and bow at the ball, She'll be wearin' a sash and bow at the ball . . . !" Put it on.

(*Tosses it over the screen. Feels his shoulders.*)

Sleeves. Sleeves . . . Sleeves? Sleeves?

(*Grins and points at two pillows on sofa, puffy like large puffed sleeves.*)

Sleeves!

(*Waves hand over pillows.*)

Dos-a-dos Promenade, go, Two puff sleeves at Your el-bow.

(*Pulls out pillows from ornate casing. Sings.*)

"She'll be wearin' sleeves that puff-puff, She'll be wearin' sleeves that puff-puff, She'll be wearing sleeves that puff-puff at the ball." Put 'em on!

(*Throws them over the screen.*)

How do you look? Like first prize at the horse show, like a girl on the calendar, or like a bride at her wedding?

CINDY: (*Shouts.*) I—I need—the dress needs—something around the neck.

TOBY: Around the neck. Something around the neck. Dog collar? Horse collar? Cow bell?

CINDY: I know! The dress needs—a ruffle of flowers!

TOBY: A ruffle of flowers! A ruffle of flowers? (*Toby looks around.*)

A ruffle of flowers? Flowers! Flowers! I've found a garden of them!

(*Rips off a ruffle of artificial flowers which edge the lampshade. Holds it to his neck. Sings.*)

"She'll be decked and dolled with flowers at the ball, She'll be decked and dolled with flowers at the ball . . ." Put 'em on!

(*Throws it over screen.*)

Now, how do you look?

CINDY: (*Shouts, excited and loud.*) OH! Oh, quick! It's falling! I need a pin!

TOBY: A pin?

CINDY: (*In panic.*) A big one! A safety pin! QUICK!

TOBY: Hold everything! (*Frantically feels himself, takes big safety pin which fastens his only and one suspender on his pants.*) A pin . . . a pin . . . a big pin . . . Ah! (*Sings.*) "She'll be pinned UP tight and right She'll be pinned UP tight and right . . ." Take it.

(*Hands her pin. Her hand reaches for it.*)

"She'll be pinned UP tight and right at the ball."

(*Gives a pull to keep his pants up.*)

CINDY: I think—I think I am all ready.

TOBY: If you're ready, we're ready. Get set. One—out of the shed! Two —straight ahead! Three—knock us dead! (*Cindy floats out from around the screen, a vision of loveliness in her lace, ruffles, and puffs and flowers. She has put on a beautiful dress, which has the same material and trimmings which Toby collected. Her mop cap is gone and her hair hangs loose and shining. Toby gives a loud whoop and continues it until she completes a circle, showing off her dress.*)

TOBY: Hoo-oo-oo-oo! You look like a princess!

CINDY: Do I?

TOBY: All you need is a crown. A crown . . . a crown . . . (*To audience.*) Anybody got a crown? A gold crown? Silver crown? (*Looks around room.*) A crown . . . a crown . . . (*Points at ornate birdcage by plants.*) A crown! (*Takes off the top ornament of the cage, which makes a perfect crown. Puts it on her head. Sings.*) "She'll be wearing a golden crown, She'll be wearing a golden crown, She'll be wearing a golden crown at the ball."

CINDY: Am I a—razzle-dazzle?

TOBY: You're a whiz-dinger! A ripsnorting whooper-dooper! (*Toby pulls up pants.*)

CINDY: And I'll dance . . . yes, I'll dance with the Prince . . .

TOBY: (*Like a square-dance caller.*) Oh, swing your partner . . . (*They start to square dance.*) Bow to your corners all, Bow to your partners all; To the left go around the hall. (*Cindy stops and calls loudly.*)

CINDY: I'll dance until—bananas split! (*Toby stops and shouts.*)

TOBY: Until bees get hives! (*Calls and they dance again.*) Dos-a-dos your corner, Back to back around you go. (*Cindy stops and calls loudly.*)

CINDY: Dance until table legs wear stockings!

TOBY: Until CATFISH have kittens! (*They dance again.*) Dos-a-dos your partner Go around, heel and toe. (*Cindy stops and calls.*)

CINDY: Dance until trees pack their trunks.

TOBY: Until meatBALLS bounce! (*His pants start to fall. Cindy sees them and points.*)

CINDY: Until Niagara Falls!

TOBY: Whoa! Hold the horses! (*His pants fall, showing his bright red long underwear. He desperately tries to pull them up. They fall again. Orchestra plays loud music: "She'll Be Comin' Round the Mountain" for fast curtain.*)

END ACT TWO

BETWEEN ACT TWO AND ACT THREE

(*Toby appears in front of the main curtain, lighted by a follow spot. He is fastening up the one suspender to his trousers. He laughs.*)

TOBY: Well, that was a hustle and a tustle! But we got her dressed. Yessirree! even if I got UNdressed. (*Laughs.*) But everything's all hitched up again, hitched up tight and right and out of sight! (*Laughs.*) And there's L—O—T—S MORE to come! Right now it's time for some more dancing and singing. Proudly I present for your pleasure, vocalizing, and harmonizing—Pete and Repeat! (*He exits as entertainers enter at opposite side.*

After the main curtain has closed on the second specialty number, Toby appears in front of it. He is lighted by a follow spot, and enters with run-on music. He comically imitates the last number, or applauds it, then begins his curtain speech for Act Three.)

TOBY: That sure was some high kicking and fancy stepping! Now that you've had a jiggle and a wiggle, it's time for the third and last act of our Toby Show. So keep your eyes open, your ears open, and your mouth open, 'cause before you can say, "Toby-took-a-tumble-in-a-tub-of-tom-turkeys," we're going to start. And you can bet your wooden pickle, I mean—I mean your puddin' nickel. I mean your tickle-fickle-nickel-wooden-pickle—(*Laughs.*) Any who—any HOW—if you've got

a wooden nickel you can bet that in the last act of our play, the fiddles
will be playing and the dressed-up folks a-dancing. And we're going to
see IF Cindy gets the Prince, and—and IF I don't stop talking we'll
never get to the party. So button on your dancing shoes and we'll cut a
caper.

ACT THREE

*Ballroom music begins. Toby exits at side. Curtains open. Scene: the
same, and a moment of beauty. At the back, the terrace is a fairyland
of colored lanterns and masked couples dancing in colorful costumes.
Music continues during the following scene of pantomime. Toby enters
from L, turns on a light. Stage is bright for the rest of the act. He motions for Cindy to enter. She enters L, beautiful in her princess costume and carries a half-mask. They stop at C. Toby smiles and nods to
assure her the moment is right for her entrance. He motions for her to
go ahead. She nods, starts to back, but stops, suddenly frightened. He
motions for her to go ahead. She shakes her head and turns to go back
to L. He grabs her hand and turns her around, motions for her to go to
the ball. In fact he shows her what to do. He imitates her walking into
the crowd, nodding to the Prince, putting her arms in dance position,
and dancing with Prince, stops, curtsies like her, steps to side, bows like
Prince, offers his arm. She accepts and they dance. He laughs. She goes
to back ready to make her entrance at the ball. He stops her. He
mimes zipping his lips and puts finger in front of his mouth signaling
her not to talk. She nods, puts finger to her lips and starts again. He
stops her. He holds up ten fingers and then two more (twelve o'clock)
then with two fingers running reminds her when she must leave. She
nods and starts. He stops her. He grins, takes horse shoe from hip
pocket, spits on it, shines it with his sleeve, then presents it to her for
good luck. She takes it, nods happily, puts mask on, and runs off at
back at L. Burtock who is dressed like a handsome fairytale prince and
wearing a half-mask enters from R at back with Mauderina who is
dressed in elegant gypsy costume and wearing a half-mask. They stop
dancing.*

PRINCE: Shall we? It is quieter in here. (*They move down. Toby is hiding by proscenium arch.*)

TOBY: It's the Prince and all dressed up like—like a prince! (*Mauderina sits.*)

BURTOCK: You are . . . you are?

MAUDERINA: Guess. Guess.

BURTOCK: Mauderina? (*Mauderina pushes up her half-mask.*)

MAUDERINA: Yes! Yes! And WHO Are YOU? (*Burtock raises his half-mask.*) The Prince. I KNEW.

BURTOCK: I have something I must say. I—I—there is a question I must ask. The question is—(*Burtock kneels.*)—will you be my—(*Burtock swallows.*)

TOBY: Hold the horses! She's the wrong one.

BURTOCK: I, Prince Burtock, ask you—if you will—to be—to be—my—(*Turns away with distressed look.*) I cannot do it.

MAUDERINA: Continue your ADDRESS. My answer will be. . . .

BURTOCK: My question is: (*Holds out hand.*) Can you read my palm? A gypsy fortune-teller should read it well.

MAUDERINA: I thought the question would BE, "Will you marry ME?" (*Dance music starts.*)

BURTOCK: Shall we dance? (*They dance off at back.*)

TOBY: Jumping jack-rabbits and leaping lizards, that was a close one! He can't ask her to jump the broomstick. He has to ask—Oh, oh! (*Shakes his head, dizzy.*) Out again, in again, gone again—he's here again! (*Quickly runs to side proscenium. Burtock enters at back with Sophia, who is dressed in an elegant native Swiss costume. They stop at C.*)

SOPHIA: O-o-o-o! We are all alone.

TOBY: It's Soffee, braying like a donkey.

BURTOCK: I have something I must say—something to ask you.

SOPHIA: Me-e-e-e?

BURTOCK: Yes, you-oo-oo. You!

TOBY: He's going to do it again.

BURTOCK: You are—Sophia? (*Sophia raises mask.*)

SOPHIA: How did you know? (*Burtock raises mask.*)

BURTOCK: I am Burtock.

SOPHIA: Oh, your highness. (*Burtock kneels.*)

BURTOCK: I must ask you—ask you—will you—will you be—will you be —(*Burtock swallows.*)

TOBY: Hold the horses! You're barking up the wrong tree!

BURTOCK: Will you be—(*Burtock makes a painful face and painful sound.*) U-u-ugh. I cannot do it.

SOPHIA: Be-be-c-d-e-f-g-h-I—will.

BURTOCK: My question is: Dressed like a Swiss Miss, can you yodel?

SOPHIA: Yodel? I thought he would propose! (*Sophia suddenly starts to yodel loudly.*)

SOPHIA: Yodel-lay-hitteos-who, etc.

BURTOCK: Shall we dance? (*They dance off R.*)

TOBY: (*Imitates yodel.*) Yodel-lay-etc. He flew that coop just in time! (*Toby looks off L.*) Oh, oh, somebody else was listening at the key-hole. It's Mrs. Van MESSEDUP all DRESSEDUP like the Queen of Hearts, and the Colonel, looking like Napoleon. (*Mrs. V and the Colonel peek in at the doorway at L, then enter. She is dressed in an elegant Queen of Hearts costume with much sparkling jewelry. He is dressed like Napoleon.*)

MRS. V: The Prince was talking to each girl.

COLONEL: Eh?

MRS. V: Talking, I'm sure, of wedding bells, rice and mating.

COLONEL: Ice skating?

MRS. V: Is he trumping up to elope?

COLONEL: Jumping a rope?

MRS. V: If we only knew—knew that he did propose.

COLONEL: If he blew his nose!

MRS. V: No! If he did propose!

COLONEL: Without any clothes!

MRS. V: Oh, Colonel, our victory is won.

COLONEL: Victory!

MRS. V: Toby! Toby! (*Toby steps into scene.*)

TOBY: Yes m'am.

MRS. V: That was quick. Tell the orchestra—where are your white gloves? (*Toby holds up hands, looks at them.*)

COLONEL: The victory waltz! Shall we dance! (*Colonel turns and steps into Toby's arms. They dance off R, Colonel singing. Toby is surprised, then laughs and dances wildly. Sophia runs in from back.*)

SOPHIA: Ma-maw! Oh, Ma-maw, Ma-maw! A new girl has arrived.

MRS. V: A new girl?

SOPHIA: A princess, and—and she is so beautiful. (*Mauderina runs in at back.*)

MAUDERINA: Oh, Ma-maw, YOU, YOU, YOU, Must DO, DO, DO—Something! A new girl in a pink GOWN, With a golden CROWN—

MRS. V: Who? Who is she?

SOPHIA: We don't know. No one knows.

MAUDERINA: She BORES US. He IGNORES US.

MRS. V: Where is she? She will not spoil my plans. (*Mrs. V goes to back. Girls follow. Burtock and Cindy dance by on terrace.*) There he is.

SOPHIA: There SHE is.

MAUDERINA: Stick her with a PIN! Kick her in the SHIN!

MRS. V: I will report this to the Colonel. The Prince may dance with her, but the Prince will marry you—or you! (*Mrs. V exits R.*)

SOPHIA: I am the one he will choose.

MAUDERINA: You will SEE. It will BE—ME! (*Mauderina sticks out her tongue.*)

SOPHIA: Don't stick your tongue out at me! Miss Bug-eyed! (*Sophia hits Mauderina with evening bag.*)

MAUDERINA: Don't you hit me, Miss Owl-eyed! (*Mauderina hits Sophia with tambourine.*)

SOPHIA: Shifty-eyed! (*Hits.*)

MAUDERINA: Wall-eyed! (*Hits.*)

SOPHIA: Pie-eyed! (*Hits.*)

MAUDERINA: Cross-eyed! (*Hits.*) (*Mrs. V enters quickly from R, between the girls. They hit her at the same time.*)

MRS. V: GIRLS! We must find the Colonel. March. (*Girls exit R.*) This is War! (*Mrs. V exits R. Cindy, wearing half-mask, enters from back with Burtock.*)

BURTOCK: Shall we rest this dance? (*She nods.*) You dance beautifully. (*She nods.*) But you don't speak. (*She shakes her head.*) I have asked you a dozen questions . . . who are you? . . . what is your name? . . . where did you come from? . . . and you only smile. Shall we take off our masks? (*He raises his. She shakes head.*) You can talk? (*She nods.*) Then why don't you? (*She gestures helplessly.*) Are you shy? (*Shakes her head.*) Are you afraid? (*Shakes her head.*) Are you playing a game? (*She is surprised. He smiles.*) Ah, you are. Well, I can play that game, too. You don't talk. I don't talk. When you speak, I will speak. (*He takes an independent stance. She is confused. She motions wildly with her hands. He looks at her and smiles. She sits on sofa. He sits. She stands. He stands. She sits, stands, sits. He quickly follows her, doing the same, ending with them both standing. She laughs. He laughs. He bows and offers his arm. Music starts. She rises and steps into his arms. Pause. He gives a big wink to the audience. They dance off at back.*

Toby enters L, and recites romantically.)

TOBY: Roses are red, Violets are blue; He wrote on her slate, "I (*Spells.*) l--o--v--e you!" Yessirree! Those two are heading straight for the hitching post! Things are sure happening fast! It's got me all tuckered out! (*Takes pink napkin from pocket and wipes forehead.*) Where did I get this napkin? And a lot more things are going to happen before the clock strikes twelve. (*Takes out blue paper will and fans himself.*) Where did I get this piece of paper? And what the heck is it? (*Reads.*) "The last will of Charles Van Undersquire!" That's Cindy's Pa. This is his will! "I hereby do give this house to my only daughter, Lucinda . . . !" To Cindy! This is her house. It's not Mrs. Van

UnderSTAIRS. "And I do give all the family jewels, a diamond necklace, a ruby . . ." All the jewelry Mrs. Van UnderNEATH is wearing belongs to Cindy! Well, I'll be hornswaggled! It's enough to get your dander up—and mine's getting up pretty high! She sure is Mrs. Van UnderHANDED. She may have HIGHFaluting ways, but the truth is—she is a LOW down, sneaking, stealing, no count horse thief! (*Waves will.*) Stealing this house, stealing Cindy's jewels, making Cindy do the work! Right's right, and wrong's wrong, and this wrong I'm a-going to make right! Right? You're darn tootin' that's right! (*Cindy runs in from back carrying mask.*)

CINDY: Oh, Toby, it's a wonderful party. It's the best night of my life. (*Cindy sits, kicks off shoes, wiggles toes.*)

TOBY: And you can bet your life that YOUR life is going to get better. Where'd he go?

CINDY: To get two glasses of punch.

TOBY: Punch or lunch. Here he comes.

CINDY: Isn't he wonderful?

TOBY: Yup, she's found her knight in shining armor. (*Burtock enters at back and comes to Cindy, as Toby goes to proscenium, outside of set. Cindy quickly puts on her mask. Burtock gives one cup to Cindy. They hold cups for toast, then sip. Burtock takes cups and puts them on table.*) Now you watch. In about a minute the clock is going to start striking twelve. And when it does things are going to start popping like popcorn in a skillet. (*Twelve slow, loud strikes of a clock are heard. Cindy freezes, looks about in panic.*)

BURTOCK: What is it? What's wrong? It is just the clock striking—striking twelve. (*Cindy starts to R.*) Where are you going? (*He blocks her way. She runs to back. He blocks her. She runs to L.*) Why—why are you running away? Stop! (*He grabs her. She struggles, pushes him away, and he comically falls into chair, and she runs L, exits.*) Wait! Wait! (*He quickly starts after her, but is stopped by Colonel, who enters L.*)

COLONEL: Burtock!

BURTOCK: Out of my way! (*They dodge side to side.*)

COLONEL: Eh?

BURTOCK: Out of my way!

COLONEL: Play croquet? (*Burtock takes Colonel by shoulders, lifts him and puts him aside, or turns Colonel around.*)

BURTOCK: Step aside! Aside! (*Burtock exits.*)

COLONEL: Bride! Bride! Picked your bride! He has picked his bride! Ah, his fortune is saved. I will call the family. Oh, we will sing a wedding song, and the wedding bells will ring. . . . (*He pulls with right hand an imaginary bell rope.*)

TOBY: (*Loud and funny.*) Ding—dong. (*Colonel, pleased, pulls rope with other hand.*) Dong—ding! (*Colonel, elated, pulls rope with fast short movements, as he exits R. Toby enjoys it all.*) Ding-dong-ding-dong-ding-dong. (*Laughs.*) (*Burtock rushes in L.*)

BURTOCK: She's gone. Not a trace of her—nothing. (*Toby points to slippers.*)

TOBY: (*Whispers.*) Her slipper . . . her slipper. (*Toby creeps to them. Burtock sits at L.*)

BURTOCK: She disappeared—like that. But where? Where? Where? (*Toby puts slipper at left of Burtock, who ignores it. He rises.*) Where IS she? And who—who is she? (*Burtock sits at R. Toby cautiously puts slipper at R by Burtock. He rises.*) How can I find her if I don't know —who! I don't know her name. I don't have a clue. I don't have— (*Toby throws the slipper in front of Burtock. He sees it. Smiles at audience.*) Her slipper! Her golden slipper. (*Picks it up.*) Is there a name inside, an initial? Let me see. (*He goes to back, holds shoe up to light. Cindy runs in from L, without her mask. Toby, at R, sees her and motions her to leave. She does not see him, but searches for her shoes. She sees one, picks it up. Burtock sees her, comes DC, stands by her. She looks up, sees Burtock standing by her.*

Cindy *covers her face, runs off L with shoe.*)

CINDY: Oh—oh—OH!

BURTOCK: Cindy! Of course, the princess is Cindy! (*Colonel enters R, followed by Mrs. V, Sophia, and Mauderina. They stop in single line, each facing front.*)

COLONEL: Forward march. Hep, hep, hep, hep . . . Burtock, we are here.

MRS. V: Here.

SOPHIA: Here.

MAUDERINA: Here. (*Toby has joined the end of the line.*)

TOBY: Here. (*They turn and look at him. There is loud dog barking. Toby turns and pets imaginary dog in line beside him.*
Colonel rocks back and forth. Mrs. V looks at him, then rocks with him. Each girl looks, then rocks. Toby looks and rocks, all of them in unison.)

COLONEL: We have come . . . we have come . . . and we are waiting . . . we are waiting . . . are waiting . . . waiting . . . waiting . . . (*He goes to sleep, snores, and whistles. He and all continue to rock, but in comic disorder, out of rhythm.*
Toby finally stops the rocking by pulling imaginary rope.)

TOBY: Ding—dong!

COLONEL: We are waiting for you to name your bride. Have you chosen, have you selected, have you—

BURTOCK: I HAVE! (*Mrs. V and daughters break the line and exclaim with eager anticipation.*)

MRS. V: Who?

BURTOCK: The girl I will marry is—very beautiful. (*Daughters react.*) She is clever and witty. Kind and helpful. She is one alone and the only one for me.

COLONEL: But which one?

BURTOCK: The one whose foot will fit this golden slipper.

COLONEL: Dipper? Put her foot in a dipper? (*Mrs. V grabs slipper.*)

MRS. V: Girls! Put it on! (*They pull at slipper.*)

SOPHIA: Let me!

MAUDERINA: I—I—I Will TRY—TRY—TRY.

MRS. V: Girls! The oldest first. Sophia, put it on! (*Sophia sits. All watch as she comically with grunts, struggles to put it on.*)

SOPHIA: Uh! OOO! Ugh! Ow! (*Toby acting as referee, kneels, and takes shoe.*)

TOBY: Her foot's too long, longer than a horse trough! (*Laughs.*) Next!
(*Mauderina grabs slipper, struggles and grunts comically to put it on.*)

MAUDERINA: O-o-o-o! Hu-hu-uh-uh! Aw!

TOBY: Her foot's wide, wider than a barn door. (*Laughs.*) Next girl!

MRS. V: There is no other.

BURTOCK: Yes, there is. She is in the kitchen.

TOBY: Now he's whetting the grindstone!

BURTOCK: Toby—call Cindy.

TOBY: You're darn tootin' I'll call. I'm the best hog-caller in the
county. (*Crosses, comically gives a prize-winning hog call, ending with
a loud "Cindy." Cindy runs in L, wearing maid's dress and cap.*)

CINDY: Did someone call?

BURTOCK: It is your turn to try on the slipper.

TOBY: Sit. (*Cindy sits.*)

SOPHIA: It won't fit HER foot.

MAUDERINA: Never, NEVER, Ever, EVER. (*Prince kneels and dramatically puts slipper on Cindy's foot.*)

TOBY: It fits!

BURTOCK: Cindy, will you . . . ?

COLONEL: No, NO! She's the maid. You will lose your fortune!

BURTOCK: Yes, I will lose a fortune, but I will gain a princess. Cindy,
will you marry me?

CINDY: Yes!

COLONEL: NO! You must marry a daughter of Mr. Van—Van Undersquire!

TOBY: Hold the horses! Lightning has just struck twice! Prince, you got
the right bride AND your fortune. Cindy is Mr. Van Undersquire's
REAL daughter.

MRS. V: Out! Out! Out! You are discharged. You meddling country
bumpkin, you uncouth hayseed, you—

TOBY: And one more thing!

MRS. V: Out! Out of my house!

TOBY: Your house? (*Toby takes blue paper will from pocket.*)

TOBY: I happen to have in my hand—

MRS. V: What is that?

TOBY: The last will of Mr. Van—

MRS. V: Give it to me. Thief! (*She grabs for it, but Toby hands it to Burtock, who reads it.*)

TOBY: No, I ain't no thief. The thief is—Mrs. Van UnderCLOTHES!

MRS. V: Oh!

TOBY: You stole this house. You stole them jewels. Everything belongs to Cindy. It's all writ there—in the will.

BURTOCK: It is true, Cindy. You are your father's only legal heir.

MRS. V: Out! Out! Out!

TOBY: No m'am. You got the cart hitched to the wrong horse. This time it's you and your mangey brood that's going out—out—out. (*To Sophia.*)

TOBY: YOU—to the kitchen—and wash the dishes. Start galloping! (*Sophia comically gasps, cries, and runs off L.*) YOU—to the kitchen —and scrub the floor. Start trotting! (*Mauderina comically gasps, cries, and runs off L.*) And you—(*Mrs. V draws herself up haughtily.*) YOU —DUMP THE GARBAGE! (*He points to kitchen. Mrs. V does not move. Toby shouts.*) Ulysses! Ulysses! (*He whistles for dog. Dog barks are heard.*) Sick'em, Ulysses. Go get her. Sick'em, Ulysses. (*Loud dog barks continue.*

Mrs. V suddenly yells, runs toward doorway at L, grabs back of dress, shakes hips, as if attacked by dog.)

MRS. V: Help! Help! Oh! Oh! Oh! Oh! (*She runs off, with dog barking.*)

COLONEL: (*To center.*) Victory! Come, Ulysses. Forward march. Hep (*Dog bark.*), hep (*Bark.*), hep (*Bark.*) . . . (*Colonel marches off R.*)

BURTOCK: (*To center.*) It's waiting. Your white horse is waiting. (*Cindy runs to him.*) I'll start the propeller. (*Offers his arm to Cindy*

She takes it and they run to back. They stop. Cindy waves to Toby. They exit.)

TOBY: Off they fly—to live happy as the dickens! And me, I'm going back to the farm and the chickens. (*Orchestra starts playing "Turkey in the Straw!" Toby dances.*) "Turkey in the straw, haw, haw, haw; Turkey in the Hay, hay, hay, hay. We gotta go and you gotta go. 'Cause this is the end of our Toby Show." (*Main curtain closes. He is in front of it in follow spot. Music continues. He waves and shouts, "Good-bye."*

Curtain calls. Toby takes his place in the center of the cast line. All bow for a final time. Toby steps forward and takes a bow alone. Curtains close behind him, in follow spot, he waves and calls "Good-bye," and exits at side.)

CURTAIN

Wiley and the Hairy Man
Jack Stokes

Adapted for the stage by Alice Molter

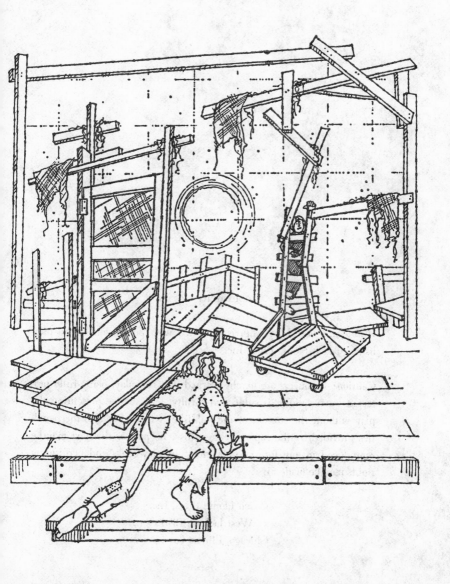

Wiley and the Hairy Man by Jack Stokes and Alice Molter is based on an old American folk myth told by regional characters of the South. The play, which combines plot with choric speaking and movement, is short by average standards, playing approximately thirty minutes.

The plot is the story of Wiley's confrontations with the dreaded Hairy Man. Three times Wiley must outwit the spell-casting terror to be assured that he will no longer be bothered by him. His Mammy, who also deals in magic, is Wiley's confidante and advisor in the conflict. The suspense mounts as Wiley wins first one and then two episodes of trickery with the Hairy Man. The final victory belongs to Mammy, however, for whom it is a particularly sweet revenge. Years ago the monster's treachery had forever captured her husband.

The language of the play is derived from a southern dialect. Written in a framework of poetry, the lines are in constant flux. They are short and long; rhymed and unrhymed; repeated and overlapping; spoken by several characters together and then by some alone; punctuated by pauses; quickly rushed and ominously slowed to reveal the emotions. They form a structure that emphasizes the shifting moods of fear and joy of the story line that must be staged to shine through the enveloping language.

The play is a work of sound and movement. All of the characters will participate in the action. Wiley, Mammy, and the Hairy Man move to enact the plot and are aided by the chorus as they comment on the main characters' situation.

The technical support necessary is minimal. The swamp and Mammy and Wiley's cabin may be suggested with a few simple set pieces: a bed and other furniture for the cabin; trees heavily hung with foliage, and moss for the swamp. Animal sounds further enhance the swamp locale. Costumes for all, even the Hairy Man, may be selected from old garments customarily worn for hard work in rural areas. The original cast wore blue denim work clothes or overalls—the Hairy Man also wore a woolly vest dyed dark brown.

WILEY AND THE HAIRY MAN

CHARACTERS

Wiley
His Mammy
The Hairy Man
Three Chorus Members (*flexible*)

SETTINGS

Wiley and Mammy's cabin.
A swamp.

Opening: The actors, except for The Hairy Man, are mingling and talking with the audience. One by one they begin to make "swamp creature" sounds (frogs, crickets, jackals, etc.), add movement to fit the sounds, and assemble onstage, beginning with the 1st Chorus Member.

1st: Now this here the story of the Hairy Man,
  How Wiley and his Mammy made the Hairy Man
  Stomp
  And rage
  And guh-nash his teeth,
  Guh-nash his teeth.

(*Hairy Man enters, also imitating a swamp creature.*)

1st: Poor Wiley's Pappy had a-fallen in the hands
    of the Hairy Man.
  A dancer and a dreamer, Wiley's Pappy was he,
  And he fell in the hands of the Hairy Mannnn.

ALL: Hairy Mannnn.
  In the hairy, scary hands of the Hairy Mannn

1ST, 2ND: (*Intense whisper.*) Hairy Mannnn! (*Cast transforms from swamp characters into country folk.*)

2ND: And Wiley's Mammy said to Wiley,

MAMMY: Wiley, Wiley!

2ND: said she.

MAMMY: Wiley!

WILEY: Yasm.

MAMMY: Wiley!

WILEY: Yasm.

MAMMY: He done got yo Pappy,

3RD: said Mammy, said she.

MAMMY: You better be keerful—

WILEY: Or he gonna git me . . . Yasm (*Scene changes to woods; 1st and Hairy Man become hound dogs, 2nd becomes tree.*)

3RD: So Wiley, wherever he went, took his dogs,

2ND: Cause the Hairy Man sho cain't stand no dogs.

1ST, HAIRY MAN: Everbody knows that . . .

1ST, 2ND, 3RD, MAMMY, WILEY: everbody knows that.

MAMMY: But one day Wiley, his ax in hand,
   Went down to the trees in the old swamp land,

WILEY: To cut down a tree
   For a henroost, see,

1ST: And his hound dogs,

1ST, 2ND, 3RD, MAMMY: they went too.

2ND: Cause the Hairy Man sho cain't stand no dogs.

3RD: Everbody knows that . . .

1ST, 2ND, 3RD, MAMMY, WILEY: everbody knows that.

MAMMY: But Wiley no more than started to swing
   Than his hounds lit out a-chasing a rabbit—

HAIRY MAN: It looked like a rabbit.

3RD: A-chasing a thing

2ND: That looked like a rabbit,

1ST: but it warn't a rabbit

2ND: Cause rabbits don't have no tail as a habit.

WILEY: Anyone knows all that, dagnabit!

1ST, 3RD: (*Speaking slowly.*) And they run so fur that round about dark

MAMMY: You couldn't even hear them hound dogs bark. (*All but Wiley huddle—frightened. Hairy Man hides behind them and transforms into his "Hairy Man" role.*)

1ST: Don't like the looks, like the looks of this,
Cause the Hairy Man comes at times like this.

WILEY: Oh me, oh my,

3RD: Said Wiley with a sigh,
As he blinked his eyes at the look of the sky.

WILEY: Ah sho do hope, oh me, oh my,
The Hairy Man ain't nowhere nearby.

(*Pause, freeze in positions.*)

1ST: (*Whispering.*) Cause they warn't no sound,
No sound aytall,
Cept Wiley's breathin,
And a cricket call.

MAMMY: So he picked up the ax.

1ST, 2ND, 3RD, MAMMY: Be keerful, Wiley.

2ND: And he started his whacks.

3RD: (*Pointing toward audience.*) Oh, lookee there, Wiley.

1ST: And then he looked up—
And what did he see a-coming through the trees,

1ST, 2ND, 3RD, MAMMY: A-coming through the trees,

1ST: What did he see a-coming through the trees?

2ND: He saw the Hairy Man,

1ST, 2ND, 3RD, MAMMY: The Hairy Man,

MAMMY: He saw the scary face of the Hairy Man.

1ST: He saw the scary,

2ND: stary,

3RD: very hairy and unmerry,

MAMMY: most unordinary face

1ST, 2ND, 3RD, MAMMY, WILEY: Of the Hairy Man, Hairy Man. (*Hairy Man enters from behind the huddling cast by splitting the group.*)

MAMMY: Hair, hair, everywhere.
He was just plumb hairy all over.

2ND: Hairy, hairy,
Everywhere he
Wuz.

3RD: Eyes that burn
Like fire
Does.

1ST: Teeth that gleam
Like teeth in a dream
Does.

(*Wiley pantomimes climbing a tree.*)

WILEY: Hairy Man,

2ND: said Wiley, scrunching up to the tree,

WILEY: You go on and git away from me!

1ST: But the Hairy Man,
The Hairy Man,

1ST, 3RD: He just kep a-comin with a scary kind of hummin,
A-grinnin and a-spinnin and a-comin and a-hummin

2ND: Through the trees.

MAMMY: Fling that ax away, Wiley,

1ST, 2ND, 3RD, MAMMY: and climb that tree!

2ND: And the Hairy Man, he
Just stood below
That big bay tree
With eyes that glowed.

1ST: He was just plumb put out about the whole thing.

HAIRY MAN: Wiley—

WILEY: Yeah, Hairy Man?

HAIRY MAN: Wiley, you mighty quick to climb trees.
Huccum you got that sudden yurge?

WILEY: What you think, Hairy Man?
If you was me and I was you,
Wouldn't you climb this bay tree, too?

1ST: The Hairy Man thought about this for a while.

HAIRY MAN: I reckon I would,

1ST: he said with a smile.

HAIRY MAN: Cause I bout the scariest—
And also the hairiest—
Hairy Man around for more than a mile!

3RD: The Hairy Man always brags a lot

1ST: Trying to be a lot he's not.

2ND: But that's the Hairy Man's hairy style.

WILEY: You go on and leave me alone, Hairy Man!

3RD: said Wiley.

HAIRY MAN: Ha!

3RD: said the Hairy Man.

1ST: Now the Hairy Man picked up Wiley's ax
And give that bay-tree four-five mighty whacks.

3RD: And Wiley, who was smart in conjure spell,
Rubbed his belly agin that tree and started to yell:

WILEY: (*Rubs "tree."*) Chips that's chopped, don't fall to the ground;
  Fly yo self around and around.
  Around and around and back to the tree
  From whence you come, for Mammy and me,
  For Mammy and me,
  For Mammy and me.

MAMMY: The chips flew back to whence they come,

3RD: And makin a face and cussin some,

2ND: The Hairy Man swung—

1ST, MAMMY: Chip,   Chop!

1ST: And the ole ax rung—

1ST, MAMMY: Klip,   Klop!

1ST: And Wiley started hollerin fast
  Trying to make that bay-tree last.

3RD: And all afternoon things kept a-hoppin
  With Wiley hollerin and the Hairy Man choppin.

WILEY: Chips that's chopped, don't fall to the ground (*Chorus members and Mammy speak softly in the background.*)

1ST, MAMMY: Chip, Chop,

2ND, 3RD: Klip, Klop.

WILEY: Fly yo self around and around—

1ST, MAMMY: Klip, Klop,

2ND, 3RD: Chip, Chop,

WILEY: Around and around and back to the tree
  From whence you come, for Mammy and me—

1ST, MAMMY: Chip, Chop,

WILEY: For Mammy and me.

2ND, 3RD: Klip, Klop,

WILEY: For Mammy and me. (*Background rhythm ends, all are exhausted.*)

MAMMY: Bout sundown,

HAIRY MAN: tired of sweatin and cussin,

MAMMY: The Hairy Man heard them hound dogs fussin
Away in the distance—(*1st bays: "ow-ow-owwwww"*)

2ND: But comin nearrrrr.

3RD: So, cussin and damnin, he flung down the ax

1ST: And, yelpin and screechin, started makin tracks,

2ND: With them hound dogs behind him—

1ST, 2ND, 3RD, MAMMY, WILEY: A-chompin his rearrrrr.
Run, Hairy Man, run, Hairy Man, the
dogs'll eat you up, Hairy Man!

(*Hairy Man exits quickly, and hides behind audience.
Mammy and Wiley at home.*)

1ST: When Wiley told his Mammy bout climbin a tree,
She shook her head hard.

MAMMY: Wiley, Wiley!

1ST: said she.

MAMMY: Wiley!

WILEY: Yasm.

MAMMY: Wiley!

WILEY: Yasm.

MAMMY: Now, when the Hairy Man a-starts a-comin your way
see,
Don't you go agin and climb no bay tree.

WILEY: No, Ma'am, I won't, I won't climb any—
Cause bay trees they just plumb too skinny.

MAMMY: Don't you climb
No trees no time.
Just walk up to the Hairy Man and say:
"Hel-lo, Hairy Man"—now try it that way.

WILEY: Hel-lo, Hairy Man.

MAMMY: Just say, "Hel-lo, Hairy Man—"
　　And then you do what ah tell you.

　　(*Mimes whispering with lots of gesture.*)

3RD: And she told him . . .
　　And the next time Wiley went down for wood,

　　(*2nd becomes tree, 1st and 3rd become swamp creatures.*)

1ST: He tied his dogs up with a rope real good,
　　Cause the Hairy Man sho don't favor dogs.
　　Everbody knows that . . .

ALL: everbody knows that. (*Mammy joins chorus and becomes a swamp creature.*)

MAMMY: But Wiley no more than got to where
　　He was goin than somethin filled the air.

　　(*Creature noises.*)

1ST: Don't like the sound, like the sound of this,
　　Cause the Hairy Man comes at times like this.

WILEY: Oh my, oh me,

3RD: Said Wiley, said he,
　　As he hugged hisself up to the trunk of the tree,

　　(*Wiley hugs tree.*)

WILEY: Ah sho do hope, oh my, oh me,
　　The Hairy Man ain't around—oh gee!

　　(*Noises stop.*)

1ST: Cause they warn't no sound,
　　No sound aytall,
　　Cept Wiley's breathin
　　And a cricket call.

3RD: And then he looked up—

1ST: And what did he see a-comin through the trees, (*Hairy Man begins entrance through audience.*)

1ST, 2ND, 3RD, MAMMY: A-comin through the trees,

1ST: What did he see a-comin through the trees?

2ND: He saw the HAIRY MAN,

1ST, 2ND, 3RD, MAMMY: The HAIRY MAN,

MAMMY: He saw the scary face of the HAIRY MAN.

1ST: He saw the scary,

2ND: stary,

3RD: very hairy and unmerry,

MAMMY: most unordinary face

1ST, 2ND, 3RD, MAMMY: Of the HAIRY MAN,

HAIRY MAN: (*Onstage.*) HAIRY MAN!

MAMMY: Hair, hair, everywhere.
Hairiest dern thing you ever seen.

2ND: And Wiley, he was scared—
Mighty, mighty scared—

3RD: So scared he purty nearly—
Oh yes, he purty nearly—

1ST: He purty nearly nigh forgot what Mammy said,
And purty nearly nigh climbed up a tree instead.

MAMMY: But he didn't.

1ST, MAMMY: No, he didn't. (*Mammy pushes Wiley toward Hairy Man.*)

MAMMY: He went up to the Hairy Man and said:

WILEY: *Hel*-lo, Hairy Man

HAIRY MAN: *Hel*-lo, Wiley.

WILEY: Hairy Man—

HAIRY MAN: Yeah, Wiley?

WILEY: What you got in that gunny sack?

HAIRY MAN: Ain't got nuthin . . . *yet!*

WILEY: Gulp,

1ST: said Wiley.

WILEY: Hairy Man—

HAIRY MAN: Yeah, Wiley?

WILEY: What you a-takin that gunny sack offn your shoulder for?

HAIRY MAN: So's ah can open it . . . *up!*

WILEY: Gulp,

2ND: said Wiley.

WILEY: Hairy Man—

HAIRY MAN: Yeah, Wiley?

WILEY: What you a-openin that gunny sack for?

HAIRY MAN: So's ah can put somethin . . . *in it!*

WILEY: Gulp,

3RD: said Wiley,

WILEY: (*Hiding.*) Gulp.

HAIRY MAN: Wiley,

2ND: said the Hairy Man, lookin around,

HAIRY MAN: Ah keep a-hearin this gulpin sound.

3RD: And the Hairy Man grinned a grin so wide

3RD, MAMMY: That two little bugs just up and died.

1ST: Cause nothin makes the Hairy Man
  Scarier,

2ND: Or hairier

1ST, 2ND, 3RD, MAMMY: Than knowin he's scarin you out of your hide.
(*Chorus pushes Wiley out of hiding and toward the Hairy Man.*)

WILEY: Hairy Man—

HAIRY MAN: Yeah, Wiley?

WILEY: My Mammy she say
  She one of the best
  At castin spells
  In the whole Southwest.

HAIRY MAN: Huh!

2ND: said the Hairy Man.

HAIRY MAN: Yo Mammy is a gabby woman. (*Chorus restrains Mammy, who gets riled by the above statement.*)

WILEY: My Mammy, she say you a gabby Hairy Man.

HAIRY MAN: Wiley,

2ND: said the Hairy Man, lookin wild,

HAIRY MAN: You gonna mess around and git me riled.

WILEY: My Mammy, she can turn into somepin she ain't.

HAIRY MAN: Shoot, that nuthin,

1ST: said the Hairy Man.

WILEY: Ah reckon,

MAMMY: said Wiley,

WILEY: ah reckon you cain't.

HAIRY MAN: Ah reckon,

3RD: said the Hairy Man,

HAIRY MAN: ah reckon ah can. (*Chant begins for "casting a spell."*)

MAMMY: The Hairy Man twisted,

3RD: The Hairy Man turned,

1ST: The Hairy Man breathed with a breath that burned—

3RD: And turned hisself—

2ND: Into a—(*Hairy Man, riding on the shoulders of two Chorus members, becomes a Geeraff.*)

HAIRY MAN: Gee-raff!

WILEY: Ah reckon you ain't nowhere near to turnin yo self
    into no—
  Al-ligator!

HAIRY MAN: Ah reckon ah am!

MAMMY: The Hairy Man twisted,

3RD: The Hairy Man turned,

1ST: The Hairy Man breathed with a breath that burned—

2ND: Leaped high in the air
And landed on his knees,

1ST, 2ND, 3RD, MAMMY: Did a little jig all through them trees.
And turned hisself—

2ND: Into a—(*Chorus becomes Alligator, with Hairy Man as one jaw.*)

HAIRY MAN: *Al*-ligator!

WILEY: My Mammy, she say the hardest thing to do
Is turn yo self into somepin smaller than you.

HAIRY MAN: Ah reckon it is.

WILEY: Ah speck you ain't about to turn yo self into somepin like a—
Possum!

HAIRY MAN: Ah reckon ah am.

2ND: The Hairy Man took four-five great big breaths,
Looked round the woods like a hundred deaths.

1ST, 2ND, 3RD, MAMMY: And then—

MAMMY: The Hairy Man twisted,

3RD: The Hairy Man turned,

1ST: The Hairy Man breathed with a breath that burned—

2ND: Leaped high in the air
And landed on his knees—

1ST, 2ND, 3RD, MAMMY: Did a little jig all through them trees.
Swore and raved and kicked his own shin,
Shinnied up a tree and down agin—
And then—

1ST: with a whole lot of sweatin

2ND: And fussin—

HAIRY MAN: And some cussin—(*Hairy Man in center, as Chorus swirls around him.*)

3RD: Turned hisself—
Into a—

(*Chorus forms line, Hairy Man hides behind it.*)

MAMMY: (*Small voice.*) Pos-sum!

2ND: And Wiley grabbed it and throwed it in the sack!

3RD: Wiley, Wiley, that's the first time you fooled 'im,

MAMMY: The first time you fooled the Hairy Mannnnn,

1ST, 2ND, 3RD, MAMMY: Hairy Mannnnn.

1ST: Fool 'im two more times—
And he'll leave you alone,

1ST, 2ND, 3RD, MAMMY: Alone.

2ND: And Wiley took that sack of possum
And flung it in the river—

1ST, 2ND, 3RD, MAMMY: Yossum!

WILEY: Good-bye, Hairy Man. (*Scene changes, as Chorus begins swamp creature sounds.*)

1ST: And then he started home through the swamp—

3RD: And then he looked up—

1ST: And what did he see a-comin through the trees,

1ST, 2ND, 3RD, MAMMY: A-comin through the trees,

1ST: What did he see a-comin through the trees?

2ND: He saw the HAIRY MAN,

1ST, 2ND, 3RD, MAMMY: The HAIRY MAN,

MAMMY: He saw the scary face of the HAIRY MAN.

1ST: He saw the scary,

2ND: stary,

3RD: very hairy and unmerry,

MAMMY: most unordinary face

1ST, 2ND, 3RD, MAMMY: Of the HAIRY MAN, (*Hairy Man joins Chorus.*)

HAIRY MAN: HAIRY MAN.

1ST: Hair,

2ND: hair,

3RD: every

MAMMY: where.

1ST: He was hairy, right hairy.

3RD: And mighty scary.

WILEY: Hairy Man, how'd you git out of that sack!

HAIRY MAN: Ah smart, Wiley.
Ah turned myself into a cyclone
And ah
BLEWWWWWWWW
Myself out!

WILEY: Oh, Hairy Man.

HAIRY MAN: And, Wiley, ah gone set right chere
Till you belly git the hongry-grumbles—hear?
Just so ah can see
You fall outa that tree!

3RD: Cause sho nuff, Wiley was up that tree agin!

1ST, 2ND, 3RD, MAMMY: Hug that tree trunk, Wiley!

WILEY: Well, Hairy Man,

1ST: said Wiley.

WILEY: You purty good at changin faces,
But how good are you at changin places?

HAIRY MAN: Whaddaya mean?

2ND: said the Hairy Man.

WILEY: Can you take a thing that's really here,

MAMMY: Said Wiley,

WILEY: and make it disappear?

HAIRY MAN: Huh!

2ND: said the Hairy Man, blowin on his nails
And shinin 'em, real stuck up, on his chest.

HAIRY MAN: That there is just my spe-ci-a-li-tee—
   Take a look at that ole birdnest!

3RD: And sho nuff,

2ND: When Wiley looked,

1ST, 2ND, 3RD, MAMMY: It was gone.

MAMMY: But Wiley, he look skepatickle,

HAIRY MAN: Now take a look at yo shirt.

3RD: And sho nuff,

2ND: When Wiley looked,

1ST, 2ND, 3RD, MAMMY: It was gone.

MAMMY: But Wiley, he look skepatickle.

HAIRY MAN: Wiley, you a-lookin mighty skepatickle,

3RD: said the Hairy Man.

WILEY: Hairy Man, ah *is* mighty skepatickle,

1ST: said Wiley.

HAIRY MAN: What ah gotta do to make you *less* skepatickle,

3RD: said the Hairy Man.

WILEY: Well,

1ST: said Wiley,

WILEY: You see this rope tied round my pants?
   Ah know it's here.
   Well, ah bet you cain't make this rope here
      disappear.

HAIRY MAN: Huh. Ah can make the rope for miles around
   go way.
   Cause this my county, and what ah says goes.

WILEY: Ah is skepatickle,

2ND: said Wiley.

1ST: Well, the Hairy Man he was plumb put out—

3RD: Cause the Hairy Man he cain't stand no doubt.

2ND: Everbody knows that . . .

1ST, 2ND, 3RD, MAMMY: everbody knows that.

1ST: So he hollered so loud the air turned blue,

3RD: And a bird on a limb just popped in two.

2ND: And he yelled:

HAIRY MAN: (*Casting spell.*) Rope, rope, wherever you are,
Go away to ah don't know whar.
Rope, disappear!
Git away from here!

WILEY: Ah reckon that in-cludes ropes that holds pants up.

HAIRY MAN: Ah said, All rope!

1ST: Wiley grabbed at his pants. (*All grab at their pants.*)

WILEY: Ah reckon that *in*-cludes ropes that dangles buckets in wells.

HAIRY MAN: Ah said, All rope!

2ND: All over the county buckets fell in wells.

WILEY: Ah reckon that *in*-cludes ropes that ties dogs up!

1ST: Wiley grinned at the Hairy Man,

3RD: But the Hairy Man wasn't grinnin:

MAMMY: He was too busy turnin green.

HAIRY MAN: Whoops,

2ND: said the Hairy Man, real soft

WILEY: Hyeah, dogs!

2ND: yelled Wiley. (*Hairy Man exits, behind audience.*)

1ST, 2ND, 3RD, MAMMY, WILEY: Run, Hairy Man; run, Hairy Man,
The dogs'll eat you up, Hairy Man!

MAMMY: Wiley, Wiley, that's the second time you fooled 'im,
The second time you fooled the Hairy Mannnnn,

1ST, 2ND, 3RD, MAMMY: Hairy Mannnnnn.

1ST: Fool 'im one more time—
And he'll leave you alone,

1ST, 2ND, 3RD, MAMMY: Alone.

1ST: Then Wiley run home,

2ND: and Mammy got a chair

3RD: And set herself down and started to stare—

1ST, 2ND, 3RD: Studyin, studyin.

1ST: And Mammy said to Wiley,

MAMMY: Wiley, Wiley!

1ST: said she.

MAMMY: Wiley!

WILEY: Yasm.

MAMMY: Wiley!

WILEY: Yasm.

MAMMY: Ah gonna set right chere and study out a way
How to fool that Hairy Man a third time today.

1ST: And Wiley took his dogs, tied one at the *front* door

3RD: And one at the back—

2ND: and wished he had *two* more.

1ST: Then over the winder
He crossed a broom

3RD: And the handle of an ax,
Went back in the room,
And built a fire in the fireplace grate.

2ND: Then he went in
And set in a chair
And helped his Mammy meditate.

1ST, 2ND, 3RD: Studyin, studyin,
The wheels go round;
Studyin, studyin,
Without a sound.

1ST: Then Mammy said to Wiley,

MAMMY: Wiley, Wiley!

1ST: said she.

MAMMY: Wiley!

WILEY: Yasm.

MAMMY: Wiley!

WILEY: Yasm.

MAMMY: You go down to the pigpen, see,
And bring that suckin pig to me.

2ND: And that's what he done,

1ST, 2ND, 3RD: And *then—*

MAMMY: *Now*, Wiley . . .
Put that pig in your little bed
And cover him from hoof to head.

2ND: And that's what he done,

1ST, 2ND, 3RD: And *then—*

MAMMY: *Now*, Wiley . . .
You go spend the rest of the night
Up in the attic out of sight.

2ND: And that's what he done,

1ST, 2ND, 3RD: And *then—*

3RD: *Oh, man, and then—*

1ST: They warn't no sound,
No sound aytall
Cept Wiley's breathin
And a cricket call.

(Begin a build in excitement, from soft cricket call.)

1ST: And then—

3RD: That cricket call it got so loud
That what was sound became a cloud.

2ND: Everything was turned around:
Things you saw were turned to sound.

1ST: In Wiley's world, for just a minute,
What was heard had color in it.

(*Chorus members become an enclosure, Wiley hides inside.*)

MAMMY: And Wiley scrunched agin the wall
Listenin to that cricket call.

(*Wiley peers and listens through a "knothole" made of 1st's hands.*)

3RD: Then Wiley looked out of a knothole,
And what did he see on the ground?

1ST: One of his hound dogs standin up,
With his lips drawn back and jumpin around.
And an animal big as a mule—

MAMMY: Big as a mule,

1ST: but it wasn't a mule,

3RD: Cause mules don't have no horns as a rule—

WILEY: Anyone knows that, any ole fool!

1ST: —Saw an animal big as a mule
Run out of the woods with a look at the house.

(*Chorus, hiding behind each other, in sequence . . .*)

3RD: I know what it is,

2ND: I know what it is.

MAMMY: Cause a thing that can turn itself into a critter as small as a possum

1ST: Can certainly turn itself into one large as a

1ST, 2ND, 3RD, MAMMY, WILEY: Yossum!

1ST: I know what it is,

3RD: I know what it is.

MAMMY: And the dog jumped and jerked at his noose,

WILEY: But he couldn't git loose.

2ND: I know what it is,

1ST: I know what it is.

3RD: Then an animal bigger than a dog,

1ST: with a snout
  And great big teeth that stuck way out—

WILEY: I know what it is.

2ND: —Run out of the woods with a growl at the house.

MAMMY: Then suddenly both of the ropes that were holdin the hounds went slack,

1ST: As the dogs broke loose and, yelpin, chased, round to the back.

WILEY: (*Rapid pace begins.*) An animal that could have been—

3RD: A *pos*-sum.

1ST, 2ND, 3RD, MAMMY, WILEY: Yossum.

MAMMY: Only it wasn't.

2ND: Only it wasn't.

3RD: (*Ominous.*) I know what it is.
  And all at once on the roof he heard sompin big as a cow,

1ST: A-flappin its wings around like a bird,
  Startin to come down the chimney,

2ND: But cussin and damnin when it found
  A fire in the grate. It jumped to the ground,

1ST: And then, as big as you please, come round
  To the door, where it knocked

1ST, 2ND, 3RD, MAMMY, WILEY: Till the whole house rocked.

MAMMY: I know what it is.

WILEY: It's the Hairy Man. (*Hairy Man enters; Chorus hides behind Mammy with Wiley behind all the rest.*)

HAIRY MAN: Mammy,

2ND: said the Hairy Man.

HAIRY MAN: Ah is come!

1ST: He done got yo Pappy—and he gonna git—

HAIRY MAN: Mammy! Come for yo baby, Mammy!

MAMMY: Well,

3RD: said Mammy,

MAMMY: you ain't a-gittin him.

HAIRY MAN: Ah better git him,

2ND: said the Hairy Man
Lookin as mean as the Hairy Man can,

HAIRY MAN: Or: ah'll turn into a spider and bite you.

3RD: And Mammy said,

MAMMY: Ah'll turn into a flice water and smite you.

2ND: And the Hairy Man said,

HAIRY MAN: Ah'll make the lightnin
burn yo house!

1ST: And Mammy said,

MAMMY: Ah'll call the rain the house
to douse!

3RD: And the Hairy Man growled a cuss in the air.

HAIRY MAN: Some mighty fancy rhymin, Mammy, there—
Ah'll—ah'll—

1ST: It's all he could say,
Cause for once that day
The Hairy Man ran out of mean things to say.

HAIRY MAN: Ah'll—ah'll—
Ah'll make yo teeth turn black

And yo hair fall out,
And yo shape turn skinny—
and—and—put a red bump right on the end of yo
    big ugly nose!

MAMMY: Hairy Man,

2ND: said Mammy, who'd forgot what a rat
The Hairy Man was,

MAMMY: you wouldn't do that—
That's plumb underhanded!

HAIRY MAN: Ah'm a plumb underhanded man,

1ST: said the Hairy Man,
real proud.

3RD: So Mammy said to Hairy Man,

MAMMY: Hairy Man!

3RD: said she.

MAMMY: Hairy Man!

HAIRY MAN: Yasm.

MAMMY: Hairy Man!

HAIRY MAN: Yasm.

MAMMY: If ah let you have mah baby,
Will you leave us alone—maybe?

(*Chorus gasps, protects Wiley, Mammy shushes Chorus.*)

HAIRY MAN: Mammy, ah swear the Hairy Man oath
That's just what ah'll do!

MAMMY: Oh, the Hairy Man oath is a terrible oath,
And it goes like this:

(*All but Hairy Man jump to attention.*)

HAIRY MAN: Ah swear, ah swear,
Ah swear by mah hair—

(*Begin soft chant to back-up Hairy Man oath.*)

1ST, 2ND, 3RD, MAMMY, WILEY: Terrible, terrible, the Hairy Man oath—

HAIRY MAN: If ah don't do what ah swear to here,
  Let little crawly things climb in mah ear.

1, 2, 3, M, W: (Terrible, terrible, the Hairy Man oath—)

HAIRY MAN: If ah don't do what ah say ah will,
  Let mah eyes pop out and roll down a hill.

1, 2, 3, M, W: (Terrible, terrible, the Hairy Man oath—)

HAIRY MAN: If ah don't do what ah say ah'll do,
  Let mah face turn green and mah nose turn blue.

1, 2, 3, M, W: (Terrible, terrible, the Hairy Man oath—) (*Chorus reacts to each of the following oaths.*)

HAIRY MAN: If ah don't do,
  What ah promise to do,
  Let crows
  Peck mah toes.
  Let a bear
  Eat mah hair.
  Let flies
  Sting mah eyes.
  Let the sun
  Cook me done.
  Also let me git the biggest toothache ever!

(*Chorus dumbfounded by the final oath—"Ugh!"*)

1ST: Now there's just one thing:

2ND: The Hairy Man oath don't mean a thing.

3RD: All it does is cloud up the sky
  And kill the grass,

MAMMY: Cause everybody knows that the Hairy Man
  Always crosses his fingers behind his back.

1ST: Mammy knowed this,
  And she knowed that the only way

3RD: To make that Hairy Man go away
  And never come another day

2ND: Was to fool him one more time.

1ST, 2ND, 3RD: Soooo,

1ST: Mammy said to the Hairy Man,

MAMMY: Hairy Man!

1ST: said she. (*Duel begins between Mammy and Hairy Man.*)

MAMMY: Hairy Man!

HAIRY MAN: Yasm.

MAMMY: Hairy Man!

HAIRY MAN: Yasm.

MAMMY: Come on in; he's there in the bed.

2ND: The Hairy Man come in and went to the bed

3RD: And pulled back the covers.

HAIRY MAN: Hey!

3RD: he said.

HAIRY MAN: Hey!

1ST: he said, swelling up real big,

HAIRY MAN: They's nuthin here but a little ole pig!

MAMMY: Well,

2ND: said Mammy,

MAMMY: ain't it a baby?

HAIRY MAN: Well,

3RD: said the Hairy Man,

HAIRY MAN: ah reckon—*maybe.*

MAMMY: And ain't it mine?

HAIRY MAN: That ah ain't denyin.

MAMMY: Well,

1ST: said Mammy,

MAMMY: like ah said,
That there's mah baby in that bed.

1ST, 2ND, 3RD, MAMMY, WILEY: Well . . .

1ST: The Hairy Man raged—

MAMMY: And the Hairy Man yelled—

2ND: And the Hairy Man stomped—

3RD: And the Hairy Man *guh*-nashed his teeth.

ALL: *Guh*-nashed his teeth.

WILEY: Then he grabbed up the pig
And he swore with a roar
As he tore out the door,
And the path that he made
In his wrath through the glade
Never growed no trees no more,
Never growed no trees no more.

(*Exit Hairy Man through audience; Chorus sings a reprise of the last
two lines to the tune of "It ain't gonna rain no more."*)

1ST: Then Wiley he come down from the attic
And hugged his ole Mammy, and said,

WILEY: Mammy, Mammy!

1ST: said he.

WILEY: Mammy!

MAMMY: Yassuh.

WILEY: Mammy!

MAMMY: Yassuh.

WILEY: Ah reckon that ole Hairy Man won't never be comin round
here no mo.

3RD: And I reckon he never did.

1ST: Cause Wiley and his Mammy.
Had fooled that Hairy Man three times.

(*All celebrate in dance and song. Noise from Hairy Man stops cele-bration. Hairy Man begins to approach stage.*)

1ST: But—if you're ever out in the woods,

3RD: And you happen to look up—

1ST, 2ND, 3RD, MAMMY, WILEY: Don't be surprised if you happen to see,
A-comin through the trees,
A-comin through the trees,

(*Whisper.*)

Don't be surprised if you happen to see

2ND: The Hairy Man,

3RD: The Hairy Man,

WILEY: The hairy, scary face of the Hairy Man,

1ST: The scary,

2ND: stary,

3RD: hairy,

WILEY: very hairy

3RD: and unmerry,

MAMMY: most unordinary face (*Hairy Man enters.*)

HAIRY MAN: Of the Hairy Man,

MAMMY, WILEY: the Hairy Man,

ALL: The hairy, hairy, HAIRY MAN!

CURTAIN

Johnny Moonbeam
and the Silver Arrow
Joseph Golden

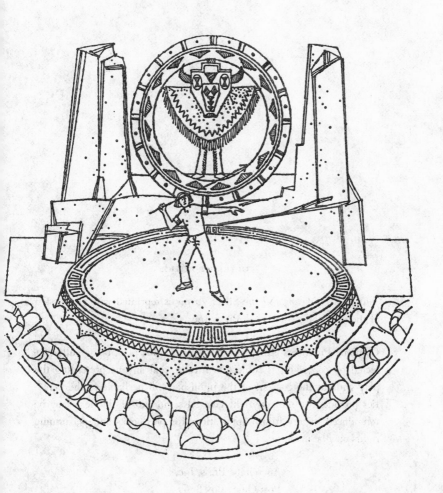

Joseph Golden's *Johnny Moonbeam and the Silver Arrow* is the story of an Indian boy's efforts to earn the coveted silver arrow of his tribe. The plot is told in two ways: through the voice of the only speaking character, a narrator; and through dance and mime that is performed by Johnny, a Medicine Man who gives him his instructions, and three Indian gods who test him. In the ceremony that begins his test, Johnny learns from the Medicine Man that he must make a long journey alone to find the gods and from them he must win rain, fire, and maize.

After three increasingly difficult confrontations Johnny indeed wins the prizes, but on the long trip home the boy is approached by three needy beggars to whom he gives his awards. As he faces the Medicine Man empty-handed, three beggars appear and throw off their ragged cloaks to reveal that they are the gods. The Medicine Man proudly presents Johnny with the silver arrow, for he is now a man, whose tribe admires not only his courage but his concern for the suffering of his fellow men.

Although no specific tribe is named, the story seems to have been derived from the lore of the nomadic Plains Indians. As the narrator speaks, the actors create the plot through mime and dance. The movement can be choreographed to suggest Indian rituals, from the intense, formal scenes with the Medicine Man that are accompanied by insistent drumbeats, to the scenes of physical combat between Johnny and each god that are accented by percussion and threatening shouts. The narrator, a frontiersman or trapper, watches and encourages the Indian boy in his quest, and may occasionally become so involved in the action that he moves deeply into the acting area.

The production will be improved by eliminating anachronistic terms such as *hot dog, 12-alarm fires, furnace, etc.* Substitution of the word *Indian* for *Injun* is also desirable.

The play can be performed on a bare stage enhanced by lighting, and the tension can be greatly increased by accompanying drumbeats and music. Except for the narrator's garments, the costumes should be based on authentic Indian clothing, both ordinary and ceremonial.

JOHNNY MOONBEAM AND
THE SILVER ARROW

CHARACTERS

Narrator
Johnny Moonbeam
Medicine Man
Rain God
Fire God
Earth God

SETTING

Indian village and surrounding countryside.

TIME

The nineteenth century.

The curtain opens slowly, accompanied by a distant and incessant throb of drums. For a moment the stage is in darkness, with only the sound of the tom-toms breaking the emptiness. A sharp shaft of white light slowly dims up revealing the Narrator, who is perched on the stage apron. His dress may be an odd combination of costumes. It is meant to suggest that while he is essentially a part of the stage picture, fully capable of thrusting himself into the heart of the action on Johnny's behalf, he is also identified with the audience. He is a virile, earthy character, but he can consort with moonbeams, moving nimbly among them, because he spins the dreams common to all boys. When the beam of light is up full he gestures to indicate that he is listening intently.

NARRATOR: Sh-sh! Listen!

(He listens intently again, turning his head fully to all sides to indicate that the sound of the drums is all around him.)

Ya hear that? Injuns! All around us. Ya can't take five steps in any direction but you'll run smack into an Injun standin' there with a head full of feathers, all proud and strong, with a tomahawk in his hand, and a quiver full o' arrows. He'll be searchin' the night sky, or countin' stars, maybe, just like you do. Or he'll be settin' in a cool beam o' moonlight, like I'm doin' right now feelin'—oh, I don't know, sorta lonely maybe, but also feelin' kinda strong and proud 'cause he's got this beam o' moonlight all to himself. Like livin' in a small, round, white house with a great big dark outside.

(The drums stop suddenly. Narrator tries to peer into the darkness around him. Suddenly a voice, apparently from nowhere in particular, breaks the silence. It is a male voice, chanting a strange incantation. It is a powerful voice, rich and melodic.)

There. You hear? The ceremony's 'bout to begin. So hold on tight to your seats 'cause only Injuns are supposed to know about this. It's a strange sort of ceremony . . .

(A blue light begins to dim up slowly at center stage, revealing a boy kneeling before a grotesquely ornamented Medicine Man.)

. . . strange and powerful. Happens only once a year in this tribe and then only when the moon gets hooked on a crag of one of those steep cliffs out there on the horizon. And when the prairie is dark and cool on such a night, the chief Medicine Man sets up a lonesome kind of music—just like you hear him doin' right now . . .

(The Medicine Man's arms are raised and are describing arcs in the air, slowly, eerily. On the circle of light are four—or any number— other persons, barely visible.)

What's it all about? Well, if you're not an Injun it might be hard to understand, 'cause you and me, well, we act and think different. But this is the night when Johnny Moonbeam's gotta go in search of the Silver Arrow!

(The chanting stops abruptly. The Medicine Man is handed a small colored wooden bowl. During the following speech by the Narrator, the Medicine Man holds the bowl aloft over Johnny's head, weaving

intricate patterns with a free hand. He then places the bowl on the ground and begins to dance around the boy, shaking feathery sticks and rattles.)

Well, it's not exactly a search. But it's a way the tribe has of makin' a twelve-year-old boy prove he's ready to be treated like a man. The Silver Arrow is . . . well, it's sort of a symbol, kind of a sign you get if everything's done all right. And this is the night for Johnny Moonbeam. It's gonna be a big night, a lonely night. A night full of danger for Johnny Moonbeam. He's got things to do. Not easy things like pickin' a quart of blueberries, or jumpin' off a tree, or wrasslin' with a tiger. Why any good Indian can do that! What Johnny's got to do is . . . Oh-oh! Watch. The Medicine Man's gonna give him final instructions.

(The drum starts again, slowly and softly at first, and gradually building up as the three assignments are given. The Medicine Man dips his hands into the bowl and scatters droplets of water up into the air. He repeats this three times whirling about each time he flicks the water off his fingers. Suddenly, he reaches out and snatches at an imaginary falling drop. He clutches it to his chest, bends over to conceal it, then turns and twists within the group to suggest that he has stolen something and is running away with it. He stops abruptly—as do the drums —and points at Johnny.)

Oh-oh! 'Fraid of that. Johnny's gonna have to search the land, and the mountains, and behind all the clouds in the sky he can grab hold of. Johnny's gonna have to search all the dark corners of the night. He's gonna have to find the Rain God!

(Johnny shakes his head "no" and rises to one knee, a fearful and perplexed look on his face.)

Not only find 'im, but steal rain from the Rain God!

(The drums start again, a bit louder this time. The Medicine Man crouches opposite Johnny and begins to collect bits of wood from the ground. He is building an imaginary fire.)

Do ya think Johnny knows where the Rain God lives? Not a bit! Why, he could live where the water trickles out of the sides o' mountains, or up where icebergs melt, or where fierce dark clouds seem to hang like a scary roof at the tops o' trees. Anywhere at all. Wherever there's water. But Johnny's gotta find 'im and steal the rain away from 'im! It's a big thing to do for one Johnny's age . . . but it's only the first thing. To get the Silver Arrow is like learnin' to start your life all over again. Watch now. The Medicine Man is showin' Johnny the second thing he's gotta do.

(*The Medicine Man has finished assembling and stacking the wood for the "fire." He stands back slightly and sets a "torch" to it. With gestures and movements of his body, he indicates the upsweep of the flames, their heat and awesomeness. He stalks the fire, suddenly lunges at it, seems to encircle the flame with his arms, tears it from the wood, and runs off with it. He abruptly turns to Johnny and points. The drums stop.*)

Whoever heard of such a thing? Whoever in this world! You saw it. You saw what that Medicine Man expects Johnny to do. That boy's gonna have to dig deep into the earth, or twist the tail of a lightnin' bolt or shut the blazin' sun up in a bottle. 'Cause he's gotta go out into the gloomy forest and find the Fire God!

(*Johnny rises from his kneeling position, stumbles back a step, and falls into a sitting position. Again shaking his head.*)

And he's gotta *steal* the fire from the orangey scorching hands of the Fire God and bring it back. First the rain, now the fire. Why, that's like tryin' to steal the purr from kittens or the nose right off the elephant's face! But the Silver Arrow's mighty important to Johnny. And if it takes him all the days and all the nights and all the cool breezes that blow across the prairie, why he'll have to do it! And bring back the rain, and bring back the fire. And then he'll—

(*Drums again. Stronger and more insistent. The Medicine Man starts by making wide gestures with his arms, as if indicating the shape of the earth. He is handed a second bowl. He follows this with movements suggesting the sowing of seeds. He traces the fall of a single seed, kneels beside it, and by a series of hand motions, urges it to sprout. It does, very quickly, and he follows its growth upward until it becomes a tall sturdy plant. He looks about furtively, takes the "plant" in both hands, wrenches it from the ground, and suggests that he is running off with it. He again turns to Johnny and points sternly. The drums have reached their climax here and stop suddenly.*)

Well, I never saw the like! Never since this old hat I got holdin' my hair down got dented and bent. And that was a long time before you got born. But there it is. The third thing Johnny's got to do to win the Silver Arrow. In every furrow a farmer turns in his earth, deep in the roots of giant trees, wherever a tiny seed warms itself and explodes in the brown soil, there Johnny will have to search for the Earth God!

(*A man and a woman, apparently Johnny's mother and father, kneel beside him to comfort him.*)

The Earth God! Wouldn't ya know it! There'll be a lot of stones to turn, Johnny, a lot of valleys and meadows and green slopes to climb. A lot of ups and downs, Johnny, 'cause the Earth God is wherever you are, and never all where you are. And when you find him, Johnny, you gotta steal the maize that grows in the earth!

(*The drums again, to the rhythm of the following lines. The Medicine Man starts some gyrations. The man and woman raise Johnny to his feet. The boy is brought to Center and is gradually left alone, the pool of light slowly narrowing around him.*)

Wet is the Rain God—
Rain you must steal, Johnny.
Warm is the Fire God—
Fire you must steal, Johnny.
Green is the Earth God—
Corn you must steal, Johnny!

Where is the Rain God?
Rain God's above the earth.
Where is the Fire God?
Fire God's within the earth.
Where is the Earth God?
Earth God's around the earth.

(*The drums stop.*)

Darts and spears and rods of steel
Will fright the morning sparrow,
    Johnny,
And blades of wicked point will mark
    the warrior,
But a *man* holds the Silver Arrow,
    Johnny!

(*Johnny is now completely alone in the pool of light. A flute is heard distantly, playing a strange melody. NOTE: Debussy's "Syrnx Suite for Solo Flute" is suggested here. Johnny begins to turn slowly peering apprehensively into the darkness surrounding him.*)

Nothin' out there but the night and the forest, Johnny. And it's all waitin' for ya. Not much moon tonight to help. Just the one beam you're standin' in. That one's yours. And it'll be waitin' for ya when ya come back. So ya better get started.

(*Johnny steps gingerly out of the protection of the moonbeam, is overcome by the darkness again, and hops back in.*)

And don't be scared of shadows, Johnny. They're awful good to hide in. So go ahead, boy!

(*The music stops. With a determined look Johnny darts off into the darkness. No sooner does he vanish than there is a low rumble of thunder, and a light flicker of lightning. The Narrator glances suspiciously off into the distance. He sets his hat a little more firmly on his head and turns up his collar.*)

I wouldn't want to be Johnny Moonbeam tonight. No, sir! Not at all. Not for a free ride on a kangaroo! Hear that rumble up in the sky? Know what it is? Thunder, you say? I guess you're right, but it's more'n that. It's that ole Rain God. He must've been squattin' on his black cloud, thinkin' o' where to shake his wet hands on next. And he must've heard the Medicine Man tell Johnny to steal the rain. Now, I know the Rain God. He can be like your best friend, the kind you'd invite into your backyard for a cold drink on a hot day. But he can also be—

(*There is a sudden clap of thunder, and another flicker of lightning.*)

There! Hear that? He's got a temper, that Rain God! As fierce and fearful as you ever saw or heard. And he's not one t' hide from the likes of a twelve-year-old boy. No, sir! He's movin' in, and he's mad . . . (*Thunder again.*) and he'll set that black cloud o' his right down on Johnny's head so's that he like to swallow up Johnny!

(*Sounds of wind and rain are heard, faintly, but steadily growing louder during the ensuing scene. Johnny's moonbeam pool begins to fade.*)

Hey, you Rain God! Leave that alone. Johnny needs that moonbeam t' find his way back! Move on! Move away! Leave the boy some light!

(*He is answered by another clap of thunder and a brighter flash of lightning. The remaining pool of light snaps off.*)

Well, looks like there's nothin' for a fella like me to do when it's rainin' but try to protect his own body a bit.

(*He reaches behind himself and picks up an umbrella. Quickly opens it. He sets it into a slot, becoming a self-supporting canopy against the "rain."*)

Johnny! Where are ya now, boy? How're you doin'? We'll find you and watch you, Johnny! We'll go where you are, 'cause we got eyes like magic lanterns and we can flash a picture of you movin' through the shadows with all the color that drips from the trees and glimmers off the rivers. Where are ya, Johnny?

(*Thunder. Suddenly the stage is bathed in blue light. It reveals two elevations on either end of the stage. Each is an irregularly stacked group of platforms representing a pile of boulders or small hills. At the peak of each there is an opening, although not immediately visible to the audience. The opening should be large enough to permit a person to rise out of the "hills." Johnny enters from L showing signs of straining against the mounting wind. The sound of rain has increased and the thunder and lightning continue intermittently. Johnny stumbles to C and tries to study the terrain.*)

Johnny, Johnny, why'd ya pick this place? Devil's Mountain just is no place for a boy! And the wind, Johnny, and all that thunder and lightnin'! Why, Satan himself wouldn't set foot on this spot!

(*Johnny starts to move curiously toward the mound at stage R. Fighting the wind and rain, he comes to the foot of it, removes a small tomahawk from his belt, and starts to circle it cautiously and apprehensively.*)

Careful, Johnny! Easy! That Rain God is everywhere! He'll streak down a gulley before you can count the ears of a rabbit. He lives in the sea and roams in the sky and visits the earth. He'll tickle the end of your nose and turn a brook into a wild thing at the same time!

(*Johnny has started to mount the mound at R, his tomahawk poised. He reaches the top and looks around. He begins moving along the edge of the uppermost level, but moving gingerly, almost fearfully, carefully placing each step and looking down as if it were a long way to the bottom.*)

Step easy, Johnny! Step easy! That's a mighty steep cliff.

(*Johnny wavers a bit.*)

Look out, boy! (*Johnny rights himself.*) Whew!

(*Johnny continues his perilous search of the hill. He has reached the summit when—suddenly—thunder, lightning, and rain cease abruptly. There is an ominous calm. Johnny drops to a kneeling position and looks fearfully around. From the hole in the L hill, a bluish white light appears, first faintly, then growing brighter. NOTE: it perhaps would be more effective if the light shone from inside the hill, but a shaft from above or behind would do equally well.*)

(*Whispering.*) Johnny! Behind ya! He's here!

(*Johnny whirls and crouches on one knee.*)

Oh, the Rain God's a clever one! He made the raindrops stream down the side of the hill, knowin' all along you'd follow it up to the top. Ya got 'im now, Johnny—or he's got you. What'll ya do now, boy?

(*Johnny quickly returns the tomahawk to his belt and removes a hunting knife. He starts to move slowly down the side of the hill in the direction of L.*)

Don't ya be a little fool, Johnny! Go carve a piece of wood with that knife or clean a buffalo skin, but you try and cut water and all you got is a rusty blade! Throw it away, boy, before it's washed clean out of your hands!

(*Johnny hesitates, looks at the knife. He discards it. At that moment, there is a low steady rumble of thunder and the Rain God begins to emerge from the top of the hill L. The Rain God is a tall, slender, impressive creature whose dress seems to sparkle and shimmer with droplets of water, all silver and blue. An expressionless mask covers his face. A glistening cape stands out from his shoulders as though in a perpetual state of being blown by a gust of wind. On his head a crown, with jagged lightning bolts as points. His hands are covered by gauntlet-type gloves that come almost to the elbows. Johnny crouches low to avoid being seen. Suddenly the sound of thunder stops. Johnny looks around surprised and curious. The Rain God actually turns away from Johnny. The boy rises slowly and starts moving cautiously toward the hill L.*)

Careful! Careful! (*Whispering.*) I told you he's a clever one! Playin' possum, that's all. He knows you're here. Think he turned off his lightnin' and rain just to make it easy for ya to sneak up on him? He's just not that kind, Johnny!

(*Johnny pauses, then drops low on all fours and begins a deliberate and determined approach to the hill.*)

I warned ya, Johnny. Can't say that I didn't boy! But go to it. And not a sound! Crawl without touchin' the ground. Move every muscle slow . . . slow, that's it! If ya let one eyelash bat against another, he'll soak ya, all over and right through, too. Make the body float on the earth, Johnny. Pull ahead again, boy . . . again, pull slow and soft!

(*Johnny has reached the base of the hill and has started to pull himself up it.*)

If ya gotta breathe, people, breathe, but don't open your mouth to make a sound.

(*Johnny is almost at the top and could, if he wanted to, touch the heels of the Rain God.*)

It's that satchel, or bag, or whatever it is hangin' 'round his neck that you want, Johnny. That's the life and power of the Rain God. A million raindrops and more are in that satchel. Easy! Easy! First try to get that rod he's holdin'. When he points it up, there's lightning. If he points it down, there's rain.

(*Johnny is making the last excrutiating reach in the hope of snatching the pouch from the Rain God. The reach seems to last forever. As his fingers are about to touch the rod, there is a sound of a sudden strong gust of wind, following by low rumbles of thunder which mount to a crescendo. The Rain God whirls on Johnny, throwing his arms up and wide as he does so. The wind increases. As the Rain God describes strange motions with the rod and seems to be rocking to and fro with laughter, the sudden gust of wind knocks Johnny off his perch and hurtles him, fighting all the way, to the opposite side of the stage.*)

Now you'll have to fight it, Johnny! Why, he's even laughin' at you! I warned ya, Johnny! And I can't blame him for laughin'. What's a twelve-year-old boy doin' fightin' with the Rain God! Go home, boy! You still got time! You might be riskin' your life t' get that Silver Arrow. A whole basket full o' silver arrows wouldn't be worth it! Go home, Johnny!

(*Johnny stares at the Rain God for a moment as if trying to determine his course of action. Out of the corner of his eye, he catches sight of the knife he threw aside. Suddenly, he lunges for the knife and, despite the strong wind, makes an effort to cross toward the Rain God.*)

No, Johnny! Put the blade away. You can't fight him with steel! All you'll do is make him—

(*As though to complete the sentence, there is a clap of thunder. The Rain God freezes into a position of defiance and anger. Slowly his arm sweeps around as he gradually brings the rod to point directly at Johnny. As the arm moves, the thunder quickly subsides and the sound of rushing water is heard.*)

I told ya, Johnny! I told ya! He's boilin', rushin' mad, and he'll tear open the heavens and fill this place with water so deep you'll think you're a fish sleepin' on the bottom of the sea!

(*The sound of water a little louder. Johnny looks around apprehensively and begins to slosh his way heavily through the quickly rising "water."*)

It's gettin' deeper fast, Johnny! It's up to your belt already. I might have to be gettin' out of here pretty quick myself! Save yourself, boy! Climb up on that hill.

(*Johnny is struggling against the rushing water, but instead of heading for the hill, "dives into" the water and tries to swim across toward the Rain God. His struggle is Herculean. With each sweep of the Rain God's arms and point of his rod, the sound of rushing water gets louder. The blue light that bathes the stage flickers, as though to reinforce the swell and churning of the water. Johnny's strokes are strenuous, he rolls, goes under sometimes, but keeps thrashing away, trying to reach the Rain God's hill.*)

If I ever tell the story of Johnny Moonbeam and the Silver Arrow again, nobody'll believe me. That water's foamin', and churnin' and twistin' like a wild panther, billowin' and kickin' like a horse stung by a bee! And that boy's in there swimmin' for his life just to steal the rain from that ornery Rain God! Well, if you must, then swim, boy, swim for your life! He's got plenty of rain, but you got the fight of a wild elephant!

(*Johnny continues the fight and is within two or three strokes of the hill when—*)

Johnny! Comin' down the gully behind ya! It's a big hunk of tree torn out by the storm! Comin' at ya, boy! Look out!

(*Johnny thrashes his arms to look behind him, sees what's coming, starts to dive under the water, twists and turns, but it's apparently too late. After trying to ward off the tree wih his arms, he seems to be hit by it, holds his head, moves dazedly, crumples to his knees, then rolls onto his back. He lies there motionless. With a sharp gesture, the Rain God lowers his arm. The sound of water quickly diminishes . . . Low distant wind. A trace of thunder.*)

Johnny! Johnny! Get up, boy. That hunk o' tree! I thought it was going to miss you, boy. Ya just gotta get up, Johnny. I got more to say! This story's not over yet! Johnny . . . you all right?

(*The Rain God starts moving down the side of the hill toward the fallen boy.*)

Look here, you Rain God! I don't care if you're the god of puppy dogs, or rattlesnakes or of all the Indian gods rolled up into one big ball! If you harmed that boy I'll just plain stop talkin' and start doin'! Y'hear?

(*The Rain God flicks his hand in the general direction of the Narrator and there is a sharp rumble of thunder.*)

Well, come ta think of it, I'm not much good at doin'. But I'm boilin' mad!

(*The Rain God has reached Johnny and slowly kneels beside him.*)

I'm sorry, Johnny. I know what that Silver Arrow meant to you, boy. But I'm proud just the same. You got closer to that demon Rain God than anybody ever did. Why you—

(*As the Rain God is about to touch Johnny, the boy suddenly rolls over, snatching the rod from the God's hand as he rolls.*)

What—! Well, I'll be—! I knew this story wasn't over yet! Now drive him back, Johnny!

(*Johnny leaps to his feet, runs to take up a position on the hill R. The Rain God starts to lunge toward the boy, but Johnny brandishes the rod at him.*)

Up, boy! Hold it up! Straight to the sky! Make those black clouds gnash their teeth together and spit a little lightning!

(*Johnny's arms shoot upward and he waves the rod frantically. The lights flicker and there is a sharp roll of thunder. The Rain God stops abruptly and bends slightly as though in pain. He rubs his hands over his arms and shoulders and chest. He turns, bent a little further and begins to stagger and reel slightly in the direction of his hill. There is heard a crackling, breaking sound.*)

You got him goin', boy! And listen! Hear that? Why that Rain God is dryin' up inside, like a dried up old log! Ya beat him, Johnny!

(*The Rain God is working his way up to the hole from which he emerged, stumbling and groping as he goes.*)

(*Suddenly.*) Great serpent-tail comets, Johnny! Don't just stand there. That stick in your hand only *makes* the rain, but you ain't got the rain itself!

(*Johnny quickly lowers the rod and is ready for action again, but doesn't quite know where to act.*)

You think you can *drink* that stick you're holdin'? Or float a canoe on it? The Medicine Man said to get rain! Find it, boy, hurry up!

(*Johnny runs down off the hill toward the Rain God and, somewhat apprehensively, tries to examine him at close range. The God has reached the peak of his hill and is starting to lower himself back into his hole. Johnny is becoming frantic. As the Rain God is about halfway down, Johnny's hand suddenly comes upon the small raindrop-shaped pouch hanging from the Rain God's neck.*)

That's it! That's it! Snatch it off, boy! If that Rain God gets swallowed up in the belly of that mountain, you're done! He's not goin' *into* the mountain, he's startin' to *be* the mountain! Only his head and neck are left. Get it, boy!

(*Johnny is struggling to remove the pouch from around the Rain God's neck but is having an awful time doing it. The neck and then the head of the Rain God are slowly swallowed up so that Johnny has to reach deep into the hill, grunting and panting and thrashing his feet. Finally, triumphantly, he pulls out his hand, stands, and holds the pouch high. The bluish white light from the hill vanishes.*)

Oh, Johnny, ya have no idea what it's like for a mortal man like me to see and tell what you just done! Stealin' the rain from the Rain God. Imagine! Why, men have been scared right out of their wits and

washed right out of their homes by the Rain God. But you didn'
scare, Johnny! No, sir! Ya hunted 'im, ya found 'im, and ya stole th
rain from the Rain God!

(*With an ecstatic leap, Johnny returns to the ground, leaping and skip*
ping about like a twelve year old might when something exception
has happened to him.)

Whoa down, boy!

(*Johnny stops and cocks his head to listen.*)

You stole the rain, sure enough. But when you took it from the Rai
God, didn't ya steal it from *everybody*?

(*Johnny looks puzzled and a bit confused. He studies the rod an*
pouch a moment. He quickly rejects his troubled feeling. For a few m
ments he revels in what he has accomplished. He takes a little sip fro
the pouch, then a long drink, and it very obviously satisfies him. H
enjoys the power of the rod by flashing it around, pointing to differer
parts of the heavens and causing lightning to flicker in the sky. And i
a cocky display, he falls to the floor and holds the rod between his fee
pointing it and sweeping it across the sky.)

All right, boy. Enjoy it! Ya worked hard enough, dodgin' lightni
bolts, swimmin' in that boilin' flood, bein' knocked around by a win
that slapped ya like a giant's hand!

(*Johnny suddenly sits up, places the pouch around his neck, tucks th*
rod in his belt. He gets to his knees and looks around. Everything is s
lent. He wipes his forehead as though becoming very warm. He press
his hands against the earth, and withdraws them quickly as if the eart
were hot to the touch. He rises and peers into the bluish darkne
around him. A faint sound of crackling, as though from a distant fir
begins to be heard.)

You're right, boy. I feel it, too. Like someone opened the door of a b
furnace and you put your face near it. (*Mopping his brow.*) Whev
All this umbrella is doin' is makin' the heat collect in one place! (*H*
takes it out of its socket and closes it.)

(*The bluish light begins to fade slowly and is gradually replaced by*
reddish glow. Johnny moves left, examining the earth and rocks, sti
finds it hot and getting hotter.)

Hoo! I'm beginnin' to feel like a pancake ready to be flipped over and browned on the other side! Well, I suppose you know, boy. You know who's nearby.

(*Johnny turns abruptly and begins searching with more fear and energy. The reddish glow is becoming more intense. Johnny is looking everywhere.*)

It's the Fire God, Johnny! Fire and water don't mix. But these Indian gods stick together. You hurt one and the other'll come a runnin'. And you sure hurt one of 'em. Whew! I don't know if I can take much more o' this! (*He picks up a fan and tries to cool himself.*)

(*Johnny, after searching L, is backing toward R.*)

This is why ya came out alone into the night, Johnny Moonbeam. Alone in this fearful dark forest. Ya got three of your gods to face. Ya ready for the second?

(*Johnny has backed up till he is at the foot of the hill L. At this moment, as the crackling sound becomes louder, the whole of the L hill seems bathed in glowing red light, much more strongly than the rest of the stage. A torch, on a long black rod, is suddenly thrust from the hole on top of the hill. And as quickly, the Fire God emerges. Of medium height, slender, wiry, the Fire God seems clad in flame that is reaching upward. He is masked also and wears a crown with yellow, orange, and red points that seem to swirl together. In the center of his chest is a large red stone, hanging like a pendant.*)

Johnny, if ya move a muscle, he'll scorch your ears off!

(*Johnny freezes, afraid to look over his shoulder. The Fire God bends and twists, as a flame itself might, to study the boy more closely. Slowly he raises his torch and points it at Johnny as though preparing to hurl a spear.*)

He's gettin' ready to throw fire at ya, boy. The heat of a dozen suns is in his torch. It'll turn a mountain into a boilin' stream of yellow jelly. You'll just go poof! and there won't be any more Johnny Moonbeam. He's rared back! Look out, Johnny! Duck!

(*Johnny ducks. The shaft goes over his head and lands in the center of the stage. Johnny scrambles away, then leaps to grab the torch for himself. He scarcely has his hands on it than the heat of the staff causes him to drop it. The Fire God leaps from the hill and proudly reclaims the torch.)*

Try to tie the tails of wildcats or make an elephant sit on a teacup, but ya just can't hold fire, Johnny!

(Pointing the torch at Johnny, the Fire God moves gracefully yet menacingly toward him. Shielding his face with his arms, Johnny recoils, turns, stumbles in his efforts to escape the determined thrusts of the torch.)

Keep away from it, Johnny! Bend and twist and jump for your life! Don't wave your arms, boy! You'll just fan the flame and make the Fire God hotter than before!

(Johnny continues to dodge the thrusts of the torch. He stumbles and falls at C, dazed and helpless from the heat. Weaving a simple pattern of encirclement, the Fire God dances grotesquely around the fallen boy, touching the torch to different parts of the floor—stones or small mounds—causing glowing fires to start. Johnny looks up, sees what is happening, struggles to his feet and tries to beat out a few of the lesser blazes with his feet.)

Oh, Johnny, you're wastin' your strength! Those ain't little fires you're tryin' to beat out, that's all the fire on the earth, and all the fire in the earth. They're sunspots, Johnny, volcanoes, 12-alarm fires!

(The Fire God has completed his circle of fire and starts to approach Johnny directly.)

You'll never get it now, boy! You'll never get that red stone that's hangin' in the middle of his chest. That's where the fire starts. That *is* fire. You just can't steal it from him!

(Johnny crouches and makes a determined lunge at the Fire God. The God sweeps the torch near him, sending Johnny rolling away toward the hill L. A few whirls and leaps and the Fire God has Johnny pinned down to the side of the hill.)

Keep movin', boy! You're gonna end up like a hotdog on the end of a stick unless ya keep movin'! Higher! Get up higher!

(Once again Johnny scrambles away from the Fire God and stands breathlessly at the top of the hill. The Fire God, now no longer playing with his prey, moves in.)

Oh, Johnny, your dream of that Silver Arrow is goin' to go up in a puff of smoke, and you're gonna go up with it! That Fire God made this earth, Johnny. He melted rock and caused mountains to split the crust of the earth and shove craggy shoulders into the sky! He burns and rages through the world with a fierce anger that makes whole cities tremble! There's nothin' to stop him, Johnny! Nothin' in the whole world!

(*Johnny cowers on his knees at the top of the hill, his arms covering his face. The Fire God is almost upon him and is ready to bring his torch down on his head.*)

That Fire God is gettin' me all burned up too! There is somethin', Johnny. Drown him! You've stolen rain! Drown him! Douse him and his fire in a great ocean of water!

(*Johnny just barely escapes the falling torch as he pulls the Rain God's rod from his belt and waves it in circles in the air. Flashes of lightning and rumbles of thunder.*)

Use your head, boy! before he singes your nose! Fire and lightnin' are old friends. Drown him! Point that stick down!

(*Dodging another lunge by the Fire God, Johnny points the stick down. The flashes and thunder stop. Abruptly, the sound of water is heard. The Fire God hesitates, looks around fearfully. Somewhat successful, Johnny continues to thrust the rod downward and the sound of water increases. The Fire God dashes off the hill and by his chaotic movements we see him caught in an eddy of rushing "water." He flails about, trying to hold the torch aloft. Suddenly, we hear a hissing sound, the sound of fire being quenched by water. The Fire God writhes in agony.*)

What a sweet sound! Hear it! That old Fire God is sputtering and sizzling, and burnin' out! You're drownin' him in the drops of the Rain God! Soak him, Johnny!

(*Johnny continues to point the rod down and finds he has to retreat to a bit higher on the hill to escape the water himself. The torch drops from the Fire God's hand and Johnny leaps into the water to grab it. With the sound of hissing continuing in the background, the Fire God struggles to return to the top of the hill from whence he came.*)

Don't let him get too far, Johnny! That stone! That red stone on his chest! There'll be no Silver Arrow for Johnny Moonbeam without the red stone. Get it fast, boy, before he turns into a puff of purple smoke!

(*Johnny scrambles after the Fire God and reaches him as he is about to reenter the hole at the top of the hill. He places his hand on the stone and withdraws it abruptly, thrusting his fingers in his mouth to show that the stone is still hot.*)

He got a little fire in him yet, eh? You still got all the water in the world, Johnny!

(*Johnny leaps off the hill, scoops up a handful of water and returns just in time to spill it on the chest of the rapidly sinking Fire God. As the water hits the stone, there is a large hiss, and the God disappears, leaving Johnny alone on the hill, holding the large red stone. The sound of hissing stops.*)

Johnny, you're holdin' in your hand a fierce and frightful thing.

(*Johnny looks up curiously.*)

You stole the fire. It's just a little stone to you . . .

(*Johnny looks at it proudly, then hangs it around his neck.*)

but it's somethin' to read by, somethin' to warm up with, somethin' to make great engines pound and heave and turn a chunk of stone into a great steel bird that makes the clouds shiver. You stole fire, sure enough. But when ya stole it from the Fire God, didn't ya also steal it from *everybody?*

(*Johnny looks quizzically in the direction of the Narrator. A low, distant sound of wind is heard.*)

That wind, Johnny. It's blowin' over all the earth now and pickin' up dry leaves and velvety soft flowers turned all to dust. Rivers and lakes are bein' sucked dry and all the oceans from here to India and back are becomin' dusty fields. And it's a cold wind, boy. 'Cause you stole the rain and stole the fire. Not since the world was made, Johnny, have things changed so much!

(*Johnny moves about, troubled. He listens to the wind for a moment. He looks at the rod and the torch. He shrugs airily and ignites a small red glow with the torch and indicates his pleasure at this feat. He then points the rod at it, and it goes out. Tucking the rod and torch back into his belt, Johnny begins stalking and searching for this third assignment.)*

One more thing to do. One more of his Indian gods to track down, the Earth God. So step easy, Johnny. 'Cause every step ya take brings ya closer to him. With every step, you're walkin' on him!

(There is a low rumble. The disturbance is strong enough to cause the Narrator's stand to tremble and Johnny to stagger and drop to one knee. Another rumble, throwing Johnny to the floor and making him hold on to the base of the hill L.)

Hey! Hold on! Calm down! You're about to shake me clean off my chair. It's the Earth God, Johnny. You can bet he's hurt and angry. Without rain and fire, he's limpin' along but got enough fight to make a mountain sink or cause an—

(Another deep rumble.)

Like that! Cause an earthquake! He won't drown ya or burn ya! No, sir. That Earth God is gonna rip open a seam down the side of the earth and swallow you up. Oh, that Medicine Man sure set you a task, Johnny. Playin' tag with a wild horse'll seem like baby stuff to ya after tonight!

(Johnny runs to R in search of the Earth God. As he peers into the darkness, the Earth God appears from behind the hill L, accompanied by a low rumble. Earth God is a sturdy creature, wearing deep green and brown, with seared branches and twigs growing out from all parts of his body so that, if motionless, he looks like a blasted tree. Around his neck, like a pendant, he wears a small ear of Indian corn. He carries a forked stick in his hands, like a divining rod. He sees Johnny and freezes, so that one might almost think him a peculiarly shaped and twisted tree standing on a double trunk. Continuing his search, Johnny backs into the Earth God, getting prodded in the back by one of the protruding branches. Johnny whirls, stares at the figure, and studies him closely.)

Funny trees grow in this forest, don't they, Johnny? Take that one you're starin' at. Looks so bleak and blasted, like a cold and dried up sassafras bush. Be careful, boy. Looks a little suspicious to me.

(Johnny takes hold of one of the branches on the Earth God and is about to chop at it with his tomahawk, when the Earth God suddenly

breaks his position causing Johnny to be thrown off balance and fall to the ground.)

Look out for him, Johnny. He can tear open holes in the earth or make mountains crumble into little pieces and roll down on your head.

(*Johnny scrambles to his feet and momentarily retreats. The Earth God removes the corn from his neck and dangles it enticingly before Johnny, moving in slow circles, provoking Johnny into action.*)

He wants ya t' come after him, Johnny. Lookit what he's holdin'. That's what ya come for, boy. That ear o' corn. Of all that the Earth God holds, nothin's stronger or greater than his power to push green stalks of corn out of the ground and feed a million mouths. But watch that stick he's carryin'. Watch it, boy!

(*Still taunting Johnny, the Earth God moves in closer to the boy. Johnny's courage grows, and he moves into position for the battle. Now only a few feet apart, Johnny is set to lunge. As he does so, the Earth God sweeps the stick in front of him, close to the ground. There is a terrific rumble and Johnny falls into a deep "pit." The Earth God quickly steps aside and peers down at the boy triumphantly.*)

He did what I warned ya he'd do, Johnny. He made the earth open and swallow a mouthful of Johnny Moonbeam. (*Straining forward on his stool.*) Can ya crawl out of there, boy? Hurry up or he'll make that mouth snap shut!

(*Johnny starts to climb out of the hole. The God, alert for more action, prepares himself for another earth splitting. Johnny makes a series of lunges, but all to no avail, for the rod of the Earth God is swift and the boy falls into two or three crevasses. The God mounts one of the hills, tears loose a few "boulders," and hurls them at Johnny who frantically dodges each one. Johnny begins to back away, putting on a great act of being frightened by the Earth God.*)

Johnny! Ya stole rain, and ya stole fire! You're not gonna let a few holes in the ground or a few rocks and boulders stop ya now, are ya? That Silver Arrow's not for cowards, boy! Ya gotta stand up, even if it means fallin' down a few times!

(*But Johnny continues to back away, running from the Earth God first in spurts and then in long dashes, the God in hot pursuit. On one such dash, Johnny suddenly drops to his knees, causing the God to stumble and fall over the boy. Before the Earth God can regain his stand,*

Johnny pounces on him and snatches the stick and ear of corn. With the prizes in his hand, Johnny runs quickly to hill L to see what effect he has had on the Earth God.)

Oh, that was clever and sly, Johnny! Even a God'll stumble on the prank of a twelve year old! Ya outdid him, and ya stole the maize. Don't stand around now. There are gulleys and hills and dark plains to cross before you get back to that Medicine Man and show him what ya done.

(But Johnny chooses to linger a moment and watch as the Earth God, now stripped of rain, fire, and plant life, makes a feeble effort to regain his power. But it is useless. He seems to shrink, and plants protruding from his body bend and droop. As a last flourish of triumph, Johnny brandishes the stick at him and with a low rumble, the Earth God staggers off. The green light snaps off, leaving the stage in a bluish white light. Johnny is exultant.)

He's gone now. And ya got no more gods to face. Rain, fire, and maize are in your hands, Johnny. All the things, all the forces that suck the breath of life. You're the strongest boy in the world, now, Johnny!

(In his glory, Johnny runs off the hill to bathe in his moonbeam, a shaft of light that has crept up at C. The sound of drums begins to be heard, faintly.)

You are rain and you are the fire, and you are the corn that ripens and points to the sun. You're all the gods rolled up into one. I just can't believe it! For a boy your age, Johnny, all those gods sure roll up nice and neat.

(The drums become a bit louder, attracting the attention of Johnny and the Narrator.)

They know, Johnny. Hear it? Medicine Man's waiting. Ya got rain, fire, and maize. But that Silver Arrow's still waitin'. So run, boy! A lot of night will seem mighty short when ya tell 'em about the gods ya faced. So run!

(With a quick look of triumph, Johnny darts off L. His moonbeam remains.)

(Looking up at the shaft of light.) Just us two, huh? Left alone in this gloomy corner of the world, marvellin' at that boy. You know him better'n I do, moonbeam. You proud of him, too?

(*The shaft of light blinks three times.*)

Knew you would be! So am I. But aren't ya just a little worried?

(*Again the light answers by three blinks.*)

'Fraid of that. I know you can't say too much, moonbeam. Just yes 'n
no. But tell me: think Johnny can handle all that power he's got?
(*Pause.*) Well, now, don't be afraid to answer. I only last long enough
for this story to be told, and I sure won't tell anybody what you said.
How about it? Can he handle it?

(*The light blinks twice: no.*)

Thought so. I don't think so either. But tell me . . .

(*The light disappears.*)

Hey, come back! No, guess you won't come back. That moonbeam
may not agree with Johnny, but he's gotta go where Johnny is. Oh,
that boy! Where are ya now, Johnny? Night, blink an eye and show us
Johnny. Wind, clear all the fuzz and mist from space and show us
Johnny Moonbeam.

(*Drums have stopped, Johnny enters running. The stage, except for
the Narrator's light, is very dimly illuminated. Music: [suggested] "Big
Brave Dance" from* Reflections of an Indian Boy *by Fischer.*)

There he is! Johnny, hold on tight to the things ya stole. Don't stop or
stumble or even pause t' count fireflies. Move along, they're waitin'.

(*Johnny starts to move away, when a sharp, small beam of light comes
up quickly revealing a dark, cloaked figure huddled on the floor. There
is nothing to identify the figure as even human except for an extended
hand holding a bowl. It is the same bowl the Medicine Man used to
describe the Rain God test earlier. Johnny stops to look at the figure,
becomes curious, and moves closer to it, dropping to one knee.*)

Don't pay it no heed, Johnny! Must be one of those beggars the forest
is full of. Don't stop for him, boy! He can find water to put in that cup
of his someplace else. Get along, hurry!

(*Johnny starts to go, but stops again. The extended arm and cup are
gesturing for water pitifully. The boy is struggling with a big decision.
Suddenly, impulsively, he removes the Rain God's pouch from his
neck, and drops it in the cup. The music surges up for a moment, and
then drops.*)

Oh, Johnny, that sure was a foolish thing to do! What d'ya think that Medicine Man is gonna say now? Givin' all the rain to a beggar!

(*Johnny stands with his head bowed, his fist clenched.*)

All right, all right! Maybe the Medicine Man won't mind so much. After all, stealin' the fire and maize from those two fierce gods wasn't exactly like pickin' pansies. Ya still might qualify, so get along, and move, boy!

(*With a last glance at the dark figure, who is moving quickly off, Johnny sets out again. Another spot of light comes up in another part of the stage, revealing another huddled figure. The figure is shivering, and holds out a stick of wood to indicate he has no warmth. Johnny pauses to look at him.*)

Johnny, everybody gets a little cold at this time o' night! That's probably just one of your friends tryin' to trick ya. Don't even look at him. Let him rub a couple of trees together or scratch some stone. You need that fire to win the Silver Arrow.

(*Again Johnny starts away, but a glance back at the cold figure is too much for the boy. He removes the red stone and gives it to the figure. The music swells up again, briefly. The figure stops shivering and exits quickly.*)

I just don't know what to say, boy. All that terror and fright. Crawlin' on an earth so blazin' hot it almost fried your shoes. And you go givin' it away to some lazy beggar who'd probably jump at the name of the Fire God. I hope you're thinkin' up some mighty good excuses!

(*The light spot vanishes, and Johnny circles the stage and stumbles over a third crouched figure. A spot comes up on it. Again a dark and shrouded figure, with only one hand showing, holding an empty bowl.*)

Well, I guess that does it! You cut through the night and nearly got gulped down into the belly of the earth to tear the maize from the neck of the Earth God. And a hungry hand holds out an empty bowl and you . . . Go ahead, boy. Finish it up.

(*Johnny drops the ear of corn into the bowl. The music swells again for a moment. The third figure leaves.*)

Empty hands or full, Johnny, you gotta go back and face 'em. They'll listen, Johnny. Maybe they won't believe and maybe they won't like it, but they'll listen. All nature might have been your toy, your plaything.

Ya could have made pools to splash around in when it pleased ya. Ya might have used fire to light up all the heavens when ya hunt at night. You might have had feasts and banquets the like of which a chief or king never saw, with all that corn—and ya might have won the Silver Arrow. But what might be never will! Ya held the earth in your hands, and ya let it roll away!

(*Johnny presses his fists to his face and, thus distraught, runs off. The music stops. His moonbeam quickly reappears.*)

(*Happily.*) Well, moonbeam, what'd ya think of *that?*

(*The moonbeam flickers rapidly for a few seconds, then stops.*)

Well, I guess I have to agree with you. That Johnny Moonbeam's not a *boy,* is he?

(*Two blinks.*)

If I never tell this story again, at least I'll have lived through it once. You know what's gonna happen now? Wait! Don't answer. He's comin' back!

(*The moonbeam goes out. Drums start, low, in the background. Music: [suggested] "Squaw's Lament" from* Reflections of an Indian Boy. *Johnny enters, despondent. He reaches the center and drops to his knees. He raises his head, then his arms slowly. Some light suddenly illuminates the top of hill L, revealing the Medicine Man. Johnny looks around and sees the figure and responds to the beckoning gesture by moving to the base of the hill. The Medicine Man holds out the rain cup and asks if he has any rain to fill it. Johnny shakes his head. The Medicine Man holds out the stick of wood and asks if he has fire to light it. Again "no" from Johnny. The maize bowl is extended. A third time a negative reply. The Medicine Man stares intently at the boy, then with a sudden gesture points off into the darkness behind Johnny. The boy turns quickly and sees the three shrouded figures moving in toward him from different directions. His first reaction is fear. When they arrive fairly close to the boy, each of the three figures, in turn, thrusts out an arm. The first holds the rod of the Rain God, the second the torch of the Fire God, the third the forked stick of the Earth God. As each symbol is shown, the black cloaks drop from the figures, revealing the three gods we have met before. They raise Johnny to his feet and turn him to face the Medicine Man. Each god points his symbol of authority toward the sky in the area above the Medicine Man's head. The blue light returns, then the red, then the green. The Medicine Man holds both hands high above his head and there descends into them the large, glistening, Silver Arrow. He presents it solemnly to Johnny. The three gods back away and vanish into the darkness, their representative colored light leaving with them. The light on the Medicine Man also goes out and he, too, leaves. The Moonbeam returns at C. Music stops. Drums continue to throb in the background. Johnny is momentarily dazed by the arrow and slowly turns and reenters his beam of light.*

Johnny's parents or friends enter the fringes of light. He kneels before them, proudly showing the arrow.)

Ya see, Johnny. That old Medicine Man is a pretty smart fella. Stealin' the rain, and stealin' the fire, and stealin' the maize wasn't the real test. Why, that only got ya warmed up. Holdin' all the power of the earth is one thing, but how ya handle it is somethin' else. And you handled it right, boy! (*Looking up.*) Didn't he?

(*The beam blinks three times. Parents and friends move off, leaving Johnny alone in the pool of light.*

Flute music is heard again.

Johnny starts to rise slowly from the kneeling position, raising the arrow high into the beam of light, as if showing it to a dear friend. The light slowly fades out on the Narrator. Still holding both hands and the arrow high, the image of Johnny also fades slowly as the beam of moonlight diminishes and finally disappears. The flute continues in the darkness for a few seconds, then—)

CURTAIN

Step on a Crack
Suzan Zeder

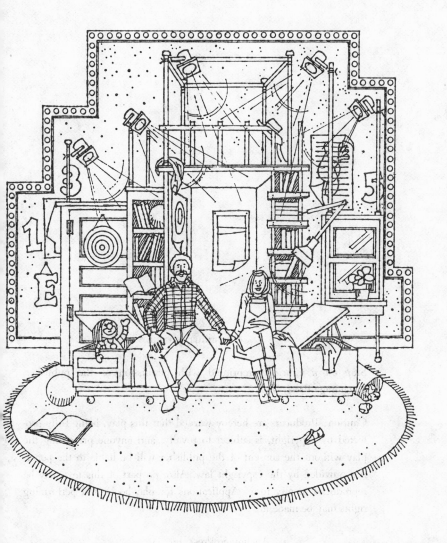

Step on a Crack is a modern play by Suzan Zeder about a ten-y
girl's adjustment to a new stepmother and, on a deeper level,
ceptance of herself. It is a play about crisis and change in a fam
about learning to face reality.

Ellie, the child, is the center of the play, and the scenes alternate between her real life and her fantasy life. As the play begins, her real life
has just been disrupted by the arrival of a new stepmother whom she
views as beautiful, talented, tidy, and intelligent. Since she considers
herself totally lacking in such attributes, acceptance of Lucille, who
Ellie believes has become her replacement in her father's affections, is
impossible. Ellie is forced to flee to her fantasy-life companions: Lana,
a glamorous, confident movie star, and Frizbee, a lovable clown who always does as Ellie bids.

Max, Ellie's father, deeply loves his daughter, but he is weak and
vacillating when discipline must be imposed. Lucille sees that Ellie
needs rules to govern her life, but her attempts to establish them are
met with loud rebellion from the unhappy Ellie. Throughout the play
"Voice," Ellie's alter-ego, speaks aloud the dark doubts, fears, jealousy,
and dislike she feels.

The situation seems to be at an impasse until Ellie sees both of her
parents desperate and sick-at-heart when they believe she has run away.
Her self-image begins to improve, she learns to control her fantasy life
as well as her deepest insecurities expressed by "Voice," and finally, she
is able to initiate a new relationship with her stepmother. She has
begun to accept herself and to risk being dependent and vulnerable.
The message that children *can* make choices that affect their lives and
can learn to like themselves is a mature one and quietly stated within
the subtext of Ellie's change.

The real characters' portrayals are enriched by the choice of language. Each one's lines clearly distinguish him from the other characters, particularly in the choice of vocabulary. Such careful delineation
does not exist, nor is it so essential, for the less developed fantasy characters.

The play requires a double setting that is comprised of Ellie's chaotic room and the family living room, which is considerably neater. The scene in a bowling alley may be pantomimed and the setting is created with lighting and sounds of the balls rolling and pins falling. The modern-dress clothing should reflect the changes in the attitudes and thinking of the three main characters, particularly Ellie. The costumes of Ellie's two imaginary companions will allow a wide leeway of choice.

STEP ON A CRACK

CHARACTERS

Ellie Murphy: A ten-year-old girl
Max Murphy: Her father, about thirty-seven
Lucille Murphy: Her stepmother, about thirty-five
Lana: Ellie's imaginary friend
Frizbee: Another imaginary friend
Voice: Ellie's alter-ego

SETTING

Ellie's house.
A bowling alley.
The streets.

TIME

The present.

The main playing space consists of two areas: Ellie's bedroom and a living room. A free-standing door separates the two areas. The set should be little more than a brightly colored framework. Each space has a ladder which is hung with the various costumes and props used throughout the play.

*Ellie's room is the larger of the two spaces. It is outlandishly deco-
rated with old pieces of junk, flags, banners, old clothes, etc., which
have been rescued by Ellie from her father's junk yard. The room is a
mess, strewn with piles of clothes and junk. Up center is a larger box
marked "Toyz." At the far side of the room there is a stool surrounded
by a simple frame. This frame indicates a mirror. This is Voice's area.
Voice never moves from this spot until the very end of the play. It
would be helpful to have a microphone and P.A. speaker here. Voice
will make all of the sound effects used during the play.*

*The living room, Max and Lucille's space, is conspicuously neat. A
coffee table and a few chairs indicate this area.*

*At Rise: Ellie, Max, Lucille, and Voice are onstage. Max holds one
end of a jumprope, the other end is tied to the set. Voice sits on the
stool. Lucille sits in the living room area. Ellie jumps as Max turns the
rope for her. She jumps for a few seconds to establish a rhythm.*

MAX: Cinderella . . . Dressed in yeller . . . Went downtown to meet
her feller. Cinderella . . . Dressed in yeller . . . Went downtown to
meet her feller. (*Max continues to chant and Ellie to jump as Lucille
speaks.*)

LUCILLE: Grace, Grace . . . Dressed in lace . . . Went upstairs to wash
her face. Grace, Grace . . . Dressed in lace . . . Went upstairs to wash
her face.

VOICE: (*Joins in.*) Step on a Crack . . . Break your Mother's back.
Step on a crack . . . Break your Mother's back. Step on a Crack . . .
Break your Mother's back! (*Ellie jumps out of the rope and hops four
times firmly.*)

ELLIE: CRACK! CRACK! CRACK! CRACK! Step on a crack, break
your STEPmother's back!

VOICE: Red Light! (*All freeze.*)

VOICE: Ellie Murphy used to be a perfectly good little girl. Green
Light! (*All come to life for a second. Max and Ellie take a few steps
toward each other.*)

VOICE: Red Light! (*All freeze.*)

VOICE: Her mom died when Ellie was just four years old, and everybody felt so sorry for her. They said "Oh you poor little girl." And they
brought her extra helpings of cake and lots of presents. Ellie lived with

her Pop, Max Murphy, boss of Murphy's Wrecking and Salvage Company. Green Light! (*During the next few lines Max and Ellie play a game of:*)

ELLIE: Not it!

MAX: Knock, knock . . .

ELLIE: Who's there?

MAX: Banana.

ELLIE: Banana who?

MAX: Knock, knock . . .

ELLIE: Who's there?

MAX: Banana.

ELLIE: Banana who?

MAX: Knock, knock . . .

ELLIE: Who's there?

MAX: Orange.

ELLIE: Orange who?

MAX: Orange you glad I didn't say banana?

VOICE: Red Light! (*All freeze.*)

VOICE: They played tag and went bowling; they ate TV dinners and practiced baseball for six years and they were very happy. Green Light! (*Ellie and Max mime practicing baseball.*)

MAX: Listen Midget, if I told you once I told you a million times, you gotta keep your eye on the ball. (*He throws an imaginary baseball, Ellie hits it and Max follows the ball with his eyes and sees Lucille.*)

MAX: Fantastic!

VOICE: Red Light! (*All freeze.*)

VOICE: About two months ago Ellie went to camp and Pop met a pretty lady who taught music. Green Light! (*Ellie and Max hug goodbye. Ellie moves up her ladder and scratches her bottom, she mimes writing.*)

ELLIE: Dear Pop, Today we went camping in the woods and guess where I got poison ivy? (*Max moves over to Lucille.*)

MAX: (*Shyly.*) Hi, my name is Max, Max Murphy.

LUCILLE: Pleased to meet you Max, I'm Lucille.

VOICE: Red Light! (*All freeze.*)

VOICE: And Pop liked Lucille and Lucille liked Pop. Green Light! (*Ellie puts a blindfold over her eyes.*)

ELLIE: Dear Pop, I can't go swimming today cause I got pink eye.

VOICE: Ellie came back from camp and everything in her whole life was different. (*Ellie, Max, and Lucille play blind man's bluff.*)

ELLIE: 5, 4, 3, 2, 1 . . . Ready or not here I come.

MAX: We're over here.

ELLIE: Where? Am I getting warmer?

MAX: Naw, you're a mile off.

ELLIE: Am I getting warmer?

VOICE: Red Light! (*All freeze.*)

VOICE: Pop and Lucille got married. Green Light! (*Max and Lucille move into wedding positions. They mime an exchange of rings and kiss.*)

ELLIE: I said am I getting warmer? Hey Pop where did you . . . (*Ellie takes off the blindfold and sees them kissing. She claps her hand over her eyes and giggles.*)

VOICE: Red Light! (*All freeze.*)

VOICE: Everything was different. Lucille cooked well-balanced meals with vegetables. She kept the house neat and sewed buttons on all Ellie's clothing. Pop liked Lucille a lot, he wanted Ellie to like her too but somewhere deep inside Ellie's head this little voice kept saying . . . Look how pretty she is . . .

ELLIE: Look how pretty she is.

VOICE: Look how neat she is . . .

ELLIE: Look how neat she is.

VOICE: Pop likes her much better than he likes you.

ELLIE: No!

VOICE: Oh yes he does! (*Ellie turns away.*)

VOICE: Ellie Murphy used to be a perfectly good little girl. Green Light! (*Max exits. Ellie moves into her room and picks up a Whammo paddleball. Lucille moves into the living room area and sets up a music stand and practices singing scales. She has a beautiful voice.*)

ELLIE: (*Hitting the paddleball.*) 235, 236, 237, 238, 239, 240, 241, 242, 243, 244, 245, 246 . . . (*Ellie misses, sighs, and starts again.*)

ELLIE: 1, 2, 3, 4, 5, 6, 7, 8, 9, 10, 11, 12, 13, 14 . . . (*Ellie misses, sighs, and starts again.*)

ELLIE: 1, 2, 3, 4, 5, 6, 7, 8, 9, 10, 11 . . . (*Ellie misses.*)

ELLIE: I'll never make 300! 1, 2, 3, 4, 5, 6 . . . (*Ellie misses. She crosses to the mirror. Voice mimes her gestures.*)

ELLIE: If I could make 300 I'd be famous. I'd be the world's champion. I'd be rich and famous and everyone in the whole world would come up to me and . . . How de do? Yes, it was very difficult, but I just kept practicing and practicing. No, it wasn't easy. (*Lucille sings louder.*)

VOICE: Considering all the racket SHE was making.

ELLIE: Considering all the racket SHE was making.

VOICE: How could anyone expect to concentrate with all that toot toot de doot.

ELLIE: How could anyone expect to concentrate with all that toot toot de doot.

VOICE: What does she think this is Grand Opree or something? (*Ellie clutches her throat and mimics Lucille; she warbles offkey.*)

ELLIE: Laaaaa . . . Laaaaaaa, Laaaaaaa, Laaaaaaa. (*Lucille hears her and stops.*)

LUCILLE: Ellinor? Did you call me?

ELLIE: No. (*Lucille resumes the scales. Ellie gets an idea. She crosses to the toy box and pulls out a weird assortment of junk; a couple of old hats, a black cloak, a deflated inner tube, silver shoes, and a set of*

Dracula fangs. Ellie dresses herself and makes a couple of menacing passes at the mirror. Voice mimics her action. Ellie sneaks out of the room and up behind Lucille.) I am Count Dracula and I have come to suck your blood!

LUCILLE: (*Startled.*) Oh my!

ELLIE: Did I scare you?

LUCILLE: You startled me.

ELLIE: What are you doing anyway?

LUCILLE: I am just running through a few scales.

ELLIE: Do you have to?

LUCILLE: Well, yes. The voice is just like any other instrument, you have to practice every day.

ELLIE: You call that MUSIC? All that toot toot de doot?

LUCILLE: Well, scales aren't exactly music but . . .

ELLIE: (*Singing very offkey.*) "Everybody was Kung Fu Fighting." Uh . . . uh . . . uh . . . uh . . . hu!*

LUCILLE: Well, ummm that's very nice but . . .

ELLIE: (*Lying on her back with feet in the air.*) "I've got tears in my ears from lying on my back crying out my eyes over you."

LUCILLE: Ellinor, what in the world are you wearing?

ELLIE: Pretty neat huh? I got this stuff from Pop, it's from the yard. He said I could keep it. You should go down there, he's got some great stuff.

LUCILLE: Oh Ellinor, you have such a nice room and so many lovely toys. Why do you keep bringing home all this junk?

ELLIE: This isn't junk! It's perfectly good stuff!

LUCILLE: But people have thrown it away.

ELLIE: That doesn't mean it isn't any good! How would you like to be thrown away?

* These songs should be constantly changed to songs that are currently popular.

LUCILLE: When I was your age I had a collection of dolls from all over the world. I used to make clothes for them and make up stories about them. You know I still have those dolls. I gave them to my brother for his children, maybe I could write to him and we could . . .

ELLIE: Dolls! Ugghhh! I like this stuff better. Besides most of it isn't mine. Most of this belongs to Lana and Frizbee.

LUCILLE: Oh?

ELLIE: This tire is for Frizbee's motorcycle and these hats and beautiful shoes are for Lana. She's a movie star and she needs these things in her work.

LUCILLE: I thought you told me she was a Roller Derby Queen.

ELLIE: She's both! Oh, the Dracula fangs . . . they're mine.

LUCILLE: Just put them away when you are through. Have you finished cleaning up your room yet?

ELLIE: Ohhh, I have been busy.

LUCILLE: You promised to do it before your father came home.

ELLIE: Pop doesn't care. He never used to make me clean up my room.

LUCILLE: Look, why don't I give you a hand. Together we can do it in no time.

ELLIE: No way! You'll just make me throw stuff out. (*Ellie walks back to her room and stands in her doorway.*)

ELLIE: Nobody gets in my room without a pass! (*She slams the door, Lucille sighs and turns back to her music.*)

VOICE: Red Light! (*All freeze.*)

VOICE: She doesn't like you. (*Ellie is drawn to the mirror.*)

ELLIE and VOICE: Pick up your room you messy little girl. Why don't you play with dolls like normal children? You're freaky and you like junk. You could have such a lovely room if it wasn't such a mess.

VOICE: She could never like a messy little girl like you. Green Light! (*Lucille resumes her scales. Ellie listens for a second and begins to mimic her. Ellie leaps to the top of the toy box and warbles in a high squeaky voice. Frizbee pops up from under a pile of dirty clothes.*)

FRIZBEE: Bravo! Bravo! What a beautiful voice you have! You sing like an angel! You sing like a bird, only better. I kiss your hand. May I have your autograph?

ELLIE: Why certainly young man! (*Ellie scribbles on his back.*)

ELLIE: "To Frizbee from Ellie, the world's greatest opera singer."

FRIZBEE: I will treasure this forever. Here this is for you! (*Frizbee pulls a flower from nowhere and presents it to Ellie.*)

LANA: (*Her voice comes from the toy box.*) Everybody out of my way. (*Ellie jumps off the box, the lid flies open and Lana pops out.*)

LANA: Ellie Murphy, the great opera singer, do you have anything to say to our viewers at home?

ELLIE: How de do.

LANA: How did you get to be such a great opera singer?

ELLIE: Oh it was very difficult. The voice is just like any other instrument you have to practice every day. (*Frizbee presents her with a bowling pin.*)

FRIZBEE: Ellie Murphy I am pleased and proud to present you with this singer of the year award.

ELLIE: Dear friends, I thank you and I have only one thing to say, I deserved it. I practiced every day . . . (*Lucille starts to sing a beautiful melody. Ellie moves toward the mirror.*)

ELLIE: I practiced until my throat was sore from singing and . . .

VOICE: Red Light! (*All freeze.*)

VOICE: You'll never be as good as Lucille. (*Voice snatches the pin away from her.*)

VOICE: She's a much better singer than you are. Green Light.

ELLIE: (*Grabs for the pin.*) This is MY prize and I deserve it! (*They struggle with the pin.*)

ELLIE: (*To Lana and Frizbee.*) Hey you guys! (*They rush to her aid. The pin is tossed in the air and Frizbee catches it.*)

FRIZBEE: Ellie Murphy, I am pleased and proud to present you with this singer of the year award.

ELLIE: Thank you for my prize. It is neat! (*There is the sound of thunderous applause. Lucille crosses to Ellie's door and knocks. The applause stops instantly.*)

LUCILLE: Ellinor? (*Lana and Frizbee freeze.*)

ELLIE: Who goes there?

LUCILLE: May I come in?

ELLIE: What's the password?

LUCILLE: Please?

ELLIE: (*Peeking out.*) Have you got a pass? (*Lucille enters and looks around.*)

LUCILLE: Who were you talking to?

ELLIE: Lana and Frizbee.

LUCILLE: (*Playing along.*) OH! Are they still here? (*Frizbee pops his head up and makes a rude sound, then disappears into the box.*)

ELLIE: Sure, Frizbee just did a raspberry.

LUCILLE: Oh? (*Lana crosses in front of Lucille making ugly faces at her.*)

ELLIE: And Lana's making faces . . . like this and this and this. . . . (*Lana goes into the toy box. Lucille crosses to the middle of the room crouches down and speaks into empty air.*)

LUCILLE: Were you two helping Ellie clean up her room?

ELLIE: Lucille, they're not here. They went into the toy box.

LUCILLE: (*Playing along a bit too much.*) Oh I see. Do they live in the toy box?

ELLIE: (*Nonplussed.*) It's too small to live in there. They just sit there sometimes.

LUCILLE: Oh. Please Ellie, let me help you. We'll have this place cleaned up in no time. Now where does this go?

ELLIE: No deal! You throw out too much! (*Ellie starts putting things away.*)

LUCILLE: Oh Ellinor, you've lost another button. I just sewed that one on too.

ELLIE: It is a scientific fact that some people are allergic to buttons. (*Ellie looks hard at Lucille.*) Hey, Lucille, how old are you?

LUCILLE: (*A bit taken aback.*) Uhhh, well, I'm thirty-five.

ELLIE: (*Very serious.*) Boy that's old.

LUCILLE: Well, it's not that old.

ELLIE: Do you use a lot of makeup?

LUCILLE: I use some.

ELLIE: A lot? Do you put that goopy stuff on your eyes to make them look big?

LUCILLE: Would you like me to show you about makeup?

ELLIE: Uhhhgg. NO! Makeup is for girlies and OLD people.

LUCILLE: Come on Ellinor, let's get this room done before your father gets home. (*Max enters with a football helmet and a feather duster for Ellie.*)

MAX: Anybody home?

ELLIE: Too late! (*Ellie runs to greet him and jumps into his arms. He gives her the helmet and duster, as Lucille enters Ellie hides them behind her back and sneaks them into her room.*)

MAX: Hey Midget.

ELLIE: Neato. Thanks. (*Lucille approaches to hug him.*)

LUCILLE: Hello dear, you're early.

MAX: Be careful, I'm a mess. I gotta wash up. (*Lucille gets him a rag. He wipes his hands and then kisses her. He sits down to take off his boots. Ellie enters with his house shoes.*)

MAX: Hey Ellie, what's the matter with your shirt? (*Max points to an imaginary spot on her shirt, Ellie looks down and Max tweaks her nose.*)

MAX: Ha! Hah! Gotcha! Can't have your nose back. Not till you answer three knock knocks . . . Let's see . . . Knock, knock . . .

ELLIE: (*With her nose still held.*) Who's there?

MAX: Dwain.

ELLIE: Dwain who?

MAX: Dwain the bathtub I'm dwouning.

ELLIE: Hey, I got one. Knock, knock.

MAX: Who's there?

ELLIE: De Gaulle.

MAX: Degaulle who?

ELLIE: (*Crossing her eyes.*) De-gaulle-f ball hit me in the head and dats why I talk dis way.

MAX: Ohhhh.

ELLIE: Oh I got another one Pop. Knock, knock . . .

LUCILLE: (*Jumping in.*) Who's there? (*Ellie shoots her a nasty look and turns away.*)

ELLIE: Nobody.

LUCILLE: (*Puzzled.*) Nobody who?

ELLIE: (*Insolently.*) Just nobody that's all! (*Max and Lucille exchange a look.*)

MAX: I've still got your nose.

ELLIE: (*Back in the game.*) Give it back you Bozo.

MAX: Nope you gotta get it. (*Max pretends to hold her nose just out of reach. Ellie jumps for it. Max tosses it to Lucille.*)

MAX: Here Lucille, catch! (*Lucille, confused, misses it.*)

LUCILLE: Huh? Oh I'm sorry. (*The game is over and Ellie scowls.*)

ELLIE: Pop, do I have to clean up my room? Can I get you a beer? Can I watch TV? Do I have to throw out all my good stuff?

MAX: Whoa! What's going on?

ELLIE: Can I watch TV?

MAX: Sure.

LUCILLE: Max, I have been trying to get her to clean up her room for days.

MAX: Awww it's Friday afternoon.

LUCILLE: Max.

MAX: Clean up your room Ellie.

ELLIE: Awww Pop, you never used to make me.

MAX: Sorry Midget. This ship's got a new captain.

ELLIE: Awww Pop!

MAX: Do what your mother says.

ELLIE: (*Under her breath.*) She is not my real mother.

MAX: What did you say?

ELLIE: Nothing.

MAX: Hey, maybe later we'll do something fun.

ELLIE: Can we go bowling?

MAX: Maybe.

ELLIE: Oh please, oh please, oh please! We used to go all the time. Pop and me, we were practically professional bowlers. We were practicing to go on Family Bowl-O-Rama, on TV.

MAX: Clean up your room and we'll talk about bowling later. (*Ellie trudges into her room. Max sits down and Lucille massages his back.*)

LUCILLE: You're early.

MAX: Yep, and I have a surprise for you.

LUCILLE: For me, Max? What is it?

MAX: You gotta guess. It's something we've been talking about. (*Ellie interrupts. She is wearing a long black cape, a tall hat, and a scarf. She holds a piece of metal pipe.*)

ELLIE: Ta Dah! Presenting the Great Mysterioso! You will see that I have nothing up my sleeve. See this pipe? See this scarf? Here hold this hat lady. (*Ellie hands the hat to Lucille.*)

ELLIE: Now I take this scarf, just an ordinary everyday magic scarf, and I put it over this piece of pipe. Now you both will blow on it. (*Max and Lucille blow on the scarf.*)

ELLIE: I say some magic words. OOOOOBLEEEDOOOO OBBBBB-LEEEDAY ZOOOOOBLEEDA! Zap! Zap! Zap! (*Ellie flips the pipe over her shoulder, it lands with a loud crash. She grabs the hat and places the scarf in it.*)

ELLIE: Presto! No more pipe! Ta Dah! (*Ellie displays the empty scarf. Max and Lucille clap.*)

MAX: I thought you went to . . .

ELLIE: I found this stuff while I was cleaning. Pretty neat huh?

LUCILLE: That was very nice Ellie.

MAX: Ellie, Lucille and I are talking.

ELLIE: What about?

MAX: ELLIE!

ELLIE: I'm going. I'm going! (*Ellie goes back to her room. Max takes some folders out of his pocket.*)

MAX: Do you remember that travel agent I said I was going to talk to?

LUCILLE: Oh Max, do you mean you did it?

MAX: Did I talk to him? Ta Dah! Little lady, you and I are going on a honeymoon. We are going to Hawaii.

LUCILLE: Hawaii? Oh Max!

MAX: Just look at this, "American Express twenty-one day excursions to Honolulu and the islands." That's our honeymoon, that is if you want to go.

LUCILLE: Want to? I have always wanted to go to those places. But can we? I mean should we? Right now?

MAX: Why not? I've been saving for a trip and I think I can take about three weeks off. Now's as good a time as ever.

LUCILLE: I'm not so sure we ought to leave Ellie right now.

MAX: She'll be fine. I can get someone to stay with her and after all she's in school. There is this lady, Mrs. Dougan, she used to stay with Ellie when I'd go on hunting trips. I'll call her tomorrow.

LUCILLE: I just don't want her to think that we are running off and leaving her.

MAX: Don't worry, I'll talk to her.

LUCILLE: Right away . . . that is if you are serious.

MAX: You bet I'm serious. I got all this stuff didn't I? Look at some of these tour deals. You get everything: air fare, meals, hotel, an air-conditioned bus . . .

LUCILLE: Oh look at that sun, and all that sand. What a beautiful beach. (*Ellie enters clutching a* TV Guide.)

ELLIE: Guess what! Midnight Spook-a-thon has a double feature tonight! *The Curse of Frankenstein* and the *Return of the Mummy's Hand!* Isn't that neat? Can I watch it, Pop?

MAX: (*Hiding the folders.*) Uhhh sure, why not.

LUCILLE: What time does it come on?

ELLIE: (*Nonchalantly.*) Oh early.

LUCILLE: What time?

ELLIE: (*Quickly.*) Eleven-thirty.

LUCILLE: That's awfully late.

ELLIE: Tomorrow's Saturday. And besides, Pop said I could.

LUCILLE: We'll see.

ELLIE: You always say that when you mean no. What are you guys doing?

MAX: We're talking.

ELLIE: (*Seeing the folders.*) What's this? (*Lucille starts to show them to her and Max snatches them away.*)

MAX: Papers, papers of mine. Ellie, is your room cleaned up yet?

ELLIE: No! Gee whiz! I'm going. I'm going! (*Ellie crosses back to her room.*)

LUCILLE: Max, why didn't you talk to her?

MAX: Oh I don't know, I just hate it when she yells.

LUCILLE: Yells? I thought you said it was going to be all right.

MAX: It is! I just have to kind of talk to her about it . . . when she's in a good mood.

LUCILLE: If you really think it is going to upset her, let's not do it now. We can always go later.

MAX: I said I was going to talk to her and I will . . . (*Max crosses to Ellie's room, Lucille follows slightly behind.*)

MAX: Ellie . . . uhhh.

ELLIE: I'm not finished yet but I'm cleaning!

MAX: Looks like you are doing a good job there. Want any help?

ELLIE: Huh? (*Ellie finds the duster and dusts everything and then starts dusting Max.*)

MAX: Ellie, umm Lucille and I . . . uhhh we were thinking that it might be a good idea if . . . if . . . we went . . . bowling! Tonight!

ELLIE: Hey, neato!

MAX: After you clean up your room.

ELLIE: I'll hurry. I'll hurry. (*Max leaves the room with Lucille shaking her head.*)

LUCILLE: Why didn't you tell her?

MAX: Let's wait until we know exactly when we're going.

LUCILLE: I don't want her to think that we are sneaking around behind her back.

MAX: I'll tell her. I just want to pick my own time. (*Ellie starts out the door.*)

VOICE: Red Light! (*Ellie freezes.*)

VOICE: Something fishy's going on. They don't want you around. They're trying to get rid of you . . . Green Light. (*Ellie stares into the mirror.*)

MAX: So that's your surprise. How do you like it?

LUCILLE: Oh Max! (*Lucille hugs him. Ellie enters.*)

ELLIE: Ahem!

MAX: What do you want?

ELLIE: I just came to get a shovel.

LUCILLE: What do you need a shovel for?

ELLIE: I'm cleaning! I'm cleaning! (*Max turns her around and marches her back into the room.*)

LUCILLE: Please Max! (*They all enter the room.*)

MAX: Ellie, I want to talk to you . . . (*Ellie shines his shoes.*)

MAX: ELLIE! (*Ellie looks up at him and gives him a goofy look.*)

MAX: I just want to tell you. . . . I tell you what! If you clean up your room right now then we'll all go get ice cream or something!

LUCILLE: (*Exasperated.*) I have to stop at the market anyway. I'll go make a list. (*Lucille exits.*)

MAX: And now once and for all . . . listen here, tough guy . . . you is gonna clean up that room. Okay?

ELLIE: (*Tough guy.*) Oh Yeah? Who is gonna make me?

MAX: I am Louie, cause I am da tough cop in dis town. Now you is gonna get in dat cell and you is gonna clean it up, or else I is gonna throw you in solitary . . . see? (*They tussle for a moment, Max pulls her cap over her eyes.*)

MAX: An I don't want to see you outta there till you is done. (*Max shuts the door and exits.*)

ELLIE: Darn! Lately this place is really getting like a prison.

VOICE: Red Light! She keeps you locked up like some kind of prisoner.

ELLIE: Yeah! A prison with walls and bars and chains. A dungeon with cold stones and bread and water and rats. Solitary confinement . . . The walls are closing in. You gotta let me out . . . You gotta let me out . . .

VOICE: Green Light! (*Suddenly the toy box lid flips open and a shovel full of dirt comes flying out. A shovel appears and on the other end of the shovel is Lana.*)

LANA: Hi yah, Sweetie!

ELLIE: Lana!

LANA: Who else? You think we wuz gonna let you take a bum rap? We dug this tunnel t'bust you outta here.

ELLIE: We?

LANA: Frizbee and me! Right Frizbee? Frizbee? He was right behind me in the tunnel. He must be here someplace. (*They look for Frizbee. Lana looks in the toy chest and slams the lid.*)

LANA: Oh no!

ELLIE: What?

LANA: Don't look!

ELLIE: Why not?

LANA: Cave in! The tunnel's caved in.

ELLIE: Oh NO!

LANA: The whole thing. . . . Squash!

ELLIE: Poor Frizbee!

LANA: What are we gonna do?

ELLIE: There is only one thing we can do!

LANA: Yeah?

ELLIE: Blast!

LANA: Blast boss?

ELLIE: It's the only way. You get the dynamite and I'll get the fuse. (*They gather together junk to make a blasting box, fuse, and plunger.*)

ELLIE: First you gotta make the box. Then you gotta put the dynamite in and then stick your fingers in your ears, and count down 10, 9, 8, 7, 6, 5, 4, 3, 2. . . . 1 BARRROOOOOOOM. (*Voice makes the sound of the explosion. The lid flies open, a puff of smoke comes out. Frizbee's arms and legs hang out of the box.*)

FRIZBEE: (*Weakly.*) Hey you guys . . . (*Lana and Ellie rush to Frizbee and lift him out of the toy chest.*)

LANA: Are you all right?

FRIZBEE: Sure.

ELLIE: The tunnel collapsed on you.

FRIZBEE: I thought it got dark all of a sudden.

ELLIE: Okay. Youse guys we gotta blow this joint. (*Frizbee pulls a handkerchief out of costume and blows his nose, as he pulls another handkerchief comes out and a whole string of handkerchiefs follow to Frizbee's amazement.*)

ELLIE: Great idea, Frizbee. Here, Lana, you take one end and go first, I'll hold this, and Frizbee, you bring up the rear. Good-bye cruel cell. (*Lana and Ellie dive into the box.*)

FRIZBEE: Good-bye cruel ceeeeeeee . . . (*Frizbee is pulled in after them. Lucille enters wearing a police hat and badge.*)

LUCILLE: Calling all cars. Calling all cars. This is the warden speaking! Ellie-the-mess-Murphy has just escaped from solitary confinement. She is messy and extremely dangerous. After her! After her! (*There is a chase. Lana and Ellie crawl under the bed, and around the stage. Lucille crouches behind the bed.*)

LANA: We made it!

ELLIE: Free at last.

LANA: Wow that was close. (*Lucille appears.*)

LUCILLE: Have you cleaned up your room yet?

ELLIE and LANA: EEEK! (*There is a short chase. Lucille lassos Ellie and Lana with the scarfs and drags them over to one side of the stage where she crouches down and Voice makes the sound of a car. Lucille mimes driving the paddy wagon. Frizbee finally makes it out of the tunnel, sees what's going on, disappears for a second, and reappears wearing the football helmet. Voice makes the sound of a siren. Frizbee mimes riding a motorcycle. Lucille puts on the brakes. Frizbee gets off the motorcycle, pulls an imaginary pad out of his pocket, licks an imaginary pencil.*)

FRIZBEE: Okay girlie, where's the fire?

LUCILLE: I'm sorry officer, I . . . just wanted her to clean up her . . .

FRIZBEE: Let me see your license. I'm gonna give you a ticket.

LUCILLE: But officer I . . .

FRIZBEE: But first I'm gonna give you a . . . tickle. (*Frizbee tickles Lucille, she laughs helplessly, Lana and Ellie escape.*)

LUCILLE: You can't do that!

FRIZBEE: Oh yeah? I just did!

ELLIE: To the hideout! (*Lucille chases them off. Ellie, Lana, and Frizbee race back to Ellie's room. They overturn the benches to make a barricade. Ellie rifles through the toy chest throwing junk everywhere; they put on guns and helmets.*)

ELLIE: Get the ammo and take cover.

VOICE: Come out with your hands up.

ELLIE: Let 'em have it. (*Imaginary battle takes place. They throw things all over the room. Frizbee uses a toilet paper roll like a grenade. Ellie clutches a grease gun like a tommy gun. All make sounds. Lucille enters dressed in regular street clothes. She is not part of the fantasy.*)

LUCILLE: (*Approaching the door.*) Ellinor, are you ready?

ELLIE: You'll never take us copper! (*Lucille opens the door. All sound effects stop. Lana and Frizbee freeze. The room is totally destroyed. Ellie pretends to be oiling the bed.*)

LUCILLE: (*Dumbfounded.*) Ellinor.

ELLIE: I . . . I . . . I uh, was just cleaning my room.

LUCILLE: Ellinor.

ELLIE: I didn't do it all. Lana threw the grenade.

LANA: I did not!

LUCILLE: I certainly hope you don't mean to tell me that Lana and Frizbee made all this mess.

ELLIE: What are you hoping I'll tell you?

LUCILLE: Oh Ellinor.

ELLIE: They made most of it.

FRIZBEE: We did not!

LUCILLE: Are they supposed to be here now?

ELLIE: (*Gesturing with grease gun.*) They're right over . . .

LUCILLE: Ellinor, that's a grease gun . . . don't . . . (*Ellie squeezes a glop of grease on the floor.*)

VOICE: Glop!

ELLIE: Uh oh!

LUCILLE: The carpet! A brand new carpet! Grease is the worst possible stain. Oh my Lord.

ELLIE: I thought it was empty.

LUCILLE: Now which is it hot water or cold? . . . Oh my Lord. (*Lucille rushes off to get a rag.*)

LANA: Uhhhh so long, boss.

FRIZBEE: Be seeing you around.

ELLIE: Where are you going?

LANA: I just remembered something I gotta do.

FRIZBEE: Yeah and I gotta do it with her . . . Whatever it is . . . (*They exit into the box. Lucille enters and rubs frantically at the spot.*)

LUCILLE: It just gets worse and worse . . . It's ruined. A brand-new carpet.

ELLIE: Well, I'm your brand-new kid.

LUCILLE: Ellinor, I knew something like this would happen. This is the last time you bring junk into your room. Oh it just gets bigger and bigger. (*Max enters, and rushes to help.*)

MAX: What in the world . . .

LUCILLE: Oh Max, Ellinor spilled grease on the carpet.

ELLIE: I didn't mean to.

LUCILLE: The more I rub the worse it gets.

ELLIE: It's not my fault.

MAX: Did you try cold water?

LUCILLE: No, it's hot water for grease.

ELLIE: Hey listen, I don't mind that spot.

MAX: No, I'm sure it's cold water.

ELLIE: Honest, I like that spot just the way it is.

LUCILLE: Max, it's hot water for grease and cold water for blood stains and ink.

MAX: I've got this stuff in my car.

LUCILLE: Oh it's no use!

ELLIE: (*Shouting.*) Would you leave it alone! I like that spot. (*They both stop and stare at her.*)

ELLIE: This is MY room.

LUCILLE: But it is a brand-new carpet.

ELLIE: BIG DEAL.

MAX: Ellie, don't talk that way to your Mother.

ELLIE: She is not my real mother. (*There is a stiff pause. Lucille is obviously hurt and upset.*)

LUCILLE: (*Covering.*) Well if we are going to the market I better get my coat. (*Lucille exits. Max is angry and very depressed.*)

MAX: That was nice . . . that was really nice.

ELLIE: It's not my fault.

MAX: You hurt her feelings.

ELLIE: I have feelings, too, you know. Just because you're a kid doesn't mean you're junk!

MAX: Come off it, Ellie.

ELLIE: That spot is almost out.

MAX: (*Really down.*) Yeah!

ELLIE: Maybe we could put something over it.

MAX: Yeah.

ELLIE: With a sign that says "Don't look here."

MAX: (*With a slight laugh.*) Sure.

ELLIE: (*Trying to get him out of his mood.*) Knock, knock.

MAX: Not now, Ellie.

ELLIE: Let's wrestle.

MAX: Uh uh! You're getting too big for me.

ELLIE: Do you think I'm too fat?

MAX: You? Naw you're fine.

ELLIE: Hey Pop, do you remember the time we went camping and you drove all afternoon to get out to the woods? It was dark when we pitched the tent and we heard all those funny sounds and you said it was MONSTERS. Then in the morning we found out we were in somebody's front lawn.

MAX: (*Responding a bit.*) I knew where we were all the time.

ELLIE: Or when we went to the Super Bowl and I got cold, and you said yell something in your megaphone.

MAX: Yeah, and you yelled "I'm cold and I want to go home." (*They both laugh.*)

ELLIE: (*Tentatively.*) Hey Pop, tell me about my real mother.

MAX: How come you want to hear about her all the time these days? (*Ellie sits at his feet and rests against his knees.*)

ELLIE: I just do. Hey do you remember the time it was my birthday and you brought Mom home from the hospital, and I didn't know she was coming that time? I remember I was already in bed and you guys wanted to surprise me. She just came into my room, kissed me good night and tucked me in, just like it was any other night.

MAX: (*Moved.*) How could you remember that? You were just four years old.

ELLIE: I just remember.

MAX: Your mother was a wonderful person and I loved her very much.

ELLIE: As much as you . . . like Lucille?

MAX: Ellie.

ELLIE: Was she pretty?

MAX: She was beautiful.

ELLIE: Do I look like her?

MAX: Naw, you look more like me, you mug.

ELLIE: (*Suddenly angry.*) Why does everything have to change?

MAX: Hey.

ELLIE: How come Lucille is always so neat and everything? I bet she never even burps.

MAX: She does.

ELLIE: HUH!

MAX: I heard her once.

ELLIE: Do you think I'd look cute with makeup on?

MAX: You? You're just a kid.

ELLIE: But Lucille wears makeup. Lots of it.

MAX: Well she's grown up.

ELLIE: Hey do you know how old she is?

MAX: Sure. Thirty-five.

ELLIE: How come you married such an old one?

MAX: That's not old.

ELLIE: Huh!

MAX: Why I am older than that myself.

ELLIE: You are?

MAX: Ellie, you know how you get to go to camp in the summer. You get to go away all by yourself.

ELLIE: Yeah but I'm not going anymore.

MAX: You're not?

ELLIE: Nope, look what happened the last time I went. You and Lucille get to be good friends, then as soon as I get back you get married. Who knows if I go away again I might get back and find out you moved to Alaska.

MAX: We wouldn't do that.

ELLIE: You might.

MAX: Ellie, kids can't always go where parents go. Sometimes parents go away all by themselves.

ELLIE: How come ever since you got married I am such a kid. You never used to say I was a kid. We did everything together. Now all I hear is, "Kids can't do this," "Kids can't do that," "Kids have to go to bed at eight-thirty." "Kids have to clean up their rooms." Why does everything have to change?

MAX: Nothing's changed. I still love you the same. Now there's just two of us who love you.

ELLIE: HUH!

MAX: I just wish you'd try a little harder to . . .

ELLIE: To like Lucille? Why should I? She doesn't like me. She likes cute little girls who play with dollies.

MAX: Well she got herself a messy little mug that likes junk. (*Ellie pulls away.*)

MAX: I'm just kidding. She likes you fine the way you are.

ELLIE: Oh yeah, well I don't like her.

MAX: Why not? (*Lucille enters and overhears the following.*)

ELLIE: Cause . . . Cause . . . Cause she's a wicked stepmother . . . (*Ellie giggles in spite of herself. Max is really angry.*)

MAX: That's not funny!

ELLIE: You shout at me all the time!

MAX: (*Shouting.*) I'm not shouting!

LUCILLE: (*Breaking it up.*) Is everybody ready to go?

MAX: Ellie, get your coat.

ELLIE: I'm not going.

MAX: Get your coat. We are going for ice cream!

ELLIE: (*Pouting.*) I don't want any.

MAX: Okay. Lucille, let's go. Ellie, you can just stay at home and clean up your room.

LUCILLE: Max . . .

MAX: I said let's go!

ELLIE: See if I care. (*They leave the room. Ellie pouts.*)

LUCILLE: Was it about the trip?

MAX: What?

LUCILLE: Were you arguing about the trip?

MAX: Are you kidding, I didn't even get that far. Come on. (*They exit. Ellie pouts for a moment then changes her mind and runs after them.*)

ELLIE: Hey, wait a minute . . . Wait, I changed my mind. I want to go. (*They have gone. Ellie turns back.*)

VOICE: Red Light! It's all her fault! She didn't want you to go. SHE made it so you couldn't go. (*Ellie is drawn to the mirror.*)

ELLIE and VOICE: Pick up your toys. Make your bed. Do what we say or you won't be fed.

ELLIE: I'll never be pretty. Ugly face, ugly hair, and squinty little eyes. If I had my real mother I'd be pretty.

VOICE: You'll never be as pretty as Lucille. Green Light!

ELLIE: They dress me in rags. They make me work all day.

VOICE: Ugly Ellie.

ELLIE: Ugly Ellie, Ugly Ellie . . . (*Ellie sits on the bed and pulls her cap over her face dejectedly.*)

FRIZBEE: (*Inside the toy box.*) Cinderelli, Cinderelli, Cinderelli . . . (*Lid to the box opens and out pops Frizbee wearing Mickey Mouse ears and singing the Walt Disney song.*)

FRIZBEE: Cinderelli, Cinderelli, Cinderelli, Cinderelli . . .

ELLIE: What are you supposed to be?

FRIZBEE: I am just a little Mouse. Who lives inside this great big house. Oh Cinderelli kind and dear, I see what's been going on right here. Your wicked stepmother cruel and mean, Makes you wash and wax and clean. Now she's gone to the ice cream ball, And left you here with nothing at all.

ELLIE: Dear little Mouse, you've seen everything?

FRIZBEE: Oh Yes! Everything and more.
    Ever since your stepmother came to stay,
    I have seen you slave all day.
    She gives you crusts of bread to eat.
    She pinches your elbows and stamps on your feet.
    She gives you rags and paper towels to wear.
    She calls you names and tangles your hair.

ELLIE: But what are we to do? I want to go to the ball but I have nothing to wear, my hair is dull, dull, dull, and my face is blah!

LANA: (*From the toy box.*) Perhaps there's something I can do. (*Toy box opens again, we see Lana's feet waving in the air. Ellie and Frizbee pull her out, she is outlandishly dressed in a gold lamé dress, blond wig, tiara, and silvery shoes.*)

LANA: I am your fairy godmother and I have come to make you a star. We have much to do, after all, stars are made not born.

ELLIE: Are you going to do a spell?

LANA: Oh no, spells are old-fashioned. Today we have something much better . . . money! (*Lana throws a fistful of money in the air.*)

LANA: First we need a dress.

ELLIE: Hey, I got an idea. Come with me . . . (*Ellie leads them out of her room to Lucille's ladder, where she gets an elaborate party dress.*)

LANA: Perfect!

FRIZBEE: But that's Lucille's.

LANA: Not anymore. We just bought it. (*Lana spears a bill on the hanger and helps Ellie on with the dress over her clothes.*)

LANA: And now the hair! Give her something that simply screams glamour. (*Frizbee becomes the hairdresser.*)

FRIZBEE: Would Madame care for a flip? (*Frizbee does a flip.*)

LANA: The hair, you dolt! (*Lana clobbers him. Frizbee makes an elaborate production of messing up Ellie's hair.*)

LANA: Makeup! (*Frizbee slaps makeup on Ellie and shows her how to blot her lipstick by smacking her lips. He gets carried away with the smacking and gives Lana a big kiss.*)

LANA: Oh gross! (*Lana clobbers him.*)

LANA: And now the coach. (*Frizbee puts on the football helmet and jumps around being a coach.*)

LANA: THE CARRIAGE! (*Frizbee gets a broomstick horse.*)

LANA: And last but not least . . . your public! (*Lana throws a fistful of money in the air and there is tumultuous cheering.*) (*Ellie, Frizbee, and Lana exit in procession. A fanfare is heard. Frizbee enters with a roll of paper towels which he rolls out like a red carpet. He stands at attention at the end of the carpet. Lana swirls on and down the carpet, she curtsies to Frizbee.*)

VOICE: Ladies and gentlemen, the Prince. (*Max enters dressed in a frock coat over his regular clothes. He bows and stands at the end of the "carpet."*)

VOICE: And now, ladies and gentlemen, the moment we have all been waiting for, the star of stage, screen, and television . . . the Princess Cinderelli! (*Music plays the "Sleeping Beauty Waltz," Ellie enters, a spotlight catches her, she sweeps down the carpet to Max, who bows. They dance.*)

LANA: (*As they waltz by her.*) Remember darling, your contract is up at midnight. (*Voice begins to bang on a pot with a spoon, twelve times in all. On the stroke of twelve Lucille appears, sweeps down the "carpet." Max turns and bows to her and dances off with her, leaving Ellie.*)

ELLIE: Hey wait a minute, what do you think you're doing? (*Lana and Frizbee exit.*)

ELLIE: Hey, I'm supposed to be the Princess around here. Hey, I'm Cinderelli! Come back. All right see if I care. I don't need any stupid old prince. I can have a good time all by myself. (*Ellie sings and dances all by herself. Music out, Ellie, obviously upset, dances faster and faster. Max and Lucille enter with groceries. They stop at her door and*) *watch. Max bursts out laughing. Lucille elbows him. Ellie stops, mortified at being caught.*)

ELLIE: Well, what are you staring at?

MAX: What is this, Halloween?

ELLIE: What's so funny?

LUCILLE: I think you look very pretty.

ELLIE: (*Defensive.*) Well, I wasn't trying to look pretty! I was trying to look dumb and funny, like this . . . and this . . . and this . . . (*Ellie makes faces.*) Since I can't be pretty I might as well be funny and dumb. (*Ellie capers around wildly until she stubs her toe.*)

ELLIE: Owwwwwwww!

LUCILLE: What's the matter?

ELLIE: I stubbed my dumb toe. (*Ellie sits and buries her head in her hands. Max starts to go to her. Lucille stops him by shoving her sack of groceries into his arms.*)

LUCILLE: Max, will you put these in the kitchen for me? (*Max gives her a look, she waves him away, and he exits. Lucille goes to Ellie and helps her out of the dress.*)

LUCILLE: You okay? (*Ellie pulls away and sits on the bed. She shrugs.*)

LUCILLE: Ellinor, if I asked you to help me with something, would you do it?

ELLIE: I didn't clean up my room.

LUCILLE: So I see, but that's not what I am talking about. I want you to help me with something else.

ELLIE: Huh! I don't see what I could help you do.

LUCILLE: (*Tentatively.*) Well, I've never had any children . . . and lots of times I'm not too sure what mothers are supposed to do. So I wanted you to help me.

ELLIE: How should I know? I never really had a mother, not one I remember real well.

LUCILLE: Well, maybe we could help each other. (*Ellie shrugs.*)

LUCILLE: You see, my mother was very strict. She made me pick up my room and practice my voice every day and I loved her.

ELLIE: She was your real mother.

LUCILLE: Yes.

ELLIE: That makes a difference. You have to love your real mother and your real kids.

LUCILLE: But you can choose to love your stepchildren.

ELLIE: But nobody can make you.

LUCILLE: (*Pause.*) That's right.

ELLIE: Well, I can tell you a couple of things mothers shouldn't do. They shouldn't try to make their kids different from the way they are. Like if the kid is messy, they shouldn't try to make them be neat. And mothers shouldn't make their kids go to bed at eight-thirty, especially when there's good movies on TV.

LUCILLE: But what if the mother wants the child to be healthy and she thinks the child should get some sleep?

ELLIE: Who's supposed to be doing the helping around here, you or me?

LUCILLE: Sorry.

ELLIE: Mothers should love their kids no matter what. Even if the kid is funny and dumb and looks like a gorilla; Mothers should make them think they are beautiful.

LUCILLE: But what if the . . . kid won't let the mother . . .

ELLIE: Mothers gotta go first! That's the rules.

LUCILLE: Ellie . . . I . . . .

ELLIE: (*Turning away.*) What's for supper?

LUCILLE: Huh?

ELLIE: I'm getting hungry. What's for supper?

LUCILLE: I thought I'd make a beef stroganoff.

ELLIE: What's that?

LUCILLE: It's little slices of beef with sour cream and . . .

ELLIE: SOUR CREAM! UHHHHHH! Mothers should never make their kids eat SOUR CREAM! (*Ellie clutches her throat.*)

LUCILLE: (*Laughing.*) You should try it.

ELLIE: I know, Why don't I make dinner tonight? I used to do that all the time. Pop and I had this really neat game we'd play. First we'd cook up a whole bunch of TV dinners and then we'd put on blindfolds and try to guess what we were eating.

MAX: (*Entering.*) Did I hear somebody mention food?

LUCILLE: I just had a great idea! Why don't we eat out tonight?

ELLIE: Knock knock . . .

MAX: Who's there?

ELLIE: Uda.

MAX: Uda who?

ELLIE: (*Singing.*) "You deserve a break today" . . .

MAX: (*Joining in.*) . . . "So go on and get away to McDonald's."*
(*Max encourages Lucille to join in.*)

LUCILLE: But I don't know the words.

ELLIE: It's simple. But you can't sing it in that toot toot de doot voice. You gotta do it like this . . . (*Ellie belts it out.*)

ELLIE: "You deserve a break today. So go on and get away to McDonald's."

LUCILLE: (*Belting.*) Like this? "You deserve a break today. So go on and get away to McDonald's." (*They all join in on the last line.*)

ELLIE: Not bad, for a beginner.

MAX: Let's go.

LUCILLE: Wait a minute, I have to put the meat in the freezer. (*Lucille exits.*)

MAX: Hey Ellie, after supper how about a little . . . (*Max mimes bowling.*)

* This jingle should be constantly updated to any popular theme song of a fast-food chain.

ELLIE: Great! Just you and me, like the old days?

MAX: Ellie?

ELLIE: Oh I bet Lucille doesn't even know how to bowl. I bet she thinks it is a dirty smelly sport.

MAX: Oh, come on.

ELLIE: Oh, I guess she can come.

MAX: If she doesn't know you'll have to teach her.

ELLIE: Yeah, I could. Cause if there is one thing I do know it is bowling. (*Lucille enters.*)

MAX: Lucille, would you like to go bowling after supper?

LUCILLE: Oh Max, I was hoping we could all come back here and. TALK.

MAX: (*Ignoring the hint.*) Oh yeah, yeah. We can do that afterward.

LUCILLE: Maybe just you two should go. I've never bowled before and I wouldn't want to slow you down.

MAX: Baloney! There's nothing to it. We'll show you. Right Midget? (*Ellie shrugs and Max elbows her.*)

ELLIE: Sure, sure, it just takes practice, to get good that is. I'll show you.

MAX: Let's go. (*They start out.*)

ELLIE: Wait a sec, let me get my shoes.

MAX: We'll meet you in the car. (*Max and Lucille exit. Ellie gets her bowling shoes from under the bed and starts out.*)

VOICE: Red Light! (*Ellie freezes.*)

VOICE: You aren't going to fall for all that stuff are you?

ELLIE: Huh?

VOICE: All that "Help me be a mother" stuff?

ELLIE: Well . . .

VOICE: Stepmothers always say that . . . to soften you up. They don't really mean that. And now she's going bowling with you. And after you teach her you know what will happen? She and Pop will go and leave you home . . . alone. Green Light!

MAX: (*Offstage.*) Come on, Ellie! (*Ellie hesitates and exits. By minor adjustments in the set it switches to the bowling alley. The sound of balls rolling and pins falling can be heard all through the next scene. As soon as the scene is shifted Ellie, Max, and Lucille enter. Ellie munches a bag of french fries, they cross to benches set up to indicate their alley. Max sets up a score sheet, changes his shoes. All bowling should be mimed.*)

MAX: Why don't we take a couple of practice shots? Will you show Lucille how to hold the ball while I get us squared away?

ELLIE: (*Licking her fingers.*) Okay, first you get a ball . . . (*Ellie points, Lucille looks a bit apprehensive but she gets a ball.*)

MAX: (*Under his breath.*) Ellie, I want you to be nice.

ELLIE: (*Slaps on a huge smile.*) I am being nice . . . SEE? Now you hold the ball like this with three fingers . . . That's good . . . very very good! And you look right at that center pin and bring your hand straight back . . . like this and you just swing through . . . See?

LUCILLE: (*Gamely.*) Sure I think so . . .

ELLIE: Well go ahead . . . Try one. (*Lucille follows all Ellie's instructions but the unexpected weight of the ball throws her off-balance. Finally she manages to bowl one ball but very badly. There is the sound of a gutterball.*)

ELLIE: (*Much too nice.*) Good! VERY GOOD, Lucille. (*Ellie smirks.*)

MAX: Lucille, that's called a gutterball, and it's not good. Ellie, I'll show her. Why don't you take your turn?

ELLIE: Can I have a Coke?

LUCILLE: You just finished dinner.

ELLIE: Pop?

MAX: Yeah sure, here's fifty cents. (*Ellie walks away a few steps. Max moves over to Lucille and shows her how to hold the ball, very cozily. Ellie returns.*)

ELLIE: AHEM! I believe it is MY turn. (*Ellie takes a ball and goes through a very elaborate warm-up.*)

MAX: (*Quietly.*) Now you see you just bring the ball straight back and . . .

LUCILLE: Where is the aiming? (*Ellie bowls just as Lucille is talking she slips a little and is thrown off. There is the sound of a few pins falling.*)

ELLIE: No fair! No fair! You're not supposed to talk! You threw me off!

MAX: (*Writing down the score.*) Uhhh, three! A little to the left.

ELLIE: That's not fair.

MAX: Oh go on, you've still got another ball.

ELLIE: This time NO talking. (*Ellie bowls. All pins fall.*)

MAX: Fantastic.

LUCILLE: Nice aiming, Ellinor. That was a good shot wasn't it, dear?

ELLIE: (*Cocky.*) You bet. That's what you call a spare. It is just about the best you can do. Of course it takes hours and hours of practice.

MAX: Nice one Midget! Okay Lucille, it's all yours. Just relax and concentrate. (*Lucille starts into the backswing.*)

ELLIE: Hold IT! (*Lucille stops clumsily.*)

ELLIE: This is the foul line. If you step over it nothing counts . . . I was just trying to help! (*Lucille bowls, very awkwardly. Sound of ball rolling very slowly.*)

ELLIE: (*Watching the ball.*) Don't expect too much, not right at first. After all there is only one thing better than a spare and that's a . . . (*Sound of pins falling domino effect. Ellie's face contorts in utter amazement.*)

ELLIE: A STRIKE?????

MAX: Fantastic!

LUCILLE: Is that good?

MAX: You bet it is!

ELLIE: I think I'm going to be sick!

LUCILLE: What does that little X mean up there?

ELLIE: (*Nasty.*) It means a strike!

MAX: Not bad, old lady, not bad at all. (*Ellie starts coughing real fakey.*)

LUCILLE: Beginner's luck.

MAX: Let's see. My turn now. (*Ellie coughs.*)

MAX: What's the matter with you?

ELLIE: I don't feel so good.

MAX: Well lie down for a minute.

ELLIE: I don't exactly feel like bowling. (*Max shoots her a look which silences her. Max picks up the ball and lines up the shot, very machismo. Just as he bowls Ellie coughs and throws him off. He gets a gutterball.*)

MAX: Ellie!

ELLIE: (*Innocently.*) Sorry.

LUCILLE: What's the matter, Ellinor?

MAX: Nothing's the matter. She's just got a bad case of fakeitus, that's all!

ELLIE: By the way, Lucille, that's called a gutterball, it's not good.

MAX: Now, no more talking, noisemaking, sneezing, coughing or anything. (*Max lines up the shot and Ellie yawns.*)

MAX: One more noise out of you and it's out to the car. (*Max takes his time lining up the shot, Ellie picks up her Coke can, which she opens just as he bowls. The can explodes in a spray of Coke. Max tosses his ball over several lanes. He is furious.*)

ELLIE: Ooops!

MAX: ELLIE!

LUCILLE: Good Lord, it is all over everything!

ELLIE: I couldn't help it.

MAX: You did that on purpose 'cause you're a rotten sport.

ELLIE: I did not.

MAX: Out to the car!

ELLIE: POP!

MAX: I said out to the car!

LUCILLE: Dear!

MAX: I am not going to have her wreck our game just because she's a lousy sport.

LUCILLE: Let's go home.

MAX: WHAT?

LUCILLE: I don't really care about bowling.

MAX: Well I do. Ellie, out to the car. I said it and I meant it.

LUCILLE: You can't send her out there to wait in a dark parking lot.

MAX: Oh yes I can. We are going to finish this game, and Ellie is going to wait for us out in the car. If there is one thing I can't stand it is a rotten sport.

LUCILLE: I will not permit you to send that child out there alone.

MAX: It's just out to the car, do you want me to hire a babysitter?

ELLIE: (*Embarrassed.*) Pop!

LUCILLE: Max, keep your voice down. We'll settle this when we get home.

MAX: Are you telling me how to discipline my kid?

LUCILLE: You? You're a fine one to talk about discipline. Why you're a bigger kid than she is. Why we should all be sitting at home right now having a family discussion. But Oh no! We have to get ice cream. We all have to go bowling first . . . all because you can't even talk to your own child . . .

MAX: (*Impulsive.*) Oh you don't think I can tell her . . . (*Max crosses to Ellie, Lucille tries to stop him.*)

LUCILLE: Max, not here and not now . . . Let's go home.

MAX: (*To Ellie.*) Ellie, we are going to Hawaii! (*To Lucille.*) There! Now are you satisfied? (*Lucille is horrified. Max realizes instantly that he has really blown it.*)

LUCILLE: Oh MAX!

ELLIE: What are you guys talking about?

MAX: (*Fighting his way out.*) Uhhh, Ellie, we are going away . . . We're going to Hawaii.

ELLIE: HAWAII?

MAX: Yeah, for about three weeks.

ELLIE: Neato! Do I get to get out of school?

MAX: No Ellie, just Lucille and I are going. I was gonna tell you all about it when we got home tonight, well now you know.

ELLIE: What . . . What about me?

MAX: Well you kind of like Mrs. Dougan and I thought maybe she'd come and . . .

ELLIE: You are going away and leaving me.

LUCILLE: Ellie . . .

ELLIE: (*Getting mad.*) So that's what all that sneaking around was about! So that's what all those papers and secret stuff was about. You guys are going away and leaving me.

LUCILLE: Ellinor, that's not . . .

ELLIE: (*Turns on her.*) And YOU! All that "Help me be a mother" stuff! That was just to soften me up. Well I'll tell you one thing mothers shouldn't do, mothers shouldn't lie to their kids about all that love stuff and then dump them.

MAX: Ellie, stop shouting.

ELLIE: I should have known. I should have known you didn't really like me. You just wanted to have POP all to yourself. Well go ahead! See if I care!

MAX: Ellie, we are going home. Take off your shoes and wait for me in the car.

ELLIE: You can't just throw me out like the trash you know.

MAX: ELLIE, OUT TO THE CAR! (*Ellie starts to run out. Max stops her.*)

MAX: Ellie, your shoes! (*Ellie, furious, takes off her shoes and throws them at him and runs out. Lucille looks at Max for a minute.*)

LUCILLE: Well you certainly handled that one well.

MAX: Lay off! Oh I'm sorry, I didn't mean for this to happen.

LUCILLE: I should hope not. Max, discipline isn't something you turn off and on like hot water.

MAX: I know.

LUCILLE: (*Taking off her shoes and exiting.*) We were just beginning. After two months we were just beginning. (*Lucille exits. Max sits for a minute. He picks up the score sheet and crumples it. He starts out when Lucille enters at a run.*)

LUCILLE: Max, she isn't there! She's gone!

MAX: What?

LUCILLE: She's run away. She left this note on the windshield. (*Lucille hands Max a note.*)

MAX: (*Reading.*) "You win Lucille."

LUCILLE: (*Panicking.*) Where could she have gone?

MAX: Anywhere! Let's go, she can't have gotten too far. (*Lucille sees Ellie's shoes.*)

LUCILLE: Oh Max, she hasn't even got her shoes on.

MAX: Come on. (*Max and Lucille exit. Weird sounds begin, the recorded voices of Lana, Frizbee, and Voice are heard chanting "Run away." The following scene is a mixture of fantasy and reality. A sound collage of voices and scarey music form the background.*)

VOICE, LANA, and FRIZBEE: Run away . . . Run away . . . Run away . . . Run away . . . (*Ellie enters at a run. Lana and Frizbee enter also but they appear as strange menacing figures, such as a stop sign that is knocked over, a staggering drunk, a car that nearly runs Ellie down.*)

VOICE, LANA, and FRIZBEE: Run away. Run away. Run away. Run away. There's a fact you've got to face . . .
Run away. Run away.
That she's taken your place . . .
Run away. Run away.

VOICE, LANA, and FRIZBEE: (*Recorded.*) And there's nothing you can do . . . Run away, Run away. Cause he loves her more than you . . . Run away, Run away.

ELLIE: I'll show you. Boy will you be sorry! I'm never going home. (*A cat yeowls and Lucille appears dressed in a long black cloak.*)

LUCILLE: (*Recorded.*) Mirror, mirror, on the wall, who's the fairest of them all?

ELLIE: I am, you wicked old stepmother! (*Ellie runs into Frizbee, who holds a newspaper in front of his face.*)

FRIZBEE: Go home little girl.

ELLIE: I'm never going home. I'll find some new parents. (*Ellie runs over to Lana, who is wearing a farmer's hat and mimes churning butter.*)

ELLIE: Will you adopt a poor orphan child?

LANA: (*Malevolently.*) My lands, who is this child?

ELLIE: I am just a poor orphan with no father or mother.

FRIZBEE: (*Also wearing a farmer's hat.*) I see the mark of the princess Cinderelli upon her cheek. We will adopt you.

ELLIE: I am not the princess, I'm just Ellie, Ellie Murphy.

FRIZBEE: Well, if you are not the princess then get lost. (*Ellie staggers away from them.*)

ELLIE: I'm not scared. I'm not scared. I'm not scared. Oh, my feet are so cold. (*Max enters slowly with his back to the audience. He wears a raincoat with a hood. Lucille enters with her back to the audience, she too wears a long coat.*)

ELLIE: Pop! Is that you, Pop? Hey!

MAX: (*Still with his back to her.*) I beg your pardon?

ELLIE: Pop! It's me, Ellie.

MAX: I'm sorry but I don't believe I know you.

ELLIE: Pop, it's me, your daughter! Ellie!

MAX: Who?

ELLIE: Hey Lucille! It's me, Ellie.

LUCILLE: (*Still with her back to her.*) I beg your pardon?

ELLIE: Look at me! It's Ellie!

LUCILLE: I don't believe I know you. (*Slowly they turn to look at her. They wear half-masks which are transparent.*)

LUCILLE: Do you know this child?

MAX: No, I'm sorry, little girl.

LUCILLE: Come dear, we have a plane to catch.

MAX: Oh yes, we mustn't be late.

LUCILLE: (*As they exit.*) What a strange little girl.

ELLIE: Don't you know me? I'm your child! (*Strange music and recorded voices begin again. Lana and Frizbee step in and out of the shadows moving in slow motion.*)

VOICE, LANA, and FRIZBEE: (*Recorded.*) You're alone . . . You're alone.

LANA: (*Like a cat yeowl.*) Hi ya Sweetie . . .

VOICE, LANA, and FRIZBEE: (*Recorded.*) Can't go home . . . Can't go home . . .

ELLIE: Doesn't anybody know me?

LANA: Hi ya, boss . . .

ELLIE: I'm not the boss. I'm . . .

VOICE, LANA, and FRIZBEE: (*Recorded.*) You're alone . . . You're alone.

FRIZBEE: Singer of the year . . .

ELLIE: I don't want to be . . .

VOICE, LANA, and FRIZBEE: Got no home . . . Got no home . . .

ELLIE: I don't want to be an orphan.

VOICE, LANA, and FRIZBEE: You're alone . . . You're alone . . . All alone . . . All alone . . .

ELLIE: I just want to go home. (*Ellie runs around the stage, as she does the scene is shifted back to her house. Ellie enters the living room area and looks around.*)

ELLIE: I'm home! Hey Pop? Lucille? I'm home. I don't want to be an orphan. Pop? LUCILLE? (*Ellie sighs and goes into her room. She throws herself down on her bed and falls into a deep sleep.*) (*Soft music begins, a lullabye played on a music box. Ellie dreams and in her dream Max and Lucille enter wearing dressing gowns. Lana and Frizbee enter. They carry windchimes which tinkle softly. During this scene the words must tumble and flow like a waterfall, nothing frightening. It is a soft and gentle dream.*)

LUCILLE: Shhhhh. Don't wake the baby . . .

FRIZBEE: What a beautiful baby . . .

LANA: What a good baby . . .

MAX: Daddy's beautiful baby girl.

ELLIE: (*Recorded.*) I never had a mother, not one I remember real well.

LANA: Sleep . . .

FRIZBEE: . . . Dream.

ELLIE: (*Recorded.*) Mother? Mother? Where are you? It's dark. I'm scared. (*Lucille billows a soft coverlet and covers Ellie.*)

LUCILLE: Shall I tell you a story? Shall I sing you a song?

ELLIE: (*Recorded.*) I can't see myself. I'm messy. I'm mean.

LANA: Sleep . . .

FRIZBEE: . . . Dream.

MAX: Daddy's pretty Ellie.

ELLIE: (*Recorded.*) Mother, tell me a story. Mother, sing me a song. (*Lucille begins to hum softly.*)

LANA: Sleep . . .

FRIZBEE: . . . Dream.

ELLIE: Can you be my mother?

LUCILLE: Sleep . . .

ELLIE: Please be my mother.

MAX: . . . Dream.

ELLIE: I want to have a mother!

LANA: Shhh. Don't wake the child.

FRIZBEE: What a beautiful child.

MAX: Daddy's beautiful girl.

LUCILLE: Pretty Ellie . . .

MAX and LUCILLE: (*Recorded.*) Pretty Ellie . . . Pretty Ellie . . . Pretty Ellie . . . Pretty Ellie. (*All exit slowly as the recorded music and sound continue for a moment. Ellie tosses and turns on the bed. The dream fades and the house returns to normal. Max enters the house dressed as he was at the bowling alley. He is upset and in a hurry.*)

MAX: I know I have a recent photograph around here somewhere. Lucille, you call the police; say you want to report a missing person. (*Lucille enters.*)

LUCILLE: I just don't understand how she could have gotten so far so quickly. Oh Max, what are we going to do?

MAX: I know we had some pictures taken at Woolworth's right before she left for camp. Where did I put them?

LUCILLE: She's been gone two hours. Anything could have happened.

MAX: Take it easy. We'll find her. She's probably just hiding in a restaurant or something. You call the police. I'll go back to the bowling alley.

LUCILLE: I can't help feeling this is all my fault.

MAX: Maybe they are in her room. Call the police. (*Max enters Ellie's room. He stops dead when he sees her asleep. He is unable to speak for a second and sighs in relief.*)

MAX: (*Very calmly.*) Lucille. (*Lucille crosses to him. He points to the sleeping figure. Lucille crouches by the bed.*)

LUCILLE: Thank God.

MAX: Let's let her sleep. She must be exhausted. (*They leave the room and close the door behind them.*)

LUCILLE: She must have walked all this way.

MAX: She must have run.

LUCILLE: (*Still slightly hysterical.*) Thank God she's all right. Anything could have happened to her. I don't know what I would have done if . . . (*Ellie wakes up, sits, and listens.*)

MAX: Hey, calm down. Everything is all right now.

LUCILLE: She could have been killed. What if she'd gotten hit by a car?

MAX: (*Firmly.*) Lucille, it is all over now. Take it easy. She's home. I'll get something to relax you, just a minute. (*Max exits. Ellie gets out of bed and starts toward the door.*)

VOICE: Red Light! (*Ellie freezes.*)

VOICE: Where are you going?

ELLIE: Out there.

VOICE: Why?

ELLIE: To tell them I'm . . .

VOICE: You could have been killed and it's all HER fault. She almost got rid of you once and for all.

ELLIE: But she really sounded worried.

VOICE: You aren't going to fall for that stuff again, are you? She just said that so Pop wouldn't be mad at her. She's trying to get rid of you.

ELLIE: Aww that's dumb.

VOICE: You could have been killed and she'd live happily ever after with Pop. That's how wicked stepmothers are, you know.

ELLIE: But . . .

VOICE: You could have been killed. Green Light! (*Sound of sirens. Lana and Frizbee enter dressed as doctors. They pull a wagon with a red flashing light on it. They cross to Ellie, push her into the wagon and wheel her to the bed.*)

ELLIE: Hey, wait a minute.

FRIZBEE: Be quiet, you are the patient.

LANA: Is there a doctor in the house?

FRIZBEE: Dats me, you Dumkoff! I am der doktor. I say it is hopeless, but let's cooperate anyways! (*They lift her to the bed. Frizbee crosses to Voice, who becomes a heart machine with a flashlight moving up and down for the heartbeat. Frizbee turns the machine on.*)

FRIZBEE: Scalpel.

LANA: Scalpel.

ELLIE: Scalpel?

FRIZBEE: Be quiet, you're the patient!

VOICE: Beep . . . beep . . . beep . . . beep . . . beep . . . beep . . . beep . . .

FRIZBEE: Clamp!

LANA: Clamp.

FRIZBEE: Sponge.

LANA: Sponge.

VOICE: Beep . . . beep . . . beep . . . beep . . . beep . . .

FRIZBEE: Brillo.

LANA: Brillo.

ELLIE: Brillo?

VOICE: (*Drawing a straight line with the light.*) Beeeeeeeeeeeee . . .

LANA: It's all over.

FRIZBEE: We did what we could.

LANA: Curse you, wicked stepmother!

ELLIE: This is dumb.

FRIZBEE: You aren't supposed to say that.

ELLIE: Why not?

FRIZBEE: Cause you're dead!

ELLIE: Oh. (*Max enters with a drink for Lucille. Lana, Frizbee, and Voice freeze.*)

MAX: Here, this will calm you down. Everything is going to be all right.

LUCILLE: Thanks. I've been thinking, Max, maybe I should go away.

MAX: What?

LUCILLE: Maybe I should just let you and Ellie work things out alone. I kept hoping that it was just a matter of time. I kept hoping that gradually she would come to accept me.

MAX: You are just upset.

LUCILLE: I love both of you too much to see you destroy what you had together. Maybe I should just leave for a while.

MAX: That's crazy. We are a family now and we are going to work through this thing, all of us, together. Your leaving isn't going to help.

LUCILLE: I don't know.

MAX: Well I do.

LUCILLE: She must have loved her real mother very much to hate me so.

MAX: She doesn't hate you. She's just mixed up right now. It's late and we are tired. Let's talk about this in the morning.

LUCILLE: No, I really think it would be best for me to leave you two alone for a while to work things out whatever way you can. (*Max and Lucille exit. Ellie is disturbed by this and she starts out the door after them.*)

ELLIE: Hey you guys . . .

VOICE: Red Light! (*Ellie freezes.*)

VOICE: Congratulations! You won!

ELLIE: But she's leaving.

VOICE: That's what you wanted, isn't it? Now you and Pop can go back to having things the way they used to be.

ELLIE: Yeah but . . .

VOICE: After all, she wanted to get rid of you. She wanted you to get killed, and then you could have had a funeral.

ELLIE: A funeral?

VOICE: Yeah a funeral. At funerals everybody is real sorry for all the mean things they ever did to you. Everybody just sits around and says nice things about you and they cry and cry and cry. (*Frizbee starts to sniffle.*)

ELLIE: What about Pop?

VOICE: He cries the loudest of all. (*Frizbee bursts into sobs.*)

ELLIE: What am I supposed to do?

VOICE: Well, first you gotta have a coffin. (*Lana and Frizbee move the toy box forward for the coffin.*)

VOICE: You just lie there.

ELLIE: Suppose I want to see what's going on.

VOICE: No, you gotta just lie there.

ELLIE: That sounds stupid. Hey, I got an idea. Why don't you lie there and be me in the coffin.

VOICE: No, I stay right here.

ELLIE: Get in that coffin!

VOICE: Okay . . . Okay . . . Green Light. (*Voice lies on the box and Ellie takes charge of the microphone.*)

ELLIE: Okay ladies and gentlemen. Let's get this show on the road. Ellie Murphy's funeral . . . Take One! (*Lana and Frizbee clap their hands like a claque board.*)

ELLIE: Now the parade starts over there. I want a black horse with a plume. (*Frizbee puts a plume on his head and neighs.*)

ELLIE: Fantastic! I want music, drums sad and slow! That's right. (*Lana wearing a long black veil falls into a procession behind Frizbee and they both wail.*)

ELLIE: Now start with the nice things.

LANA: She was so young and so beautiful . . .

ELLIE: Cut! Lana, honey, more tears . . . that's right cry, cry, cry. Now throw yourself over the coffin. Preacher that's your cue. (*Frizbee becomes the preacher.*)

FRIZBEE: Poor Ellie Murphy! Why didn't I tell her how cute she was and what nice straight teeth she had.

ELLIE: Come on preacher, nicer things!

FRIZBEE: Poor Ellie Murphy. Why didn't I tell her how pretty she was, what a good voice she had. She was the best bowler I ever saw!

ELLIE: Pop! You're on! (*Max enters wearing pajamas and a high silk hat, and black arm bands.*)

MAX: I'm sorry, Ellie.

ELLIE: More feeling, Pop!

MAX: I'M SORRY, ELLIE!!!! How could I have been so blind? I never needed anyone but you. Now my life is empty, bleak, bland . . .

ELLIE: From the bottom of your heart, Pop!

MAX: What a fool I have been and now it is too late!!!

ELLIE: And now for the final touch! Lucille enters up right, rubbing her hand and laughing. (*Ellie indicates up right. Nothing happens.*)

ELLIE: I said, the grand finale . . . LUCILLE enters up right, rubbing her hands and laughing. (*Ellie indicates up right again and Lucille enters up left. She wears a coat and carries a suitcase.*)

LUCILLE: I have been thinking, Max, maybe I should go away.

ELLIE: No, CUT! Lucille enters up right, rubbing her hands and laughing.

LUCILLE: Maybe I should let you and Ellie work things out alone.

ELLIE: I said, up right!

LUCILLE: I kept hoping that it was just a matter of time.

ELLIE: Cut! Cut! You are not supposed to be saying that!

LUCILLE: I kept hoping that gradually she would come to accept me.

ELLIE: You are supposed to be glad that I'm dead.

LUCILLE: I love both of you too much to see you destroy what you had together. Maybe I should just leave . . .

ELLIE: You are not supposed to be saying that!

LUCILLE: She must have loved her real mother very much to hate me so. So I'm leaving. (*Lucille exits.*)

ELLIE: Hey wait, Lucille! Wait! I didn't mean for it to go this far.

VOICE: Red Light! (*Ellie freezes.*)

VOICE: Don't call her back. You've won! Now things will be the way they always have been.

ELLIE: Why don't you shut up! You are supposed to be dead! I want a mother and she's a perfectly good one.

VOICE: But she's a wicked step. . . .

ELLIE: RED LIGHT! (*Voice freezes.*)

ELLIE: Lana, Frizbee, take that thing away. Green Light! (*Lana and Frizbee move like puppets. They move Voice back to the stool and move the toy box back into its place.*)

ELLIE: Now get in. (*Ellie helps them both into the toy box. She closes the lid and sits on the box for a second.*)

ELLIE: Lucille! Lucille! Come back! (*Ellie moves back into bed as Lucille and Max enter her room. They both wear the dressing gowns seen in the dream scene.*)

MAX: (*Entering first.*) Ellie? What's the matter?

ELLIE: Where is Lucille?

LUCILLE: (*Entering.*) Right here. What's the matter?

ELLIE: (*Relieved.*) Oh . . . uhhh, nothing. I must have had a bad dream.

MAX: Do you want to tell me about it?

ELLIE: I don't think you'd like it.

MAX: Is it all right now?

ELLIE: Yeah. I guess so.

MAX: Well, good night, Midget. (*Max kisses her on the forehead.*)

ELLIE: Good night, Pop. (*Max and Lucille turn to leave.*)

ELLIE: Uhhh Lucille? (*Max stays in the doorway and Lucille crosses to her.*)

LUCILLE: Yes?

ELLIE: I'm . . . sorry I ran away.

LUCILLE: So am I.

ELLIE: Well, I'm back now.

LUCILLE: I'm glad.

ELLIE: So am I. (*Pause.*)

ELLIE: Uhhh Lucille, I'm cold.

LUCILLE: Well no wonder, you kicked your covers off. (*Lucille billows the covers over her and tucks her in. Ellie smiles.*)

ELLIE: Uhh Lucille, knock, knock . . .

LUCILLE: Who's there?

ELLIE: Sticker.

LUCILLE: Sticker who?

ELLIE: Sticker-ound for a while, okay?

LUCILLE: Okay. Good night, Ellie. Sleep well. (*Lucille moves away a few steps and crouches.*)

LUCILLE: Good night, Lana. Good night, Frizbee.

ELLIE: Uhhh Lucille, they're not here.

LUCILLE: Oh. (*Lucille crosses to Max and turns back.*)

LUCILLE: Good night, Ellie.

ELLIE: (*Pulling the covers up and turning over.*) See ya in the morning.

CURTAIN

I Didn't Know That!

*Louis Moloney, Johnny Saldaña,
Joyce Chambers Selber,
Rachel Winfree*

I DIDN'T KNOW THAT!
A Light-hearted Revue of
First Facts, Selected Oddities, and World Records

book, music, and lyrics
developed through improvisations by
Louis Moloney,
Johnny Saldaña,
Joyce Chambers Selber,
Rachel Winfree

musical arrangements by
Johnny Saldaña

All factual statements and material based for selected vignettes followed by an asterisk (*) are from the *Guinness Book of World Records* © 1979 by Sterling Publishing Co., Inc., New York. Reprinted by permission.

Vocal and instrumental arrangements for
I DIDN'T KNOW THAT!
are published in the acting editions scripts.

I Didn't Know That! is a three-part collection of humorous vignettes described in the script as "first facts, selected oddities, and world records," and created through improvisations by Louis Moloney, Johnny Saldaña, Joyce Chambers Selber, and Rachel Winfree.

Performed by four actors and accompanied by a narrator on various musical instruments, the unusual information is dramatized in speech, song, movement, and dance. There is no sustained plot, but a series of short, complete scenes played in rapid succession. The revue is very demanding physically for the actors because their bodies and voices must become more than characters in a play: they become properties, set pieces, and sound effects as well. Although stage directions are included throughout the script, actors preparing the play should be encouraged to use improvisation to create the most effective staging and choreography for their production.

Interspersed within the spoken lines are short verses of sense and nonsense that are chanted and repeated in a style similar to jumping rope rhymes. Other verses are sung to short familiar tunes unaccompanied except by the percussion instruments that emphasize the rhythms.

The element of technical production of greatest importance is the instruments for the sound effects. The narrator/accompanist who sits at one side, observing the action and commenting, uses various instruments to punctuate the action and to signal the beginning and end of each scene. Production Notes from the original production immediately precede the script.

PRODUCTION NOTES

I Didn't Know That! depends on the performer's body and voice to create a multitude of pantomimic and sound effects. It is a physically demanding play; the swift changes from fact to fact require versatility, concentration, and coordination. As a presentational revue, there is direct address to the audience and a stylish, almost vaudevillian flair to the piece.

Aside from the lively tempo and vigorous energy required, the actors should allow their own creativity to flourish. The stage directions in the playscript are from the original production. Other companies can improvise on the staging and choreography. In fact, that was how the entire script evolved: through creative play.

The original company discovered that younger children seem fascinated by the constant change of movement and aural effects. Older children take an interest in the text itself and the staging techniques. After each show, the actors took questions from the children; the one they most often asked was: "Is it true?" With a bit of leeway for dramatic license, all the facts in *I Didn't Know That!*, bizarre as they may seem, are true.

The Playscript

For clarity in the printed script, dates and statistics are in Arabic numerals. "March 19, 1831" is spoken as "March nineteenth, eighteen thirty-one." "5,750" would, of course, be said as "five thousand seven hundred and fifty," and "27½'" as "twenty-seven and one half feet."

Dates, places, and numbers are perhaps the most difficult to memorize, but they should, at all times, be accurately presented. Production companies are asked to check the most recent edition of the *Guinness Book of World Records* to make certain that records in the playscript are still valid. If they've been broken, substitute the current information. Hopefully, the basic structure of the vignette will require no change at all.

When performing *I Didn't Know That!* the actors should use their own names in the dialogue, when needed.

The play grew out of a childlike fascination for rhythm, music, and dancing. Therefore, the chants and songs in the playscript are reminiscent of jump rope rhymes and are sung *a cappella* with only percussion accompaniment. The musical arrangements are found at the end of the book.

Scenery

A bare stage with a simple backdrop works most effectively for the play. Since the show was originally designed to tour and adapt itself to any available space, the staging relied on creating spectacle with physical movement rather than with scenic devices. Individual groups may wish to experiment with platforms or movable blocks. But the inventiveness of the play must come from the movement of the actors themselves. Their bodies and voices are the real "scenery," creating anything from trains and rocket ships to mirrors and lightning.

PROPERTIES

The only hand properties required for the show are three pairs of old-fashioned wire-rim eyeglasses.

COSTUMES

Since the play is an "ensemble" piece, the actors can all wear the same type of basic outfit with individualized accessories. Drawstring pants and T-shirts, both one color for each actor, can be satisfyingly simple and comfortable for the rigorous movements demanded. The original company wore a variation of the traditional "newsboy" garb: knee-length pants with knee socks, muslin shirts, soft caps, scarves, and gymnastic slippers. Each actor wore either a vest or suspenders for variety. In addition, each player's costume had its own set of two colors with pastels and plaid patterns to unify the designs.

MUSICAL INSTRUMENTS

These are perhaps the most important "devices" for the revue. The range of sound effects enhances not only the action, but punctuates the beginning and ending of each vignette. Many of the percussion instruments listed can be found in any toy shop. Unusual instruments, such as a "vibra-slap" or an "afuche," are relatively expensive and found only at music stores. Though delightful to have, they are not necessary. Each production group can use other available percussion, or create their own musical instruments. Whatever the solution, the collage of sounds creates an amusing effect and fascinates the children both aurally and visually.

Basic Percussion:

    1 small snare drum

    1 small tenor drum

    3 drumsticks
    1 drum mallet

Hand Percussion:

    1 pair of claves
    2 tambourines
    6 finger cymbals
    1 pair of small cymbals
    1 cowbell
    1 woodblock
    1 ratchet
    1 triangle and mallet
    2 sets of castanets (or hand-held clackers)

Effects Percussion:

    3 kazoos
    1 vara-tone
    1 whistle
    1 slide whistle
    1 siren

Special Percussion/Instruments:

    1 vibra-slap
    1 kalimba
    1 afuche

The instruments are pre-set on the stage for each actor, as needed. In some cases, the instruments are borrowed from the narrator's table or returned to the narrator when an actor is finished with them.

I DIDN'T KNOW THAT!

CHARACTERS

Beryl
Rachel
Louis
Johnny
Joyce

A bare stage with a backdrop; the instruments required for the players are pre-set on the stage floor; Beryl, the narrator/accompanist, sits on a stool at the downstage right corner of the acting area; her instruments are laid out on a small table; the players, Joyce, Rachel, Johnny, and Louis, form a tableau in the center of the stage. The curtain rises and lights raise to the above scene; all smile at the audience.

BERYL: (*Triangle hit.*)

RACHEL: (*Music Cue 1. Rachel strikes the claves together as the other players get into position: Rachel at center, Joyce downstage left, Johnny stage right, Louis upstage left; Rachel skips to the beat and stops.*) Did you know that over 235,000,000 Coca-Colas are sold every day?*

LOUIS: (*Turning to Rachel.*) Well, I didn't know that! (*Music Cue 2. Louis, with a tambourine, joins Rachel in a rhythmic beat as they dance across the stage; they stop.*) Did you know that the largest popsicle in the world weighs 5,750 pounds?*

JOHNNY: (*Turning to Louis.*) I didn't know that!

LOUIS: It's true! (*Music Cue 3. Johnny, with a vibra-slap, joins Rachel and Louis in a rhythmic beat as they dance across the stage; they stop.*)

JOHNNY: Did you know that the toothbrush was invented in China in 1498?

JOYCE: (*Turning to Johnny.*) I didn't know that!

JOHNNY: M-hm. (*Music Cue 4. Joyce, with finger cymbals, joins the others in the rhythmic beat and dance; all stop.*)

JOYCE: Did you know that bees can dance?

RACHEL/JOHNNY/LOUIS: (*To each other.*) I didn't know that!

JOYCE: And ants have 5 noses.

LOUIS: (*To audience.*) And a flea can jump 130 times its own height.*

RACHEL: (*To audience.*) And tortoises are the longest-living animals.*

JOHNNY: And the largest watermelon ever grown weighed 19 pounds.* (*Music Cue 5. All chant to each other, then to the audience.*)

ALL: I didn't know that,
   I didn't know that,
   I didn't know that,
   I DIDN'T KNOW THAT!

LOUIS: (*As an announcement.*) I DIDN'T KNOW THAT!—A light-hearted revue of . . .

JOYCE: First facts.

RACHEL: Selected oddities.

JOHNNY: And world records.

LOUIS: FIRST FACTS! (*Rachel strikes the claves twice to begin the beat for Music Cue 6. The players speak to each other.*)

JOHNNY/LOUIS: When was it created?

JOYCE/RACHEL: When was it invented?

JOHNNY/LOUIS: When was it created?

JOYCE/RACHEL: When was it invented?

ALL: (*Dancing with hands waving in the air.*)
   It's a First Fact,
   It's a First Fact.
   It's a first in the world,
   It's a *First Fact!*

BERYL: (*Triangle hit.*) The invention of soap. (*The players move into position; Joyce downstage left, Louis, Johnny, and Rachel in center; the three pantomime bathing as Joyce speaks to the audience.*)

JOYCE: Long ago, people rarely took baths. They either had their own private tub, (*Rachel gets in an imaginary tub.*) took a swim in the river (*Johnny makes a splashing noise and dives to floor; he "swims."*) or else sprayed themselves with perfume. (*Louis uses an imaginary atomizer on his neck.*) But even with all the perfume people used, they still smelled bad. (*Johnny rises and crosses to Louis; they shake hands.*)

LOUIS: How are you doing, Johnny?

JOHNNY: Fine. (*The men get too close and turn away from each other in disgust at the smell.*)

LOUIS: Ooh, stinky!

RACHEL: Johnny! (*She and Johnny approach each other and kiss each other's cheeks; they gag from the smell.*)

JOYCE: No one knows who invented it, but in the year 1259, in England, a thing called "soap" was invented. (*She passes an imaginary cake of soap to Louis; he uses it, then it slips out of his hands and into Johnny's, who rubs it on himself and passes it to Rachel.*) It was a greasy but sweet-smelling cake that people used to scrub themselves with while bathing. And the perfume in the soap stayed on their bodies, making people smell *much* nicer. (*Louis, Johnny, and Rachel approach each other with caution; they place their arms around each other and inhale; they exhale with delight.*)

RACHEL/JOHNNY/LOUIS: Aaaahhh!

BERYL: (*Triangle hit.*) The invention of eyeglasses. (*Johnny crosses downstage right; Joyce, Rachel, and Louis get pairs of old wire-rim glasses; the earpieces are folded in, so the players hold them to their eyes with their hands; portraying aged people, they fumble with the glasses, read, walk, bump into each other, and mutter.*)

JOHNNY: Eyeglasses were first created in Italy in 1287. They were used primarily by the elderly when their own eyesight began to fail.

RACHEL: I just love my new glasses!

JOHNNY: The only problem was, they kept slipping off their noses.

JOYCE: Confounded glasses!

JOHNNY: It wasn't until 1727 that an Englishman, Edward Scarlet, created sidepieces to help keep the glasses resting on the nose. Take it away, folks! (*Joyce, Rachel, and Louis open the sidepieces of the glasses and exclaim with delight and amazement; they wear them, place their arms around each other for a chorus line, and kick up slowly and stiffly.*)

JOYCE/RACHEL/LOUIS: (*Music Cue 7.*)
Me and Grandma Moses
Are kickin' up our toeses,
'Cause now we got some glasses
To stay upon our noses.

LOUIS: Faster! (*The three kick up with energy and speed.*)

JOYCE/RACHEL/LOUIS: Me and Grandma Moses
   Are kickin' up our toeses,
   'Cause now we got some glasses
   To stay upon our noses.

   (*They laugh with delight.*)

BERYL: (*Triangle hit.*) The first sandwich. (*Joyce, Rachel, and Johnny assemble in center, pantomiming a game of cards; Louis, as a servant, pours tea for them.*)

RACHEL: The first sandwich was invented completely by accident.

JOYCE: In London, in the year 1762, members of royalty played a card game . . .

LOUIS: That lasted 24 hours! (*All yawn; Louis crosses stage right.*)

JOHNNY: One of the players, John Montagu—the Earl of Sandwich—was so involved with the game that he refused to leave the table to eat. (*He snaps his fingers; Louis rushes to him.*)

LOUIS: He ordered a servant to bring him (*Johnny demonstrates through pantomime; Louis speaks in puzzled amazement.*) a piece of meat in-between two pieces of bread? (*Louis crosses stage right to an imaginary banquet table.*)

RACHEL: That way he could hold on to the meat without getting his hands dirty.

JOYCE: And still stay in the game. (*Louis brings Johnny the sandwich; Johnny takes a bite out of it and exclaims satisfaction.*)

LOUIS: The idea caught on.

RACHEL: Oh, bring me one of those things!

LOUIS: What things? (*All look at each other in puzzled expressions.*) And it was called . . .

ALL: A sandwich.

JOHNNY: Because *that* was the name of the town where John Montagu —the Earl of Sandwich—lived. (*He takes a bite out of the sandwich.*)

BERYL: (*Triangle hit.*) The first ballet. (*Johnny and Joyce as audience members down left; Rachel as a dancer up center; Louis as a dancer down right.*)

LOUIS: The first ballet in America was on February 7, 1827, at the Bowery Theatre in New York City. (*Louis hums a classic ballet tune as Rachel spins and imitates a ballet dancer; it is a comic sight as Louis has difficulty lifting his partner.*)

JOHNNY: (*As Louis and Rachel dance downstage.*) One of the dancers, Madame Fransiquy Hutin, who introduced modern ballet to America, wore a dress made out of . . . (*The dancers spin to him.*) sheer see-through gauze . . . (*He approaches Rachel to get a closer look.*)

LOUIS: Similar to the tutus of the day.

JOYCE: (*Looking on with disgust.*) And the initial reaction of the ladies in the audience was *shock*—and *terror!* They fled from the theatre . . .

JOHNNY/JOYCE: (*Still looking at Rachel dancing, he sighs ecstatically; Joyce, having left her husband, returns and pulls him away.*) Taking their husbands with them! (*She drags him off right.*)

BERYL: (*Vibra-slap hit.*) The first bank robbery. (*Joyce and Johnny up center, standing sideways to represent two doors, their hands out as doorknobs; Joyce has a drumstick in the other hand, Johnny a woodblock in his other hand; Rachel up left, back to audience with a whistle in hand; Louis sneaks upstage to the doors.*)

LOUIS: The first bank robbery in America was on March 19, 1831, when two doors of the City Bank, (*He "opens" Johnny, who turns to the audience while making a squeaking sound.*) New York City, (*He "opens" Joyce, who does the same; Louis enters and pantomimes stealing money in a sack.*) were opened by duplicate keys. (*Beryl strikes two finger cymbals together.*) And the bank was robbed of . . .

JOYCE/JOHNNY: $245,000.00! (*Louis laughs villainously and goes the other way; Rachel spins around and blows the whistle twice.*)

RACHEL: Edward Smith was immediately arrested and brought to court! (*She pushes Louis to his knees, now before the "court": Rachel, Johnny, and Joyce standing erect as judges.*)

JOYCE: (*Hitting the woodblock in Johnny's hand with the drumstick 3 times.*) Court in session.

JOHNNY: Edward Smith—(*Louis makes a different face for each name.*)—alias Jones—alias James Smith—alias James Honeyman was indicted by the Grand Jury and arraigned at the Court of General Sessions.

JOYCE: And on May 11, 1831, was sentenced to . . .

JOYCE/RACHEL/JOHNNY: (*All pointing a finger at Louis on each word.*) *Five years hard labor at Sing-Sing!* (*Louis weeps hysterically and saunters down right; he pantomimes breaking rocks with an ax, striking on the woodblock hit of Music Cue 8, a requiem.*)

Ta-da-da-da-da, ta-da-da-da-da,
Da-da-da-da, da-da-da-da.

RACHEL: Which proves once again that . . .

ALL: *Crime doesn't pay!*

BERYL: (*Ratchet turn.*) The first bicycle. (*Joyce and Rachel stage left; Johnny in center, pantomiming the construction of a bicycle; Louis up right.*)

LOUIS: The first bicycle was invented by Kirkpatrick Macmillan . . .

JOHNNY: An Englishman . . .

LOUIS: In 1839. (*Johnny pantomimes a struggle to lift the bicycle.*) The first bicycle had wheels . . .

JOHNNY: That were made out of solid iron! (*Johnny pantomimes getting on the bicycle and struggling to ride it stage left; Rachel and Joyce, as bystanders, look on in amazement.*)

RACHEL: And since it was so new to the world . . .

JOYCE: It was called a . . . (*Johnny loses control of the bicycle and heads for the girls.*)

LOUIS: Look out!

JOYCE: *Terror on wheels!* (*Johnny, racing with the bike, chases Joyce and Rachel around the stage; they dodge each other.*)

LOUIS: The inventor also had the first bicycle accident . . . (*Johnny rushes in between Rachel and Joyce, knocking them to the floor; Johnny stumbles off the bicycle; all scream.*) when he ran over . . .

RACHEL: (*Angrily.*) A child in the street!

JOHNNY: (*To Rachel.*) I'm sorry, I'm so sorry!

LOUIS: (*Goes to Johnny and grabs him by the back of the shirt.*) And was fined 5 shillings by the police! (*Johnny moans.*)

BERYL: (*Triangle hit.*) The first policewoman. (*Joyce at center, Johnny next to her, Rachel and Louis with their backs to the audience up left.*)

JOYCE: The first policewoman in America was Alice Stebbins Wells.

JOHNNY: She was appointed to the Los Angeles Police Department on September 12, 1910. (*He places a whistle around Joyce's neck and they salute; Joyce turns and pantomimes writing out a ticket; Johnny crosses up right and searches for someone; Rachel and Louis turn around and dance closely together.*)

RACHEL: Part of Miss Wells's job was to keep . . .

RACHEL/LOUIS: Law and order . . .

LOUIS: In such places as . . .

RACHEL/LOUIS: Dance halls. (*They dance toward center and bump into Joyce; she clears her throat warningly; Rachel and Louis cross back left.*)

LOUIS: Oh, it's that lady cop!

RACHEL: I'm so embarrassed! (*Joyce returns to her work, checking a photo file.*)

LOUIS: (*To Rachel.*) C'mon, baby, let's get outta here.

RACHEL: No.

LOUIS: I said let's go!

RACHEL: No!

LOUIS: Don't give me no trouble! (*He pantomimes throwing his fist across Rachel's face, making her spin and fall unconscious into Louis' arms; he drags her to the upstage center area; Johnny, still searching, goes to where Rachel was struck.*)

JOYCE: She also searched for missing persons.

JOHNNY: (*To Joyce.*) My girlfriend is gone!

JOYCE: (*Blows her whistle.*) Follow me! (*They go upstage where Rachel has been stretched out on the floor; Louis hides behind Beryl.*)

JOHNNY: There she is! (*He pulls Rachel up; she looks confused.*) Darling, who did this to you? (*Rachel points to Louis; Joyce blows her whistle.*)

JOYCE: She also had powers of arrest! (*Music Cue 9. Johnny and Rachel sing as Joyce chases Louis around the stage; he attempts to strike her, but Joyce punches him in an elaborately staged fight; he groans with each blow.*)

RACHEL/JOHNNY: Ta-ka-ta-ka-ta, ta-ka-ta-ka-ta, ta-ka-ta-ka-ta-ka-ta-ka-ta-ka-ta-ka-ta. Ta-ka-ta-ka-ta, ta-ka-ta-ka-ta, ta-ka-ta-ka-ta-ka-ta-ka-ta-ka-ta-ka-ta. Ta-ka-ta-ka-ta, ta-ka-ta-ka-ta, ta-ka-ta-ka-ta-ka-ta-ka-ta-ka-ta-ka-ta. (*Joyce kicks Louis in the rear; he flies through the air as Beryl blows a siren whistle to match his flight and fall; Rachel and Johnny point to Joyce, as if to say "our hero."*) Alice Stebbins Wells!

LOUIS: (*In pain.*) The first policewoman!

BERYL: (*Cowbell.*) The first flying cow! (*The players looks at her questioningly.*)

ALL: *What?!*

BERYL: (*Sheepishly.*) Or rather, the first cow to fly in an airplane.

ALL: (*They understand now.*) Oh! (*Louis crosses down left; Joyce upstage with her arms outstretched to form the wings of an airplane; Johnny as the cow, is led into the plane by Rachel, the pilot; Johnny "moos" now and then; Rachel spins the propeller to start the plane, then sits downstage to fly it.*)

LOUIS: All right, everyone, let's climb aboard. (*He gets into the plane; all bounce and swerve together as if flying; Louis interviews Johnny.*) After a bumpy takeoff, in 1930, er—what's your name?

JOHNNY: (*In a "mooing" effect.*) Elm Farm Ollie.

LOUIS: Elm Farm Ollie was the first cow to fly in an airplane. How are you doing? (*The plane swerves to the left; Johnny moos in pain and holds his stomach.*) Something seems to be the matter. (*The plane swerves right; Johnny moos.*) Stomach ache? (*Johnny moos a "no" and points to his stomach.*) I think she needs to be milked! (*Johnny moos in relief; Louis pantomimes milking the cow.*) Yes sir, folks, on that historic flight, Elm Farm Ollie was milked. The milk was put in paper containers and parachuted over . . . (*Louis pantomimes throwing the containers out.*) St. Louis, Missouri. (*All swerve to watch the containers going down while they make a "falling" noise descending in pitch by whistling or mooing; Beryl accompanies the "drop" by blowing a slide whistle down in pitch.*)

ALL: *Splat!*

BERYL: (*Triangle hit.*) The first space flight. (*Johnny goes down right; Joyce, Rachel, and Louis stand together with their arms raised to form a rocket ship.*)

JOHNNY: The first space flight, oddly enough, wasn't done by people—it was done by monkeys! (*All move and screech like monkeys; they line up.*) In 1951, four monkeys with the code names: (*All in a screeching voice; each one scratches the head of the next monkey.*) Albert 1 . . .

JOYCE: Albert 2 . . .

RACHEL: Albert 3 . . .

LOUIS: (*Scratching his armpit.*) Albert 4 . . .

JOHNNY: (*Normal voice.*) Were launched 85 miles into the stratosphere in a V-2 rocket. (*Music Cue 10. All dance like monkeys; Beryl on claves.*)

ALL: Ooh! Ooh! Ooh!

RACHEL/LOUIS: Oh-ho, the first space flight . . .

JOYCE/JOHNNY: Oh-ho, the first space flight . . .

RACHEL/LOUIS: By living creatures . . .

JOYCE/JOHNNY: Living creatures . . .

RACHEL/LOUIS: Wasn't done by people . . .

JOYCE/JOHNNY: No civilized, humanized, bug-eyed, people . . .

ALL: No! But by monkeys!
    Ah-ooh-ah-ooh-ah-ooh!
    Monkeys . . .

JOHNNY/LOUIS: In '51.

JOYCE/RACHEL: Yessiree, 1951.

JOHNNY/LOUIS: Four adorable monkeys . . .

JOYCE/RACHEL: Adorable monkeys . . .

JOHNNY/LOUIS: Were sent in flight.

JOYCE/RACHEL: How did we earn this right?

JOHNNY/LOUIS: Launched 85 miles . . .

JOYCE/RACHEL: Into the stratosphere.

ALL: They flung us in space,
Right out of this place
In a . . .

JOHNNY/LOUIS: V . . .

JOYCE/RACHEL: 2 . . .

JOHNNY/LOUIS: V . . .

JOYCE/RACHEL: 2 . . .

ALL: V-2 rocket ship!
Ah-ooh-ah-ooh!

(*All screech.*)

BERYL: (*Vara-tone effect. Eerie voice.*) SELECTED ODDITIES. (*All players move in haunting, eerie fashion, and speak ominously.*)

RACHEL/JOHNNY: Selected . . .

JOYCE/LOUIS: (*Echo effect.*) Selected, selected, selected, selected, selected . . .

RACHEL/JOHNNY: Oddities . . .

JOYCE/LOUIS: Oddities, oddities, oddities, oddities, oddities . . . (*They line up stage left, facing right and staring ahead.*)

BERYL: (*Tambourine hit.*) The world's smallest man-eating fish.

ALL: (*Turning to audience sharply; each has one hand on their stomach, the other on the small of their back, like a flamenco dancer; they speak in a harsh whisper.*) Piranha! (*They dance in flamenco fashion; Beryl on castanets; Music Cue 11.*)

In the waters of South America,
There's a fish they call "piranha."
They swim in schools of a thousand.
And they eat whatever they wanna.

(*They break apart and dance in the style of "La Cucaracha" with Rachel and Louis as partners, Joyce and Johnny the same.*)

P-p-piranha,
P-p-piranha!
They eat whatever they wanna!
P-p-piranha,
P-p-piranha!
They eat whatever they wanna!

(*Joyce crosses down left; Rachel, Johnny, and Louis cross upstage with their backs to the audience.*)

JOYCE: Piranha are very small fish, about the size of a human hand. And when swimming in schools of a thousand, they can devour a horse within minutes, and a man within seconds. (*Rachel, Louis, and Johnny turn around and "swim" to Joyce with facial expressions like the piranha; Joyce does not notice them and dances; Music Cue 12.*)
    P-p-piranha,
    P-p-piranha . . .

RACHEL/JOHNNY/LOUIS: We eat whatever we wanna.

JOYCE: (*Seeing them, cowers in fear; they close in.*)
    P-p-piranha!
    P-p-piranha!

RACHEL/JOHNNY/LOUIS: For you, there is no mañana! (*They cover her head; Joyce screams; they speak in a terse whisper.*) Piranha!

BERYL: (*Cymbal crash.*)

ALL: (*Dancing in different shapes, forming sizes with bodies; Music Cue 13.*)
    Shapes and sizes,
    Shapes and sizes.
    Everybody everywhere's
    Diff'rent sizes.
    Shapes and sizes,

Shapes and sizes.
Everybody everywhere's
Diff'rent shapes and sizes!

BERYL: (*Triangle hit.*) The world's tallest man.* (*Louis and Johnny go upstage, squat with backs to audience; Joyce in center, pantomiming a baby in her arms; Rachel down left.*)

RACHEL: The world's tallest man was Robert Pershing Wadlow. When Pershing was born, he weighed 8½ pounds—and his mother thought she had a perfectly average baby. (*Johnny "cries" like a baby; Joyce tickles the "baby."*) But Pershing's growth began almost immediately. (*Joyce picks up Johnny by the hand, his thumb in his mouth.*) At age five, Pershing weighed 105 pounds and was 5′ 4″.

JOYCE: (*Trying to pull the thumb out of Johnny's mouth.*) Pershing, no sucking thumb! (*She pulls it out; they spin around from the effort; Johnny stands on tip-toe while Joyce slumps down in height.*)

RACHEL: When he was 10 years old and in the 4th grade, he was 6′ 5″ and weighed 210 pounds.

JOHNNY: (*Low voice.*) Hi, mom.

JOYCE: (*As Johnny puts his arm around her; dumbfounded.*) Oh, Pershing—you're growing so fast!

RACHEL: And when he was 22, he reached his full height of . . . (*Louis gets between Johnny's legs and lifts him up on his shoulders; Joyce stares at his height; Beryl blows a slide whistle up in pitch as Johnny "grows."*) 8′ 11″!

JOYCE: (*Proudly.*) That's my little Pershing! (*Johnny lays his hand on her head.*)

BERYL: (*Triangle hit.*) The world's longest earthworm.* (*Louis stage left, facing left; Johnny and Joyce up right; Rachel center.*)

RACHEL: The longest species of earthworms can be found in South Africa, with an average length of 4′ 6″.

JOHNNY: (*Joining Rachel and standing next to her; he places his hand on her shoulder.*) Although some species of earthworms have been known to reach 11′.

JOYCE: (*Joining Rachel and Johnny, standing next to him, her hand on his shoulder.*) And some earthworms, when extended to their full length, can reach up to 21′. (*The three "stretch out," their arms extended and holding hands to form a "worm"; Louis imitates a bird and dances to the center; Beryl accompanies on a kazoo; the earthworm follows him; Music Cue 14.*)

LOUIS: Oh, the early bird catches the worm.
The early bird catches the worm.
C'mon ya slimy little worms,
I'm gonna eat you up, 'cause
The early bird catches the worm.

JOYCE/RACHEL/JOHNNY: (*Closing in on the bird.*)
The biggest worm catches the early bird.
The biggest worm catches the early bird.

(*Louis tries to escape; the worm surrounds and devours him.*)

Slurp! Slurp! Slither and slime! 'Cause
The biggest worm catches the early bird!

(*Louis sticks his head out and screeches; the worm pushes it back in.*)

BERYL: (*Ratchet turn.*) The longest fast.* (*Joyce in center; Rachel, Johnny, and Louis mutter "Fat, fat, fat . . ." and surround her to form a large waddling body; Beryl on slide whistle as it moves.*)

JOYCE: The longest time anyone has ever gone without food has been 382 days. (*The "fat" cries out.*)

RACHEL: Give me something to eat!

LOUIS: Food!

JOHNNY: I'm hungry!

JOYCE: (*Moves right; fat waddles with her; she speaks to it.*) No food, no food! (*To audience.*) That's longer than a year. Surviving solely on tea, coffee, water, soda water, and, of course, vitamins—

RACHEL: Chocolate cake!

LOUIS: Food!

JOHNNY: Pizza!

JOYCE: (*Moves to center, the fat with her.*) Oh, no food!—that person lost down from 472 pounds . . . (*The "fat" begins to slowly drop to the floor.*) to 178—a total loss of 294 pounds. (*All groan "Food" chant as Rachel and Joyce go up right, Louis and Johnny stage left; Music Cue 15.*)

ALL: Food, food, food, food, food, food, food, *food!*

JOYCE/RACHEL: (*Dancing to center.*) Food, food, food, food, food, food, food, food. Boy, oh how I love that food food. (*Johnny and Louis join them.*)

JOYCE/RACHEL:	(*Together.*) JOHNNY/LOUIS:
Food, food, food, food,	Bring on the chow!
Food, food, food, food.	Bring on the chow!
Boy, oh how I	Come on, mama, and
Love that food food.	Bring on the chow!
	Crunch! Munch! (*Rubbing stomach.*)
	Mm—mm—mm!
Food, food, food, food,	Bring on the chow!
Food, food, food, food.	Bring on the chow!
Boy, oh how I	Come on, mama, and
Love that food food.	Bring on the chow!

ALL: Bring on the chow!
Bring on the chow!
Come on, mama, and
Bring on the chow!

BERYL: (*Triangle hit.*)

LOUIS: The world's largest hamburger.* (*All join in center and stretch out to the corners of the stage, holding up the "hamburger."*) The world's largest hamburger was 27½' in circumference, and weighed 2,859 pounds. (*All collapse from the weight of the hamburger.*) Dig in! (*A slow motion "food fight" as they eat the burger.*)

JOYCE: Give me the tomatoes!

RACHEL: I want all the pickles! Look! Here's a great big pickle!

JOHNNY: (*Taking it away from Rachel.*) Give me that pickle! (*He swats it in Joyce's face.*)

LOUIS: Have some mustard! (*He throws it in Johnny's face; all make a "splat" sound; Beryl hits the triangle.*)

JOHNNY: The world's largest pizza.* (*Joyce, Rachel, and Louis pantomime making a pizza.*) The world's largest pizza ever created was 80'

1″ in diameter, weighed 18,664 pounds, with 60,318 slices served. (*All walk on the pizza getting their feet stuck in the cheese; Johnny sings, Music Cue 16.*)

Santa Lucia, sausage and mushrooms,
Cheese and onions, hot jalapeños.

(*All pantomime a burning taste in their mouths; Beryl blows the siren.*)

RACHEL: The world's longest banana split.* (*All gather in the center; Rachel and Johnny together, Joyce and Louis together.*) The world's longest banana split was . . . (*Rachel and Johnny go left, Joyce and Louis go right; they separate to show the length of the "bowl."*) 1 mile, 99 yards long . . . (*All wave and say "Hello" to each other as if far away.*) Encompassed 11,333 bananas . . . (*They peel bananas, drop them in the bowl, moving toward the center; they sing in calypso fashion.*)

ALL: See the boat with the big banana.

RACHEL: 34,000 scoops of ice cream . . . (*The players pantomime scooping and throwing ice cream into the bowl; they separate again.*)

RACHEL/JOHNNY: Scoop, scoop . . .

JOYCE/LOUIS: Ice cream!

RACHEL/JOHNNY: Scoop, scoop . . .

JOYCE/LOUIS: Ice cream!

RACHEL: 260 imperial gallons of gooey topping . . . (*They pantomime pouring it in, disgusted with the stickiness; all join center again.*) 150 pounds of chopped nuts . . . (*All throw in nuts, acting like "nuts," and separate.*) And 100 gallons of whipped cream! (*They pantomime squirting whipped cream from fire hoses, while creating the sound; they join in the center.*) It certainly is *big!*

LOUIS: Well, let's eat it up!

JOHNNY: I don't think I can.

JOYCE: Well, *I* can!

JOHNNY: (*To audience, pointing out.*) What about giving it to them?

LOUIS: (*To audience.*) You want to help us eat it?

(*If audience says "yes":*)	(*If audience says "no" or is silent:*)
ALL: All right—here it comes! Whoa!	ALL: No? Well, you're going to get it, anyway! Whoa!

(*In either case, the players "push" the banana split to the edge of the stage into the audience; Beryl crashes the cymbals; Music Cue 17.*)

ALL: (*Dancing upstage; the players shape their bodies to suit their individual lyrics.*)
Hey, hey, whaddaya say
About the words you hear today?

RACHEL: Big words . . .

JOHNNY: Little words . . .

LOUIS: Long and . . .

JOYCE: Skinny.

ALL: You should know that
There are many.

JOYCE: Moan . . .

LOUIS: Groan . . .

RACHEL/JOHNNY: Ice cream cone . . .

LOUIS: Chase . . .

JOYCE: Base . . .

RACHEL/JOHNNY: Haste makes waste . . .

RACHEL: Heart . . .

JOHNNY: Head . . .

LOUIS: Body and . . .

JOYCE: Soul.

RACHEL: Come on, y'all, and let it be told! (*Johnny crosses behind Beryl; Joyce, Rachel, and Louis upstage with backs to audience; they turn and cross downstage when they speak; they act like contestants in a beauty contest and deliver their words with charm and grace.*)

JOHNNY: The 10 most beautiful words in the English language. (*Beryl accompanies with delicate melodies on a kalimba.*)

RACHEL: Golden. Dawn.

JOYCE: Lullaby.

RACHEL: Chimes.

JOYCE: Luminous.

LOUIS: (*With comic parody as a contestant.*) Melody.

JOYCE: Hush.

LOUIS: Mist. Murmuring. (*Johnny, with a tambourine and ratchet in hand, crosses to Joyce, shaking the tambourine over her head; the intent is to determine the winner; he crosses to Rachel and does the same, then goes to Louis and sets the tambourine over his head.*) Tranquil. (*Johnny turns the ratchet; all react to the noise.*)

JOHNNY: The five ugliest words in the English language are . . . (*All speak with harsh tones and gang up on Louis.*)

RACHEL: Treachery!

JOYCE: Gripe!

RACHEL: Sap!

LOUIS: Cacophony!

ALL: (*Pushing Louis to the floor as Johnny turns the ratchet.*) Crunch! (*The players rush about madly, as if being haunted; Music Cue 18.*)
   Superstitions, superstitions,
   What kind of word is "superstitions"?
   Superstitions, superstitions,
   Four common signs of superstitions!

   (*Joyce and Johnny upstage; Rachel and Louis center.*)

RACHEL: Superstition number 1. (*Louis sneezes.*) Gesundheit.

LOUIS: "Gesundheit"? What kind of word is "gesundheit"?

RACHEL: Well, primitive man used to believe that when a person sneezed, it opened up a passage for evil spirits to enter and take away his soul. (*Joyce and Johnny, creeping like "evil spirits," approach Louis from behind.*)

LOUIS: Aw, evil spirits! (*He laughs.*)

RACHEL: So people said "gesundheit" to frighten the evil spirits away. (*Louis continues to laugh as the "evil spirits" approach; his laughter turns into a loud sneeze.*)

LOUIS: AH-CHOO! (*Johnny and Joyce prepare to strike.*)

RACHEL: Gesundheit.

JOYCE/JOHNNY: (*Screaming and falling to the ground from the word.*) AUGH!

RACHEL: But it's just a silly superstition. (*Beryl hits the vibra-slap.*)

LOUIS: Superstition number 2. (*Louis goes upstage of where Joyce fell, Rachel upstage of Johnny; they stand with their arms extended to represent headboards of a bed; Joyce and Johnny remain lying down.*)

RACHEL: Getting up on the right side of the bed. (*During Rachel's monologue, Johnny and Joyce "rise" out of bed on the left side and stumble around; Beryl plays a Mexican "fish" to accompany their movement.*) Getting upon the left side of the bed is bound to make you have a rotten, crummy, horrible day—and it's bound to be filled with hardship and misfortune. (*Johnny and Joyce growl at each other.*)

LOUIS: To reverse the situation, walk calmly backwards over the same path . . . (*Johnny and Joyce reverse their movements; Beryl accompanies by blowing a slide whistle up in pitch.*) return to your bed . . . (*Johnny and Joyce lie down as before.*) and begin anew.

RACHEL: (*Johnny and Joyce, refreshed, do what she says.*) Now, get up on the right side of the bed with your right foot first. Stand up, stretch, and have a . . . (*Johnny and Joyce embrace.*)

RACHEL/LOUIS: Bright and happy day! (*Beryl hits the triangle.*)

JOYCE: Superstition number 3.

JOHNNY: Breaking a mirror. (*He and Joyce go upstage, using the outstretched arms of Louis and Rachel as turnstiles, and cross up left; Louis and Rachel spin once; Louis frames his head with his arms as if making a mirror; Rachel stares at him.*)

RACHEL: (*With arrogance; Louis mocks her face.*)
Mirror, mirror, on the wall,
Who is the fairest, most beautiful girl of all?

LOUIS: Not *you!* (*Rachel shrieks and "breaks" the mirror by striking Louis; he crumples to the ground making the sound of shattering glass as Beryl accompanies the breaking by clashing the cymbals.*)

JOHNNY: (*Pointing to Rachel and speaking like a "voice from above."*) You are sentenced to 7 years' bad luck! (*Louis rises like a ghost and taunts Rachel; he laughs wickedly as Joyce and Johnny sing Music Cue 19.*)

JOYCE/JOHNNY: Ta-da-da-da-da, ta-da-da-da-da.
  Da-da-da-da, da-da-da-da.

  (*Joyce rushes in between Rachel and Louis; Johnny crosses down left.*)

JOYCE: *Stop!* (*All comes to a standstill.*) To avoid this situation, you must first remove the mirror from your house and *bury it.* (*Johnny pantomimes digging a hole with a shovel; Louis stares in horror.*)

JOHNNY: (*A rhythmic beat as he digs; Music Cue 20.*) Sh-sh, sh-sh, sh-sh, sh-sh. (*Joyce and Rachel fling Louis to the "hole"; he falls to the ground as Johnny shovels the dirt on top of him; Louis grunts and groans in panic as if eating dirt; on the final beats of Johnny's shoveling, Joyce and Rachel join him; Music Cue 21.*) Sh-sh, sh-sh, sh-sh, shew-shew . . .

JOYCE/RACHEL/JOHNNY: (*Dancing as a 1950s backup group parody.*)
  Shew-wap-du-wadda-wadda,
  Shew-wap-du-wadda-wadda,
  Shew-wap-du-wadda-wadda,
  Shew-wap-du-wadda-wadda.

LOUIS: (*Rises, crosses up right.*)
  Superstition number 4.
  I say Salt!

JOYCE/RACHEL/JOHNNY: Salt!

LOUIS: Salt!

JOYCE/RACHEL/JOHNNY: Salt!

LOUIS	(*Together.*)	JOYCE/RACHEL/JOHNNY
Salt was a rare and		Shew-wap-du-wadda-wadda,
Costly item, and		Shew-wap-du-wadda-wadda,
If you wasted it, it		Shew-wap-du-wadda-wadda,

Brought bad luck.
Now take it away,
2, 3, 4 . . .

Shew-wap-du-wadda-wadda,
Shew-wap-du-wadda-wadda,
Shew-wap-du-wadda-wadda.

JOYCE/RACHEL/JOHNNY: Salt and pepper in a
Shaker and a holder.
If you spill some salt,
Throw it over your shoulder.

LOUIS: I say Salt!

JOYCE/RACHEL/JOHNNY: Salt!

LOUIS: Salt!

JOYCE/RACHEL/JOHNNY: Salt!

ALL: Salt and pepper in a
Shaker and a holder.
If you spill some salt,
Throw it over your shoulder.
Salt!

BERYL: (*Triangle hit; players come to attention.*) WORLD REC-
ORDS!

ALL: (*The players run around the stage as if in a race; Music Cue 22.*)
Who can set a record,
Set a record, set a record, yeah,
Who can set a record,
Set a record today?
Who can set a record,
Set a record, set a record, yeah,
Who can set a record,
Set a record today?

(*Rachel and Johnny finish upstage; Joyce and Louis downstage.*)

BERYL: (*Triangle hit.*) The world record for handshaking.* (*Rachel
and Johnny on kazoos; Music Cue 23; humming "Hail to the Chief,"
they march center, then downstage; Louis joins them, waving and
smiling at the audience.*)

JOYCE: The world record for handshaking was set by President Theodore
Roosevelt on January 1, 1907. (*Louis, as Roosevelt, shakes hands with*

Rachel and Johnny as they continue to hum on the kazoos; he shakes their hands alternately as the speed picks up frantically.) At a New Year's Day White House presentation, the President shook hands with 8,513 people. (*The handshaking, a feverish pace by now, runs down; the kazoos screech down in pitch, the hands and arms a tangled mess.*)

BERYL: (*Vibra-slap hit.*) The strongest teeth in the world.* (*Joyce and Rachel up right; Johnny in center, gritting his teeth and pointing to them; Louis down left.*)

LOUIS: The strongest teeth in the world belong to "Hercules" John Massis of Belgium. (*Johnny smiles, shows off his teeth.*) How are you doing, John?

JOHNNY: (*To audience through clenched teeth.*) Fine, thank you very, very much. (*He massages his jaw.*)

LOUIS: Ol' talkative Johnny, there. Is the locomotive ready? Bring it on the tracks. (*Rachel and Joyce, as a train, come up center; they "choo-choo" with Beryl accompanying on an afuche; the train whistles to a stop; Johnny pretends to connect a cable from the "train" to his teeth.*) The track looks level and he's got the bit in his mouth. (*The train chugs backwards and Johnny is pulled forward; he pulls and the train chugs forward, picking up speed with Joyce and Rachel creating train sound effects with Beryl's afuche accompaniment.*) November 8, 1978, "Hercules" John Massis pulled a locomotive and a truck weighing 140 tons . . . (*The speeding train and John Massis head toward Louis; he sees the imminent crash.*) with his teeth! (*The players crash into one another and freeze.*)

BERYL: (*Triangle hit.*) The world record for leap-frogging.* (*Rachel down left; Joyce, Johnny, and Louis limber up with energy and begin to play leap-frog.*)

RACHEL: The world record for leap-frogging was set by a group of students in 1978, going for 555.25 miles in just 6 days. On that first day, they had energy, vim, and vigor!

LOUIS: *Energy, vim, vigor!* (*The others cheer.*)

RACHEL: On the third day, they had vim and vigor. (*The leap-frogging goes slower; the players moan in pain.*) On that fifth day, all they had was vim. (*The leap-froggers collapse in a heap and groan.*) Congratulations, world champion leap-froggers, for going 555.25 miles in just 6 days! (*The leapers raise their heads.*)

JOYCE/JOHNNY/LOUIS: (*Like frogs, Louis flashing his tongue.*) Ribit—ribit—ribit. (*They drop their heads.*)

BERYL: (*Triangle hit.*) The world's worst gas fire.* (*Joyce and Louis form an operable oil rig stage center; Rachel and Johnny down left.*)

RACHEL: The world's worst gas fire happened in the Algerian Sahara . . . (*She crosses to the rig.*) when one of the oil rigs *erupted!* (*Beryl blows the siren; Rachel, Joyce, and Louis make an exploding effect and all use their bodies to create flames.*)

LOUIS: The flames reached 450′ in the air!

JOYCE: And the smoke billowed 600′.

JOHNNY: The fire, that burned for over 5 months, was eventually extinguished by Red Adair of Austin, Texas. (*He sets up a dynamite charge.*) Red used 550 pounds of dynamite. (*Johnny places his hands on the imaginary charge box.*) Three, two, one . . . (*He pushes the charger down; all shout "Boom!" and jump in the air; the "flames" collapse on the ground.*) How much was he paid for the job? $1,000,000.00! (*He clicks his heels in the air.*)

BERYL: (*Vibra-slap hit.*) The world's worst diseases.* (*Joyce and Johnny cross up right, Rachel and Louis center; all have their backs to the audience.*) The world's worst noncontagious disease afflicting 53 percent of the population in America is . . .

RACHEL/LOUIS: (*Turning around; wickedly.*) Tooth decay! (*Music Cue 24; they dance a macabre tango.*)
Make way for tooth decay,
Make way for tooth decay,
Make way for tooth decay!

JOYCE/JOHNNY: (*Turning around; smiling and dancing with excessive sweetness to center.*)
We're new teeth and we're proud about it!
We're new teeth and we love to shout it!
We're new teeth and we can't be beat, yeah,
We're new teeth and we love to eat!

(*Rachel and Louis dance to the teeth as Joyce and Johnny sing and smile.*)

RACHEL/LOUIS: (*Together.*)   JOYCE/JOHNNY:
Make way for tooth decay,   Da-da-da-da-da-da-da-da,
Make way for tooth decay!   Da-da-da-da-da-da-da-da . . .

LOUIS: (*Suggestively to the teeth, with an imaginary lollipop.*)
Want some—*candy?*

JOYCE/JOHNNY: (*Ecstatic.*) *Oh, boy!* (*Rachel feeds Johnny, Louis feeds Joyce; the "tooth decay" stuffs the "new teeth" with candy.*)

JOYCE/JOHNNY: We love sweets and lots of candy!
    Love the stuff 'cause it's so dandy!

(*The feeding goes faster; Joyce and Johnny sing as though their mouths are clogged with candy.*)

We love sweets and loth of cahdi!
Luh the stuh '*cuh ith tho dahdi!*

(*Rachel and Louis cover the teeth of Joyce and Johnny; they laugh wickedly and dance around them.*)

RACHEL/LOUIS:
    Make way for tooth decay,
    Make way for tooth decay!

LOUIS: (*Grabbing Johnny.*) You didn't use the brush . . .

RACHEL: (*Grabbing Joyce.*) Now your teeth are mush!

LOUIS: (*Throwing Johnny to the ground.*) You didn't use the floss . . .

RACHEL/LOUIS: (*Rachel throws Joyce to the ground.*) Now *we're* the boss! (*They laugh.*)

ALL: Tooth decay!

BERYL: (*Vibra-slap hit.*)

LOUIS: The world's rarest disease.* (*Louis crosses down left; Joyce, Rachel, and Johnny in center; they pantomime eating each others' brains; Beryl "laughs" on a kazoo.*) The world's rarest disease is Kuru. Kuru is transmitted by the cannibalistic practice of eating human brains. Kuru causes laughing sickness. (*The three cannibals giggle and laugh hysterically.*) It is affected only by the Fore tribe of eastern New Guinea. Fortunately, Kuru is 100 percent fatal. (*The cannibals' laughter turns into shrieks; they "die" instantly.*) Kuru.

BERYL: (*Triangle hit.*)

LOUIS: The world's most common contagious disease is . . .* (*Johnny rises and sneezes loudly.*) acute nasopharyngitis, or . . . (*All rise and form a line in center.*)

ALL: The common cold. (*The players sing and dance in a backup group parody; Music Cue 25.*)
When you got the chills and the fever,
When you got the chills and the fever,
When you got the sniffles and the sneezes
And the shivers and the shakes,
You better not go for a swim in the lake.

LOUIS: 'Cause you got that . . .

ALL: Nasopharyngitis.

RACHEL: (*Hiding her face behind Louis as he mouths the words—she uses a high-pitched screech.*) You got that . . .

ALL: Nasopharyngitis.

LOUIS: What's that?

ALL: Better known as the common cold, cold, cold, cold! Yeah!

BERYL: (*Triangle hit.*) The world's most uncomfortable facts. (*All wander around the stage with their affliction; when speaking, they come center; Rachel yawns, Joyce sneezes, Louis snores, Johnny hiccoughs.*)

RACHEL: (*Yawning throughout.*) A girl in England, 15 years old, yawned for 5 weeks straight.*

JOYCE: (*Trying to hold back sneezes.*) June Clark, of Florida, sneezed for 155 days.* (*She sneezes.*)

LOUIS: (*Snoring.*) Research has shown that the loudest snore can reach 69 decibels—that's comparable to a pneumatic drill.* (*He "drills" and snores at the same time.*)

JOHNNY: (*Hiccoughing throughout.*) Charles Osborne, of Iowa, has been hiccoughing for the past 58 (*hic*) years.* (*The others look at him and say "Aw," in pity.*)

BERYL: (*Vibra-slap hit.*) The world's human lightning rod.* (*Louis center; Joyce up right, Rachel up center, Johnny up left, with backs to audience.*)

LOUIS: The world record for being struck by lightning is held by park ranger Roy C. Sullivan—who has been struck 7 *times*. (*Joyce, Rachel, and Johnny spin around and extend their arms like lightning bolts; they make a "thundering" noise; Beryl on slide whistle each time they strike.*) His attraction for lightning began in 1942, when . . .

JOYCE: (*Rushing forward and striking Louis on the foot with her arm like a thunderbolt.*) He was struck on the foot and lost his big toenail! (*She rushes back to place.*)

LOUIS: Ow! Then in 1969 . . .

JOHNNY: (*Rushing to strike Louis on the forehead.*) He lost his eyebrows! (*He rushes back to place.*)

LOUIS: Ow! Then in 1970 . . .

RACHEL: (*Rushing to strike Louis.*) His shoulder was seared! (*She rushes back to place.*)

LOUIS: Ow! Then in 1972 . . .

JOYCE/RACHEL/JOHNNY: (*All rushing to strike Louis on the head, their fingers like flames.*) His hair caught on fire!

LOUIS: Ow! (*Joyce, Rachel, and Johnny go left; they place their arms around each others' shoulders and revolve in a low circle.*) Then, again, in 1973, as he was driving down a lonely road, out of a small low-lying cloud came . . .

RACHEL: (*Breaking apart from the circle to strike Louis.*) A bolt of lightning that knocked his hat off . . . (*Goes right, crosses upstage to left.*)

LOUIS: Ow!

JOYCE: (*Breaking apart, rushes to Louis.*) And set his hair on fire again . . . (*Goes right, crosses upstage to left.*)

LOUIS: Ow!

JOHNNY: (*Rushes to Louis, grabbing him.*) And knocked him 10′ out of his car! (*He throws Louis right and joins the other "lightning."*)

LOUIS: Ow! (*Rushes center, pantomiming a bucket over his head.*) He had to pour a pail of water over his head to cool off. (*The lightning rushes to Louis and surrounds him.*)

RACHEL: He was struck again in 1976! (*The lightning strikes him; he shakes his head.*)

LOUIS: Ow!

JOYCE: And, again, in 1977! (*The lightning strikes him; he shakes his rear.*)

LOUIS: Ow! (*He rushes down right.*) *But*—he lived to tell his story. (*He gives the "thumb to nose" gesture to the lightning.*) Nyah! (*The lightning "flashes" angrily at him.*)

BERYL: (*Vibra-slap hit.*) The world record for egg laying.* (*Joyce and Louis up left, Rachel down center; they cluck like hens while getting into place; Music Cue 26.*)

JOYCE/RACHEL/LOUIS: (*Arms at sides like the wings of hens.*)
   Ba-buk-ba-buk-buk-ba,
   Ba-buk-buk-ba,
   Ba-buk-ba-buk,
   Buk-ba-buk,
   Buk-buk-buk.

   (*Johnny comes center, holding a small drum as a basket; he collects the "eggs" from Louis and Joyce.*)

JOHNNY: (*Southern dialect.*) Well, hello, how are all my little chickies today? (*Joyce and Louis "cluck" with happiness; he turns to Rachel angrily.*) Now, Penny, this is the seventh day you've gone without laying an egg—*what's wrong?* (*Rachel "clucks" and shrugs her shoulders.*) I want you to start making up for all the time you've lost. Now I want to see seven eggs by *tonight*, or else *you're* going to be fried chicken for *my* Sunday dinner! (*He stalks away and sits behind Beryl; the chickens cluck in panic.*)

RACHEL: (*Southern dialect.*) *I don't wanna be no fried chicken!*

LOUIS: (*Music Cue 27.*)
   There was an old chicken,
   Her name was Penny,
   She had to lay 7 eggs
   In just one day.

   (*Rachel scratches the ground to prepare for laying eggs.*)

JOYCE: Clear out the henhouse,
   Throw in the hay.

Come on, Penny, so
You can lay.

LOUIS: (*Rachel jerks as the eggs are laid; Johnny beats a drum as each egg comes forth.*) Here comes the first egg . . .

JOYCE: Here comes the second egg . . .

LOUIS: Here comes the third . . .

JOYCE: And the fourth's on its way.

LOUIS: Here comes the fifth egg . . .

JOYCE: Here comes the sixth egg . . .

LOUIS: One more egg and you're OK. (*Rachel strains for the final egg as Beryl begins a drum roll.*)

JOYCE/JOHNNY/LOUIS: *Come on, Penny,*
  Lay that egg!
  Come on, Penny,
  Lay number 7!

(*The drum roll continues as Rachel strains; the roll builds to a climax, then a final bang as Rachel lays the seventh egg; she sighs with relief as Johnny comes to collect the eggs.*)

JOYCE/LOUIS: Farmer Lee,
  He came to see . . .

RACHEL: How many eggs been laid by me!

JOHNNY: (*Amazed.*) Seven eggs!

JOYCE/JOHNNY/LOUIS: (*As Rachel proudly struts.*)
  Penny, Penny,
  Rhode Island Red,
  She laid 7 eggs
  In just one day.

RACHEL: Come this Sunday,
  Farmer Lee
  Ain't gonna make
  Fried chicken outta me!

(*Drum beat; all "cluck" and "crow."*)

BERYL: (*Cymbal crash.*)

ALL: (*Joining together for the finale; they dance downstage; Beryl on claves; Music Cue 28.*)

    Who can set a record,
    Set a record,
    Set a record, yeah,
    Who can set a record,
    Set a record today?

    You can set a record,
    Set a record,
    Set a record, yeah,
    You can set a record,
    Set a record today.

    You can be the first,
    Be the first,
    Be the first, yeah,
    You can be the first
    In the universe.

JOHNNY/LOUIS: You can be the fastest,
    Be the tallest,
    Be the smallest, yeah,
    You can set a record,
    Set a record today.

LOUIS: You can be the biggest . . .

RACHEL: Be the boldest . . .

JOYCE/JOHNNY: Be the oldest . . .

ALL: Yeah, you can set a record,
    Set a record today.

    (*Softly.*)

    Who can set a record,
    Set a record,
    Set a record, yeah,
    Who can set a record,
    Set a record today?

JOHNNY/LOUIS: (*Loudly.*) Who can?

JOYCE/RACHEL: (*Loudly.*) She can!

JOHNNY/LOUIS: Who can?

JOYCE/RACHEL: He can!

JOHNNY/LOUIS: Who can?

JOYCE/RACHEL: We can!

JOHNNY/LOUIS: Who can?

ALL: *You can!* (*Beryl accompanies with a tambourine for the "grand finale."*)
  You can set a record,
  Set a record,
  Set a record, yeah,
  You can set a record,
  SET A RECORD TODAY!

(*All bow; they run offstage chanting the finale and waving to the audience; Beryl follows the group off.*) (*Lights dim.*)

CURTAIN

Part Two:

Plays for Children to Perform

Introduction: An improvisational approach to staging

When children stage plays for other children, the watchword for the adult leader is to "evoke." The leader should act as a guide, providing encouragement, thought-provoking questions, and enthusiasm—as well as steady nerves for settling disputes. But unlike the stage director in the traditional sense, he *should not direct*. The adult must present an atmosphere in which children can create. And they will gradually do just that as they begin to make decisions about how to enhance their production.

Children naturally want to create a production that they are happy with and that is entertaining. But the leader must be there to guide them, and he must always remember that his primary responsibility is the participants' learning. The process of producing the play is more important than the performance itself.

This approach to producing plays with children is based on an extensive use of creative drama or improvisation: The children hear the plot told as a story, or several of them read the play aloud to the group. Then without reading lines but using their own words, the entire group should enact the story several times in order to absorb and understand it. They should switch roles; expand and lengthen the play through character action; discover different movements and setting arrangements; locate doors; and arrange props, boxes, platforms, steps, etc. to create a variety of heights in the acting area. Then through discussions they should analyze their improvisations, deciding what to keep and what to discard. The adult serves as a catalyst to bring out their ideas.

Using this method will enable everyone in the group to gradually absorb and understand the whole play. As they learn the story of the play by acting it out and creating the characters' lines in their own words, they also become aware of the rudiments of dramatic form. They should be able to see that the plot is created by a closely woven series of action units; the theme, if there is one, is the underlying message of the play; and the characters behave, react, and speak in certain ways which should suggest the appropriate costumes. The settings don't have to be exact, they can be suggested by a prop or a piece of scenery or by the pantomime of an actor. Some settings can simply be "atmospheric," created by background sounds, musical effects, or lighting.

Although ten is recommended as the youngest age for participants in a dramatic production, there are always exceptions. Some children as young as six have the ability and desire to sustain their concentration through the many weeks of rehearsals, but they are rare.

The improvisational approach is particularly useful with children and teenagers. The young participants learn to think and create together. Because everyone understands the sequence of the plot thoroughly, a forgotten line can easily be replaced with a similar one. This approach to a script will help young actors to eliminate excessive stage fright during performances. Using creative drama throughout rehearsals helps keep the actors thinking and will keep the performance spontaneous. This spontaneity will avoid the stiffness of a performance that is too programmed by a director.

SELECTING THE PLAY

Having everyone in the group involved in choosing what they will perform will help to give the children as much control over the production as possible. But the leader must exercise his responsibility as the adult. He should narrow the options, and then guide the children in their choice. To younger groups, the leader may suggest two possible choices, and to older, more mature groups the leader may suggest as many as four or five. If none of these strikes a spark of interest, it is always possible to introduce others later on.

First the leader should read as many plays as possible and select those that will have appeal for his group based on two criteria: a length that

can be prepared within the given amount of rehearsal time; and a cast large enough to use most of the children. If the group is young, say ten or eleven, and inexperienced, the leader is wise to choose either *Hands Off! Don't Touch!, Ma and the Kids,* or one or two tales from *In One Basket.* These are short, simple, and easily improvised. Success with these builds the confidence to try more complicated pieces next, such as the *Yankee Doodle Dandies, Jack and the Beanstalk, Punch and Judy, The Fisherman and His Wife,* or *Pinocchio and the Fire-Eater. The Buffalo and the Bell,* because of its derivation from a theatrical tradition unfamiliar to American children and *Ming Lee and the Magic Tree,* because of its length and formal style, will require more rehearsal and a longer period of concentration.

Next the leader decides how to present the plays to the children for consideration: either by telling the story of the plot or by having the group read the play aloud together. With either approach the leader will need to do more than a cursory reading in advance. He must have thoroughly absorbed the play: its plot, characters, and setting.

READING THE PLAY ALOUD

Several children taking turns reading the play aloud should only be considered if there are strong readers in the group. A poor reading of the play in which the children stumble and hesitate can destroy the play's potential in the minds of the listeners. And keep in mind that since reading aloud takes much longer than a telling, it is usually impossible to consider more than one or two suggested plays in one session. To keep everyone interested while the play is being read, the leader should stop the reading now and conduct some improvisation and discussion of the scene just read aloud.

STORYTELLING

If the leader chooses storytelling to introduce the plays, the telling should be smooth and confident and should move straight through the action to the end. Preparation for storytelling means outlining scenes to learn the basic units of action and memorizing the sequence of the units. Practicing the story is advisable so the teller becomes accustomed to re-creating it extemporaneously based on his memory of the action. Word-by-word memorization is to be avoided, because if the teller forgets and loses his place, the stumbling will definitely lose the children's attention.

Telling the plot as a story differs in an important respect from reading a play aloud; it is best not to interrupt the storytelling with improvisations. If the story is well told, the group will be caught up in it and will not want to stop for improvisation. Tell the entire story in no more than ten minutes, and then guide the children in acting it out.

IMPROVISATION

Their first improvisation will be brief, with a minimum of action and dialogue. Discussion should encourage suggestions of what might be added to expand the playing. Remember to consider what additional parts—animate or inanimate—might be included. By playing the story spontaneously in their own words several times, the children become much more aware of the progress of the plot than if they have just heard or read it. Later in the discussion they will be better able to remember and evaluate each play as a possible one for them to produce.

Unanimous agreement on a play is rare, so the group must be willing to accept the decision of the majority. If rehearsal time is adequate, it might be a good idea to choose two or three very short plays for production; this will allow more leeway when making a final decision and can help prevent initial divisions within the group. In the face of a deadlock, of course, the leader must decide. Once the choice has been made, the decision should be considered final and the energy and attention of the group directed toward bringing the play to life.

Occasionally it is impossible to offer them a choice of plays, such as at Christmastime when the traditional story of the holiday is the only one suitable for a particular program. At those times, the leader simply presents his selection by storytelling or by the group reading the play aloud, and proceeds as just described.

The leader and the group may want to use a play from the section recommended for adult performers. The most important requirement here is that the choice have a dominant, easy to understand plot, such as that in *The Sleeping Beauty*, *A Toby Show*, *Tom Sawyer*, *Snow White and the Seven Dwarfs*, and *Androcles and the Lion*. One way to handle these longer, more difficult productions is for the children to perform several scenes from the play and then, because children are much more satisfied by a whole story than by a group of isolated scenes from a play, narration can supply the missing sections to complete the plot. Plays of character study such as *Step on a Crack* and *Birthday of the Infanta* or those in which the lines must be memorized exactly such as in *Wiley and the Hairy Man, I Didn't Know That!,* and *Johnny Moonbeam and the Silver Arrow* are better prepared by an older group using the more traditional, directed and staged approach.

REHEARSALS

The length of preparation time will determine what can be accomplished. The most effective use of time is to schedule rehearsals in a way that reduces the total number of weeks required to a minimum. A three- to four-week preparation period with three to five rehearsals per week is preferable. But that kind of intensive scheduling is not always possible. Below is an example of how the necessary one-and-a-half-hour rehearsals might be planned over a longer period.

			Total Number of Rehearsals
Sleeping Beauty	6–8 weeks	4 rehearsals weekly	24–32
Ming Lee, Pinocchio and the Fire-Eater, and *The Fisherman and His Wife*	6 weeks	3 rehearsals weekly	18
Buffalo and the Bell, Yankee Doodle Dandies, Punch and Judy, Christmas Pageant, and Plays from *In One Basket*	6 weeks	2 rehearsals weekly	12
One or more tales from *In One Basket, Ma and the Kids, Don't Touch!,* and *Jack and the Beanstalk*	8 weeks	1 rehearsal weekly	8

As soon as you begin the project, everyone should be given a copy of the rehearsal schedule that also includes the dates of the actual performances. The participants need to know what is required in terms of time and dates. It is better to schedule more sessions than seems necessary and cancel the extra ones if work progresses well, than to underestimate the number of rehearsals and then later call additional ones. If possible, the group should present more than one performance.

DISCIPLINE

Since theatre production is a group effort and depends on everyone's cooperation, it is necessary for the leader, either alone or with the group, to decide on some ground rules and, at the same time, the consequences for those who violate them. Tardiness, absences, and rowdiness are areas that need specific guidelines. These guidelines should be set at the first meeting and punishments for misconduct can be decided upon with the children. Examples of questions that will need firm answers are:

What happens if someone is late?

What is an acceptable reason for absence?

How many times may someone be late or absent before a penalty is leveled?

What happens if someone disturbs those who are rehearsing?

If the rules are later found to be too harsh or too lenient, they can be adjusted by halting rehearsal for a group discussion.

But it is important that rules be made clear early in the rehearsals, and that they be enforced consistently. Children may look at rehearsals for a play as a time for roughhousing. It cannot be, if a show is to be created.

The young participants must also understand that there will be times in rehearsal when they will not be directly involved in a scene or a task related to the production. Obviously not everyone can be rehearsing every minute. But each member has a responsibility to the group to contribute ideas and to encourage each other. Attentive, conscientious observing when not otherwise participating is a form of self-discipline that everyone must learn. The efforts of the actors are thus never disturbed but in fact enhanced by the reactions of the observers.

The leader's own enthusiasm for the play and his desire to help the group bring it to life will do much to kindle the enthusiasm and loyalty of each participant. The leader creates the atmosphere by expecting and then welcoming the magic the children make.

UNDERSTANDING THROUGH IMPROVISATIONS

After the preliminary business of choosing a play, defining the rules, and planning the rehearsal schedule, the leader's next task is to make certain that every child in the group thoroughly understands the play. Unless the children have read the play together, none of them has yet seen a script, and no parts have been assigned. Before the casting, everyone should have a chance to play various roles. These early rehearsals are a time for exploring through improvisation.

Plays are created out of a series of dramatic action. Something happens and because it did, something else happens. The first step toward understanding is to analyze the progression of the dramatic action. As the group discusses and plays out the plot unit by unit, the children should write out a summary of the units either on a chalkboard or large paper that can be posted for later reference by those who need to check it. The action of *The Three Wishes* from *In One Basket* can be described as follows:

Unit One: When her husband rejoices at their good fortune in life, the wife counters that she thinks their lot in life could be greatly improved.

Unit Two: Fairy Fortunata magically appears and grants three wishes: one to him; one to her; and one to both of them.

Unit Three: When they begin imagining all the wishes they could make, the wife accidentally uses hers for a pudding.

Unit Four: Her husband is furious because she has wasted her wish, and he wishes the pudding stuck to her nose.

Unit Five: The pair argue vehemently about how to use their final wish: he wants great wealth and she wants the pudding removed. They finally agree that the pudding must go.

Unit Six: The fairy returns and grants their wish, and they are left exactly as they began; but with the realization that happiness does not come from having wishes granted.

The resulting list that the group makes should closely resemble the one the leader made for himself originally when preparing to tell the story.

In order to make sure the children realize the interlocking action of the play, the leader should ask these questions:

How does our play start?
What characters are on stage? Who are they?
Where are they?
When do you think this play takes place—now? —a long time ago?
Why do you say that?
What happens?

The leader then selects a group to play that scene. What happens next? Why? As the talk and dramatizations continue and the action of the plot is recorded, the group can readily see the underlying design of the play.

Because characters in plays for children are usually drawn rather sketchily, questions about the characters such as those below encourage the children to extend their understanding. Answers will come through the discussion and in the playing. The leader must be receptive to new ideas and flexible in his questioning. Actually, his questions should depend on the responses he is getting from the group. Of course, if their additions or interpretations take them too far from the playwright's conception of the characters or plot, the leader must bring them back, keeping as many of their contributions as possible.

How old is the character?
What in the play angers (pleases, astonishes, scares, etc.) him?
How does the character react to other characters?
How would he move? Slowly or quickly? Often or infrequently?
How much space would he keep between himself and others?
What kind of job might he have?
Where might the character live?
What might the character wear?
If you were to choose one article of clothing to suggest the character, what would it be?
What extra character might be added to the play?
Exactly what could he do to improve but not change the play?

Only after everyone is thoroughly familiar with the play through improvisation are the roles cast and that may take as long as the first 25 percent or more of the total number of rehearsals scheduled. Once the cast is chosen and the lines are memorized, the young actors are still required to think of the meaning of what they are saying, rather than spieling off the words by rote. Because they have begun their work on the play through improvisation, they are more likely to continue their patterns of concentration, particularly if the leader helps them add appropriate movement and new stage business to enhance their characterizations.

STAGING THE PLAY

The decisions about using space in staging the play will probably be made naturally within the course of the improvisations. To make the participants aware of the setting of the play, the leader may want to ask questions such as the following:

In how many places does the plot take place? What are they?

Where are we to locate the exits and entrances?

How will we suggest doors if they are important in the action?

How can we plan the acting space so one scene can follow another without stopping for scenery pieces to be shifted and rearranged?

How many characters will act in each setting?

How can we plan the whole space to allow large enough areas for the scenes with many characters?

Which scenes might be played on a platform?

Do any scenes need steps or two levels? Why?

The best place for preparation and performance is an *empty room*, three or four times larger than an ordinary classroom. From the very first improvisations of the play, the leader should encourage the group to expand into as much space as possible. Just as their imaginations recreate the plot and build the characters, their physical movements should push outward into whatever space is necessary to produce the play. Later, the audience can simply sit in whatever space is available around the acting area.

The children will now need to discover a way to enact the action without interruption. If there are several settings, they may be placed side by side and arranged before the performance begins so that the actors may move from place to place as the script demands without having to stop to change scenery. For example in *Jack and the Beanstalk*, the opening scene in his mother's cottage may be set next to the place which will become the road to the village where Jack trades the cow for the magic beans. The spot for the "growing" beanstalk may be placed on the other side of the cottage. The Giant's house will be located in still another area. These locations remain permanently situated during the action.

The reason for this type of production in which all settings are visible at once is that it is easier to maintain the young audience's attention if the plot can proceed to its conclusion uninterrupted by scenery shifts. Using simultaneous settings avoids breaks in mood and story progression. The group may even decide to place individual settings some distance from each other in the room with the audience sitting between them. The audience members will simply shift their positions to follow the actors' movements and voices as they proceed from one setting to the next.

In order for the entire audience to have a good view of the action, it might be good to have the younger members sit on the floor. A few chairs may be set at the back for the adults who prefer them. Aisles through the audience for actors' entrances and exits must be carefully demarcated by tape and should be considered an extension of the acting area. Any audience members who sit in the "aisle" should be shifted to the audience area before the play begins. The closeness of the audience can cause problems if boundaries are not set up ahead of time.

Movable platforms, wooden boxes, and steps are particularly useful items for improvisational staging because they can be placed and adjusted as the participants discover what the play demands. A performance on a variety of levels is not only more interesting to watch for the audience, but more exciting to plan and perform for the actors. If platforms and steps are unavailable, the acting area will be a section of the floor.

If the group does not have access to a large empty room, the leader must consider alternatives and make the necessary adjustments. A gymnasium with its high ceiling tends to swallow the young actors' voices and movements in its excessive space, but if that is the only available place, plan to use only one end or corner of the total area. A cafeteria or lunchroom may be a better choice, but there are disadvantages in using a space that is in daily use for other activities. The furnishings of the room will have to be rearranged before and after every rehearsal. Also, rehearsals must be specifically scheduled in advance to avoid conflicts with other groups who also use the space.

Using a stage for performances by very young actors is not advisable. Their voices are usually not strong enough to carry far enough into the audience without amplification. Their movements will have to be more carefully "directed" so the audience is sure to see the important action. And again, the more "direction" the children receive, the less spontaneity and concentration there will be in the production. They will perform their roles by rote. The result is a weakened performance, much less interesting to the audience and less satisfying to the actors.

If the group *must* use a stage, the players should never think of themselves as being "onstage," restricted to a small rectangular space and encased behind a "picture frame." Use the space directly in front of the stage arch as part of the acting area, both the area onstage in front of the main curtain and the floor in front of the stage. The acting area on the floor in front of the stage may be elevated by platforms slightly lower than the stage height. The two levels of stage and platform increase visibility, especially of actors who during a scene move upstage behind the proscenium arch.

If the curtains must be closed for a scenery change, let the next scene of the play continue on the forestage in order to keep the audience's attention. Closing a curtain onstage to change a setting can trigger a period of noise and restlessness among the audience members, if the action of the play has been stopped.

SELECTING PROPS

Along with a consideration of space in settings is the selection of furniture and set pieces, such as a large rock, a well, or a pier, to specify the location of a setting. Encourage the children to think in terms of a few pieces to define a particular place; their acting and pantomime will add the details. The key word is *suggestion* not complete realistic representation. Questions for deciding on furniture or other stage properties might take the following form:

What should be on the setting to indicate what kind of place is being represented?

What pieces of furniture or other set pieces are required by the action?

If we do not use real furniture on stage, what could be used to suggest it? How could large cartons be made to suggest a table, chairs, etc.?

Which small props that the characters use in the action are essential? If the real objects are unavailable for the production, what can be substituted to represent the props?

How could we pantomime using the objects so that the audience knows what we are doing?

Obviously in a production staged by young performers, all efforts toward elaborate technical production are to be avoided and the emphasis kept on the acting. The children can act the story well, but achieving an equivalent level of expertise in creating scenery, costumes, and lighting effects requires the specialized training of the leader, the skills of adults, and the necessary equipment. Even when such expertise and facilities are available, the technical effects should be minimal so as not to overwhelm the efforts of the young performers.

CASTING AND ASSIGNING DUTIES

Delaying the decision about casting until a quarter of the rehearsals has elapsed gives the children time to understand the play and consider how they will produce it. They should see the play as a whole first— how the story of the plot can be acted out, how a given space becomes its settings, who its characters are and how they might dress. Each member should have had a chance to act several roles in improvisations. Those who are at ease, talkative, and creative during improvisation are the ones to consider first for major roles. Do not cast on the basis of reading tryouts. A child's ability to read the script aloud is not always a reliable determinant of his strength as an actor.

The delay in casting also gives the leader valuable time in which to observe the members of the group, and thus make his assignments more wisely. The production of the play is the culmination of everyone's efforts. Each person's individual assignment is equally important to create the complete production.

Another consideraton in the final casting is whether or not the physical appearance of an actor is compatible with the requirements of the role. A thin, undersized boy with a young voice should not be cast as an evil giant or fire-eater, nor should the characters of younger children be played by actors who are larger than those portraying their parents. The leader cannot expect a perfect match between the physical presence of an actor and the ideal one for the character, but he must not ignore their relationship either. Young actors who are vastly miscast physically are usually very uncomfortable in the roles. Furthermore, the leader has a responsibility not to risk exposing the children to ridicule by insensitive casting.

A leader should cast major roles with dependable, cooperative participants. Children who are less self-disciplined than the others should have smaller roles. In the next production the leads should be changed to give others a chance. When the children realize that that will happen, the possibility of playing a major role in the next production is a strong motivation for them to conform to the group's expectations.

Casting two people in the same role gives twice as many the opportunity to perform, and the leader may find security in the knowledge that two actors know each part. Any illness or unforeseen crisis that removes a cast member from the production is covered by having a prepared substitute. Even so, doublecasting is certainly not recommended for an inexperienced group's first attempt at theatrical production. A leader and the group members must learn how long it takes one cast to prepare a production in their situation before considering doublecasting. Since each doublecast pair will need an equal amount of time to rehearse, the leader must plan the schedule to make that possible. It is also important that there are an even number of performances so that they may be fairly divided between the doublecast pairs.

Even if an actor is removed from a cast as a disciplinary measure or for some other reason such as illness, the entire group's familiarity with the play and its characters will make it easy to train the replacement. (A young actor should *never* be removed from a role because the leader later decides that he is lacking the necessary talent for the part. Such a decision is inexcusable because the child will be cruelly humiliated. A "better show" gained at the expense of the participants is a hollow reward, indeed.)

Another variation of casting more than one person in a role is to use understudies; a method certainly not recommended. This method of casting begins with the permanent role assignments, and then in addition, the naming of an alternate cast. Each member of the second cast learns his role, but has no chance of performing unless the original actor becomes ill or is otherwise indisposed. The use of understudies can be discouraging to young actors who prepare a role that they probably will never get to perform. The practice of using understudies also has an unwelcome side effect: it creates a climate of rivalry and envy among the participants that can destroy the necessary cohesion of the group.

Even if it is possible to add a minor role or two to the playwright's cast of characters, some of the group will undoubtedly have to be omitted from the casting. In the beginning when everyone is getting acquainted with the script the leader may notice that some children

pay special attention to technical production problems. Some may express an interest in creating certain properties, set pieces, or sound effects instead of acting a role. During earlier discussions the leader may have observed a special ability in a youngster to transform ideas about characters into inventive ideas for their costumes, but the child has given no indication that he is interested in the responsibility of costume coordinator. The leader, in suggesting that such children assume the appropriate technical posts, should mention how they have previously provided good ideas about costumes, scenery, or sound effects. In all instances, the technical production assignments must be given the same importance as the acting roles.

In each production the technical assignments will be determined by the script and the group's interpretation of it. If the group decides to use several set or furniture pieces that will need to be created, most of those not cast will become setting coordinators. When the group does a play with special costume requirements such as a Chinese story, the participants may decide to make simple T-shaped garments for everyone. Appropriate accessories may then be added by the actor to identify the character wearing it.

Here is a description of the general duties required of those not among the cast:

Assistant to the leader   Number of children: 1

When the leader doesn't want to interrupt the performers rehearsing a scene, the assistant makes notes as the leader whispers them, and they are discussed later. These notes will be about the interpretation of the play, characters, or individual lines; movement of the performers; reminders to concentrate, etc. The assistant also follows the words of the script to prompt if necessary when actors are trying to memorize their lines.

Setting coordinators   Number of children: 1 to 4

They are responsible for creating or finding and borrowing the set pieces, furniture, and hand properties (any object necessary to the action). After getting or making the items that furnish the setting, the coordinators are responsible for placing them on the sets for rehearsal and performances, and for storing them away afterward.

Costume coordinators   Number of children: 1 to 3

The responsibilities in this area will depend on how much each actor is able to do on his own and how complicated the costumes are. Since simplicity is the recommended approach, each performer will probably assume most of the responsibility for creating his costume with advice and assistance offered as necessary by the coordinators. They should be responsible for keeping the garment and fabric collection intact and neat. As actors choose pieces to use, the actors themselves should temporarily mark them with their names and assume full responsibility for putting them away after working in them. The coordinators may need to create more than one of the same piece of clothing especially if several characters must be alike in some way. Or they might make a special item that a character should have, such as an ornate headdress or padding to make the actor larger.

Sound effects coordinator   Number of children: 1 or 2

The duty of the sound effects coordinator is to tape-record either real or simulated sounds that cannot be produced by the actors themselves during the course of the action. During rehearsals and performances one coordinator will be responsible for playing the tape when necessary. The coordinator will also be responsible for finding possible music to be played before or after the performance according to what the group decides is best.

All of the areas of technical responsibilities should overlap. The actors and coordinators may all work together on a sound effect or a set piece. Several actors may help another choose a costume. The production is a group effort, and although general areas of responsibility are assigned to coordinators, everyone works to create the whole.

But remember: It is essential that the entire group realizes that these coordinators and assistants are just as vital to the production as the actors and their contributions should be treated with equal respect and importance. When everyone takes their bows, it would be nice to introduce these vital, hardworking helpers.

COSTUMING THE PLAY

Again the cardinal rule is: *suggest* the complete costume for a character rather than create one. Only then can a young person actually make the costume. The final costume may initially seem incomplete or inappropriate to the leader, but the choice may in fact be quite acceptable to the performers and to the audience. If the participants can reasonably defend their costume selections based on their knowledge of the play and its characters, the leader must be content to let their decisions stand.

Since the basis of any costume is the understanding of the character who wears it, begin the process of costuming with questions that apply their knowledge of the characters to clothing:

How old is the character? What would a person that age wear?
How much can he spend on his clothes?
What colors and fabrics would this character choose to wear?
Would clothes be important to the character? Why?
What does the character do in his clothes during the play?
How would you describe his clothes? Neat, sloppy, dirty, torn, matched, mended, etc.?
When in history and in what country does the story take place?
What did people wear in that place at that time?

The search for the garments can be started with a box of miscellaneous articles of clothing brought from home which includes the

usual basic items of shirts, long pants, blouses and skirts, plus hats, scarves, belts, shoes, capes, jewelry, wigs, feathers, spectacles, and full-length skirts. Then add different pieces of fabric, at least four or five yards in length. The pieces should be of various colors, textures, and weights, such as wool, velveteen, corduroy, chiffon, homespun, vinyl, tulle, terry cloth, velour, taffeta, and metallic fabrics. Although cheap and easily washed, broadcloth, sheeting, and muslin are undesirable because their surfaces are so flat and uninteresting. If imaginations are to function, they must be fueled with a rich array of materials. Have the children experiment in creating simple garments on the body by draping, belting, and pinning. There is no complicated cutting, sewing, and tailoring required with such an approach. Acceptable costumes can be fashioned and worn over the actors' street clothes. This method of costuming is really a matter of decision and choice which the participants themselves make. They will better understand their play and characters for having created their own costumes.

Sometimes a single item of clothing added to street clothes is enough to suggest a character. The leader and children could decide to make that a restriction for costuming every character in a play: each performer must find *one* garment or accessory that best suggests his character. Even an animal character may be suggested by a single identifying badge, such as horns, ears, tail, or mane.

No matter how varied and extensive the contents, the box of items will surely only be a beginning of the group members' search for costumes. Some will find exactly what they want immediately; others will still be experimenting with new combinations during the last week of rehearsal. Remind them to consider their own wardrobes and ask their families and friends to lend them items. Stores that sell old, used clothing can be a treasure trove.

The sooner the performers make their choice of costume, the more opportunity they will have to wear the unfamiliar items in rehearsal. It takes time to learn to move easily in apparel such as trains, long skirts or gowns, shoes different from his usual ones, large hats or swords. Ideally the actors should begin rehearsing in the unusual garments as soon as possible after their casting to accustom themselves and each other to their new attire. Suddenly seeing friends dressed in costumes unlike their usual clothing can be very amusing to the other participants. The humor, however, eventually subsides as the costumes become familiar to everyone. Last minute additions of new or unusual items should be avoided for two reasons: the actors may not be able to handle the new

items correctly, and precious time and concentration will be lost as the cast dissolves in laughter upon seeing the new costuming.

If the historical time or culture in which the play is set is unknown to the children, the leader may want to show them background materials before they choose their costumes. Art history and costume books are a great source for examples of clothing worn throughout history at all levels of society. Photographs in magazines and books on certain cultures or eras in history provide a complete record of twentieth-century garments. Just because the children have been shown art prints or photographs with historically accurate clothing does not mean that their choices of costumes will reflect authenticity. But it will, however, guide them toward better choices and more understanding of the time and culture of the play. The leader must always remember that it is a valuable experience for them to make these decisions themselves. The final interpretations of the characters' dress must be their own.

MAKEUP

Any makeup effects that are used along with the costumes to complete the characterization should be simple and quick to apply and be merely a suggestion of the character. A few whiskers on the cheeks for animals or a sprinkle of freckles for the character of a young child may be drawn on the face. Spots of color on the cheeks indicate puppet characters. Heightening the eyebrows into a scowl gives the impression of evil.

Keep the face natural and uncovered. Moustaches and beards are more of a hindrance than a help to characterization because in hiding so much of the face they drastically reduce communication. They also tend to look ridiculous on youngsters as does full facial makeup to simulate age. Avoid masks of any size, the faces should always be visible.

SOUND EFFECTS

Sound effects are yet another aspect of theatrical production which the children may use to enhance their work. Many of the sounds necessary to the action can and should be made by the actors as they perform. Whether it is a barking dog, the beating of a gong, blacksmith and tinsmith noises, or the singing of entertainers, sounds created on the spot by the actor as he needs them are by far the preferred method. Even when noises must be made offstage to augment the action, these, too, should be live and fitted into each performance by the person or persons responsible for sound effects.

When the live sound effect is impossible, the alternative is by mechanical means. Avoid using a record player because it allows so little control. Instructing someone to place the needle at an exact point on a record is expecting the impossible, and even using music played from the beginning of a record is risky—needles get stuck, records scratched, and phonographs bumped, particularly if they are in the midst of the action backstage. The tape recorder is a more reliable instrument, but coordinating the taped sounds with the action onstage takes much rehearsal. Occasionally the time spent for that is really worth the effort; many times it is not.

For some productions, the addition of music before and after the performance helps create the desired atmosphere, and that will need to be tape-recorded. Music is especially effective when the group is producing a play that is rooted in another culture or country. Chinese music for *Ming Lee and the Magic Tree* and Thai music for *The Buffalo and the Bell* are important for creating the proper atmospheric background for the audience. Other plays may not actually require music before and after the performance, but its use may extend the mood of the play, provided the selections have been carefully chosen to enhance that specific script.

If sound effects are desired, the participants should make the decisions about what is to be used. The following questions will help to guide them:

What sound effects are necessary?
How can we create them?
Which sound effects should be live and which recorded on tape?
If it is impossible to tape-record the real sound of a necessary effect, what would be a possible substitute sound?
Would music played before the play begins be desirable?
What kind of music should be played?
Would the addition of music enhance any of the scenes? Which ones? How would it do so?

Part of the decision process is experimentation. Encourage the group to listen as the selections are played during rehearsals to be sure that they are the right ones. Be ready to help them search further if necessary.

CONCLUDING REHEARSALS

After the roles and technical positions are assigned, the scripts are distributed. The full play is read aloud and then improvised by the cast, who try to remember and include as many of the playwright's lines as possible. The group next concentrates on the play as a series of brief scenes. Each scene is repeatedly rehearsed as follows: Reading from the scripts followed by an improvisation. Each succeeding attempt should include more memorized lines. There should be discussions to evaluate the work in progress and to reconsider the characterizations and settings if necessary. By continuing to rehearse through improvisation and discussion, the young players are more likely to preserve the spontaneity of their acting as they gradually memorize their lines.

Sometimes it may be necessary to set aside part of the rehearsal for memorizing lines. The actors may combine in pairs or trios to cue each other. Those who are busy with technical assignments can also take a break to read lines with the actors who are trying to memorize their parts.

The movements of the characters will become more final as rehearsals progress, but since the actors are being encouraged to *think* as they act and to *become* the characters, they should still continue to move as their thinking motivates them.

Since the group will have developed the plot in a manner meaningful to them, the actual stage directions from the script may not always be appropriate for their interpretation. The group should decide which of the directions would actually enhance their interpretation and use only those.

The youngsters should also develop an awareness of the audience's presence. The dual task of concentrating on their characterizations as well as communicating to the audience makes performing difficult for many young actors, especially the inexperienced. For this reason the improvisational approach places a minimum of emphasis on producing for an audience. The group, however, must recognize its presence. How much consideration to give the audience depends in part on the type of staging used.

Communicating to the audience is a big concern when the performance is confined to a stage behind a proscenium arch. The audience is seated "out front," usually some distance from the raised stage. In a production presented from a stage, movements must be more definitely planned so that important actions are not blocked from the audience's view. Although actors should not be commanded to "face front" and "never turn your backs to the audience," they must learn to assume positions that turn out toward the invisible fourth wall, their audience. The young participants will have to be reminded to speak loud enough to be heard by everyone.

If the acting area is three quarters or completely surrounded by audience members, the participants don't have to be so aware of the observers' presence. Movements must be visible, but if the actors move frequently during the playing, the shifting of their positions will reveal most of the action to most of the audience. A normal speaking voice generally carries enough volume to be heard easily if the audience of fifty to one hundred is seated adjacent to the acting area.

Whatever the staging approach, the actors must be prepared for the reactions of an audience, which will be varied. Humor, surprise, dread, or fear may receive quite a noisy response. The actors must be taught to rehearse without being overly aware of an audience. Professional performers are aware of their audience and use the responses to intensify their own performance. Children, however, sometimes react to the audience by forgetting their characterization, looking at the audience and becoming self-conscious and sometimes even joining the audience in the reactions. Also, they must be taught to rehearse without looking at the leader and others who are not in the cast. It is important to break the habit of looking at people in the rehearsal room and losing concentration during the rehearsals. If the children are really involved as the characters, their minds will be on the plot and their attention on the other characters. Through rehearsals and discussions the actors are made aware of this important aspect of performing. If they are well prepared they will remain in character when presenting the play for an audience.

In the last few rehearsals the group will need to play the script several times from beginning to end *without* interruption for any reason. All sound effects, costumes, set pieces, and small properties should now be assembled and included in the production. New technical additions may lengthen the playing time and disturb the actors' concentration. Several run-throughs with the complete technical support will reaffirm the group's grasp of the continuity of the script.

THE AUDIENCE

Even though the leader's primary interest should be in the participants' own growth and enjoyment, the players themselves will want a receptive audience of the proper age to see their production. Usually the audience will be younger than the performers and the script will have been selected with that as a natural, guiding condition. Although young actors generally will feel more secure performing for children who are younger than they are, they will want to present the play for their own age group, too. Performing for older students is the most challenging assignment of all.

Since it is difficult for the children to perform successfully before large groups, invite only a few of the appropriate classes at a time. Presenting several performances will teach the actors that audiences vary considerably in their reactions. Another welcome benefit of repeated performances is the increased self-confidence of the actors.

ANNOUNCEMENTS AND PROGRAMS

To some groups printed programs are important. If so, one or more students may design a program. Samples from other theatrical productions can serve as models for possible program layouts and indicate what information should be included.

Posters, flyers, and announcements in the school paper and to appropriate classes or groups may be desirable if the audience is not already invited and their attendance assured. Encourage the designers of the promotional materials to use their knowledge of the play to stimulate interest in the production. The participants should restate their ideas about the play in artwork as well as in the written word.

Jack and the Beanstalk
Robert Rafferty

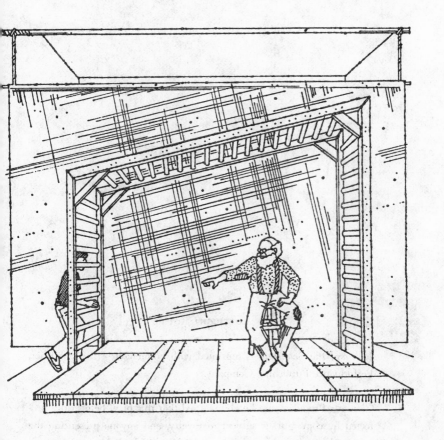

Jack and the Beanstalk by Robert Rafferty is written in story theatre form, a theatrical style that was made popular by Paul Sills's play *Story Theatre*. The characters sometimes speak as narrators; sometimes as the people in the story. The actors therefore must learn to step in and out of character and then comment on the situation as a storyteller might do.

The plot of this play is a series of gradually intensifying conflicts between Jack and the other characters. When the play opens there is a quarrel between Jack and the farmer. This conflict is increased by his mother's liaison with the farmer and is followed by a humorous scene with Jack and the cow. A potentially frightening incident with an evil giant is averted, by aid from the giant's wife and then by Jack's escape. Upon his return to the giant's house, however, Jack discovers that he has lost the support of the giant's wife and both are conspiring to catch him. Before the final resolution, the suspense builds to heighten the conflict as Jack faces the danger alone.

Suggestions:

All props are imaginary except for two stools in the giant's house. The magic beanstalk may be created by a green spotlight mounted above and controlled as the action demands. The costumes should be chosen with consideration of the characters who wear them and their relationship to one another.

JACK AND THE BEANSTALK

CHARACTERS

Mother
Jack
Mr. Farmer
Cow
The Giant
Giant's Wife

Curtain music: lively old English tune. Curtain opens on a bare stage. No furniture is used in the play except stools in the Giant's house. All props are imaginary and are indicated by the actors miming them. Mother enters L. Music out.

MOTHER: Once upon a time there was a poor widow who lived in a cottage with her only son, Jack. She thought Jack was a wonderful son. Just the kind of child every mother wants to have—a child just like each one of you.

Jack. Oh, Jack! Where are you, dear? (*Crosses L, getting annoyed.*) Jack! I'm calling you! Where are you?

JACK: (*He runs in from R, rushing past her, then hiding behind her for protection. He mimes carrying a heavy milking pail.*) Here I am, Mother!

MR. FARMER: (*He storms in from R, chasing Jack.*) That no-good son of yours was stealing apples from my tree! (*Sees Jack hiding behind Mother.*) Ah, there you are! And there are my apples in that milking pail!

MOTHER: (*Sweetly.*) Now, Jack, you know you're not to steal . . . er . . . to borrow apples from Mr. Farmer's tree.

JACK: Aw, Mother, he has a lot. He won't miss a couple.

MR. FARMER: A couple!

MOTHER: Give Mr. Farmer back the apples, Jack. (*Jack hesitatingly comes from behind his mother and edges up to within arm's length of Mr. Farmer, holding the pail behind him so neither of the others can see into it. He reaches in and hands one apple to Mr. Farmer, then quickly turns to leave, but is stopped by the stern look of his mother as she gestures for him to give back the "other" apple. Reaching into the pail he reluctantly takes out a second apple and gives it to Mr. Farmer. As he starts to leave again, Mother looks into pail.*) Jack! (*Mother looks furious and Jack quickly starts handing an imaginary stream of apples from the pail to Mr. Farmer, who can't take them all in his hands so makes a cradle of his arms as Jack continues to pile on the apples until he empties the pail.*)

MR. FARMER: (*Struggling to keep the apples from falling, crosses R.*) You better do something about that no-good son of yours, or he'll come to a bad end. (*Exits R.*)

MOTHER: I don't know what I'm going to do with you, Jack. I send you to milk the cow and you go off stealing apples. (*Cow enters L, and as she drifts toward them, Jack goes to meet her.*)

JACK: I was hungry. We never have enough to eat. Besides, this old cow didn't give any milk. She's gone dry.

MOTHER: If we don't have milk to sell, we'll starve. Oh, what's to become of us?

JACK: (*Crosses to her.*) Don't worry. I'll get a job.

MOTHER: You're just a boy.

JACK: Then what will we do?

MOTHER: We'll just have to sell the cow for some money. You take her to market. (*Crosses and smacks Cow on rump, driving it to Jack.*) And you get a good price for her. And be quick about it. (*Exits L.*)

JACK: Aw, Mother . . . aw, all right. (*He pantomimes putting down pail and takes Cow's imaginary halter and turns and starts to walk. But Cow doesn't move and when he comes to end of halter Jack is pulled up short. He turns on her and starts to pull hard on halter.*) Come on, you lazy thing! (*Cow doesn't budge. He picks up an imaginary stick and holds it threateningly.*) You see this stick? Now you come on before I . . .

COW: (*Lowers head and paws ground as if getting ready to charge.*) Moooooooooooo! (*Cow starts to charge, but is slow and clumsy. Jack starts to back away, going clockwise. The Cow chases after him.*)

JACK: Ooooooh! Mother! (*They go around the stage one time, then Jack stops suddenly, sidesteps the charging Cow with a little bullfighter's pass, and the Cow lumbers by.*) Ah, ha! (*Jack starts running counterclockwise as the Cow continues clockwise and they head for each other on a collision course. As they meet the Cow lowers her head to butt him and Jack leap-frogs over the Cow's back, landing behind her. Cow pulls up, panting and worn out. Jack stops, looks at her, and grins in triumph. He strides toward her.*) Now we know who's the cow and who's the master. (*Jack picks up imaginary halter.*) So Jack started to take the cow to market.

OLD MAN: (*Enters R. They meet.*) On the way he met an Old Man. Good morning to you, Jack.

JACK: Morning. (*Puzzled.*) How do you know my name?

OLD MAN: Oh, I know lots of things. I know that you are a smart boy and a sharp trader. And you're going to market to sell your cow. And because you're a sharp trader I'm going to give you a wonderful price for your cow. But first, tell me, Jack, do you know how to count? (*Jack nods.*) Then tell me, how many beans make three?

JACK: That's easy. (*Stops and thinks.*) Er . . . one in each hand and one in the mouth make three.

OLD MAN: (*Taking imaginary beans from pocket.*) Ah, right you are! And here are the very beans themselves. (*He puts one in each of Jack's hands.*) Here's one in each hand, now take this one in your mouth and we'll make the swap.

JACK: Swap! Swap what? Swap three beans for my cow? Three common beans for a cow! Ha! (*He jams the beans back in the Old Man's hands.*)

OLD MAN: Ah, but lad, these aren't just common beans. If you plant these beans and water them they'll grow . . . and grow . . . and grow right up to the sky!

JACK: (*Intrigued, but not sure of himself.*) Right up to the sky? Aw, you're funning me.

OLD MAN: (*Putting beans in each of Jack's hands again.*) Wouldn't you like to climb up . . . up . . . right up through the clouds and find out what's way up there in the sky? (*Jack is wide-eyed at the idea, his mouth drops open as he looks up at the sky, and the Old Man pops the third bean into his mouth. Startled, Jack closes his mouth.*) Chew it, Jack! Chew the magic bean. It'll give you magic. Chew it, Jack! (*Jack chews. Magic music up. Psychedelic lights on. Reach peak when he swallows. Lights fade, but not off. Music down and under.*) That's it! Now you have your three beans, so I'll just take my cow. (*He takes Cow by halter and leads her R.*) You mind what I told you, Jack. Those beans will grow up to the sky. (*Exits R. Offstage.*) Up to the sky. (*Jack crosses L, in a daze. Music out.*)

MOTHER: (*Enters L and crosses to meet him.*) Back so soon, Jack. How much did you get for the cow?

JACK: You'll never guess what a bargain I got, Mother!

MOTHER: Five pounds? (*Jack shakes his head.*) Ten pounds? (*Shakes his head.*) Twenty pounds?

JACK: I told you you couldn't guess! (*Holds out both hands, shows beans.*) Here! These are what I got for her!

MOTHER: Beans? Two beans?

JACK: I got three, but I ate one of them.

MOTHER: Three beans for our only cow! (*Cries.*) We'll starve for sure.

JACK: No, Mother, these are magic beans. The Old Man said if we plant them and water them they'll grow . . . and grow . . . right up to the sky!

MOTHER: (*Angry.*) Give me those beans, you foolish boy! (*She grabs one from each hand and throws them into the garden.*) There! Oh, three beans for a cow! Heaven help us! Now you march right off to bed without supper! (*She exits L, crying. Lights start to dim.*)

JACK: (*Mimes action.*) So Jack started to go up to his little room in the attic. But before he did, he got the watering can and watered the garden where the beans had been thrown. Then he climbed the ladder to the attic . . . and looked out the tiny window to see if a beanstalk had grown. Nothing! Now he felt foolish to have traded a cow for a few beans. Mother was right. They weren't magic. He tried to sleep, but he was very hungry. (*He stands still, his head drooping. Gradual blackout.*) But, at last, he dropped off to sleep. (*Magic music up. №1 green spotlight from grid on, focused on floor outside Jack's window where beans were thrown. Light starts pencil thin and grows in intensity and size until on full, making a green shaft of light—a beanstalk. Lights gradually up to dawn. Sound effect: cock crows. Music out.*) Early the next morning Jack woke up. (*Mimes action.*) He opened the tiny window and looked out. A beanstalk! Growing clear up to the sky! The Old Man was right! I can't see the top. Mother! It's there! One of the beans grew! Mother! (*He climbs down ladder and runs outside and stands at foot of beanstalk looking up.*)

Mother! Come quick!

MOTHER: (*Rushes in from L, looks up in awe.*) Oh my, oh my, oh my!

JACK: (*Testing the imaginary stalk.*) It's strong enough to climb. I'm going to climb it . . . up to the sky!

MOTHER: No, Jack, no! It's too dangerous!

JACK: (*Jack mimes climbing the beanstalk. Mother slowly backs away toward L. She gestures for him to come down.*) It's easy to climb, Mother!

MOTHER: You don't know what's up there! (*She backs off L. Offstage voice becomes more and more distant.*) Please, Jack! Please come back! Jaaaack.

JACK: Jack climbed and climbed until everything below looked smaller and smaller, and still he climbed up . . . up . . . up through the clouds. He climbed so high he was scared to look down. By the time he got to the top he was very tired. (*As he reaches top of beanstalk, the green spot gets thinner and thinner. Jack steps off. Lighting value changes to indicate this is a fantasy world.*) He was in a strange new land. He saw a winding road and started to follow it. (*Walks winding path around stage. Beanstalk light out.*) Soon he came up on a great, big, creepy-looking, old house. (*As he passes R, the Giant's Wife, a cyclops, enters and sneaks along beside him.*) It had a huge front door. (*Crosses to C and turns to face C as if facing the huge doors. Shaking with fright.*)

It's too scary. I'll find another house.

WIFE: (*He backs away from door into arms of Giant's Wife.*) Ah, ha! I got you! And I won't let you go!

JACK: Who . . . who are you?

WIFE: I'm the Giant's Wife. And you are going to be my servant. (*Holding him with one hand, she opens the huge door with other, drags him inside, and closes the door. Sound effect: big door creaking open and shut.*) The Giant makes me do all the work. I should have a servant like all the other wives. Now you'll do the work while I sit and look pretty. But when my husband comes home I'll have to hide you. Everytime I catch a servant he eats them. He likes tender little boys and girls.

JACK: Jack was never so scared in his whole life. The Giant's Wife was so big and strong! "I'll do whatever you want, ma'am, just don't let him catch me." (*Sound effect: heavy footsteps of the Giant. Jack and Wife tremble as if ground is shaking.*)

WIFE: Oh, jiggle-my-thumbs! Here he comes now. Quick, hide! Here—in the oven. (*Sound effect: oven door opening. Jack climbs into imaginary oven. The Giant enters L. Sound effect: fast creaking as door opened quickly and then boom as it's slammed shut.*)

And the Giant's Wife closed the oven door . . . (*Sound effect: oven door closing*) . . . just as the Giant entered.

Good day, husband. How did the hunting go today?

GIANT: Baah! Couldn't find even one person to eat. (*Sniffs air.*) What do I smell? Fee-fi-fo-fum, I smell the blood of an Englishman. Be he alive or be he dead, I'll grind his bones to make my bread.

WIFE: But the Wife didn't want to lose her new servant . . . Nonsense! The older you get the worse your smeller gets. You smell the bones of the little girl you had for supper last night. I'm boiling them for soup. Do you want me to bring your hen that lays the golden eggs before you take your nap?

GIANT: *No! Bring me my bag of gold.*

WIFE: (*Gets imaginary bag of gold from closet.*) So the Wife went to the closet and brought him his bag of gold. Here. I have to go out and get some firewood. (*She goes to door, opens it, closes it behind her, and exits L. Sound effect: creaking door opening and closing.*)

GIANT: (*Takes coin from bag and bites it.*) Ah, my gold . . . my lovely gold . . . gold . . . (*Yawning.*) Time for a nap . . . hard day hunting . . . Mmmmm, that little girl soup . . . (*Yawning.*) smells good . . . good . . . (*Gives a violent snore.*)

JACK: When Jack was sure the Giant was asleep, he crept out of the oven. (*Sound effect: oven door opening.*) Sneaked up to the Giant . . . took the bag of gold . . . (*It is heavy for him.*) and tiptoes to the door. (*Opens door. Sound effect: creaking door.*)

GIANT: (*Waking at sound of door.*) Who's there? (*Jack runs off R. Giant doesn't see him.*) Wife! Wife! Where's my bag of gold? (*Exits L. Offstage.*) Where are you wife?

JACK: (*Enters R and follows winding path.*) Jack ran back to the beanstalk . . . (*Lights dim. Beanstalk light on. Magic music on and under.*) . . . and started to climb down. (*Music out.*) But he couldn't climb with the heavy bag of gold. So he dropped it straight down through the clouds. (*Sound effect: whistling as bag of gold falls. Sound fades out.*) And then scurried down after it as fast as he could. When he reached the bottom, he found . . .

MOTHER: (*Enters L, picks up coins.*) His mother, picking up gold coins from the yard as fast as she could because, of course, the bag burst when it hit the ground. (*She sees Jack get off beanstalk, runs and hugs him.*)

Laws-a-mercy me, Jack! Wherever have you been? I was so worried. And, look! It's raining gold!

JACK: It isn't raining gold, Mother. They are coins from the wicked Giant who lives up in the sky and I threw them down the beanstalk.

MOTHER: (*Embraces Jack.*) And his mother was very pleased because Jack was safe and they had a bag of gold and wouldn't starve.

JACK: But Jack was worried. If the Giant found the beanstalk he could climb down it. So he got an ax and . . . (*He swings ax at light. As soon as he hits it, the light goes out.*)

Why, it just . . . disappeared! Now the wicked Giant can't climb down.

Jack was very happy!

MOTHER: And his mother was even happier. (*Music: lively old English tune. They dance a short lively jig. Mother exits L.*)

JACK: But Jack got to thinking. There was still one more bean in the garden and . . . (*Looks up.*) . . . the Giant had a hen that laid golden eggs. So he got the watering can and watered the garden again. (*After miming, he looks around.*)

Nothing. (*He waters more. Looks again.*) Nothing . . . Well, I guess I can't expect both beans to be magic. (*Magic music up softly. Second beanstalk light on, starting thin and growing in size and intensity.*) Maybe the other one is just . . . well, just a common bean. (*If audience calls his attention to it, he turns and looks, otherwise he turns naturally and sees it. Music up as he discovers it.*) Another one! Another beanstalk! (*He quickly climbs up and up. Music down and out.*)

Once again Jack stepped out into the land of the Giant. And once again he was very scared. It would be harder to fool the Giant a second time. Taking a deep breath he set out along the winding road . . . (*Beanstalk light out. He follows path.*) . . . until he came to the Giant's house. (*Lights up to full.*) Quietly Jack hid in the bushes near the big door and waited to see who was inside.

WIFE: (*She enters L, opens door from inside house. Sound effect: door opening as she comes out.*) After a little while the Giant's Wife came out to gather firewood. (*As she picks up imaginary wood, Jack quickly slips in open door and into kitchen. He starts to hide in oven. Sound effect: oven door opening.*)

JACK: No, not the oven. That's the first place she'll look. (*Closes oven. Sound effect: oven door closing.*) Where can I hide? (*He looks around frantically. Wife starts coming in carrying a big load of imaginary firewood in her arms.*) Behind the woodbox! (*He climbs behind the make-believe woodbox. Bends down. Pops up.*) She'll see me! (*Climbs out. Looks around for another place. The Giant's Wife enters open door and kicks it shut with her foot. Sound effect: door slamming. Jack climbs back behind woodbox.*)

Jack squeezed down behind the woodbox, trying to make himself as tiny as an ant. Lucky for him . . .

WIFE: (*Staggering under high load of wood.*) . . . the Giant's Wife had picked up such a big load of firewood she couldn't see over it. And when she dumped it in the woodbox . . . (*Sound effect: wood falling into box.*) the big pile of wood . . .

JACK: (*Ducking falling wood.*) completely hid Jack.

WIFE: Whew! I wish my husband wouldn't eat all the servants. But if I ever catch that boy who stole the bag of gold, I'll be happy to cook HIM for dinner! (*Sound effect: Giant's footsteps. Jack and Wife tremble as if ground is shaking. Giant enters L. Stops and sniffs outside door where Jack hid. Slams door open. Doesn't close it. Sound effect: door slamming.*)

GIANT: (*Sniffing.*) Fee-fi-fo-fum! I smell the blood of an Englishman. Be he alive or be he dead, I'll grind his bones to make my bread. I know I smell the blood of a boy this time. Smell him for sure.

WIFE: (*Sniffing.*) You're right, husband. I smell him too. It's that boy who stole your gold. He'll be hiding in the oven. (*They sneak up on oven and pull door open. Sound effect: oven door opening.*)

GIANT: Not there! (*She slams door shut. Sound effect: door slamming.*)

WIFE: Maybe . . . under the table.

GIANT: (*Picks up imaginary table. She bends and looks under it. Shakes her head.*) Baaah!

WIFE: The closet! (*She pulls open closet door and jumps in with arms spread expecting to catch Jack. Comes out looking sad.*)

GIANT: Baaah! I'll find him. He can't get away. You start the fire to cook him. (*Raising hand to threaten her.*) And be quick about it! (*Wife ducks hand and goes toward woodbox.*) Where are you going?

WIFE: To get firewood from the woodbox. (*Jack looks scared. She crosses to box, but keeps head turned to watch Giant, afraid he will hit her, so even as she's picking up wood she doesn't notice Jack.*)

GIANT: (*Threatens her with fist.*) I should beat you again for losing my gold.

WIFE: (*Cowering away from him.*) Sit. Sit and I'll bring you your magic hen that lays the golden eggs. That will cheer you up.

So the Wife went and . . . (*Exits momentarily, comes back with imaginary hen.*) . . . brought him the big black hen with the shiny golden comb. (*Sound effect: hen squawking.*)

GIANT: (*Takes hen, sets it down on table. Points at hen, commands.*) Lay a golden egg! (*Sound effect: hen clucking as it lays an egg. Giant picks up hen, takes imaginary egg from under it, bites to test it.*) Ahh! Pure gold. (*Puts egg down. Points at hen.*) Lay another golden egg! (*Sound effect: hen clucking as it lays second egg. Giant picks up hen, takes egg from under it, puts hen down, looks at egg.*) Ahhhh! Two golden eggs. Good! I can take my nap. (*He yawns. She yawns and sits.*) Watch my magic hen. If someone steals it, I'll kill you! I mean it. I'll kill you this time!

WIFE: (*Already starting to doze.*) Yes, husband. I'll watch it. I won't close my eye. (*They both drop off to sleep and start snoring. Jack and both of them shake with each violent snore.*)

JACK: (*Pops up.*) They're asleep. Jack climbed out of his hiding place and tip-toed to the magic hen. He picked up the two golden eggs, put them in his pocket, picked up the hen and . . . (*Sound effect: hen squawking. Jack mimes it fluttering in his arms and hard to hold.*)

GIANT: (*Wakes up.*) My magic hen! My golden eggs! You! (*Sees Jack, starts after him. Jack backs away, toward Wife, who is awake and up.*) I'll get you this time! (*Jack continues to back away. He doesn't know he's backing right into the arms of the Wife.*) Fee-fi-fo-fum!

WIFE: Fi-fo-fum-fee! (*Startled, Jack turns to face Wife. Giant and Wife both lunge at him. Jack whirls and dives through Giant's legs and Giant and Wife collide and catch each other.*)

GIANT and WIFE: I got you! (*Jack runs out door. Exits R.*)

GIANT: You! Baah! (*He picks her up by the ears, sets her aside, makes fist, and hits her a hard blow on top of head.*)

WIFE: Ooooooooh! (*She staggers off L. Sound effect: crash as she falls.*)

GIANT: (*Rushes out door, chasing Jack, exits R.*) I'll get you!

JACK: (*Enters DR.*) Jack had to take ten steps for every one of the Giant's steps, and soon . . .

GIANT: (*Enters DR.*) Ha, ha! Now I've got you! (*Jack stops short and ducks and the Giant overruns him and exits L.*)

JACK: (*Running around in a circle.*) Where's the beanstalk? I can't find it! (*Magic music up. Lights lower. Beanstalk light on.*) There it is. (*Runs to it. Starts to climb down. Music out. Sound effect: hen squawking.*)

Jack climbed down as fast as he could, but . . . (*Beanstalk light begins to shake violently. He has a hard time holding on.*) the beanstalk began to shake. (*Looks up. Scared at what he sees.*)

The Giant! He's coming down after me! (*He climbs down frantically.*)

Faster, faster he climbed . . . down until he could see his cottage and his mother.

Mother! Mother! Get the ax! Chop down the beanstalk!

MOTHER: (*Runs on from L.*) And his mother came running with an ax.

JACK: (*Reaches ground.*) Quick. Take the magic hen. Give me the ax. (*He takes ax and swings at beanstalk, but its swaying causes him to miss.*) Missed!

GIANT: (*Voice roars overhead.*) I'll get you! I'll get you for dinner!

MOTHER: (*Jack and Mother look up, frightened.*) Run!

JACK: We can't outrun the Giant!

GIANT: (*Overhead.*) Fee-fi-fo-fum. I'm going to eat an Englishman! (*Jack shakes off Mother, who backs away, looking up. He takes big breath, brings ax back, and aims, swings, and hits beanstalk. Beanstalk light out.*) Fee-fi-fo-o-o-o-o-o-o! (*Jack and Mother look up and follow with their eyes the fall of the Giant. His cry gets louder as he falls.*) Aaaaaaaaaaaaaagh!

JACK: Look out! He's falling! (*Sound effect: crash off L. Cloud of dust blows in from L, as Giant hits earth. Jack looks L.*) He's dead! The wicked Giant is dead! We're safe, Mother! And look! A hen that lays golden eggs! Watch! (*Points at hen and commands.*) Lay a golden egg! (*Sound effect: hen clucking as it lays egg. Jack picks up hen, gets egg, hands it to Mother.*)

MOTHER: Real gold! (*Sound effect: clucking of hen.*)

JACK: Yes, Mother. We'll never be poor or hungry again.

MOTHER: (*To audience.*) So ends the story of . . .

JACK: Jack and the Beanstalk. (*Sound effect: merry old English tune up. They bow and dance off.*)

CURTAIN

Ming Lee and the Magic Tree
Aurand Harris

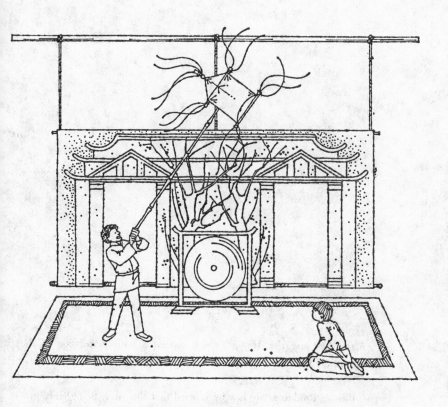

Aurand Harris's *Ming Lee and the Magic Tree* is the story of a Chinese prince's quest for a reply to the question: What makes a happy man? Set upon the search by the Jade Emperor who has transformed him into a tiger with a magic-making tail, the prince hopes the response he finds will win the Princess of the Stars as his wife. Ming Lee, a peasant, is the happy man who discovers an answer for him.

To tell the story, several Chinese theatre traditions have been adapted to suggest the culture. A silent prop man provides set pieces for the actors. He is aware of the actions and words of the other characters, and sometimes reacts to them in a wordless communication with the audience. A character named Chorus introduces the prop man and explains the staging, and then periodically describes the setting of a scene, announces a character, or comments on the plot. During most of the play, every character speaks or reacts directly to the audience, "overhearing" each other only when necessary for the plot. The primary interaction is therefore between actor and audience rather than among actors, giving a formal and ritualistic quality of traditional oriental theatre forms.

Suggestions:

Costumes and properties should be as elaborate or simple as the group desires and as the situation allows. The already large cast may be augmented by musicians who accompany the action with sound effects on instruments, such as paper wrapped over combs, cymbals, bells, gongs, toy xylophones, and drums.

MING LEE AND THE MAGIC TREE

CHARACTERS

Chorus
Property Man
Ming Lee, *a stonecutter*
Moo Yuen, *a prince disguised as a tiger*
Shing Nu, *Princess of the Stars*
Mei Ling ⎫
                ⎬ *Star Maidens*
Mei Ping ⎭
Kuan Lung, *ruler of the valley*
Kite Maker
Sun God, *ruler of the sky*
So Hi ⎫
So Lo ⎬ *three fair maidens*
So So ⎭
Rain God, *ruler of the clouds*
Bear
Monkey
God of the Mountain, *ruler of the mountain peak*
Lin Po, *a young stonecutter*
Attendants to Kuan Lung
Wedding Guests
Gong Striker
Orchestra

DESCRIPTION OF CHARACTERS
AND COSTUMES

Chorus: Perfect in manner and in speech. He wears a colorful Chinese robe and carries a large fan.

Property Man: Speaks only in mime, obeys quickly, and enjoys his duties. He wears a skullcap with a button on top, jacket, and trousers.

Ming Lee: Young and handsome. He wears a coolie hat, jacket, and trousers.

Moo Yuen: Prince Charming who is disguised as a tiger. He wears a yellow suit with black stripes and a removable tiger mask.

Shing Nu: Princess of the Stars. She is beautiful and beautifully dressed in a glittering Chinese robe.

Mei Ling, Mei Ping: Two Star Maidens. They wear beautiful Chinese robes.

Kuan Lung: Ruler of the valley. He wears a costly Chinese robe and a tall hat with a large golden badge.

Kite Maker: Humble workman. He wears a peasant jacket and trousers.

Sun God: Powerful and commanding. He wears a rich Chinese robe and carries a staff topped with gold tinsel streamers.

So Hi, So Lo, So So: Three pretty maidens. They wear flowing Chinese robes and colorful flowers in their hair. They each carry a beautiful fan.

Rain God: Strong and mighty. He wears a rich Chinese robe and carries a staff with silver tinsel streamers.

Bear: Lumbering and with a deep voice. He wears a Chinese costume and a colorful animal mask.

Monkey: Small, quick, and chattery. He wears a Chinese costume and a monkey mask.

God of the Mountain: Ancient and majestic. He wears a Chinese robe, has a long stringy beard, and his hat is the peak of the painted mountain top.

Lin Po: Youthful and energetic. He wears a coolie hat, jacket, and trousers.

Attendants, Wedding Guests, Gong Striker, Orchestra: All wear appropriate Chinese costumes.

As in the traditional Chinese theatre, there is no stage setting. The back and sides of the stage are masked with curtains. There is an entrance at R and one at L.

As the play begins, the members of the Orchestra and the Gong Striker enter and take their places on one side. On the other side there is a box for the Property Man. The Musicians wear traditional black or blue Chinese pajamas with long tops, and they carry various instruments: bells, drums, recorders, cymbals. The Orchestra plays briefly and loudly. Gong Striker strikes the gong. Chorus enters, wearing a colorful Chinese robe and carrying a fan. He is followed by the Property Man, wearing a skullcap with a button on top, jacket, and trousers. He stands at the side of Chorus.

CHORUS: I am the Chorus. I bow and say welcome to most honorable audience. (*He bows. Property Man also bows and keeps bowing until a frown from Chorus stops him. Chorus points with fan at Property Man.*) He is the Property Man. He will set the stage and help our illustrious actors. (*Property Man grins and bows.*) Although he is visible, and you will see him walk about in full view, please pretend he is— (*Snaps fan open and holds it in front of Property Man's face.*)—invisible to you. I bow again and again. (*Chorus bows to R and L. Property Man imitates him.*) Our most unworthy play will begin. (*Gong Striker strikes gong.*) In the Valley of a Hundred Flowers there lives a poor but honest stonecutter. (*Ming Lee enters, wearing a coolie hat, jacket and trousers.*) Every morning at the hour of the dragon—(*Ming Lee looks at sky.*)—he leaves his hut of mud and straw and climbs the mountain to cut stones for the royal palace.

MING LEE: (*A painted mountain moves on stage. Ming Lee walks to the mountain and stands by it.*) I am Ming Lee, a poor but honest stonecutter. With my mallet—(*Holds up right hand.*)—and my chisel—(*Holds up left hand. Property Man quickly takes mallet and chisel from property box.*)—I earn my bowl of rice. My arms are strong. My back is straight. I can lift a stone twice my weight. When I strike the mountain—tap, tap, tap, they hear the echo in the valley—clap, clap, clap.

(*Property Man puts chisel and mallet into Ming Lee's hands. Ming Lee pantomimes hitting the mountain. Property Man claps his hands in echo. He grins, clapping louder and faster, enjoying the fun. Drum beats. Ming Lee and Property Man stand silently. Loud roaring is heard and Tiger, dressed in yellow with black stripes, jumps onto the stage, looks at audience and roars.*)

CHORUS: A tiger enters.

TIGER: Do not tremble. Do not run. (*Holds up paws.*) For under this tiger's skin I am Moo Yuen, a mortal prince who seeks to wed Shing Nu, the Princess of the Stars. The great Jade Emperor—(*He looks up. Drums beat. He bows.*)—who knows best, has changed me into a tiger and sent me on a quest. Before I can marry the Princess of the Stars, the great Jade Emperor commands that I must find the answer to a question. I must find—what makes a happy man. Until then I will remain a tiger. I will roar—(*Walks and roars.*)—and shake my magic tail. Alas, magic I can make with it for others, but none for me. (*Feels behind for tail which is not there.*) My magic tail? My tail! MY TAIL!

(*Property Man quickly gets red rope tail from property box and ties it around Tiger's waist.*) Quickly I must find the answer to the question: What makes a happy man? Then quickly I may marry the beautiful Princess of the Stars.

(*The music of the Princess is heard, tinkling bells. Princess of the Stars enters, followed by Mei Ling and Mei Ping. They wear beautiful Chinese costumes and walk in a slow, stately walk, swaying the body gently.*)

PRINCESS: I am the Princess of the Stars,
   Shining—shining silver bright—
   With my maidens through the night.
   Brightly my jewel lantern burns
   Waiting—waiting—
   Until my Moo Yuen returns.
   (*Princess looks fondly toward Tiger. He looks lovingly at her. Music of the bells tinkles as Princess and maidens exit.*)

CHORUS: The sun has now climbed to his height. Ming Lee can tell by his short shadow and his long appetite.

MING LEE: I will rest and eat my cake of rice. (*Property Man returns mallet and chisel to box.*) I will walk and find a tree. I will sit in the shade it makes for me. (*He starts walking in a big circle. Property Man places a stool at C., takes from the box a colorful, flowering tree branch, stands by the stool like a tree, and waves the branch.*) Ah, here is a kind peach tree. Thank you, peach tree. Thank you for the shade you have made. (*He bows to tree. Property Man returns the bow. Ming Lee sits and smiles happily.*) It is a happy time, when you have worked your best, to sit quietly and enjoy a rest.

TIGER: What do I hear? A *happy* man is near. By my magic tail to him I will appear. (*With his hand he swings his tail in a circle behind him. Tiger takes a step toward Ming Lee and roars.*)

MING LEE: The wind is roaring like a tiger. (*Tiger takes another step and gives another roar. Ming Lee shivers.*) The wind is blowing like a tiger. (*Tiger takes a third step and gives a third roar. Ming Lee looks up.*) It is a tiger! (*Ming Lee jumps up. Tiger now purrs like a kitten and acts comically shy.*) It is a small tiger. (*Tiger and Property Man nod.*) It is a gentle tiger. (*Tiger and Property Man nod.*) It is a friendly tiger. He will not hurt me. (*Tiger and Property Man shake their heads. Tiger purrs again and holds out paw.*) He is a hungry tiger. (*Tiger and Property Man nod.*) I will share my rice cake with him.

(*Property Man with his free hand, the other hand still holds the branch, gives Ming Lee a small rice cake. Ming Lee breaks it in two and gives Tiger half.*)

CHORUS: When honorable one helps another one, then *two* people enjoy what is done. (*Ming Lee and Tiger smile at each other and chew loudly.*) Ming Lee and Tiger eat, as you can see, most politely. Their chewing is loud and clear so the gods will hear and know they are thankful.

(*Property Man adds to the sound by chewing loudly and smacking his lips.*)

TIGER: I have found a friendly man. Now, by the twist of my magic tail, I will ask if he is a happy man. (*Tiger swings his tail around.*)

TIGER, CHORUS, AND ORCHESTRA: (*Chanting.*)
O Ming Lee . . . tell me,
　　Tell me, are you
　　　　Hap—py?

MING LEE: The wind is whispering in the tree. (*Tiger, Chorus, and Orchestra repeat the chant.*) The wind asks me—am I happy? I am the strongest stonecutter on the mountain. I have rice. I have tea. The Kitchen God sends to heaven a good report of me. How—how could I happier be?
(*Gong strikes.*)

HERALDS: (*Enter and call.*)
Bow! Bow low.
Bow to the ground and stay!
Bow! Bow low.
The great Kuan Lung comes this way!

MING LEE: I bow. I bow. I obey. (*Ming Lee falls to his knees and bows to the ground. Orchestra plays as a procession enters. Leading, with trumpetlike shouts, are the Heralds, "Bow! Bow low! Bow! Bow low!" Following come the Banner Carriers, Lantern Carriers, Musicians, Nobles, Ladies, Guards, and the great Kuan Lung himself, impressive in a tall hat with a large golden badge. The procession circles and exits. Ming Lee looks after procession in awe.*) Oh, how great is the great Kuan Lung. He wears a tall hat with a golden badge. How happy he must be. (*Feels his coolie hat.*) I thought I was happy as Ming Lee. I am a mighty stonecutter, but he is the mighty ruler of all the Valley. If I could be—the great Kuan Lung—all would bow to me. Oh, then—then I know—I *know* I would be happy.

(*Cymbals clap.*)

TIGER: Happy he will be, and of this tiger's tail I will be free!
O brave Ming Lee,
You will see—
You are sitting—
Fortunately—
Under a magic tree.
A turn of my tail—swish!
You will have your wish!

(*Tiger twirls his tail and points it at tree. Property Man shakes himself and the branch violently.*)

Any wish today I will grant you.
Any wish you say will come true!
You, Ming Lee—
The great Kuan Lung shall be!
(*Gong sounds. Property Man shakes tree. Tiger runs to R, where he is handed tall hat with badge. He takes off Ming Lee's coolie hat and hands it to Property Man. Tiger puts tall hat on Ming Lee's head.*)

MING LEE: (*Amazed and pleased.*)
I made a wish . . .
To be the great Kuan Lung,
To wear a hat, tall and new.

(*With wonder feels hat on his head.*)

I made a wish . . .
My wish is coming true.

(*He looks up.*)

Surely I, Ming Lee,
Unworthy me,
Sit beneath a magic tree.
(*Property Man nods and waves branch.*)

CHORUS: Most wise audience, do not judge Ming Lee too severely. He is merely dazzled by wealth and show. He does not know that borrowed feathers will not help a rooster crow. Honorable Grandfather wisely said, "*A fine hat does not make a fine head.*"

HERALDS: (*Enter, calling.*)
Bow! Bow low!
Bow to the ground and stay.
Bow! Bow low!
The great Ming Lee comes this way.
(*Orchestra plays as the procession enters and makes a circle. The procession is the same as before, but without Kuan Lung. When the procession passes Ming Lee, he fills this space, walking proudly. The procession circles again, and Ming Lee sits on stool, with the members of the procession grouped around and behind him.*)

CHORUS: Ming Lee sits in his golden house enjoying the Garden of Sweet Smells, and watches the golden fish swim in the golden pool.

MING LEE: I am the great Ming Lee. (*Claps his hands.*) Bow. Bow to me. (*Members of the procession bow. Ming Lee nods happily.*) I have gold enough that I cannot count it all. I have firecrackers enough to make noise enough to make the good spirits happy, and to frighten the evil ones away. No man can say he is greater than Ming Lee.

TIGER: I have found the answer! To be rich makes a happy man. (*Tiger twirls his tail excitedly.*)

TIGER, CHORUS, AND ORCHESTRA: (*Chanting.*)
O Ming Lee . . . tell me,
Tell me, are you
Hap—py?

MING LEE: The wind chimes tinkle in the breeze. (*Tiger, Chorus, Orchestra repeat chant.*) The chimes ask me—am I happy? I am the ruler of the Valley. Bow, bow, I say! (*Members of procession bow.*) I speak and all obey. How—how could I be happier?
(*Cymbals clap. Members of the procession rise. Kite Maker enters.*)

KITE MAKER: I am a kite maker. With my unworthy hands, I have made a kite worthy of the richest in the land. (*Property Man takes large kite from box and gives it to Kite Maker.*) O most illustrious and industrious ruler, I bow before you. At your feet I lay my most unworthy kite, made by me for the most worthy, the great Ming Lee.

MING LEE: Attend! Let the flying of the kite begin!

HERALDS: All look! All look to the sky.
  The great golden kite will fly!

KITE MAKER: (*Holds up kite.*)
  Above the plum tree, above the mountain snow—
  To the Celestial Heavens the kite will go!

TIGER: (*To audience.*)
  By my magic tail
  I will sail
  A message on the kite in the air,
  A message to my princess fair.
  (*Tiger twirls his tail and roars. Kite Maker gives kite to Property Man, who hooks it to the end of a pole, then holds it high and moves it as if it were flying. Kite Maker pretends he is holding a string and is flying the kite.*)

KITE MAKER: Up . . . up . . . up it flies . . .
  Around . . . around . . . around. . . .

  (*Property Man goes in circles with kite.*)

  HELP . . . help . . . help. . . .
  It lifts me off the ground!

  (*Orchestra starts playing. Kite Maker, holding the imaginary string, runs after Property Man. Members of the procession join, running behind and holding on to the Kite Maker.*)

  Up . . . up . . . hold tight!

  (*All join the line of follow-the-leader, holding onto the person in front.*)

  Up . . . up . . . out of sight.
  (*All the attendants follow the Kite Maker, who follows the Property Man, who leads them off. Bells of the Princess tinkle. Princess, followed by Mei Ping and Mei Ling, enters. Property Man enters and holds kite near her ear.*)

PRINCESS: The kite brings a message to me.
  Words from my Moo Yuen it sings to me.
  (*She leans to listen to kite.*)

MEI PING: Has he learned the answer to the question?

MEI LING: Can you hear?

MEI PING: When does he return?

MEI LING: When will he appear?

PRINCESS: (*Shaking her head sadly.*)
Not soon, I fear.
Wealth and power he thinks are the answer.
Before he can return,
A better answer he must learn.

MEI PING: Oh, may it be soon . . . soon.

MEI LING: Please before another moon.
(*Bells tinkle. Princess and maidens exit, followed by the Property Man.*)

MING LEE: (*Rises and looks up.*) Up . . . up . . . the kite is out of sight. I cannot see it. The sun is in my eyes. The sun—the sun is blinding me.

SUN GOD: (*Cymbals clap. The Sun God enters, dressed in a Chinese robe. He carries a staff topped with golden streamers.*) I am the mighty Sun God, blazing, bright! Around the earth I circle, bringing light.

MING LEE: How powerful is the sun! He comes into my garden uninvited. Away! Away! The sun does not obey. The sun is greater than I. I rule only the Valley. The sun rules the sky! Oh, if I could be the sun— then I know I would be happy.

TIGER: With the twist of my magic tail, I will grant his wish! (*Twirls his tail.*) O wise Ming Lee, your wish is granted. God of the Sun you shall be!
(*Gong sounds. Property Man takes hat from Ming Lee's head. Tiger takes staff from Sun God, who exits, and puts staff into Ming Lee's hand.*)

CHORUS: A second wish is made and a foolish one. Ming Lee will not be happy when he is the God of Sun. But while he learns to be a happy man, we must wait, so—we will fan. (*Fans himself.*) Honorable Grandfather spoke truth in talk: "*Man must first stumble before he learns to walk.*"

MING LEE: I am the Sun God. Behold me in my golden glory!
From east to west I light the skies
With a fire that never dies.
My golden arrows pierce the earth.

Power is in my hand.

In an hour I can burn the land!

(*Orchestra plays, recorders, as So Hi, So Lo, and So So enter. They are three pretty maidens, dressed in Chinese robes and with flowers in their hair. They carry fans which they flutter gracefully, and they walk with quick, dainty steps.*)

SO HI, SO LO, SO SO: We are three maidens fair

SO HI: So Hi—

SO LO: So Lo—

SO SO: So So—

SO HI, SO LO, SO SO: Walking in the garden for a breath of air—

(*All flutter their fans.*)

SO HI: Through the moon gate—

SO LO: By the lily pool—

SO SO: To the pagoda—

SO HI, SO LO, SO SO: Hoping it will be cool.

(*Flutter their fans.*)

SO HI: The heat—

SO LO: The heat—

SO SO: Is oppressive.

(*They fan.*)

SO HI: The sun—

SO LO: The sun—

SO SO: Is excessive!

(*They fan.*)

SO HI, SO LO, SO SO: We go—

SO HI: Fanning high,

SO LO: Fanning low,

SO SO: Fanning oh—

SO HI, SO LO, SO SO: (*Fanning slower and slower.*) So—so—slow.

(*Orchestra plays as they exit.*)

MING LEE: With one hot breath, I will make rivers run dry, wells go thirsty, flowers crumple and cry, trees fall and die. No one—no one is mightier than I! (*Cymbals clap.*)

TIGER, CHORUS AND ORCHESTRA: (*Chanting.*)

O Ming Lee . . . tell me,

   Tell me, are you

      Hap—py?

MING LEE: The wind dares speak and disturb me. (*Tiger, Chorus, Orchestra repeat chant.*) Happy? I am the powerful one. Nothing is greater than the sun.

(*Ming Lee shakes his staff. Drums roll like thunder. Rain God enters, dressed in a Chinese robe. He carries a staff topped with silver streamers.*)

RAIN GOD: I am the God of Rain—

Rumbling, tumbling across the sky.

Through my fingers water falls, hail, snow—

Blizzards blow!

Across the blue ceiling of the world I go,

Making a giant shadow below.

MING LEE: Someone dares come near the sun!

RAIN GOD: O burning ball of fire, you are high.

You are blazing hot.

But I,

The great Rain God,

With thunder shout:

I can blot you out!

MING LEE: No shadow can turn day to night!

RAIN GOD: (*Taking one threatening step.*) Fight!

MING LEE: No dragon of darkness can steal my light!

RAIN GOD: (*Taking another step.*) Fight!

MING LEE: Fight!

(*Drums beat. Ming Lee and Rain God duel with staffs, using large swinging movements. Rain God forces Ming Lee's staff to the ground and holds it there. Cymbals clap. Rain God triumphantly holds up his staff, then stands in front of Ming Lee, arms spread, blocking him out.)*

CHORUS: The heavens are still. The battle is done.
The God of Rain has eclipsed the sun.

MING LEE: (*Rain God steps aside.*) Greater than the ruler of the Valley, greater than the sun is the mighty Rain God. I wish—I wish I were the God of Rain. Then with mighty thunder I would roar: Ming Lee is the mighty wonder!

TIGER: With the twist of my magic tail, I will grant his wish.
With more power he will be happy, and I will be free.

(*Twirls his tail.*)

O Wise Ming Lee, your wish is granted. The God of Rain you shall be.
(*Property Man takes sun staff from Ming Lee. Tiger takes rain staff from Rain God, who exits. Tiger gives rain staff to Ming Lee.*)

CHORUS: In every moon dark days appear.
Ming Lee, unfortunately, does not see clear.
His eyes are blinded by a flash of power,
Which will need feeding every hour.
Honorable Grandfather did wisely repeat:
"*When you buy shoes, be sure to measure feet.*"

MING LEE: I am the mighty Rain God.
I stop the sun,
Make rivers run
And overflow;
Shake the earth with torrents,
Blow hurricanes below!

(*Orchestra makes whistling sounds. Ming Lee strides about, shaking his tinsel staff.*)

I will throw open the windows of the sky
And let the tears fall from my eye!
River rise! Water flood the land!
I am the master. It is my command!

(*Property Man takes long blue cloth from property box.*)

Over the Valley, like a cover the water creeps—
Higher—higher—higher—

(*Property Man stretches blue cloth on floor.*)

Like an angry dragon, the water leaps—
High—higher—higher.

(*Property Man shakes one end of the blue cloth, making it ripple in the air.*)

Trees are uprooted; animals flee.
No one is as mighty as Ming Lee.

BEAR: (*In Chinese costume and colorful mask, enters.*)
I am a bear.
When day is warm and fair,
I growl and glare.
When day is snowy and blowy,
I smile and gloat
Because—every day,
Cold or fair,
I always wear
My fur coat.
When Thunder God begins to roar
And Rain God begins to pour
Water from the sky,
I do not hide inside
Like a cricket bug.
If my coat gets wet,
I have no sneezes
Because—I
Give a big bear hug
Which squeezes
Me dry.

(*Bear gives himself a big bear hug.*)

MONKEY: (*Dressed in Chinese costume and monkey mask, enters.*)
I am a little monkey.
One day on my way
To find shady shelter,
A bamboo tree
Bowed its head
And it said,

"Welcome," just to me.
 Up the tree with a hop,
 I made my home at the top.
 Happy was I
 To live so high
 In a slender, tender
 Bamboo tree.
 But—now—
 Thunder roars in the sky,
 Rain doors open in the sky,
 Water falls out of the sky
 On me—high
 In a leaky, creaky
 Bamboo tree.
 Down I slide
 Hoping to hide
 From rain dragon in the sky.
 Rain plopping . . . plopping . . .
 I hopping . . . hopping . . .
 Rain never stopping . . .
 There must be a reason why!
 Stop!
 Stop water throwing on!
 Monkey thinks
 Some monkey business is going on!

BEAR AND MONKEY: Weather . . . weather . . . weather . . .
 Chilly, silly, cold, or hot;
 There'll always be
 For you and me
 WEATHER—
 Whether
 Or not!
 (*Bear and Monkey exit.*)

MING LEE: The world is covered with the darkness of my cloud.
 Lightning, come!

(*Property Man takes streak of lightning from box. He runs about, jabbing the air.*)

Light the sky!
 Let bolts of fire fly!

High, low. Low, and high.
Lightning flash!
Torrents splash!
Gales lash!
Thunder crash!
I—I am the mighty one!

TIGER, CHORUS AND ORCHESTRA: (*Chanting.*)
  O Ming Lee . . . tell me,
    Tell me, are you
      Hap—py?

MING LEE: Happy? All things tremble, tumble, flee. All—all now bow to me. (*Cymbals clap.*)

GOD OF THE MOUNTAIN: (*Appears behind the top of the mountain. He is an old man with a long, stringy beard, and he wears a hat the same shape as the painted mountain top.*) I am the God of the Mountain. I never tremble. I never flee. A mountain stands forever—for eternity.

MING LEE: Strike him! Strike! Shake the mountain with a lightning flash. Quake the mountain with a thunder crash. Make him bow to me!

  (*Drums beat. Property Man strikes at mountain with shaft of lightning.*)

GOD OF THE MOUNTAIN: The sun will set each day. The God of Rain will blow away. But I—the ancient mountain—stay.

MING LEE: I cannot move the mountain. The mountain is mightier than I. (*Property Man puts lightning streak and blue cloth back into box.*) I wish—I wish to be the God of the Mountain, then I know—I know I will be happy.

TIGER: With a twist of my magic tail I will grant his wish. (*Twists tail.*) O Ming Lee, your wish is granted. God of the Mountain you shall be.

  (*Cymbals clap. God of the Mountain disappears. Ming Lee goes behind the mountain.*)

CHORUS: Most honorable audience, four wishes you have seen pass. Yet Ming Lee still seeks for happiness, alas. And the Tiger still seeks for an answer. All because far-off grass looks greener. Honorable Grandfather the truth related when he stated:

"The fingers on your hand all have strength,
  But each finger is a different length."

MING LEE: (*Appears at the top of the mountain, wearing God of the Mountain's hat.*) I am God of the Mountain. Alone I stand, a mighty tower of stone. Up I reach with my snowy peak. With the gods I speak!

TIGER: (*Holds arms up, imploring.*)
  O great Jade God, the answer
  To your question I now know.
  The happy man is the mighty man,
  Ming Lee has proved it so.
  Release me now from this tiger's skin
  And let my wedding with the Princess begin.
  (*Princess' music of bells begins. Princess, followed by Mei Ling and Mei Ping, enters.*)

PRINCESS: O Moo Yuen, the truth still you do not see.
  You are as blind as poor Ming Lee.
  Power can be abused.
  Might can be misused.
  You have not yet found the simple answer.
  I fear our wedding day
  Is still far, far away.
  (*Bells tinkle as Princess and maidens exit.*)

TIGER: The great Jade God does not answer. O mighty God of the Mountain, from your lofty peak, speak! Tell the great Jade God you are a happy man.
  (*Tiger, Chorus, Orchestra chant:*
  O Ming Lee . . . tell me
    Tell me, are you
      Hap—py?*)

MING LEE: Happy? To me the earth and the heavens bow. No one can touch me now.
  (*Gong sounds. Lin Po, a young stonecutter, dressed the same as Ming Lee was, enters.*)

LIN PO: I am Lin Po, a young stonecutter. Each day with my chisel and my mallet—(*He raises his arms. Property Man takes chisel and mallet from box and puts them into his hands.*) I go to the mountain.

Each day I chip, chip, chip the stones away. (*He walks to mountain and pantomimes hitting at it. Property Man claps the echoes.*)

MING LEE: Stop! I feel a shiver which shakes my side.
Stop! I feel a quiver deep inside.
Stop!
Someone is stronger than I.
It is—a stonecutter.
Stop! Stop, I say.
He does not obey.
A stonecutter can chip-chip a mountain away.
Quick, fast—I wish I were a stonecutter,
Then I know at last—I would be happy.

TIGER: By the twist of my magic tail, I will grant his wish. O wise Ming Lee, your wish is granted. A stonecutter you shall be.
(*Ming Lee disappears behind the mountain and appears at the side. Tiger takes chisel and mallet from Lin Po, who exits, and gives them to Ming Lee. Property Man puts coolie hat on Ming Lee's head.*)

CHORUS: Most kind audience, around in a circle Ming Lee has gone and come. He—we—are back where we started from. Honorable Grandfather, with brush, wrote most truthful note:
"*Man often makes a foolish wish.*
Don't climb a tree to catch a fish."

MING LEE: I am Ming Lee, a poor but happy stonecutter. Each day I go to the mountain. Each day I proudly chip the stones away. (*He pantomimes hitting the mountain and sings. Property Man claps the echoes.*)

TIGER: (*Amazed.*) Can it be—that poor Ming Lee—is—a happy man?

MING LEE: I have learned to be myself
And do the best I can.
Yes, I am a happy man!

TIGER: O great Jade God,
I was deceived.
The answer is not,
As I believed,
Power, or wealth, or glory.
The answer is—
He who knows who he is

And does the best he can—
He—is the happy man.

(*Gong sounds. Bells of the Princess' music tinkle. Princess and maidens enter. Tiger takes off tail and mask and gives them to Property Man, who gives him his prince's hat. Prince and Princess bow to each other.*)

CHORUS: The great Jade God is pleased with the answer. He smiles and the heavens ring with wedding sounds. Bright lanterns will light the sky, twinkling ever; as the Prince and the Princess of the Stars live happily forever.

(*Orchestra plays. Prince and Princess lead Mei Ling and Mei Ping in a wedding procession. Other wedding guests enter, carrying lighted lanterns. As procession circles the stage three times in a grand march, Ming Lee slips to center of the circle and sits on stool. Property Man stands by him, holding the tree branch over him. Procession stops, forming a semicircle behind Ming Lee.*)

CHORUS: It is night and the stars shine high
Like lanterns in the sky.
And the stonecutter smiles,
Wisely,
Content to be
Himself.

(*Ming Lee bows to tree. Property Man bows to Ming Lee.*)

So ends the story of Ming Lee and the Magic Tree.

(*Cymbals clap.*)

Illustrious actors will now step forward lightly.
Honorable audience, if enjoyed, will applaud politely.

(*Actors bow as Chorus leads the audience in applauding. Chorus holds up fan for silence.*)

Honorable Grandfather leaves these words with you:
"*May your wishes all be wise—and all come true.*"
I bow and say, "Good-bye to you."
(*Chorus bows. Orchestra plays. Actors exit.*)

CURTAIN

Ma and the Kids
Judith Martin

Story devised by Judith Martin
The dialogue and action were developed by Irving Burton, Betty Osgood,
and Daniel Jahn under the direction of Judith Martin.

Ma and the Kids is a script originally created by Judith Martin and others of The Paper Bag Players. It's divided into two main episodes in which an indulgent Ma is confronted by problems with her brood of children. In the first scene, "Suppertime," the children's unreasonable demands are as zany as Ma's eager willingness to comply. The second scene, "Mother's Mistake," is created out of the confusion caused by the children's inability to remember everything they must take to school that morning. But the harried Ma inadvertently turns the tables on them by realizing that she, too, has forgotten something: today is Saturday and there is no school. The following notes are from the creators of the play:

> While this play is written for a cast of four, it may easily be adapted for a cast of six or seven simply by adding more children to the family. In "Suppertime," the extra children could ask for mustard, napkins, relish, etc. In "Mother's Mistake," the other children will need to think of more things to forget, i.e., books, carfare, ruler, etc. A large cardboard box can be used for a table. Children can use boxes to sit on, or just pretend to sit. Mother should wear a large apron. Oversize clothes on children give an amusing effect. Wigs of paper or cotton mops are not necessary, but add humor.

MA AND THE KIDS

CHARACTERS

Ma
Betty
Judy
Irving

MA AND THE KIDS by Judith Martin except for *Suppertime* which was suggested by Irving Burton. Developed by present and former Paper Bag Players Betty Osgood, Remy Charlip, Daniel Jahn, Shirley Kaplan, Irving Burton, and Judith Martin.

INTRODUCTION

(*Ma, Betty, Judy, and Irving enter.*)

MA: (*Gestures to children.*) This is Betty, the most intelligent child in her class. . . . This is Judy, a real little lady . . . And this is Irving. He's the hero of his class and he's my hero, too.

CHILDREN: (*Gesture to Ma.*) And that's our Ma, the best Ma in the whole wide world. Ma, we're hungry!

MA: Well, children, set the table.
   (*All exit.*)

SUPPERTIME

(*Enter children bringing table.*)

MA: I didn't have time to shop so we're going to have . . .

CHILDREN: Potato chips!

MA: (*Empties potato chips into one large bowl.*) Right. (*Starts to sit down.*)

BETTY: Ma, may I please have some ketchup?

MA: Of course. (*Exits and returns with bottle of ketchup.*)

JUDY: Ma, may I have some salt?

MA: Oh, I forgot the salt. (*Exits and returns with salt shaker.*)

IRVING: Ma, there's no water.

MA: Oh, isn't there any water? (*Exits and returns with glass of water.*)

BETTY: I need more ketchup, please.

MA: You do love ketchup. (*Ma begins to run back and forth moving faster and faster.*)

JUDY: Guess what, Ma? The salt shaker is empty.

MA: And I just filled it this morning. (*She continues to run back and forth bringing in more ketchup bottles, salt shakers, and glasses of water each trip.*)

IRVING: I need more water.

BETTY: I need more ketchup.

JUDY: I need more salt.

IRVING: Water.

BETTY: Ketchup.

JUDY: Salt.

IRVING: *Water!*

MA: (*Finally sits down.*) Now, children, please pass me some potato chips.

CHILDREN: Oh, Ma, there are no more.

MA: (*Sighs.*) Children, clear the table. (*Children exit taking table.*)

MA'S MISTAKE

MA: My children do have big appetites and they sometimes get a little noisy, but when they sleep they're angels.

(*Enter children standing behind sheet that they are holding under their chins. They stand still with their eyes closed as if they were asleep. Ma stands on the side of stage and calls to them.*)

MA: Wake up, children. It's time to go to school. . . . Get up, sleepyheads . . . I told you last night that if you didn't go to bed you'd be sleepy in the morning . . . I don't hear the patter of little feet and it's getting very late. . . . It's 8:29! The school bus will be here in one minute.

(*Children begin to dress.*)

IRVING: That's my tie.

JUDY: That's my shoe.

BETTY: I can't find my belt.

IRVING: Who has my shirt?

JUDY: Has anybody seen my eyeglasses?

ALL: Good-bye, Ma.
  (*Exit children.*)

MA: Just a little tidying to do and then I'll have a nice quiet day all to myself. (*Ma starts to sweep.*)

JUDY: (*Enters.*) Ma, I forgot my sneakers. Can you help me find them?

MA: Here they are.

JUDY: Thanks, Ma. Good-bye, Ma. (*Judy exits.*)

MA: Good-bye, dear. Now, what was I doing?
  (*Each time the children enter they rush across stage and disappear. They reappear with object they had forgotten, rush back across stage, and exit. Eventually all the children are loaded down with their things.*)

BETTY: I forgot my notebook.

JUDY: I forgot my report card.

BETTY: I forgot my gym suit.

MA: I'll dry the dishes.

IRVING: I forgot my violin.

JUDY: I forgot my plant for science class.

MA: Whoops, I dropped a dish!

BETTY: I forgot my hockey stick.

IRVING: I forgot my lunch.

MA: Hurry off to school, dears, or you'll be late. Now what was I doing?

CHILDREN: (*All enter.*) Ma, we forgot to kiss you good-bye.
(*All kids kiss Ma and exit.*)

MA: How sweet of them to remember. (*Calling after them.*) Good-bye, dears.

CHILDREN: (*Voices only.*) Good-bye, Ma.

MA: At last I can clean the house. Oh, dear! (*Very loud.*) Children, come back!
(*Children rush in.*)

BETTY: What is it?

IRVING: What happened?

JUDY: Did I forget something I didn't remember?

MA: I forgot something. Today is Saturday. There's no school.

CHILDREN: Hooray! Yippee! Hooray!
(*All dance around Ma.*)

CURTAIN

Hands Off! Don't Touch!
Judith Martin

Story devised by Judith Martin
The dialogue and action were developed by Irving Burton, Betty Osgood, and Daniel Jahn under the direction of Judith Martin.

Hands Off! Don't Touch! by Judith Martin of The Paper Bag Players of New York City is a novel interpretation of the old warning that all children find very familiar. Instead of an adult scolding a child, we find flowers and then butterflies scolding a human being for trying to pick or catch them! The play ends in an amusing surprise as the human being stops the hungry advances of a lion. Each of the conflicts between Man and an adversary is enlivened by the audience's repeated participation in a simple four-line song. The creators of the play have written the following suggestions for children presenting the play:

This play may be produced on a bare stage or with painted cardboard scenery representing trees and rocks. There may be many butterflies and flowers or just one of each, depending on the number of children in the group and the size of the stage.

For costumes, flowers can be made of cardboard. The stem should come to the chin of the child. The flower itself should have a hole cut for the child's face. Another possible costume might be simply hats of colored paper petals. Butterflies can also be made out of cut-out cardboard. Wings can be painted, but colored pictures from discarded magazines pasted on cardboard also give beautiful effects. Another way of making wings would be to use colored tissue paper or scarves. For Lion, an oversized cardboard box is ideal. The face can be painted on the box. Excelsior, old string, or worn-out mops all make a good mane. Man should carry a stick with any thin material attached to it to represent a butterfly net, along with an old pair of binoculars and a big book.

HANDS OFF! DON'T TOUCH!

CHARACTERS

Man
Lion
Butterfly
Flower

The cast may be expanded to include many butterflies and many flowers.

The whole play takes place in an imaginary forest. We used a blank stage but you could paint trees and flowers on a background. A Man comes on the stage. You can tell he's a butterfly collector because he's carrying a butterfly net. He's also a bird watcher and a flower collector. You can tell, because he also has binoculars and a big book that identifies flowers and animals. He walks about trying not to make any noise that would disturb the birds. He stops and looks through his glasses whenever he hears a bird whistle. You never see the bird. All the sounds come from offstage.

BIRD: Brrp. Brrrp.

MAN: That's the sound of a yellow-bellied nutcracker!

BIRD: Wreeop. Wrooop.

MAN: And that's the red-headed hoodwinker!

(*A Flower comes in. It's oversized cardboard. It takes very small and dainty steps. There is music while the Flower comes in. She almost does a dance. The Man follows her every movement. Finally the Flower stops. It looks as if she has been cornered by the Man.*)

MAN: What do I see blooming right in front of me? A double-deckered cornucopia with stamen and pistils! I must have it for my collection.

FLOWER: Pick me if you must but before you do, may I please have a few last words?

MAN: Of course.

FLOWER: (*Sings.*)
Hands off! Don't touch! I don't ask much—
Hands off! Don't touch! You'll get in dutch!

MAN: (*Amazed.*) What did you say?

FLOWER: (*Sings again.*)
Hands off! Don't touch! I don't ask much—
Hands off! Don't touch! You'll get in dutch!

MAN: (*He still can't believe his ears, asks the audience:*) What did that flower say?

AUDIENCE: (*Also sings.*)
Hands off! Don't touch! I don't ask much—
Hands off! Don't touch! You'll get in dutch!
(*While the audience is singing to the Man, the Flower tiptoes away. When the Man looks around the Flower is gone.*)

MAN: That flower talks too much anyway!
(*A Butterfly comes in and flies around the stage before it settles.*) By jove! A super cholestrol ruby-winged monarch! An entomologist's dream come true. I must have it for my collection.

BUTTERFLY: Add me to your collection if you must, but before you do, may I please have a few last words?

MAN: Of course.

BUTTERFLY: (*Sings.*)
Hands off! Don't touch! I don't ask much—
Hands off! Don't touch! You'll get in dutch!

MAN: (*In astonishment to the audience.*) What did that butterfly say?

AUDIENCE: (*Also singing.*)
Hands off! Don't touch! I don't ask much—
Hands off! Don't touch! You'll get in dutch!
(*While the Man is listening to the audience, the Butterfly tiptoes away. When the Man looks around, the Butterfly is gone.*)

MAN: That butterfly wouldn't fit in my net anyway!

(*A Lion leaps on the stage.*) By George! It's a two-legged man-eating Leo Furioso!

(*The Man is very worried and backs away from the Lion. The Lion follows him slowly around the stage. It's very slow and scary. The Lion pounces. The Man falls on his knees.*)

LION: I AM GOING TO EAT YOU!

MAN: Eat me if you must, but before you do, may I please say a few last words?

LION: GRRR—SURE—RRRR!

MAN: (*Sings.*)
Hands off! Don't touch! I don't ask much—
Hands off! Don't touch! You'll get in dutch!

LION: (*Asks audience.*) What did that man say?

AUDIENCE: (*Sings.*)
Hands off! Don't touch! I don't ask much—
Hands off! Don't touch! You'll get in dutch!

(*While the audience is singing the Man tiptoes away, offstage. When the song is over the Lion realizes the Man has gone and runs offstage after him. The Man runs back with the Lion chasing him. They run around and around. The Man escapes.*)

CURTAIN

Punch and Judy
Traditional

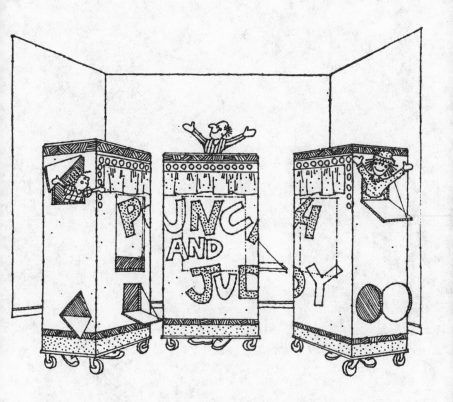

Punch and Judy, which has been adapted from the traditional puppet plays of the same title, is written for hand puppets but may also be played by actors. The play is a series of separate confrontations of Punch with his adversaries. Punch defies the shackles of being human and is victorious against a doctor, a policeman, death, and even the devil. With his whacking slapstick, he then takes on Judy, his wife, and Toby, his dog, but when faced with setbacks at their hands, Punch's good humor is irrepressible and he merrily faces his next opponent.

The play is full of physical assault that is mitigated and made acceptable by the witty repartee that mirrors it. The action of the script is limited by the movements that hand puppets can perform; the number of characters onstage at any one time is usually limited to two, again because the play is for puppets. Besides enough space for the action, the play needs a minimum of properties and costumes that mark the difference between free-spirited Punch and the staid authority figures he opposes.

PUNCH AND JUDY

A *Play for Hand Puppets*.

An adaptation by the editors of scenes from traditional Punch and Judy shows.

CHARACTERS

> Punch
> Judy
> Toby
> Doctor
> Baby
> Policeman
> Hangman
> Devil

SCENE

The stage of a Punch and Judy Puppet Theatre.

(Music. Curtains of the Puppet Theatre open. Punch enters. Music out.)

PUNCH: Hello. Hello. (*Waves to back row.*) And a Yoo and a Hoo to you, too. HELLO! (*Sings and dances.*)
Ooooooh—
Mr. Punch is a jolly good fellow,
His coat is scarlet and yellow.
He has a bump on his nose,
And a hump on his back,
And a stick to give you a smack and a whack!
Rootle-dee-tootle-dee-toot.

PUNCH WITH JUDY

PUNCH: (*Calls.*) Judy! Judy!

JUDY: (*Off.*) Yes, Mr. Punch.

PUNCH: Come up and meet—come up and greet—the children!

JUDY: (*Off.*) Wait.

PUNCH: You're late!

JUDY: (*Off.*) Ribbons and bows on my cap—

PUNCH: Judy!

JUDY: (*Off.*) Apron tied around my lap—

PUNCH: (*Raises stick.*) Judy, DEAR!

JUDY: (*Enters.*) I'm here!

PUNCH: Oh, Judy, my love, my dove. Oh, Judy, you are my beauty! (*To audience.*) She wears a wig! (*To Judy, romantically.*) Shall we dance?

JUDY: A waltz?

PUNCH: A jig!

(*Music. They do a short, fast dance and bow. Music out. Judy continues to bow. Punch gives her a whack from behind with his stick.*)

JUDY: Mr. Punch!

PUNCH: Oh, Judy, my beauty, give me a kiss.

JUDY: A kiss?

PUNCH: A big smacker.

JUDY: (*Takes stick.*) I'll give you a kiss. (*Hits him with stick.*) I'll give you a smacker! I'll give you a whacker!

PUNCH: Stop! Stop! No more kisses. No more kisses.

JUDY: Now behave yourself. I am going to tidy and didy the baby. (*Exits.*)

PUNCH: (*Wails loudly.*) Oh, Rootle-dee-tootle-dee-toot. Mr. Punch got the boot!

PUNCH WITH TOBY

TOBY: (*Off, barks.*) Rauff! Rauff! Rrrrrauff!

PUNCH: Toby!

TOBY: (*Off.*) Rauff! Rauff! Rauff!

PUNCH: (*Barks in answer.*) Rauff! Rauff! Rauff! (*Whistles, then calls.*) Come here, Toby. (*Toby enters.*) Say "Hello" to the children. (*No response.*) I think he got up on the wrong side of the dog house. Do you want to sing? (*No response.*) Do you want to dance? (*No response.*) You want to fight?

TOBY: (*Jumps and growls.*) Rrrauff! Rauauauauff! Rauff!

PUNCH: All right. Put up your paws. (*They spar in a circle.*) I'll give him a twist of my fist. (*Circle again.*) I'll give him a knock and a sock! (*Circle again.*) I'll—(*Toby leaps, barks, and grabs Punch by the nose. They struggle, pulling back and forth, with Toby barking and holding fast to the nose.*)
Help! Help! My nose! My beautiful nose! Let me go! Let me go! Oh! Oh! Oh! (*Punch flops down on playboard.*)

TOBY: (*In triumph, barks loudly, imitating Punch's song.*) Rau-rau-rauttle-dee-tootle-dee-rrrrroot! (*Exits.*)

PUNCH WITH THE DOCTOR

PUNCH: (*Sits up.*) Oh, doctor! Doctor fly! Medicine kit and koobootle! Bandage up my noodle—before I die! (*Flops down again.*)

DOCTOR: (*Enters.*) Never fear. I am coming. The doctor is here. How is the patient?

PUNCH: (*Sits up.*) Dead. (*Flops down.*)

DOCTOR: How long have you been dead?

PUNCH: (*Up.*) Three weeks. (*Down.*)

DOCTOR: When did you die?

PUNCH: (*Up.*) Yesterday. (*Down.*)

DOCTOR: Let me see your pulse. (*Holds Punch's hand.*) Five, four, three, two, one—it's stopped. Medicine! Medicine! Stand up and take your medicine.

PUNCH: (*Stands. Doctor shakes him.*) Why are you shaking me?

DOCTOR: The direction for giving medicine is always: shake well before taking. (*Grabs Punch's stick.*) Now, stand still. This will cure whatever's ill. Ready. One pill for a sneeze and a chill. (*Hits Punch.*) One dose for a shiver in your liver. (*Hits him.*) And this cure goes—from head to toes! (*Hits him.*)

PUNCH: Stop! Stop! No more medicine. I am well.

DOCTOR: Well?

PUNCH: Well!

DOCTOR: Well, pay me my doctor's fee.

PUNCH: I'll give him back his own medicine. I'll give you back every whack you gave me. Ready? This pays for blisters, bruises, and breaks. (*Hits Doctor.*)

DOCTOR: Help!

PUNCH: For sniffles and stomach aches. (*Hits him.*)

DOCTOR: Help!

PUNCH: And one to run until—you never give another pill! (*Hits him.*)

DOCTOR: Help! Help! Help! (*Exits.*)

PUNCH: (*Dances.*) Rootle-dee-tootle-dee-toot!

PUNCH WITH THE BABY

JUDY: (*Enters with Baby.*) Mr. Punch. I have a dozen things to do, undo, and re-do. Take the Baby.

PUNCH: Shake the Baby!

JUDY: Sh! He's asleep. (*Gives Baby to Punch. Sings.*)
Mama's little little boy,
Mama's little little joy . . .

PUNCH: (*Rocks Baby and sings.*)
Papa's pretty pretty little rose,
With Papa's pretty pretty nose . . .

JUDY: I'm going outside to get the potatoes and tomatoes. Oh—I'll miss him. Oh—do kiss him—for me. (*Exits.*)

PUNCH: Kissie, kissie, little Punchie. Get your nose out of the way! Kissie, kissie—SMACK! (*Gives loud smack with his mouth. Baby immediately gives a loud cry and continues to wail.*) Stop the crying! Stop the waterworks! (*Sings and rocks Baby.*)
Papa's little little boy,
Papa's little little joy . . .
Stop the racket! (*Shakes and tosses Baby.*) Judy! Are you outside the window? He's calling for you. He's bawling for you. What am I going to do? Judy! I'll throw him out to you! (*Throws Baby off. Whistle*

sound effect as Baby sails through the air. Crying stops.) What else can you do with a crying baby?

JUDY: (*Enters with Baby.*) Mr. Punch! You threw the Baby out the window!

PUNCH: (*Looks away.*) That's bad.

JUDY: I caught him.

PUNCH: (*Looks happy.*) That's good.

JUDY: You are a stupid selfish tootle-dee-toot! (*He nods.*) You are a hard-hearted, half-wit galoot! (*He nods.*) I am going to call the police! (*He shakes his head. Judy exits.*)

PUNCH: Rootle-dee-tootle-dee-toot! I think I'd better scoot!

PUNCH WITH THE POLICEMAN

PUNCH: (*Two knocks are heard off.*) Knock. Knock. Who's there?

POLICEMAN: (*Off.*) Open in the name of the law.

PUNCH: A policeman!

POLICEMAN: (*Enters.*) Mr. Punch, you are under suspicion.

PUNCH: (*Looks up.*) I am?

POLICEMAN: You have broken the laws of the country.

PUNCH: No, I never touched them!

POLICEMAN: You gave your wife a smack. You gave the doctor a whack. You threw the Baby out the window! You will hang from a *long* rope.

PUNCH: But it was a *short* baby!

POLICEMAN: Repeat after me.

PUNCH: *Eat* after you!

POLICEMAN: I am a bad and wicked man.

PUNCH: I'll have some ham with bread and jam.

POLICEMAN: (*Face to face.*) I have a note to lock you up.

PUNCH: I have a notion to knock you down.

POLICEMAN: Take your nose out of my face.

PUNCH: Take your face out of my nose.

POLICEMAN: I arrest you in the name of the law!

PUNCH: First you have to catch me. (*Punch runs, Policeman after him. Chase music. Punch drapes the puppet stage curtain around his head, speaks in a high voice. Music out.*) You won't hit an old old lady, would you?

POLICEMAN: Pardon me, madam. (*He turns away.*)

PUNCH: (*Throws off curtain, teases Policeman.*) Rootle-dee-tootle-dee-toot!

POLICEMAN: I'll get you! (*Chase starts again, with music.*)

TOBY: (*As Punch runs to R, Toby appears.*) Rauff! Rrrrauff! Rauff! (*Exits*)

DOCTOR: (*As Punch runs to L, Doctor appears.*) Fetch him! (*Exits.*)

JUDY: (*As Punch runs to R, Judy appears.*) Catch him! (*She exits. Punch starts to L and is caught by Policeman. Music out.*)

POLICEMAN: Mr. Punch, you can't escape from the law. There is no hope. You will swing on a rope from the highest tree.

PUNCH: No, no! Mr. Punch is always free! (*A rope with a noose is lowered from above.*)

POLICEMAN: Mr. Hangman?

HANGMAN: (*Off, loud deep voice.*) Yes.

POLICEMAN: Are you ready?

HANGMAN: (*Off.*) Yes, yes.

POLICEMAN: Then hang your man. (*Exits.*)

PUNCH WITH THE HANGMAN

HANGMAN: (*Enters.*) Yes, yes, yes! Swing . . . swing, rope in the air. Soon a head will swing there. (*Laughs.*) He, he, he!

PUNCH: (*Imitates Hangman's laugh, weakly.*) Me, me, me.

HANGMAN: Mr. Punch, you are going to suffer.

PUNCH: (*Scared voice.*) I don't want any supper.

HANGMAN: You are going to put your head in this loop.

PUNCH: I don't want any soup.

HANGMAN: Say your last words: Good-bye—good-bye—good-bye.

PUNCH: Good-bye—good-bye—I don't want to go by-by!

HANDMAN: Stand there.

PUNCH: Where?

HANGMAN: There. Put your head in the noose.

PUNCH: How?

HANGMAN: Now! (*Punch puts head below noose.*) No! Not below. (*Punch puts head above.*) Not above! (*Punch puts head at side.*) Not at the side! (*Punch puts hand into noose.*) Not your hand. Your head!

PUNCH: Where?

HANGMAN: There! In the noose, you silly goose! Use your head!

PUNCH: Your head?

HANGMAN: No, your head.

PUNCH: Your head!

HANGMAN: No, no, you blockhead. YOUR head.

PUNCH: That's what I said, your head.

HANGMAN: NO! NO! Look! I will show you what to do. First you bend and stoop, then put your head through the loop. (*Does action.*)

PUNCH: He's putting his head through the loop!

HANGMAN: Turn your neck, left . . . right; so the rope fits tight. Then—

PUNCH: Then pull the rope with all my MIGHT! (*Punch pulls end of rope. Hangman is pulled into the air, with a whistle sound effect as he goes up.*) He thought he'd hang MY head, but he hung himself instead! (*Dances.*) Rootle-dee-tootle-dee-toot! Good-bye, Mr. Hangman, good-bye, good-bye, good-bye. (*Hangman and rope are pulled up out of sight.*) No one can stop Mr. Punch.

PUNCH WITH THE DEVIL

DEVIL: (*Off.*) Yes there is and I am the one!

PUNCH: Who are you?

DEVIL: (*Off.*) The time has come for you to pay for all your wicked deeds.

PUNCH: Who are you?

DEVIL: I have come to get you.

PUNCH: WHO ARE YOU?

DEVIL: I am—(*Enters.*)—the Devil!

PUNCH: The devil you are!

DEVIL: The devil I am. Your time of tricks with sticks are over, Mr. Punch. You are going to Hell—where I dwell.

PUNCH: No, Mr. Punch is not like the rest. I'm free! Nobody gets the best of me!

DEVIL: Attend!

PUNCH: I'll fight to the end.

DEVIL: Begin! Pitchfork—(*Holds out pitchfork.*)

PUNCH: Against stick! (*Holds out stick.*)

DEVIL: Begin!

PUNCH: Mr. Punch will win!
(*They begin the famous fight of Mr. Punch and the Devil. The stage grows red, smoke rises, and there is fight music. Devil laughs when he is winning. Punch "Rootle-dee-tootle-dee-toot's" when he is winning. At the climactic moment, Punch wins and the Devil falls. Red light, smoke, and music stop.*)
The Devil is dead! Victory for me! (*Sings and dances.*)
  Mr. Punch is a jolly good fellow,
  His coat is scarlet and yellow.

He has a bump on his nose,
And a hump on his back,
And a stick to give you a smack and a whack!
(*Stands and announces.*) The—END. Mr. Punch says "good-bye,"
Judy says—

JUDY: (*Enters with Baby.*) Good-bye.

PUNCH: Baby says—(*Baby gives a loud, comic cry. Judy shakes it. Then they all wave.*)
Good-bye, good-bye, good-bye.

MUSIC AND CURTAIN.

Pinocchio and the Fire-Eater
Aurand Harris

Adapted from Carlo Collodi

COPYRIGHT NOTICE

Pinocchio and the Fire-Eater is from traditional sources and therefore not under copyright.

Pinocchio and the Fire-Eater is based on one adventure of the famous puppet character created in children's fiction by Carlo Collodi. In the opening scene, Pinocchio introduces himself to the audience before the action begins explaining his unusual beginning. In the midst of a protest about going to school, he hears the irresistible call of band music and the story is under way.

The major part of the action takes place as a play within a play. Although Pinocchio goes to the show intending to be in the audience, he is immediately recognized as a puppet by the performers and coaxed onto their stage. Much of the ensuing conflict of the plot is directly related to the fact that he is a puppet. Some of the performers are also puppets, but they are played by actors because of the physical action required by their roles.

A stage or performance area for the traveling players should be suggested. Costumes, particularly for the players of the troupe, will also merit special attention.

PINOCCHIO AND THE FIRE-EATER

Adapted from Carlo Collodi
by Aurand Harris

CHARACTERS

Pinocchio
Musicians
Clown
Children
    Freckle-Faced Boy
    Big Sister
    Little Brother
    Tough Boy
    First Twin Girl
    Second Twin Girl
    Big Boy
    Giggling Girl
    Others
Boy Without a Penny
Peddler
Fire-Eater
Dolls
    Marcella
    Estella
    Rosabella
Guards

SETTINGS

Scene I. A street in a small town in Italy.
Scene II. A nearby park, in front of a puppet theatre.

SCENE I

Pinocchio enters in front of the curtain at stage right and crosses, walking, talking, and whistling in a rhythm. He carries a large book.

PINOCCHIO: I'm on my way . . . I'm on my way . . . I'm on my way to school today . . . (*Whistles, stops stage center, grins, and speaks to audience.*) I'm on my way to school. My first day! I have a new hat which Geppetto made. And a new coat which Geppetto made. In fact, Geppetto made me. (*Confidentially.*) I—I am a puppet. (*Gaily and conceited.*) In fact, as Geppetto painted the tip of my nose, he said, "Pinocchio, you are the finest puppet in the land." (*Whistles and postures importantly.*) I have a book—a new one. Geppetto sold his coat to buy it for me. (*Looks at book with awe.*) It's a big, big book . . . (*Exhausted.*) and it's heavy, heavy to carry. But Geppetto said that soon my arms wouldn't be tired (*Smiles brightly.*) because soon I would be carrying the book in my head! (*Walks a few more steps to stage left.*) I'm on my way . . . to school today . . . (*Stops.*) I'm going to work and study, and Geppetto will be proud of me. Today I will learn to read and write. Tomorrow I will learn all the numbers. Then I will earn pockets and pockets full of money for Geppetto! I'll buy Geppetto a coat—a golden coat with diamonds and jewels for buttons. I'll give Geppetto . . . (*Listens off right.*) What is that? It sounds like music. A drum . . . (*Marches and makes drum sound.*) and a fife . . . (*Whistles like a fife.*) It is music. Oh, I like music! (*Confidentially.*) And music likes me. (*Pinocchio turns, whistles and marches to right. He stops with an unhappy thought.*) School! I have to go to school today. (*Looks left, turns, and trudges wearily toward left.*) Read . . . and write . . . and numbers . . . (*Stops, face brightens with a smile.*) Music! (*Looks toward right, turns and marches gaily to right.*) Drums . . . and fife . . . a band! (*Stops, looks left.*) School. (*Looks right.*) Music. (*Looks back and forth, left to right, left to right, torn between the two.*) Which way shall I go? (*Smiles happily.*) Ah, I know what I'll do! Today I will hear the band. Tomorrow I will go to school.

(*Whistling like a fife, then booming like a drum, Pinocchio joyously marches to right. He stops, grins at the audience.*) Wouldn't you? (*Pinocchio exits right.*) (*The drum and fife noises fade out as recorded music grows louder, off right. Musicians, dressed in high hats, plumes, and gold braid, march in from right, stepping high and playing vigorously. The scene is still in front of the curtain.*

The Clown, with a jump and a bounce and a cartwheel, enters right. He is followed by a group of excited school children: Freckle-Faced Boy, Big Sister, Little Brother, Tough Boy, Twin Girls, Big Boy, Giggling Girl, and Others. The Boy Without a Penny stands apart.)

CLOWN: Ladies and gentlemen (*Looks at group.*) and children, too. I bow and tip my hat to you! (*Bows, then pulls up pointed clown hat, which pops back on his head, with the aid of an elastic band under his chin.*)

To this fair city of yours today—
And tomorrow if you still will pay—
We bring for your pleasure and delight
A wondrous show, a wondrous sight.
Loudly . . . proudly, I present—
The Fire-Eater and his Puppet Tent!

CHILDREN: (*Exclaim.*) Puppets! Puppets! A puppet show! I want to go . . . etc.

CLOWN: A little music, please. (*Musicians play a few notes and Clown swings with gusto into the main part of his speech.*)

CLOWN: A puppet show! A puppet show!
With puppet dolls in a row.
They dance! They laugh! They sing!
Suspended on a magic string.
A wondrous show. A wondrous treat!
Again, I repeat . . .
Loudly . . . proudly, I present—
The Fire-Eater and his Puppet Tent!

(*Children talk to one another excitedly.*)

CLOWN: A little music, please. (*Musicians play a few more notes.*)

CLOWN: One penny, my friends, is all you pay.
One penny, my friends, pays your way.
Follow me, if you want to go.

Follow me, if you want to see
The Fire-Eater and his Puppet Show!

(*Musicians play.*)

CLOWN: Off we go
To the Puppet Show.
Come with me.
You will see
Puppets speak, puppets sing,
Puppets dance on a magic string.
Off we go
To the Puppet Show!

(*Musicians continue to play as they march off left. The Clown, like a Pied Piper, leads the excited and talking Children off left. Only the Boy Without a Penny remains. He watches the others leave and listens to the music and the happy voices die away.*

In the middle of a big sigh, he is interrupted by Pinocchio, who rushes in from right.)

PINOCCHIO: Music! Music! I hear music! (*Boy nods.*) A drum? (*Boy nods.*) A fife? (*Boy nods.*) A band! (*Boy nods.*) Come! We will follow it!

BOY: I don't have a penny.

PINOCCHIO: (*Crosses to left.*) I like music! (*Booms like a drum and marches.*) And music likes me! (*Whistles like a fife.*)

BOY: It costs a penny to see the show.

PINOCCHIO: A show? A show! I've never seen a show!

BOY: I don't have a penny.

PINOCCHIO: Please don't look so sad. I know—come and see the show and then you'll be happy!

BOY: I don't have a penny.

PINOCCHIO: I don't have one either, but I want to see the show. I . . . (*Blinks with a realization.*) Oh! You have to pay a penny to see the show? (*Boy nods.*) Oh. And you don't have a penny (*Boy shakes his head.*) Oh. And I don't have a penny. (*Pinocchio shakes his head.*) No. But if I had one, I'd give you one. But . . . I don't have one (*Boy shakes his head. Pinocchio shakes his head, then looks wistfully off left.*) What kind of a show is it?

BOY: A puppet show.

PINOCCHIO: A puppet show! A PUPPET SHOW! Oh-oh-oh! Then I must go. I must! I'm a puppet too, you know. Excuse me, we haven't been introduced. (*Tips his hat.*) Pinocchio! I've never seen another puppet. So I really must go and see the show. Come along. You'll enjoy it, too.

BOY: I don't have a penny.

PINOCCHIO: Oh . . . a penny. *I* need a penny, too. (*Smiles with an idea.*) I have a nice new hat. Would you buy my hat for a penny?

BOY: I don't have a penny.

PINOCCHIO: Oh, you don't want my hat. (*Smiles with another idea.*) Would you like my book? My new school book, which I've never used—would you like it for a penny?

BOY: (*Shouts.*) I don't have a penny.

PINOCCHIO: You don't want my book. (*Brightens with still another idea.*) Would you buy my jacket for one small penny?

BOY: (*Whispers.*) I don't have a penny.

PINOCCHIO: You don't wany my jacket. But I want a penny!

BOY: So do I.

PINOCCHIO: What are we going to do? (*Looks hopefully off right.*) How are we going to go—and see the show?

(*Offstage left is heard the singsong chant of an old clothes Peddler. He is a comic little Italian man, with a musical Italian accent. He pushes a baby carriage filled with junk. He wears a stack of hats on his head.*)

PEDDLER: Old hats . . . old hats . . .
I buya da old hats.
Worn hats . . . torn hats . . .
Good in any weather.

(*He enters left and crosses slowly to center.*)

PEDDLER: Leetla hats, beeg hats,
All stacked together.
Old hats . . . old hats . . .
I buya da old hats . . .

PINOCCHIO: Hats? Hats? Hats! (*Feels his hat, looks at Peddler, then rushes to him, stopping him by pulling on his coattail.*) Oh, Mister Peddler! Mister Peddler! Do you buy old hats?

PEDDLER: I buya da old hats. (*Starts his calling.*) Worn hats . . . torn hats . . .

PINOCCHIO: Will you buy a *new* hat?

PEDDLER: Da new hat?

PINOCCHIO: This one. (*Takes off hat.*) It's hardly worn at all.

PEDDLER: Letta me see. (*Takes hat.*)

PINOCCHIO: And my book. You may have my new book, too.

PEDDLER: Da book? (*Takes book.*)

PINOCCHIO: And my jacket.

PEDDLER: Da jacket? (*Takes jacket.*)

PINOCCHIO: You may have them all for a penny!

PEDDLER: For how mucha you say?

PINOCCHIO: A penny!

PEDDLER: Da hat, da book, da jacket for a penny?

PINOCCHIO: It's a new jacket, and the book has never been opened, and the hat has a feather in front.

PEDDLER: (*Delighted with feather.*) Ah, yes! Da feather! (*Studies it.*) Letta me think. Da jacket?

PINOCCHIO: Yes?

PEDDLER: Da book?

PINOCCHIO: Yes?

PEDDLER: Da hat?

PINOCCHIO: Yes?

PEDDLER: I buya dem all!

PINOCCHIO: For a penny?

PEDDLER: For one leetla penny.

PINOCCHIO: Sold! (*Holds out hand.*)

PEDDLER: (*Gives him money.*) Der ees one leetla penny.

PINOCCHIO: Thank you!

PEDDLER: And—here ees another leetla penny for good luck. (*Gives him another penny, then puts book and jacket in cart, and takes off his stack of hats to put Pinocchio's hat on the top.*)

PINOCCHIO: Two pennies! Two pennies! (*To Boy.*) Look! We can go. We can see the show.

BOY: I don't have a penny.

PINOCCHIO: I have one—and another one. See! One for you. One for me.

BOY: One for me? Thank you! Thank you!

PINOCCHIO: We both thank you, Mister Peddler. (*Points at his hat which Peddler has on.*) And the feather—it goes in front.

BOY: Hurry. Let's run.

PINOCCHIO: Let's go and see the Puppet Show! (*He and Boy run off left.*)

(*Peddler takes off stack of hats, puts feather in front, puts hats back on, and pushes his cart off right, calling.*)

PEDDLER: Old hats . . . old hats . . .
I buya da old hats.
Worn hats . . . torn hats . . .
Good in any weather.
Leetla hats . . . beeg hats . . .
One with a feather!
Old hats . . . old hats . . .
I buya da . . .

(*He exits right.*)

SCENE II

Puppet show music is heard. The curtain opens on a full stage. The front of a colorful puppet theatre faces the audience at stage right. The puppet stage is one step up from the ground and is large enough for three little girls, marionettes, to perform on. At the moment the puppet curtains are closed. Musicians stand stiffly in center and play magnificently. The Children sit on the ground at stage left in a semicircle. They face the puppet stage, and some have their backs to the audience. The Children are excited and active. Music stops. Musicians bow. Children applaud and cheer. The Clown's head appears between the curtains of the puppet stage.

CLOWN: (*Calls happily to Children.*) Hello.

CHILDREN: Hello.

CLOWN: Hello. Hello.

CHILDREN: Hello. Hello.

CLOWN: Hello, hello, hello, hello, hello.

CHILDREN: Hello, hello, hello, hello, hello.

CLOWN: (*Whispers.*) Hello-o-o.

CHILDREN: (*Whisper.*) Hello-o-o.

CLOWN: (*Jumps from between the curtains to ground, arms outstretched to encircle every child, and shouts.*) Hello!

CHILDREN: (*Shout.*) Hello!

CLOWN: Welcome to the Fire-Eater's Puppet Show! (*Children applaud.*)

CLOWN: The puppets are waiting and within.
    The show is ready to . . . begin!

FIRE-EATER: (*Offstage, from behind the puppet theater, his voice roars loudly.*) No-o-o-o! No! No-o-o!

CLOWN: It is the Fire-Eater. First he must say hello.

FIRE-EATER: (*Offstage, his voice roars louder.*) Hello-o-o-o-o-o! (*A big puff of smoke blows out from between the curtains. Children answer frightened "Hello." The unseen Fire-Eater laughs loudly, which is more frightening than his "Hello." Clown shakes with fright. Another puff of smoke blows out from between the curtains.*)

CLOWN: I will begin . . . again.
Introducing for your pleasure today,
The Fire-Eater's puppet play!

(*Musicians play. Clown pulls open the curtains on the puppet stage. Three pretty Puppet Dolls—little girls with strings on wrists and ankles—bow gracefully.*)

CLOWN: Presenting the Three Dainty Dancing Dolls! MARCELLA! (*Marcella bows like a ballet dancer.*) ESTELLA! (*Estella bows gently.*) ROSABELLA! (*Rosabella throws kisses with both hands to children. Children applaud. The Dolls speak in beautiful little voices.*)

ROSABELLA: We will sing for you—

MARCELLA: Sweetly—

ESTELLA: Wittily—

ROSABELLA: A favorite song

ESTELLA AND MARCELLA: Of Italy! (*Musicians play "Funiculi, Funicula." Dolls sing verse and chorus. Chorus is repeated and Dolls dance. Music stops. Dolls bow. Puppet stage curtains close. Children applaud and cheer.*)

CLOWN: Bravo! Encore! Encore! Will you see some more?

CHILDREN: (*Shouting.*) Yes . . . more . . . more . . . encore . . . (*Clown quiets them.*)

CLOWN: Presenting—Marcella, Estella, and Rosabella! (*Musicians strike up the band. Curtains open again. Dolls repeat "Funiculi, Funicula" song and dance. At the beginning of the chorus, Pinocchio and Boy Without a Penny enter left and stand watching. Marcella stops singing and points at Pinocchio. Then Estella stops and points. Rosabella stops and points. Music stops and Musicians look. Children turn and look toward where the Dolls are pointing.*)

ROSABELLA: Look!

MARCELLA: Is he true?

ESTELLA: Is he real?

ROSABELLA: You!

PINOCCHIO: Me?

MARCELLA: Are you a puppet?

ESTELLA: Are you a puppet, too?

PINOCCHIO: Yes! (*Struts proudly to puppet stage.*) Geppetto said, as he painted the tip of my nose, "You are the finest puppet in the land." I am—Pinocchio. (*Tips his "hat," which he doesn't have.*)

ESTELLA: (*With delight.*) Pinocchio!

ROSABELLA: (*With delight.*) Pinocchio!

MARCELLA: (*With delight.*) Pinocchio!!

FIRE-EATER: (*Offstage, his voice shouts.*) Silence! Silence! Who has stopped the show?

CHILDREN: (*Shout together.*) Pinocchio!

FIRE-EATER: (*Offstage, roars.*) Pinocchio?

ROSABELLA: It is the Fire-Eater!

MARCELLA: Quick! Hide by us!

ESTELLA: Quick! Hide beside us! (*Pinocchio joins Dolls on stage.*)

FIRE-EATER: (*Offstage, roars.*) Begin—again!

CLOWN: (*Quickly.*) Some music, please! (*Musicians play "Funiculi, Funicula." Dolls sing and dance. Pinocchio comically tries to kick and dance as Dolls do. An argument begins among the Children during the dance.*)

BIG SISTER: A puppet without strings!

LITTLE BROTHER: (*Hopping up and down.*) I can't see. I can't see.

FRECKLE-FACED BOY: A real live puppet—dancing and singing!

TOUGH BOY: He ain't no puppet.

BIG BOY: Yes, he is!

TOUGH BOY: No, he ain't!

FIRST TWIN GIRL: He says he is.

SECOND TWIN GIRL: He says he is a puppet.

TOUGH BOY: He ain't no puppet.

BIG BOY: He is!

GIGGLING GIRL: Of course he is!

TOUGH BOY: He ain't!

BIG BOY: He is!

TOUGH BOY: You wanta fight?

BIG BOY: I say he is!

TOUGH BOY: I say he ain't! (*Tough Boy and Big Boy begin a rough and tumble fight. Other Children take sides, cheering and jeering. Dolls become frightened but keep singing and dancing. Into the scene of confusion, the Fire-Eater stomps from behind the puppet stage. He is big and fierce looking, with a long black beard. He raises his hands and roars.*)

FIRE-EATER: Silence! Silence! (*Musicians stop. Dolls stop. Children freeze in their positions. Only Pinocchio continues dancing and singing.*)

PINOCCHIO: "Tra la la la la,
    Tra la la la—"

FIRE-EATER: Who—who is the cause of this?

PINOCCHIO: (*Continues singing.*) "Joy is ev'rywhere—
    Tra la la la,
    Tra la la—"

FIRE-EATER: (*Turns slowly and points at him.*) Who are you?

PINOCCHIO: (*Stops.*) I am—(*Jumps to ground.*)—Pinocchio. Who are you?

FIRE-EATER: I am the Fire-Eater!

PINOCCHIO: I am pleased to meet you. (*Tips his "hat," which he doesn't have.*)

FIRE-EATER: I am *not* pleased to meet you! You have interrupted my show. You are a stupid little numbskull!

PINOCCHIO: Oh, no. I am a puppet.

FIRE-EATER: A puppet?

PINOCCHIO: Yes. Geppetto said, as he painted the tip of—

FIRE-EATER: Silence! (*Walks in a half circle around Pinocchio, looking him up and down.*) So—you are a puppet?

PINOCCHIO: (*Walks around Fire-Eater, making the other half of the circle, and looks him up and down.*) Yes.

FIRE-EATER: A wooden puppet?

PINOCCHIO: Yes.

FIRE-EATER: Wood burns very easily. I am going to cook a chop to-night for supper. But I have no wood for the fire. You, my little man—my little *wooden* man—will join me.

PINOCCHIO: Oh, no. Thank you very much, but I am not hungry. No, I wouldn't like a chop for supper. (*Starts away.*)

FIRE-EATER: Stop! You wooden-headed nitwit! I am going to burn you for firewood.

PINOCCHIO: Burn? Fire? (*Looks down at himself.*) Wood! No! No!

FIRE-EATER: Yes! Yes! Seize him, men! (*Two Musicians hold Pinocchio on either side.*)

FIRE-EATER: You will crack and pop—and cook my chop! (*He laughs.*)

(*All shake with fright. Two Guards appear and grab Pinocchio, feet off the ground, as he "runs" in the air.*)

PINOCCHIO: No! No! I will not die! I will not die! Save me, Papa! I must go home. My Papa is waiting for me.

FIRE-EATER: Your Papa? (*Guards put Pinocchio's feet on ground.*)

PINOCCHIO: Yes, poor Geppetto. He is alone . . . worried . . . waiting . . . for me to come home.

FIRE-EATER: You are his little boy?

PINOCCHIO: His only little boy. He is old . . . and poor. He sold hi‑coat to buy me a book. (*Holds out "book," which he doesn't have.*)

FIRE-EATER: (*Touched.*) Only a father would make such a sacrifice. Ah ‑. . . Ah . . . (*He starts to sneeze, but doesn't.*)

PINOCCHIO: Poor Papa. I am his only pride and joy.

FIRE-EATER: His only pride and—ah . . . ah . . . ah . . . (*Sneeze comically.*)

PINOCCHIO: Bless you.

FIRE-EATER: Thank you. (*Gets large, bandanna-style handkerchief.*)

CLOWN: (*Aside to Pinocchio.*) Ah, the Fire-Eater sneezed. You have touched his heart. When some people are sad, they cry. But when the Fire-Eater is sad, he sneezes. If he sneezes once again, you are saved.

PINOCCHIO: (*With a great burst of pathos.*) Oh, poor, poor Papa. Poor Geppetto. Alone—all alone without his little boy.

FIRE-EATER: Stop your crying. No more tales of woe! They give me a-ah . . . ah . . . ah . . . (*Almost sneezes.*) PAIN in my ah . . . ah . . stom . . . stom . . . stom . . . STOMACH! (*Gives a mighty sneeze.*) ACHEW!!

PINOCCHIO: Bless you.

FIRE-EATER: Thank you. (*Wipes his eyes.*)

ROSABELLA: A second sneeze!

MARCELLA: The Fire-Eater cries.

ESTELLA: He wipes his eyes!

ROSABELLA: Pinocchio is free!

FIRE-EATER: Go back to your Papa. Go home to him and be . . . his little joy. (*Becomes loud and angry again.*) But—I still will have my supper! I still will eat my chop! I *will* have a fire of wood tonight!

PINOCCHIO: Wood?

FIRE-EATER: I will burn *another* wooden puppet!

MARCELLA: Oh!

ROSABELLA: Oh!

ESTELLA: Oh! (*Fire-Eater looks at Dolls.*)

PINOCCHIO: No!

FIRE-EATER: Guards! Seize Rosabella! Bind her securely and throw her on the fire!

ROSABELLA: Oh, no!

MARCELLA: (*Kneels.*) We beg you on our knees—

ESTELLA: (*Kneels.*) Spare her, please!

FIRE-EATER: Seize her! (*Guards go to puppet stage.*)

ROSABELLA: Help!

PINOCCHIO: Rosabella! You cannot die!

ROSABELLA: Oh, help! Help me!

PINOCCHIO: (*On knees, to Fire-Eater.*) Oh, Mister Fire-Eater, hear me. (*Crosses on knees to him.*)

FIRE-EATER: Away! No more of your weeping and creeping.

PINOCCHIO: Have pity, Sir Fire-Eater.

FIRE-EATER: I am not a Sir.

PINOCCHIO: Have pity, Sir noble Knight!

FIRE-EATER: I am not a Knight.

PINOCCHIO: Have pity, brave Commander!

FIRE-EATER: I am not a Commander.

PINOCCHIO: Have pity, Your most Excellent Highness.

FIRE-EATER: (*Pleased.*) Excellent Highness . . . (*Poses and speaks comically, imitating a king.*) What is it? What does my subject beg from me?

PINOCCHIO: I beg . . . I implore . . . I beseech . . .

FIRE-EATER: Yes, yes, speak!

PINOCCHIO: Pardon poor Rosabella. Give her back her life.

FIRE-EATER: (*Shakes his head.*) For her there can be no pardon. I have spared you. She must take your place. (*Roars.*) I will have my chop well cooked tonight!

ROSABELLA: O-o-o-o-oh! It is the end for me. (*She faints in the convenient arms of the other two dolls.*)

PINOCCHIO: (*Rises and speaks heroically.*) No, by all the smoke of Mount Vesuvius, she shall not die. I know my duty. Come, guards. Bind me. Throw *me* into the fire.

FIRE-EATER: You?

PINOCCHIO: It is not right that Rosabella should die for me.

FIRE-EATER: You are a brave boy.

PINOCCHIO: I will die for myself.

FIRE-EATER: You are a . . . ah . . . ah . . . ah . . . (*Almost sneezes.*) noble boy.

PINOCCHIO: Throw me into the fire!

FIRE-EATER: You are . . . a . . . ah . . . ah . . . ah . . . (*Sneezes.*) ACHEW!

PINOCCHIO: Bless you.

FIRE-EATER: Thank you. (*Uses handkerchief.*)

CLOWN: (*Clasps his hands in prayer.*) Please . . . please . . . one more sneeze. (*All hope with him.*)

FIRE-EATER: You are a fine son. I would be proud to be a . . . ah . . . ah . . . ah . . . Father to a . . . ah . . . ah . . . ah . . . SON like ah . . . ah . . . ah . . . ah . . . YOU. ACHEW!

PINOCCHIO: Bless you.

CLOWN: Another sneeze! Hurray!
Another puppet saved today!

FIRE-EATER: Guards, away. I grant a pardon. Rosabella shall not cook my chop.

ROSABELLA: (*Revives instantly.*) Oh . . . I live again! (*Two Guards return to positions.*)

PINOCCHIO: (*Touched, near tears.*) Oh, great Sir . . . Knight . . . Commander . . . Your Excellence! I do not know . . . ah . . . ah . . . ah . . . (*Starts to sneeze.*) what words to ah . . . ah . . . ah . . . say. ACHEW!

FIRE-EATER: Bless you.

PINOCCHIO: (*Grateful for the right words.*) Thank you!

FIRE-EATER: Here are three pieces of gold for your poor father. (*Gives Pinocchio coins.*) Tell him what you've done today—what a good boy you have been.

PINOCCHIO: Good? (*Aside.*) I didn't go to school. I sold my book and jacket and hat. I spoiled the Puppet Show. I've acted like . . . a woodenhead! (*To Fire-Eater.*) Tomorrow—instead of acting with a head of wood—I will be . . . I hope . . . like a boy who's good! (*He and Fire-Eater shake hands. Pinocchio starts off right.*)

CHILDREN: (*Chant.*) We want the show! We want the show! We want the show!

FIRE-EATER: The show will begin—again!

MARCELLA: Pinocchio, please stay . . .

ESTELLA: One last song . . .

ROSABELLA: Before you go away . . .

PINOCCHIO: (*Looks toward right.*) Geppetto is alone. I must hurry home to be his pride and joy.

CHILDREN: We want Pinocchio. We want Pinocchio. We want Pinocchio.

PINOCCHIO: (*Immediately forgetting Geppetto.*) Me? You want me?

FIRE-EATER: Stay! Sing one song to end our play! (*Pinocchio nods eagerly.*)

FIRE-EATER: Start the music. Start the band! (*Musicians stand at attention. Fire-Eater exits behind puppet stage.*)

PINOCCHIO: (*Aside.*) After all, I am the finest puppet in the land! (*Walks happily to puppet stage.*)

CLOWN: To conclude our Puppet Show—
    We present—Pinocchio!

(*Pinocchio bows grandly. Musicians play "Funiculi, Funicula." The Dolls dance and sing. The Clown leads the Children who join in the singing. Pinocchio, in front of the puppet stage, sings and dances happily. Even the Fire-Eater enters at the end of the chorus and comically joins in the singing.*)

CURTAIN

In One Basket (Tale of a Mouse, The Rich Man, Three Wishes, Gustav)

Shirley Pugh

AUTHOR'S NOTE:

Since the scenery and costumes for the four plays from *In One Basket* are so simple, only one play, *Tale of a Mouse,* has been selected for illustration.

Shirley Pugh's four short dramatizations from *In One Basket* are written in story-theatre form, a style in which actors are narrators and then become characters in the story, stepping in and out of the action and dialogue.

Suggestions:
Since the stories are brief and quickly told, a minimum of technical production support is recommended. Props can be imaginary and pantomimed. If actual articles are used, they must be readily available and promptly put aside without interrupting the story when they are no longer necessary. In *The Rich Man* even the two smiths' tools and materials of their trades may be imagined if the necessary clamor is provided by sound effects.

TALE OF A MOUSE

CHARACTERS

Lana
Stanley
Sun
Cloud
Wind
Wall

Music: "Three Blind Mice" used throughout. Mood chords and fragments of melody used in scenes with sun, cloud, wind, wall.

LANA: A beautiful young mouse named Lana—

STANLEY: (*He wears glasses.*)—lived next door to a brown field mouse named Stanley.

LANA: Good morning, Stanley.

STANLEY: Good morning, Lana. (*They each lick the back of own left paw, then right paw—then "shake paws."*) May I walk with you this summer day?

LANA: I'm afraid not, Stanley. I am off to search for a husband.

STANLEY: Oh, Lana, end your search right here and marry me.

LANA: Marry *you*? But I want to marry the greatest being on the earth, and that certainly is not you. I want to have the strongest, most powerful husband in the world, so that I will be proud of him as long as I live.

STANLEY: I would try to make you proud of *me*.

LANA: No, my husband must be mightier by far than you could ever hope to be. I will walk to the end of every road and climb to the top of every mountain, and somewhere I will find him.

STANLEY: Well, good luck, Lana—whoever he turns out to be.

LANA: Stanley, you'll meet the right one, too, some day.

STANLEY: There will never be anyone else for me but you.

LANA: Stanley, I'm sorry. (*They do the paw licking and paw shaking. Music.*)
And she began her search for the greatest being on the earth. She walked and walked, until the hour was noon. (*Sun enters.*) How brightly the sun shines down. (*Music.*)

SUN: Oh, yes. I warm all the creatures of the land, and I help the grain in the fields to grow, and I light the world with my rays.

LANA: Mr. Sun, I think you are the greatest being on the earth, and I choose you for my husband.

SUN: The greatest being on the earth? Not I. There is one much greater.

LANA: Greater than the sun?

SUN: Yes, a cloud can cover me, and hide my light and cool my rays—and I can do nothing to stop him.

LANA: Then I must marry a cloud.

SUN: Mmmmm—you do that. (*Exits.*)

LANA: And she walked on until she saw a billowing white cloud. (*Music. Cloud enters.*) Mr. Cloud, I think you are the greatest being on the earth, and I choose you for my husband.

CLOUD: It's true, I can conquer the sun by hiding his face, and also the moon. But I am not the greatest being on the earth. There is one much greater.

LANA: Who is greater than a cloud?

CLOUD: The wind. When he chooses to blow me away, then I am done for—and I can do nothing to stop him.

LANA: Then I must marry the wind.

CLOUD: Mmmmm—you do that. (*Exits.*)

LANA: And she walked on until she saw the trees swaying and heard a whistling in the grass. (*Music. Wind enters.*) Mr. Wind, I think you are the greatest being on the earth, and I choose you for my husband.

WIND: Whhhhooo, me? Whhhhyy, I can move a cloud whheeereever I desire, and whhhiiine through a snowstorm, and make the autumn leaves whhhiiirl, but there is one much greater.

LANA: I cannot imagine that.

WIND: Whhhheeether you can imagine it or not, a wall is greater than I. Whhhheeen I blow against a wall, no matter how I whhhiiiip and puff, the wall stands firm, and I cannot move it.

LANA: Then I must marry a wall.

WIND: Mmmmm—you do that. (*Exits.*)

WALL: (*Music. Wall enters.*) And she walked on until she saw a thick strong wall before her.

LANA: Mr. Wall, I think you are the greatest being on the earth, and I choose you for my husband.

WALL: Dependable I am. Yes, I remain standing even when the wind blows ferociously and tries his best to knock me down. I hold the river back—but there is one I cannot hold back, and he is greater than I.

LANA: Then tell me who that can be.

WALL: It is a mouse. When he wants to nibble a hole in my side, I cannot stop him. He may be little, but his power is greater than mine.

LANA: Is a mouse the greatest being on the earth?

WALL: Well, the sun is great, but a cloud can hide him. A cloud is great until the wind sends him away. The wind is great, but he cannot budge a wall. And yet a mouse can chew a hole right through me.

LANA: So a mouse is the one I must marry!

WALL: Mmmmm—you do that. (*Exits.*)

LANA: (*Music.*) And she walked very fast, over the hills and valleys and through the forests, and under the bridges and over the bridges—and at last she came to her own little house. (*She leans, panting.*) She ran next door and knocked and knocked—

STANLEY: —and Stanley opened his door—

LANA: Stanley! You are the greatest being on the earth, and I choose you for my husband!

STANLEY: Mercy, Lana! You gave me such a scare!

LANA: Marry me, Stanley, and I will be proud of you for as long as I live!

STANLEY: So he did.

LANA: And she was. (*They do the paw licking and paw shaking.*)

LANA AND STANLEY: (*Face audience and smile photogenically.*) Cheese!

(*Music.*)

CURTAIN

THE RICH MAN

CHARACTERS

Rich Man
Tinsmith
Blacksmith

Stage is dark. There is sudden noise of drum, cymbals, and what-have-you. Lights up. The Tinsmith is at one side of stage, pounding out a pan (Mime) and the Blacksmith is at the other side, forging a horse-shoe (Mime). The Rich Man steps front and center to speak. He waits. There is a lull.

RICH MAN: Once there was—(*Noise resumes. He waits. A lull.*) Once there was a very—(*Noise resumes. He waits. A lull.*) Once there was a very rich man who lived in a grand mansion. He ate well and drank well and slept on a bed of softest down. His life would have been perfect, except for two things. (*Noise. A lull.*)

TINSMITH: At one end of the rich man's street there lived a tinsmith who spent all his days fashioning pots and pans for the good wives of the town. (*Noise, as he works on a pot. Lull.*) This will be a sturdy kettle to cook many a tasty stew!

BLACKSMITH: At the other end of the rich man's street there lived a blacksmith who forged shoes of iron for the horses of the town. (*He forges shoe. Noise. Lull.*) There's a shoe that will travel many a rough road without breaking! (*Noise resumes. A lull.*)

RICH MAN: With the tinsmith at one end of this street and the black-smith at the other, I can hardly hear myself—(*Noise. A lull.*)—I can hardly hear myself think. If the two of them would move out of their houses, this would be a quiet neighborhood. (*Noise. Lull.*) I can bear it no longer! So he went to see the tinsmith.

(*Much noise as he approaches Tinsmith. Rich Man tries to shout over noise.*) Tinsmith! Tinsmith, I say. (*Lull. Rich Man shouts louder than ever.*) Tinsmith! (*Quietly.*) I beg your pardon, tinsmith. I have come to make you an offer.

TINSMITH: You wish to buy a skillet or a soup pot, sir?

RICH MAN: No, no. I wish to pay you a large sum of money—if you will leave this house—move somewhere else—

TINSMITH: But I've always lived in this street, sir.

RICH MAN: I know that, believe me! But if I pay you very well, would you agree to move to another house?

TINSMITH: I think I would do that, sir.

RICH MAN: Then here is a handsome sum in pieces of gold—and I will expect you to be gone from here by the day after tomorrow. (*Noise. Rich Man goes to Blacksmith. He tries to shout over noise.*) Blacksmith! Blacksmith! (*He taps Blacksmith on shoulder. Lull.*)

BLACKSMITH: Yes, sir. You have a horse that needs a shoe?

RICH MAN: No, no. I have two ears that need—

BLACKSMITH: Shoes for your ears?

RICH MAN: No! I have two ears that need a rest! I have come to make you an offer.

BLACKSMITH: What sort of offer, sir?

RICH MAN: I wish to pay you a large sum of money—if you will leave this house—move somewhere else—

BLACKSMITH: But this is where I work, sir.

RICH MAN: Heaven knows I am aware of it! But, look. If I pay you very well, would you agree to move to another house?

BLACKSMITH: Another house might suit me, sir.

RICH MAN: Then here is a handsome sum in pieces of gold—and I will expect you to be gone from here by the day after tomorrow. (*Noise. Rich Man goes home. Lull.*) What a peaceful place this will be when both of them have moved!

TINSMITH: (*Hurrying to the middle of the street.*) Wait till I tell my friend the blacksmith of this good fortune! (*They meet on the street.*) Blacksmith! You will never guess what has happened!

BLACKSMITH: Just a minute, tinsmith. I have news for you, too. The rich man has paid me to move from my house.

TINSMITH: No! And he has paid me to move from mine! When must you be gone?

BLACKSMITH: The day after tomorrow. And you?

TINSMITH: The same. The day after tomorrow.

BLACKSMITH: Where will you go?

TINSMITH: I don't know that yet. Where will *you* go?

BLACKSMITH: I don't know either.

BOTH TOGETHER: Listen, I have a good idea—
(*They whisper together and gesture toward each other's houses. They each run home and stack up tools, pans, iron scraps—noise again [Mime]—and leave their respective houses. Each wheeling a cart [Mime] they meet midway and do an Alphonse and Gaston routine in silence—"you go first," "excuse me," "you go first"—and finally make the double crossing to each other's houses, where each reestablishes himself.*)

RICH MAN: (*Simultaneously with their crosses.*) There is nothing I cannot buy with gold! The tinsmith will leave his house, the blacksmith will leave *his* house, and I will have silence at last. (*As the Rich Man ends his speech, the Tinsmith and the Blacksmith are settled in again and begin to work. Noise. Rich Man runs to Tinsmith. Shouts over noise.*) No! (*Runs to Blacksmith. Shouts over noise.*) No! (*Runs home, puts fingers in his ears and [Mimes] a horrified single word.*) NO! (*Noise continues for a moment in the dark. Lull.*)

CURTAIN

THE THREE WISHES

CHARACTERS

Husband
Wife
Dog
Fortunata

The music used throughout is "Sail Away, Ladies"—(Music.)

HUSBAND: Once there was a married man who, although poor, had worked diligently all his life on his little piece of ground. (*Goes to sit at hearth.*) Each night, after the day's work was done, the man—

WIFE: —and his wife sat before the fire—

DOG: —with their faithful dog. Ralph!

HUSBAND: Come on, boy. Down.

DOG: Ralph! Ralph! (*Holds paw up to shake hands.*)

HUSBAND: All right, all right. (*Shakes paw.*) Now, down, boy.

WIFE: Isn't it nice to sit here when the day's work is done?

HUSBAND: Yes, it is. I'm very content.

WIFE: Content?

HUSBAND: Content. What could be better than this? My wife, my fireside, my dog.

DOG: Ralph!

WIFE: Well, if it comes to that, things could be better.

HUSBAND: Oh, if we were younger—or richer—

WIFE: Or if we had a fine, large, new house.

HUSBAND: For that matter, you might as well wish we had a farm with rich, black soil.

WIFE: And a pig. A fat pig to kill, and then we'd have a good pork roast for our supper.

HUSBAND: That wouldn't be bad.

DOG: Ralph! (*Sniffs around floor.*)

HUSBAND: Looking for the bones from that roast, eh, boy?

DOG: Ralph!

WIFE: There'll be a strong, young mule to help with the plowing.

HUSBAND: As long as we're wishing for the impossible! (*A cymbal crash and a flash of red light, and Fortunata appears in the room.*)

FORTUNATA: Scarcely had he uttered these words when a strange looking woman appeared in the room.

DOG: Ralph! Yelp! Grrrr!

HUSBAND: Steady, boy.

FORTUNATA: I am the fairy Fortunata. I have come to grant you three wishes. The first wish is yours, good wife. And the second wish is for you, good husband. The third wish must be mutual and agreeable to you both. Tomorrow night I will return and you must make the third wish together. (*Cymbal and light. Exits.*)

DOG: Ralph! Ralph!

HUSBAND: Did you hear what I heard?

WIFE: I'm to make one wish—

HUSBAND: And I'm to make one wish—

WIFE: And we're to make the third wish—

HUSBAND AND WIFE: —together.

WIFE: I never dreamed of such good fortune.

HUSBAND: Let's plan very carefully what our wishes will be.

WIFE: A new house—

HUSBAND: A prosperous farm—

WIFE: A team of horses, and a carriage—

HUSBAND: A pig, a pen full of pigs!

WIFE: New clothes, suitable to our station—

HUSBAND: Your wish is the first.

WIFE: Oh, I must think. The new house, I suppose.

HUSBAND: Are you sure a new house is what you want?

WIFE: Well, you've seen the house of our neighbor. Wouldn't you like to live in such a house as that?

HUSBAND: I don't know. I've never lived in such a house as that.

WIFE: I was at their door today. In the kitchen they were making puddings! What an aroma! And how those puddings looked, bulging with fruits and almonds! It would have done you good to see them. I can smell them yet. I wish we had such a pudding here! (*Cymbal and light.*) Scarcely had she uttered these words when a pudding appeared. (*Breathes in its aroma.*)

HUSBAND: You greedy woman! You have wasted the first wish on that stupid pudding!

WIFE: (*Tasting, licking her fingers.*) And a good pudding it is, too.

HUSBAND: You glutton! I hate you—and I hate that pudding, too! I wish it were stuck on the end of your nose! (*Cymbal and light.*)

WIFE: Oh! (*Clutches pudding on her nose* [*Mime*].) The evil of your tongue!

DOG: Ralph! (*Jumps at wife to sniff pudding.*)

WIFE: Get down, you crazy dog!

HUSBAND: (*Laughing.*) Down, boy.

WIFE: Why are you laughing? You have wasted the second wish to put this lump of dough on my nose! Help me to take it off.

HUSBAND: (*Tries to pull pudding off and fails.*) It's no use. The pudding is there to stay.

WIFE: What a night for bad luck.

HUSBAND: At least we still have a third wish.

WIFE: Then we'll wish this pudding to be off my nose.

HUSBAND: No, look here, wife. We'll wish for a great fortune.

WIFE: What use is a great fortune if I have a pudding on my nose?

HUSBAND: We'll be rich. You can buy a veil of gold to wear over the pudding.

WIFE: Give me no veils of gold! We'll wish this pudding to be off my nose.

HUSBAND: Woman, think! What of the new house?

WIFE: Nothing of the new house.

HUSBAND: But the farm—what about the farm?

WIFE: You fool, what does it matter now?

HUSBAND: Will we waste the third wish, too?

WIFE: We'll wish this pudding to be off my nose.

HUSBAND: And we'll be exactly as we were before. Poor.

WIFE: Then that's what we'll be. Poor.

HUSBAND: You—you—pudding-nose! (*He walks away from her, hides his eyes with both hands, walks back to her carefully, and pulls his hands away as though the pudding might be gone.*)

WIFE: Well, what is it now?

HUSBAND: I thought it might be gone.

WIFE: It's more than a bad dream, you know.

HUSBAND: (*Tries again to wrench pudding off her nose.*) Oh! (*He laughs.*)

WIFE: I'm glad you think it's so funny.

HUSBAND: No, no. I think I'm getting used to it. It really doesn't look so bad.

WIFE: It doesn't?

HUSBAND: No. Listen, wife, for the third wish we could—

WIFE: —wish this pudding to be off my nose! (*Cymbal and light.*)

FORTUNATA: That night the fairy Fortunata returned to grant their third wish. Upon this wish you must agree—

HUSBAND: The house, wife, please—

WIFE: No!

HUSBAND: Then the farm, the farm—

WIFE: No!

HUSBAND AND WIFE: And they agreed: we wish this pudding to be off my (her) nose! (*Cymbal and light. Fortunata exits. The pudding is off.*)

WIFE: I never want to go through anything like *that* again! I am going to sit down and try to forget all about it.

HUSBAND: It's good to have peace in the house again.

DOG: Ralph!

WIFE: (*To audience.*) And so they learned that happiness does not come from the granting of wishes—

HUSBAND: (*His arm around her.*) Happiness comes when there are no wishes.

DOG: (*Nuzzling husband.*) Ralph! (*Music.*)

CURTAIN

GUSTAV

CHARACTERS

Mother
Gustav
Neighbor
1st Bandit
2nd Bandit
Dog

Music—"Turkey In The Straw" is used throughout. (Music.)

MOTHER: (*Enters and feeds chickens in [Mime].*) Once a widow lived in a poor cottage with her only son, Gustav. Whatever Gustav did, his Mother thought him always right. (*Back to chickens.*)

(*Music. Gustav carries a small stepladder on, sets it up and* [Mimes] *painting high on a barn wall, then lower and lower, until he cannot reach the bottom of the wall from his high point on the ladder. Gets off the ladder and turns it upside down.*) Gustav! Why do you turn the ladder upside down?

GUSTAV: Because it is too high. (*He steps into the ladder and paints bottom of the wall.*)

MOTHER: And so you paint the bottom of the wall! Gustav! You are always right! (*Kisses him and pats his cheek.*)

NEIGHBOR: (*Enters and stands with Gustav, admiring the wall.*) Neighbor Gustav, you did a fine job of painting that barn!

GUSTAV: Well, it's done now. Tonight I will sleep soundly on my mattress of straw.

NEIGHBOR: You have a mattress of straw? That's lumpy.

GUSTAV: Oh, I manage to sleep.

NEIGHBOR: You should have a mattress stuffed with feathers.

GUSTAV: Feathers?

NEIGHBOR: You would sleep much better on a bed of feathers.

GUSTAV: Thanks, neighbor—for the advice.

NEIGHBOR: (*As he goes off.*) Take my word—you will never sleep on straw again once you try feathers!

GUSTAV: (*Music.*) Feathers! ([Mime.] *He chases a chicken around the yard—cackling sounds—catches it and pulls one feather. Noise brings his Mother to him.*)

MOTHER: Gustav! What have you done to the hen?

GUSTAV: I wanted a feather, Mama—and I got it, too.

MOTHER: What will you do with a feather?

GUSTAV: Our neighbor says feathers are better than straw for a bed. I'll try it. And Gustav went into the house and put his feather on the floor ([Mime] *action.*) and lay down to sleep on it. (*Music.* [Mime] *sleepless night on the feather. Lights dim for night, up again for morning.*)

MOTHER: Good morning, Gustav. Did you sleep well?

GUSTAV: Sleep? My eyes were never closed. I lay on this feather the whole night through, and this morning my bones are broken. I will keep my mattress of straw—a feather bed is not for me!

MOTHER: But, Gustav! You had only one feather!

GUSTAV: Yes—and if *one* feather is so uncomfortable, imagine lying on a mattress stuffed with them!

MOTHER: Gustav! You are always right! (*A kiss and a pat.*) Later that day Gustav's Mother churned a bowlful of rich, golden butter, and she hoped to sell the butter for a good price. I will go to the town and sell this butter.

GUSTAV: Let me go to the town, Mama, you are tired. I will sell the butter.

MOTHER: Gustav! You have never even seen the town!

GUSTAV: Well, tell me how to go there.

MOTHER: But the town is on the far side of the deep woods. You will lose your way.

GUSTAV: Mama! Do you think I am a fool?

MOTHER: Well, *you* know, Gustav—all right. Walk straight through the woods, turning only once, at the giant oak tree. The town is very big. You will know it when you see it.

GUSTAV: I will sell the butter for a pocketful of gold!

MOTHER: It is very hard to sell to the town. Why, the town sometimes refuses even to talk to a stranger. Oh, Gustav—I don't know—

GUSTAV: I will sell the butter to the town and you will be pleased. (*Takes bowl [Mime].*) Turn once at the giant oak tree, right? And the town is big, right?

MOTHER: Go, then.

GUSTAV: Good-bye, Mama. (*Music.*) And Gustav set off through the deep woods.
  ([*Mime*] *walking, stumbling, making his way through the under-brush, hanging limbs; balancing the bowl of butter. While action is blocked elsewhere, the big rock is placed on the stage.*)

Is this the giant oak—or is that the giant oak? Or is it the tree over there? That must be the one. Now. *Here* I am to turn. This way—or that way? That way looks better. I should be coming to the town. Mama says it's very big—I can't miss it. And then Gustav saw a big rock ahead of him, in the sunlight. There is the biggest thing I have seen. So that must be the town. It's so big! (*He approaches the rock and begins vending.*) Town! I have rich, golden butter to sell. Creamy fine butter! Town! It is just as Mama said—the town will not talk to a stranger. Listen, town—I will let you taste this good butter. I'll put some right here (*He smears a bit of butter on the rock.*) and you will see that it is good. And the sun melted the butter and it disappeared. Gone already? Did you like it? Answer me, town! Is it not good butter. You want to buy the entire bowlful? All right—(*He smears all the butter on the rock, cleaning the bowl out carefully.*) Now you must pay me, town. I say, pay me, town. I want gold for my butter and I want it now! Well then, will you pay me if I come back tomorrow? All right, I will return tomorrow and you must give me gold for the butter. (*Leaving.*) Town, I will be back tomorrow, and then you will give me the gold.

(*Walking.*) So Gustav went home to his Mother and told her what had happened.

MOTHER: Gustav! You gave that butter to the town and you received no pay!

GUSTAV: It's all right, Mama. The town will pay tomorrow.

MOTHER: The town will never pay! How could you leave the butter and receive no gold?

GUSTAV: I am sure, Mama. The town will pay tomorrow.

MOTHER: I don't trust the town.

GUSTAV: Tomorrow—you'll see, Mama. And the next day Gustav went back to the rock. Town, here I am. Pay me for the butter. Now look. I say, pay me, town. (*He hits the rock.*) Pay me for that butter! I will count to ten. (*He counts on his fingers. Hits the rock. Enter two Bandits—very bad guys.*)

1ST BANDIT: There! That's the rock. I buried the gold under that rock.

2ND BANDIT: Who is that?

1ST BANDIT: I never saw him before. Let's wait—he'll leave.

2ND BANDIT: Maybe it's a trap!

1ST BANDIT: What's he trying to do?

GUSTAV: Now pay me, town. (*Hits rock.*) If you don't pay me, I will turn you topsy turvy. (*Pause.*)

1ST BANDIT: He knows the gold is there!

GUSTAV: I warned you, town. (*He hits and pushes the rock.*)

2ND BANDIT: It's a trap, I tell you. Let's get out of here!

1ST BANDIT: Better we lose the gold than go to prison! (*They flee.*)

GUSTAV: Topsy turvy! I will upset you, town! (*He turns the rock over and finds the gold.*) That's more like it! There's gold enough to pay me well! Thank you, town. (*Walking.*) So Gustav went home to his Mother and told her what had happened. (*Showing her the gold.*)— and the town paid me, exactly as I said it would.

MOTHER: Gustav! You are always right! (*Kiss and pat.*) Tomorrow I will give you some meat from the cow I butchered. Will you sell it to the town for me?

GUSTAV: Sure, Mama. I'm a good one to sell things, right? The next day Gustav took the meat (*Mime.*) and set off through the woods again. (*Music. Gustav in the woods.*)

DOG: Grrrr!

GUSTAV: Get away, you old dog!

DOG: Grrrr! Bark! Bark!

GUSTAV: Get away from this meat, dog!

DOG: Bark! Bark!

GUSTAV: Oh, I see! You want to buy the meat!

DOG: Rrrrrrright!

GUSTAV: I might as well sell it to you as to anyone. Here, take it.

DOG: Rrrrreally? (*Tears and snarls and eats all the meat.*)

GUSTAV: I'm waiting for you to pay me, dog.

DOG: (*Looking for more meat.*) Sniff, sniff—

GUSTAV: I have no more meat. You must pay me for what you ate.

DOG: Bark! Bark-bark-bark-bark-bark-bark-bark!

GUSTAV: You will pay me tomorrow?

DOG: Grrrreat!

GUSTAV: All right, then I will return tomorrow. (*Walking.*) So Gustav went home to his Mother and told her what had happened.

MOTHER: And the dog will pay you tomorrow?

GUSTAV: (*Nodding.*) Just as the town paid for the butter.

MOTHER: Then that will be fine. And the next morning Gustav set off for the woods again. Good-bye, Gustav.

GUSTAV: Good-bye, Mama. (*Exits.*)

NEIGHBOR: Where is Gustav going?

MOTHER: He has some business on the far side of the woods.

NEIGHBOR: Gustav? Then he will come home with another sad story.

MOTHER: Gustav will come home with a pocketful of gold. Even you will smile.

NEIGHBOR: Smile? When he tells of his latest adventure, I will no doubt weep for sorrow.

MOTHER: Oh, no. Gustav will make you smile.

NEIGHBOR: In this bag I have a hundred pieces of gold. If Gustav makes me smile, the gold is yours. No—he will come home with another sad story. And that evening, Gustav returned.

MOTHER: Gustav! My clever boy! Bringing me a pocketful of gold!

GUSTAV: (*Sadly.*) No, Mama. I bring you no gold at all.

NEIGHBOR: What did I tell you? Another sad story!

MOTHER: Didn't you find the dog in the woods?

GUSTAV: I found the dog, but that did me no good.

NEIGHBOR: Dog? His business was with a dog?

GUSTAV: I said to the dog, "You promised to pay me today, for the meat you ate."

NEIGHBOR: A dog promised to pay him?

MOTHER: And what did the dog do?

GUSTAV: Well—he barked, and he growled and he ran around in circles (*Gustav [Mimes] each action of the dog.*)—but he did not pay me. I spoke to him firmly. I hit him and I pushed him—the same things I did to the town—and finally I said, "Dog, if you do not pay, I will turn you topsy turvy!" And I knocked him over on his back—just like the town—and he waved his legs in the air and rolled on the ground and barked—(*Gustav [Mimes] the dog's actions.*)—but he did not pay me.

NEIGHBOR: (*Grinning.*) Oh, Gustav, that is a very sad story.

MOTHER: And yet you smile.

NEIGHBOR: (*Bursting into laughter.*) That story is *worth* a hundred pieces of gold! (*Gives gold to Mother.*)

GUSTAV: So Gustav and his Mother lived very well all winter—(*He scratches his head in puzzlement.*)

MOTHER: (*Kisses Gustav and pats his cheek.*) One way or another— Gustav is always right!

CURTAIN

The Fisherman and His Wife
Lowell Swortzell

Adapted from the Brothers Grimm

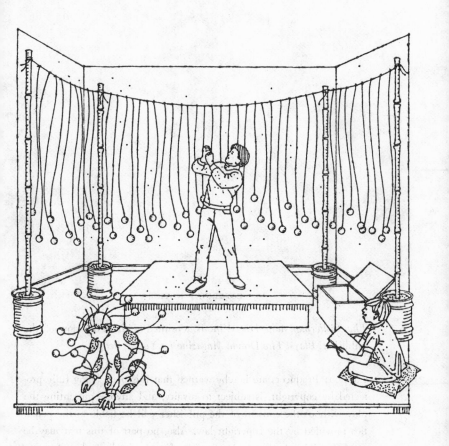

Lowell Swortzell's *The Fisherman and His Wife* is essentially a dispute between a fisherman's wife and a talking, magical fish. The woman and the fish never meet face-to-face but carry on their increasingly heated communication through the fisherman. The two-character scenes between fisherman and wife, and then fisherman and fish, are set off by the comments of a narrating storyteller (who remains uninvolved in the action) as well as brief scenes of dance representing the movement of sea and wind. A brewing storm reflects the growing antagonism between the characters.

Suggestions:

Costuming the characters offers a challenge. First, the dancers need swirling garments to enhance their movements and suggest ocean and wind. The fisherman, his wife, and the fish must have costumes that make their characters known. The fish must be commanding; clothed in a way that says "fish" and simultaneously hints at the latent strength that will eventually be revealed in the final scene. The fisherman's clothing may reveal some surge in personal wealth through the addition of extra pieces, but the greatest changes should be reserved for his wife's dress, because it is she who would be sure to benefit from their swelling fortune. The wife's gradually added costume pieces should mirror her increasing greed, arrogance, and wealth.

If the play is performed on a stage, a large four-sided box may be painted with a depiction of each of their four dwellings. The sea/wind dancers can then turn the box to the appropriate side for the next scene. All technical support must be done swiftly, without loss of momentum.

THE FISHERMAN AND HIS WIFE

CHARACTERS

Storyteller
Fisherman
Fisherman's Wife
The Fish
The Sea, dancers
The Wind, dancers

AT RISE: *The Storyteller enters and stands at one side of the stage.*

STORYTELLER: Our play takes place by the sea. But, of course, we can't have the sea here except in our imaginations. Or can we? Listen, I think I can hear it. Yes, the waves lap and roll and roar. (*A chorus of dancers, representing The Sea, enters, moving in patterns like waves. Their arms flow up and down as they fill the stage, and they murmur softly, making the sounds of the sea.*) The sea is driven by the wind. (*Another chorus, representing The Wind, enters, blowing and puffing. The Sea dancers spread out, their movements becoming more rapid but still graceful. The Wind dancers drive them about the stage.*) It is the wind that makes this seaside cold, and makes life hard. (*The Sea dancers stand near center, still moving gracefully, as The Wind dancers move around them.*) In fact, it is so bleak, that only this fisherman and his wife live here. (*Fisherman and Fisherman's Wife enter, carrying a large cardboard box which they place near The Sea. They also bring a feather duster, candle, and crown which they place behind box. On the side of the box visible to the audience is painted a wretched hut of sticks, hung with fishing nets.*) They live in this hut. Even though it is small and shabby, they are happy.

FISHERMAN: (*Working on the roof of the house.*) There. The roof is as good as new.

FISHERMAN'S WIFE: Will it keep the wind out?

FISHERMAN: Yes. Just watch. (*The Wind dancers dance about the house, attempting to touch the roof, but unable to.*) You see, wife, the house is sturdy and tight. (*The Wind dancers give up and go to one side of the stage.*) Now you will be warm and cozy while I am fishing.

WIFE: I will cook you a surprise for supper, a special treat to celebrate our new roof. Now go, and keep your scarf wrapped snugly around your neck.

FISHERMAN: I will.

WIFE: And, good husband, catch a great fish. (*She waves good-bye, and disappears behind the house.*)

FISHERMAN: I will, good wife. (*He walks briskly to The Sea.*)

STORYTELLER: And so he did. (*In pantomime, the Fisherman casts an imaginary line out into the water. The Sea dancers move about it, while one dancer pretends to pull the line, as the others encircle the Fisherman, who pulls and tugs. Some of the Wind and Sea dancers go to the side of the stage, and surround The Fish, as he enters unseen by Fisherman or audience. Then they move back to Fisherman.*)

FISHERMAN: I may be pulled into the sea. (*He almost loses his balance, as The Wind and Sea dancers push him back and forth.*) What can be so heavy on my line?

THE FISH: (*Jumping up to reveal himself, but still surrounded by The Sea.*) Why, a fish, naturally. You don't catch a train in the sea, do you? You don't catch a disease either. No, you catch a fish. I am a fish, you have caught me, and I don't like it one little bit.

FISHERMAN: A talking fish? I don't think I like it either.

THE FISH: Very well, then, you'd best let me go. Break the line and I will swim away.

FISHERMAN: Well, I don't know. What kind of fish are you?

THE FISH: No ordinary fish, that should be evident. Besides talking, I do other unusual things.

FISHERMAN: I can't imagine what.

THE FISH: No, you can't. So, I will tell you. I grant wishes.

FISHERMAN: You must be joking.

THE FISH: Of course not. Oh, I am good at jokes, too, but now I am serious. Have you a wish?

FISHERMAN: Let me see. No, I can't think of anything to wish for. But thank you just the same. Here, I will set you free. (*He pretends to break the line.*)

THE FISH: Much obliged, good fisherman. And if ever there is anything you wish, let me know. Now, to the depths of the sea with me. (*Encircled by The Sea dancers, he moves away quickly and exits. The dancers then return.*)

FISHERMAN: A talking fish? I must be dreaming. (*He pinches himself.*) Oww! No, that hurt. (*He calls toward the house.*) Wife, wife.

STORYTELLER: And the fisherman ran home to describe the fish to his wife.

FISHERMAN: (*Running to house, out of breath.*) I have something to tell you, wife.

WIFE: (*Entering from behind the house.*) Is it about the one that got away? (*She laughs.*)

FISHERMAN: Yes, it is, but I *let* this one get away.

WIFE: Why, good husband?

FISHERMAN: It asked me to.

WIFE: It did *what?*

FISHERMAN: The fish spoke to me.

WIFE: Husband, I have heard many fish stories in my life, but this sounds the fishiest. Now, what really happened?

FISHERMAN: A great fish came out of the sea and spoke to me. The strangest fish I've ever seen.

WIFE: (*Excitedly.*) Yes, yes, go on—what did it say?

FISHERMAN: It said it granted wishes, and asked me if I had any. I said no, and set it free. And that is the truth, dear wife.

WIFE: Very well, I believe you. But . . .

FISHERMAN: But what?

WIFE: It seems to me you missed a rare opportunity. If this fish grants wishes, you should have asked for something.

FISHERMAN: For what? (*Gesturing.*) We have everything we wish right here.

WIFE: That is true. But . . .

FISHERMAN: But what? What could I ask for?

WIFE: Why, you silly man, you could ask for—(*She looks around.*) I have it! Ask for a new house. Nothing elaborate, just a freshly-painted seaside cottage instead of this hut we call home.

FISHERMAN: We are happy here; I would hate to leave.

WIFE: Yes, but . . .

FISHERMAN: But what?

WIFE: I would leave for something better. Find your fish and get your wish.

FISHERMAN: He seemed in a hurry. I hate to bother him.

WIFE: Do as I say! Now go! (*She pushes him toward The Sea.*) And tell him the curtains should be red. (*She disappears behind the house, as he stands near The Sea.*)

STORYTELLER: The fisherman had never seen his wife in such a temper, so he went to the sea again, but he noticed the water was not as quiet as before, and the color had changed from blue to green. Still, he cast his line just as he had earlier in the day.

FISHERMAN: (*Pretending to cast line and calling.*)
Great Fish of the Sea,
My wife has a wish.
Please listen to me,
Great Fish of the Sea.

(*Moving faster than before, The Sea dancers swirl about The Fish as he enters and hurries to the Fisherman.*)

THE FISH: Yes, what is it?

FISHERMAN: My wife . . .

THE FISH: Yes, I know all that. What does she want?

FISHERMAN: Suddenly our house no longer suits her. She wants a cottage with a red curtain or two.

THE FISH: She shall have it by the time you get home. Now I must be on my way. Nice to see you again, friend. (*The Sea dancers escort The Fish off as The Wind dancers turn the box to reveal a side on which is painted the cottage with red curtains at the windows.*)

FISHERMAN: (*Waving to The Fish.*) Thank you, great fish. You've made her very happy I know.

STORYTELLER: And the fisherman hurried home to tell his wife the good news. But suddenly he stopped. His house was not there. Instead he saw . . .

FISHERMAN: (*Looking at new house in amazement.*) The cottage, the very cottage she asked for. Wife, wife, is this not a great gift? (*Wife, smiling and skipping with delight, enters from behind the house, carrying a feather duster.*)

WIFE: It's better than a hut, isn't it?

FISHERMAN: Never have I seen a lovelier house. (*He runs and touches it.*) Can it be real?

WIFE: Oh, it's real, don't worry about that. And inside you will find the kitchen I've always dreamed of owning and a fireplace of stone to keep us warm.

FISHERMAN: (*Pointing to the windows.*) And lovely red curtains!

WIFE: Yes, curtains. (*She frowns.*) But—

FISHERMAN: But what, wife?

WIFE: I wish they were blue instead of red.

FISHERMAN: You asked for red curtains and red is a happy color.

WIFE: But the kitchen is crowded.

FISHERMAN: You said the kitchen had all the things you always wanted.

WIFE: But there are too many things in it, that's all. I need more room.

FISHERMAN: This house is bigger than any we've lived in.

WIFE: I tell you the cottage is too small. Go to your fish and ask for something grander. A mansion with fifty rooms should do.

FISHERMAN: But, wife, I like this house.

WIFE: No, I cannot be happy here where I must do the dusting. (*She throws the feather duster down angrily.*)

FISHERMAN: But, wife, the fish has been generous enough already. I cannot trouble him again.

WIFE: Of course, you can.

FISHERMAN: He is such a kind fish.

WIFE: That's all the more reason he'll be glad to take care of our request. Not another word, silly man. Find your fish and get your wish.

FISHERMAN: Yes, wife. I will go. (*He walks slowly toward The Sea as Wife goes behind house.*)

STORYTELLER: This time, the fisherman walked with heavy steps because he did not want another house. And most of all, he did not want to disturb the fish again.

FISHERMAN: The sea is getting rougher. A storm is coming, I fear. (*The Sea dancers move about more rapidly, and The Wind dancers make loud wind sounds as they circle around and through The Sea.*) I am not certain the fish will be able to hear me. (*Shouting.*)
Great Fish of the Sea,
My wife has a wish.
Please listen to me,
Great Fish of the Sea.

(*The two groups of dancers move to the side and surround The Fish, who enters and moves with them to Fisherman.*)

THE FISH: What is it this time?

FISHERMAN: I am sorry, but my wife doesn't think the cottage will do, and wonders if you have anything in the way of a mansion. I do hate to ask you for this.

THE FISH: Yes, I know you do, but she shall have her mansion just the same. Now I must be on my way before the storm comes. Take care of yourself, good fisherman. (*The Sea dancers escort The Fish out.*)

FISHERMAN: (*Calling after him.*) You do the same, and thank you You've made her very happy I know.

STORYTELLER: And the fisherman hurried home to tell his wife the good news. (*The Wind dancers turn the box to show a side painted like the mansion with fifty windows with a candle in each.*)

FISHERMAN: (*Stopping before mansion.*) The mansion, just as the fish said. (*Calling.*) Oh, wife, how happy you must be. (*Wife, again smiling, enters from behind the box, carrying a candle.*)

WIFE: It's better than a cottage, isn't it?

FISHERMAN: I've never seen a larger mansion.

WIFE: There's room for everything—galleries for our magnificent paint ings . . .

FISHERMAN: Paintings? Oh, the fish was more than kind.

WIFE: And marble staircases . . .

FISHERMAN: Imagine you and me climbing marble staircases. I hope we don't fall.

WIFE: And a ballroom with chandeliers that hold five thousand can dles!

FISHERMAN: In my whole life I've never seen five thousand candles.

WIFE: They are lovely, take my word for it. (*She frowns.*) But . . .

FISHERMAN: But what, wife?

WIFE: They do smoke and make the mansion stuffy.

FISHERMAN: We'll just open a window and everything will be fine.

WIFE: Then I'll catch cold. No, it won't do.

FISHERMAN: What do you mean?

WIFE: It has too many candles. (*She throws the candle down.*) I want something better.

FISHERMAN: But, wife, this is no mere mansion. This is truly a palace fit for a king.

WIFE: Fit for a king, did you say?

FISHERMAN: It is, thanks to the fish.

WIFE: That's what I want more than anything else.

FISHERMAN: What?

WIFE: To be king!

FISHERMAN: What?

WIFE: If I am going to live like a king, I may as well *be* the king.

FISHERMAN: You're joking, aren't you?

WIFE: (*Pointing toward The Sea.*) Go. Find your fish and get your wish.

FISHERMAN: *Your* wish, you mean. I am happy right here.

WIFE: Foolish man, do as I say. Now go.

FISHERMAN: The fish is busy.

WIFE: Nonsense! He has given you everything else. He will give you this. Ask him, I say. (*She goes behind the house.*)

FISHERMAN: What has happened to her? She used to be happy with nothing; now, with everything, she's unhappy. (*He goes toward The Sea slowly.*)

STORYTELLER: And, again, even more reluctantly than before, the fisherman sought the fish. But the sea was raging and the wind was wild as they swirled about, engulfing the fisherman, who noticed the water was becoming purple.

FISHERMAN: (*Almost losing his balance as he calls.*)
Great Fish of the Sea,
My wife has a wish.
Please listen to me,
Great Fish of the Sea.

(*The Fish hurries on, tossed back and forth by The Sea dancers, as The Wind dancers dance about wildly.*)

THE FISH: What does she want this time?

FISHERMAN: I can't bring myself to say it. (*He turns his head away.*)

THE FISH: Oh, go ahead, nothing surprises me anymore.

FISHERMAN: Very well, she wishes to be king.

THE FISH: Granted. She is king. Go and bow to her.

FISHERMAN: Thank you, fish. This certainly will satisfy her.

THE FISH: The storm is here. Go home safely, friend. (*The Fisherman waves good-bye as The Fish leaves. They both move with great difficulty, as if struggling against the wind.*)

STORYTELLER: Fighting his way through the wind, the fisherman reached his home, only to discover that it was no longer a mansion. (*The Wind dancers turn the box again to show the side on which is painted a high castle with turrets and towers, a drawbridge and iron gate.*)

FISHERMAN: A castle! She *is* king. (*Wife comes from behind the box, wearing a crown on her head.*)

WIFE: It's better than running a smoky old mansion, isn't it? Do you like my crown?

FISHERMAN: Yes, I do.

WIFE: (*Sharply.*) Yes, you do, what?

FISHERMAN: (*Puzzled.*) Yes, I like your crown and your castle.

WIFE: (*Angrily.*) You like my crown and my castle, *what?*

FISHERMAN: (*Suddenly realizing.*) I like them, Your Majesty. (*He bows low.*)

WIFE: Well, that's more like it. Oh, I love to see people bow and curtsy when I enter a room. It's so much fun. Don't you agree?

FISHERMAN: Yes, Your Majesty. (*He bows.*)

WIFE: And I've ordered magnificent robes and jewels for myself, and a nice little cloak for you.

FISHERMAN: Oh, thank you, Your Majesty.

WIFE: And I have ordered a glorious dinner.

FISHERMAN: Thank you, Your Majesty.

WIFE: And I've ordered everyone in my kingdom to come to a ball in honor of me.

FISHERMAN: Shouldn't you give the ball in honor of the fish who granted your wish?

WIFE: Don't be silly. Kings don't honor fish except by eating them. And I've ordered gardens and stables, and carriages and servants. Oh, I love to order.

FISHERMAN: Will you tell me one thing, Your Majesty?

WIFE: Very well, what is it?

FISHERMAN: Are you happy now that you have a kingdom to order?

WIFE: Of course. (*A frown comes over her face.*) But . . .

FISHERMAN: But what?

WIFE: Do you know what I would like most to order?

FISHERMAN: What?

WIFE: Something even a king can't order—the sun and the moon!

FISHERMAN: No! I don't believe it, Your Majesty.

WIFE: Yes, that is what I want: the power to make the sun rise and set as I like, the power to make the moon come and go when I say.

FISHERMAN: Your Majesty, I beg you, stop. It is not right for you to want this.

WIFE: Lowly fisherman, go to your fish and get my wish.

FISHERMAN: I will not do it. You are king, and that is enough for anyone.

WIFE: Yes, I am king, your king, and I order you to go. (*Screaming.*) I order you, do you hear?

FISHERMAN: (*Meekly.*) Yes, Your Majesty. (*He bows and backs away from his Wife, who disappears behind the box.*)

STORYTELLER: Now the sea was black, even the foam, and it looked as if it would devour the earth. The wind howled and screeched as if it were trying to blow the earth away.

FISHERMAN: (*Stumbling and falling as The Wind dancers claw at his face and The Sea dancers rush about him.*) He will never hear me in this storm. (*The storm reaches a high level of fury, as he attempts to call.*)

 Great Fish of the Sea,
 My wife has a wish.
 Please listen to me,
 Great Fish of the Sea.

 (*The Fish appears quickly.*)

THE FISH: What does she want now, for heaven's sake?

FISHERMAN: (*Crying.*) I am ashamed to tell you. (*He covers his face with his hands.*)

THE FISH: (*Sternly.*) Out with it, speak!

FISHERMAN: She seeks power over the sun and the moon. She wants to order them to do what she wishes.

THE FISH: Go. She is back in her hut. This is the reward for greed that knows no end. This is the reward for power misused. She has had everything. (*He starts to exit, but stops, and speaks more kindly.*) But remember, fisherman, that once you were happy in your hut, contented with what you had. Try to be happy again. Good-bye. (*He exits, escorted by The Sea dancers. The Wind dancers turn the box again, to the side painted like the hut. As the Fisherman crosses to the hut, all the dancers exit calmly in various directions. The Fisherman touches the hut happily, then goes behind the box, out of sight.*)

STORYTELLER: And here the fisherman and his wife lived all their days happy to be in their hut. Having learned that greed can never be satisfied, they no longer measure happiness by their possessions, but by their contentment. (*He exits as the curtains close.*)

CURTAIN

A Christmas Pageant
Traditional

The five scenes of *A Christmas Pageant* retell the well-known Christmas story. Each scene is augmented by the singing of an appropriate carol by a choir. The pageant can be presented in a church sanctuary, in a large room, or on a stage, with only a simple manger and costumes that suggest the familiar personages of the story. The Bible story is told essentially by a narrator; the brief scenes acted within the narrative serve as living illustrations.

A CHRISTMAS PAGEANT
From traditional sources

CHARACTERS

Reader
Mary
Joseph
Angel Gabriel
First Shepherd
Second Shepherd
Third Shepherd
First Wise Man
Second Wise Man
Third Wise Man
A Multitude of Angels
Other Shepherds

MUSIC FOR THE CHOIR

SCENE 1. "Once in Royal David's City" by Henry J. Gauntlett or "O Come, Emmanuel," a plainsong tune adapted by Thomas Helmore
"Gabriel's Message," a Basque carol

SCENE 2. "What Child Is This?" to the old English tune "Greensleeves"

SCENE 3. "The Snow Lay on the Ground," a traditional carol

SCENE 4. "Angels We Have Heard on High," a traditional French carol

SCENE 5. "We Three Kings" by John Henry Hopkins
"Silent Night" by Franz Grueber
"O Little Town of Bethlehem" by Lewis H. Redner or
"Forest Green," a traditional tune
(Other favorite Christmas songs may be used.)

Music selected by Frank C. Smith

Opening music: "Once in Royal David's City" or "O Come, Emmanuel."

SCENE 1. The Annunciation.
Luke I:26–27

READER: (*Enters and stands at side.*) And it came to pass that in the sixth month the Angel Gabriel (*Gabriel enters R, crosses to C.*)—was sent from God unto a city of Galilee, named Nazareth. To a virgin— (*Mary enters at L, crosses to C.*)—espoused to a man, whose name was Joseph, of the house of David, and the virgin's name was Mary.

GABRIEL: Hail, Mary, Thou are highly favored. The Lord is with thee; blessed art thou among women. (*Mary reacts.*) Fear not, Mary: for thou has found favor with God. And behold, thou shalt bring forth a son, and shalt call his name Jesus.

MARY: Behold the handmaid of the Lord; be it unto me according to thy word. My soul doth magnify the Lord.
(*Tableau: Gabriel blessing Mary. Choir sings "Gabriel's Message." Gabriel exits at the end of the song. Mary sits on the stool by the cradle.*)

SCENE 2. The Nativity.
        Luke II:1–7

READER: In those days there went out a decree from Caesar Augustus that all the world should be taxed. And all went to be taxed, everyone into his own city. And Joseph—(*Joseph enters at L, and walks to Mary.*)—also went up from Galilee unto Bethlehem, with Mary, his espoused wife, being great with child. (*Joseph stands behind Mary.*) And so it was while they were there, the days were accomplished that she should be delivered. And she brought forth her first born son, and wrapped him in swaddling clothes and laid him in a manger, because there was no room at the inn.

   (*Light goes on inside the cradle. Tableau: Mary rocks cradle while Joseph stands watching. Choir sings "What Child Is This?"*)

SCENE 3. Shepherds Watch by Night.
        Luke II:16–19

READER: And there were in the same country shepherds—(*Three, or more shepherds, enter at R, cross to C, frightened and looking at the sky.*)—abiding in the field, keeping watch over their flocks by night. And, lo, the angel of the Lord came upon them, and the glory of the Lord shone round about them; and they were sore afraid.

FIRST SHEPHERD: (*Shepherds stand at C, masking Mary and the cradle.*) 'Tis a strange night.

SECOND SHEPHERD: Thou speakest truly. Even the sheep do not lie still.

THIRD SHEPHERD: On such a night, wonders are said to happen.
   (*Gabriel enters at R.*)

SECOND SHEPHERD: Look, look! See the strange person! (*Shepherds huddle together.*)

GABRIEL: Fear not; for behold, I bring you glad tidings of great joy, which shall be for all people. For unto you is born this day in the city of David, a Saviour, which is Christ the Lord. And this shall be a sign unto you: Ye shall find the Babe wrapped in swaddling clothes, lying in a manger.

   (*Tableau: Gabriel stands, arms lifted. Shepherds kneel, backs to audi-*

ence. Choir sings "The Snow Lay on the Ground." During the song many Angels enter singing, stand in a pictorial grouping, and then exit at the end of the song. Gabriel leaves last.)

SCENE 4. Adoration by the Shepherds.
Luke II:16–19

FIRST SHEPHERD: (*Shepherds rise.*) Let us go now even unto Bethlehem, the city of David.

SECOND SHEPHERD: Yes, let us hasten to see this thing which has come to pass.

THIRD SHEPHERD: This is the thing which was foretold by the prophets of old. (*Shepherds exit at R.*)

READER: And the shepherds came with haste, and found Mary and Joseph and the Babe lying in a manger. And when they had seen it, they made known abroad the saying, which was told them concerning the child. And they that heard it wondered at those things which were told them by the shepherds. But Mary kept all these things and pondered them in her heart.

THIRD SHEPHERD: (*Shepherds enter at R.*) Did not the Holy One say we should find the Babe lying in a manger?

FIRST SHEPHERD: That is so.

SECOND SHEPHERD: (*Points to cradle at C.*) Look. Look! There is a manger over there.

THIRD SHEPHERD: (*Calls.*) Ho, stranger! Where shall we find the Infant Saviour?

JOSEPH: The Babe is here, lying in a manger, beside Mary, his mother.
(*Tableau: Shepherds kneel at R of cradle. Choir sings, "Angels We Have Heard on High."*)

SCENE 5. Adoration by the Magi.
Matthew II:9–11.

READER: Now when Jesus was born in Bethlehem in the days of Herod the King, behold there came wise men from the East to Jerusalem, led by the star which they saw in the East, and which went before them till it came and stood over where the young child was. When they saw the star they rejoiced with exceeding great joy. And when they were come into the house, they saw the young child with Mary, and fell down and worshipped him, and they had opened their treasures, they presented unto him gifts: gold, frankincense, and myrrh.

(*Choir sings "We Three Kings." On the second, third, and fourth verses the First Wise Man, the Second Wise Man, and the Third Wise Man enter from L, each carrying a gift. Each lays his gift in front of the cradle, and then kneels at L.*

Tableau: Choir sings, "Silent Night." Gabriel enters and stands behind Mary and Joseph, blessing them. The other Angels enter and form a background, with arms lifted. Shepherds remain kneeling at R. Wise Men remain kneeling at L.

The pageant ends with the end of the song. The curtains close, or all exit. After music: "O Little Town of Bethlehem" or "Forest Green.")

CURTAIN

Yankee Doodle Dandies (Johnny Appleseed, Harriet Tubman, Casey at the Bat)
Aurand Harris

Yankee Doodle Dandies is a collection of three scenes from Aurand Harris's full-length play, *Yankee Doodle,* a musical review of American history. Each of the three has a slightly different style from the other two, even though all three use narration and mime.

Johnny Appleseed is written in the story-theatre style. Although the actor playing Johnny has the far greater proportion of lines, other characters also have exchanges of dialogue and narrate the story of America's apple-tree-planting hero. Often while Johnny speaks, the others are miming his narration.

Harriet Tubman is the only one who speaks in the scene that tells her story. The others in the cast provide a background of mime and dance which symbolizes her first journey to freedom.

In *Casey at the Bat* the reader or readers present the familiar poem by Ernest Lawrence Thayer as the actors mime that crucial inning of the game in slow motion. A small group of actors performing as "spectators" may help narrate by speaking the comments in the poem which obviously are said by them.

Suggestions:

All three of these scenes demand adequate performing space. Properties may be imaginary, although the addition of actual items in *Johnny Appleseed* may clarify the meaning of the lines. Costumes may be simple and uniform. Appropriate accessories may be quickly added to identify the characters.

JOHNNY APPLESEED

CHARACTERS

John Chapman, Johnny Appleseed
Old Tree
Young Tree
First Indian
Second Indian
Third Indian
Orchard of Trees

John Chapman, Johnny Appleseed, enters and speaks to audience in story-theatre fashion.

JOHNNY: Once upon a real time—during the first year of the Revolutionary War—John Chapman was born in the State of Massachusetts. As a boy he walked in the woods and (*Walks and mimes.*) looked up at the trees. "They are my friends," he said.

(*Actor-tree enters, stands with back to audience.*)
Of all the trees, his favorite was one apple tree. An old, old apple tree. (*Tree turns around. He wears a long green beard.*) A bent and gnarled —(*Tree crooks his arm.*)—ancient apple tree. (*To audience.*) "Everyone should have an apple tree," John said. When John was eighteen he set off for the West. He said good-bye to his favorite apple tree. (*John raises his hand. Tree waves, then exits.*) And he walked toward the setting sun. He walked across the Allegheny Mountains . . . (*Mimes walking up mountain, body tilted backward.*) walked UP the east side . . . (*Mimes walking down, body bent forward.*) and DOWN the west side. And he walked until he came to Fort Pitt. There he settled on a farm, but there were no apple trees. So he went to the cider mills. (*Pantomimes the following.*) And he scooped and he scooped up sacks and sacks full of apple seeds, and planted them. He watered and cared for them. (*Actor, Young Tree, enters and sits low, back to audience.*) He watched the seeds begin to grow. Slowly . . . and the first year

there appeared a green shoot. (*Actor raises hand with green glove.*) The next year, a bigger seedling. (*Actor raises other hand with green glove.*) And it grew and grew until, in five years, there stood an apple tree. (*Actor has slowly risen to full height.*) And, lo and behold, in the spring a tiny green bud appeared. (*Actor opens his fist, which holds a big pink blossom.*) "A miracle," he said. "That happens every spring." And where the blossom had been, there, starting to grow, was a little round apple. (*Actor puts a red balloon to his mouth and blows it up, or holds a red circle of cloth he takes from his sleeve.*) The apple grew and it grew, bigger and bigger, until it was a beautiful big red apple. "It is a miracle," he said. "That happens every fall." (*Actor exits.*) Then he knew what he must do. "I will go west, not with a gun, but with sacks of apple seeds. I will plant them and they will grow—and every year a miracle will happen." As he traveled, planting orchards, he became a living legend. And they called him Johnny Appleseed.

FIRST INDIAN: (*Indians creep in.*) The Indians also watched and listened. They heard him talk to the animals.

SECOND INDIAN: They saw him walk through the snake country without shoes. They saw him plant seeds—and trees grow.

THIRD INDIAN: They knew he was brave because he carried no gun.

ALL INDIANS: "Magic," they said, and bowed low to the white medicine man.

JOHNNY: But Johnny held out his hand and said, "Friend."

SECOND INDIAN: "Come," the Indian said, and in their village they made a celebration.

FIRST INDIAN: (*He sits right. Second Indian sits at left. Johnny sits in center facing audience.*) They gave him moccasins of soft skins.

THIRD INDIAN: They gave him beads of sharp teeth and shining shells.

SECOND INDIAN: (*Standing behind Johnny.*) The Chief crowned his head with a circle of bright feathers and called him "Brother."

JOHNNY: Friend of the Indians, friend of the settlers, he tried to keep peace between them. When he heard the war drums beat (*War drums beat. He rises and comes to front.*) he ran thirty miles to bring soldiers to Fort Mansfield. When the Indians saw they were outnumbered they slipped quietly away. (*Drum stops. Indians slip out.*) On he went, and more and more of his orchards bloomed in the wilderness. (*Actors,*

Orchard of Trees, enter quickly and quietly, scatter over the stage, and stand with backs to audience. Johnny walks among them.) "I'll come back," he always said. "I'll come back in the spring." And he did, pruning and tending his trees. As he grew old, he was asked, "Are you not lonely, always walking alone?" He held out his arms to the woods. "I have a thousand friends." When he was seventy he took his last walk. He became ill with the winter plague, pneumonia, and was nursed in the house of William Worth. One morning William said, "The old man is dead." (*Soft music of a flute is heard. Actors over music, chant, "I'll come back." Music continues softly.*) Every spring his trees burst into pink and white clouds of beauty. (*Actors move their arms like branches and chant over music, "I'll come back. I'll come back."*) Every fall the branches are heavy with red and golden apples. A miracle that happens every year. (*Actors, above their heads, spread brilliant red fans which they hold. They chant with the music, "I'll come back. I'll come back. I'll come back."*) Johnny Appleseed went west without a gun. (*Tableau. A few more notes of soft music, then:*)

CURTAIN

HARRIET TUBMAN

CHARACTERS

Harriet Tubman
Chorus

Harriet Tubman enters as the Chorus, offstage, hums "Steal Away Home."

TUBMAN: I was born a slave. I can show you the scars where I was whipped. My prayer was always—let me, Harriet Tubman, be free.

(*Chorus enters and enacts in pantomime Tubman's experiences as she relates them, first a girl telling folks good-bye.*)

One night I told the cabin-folks I was going to run away north. I dared not speak the words aloud, so I sang them. (*Sings.*)

Steal away, steal away,
Steal away to Jesus.
Steal away, steal away home.
I ain't got long to stay here.

They heard and understood; steal away meant escape from slavery. When the North Star was shining bright, I slipped away on the Underground Railroad.

(*Chorus hums "Steal Away Home," and in pantomime suggest a girl hiding and traveling.*)

I hid in the attic of a Quaker lady's house. I was hidden in a potato hole for a week by a free black family. I was covered in a wagon and driven north by a farmer whose words I could not understand. I was buried safely in a haystack when the slave hunters came with their hounds and guns. I was rowed in a boat up the Choptank River. And at last—at last I crossed the freedom line into Pennsylvania. I felt like I was in heaven. I was free!

(*Chorus continues to pantomime action. For the Freedom Train, one actor stands at right, stretches out his left hand, another actor takes it, stretches out his hand, and so on, until an unbroken line of linked actors reach across the stage.*)

Now that I knew the way, I knew what I must do. I must go back. I, like Moses, must lead my people out of slavery. Let my people go—on the freedom train. Nineteen trips I made. Three hundred slaves I delivered up to freedom—always guided by the North Star and my trust in God. Oh, let it be written and be remembered that I, Harriet Tubman, never ran my train off the track and I never lost a single passenger!

(*All clap and sing "Didn't My Lord Deliver Daniel?"*)

Didn't my Lord deliver Daniel,
Deliver Daniel, deliver Daniel?
Didn't my Lord deliver Daniel,
And why not-a every man?

CURTAIN

CASEY AT THE BAT

Adapted as a pantomime in slow motion, from the poem "Casey at the Bat" by Ernest Lawrence Thayer.

CHARACTERS

Pitcher
Catcher
First Baseman
Second Baseman
Third Baseman
} The Blues

Umpire

Flynn
Blake
Casey
} The Reds

Reader (There may be more than one Reader.
There may also be a grandstand of
spectators who react to the ball
game in unison, and also say some of
the speaking parts of the poem.)

CASEY AT THE BAT

Music: "Take Me Out to the Ball Game." The Blues, wearing blue baseball caps, enter—Pitcher, Catcher, Three Basemen—and take their places, making a small baseball diamond on the stage. The Pitcher is in center, facing down right. Catcher is down right. Umpire enters and stands behind Catcher. First Baseman is down left. Second Baseman is up left. Third baseman is up right. The Reader, or Readers, stands down left of the diamond. Grandstand, seats, with spectators may also be down left.

The Blues, in slow motion, warm up throwing and catching an imaginary baseball. All movement in the entire play is done in slow motion, fitting the action to the words of the poem. There are no hand props. The ball and bat are imaginary and pantomimed.

The music dims out when Reader begins.

READER: It looked extremely rocky
    For the Mudville team that day;
    The score stood two to four,
    With but one inning left to play.

If only—if only Casey
    Could get a whack at that,
    They'd put even money now,
    With Casey at the bat.

(*Flynn, wearing Red cap, enters and goes to plate.*)

But Flynn preceded Casey,
    And likewise so did Blake,
    And the former was a pudd'n
    And the latter was a fake.

(*Pitcher warms up, winds up, throws imaginary ball. Flynn strikes, hits, runs to first—all in slow motion.*)

But—Flynn let drive a single
    To the wonderment of all.

(*Blake, in Red cap, enters, and goes to plate. Ball is pitched. He hits it, runs to first, then to second. Flynn runs to third, sliding to safety.*)

And the much-despised Blakey
    Tore the cover off the ball.

And when the dust had lifted
    And they saw what had occurred,
    There was Blakey safe at second,
    And Flynn a-huggin' third.

(*Spectators wave arms and pantomime shouting in slow motion.*)

Then the crowd begin to yell
    And arose from where it sat;
    For Casey, mighty Casey,
    Was advancing to the bat.

(*Casey enters, strutting with comic confidence.*)

There was an ease in Casey's manner
    As he stepped into his place,

There was pride in Casey's bearing
And a smile on Casey's face;

And when responding to the cheers
He lightly doffed his hat,

(*Lifts hat.*)

No stranger in the crowd could doubt
'Twas Casey at the bat.

Ten thousand eyes were on him as
He rubbed his hands with dirt,

(*Casey mimes.*)

Five thousand tongues applauded when
He wiped them on his shirt;

(*Casey mimes, crowd waves.*)

Then when the writhing pitcher ground
The ball into his hip,

(*Pitcher mimes.*)

Defiance gleamed from Casey's eye,
A sneer curled Casey's lip.

And now the leather-covered sphere
Came hurtling through the air

(*Ball is pitched.*)

And Casey stood a-watching it
In haughty grandeur there.

Close by the sturdy batsman
The ball unheeded sped;
"That ain't my style," said Casey.
"Strike one," the umpire said.

(*Umpire mimes. Crowd reacts. Catcher catches ball.*)

From the benches black with people,
There went up a muffled roar.
Like the beating of the storm waves
On the stern and distant shore.

"Kill him! Kill the umpire!"
Shouted someone on the stand

(*Casey mimes.*)

And it's likely they'd have killed him
Had not Casey raised his hand.

With a smile of Christian charity
Great Casey gave a grin;
He quieted the rising tumult,
The game began again.

(*Catcher throws ball to Pitcher.*)

He signaled to the pitcher

(*Casey mimes.*)

And once more the spheroid flew;

(*Ball is pitched.*)

But Casey still ignored it,
And the umpire said, "Strike two."

(*Umpire mimes. Crowd reacts.*)

"Fraud!" cried the maddened thousands,
And the echo answered, "Fraud!"
But one scornful look from Casey

(*Casey glares. Crowd reacts.*)

And the audience was awed;

They saw his face grow stern and cold,
They saw his muscles strain,

(*Casey gets ready.*)

And they knew that Casey wouldn't let
The ball go by again.

The sneer is gone from Casey's lips,
His teeth are clenched in hate.
He pounds with cruel vengeance
His bat upon the plate;

And now the pitcher holds the ball,
And now he lets it go,

(*Pitcher throws. Casey swings, twisting completely around, facing audience with a surprised look on his face.*)

And now the air is shattered
By the force of Casey's blow!

(*All freeze in a moving position.*)

But there is no victory shout—
Mighty Casey has struck out!

(*Casey opens his mouth wide and comically in bewildered amazement.*

Fast, loud music, "Take Me Out to the Ball Game.")

CURTAIN

The Buffalo and the Bell
Kim Wheetley

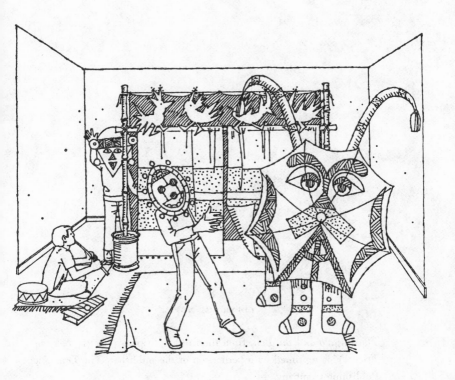

Based on a popular folktale of Indonesia, *The Buffalo and the Bell* by Kim Alan Wheetley is the story of a good-hearted bumpkin who outwits those who trick him. The trickster plot is set in a form that derives from both the Indonesian wayang kulit shadow puppet theatre and the topeng masked theatre.

Topeng is traditionally staged in front of an ornamental curtain of four or five horizontal bands of various colors and divided in the center for entrances and exits. Flanking the curtain are two large gilded ceremonial umbrellas and two tall bamboo poles with bell-tipped banners.

The gamelan orchestra is an integral part of a topeng performance. Musical effects emphasize important moments throughout the play. The quality of the gamelan sounds may be suggested by a xylophone, gong, bells, cymbals, drums, wind chime, and recorder. Other instruments for special sound effects may include a woodblock, claves, ratchet, triangle, and autoharp.

Certain theatrical traditions have also influenced the creating of the characters in *The Buffalo and the Bell*. When the trio of tricksters is on the offensive in their villainy against Pandji, the hero, they assume stances from the martial arts to heighten their threatening demeanor. The two-dimensional puppets actually become characters in the action. They are manipulated by Dalang, a silent property man, who is in full view of the audience and is ignored by the other characters.

The group will need to become acquainted with the look of Indonesian peasant dress and theatrical costume before considering how to costume the characters. Although all of the characters in topeng theatre except the property man wear half masks, young actors should perform with faces uncovered.

Since these theatrical traditions will seem very new and different to American youngsters, the group should learn the story thoroughly through improvisations, and then gradually add the Indonesian conventions, such as stances from the martial arts and frequent emphasis of dialogue with musical sounds.

THE BUFFALO AND THE BELL

CHARACTERS

Pandji (pänd-yē), a simple-minded farmer
Sukani (sōō-kän-ē), his domineering wife
Klungkung (klōōng-kōōng), a notorious cheat
Kalebet (kä-lä-bät), his clumsy confederate
Kalabuat (kä-lä-bōōt), their attractive female companion
Masak (mä-säk), the old vendor
Dalang (dä-läng), the puppeteer
The Orchestra

Three gongs. Gamelan music.

An Indonesian temple procession approaches. A Bearer leads the procession carrying a pendjo. Next comes the Dalang, shaded by a fringed ceremonial umbrella carried by an Attendant. Last come the Performers bearing puppets and masks, or balancing ornate pyramids of fruit and flowers on their heads. Gong.

DALANG: Selmat Datang. [Welcome.]
Welcome from us to you.
We come from the South Pacific,
From a realm of tall bamboo.
Our land is many islands,
Volcanic peaks in waters blue,
Crowned with rice paddy terraces
And lush forests damp with dew.

Come share our comic tale
From the land of the Indonese.
Hear the harmonies of the orchestra
Floating on the gentle breeze.

Meet the actors with their masks
Who will portray all manner of man.
And observe the puppets soon to be
Animated by an "unseen" artisan.

And now our play from Indonesia,
Full of tricks by friend and foe.
It's an age-old tale of a magic bell,
A farmer, and his water buffalo.

(*Gongs. The performers take their positions. Pandji, the farmer, enters shepherding two flocks of brightly painted "shadow puppet" ducks. The puppets are mounted on stiff wires manipulated by Dalang, the puppeteer, who goes unobserved by the performers. Pandji directs the ducks with a feather-tipped bamboo pole decorated midway with a white scarf.*

Pandji attempts to silence his quacking flock [xylophone] by hypnotizing them with the flutter of the feather on the pole.)

PANDJI: Shhh! Shhh! Be quiet, my little ducks. No more quacking. Follow the feather and you'll soon be there. Be quiet now and stay in line. Everyone ready? Follow me.

(*Pandji and the silent ducks begin to sneak across the stage. Sukani, his wife, enters behind them balancing an offering of fruit, rice cakes, and flowers on her head.*)

SUKANI: What's this? Oh, Pandji.

PANDJI: Shhh! Shhh!

SUKANI: Don't you shhh me!!

(*The startled ducks scatter, causing Sukani to trip and drop the offering. She is instantly overrun with ravenous quacking ducks.*)

SUKANI: What? What are you doing? Get out of here! Get away! Pandji! Stop eating that rice, you feather brains! Pandji! Get these scavengers out of here!

(*Pandji scurries about unsuccessfully trying to corral his charges.*)

Get away from those rice cakes! You're ruining my temple offering. Get away! Get away! Pandji, do something! Pandji! . . . Hhhaaahhh-iiieee!

(*Drum. The ducks scurry toward the cowering Pandji for protection from Sukani, who leaps into an ominous martial arts attack position. Unfortunately she smashes the offering in the process.*)

Ooohhh! Just look at this mess! You and your feather brained flock have ruined my temple offering!

PANDJI: But, wife . . .

SUKANI: I've been up since before dawn preparing these flowers and food. And now they're ruined.

(*Sukani balances the remnants of the offering on her head.*)

PANDJI: But Sukani . . .

SUKANI: And just where were you going with these greedy gluttons? Well? Speak up!

PANDJI: Sukani, dearest. I was just taking them down to the rice paddy for their morning swim.

SUKANI: Oh you were, were you. And did you forget what you were supposed to do this morning?

PANDJI: No, but I just thought . . .

SUKANI: You thought! The village dim-wit thought! Did I ask you to think? Did I? Well, did I?

PANDJI: No.

SUKANI: No, I did not. But I did ask you to do something, didn't I? Didn't I?

PANDJI: Yes.

SUKANI: And can you possibly tell me what that was?

PANDJI: You told me to sell our buffalo. But I don't want to sell him.

SUKANI: Don't be stupid. We have no money. Our roof is full of holes. Our clothes are wearing thin. And that lazy old buffalo eats all our food. I've had enough. You will take that animal to the market and sell it.

PANDJI: But wife . . .

SUKANI: It's worth at least 250 rupiahs, so don't take one rupiah less! Do you understand?

PANDJI: But Sukani, we've had the buffalo so long. I don't want to sell him.

(*Sukani grabs the pole and aims a powerful blow at him, which he and the ducks acrobatically dodge.*)

SUKANI: Hhhaaahhhiiieee!

(*Drum.*)

PANDJI: All right, wife. I'll sell our buffalo.

SUKANI: For 250 rupiahs. Don't forget that.

PANDJI: But what about the ducks? I promised them a swim.

SUKANI: Oh, very well. You take the buffalo to market and I'll tend to these scavengers . . . Move along there, you feather brains! Stay in line! (*Xylophone.*) Stop that quacking!

(*Sukani herds the flock out of sight, while Pandji exits in the opposite direction, not noticing Klungkung, who is peering through the curtain, his face partially hidden behind a huge silk fan.*)

KLUNGKUNG: So . . . Pandji plans to sell his buffalo, does he? How nice. Since he's so stupid and I'm so clever, it should be easy to cheat him out of it. Haaaiii!

(*Klungkung leaps into a dramatic threatening pose. Autoharp and drum.*
  Note: All three villains use sharp stylized movements and poses derived from the martial arts throughout the play.)

Kalabuat!

(*Kalabuat leaps out from behind Klungkung, landing in her version of a threatening pose. Autoharp and drum.*)

KALABUAT: Haaayooo!

KLUNGKUNG: Kalebet!

(*Kalebet leaps out to the other side of Klungkung, assuming his threatening stance. Autoharp and drum. Unfortunately he lands on top of Klungkung's foot.*)

KALEBET: Heeeyaaa!

KLUNGKUNG: Ooowwwhhh!

(*Grabbing his foot, Klungkung strikes Kalebet with his fan. Wood-block.*)

Good morning, my fine fellow thieves.

(*All three leap into another pose, peering over their forearms, their fans masking their lower faces. Autoharp and drum.*)

ALL: Hhhaaahhhiiieee!!!

KLUNGKUNG: Now listen carefully. I have a plan for a profitable little trick.

KALEBET: Is it sneaky?

KLUNGKUNG: The sneakiest!

(*Autoharp.*)

KALABUAT: Is it clever?

KLUNGKUNG: The cleverest!

(*Autoharp.*)

KALEBET: Is it rotten?

KLUNGKUNG: Of course.

(*Autoharp. Laughing and plotting, they "disappear" behind their fans. Pandji enters, prodding a lumbering water buffalo, a full-sized colored shadow puppet manipulated by the Dalang. Each prod from Pandji's pointed stick produces a plaintive "moo." Cowbell.*)

PANDJI: Move on there, buffalo.

BUFFALO: (*Through a kazzoo.*) Moo.

PANDJI: I'm sorry I have to sell you.

BUFFALO: Moo.

(*Kalebet and Kalabuat eavesdrop from a distance, peering over their fans, as Klungkung leaps out in his customary pose. Autoharp and drum.*)

KLUNGKUNG: Haaaiii!

BUFFALO: Moo!

PANDJI: Oh! . . . Klungkung!

KLUNGKUNG: You're out early this morning, Pandji. Where are you going?

PANDJI: To the market to sell this buffalo.

(*Cowbell.*)

BUFFALO: Moo.

KLUNGKUNG: Buffalo? What buffalo are you talking about?

PANDJI: This buffalo here.

BUFFALO: Moo.

KLUNGKUNG: Why you really must be as stupid as they say.

PANDJI: Why?

KLUNGKUNG: This is no buffalo. This is a goat!

(*Autoharp.*)

PANDJI: A goat?

KLUNGKUNG: Yes! If you're going to sell it, I'll give you 30 rupiahs for it now.

(*Rattle.*)

BUFFALO: (*Through the kazoo.*) Don't do it! Don't do it!

PANDJI: What?

BUFFALO: (*Through kazoo.*) It's a trick.

PANDJI: A trick?

BUFFALO: (*Through kazoo.*) A trick.

PANDJI: . . . No, I'd better go on to the market.

KLUNGKUNG: Suit yourself.

(*Klungkung moves off to spy over his fan.*)

PANDJI: He can't fool me. How can a buffalo be a goat? He was only trying to trick me because he thinks I'm stupid.

BUFFALO: Uh-hm.

PANDJI: What? . . . Aaahhh.

(The Buffalo and Pandji are laughing together when Kalebet appears via his leap-pose. Unfortunately he lands on top of Pandji's foot. Autoharp and drum.)

KALEBET: Heeeyaaa!

PANDJI: Ooowwwhhh! . . . Kalebet.

KALEBET: Pandji. What a healthy-looking goat you've got there.

(Autoharp.)

PANDJI: Goat? It's not a goat. It's a buffalo.

(Cowbell.)

KALEBET: It's plainly a goat. Just listen.

(Kalebet hides his attempted ventriloquism behind his fan.)

Baahh.

(Autoharp.)

BUFFALO: Moo.

(Cowbell.)

KALEBET: Baaahhh!

(Autoharp.)

BUFFALO: Moooo!

(Cowbell. Kalebet thrusts the fan across the buffalo's mouth.)

KALEBET: BAAAHHH!!!

(Autoharp. Kalebet suddenly realizes his trick has been exposed.)

Uh . . . hmmm . . . aahhh . . . how much money do you want for your goat?

PANDJI: Eh . . . the price is 250 rupiahs. Do you want to buy it?

KALEBET: Two hundred and fifty rupiahs! That's a very high price for a goat!

PANDJI: It's not a goat! Look carefully. Did you ever see a goat that big?

(Kalebet turns to find the buffalo breathing in his face.)

BUFFALO: Mooo!

(*Cowbell.*)

KALEBET: Well, you can call it what you want. Buffalo. Pig. Elephant if you like! But it's still a goat. I'll give you 40 rupiahs for it here and now.

(*Rattle.*)

PANDJI: No!

(*Pandji strides angrily away. Kalebet follows.*)

Two men in a row have called my animal a goat. But I know it's a buffalo . . .

KALEBET: Baaahhh!

(*Autoharp.*)

PANDJI: Or is it?

(*Kalebet joins Klungkung to spy behind their fans. Making sure he is unobserved, Pandji bends down to face the buffalo.*)

Baahh?

BUFFALO: Moooo!

(*Cowbell. The buffalo licks Pandji's face.*)

PANDJI: No. It's definitely a buffalo. Those two men were trying to trick me.

(*Kalabuat sidles up behind Pandji, slowly easing into her sexy pose. Autoharp and drum.*)

KALABUAT: (*Yawning.*) Haaayooo. Selamat pagi [good morning], Pandji. You're out very early. Where are you going?

PANDJI: Oh, Kalabuat . . . I'm . . . I'm going to the . . . market.

KALABUAT: Ahh. To sell your goat. How much do you want for it?

PANDJI: Aggghhh!! I'm going crazy!

(*Sukani joins Klungkung, Kalebet, and Kalabuat and they all circle about Pandji chanting. Slaps on autoharp.*)

ALL: Buffalo! Goat! Buffalo! Goat! Buffalo! Goat!

PANDJI: Stop! . . . My wife says . . .

SUKANI: It's a buffalo.

(*Cowbell. Sukani circles Pandji and disappears.*)

PANDJI: It's a buffalo. But three people in a row have called it . . .

(*Slaps on autoharp.*)

KLUNGKUNG: A goat!

KALEBET: Baaahhh!

KLUNGKUNG: A goat!

KALEBET: Baaahhh!

(*Klungkung and Kalebet circle Pandji and retreat to spy over their fans.*)

PANDJI: What am I to believe? . . . Look, I want 250 rupiahs for this . . . for this . . . for this animal!

BUFFALO: (*Through kazoo.*) Animal?

KALABUAT: No goat is worth that much. Come, I'll give you 50 rupiahs. (*Rattle.*) . . . Well, are you going to sell this goat, or not?

PANDJI: (*To buffalo.*) I think my wife has been playing a joke on me, calling you a buffalo. If I sell you now, I'll save myself a trip to the market. (*To Kalabuat.*) Yes. I'll sell the . . . goat . . . for 50 rupiahs.

(*Rattle and autoharp. They exchange money and the prodding stick. Kalabuat removes the buffalo's wooden bell and places it around Pandji's neck. Cowbell.*)

KALABUAT: Here. Keep this bell to remind you of what a good deal you made.

(*Pandji is about to bid the buffalo good-bye, but Kalabuat sends it running with a mighty prod. Drum and autoharp.*)

Haaayooo!

(*Kalabuat joins Klungkung and Kalebet for mutual congratulations. Gong.*

The scene changes to Sukani, who is rhythmically pounding rice in a large stone bowl with a long wooden pole. Pandji appears behind her.)

SUKANI: Well, this is the last of our rice. It's fortunate we had a buffalo to sell.

(*Pandji rattles the coins behind her ear. Sukani lashes out with the pole. Drum.*)

Hhhaaahhhiiieee! . . . Oh, it's you. I didn't expect you home so soon.

PANDJI: I had a stroke of good fortune.

(*Pandji rattles the money behind her.*)

I was able to sell the animal before I'd even left the village. Here is the money . . .

(*Sukani grabs it.*)

SUKANI: What's this? There are only 50 rupiahs here. Where are the other 200?

PANDJI: Two hundred? Well . . . uh . . .

SUKANI: You stupid man! Do you mean to tell me you sold a full-grown buffalo for 50 rupiahs!

PANDJI: But it wasn't a buffalo.

SUKANI: What?

PANDJI: It was a goat!

(*Sukani swings the pole at him six times as he acrobatically dodges each blow.*)

SUKANI: AAAGGGHHH! (*Drum.*) . . . You are completely crazy! (*Drum.*) . . . A grown man (*Drum.*) . . . and you don't know the difference (*Drum.*) . . . between a buffalo (*Drum.*) . . . and a goat! (*Drum.*)

(*Pandji dodges one extra time. Sukani glares at him and he smiles feebly.*)

Now you go straight back to the villain who bought our buffalo and you get another 200 rupiahs.

(*She gives him back the coins.*)

PANDJI: Another 200 rupiahs!

SUKANI: If you don't get them . . . watch out! Hhhaaahhhiiieee!

(A *final blow and she is gone. Drum.*)

PANDJI: I think . . . I think I was tricked by Kalabuat (*Autoharp.*) . . . and Kalebet (*Autoharp.*) . . . and KLUNGKUNG! (*Autoharp.*) But what can I do? They'll never give me the extra 200 rupiahs . . . unless . . . unless I can trick them. But how? Oh, think, brain, think . . . think . . .

(*As he fingers the bell around his neck, a plan begins to form.*)

Ah! The bell . . . from the buffalo . . .

(*Gong. The scene changes to Masak, an old vendor carrying two baskets of food balanced on a shoulder pole.*)

MASAK: (*Crying her wares.*) Bananas! Bananas here! Fresh, fried, boiled, or steamed! Bananas here!

PANDJI: Excuse me, my good woman.

MASAK: The name's Masak. What kind of bananas you want? Fresh, fried, boiled, or steamed?

PANDJI: No. No bananas. What I want is . . .

MASAK: No bananas, huh? How about some breadfruit? A mango? How about some coconut milk? No, huh. Ahhh, I know . . . a little palm wine.

PANDJI: No. I don't want anything to eat . . . just yet.

MASAK: Then what are you bothering me for!

(*She starts to move on, but the rattle of coins brings her back.*)

PANDJI: Now this is what I want you to do, my good woman . . .

MASAK: The name's Masak.

PANDJI: Yes. Now listen carefully . . .

(*Pandji whispers to Masak.*)

MASAK: You want me to do what? . . . When the bell rings? . . . But I can't say that I've been paid if I haven't been . . . (*Pandji gives her some money.*) paid. Why thank you very much, sir. That's very generous. Very generous indeed.

PANDJI: And you won't forget?

MASAK: You can count on Masak. —Bananas! Bananas here! Fresh, fried, boiled, or steamed! Bananas here!

(*Masak disappears. Gong. Klungkung, Kalebet, and Kalabuat enter.*)

KLUNGKUNG: I just sold the buffalo for 250 rupiahs! So we've made a profit of 200 rupiahs!

(*Their laughter ceases at the sight of Pandji, and they leap into defensive stances, Kalebet again landing on Klungkung's foot. Autoharp and drum.*)

ALL: Hhhaaahhhiiieee!

KLUNGKUNG: Ooowwwhhh!

(*Klungkung strikes Kalebet with his fan. Woodblock.*)

PANDJI: They expect me to be angry, but I'll surprise them. And I'll try to trick them.

(*He passes a hand across his face, leaving a wide forced smile. Wind chime.*)

Why, if it isn't my good . . . friends. Kalabuat (*Autoharp.*) . . . Kalebet (*Autoharp.*) . . . and, of course, Klungkung. (*Autoharp.*) I was just about to have something to eat and drink. I sold my goat this morning for 50 rupiahs, so come along with me and share my good fortune.

KLUNGKUNG: He's even more stupid than I thought.

KALEBET: Shall we accept his invitation?

KALABUAT: We took his buffalo, so why not take his money too.

KLUNGKUNG: Lead the way . . . friend.

(*They all converge on Masak. Clave.*)

PANDJI: Here we are. My good woman.

MASAK: The name's Masak.

PANDJI: Yes. Food for my friends and me. And maybe a little palm wine?

(*Masak takes the food, wrapped in palm leaves, out of one of her baskets. Pandji tosses it to Klungkung and Kalabuat, who sit on their haunches and greedily devour the food. Slaps on autoharp.*)

MASAK: Bananas?

KLUNGKUNG and KALABUAT: Yes!

MASAK: Fresh!

KALABUAT: Here!

MASAK: Fried!

KLUNGKUNG: Mine!

MASAK: Boiled and steamed!

KLUNGKUNG and KALABUAT: Owww! Hot!

(*Kalabet, meanwhile, is sneakily loading up his arms with food from the second basket.*)

KALEBET: Mangoes! . . . Breadfruit! . . . And coconut . . . (*The milk spills out through a hole in the shell.*) . . . milk!

MASAK: Care for a little palm wine?

KLUNGKUNG and KALABUAT: (*Mouths full.*) Hmmmmmmm!!

PANDJI: I trust everyone has had enough?

(*Slaps on autoharp cease.*)

KALEBET: Well . . . maybe just a bit more.

(*More slaps on autoharp. Taking a few more mangoes and breadfruit, Kalebet staggers to Klungkung and Kalabuat, and they all deviously stuff the food in their clothes.*)

PANDJI: Now my good woman . . .

MASAK: The name's Masak.

PANDJI: Yes. How much do I owe you?

MASAK: Let me see now . . . that's . . . 15 rupiahs!

(*Autoharp.*)

KLUNGKUNG: Aaahhh!

(*Pandji removes the bell, holds it above Masak's head, and rings it energetically.*)

MASAK: Thank you, sir. That's just enough.

(*Masak disappears. Klungkung, Kalebet, and Kalabuat huddle with many quizzical glances toward Pandji.*)

KLUNGKUNG: How did he do that?

KALEBET: It was magic!

KALABUAT: No, it was that bell.

KLUNGKUNG: Oh, Pandji. We were just wondering . . . How did you pay for all the food? It seemed that all you did was ring that bell?

PANDJI: Oh, you noticed that? . . . Well, it's sort of a secret . . .

KALEBET: Secret?

KALABUAT: Tell us!

PANDJI: Well . . . if you promise not to tell anyone.

KALEBET: We promise! We promise!

KALABUAT: Tell us! Tell us!

PANDJI: It's like this. When my father died, he left me this old buffalo bell, and only recently have I discovered it has magical powers.

(*Wind chimes.*)

KALEBET: I told you it was magic!

KLUNGKUNG: Quiet!

PANDJI: It has the power that when you buy something . . .

(*He rings the bell as an enticement. Klungkung grabs for the bell, but misses, leaving his arm outstretched.*)

PANDJI: . . . and the seller hears the ringing . . .

(*Kalabuat grabs and misses, leaving her arm outstretched.*)

. . . he thinks that he has already been paid.

(*Kalebet grabs and misses. Pandji raps Kalebet's knuckles with the bell, and all three villains pull their hands back in pain. Woodblock.*)

It's just as simple as that.

KLUNGKUNG: I've got to have that bell!

KALABUAT: It's the same bell that was on his buffalo.

KLUNGKUNG: What?

KALABUAT: I didn't know it was magic, so I gave it back to him.

KLUNGKUNG: You stupid fool!

(*Klungkung lunges for her, and Kalebet leaps into the fray. Slaps on autoharp. But the battle is stopped short by the sound of the bell.*)

Ah . . . I was just thinking, Pandji. Since we're such good friends . . . You could sell that little bell to me. I'll give you 200 rupiahs for it.

(*He rattles a money bag under Pandji's nose.*)

PANDJI: Oh . . . that is a lot of money! . . . but . . . but . . . No! I don't think I could do that.

(*Pandji entices Klungkung with the bell. Klungkung then entices Pandji with the money.*)

KLUNGKUNG: But you don't understand. If you let me have it, I'll never forget you. Every day I'll send you all your needs. So you won't loose anything at all, and you'll have an extra 200 rupiahs besides.

(*Rattle.*)

PANDJI: Well . . . Yes. That sounds all right. But you mustn't tell my wife.

KLUNGKUNG: Oh, of course not.

PANDJI: And I want 250 rupiahs.

(*Klungkung hesitates, but Kalebet and Kalabuat pressure him to accept.*)

KLUNGKUNG: Oh . . . Here's the 250 rupiahs. Now give me the bell.

(*Warily eyeing each other, the exchange is made. Rattle and autoharp.*)

I've got it! It's mine!

KALEBET: Let me see! Let me see!

KALABUAT: It looks just like an ordinary bell to me.

KLUNGKUNG: Let's try it out.

(*They converge on Masak [clave] and proceed to stuff food into their mouths and clothing. Slaps on autoharp.*)

KALEBET: Look! Steamed rice and coconut oil!

KALABUAT: Vegetable salad and peanut butter sauce!

KLUNGKUNG: Sate!

(*They each take a skewer and taste the meat.*)

KALEBET: Chicken.

KALABUAT: Beef.

KLUNGKUNG: And goat!

ALL: (*Laughing.*) Baaahhh!!

KALEBET: What's this?

(*Autoharp stops. They all taste the food. Cymbals.*)

ALL: Ohhhh! Aggghhh! It's pepper sauce!

KALEBET: Milk!

KALABUAT: Water!

KLUNGKUNG: Wine!

(*Grabbing the baskets, they desperately search for something to drink. A disheveled Masak retrieves her pole.*)

MASAK: I assume you've had all you want?

KLUNGKUNG: For the moment. Tell us, how much do we owe you?

MASAK: You're sure you want to know?

KLUNGKUNG: Out with it, woman!

MASAK: The name's Masak.

KLUNGKUNG: How much! How much!

MASAK: Ninety-five rupiahs . . . sir.

(*Autoharp.*)

KLUNGKUNG: Is that all? Here you are, my good woman.

MASAK: The name's . . .

(*The bell is rung above her head.*)

KLUNGKUNG: Well, now. What shall we "buy" next?

MASAK: Just a moment. Where is the money?

KLUNGKUNG: What's the matter, are you deaf? Listen!

(*He rings the bell again.*)

MASAK: I hear the sound of a bell, not money.

(*She holds out her hand. Klungkung desperately rings the bell.*)

KALEBET: Ring! Ring!

KALABUAT: Listen! Listen!

MASAK: So you think you can make a fool of old Masak, do you?

(*She thrashes them with her pole.*)

I'll teach you to try and cheat me! (*Drum.*) . . . How dare you eat my food when you haven't any money! (*Drum.*) . . . You can't (*Drum.*) . . . pay (*Drum.*) . . . for food (*Drum.*) . . . with the sound of a stupid bell!

(*She rings the bell above them. The buffalo enters and licks Pandji's face. All freeze.*)

DALANG: And since that day no one has ever called Pandji stupid again.

(*Gong. The performers remove their masks, if worn.*)

> Now if any of you assembled here
> Be prone to playing tricks,
> Heed the beating that comes from cheating,
> The fate that follows greed.
> Share good fortune with your friends.
> Thus our tale of trickery ends.

(*Gongs. The performers wai, or bow, to the audience.*)

CURTAIN

DATE DUE			
FEB 1 '83			
APR 1 '85			
MAY 17 '88			
OCT 11 '92			
DEC 0 6 '93			
DEC 09 '96			
FEB 1 6 1998			
MAR 0 5 1999			
APR 1 7			